Current Controversies in Sports, Media, and Society

Bassim Hamadeh, CEO and Publisher
Angela Schultz, Senior Field Acquisitions Editor
Carrie Montoya, Manager, Revisions and Author Care
Tony Paese, Project Editor
Jess Estrella, Senior Graphic Designer
Danielle Gradisher, Licensing Associate
Don Kesner, Interior Designer
Natalie Piccotti, Director of Marketing
Kassie Graves, Vice President of Editorial
Jamie Giganti, Director of Academic Publishing

ISBN: 978-1-5165-2276-7 (pbk) / 978-1-5165-2277-4 (br)

3970 Sorrento Valley Blvd., Ste. 500, San Diego, CA 92121

Current Controversies in Sports, Media, and Society

First Edition

Cynthia M. Frisby, Ph.D.

cognella®

SAN DIEGO

Brief Contents

Detailed Contents

1

The History of Sports

LEARNING OBJECTIVES

After completing this chapter, students should be able to:

- define sports and identify the activities that are described as sports in American culture;
- understand history when studying the interplay of race, gender, media, and sports in society;
- use the history of sports to understand sports and the interaction of race and gender in sports today; and
- understand why we study sports and culture, and their role in society.

Definitions of Sport

This chapter begins with a clear definition of what criteria is used to qualify a sporting activity. Listed next are a few of the definitions found online:

> "An activity involving physical exertion and skill in which an individual or team competes against another or others" (Wood, 2008).

> "A human activity capable of achieving a result requiring physical exertion and physical skill, which, by its nature and organization, is competitive and is accepted as being a sport" (Australian Sports Commission, 2010; Wood, 2008).

> "An activity involving physical exertion and skill that is governed by a set of rules or customs and often undertaken competitively" (Wood, 2008).

Sport Criteria

After careful consideration of the earlier definitions of what constitutes a sport, we gather three basic criteria that are used to differentiate a sport from an extracurricular activity. We learn that to be identified as a sport, the activity must involve some sort of physical ability and

According to *TopEnd Sports*, sport is defined as activities that involve both physical and mental effort. While we are unable to find a definitive, legitimate definition of what sport is, we know that some scholars believe that for a sport to be classified as a sport, the activity must be guided by organizational rules or sanctions and involve an element of competition. (Wood, 2008).

In our culture, several pastime activities are often debated as to whether or not they are sports. Activities such as golf, bowling, fencing, dodgeball, dancing, and snooker pool, to name a few, are often described as "hobbies" and not considered actual sports. Using the three criteria listed earlier, we will determine whether these are considered "games" in Western culture. According to the criteria, cheerleading easily fits the definition of sport, especially when it is competitive and achieves a particular outcome. For some individuals, activities such as fishing and dancing are often considered hobbies or extracurricular activities. However, within both of those activities, there are competitions that ultimately would classify them as sports, especially regarding individuals or teams competing against others.

The History of Sports

The history of sports in American culture lays a foundation that enhances understanding of how Americans live with ethnic and gender disparities in a culture that is often described as a "melting pot." For more than 100 years, sports have served as one of America's most dominant unifying variables. In fact, we know from studying American history that sports in this culture are the one factor that can unite Americans from diverse cultures, and they are also instrumental in helping define American identity. Regarding diversity and a society struggling with racial tensions, the importance of sports in our society cannot be ignored. For many Americans, whether they are participants or fans, sports have given them opportunities for escape from everyday life and served as a pastime used to entertain and relax, but, more importantly, games give Americans an opportunity to connect and unite with people from different racial, ethnic, and other demographic backgrounds.

Take a favorite sporting event like the Super Bowl. The Super Bowl serves as an excellent example of a sporting event that brings millions of Americans together for three or four hours a year. In fact, advertisers have found the Super Bowl to be the venue by which they can introduce new commercials and market products and services around the cultural ritual of watching the game and the half-time entertainment. The Super Bowl and its rise in popularity in American culture allows us to examine how we live and entertain, and provides us with the opportunity to gather together to celebrate and affirm our identity as Americans.

FIGURE 1.1   *The Legendary Babe Ruth, Boston Red Sox*

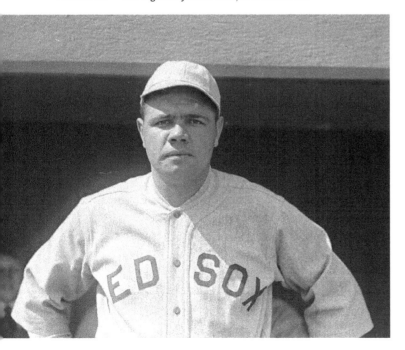

In addition to the Super Bowl, two other American sports offer opportunities that allow us to unite and affirm our identity as Americans; professional boxing and baseball. These two sports, for instance, have become important vehicles by which individuals from all over the world can integrate and progress in American society. These two sports, according to history books, were known to spread in popularity in American culture through the mass media. Newspapers and radio allowed people to enter America and integrate by participating in these two popular cultural sporting events. Rocky Marciano, as well as the iconic baseball players Babe Ruth (Figure 1.1) and Joe DiMaggio, became symbols of potential. These baseball players, specifically, made it possible for Italian, Jewish, and Irish Jewish Americans to become sports heroes and gain popularity and acceptance in American culture.

As sports evolved in America, they became a significant influence in racial discrimination. In 1930, for example, track and field, along with boxing, introduced young African American athletes to the sporting world, including Jesse Owens and Joe Louis. Just as Rocky Marciano and Joe DiMaggio did for Italian, Irish, and Jewish Americans, Jesse Owens and Joe Lewis brought notoriety to African Americans when they went up against athletes from Nazi Germany. As history notes, it was this time in our culture when Germany was most known for its cruel acts against non-whites. However, the stigma of being African American athletes did not deter Owens and Lewis. It was at the 1936 Berlin Olympics when Jesse Owens's won four gold medals (Figure 1.2). Then, in 1938, Joe Louis was victorious over Max Schmeling at Yankee Stadium. These two moments in the history of sports set the stage for colleges such as New York University to recruit top African American athletes to join football, basketball, and baseball teams. Coaches were now "free" to address the segregation that before this time ran rampant in sports.

Concerning gender in sports, breaking down barriers in sports took a bit of a different path. For female athletes, unlike much of the story about athletes of color, the issue was more about the institutional sexism that insisted that participation in sports by women be deemed inappropriate because it would masculinize women. Very early on in American culture, women and girls were taught that competitive sports were a "for-men-only" activity. Women during this era were given few opportunities to develop their athletic talents. Then in 1948, the All-American Girls Professional Baseball League (AAGPBL) (Figure 1.3) was started. This new

FIGURE 1.2   *August 1936: Jesse Owens of the USA starts the 200-meter event at the 1936 Olympic Games in Berlin*

professional baseball league consisting of women was created so that baseball could remain a favorite American pastime while men were away fighting in World War II. The league was in existence from 1943 through 1954, and records show that over 600 women played in the league, attracting attendance that peaked at over 900,000 spectators.

Not until the approval of Title IX of the Civil Rights Act of 1964 were female athletes able to consider their participation in a sport as a feminist or women's rights issue. Because of Title IX, women started to insist that they were afforded the same opportunity to participate in sports as men. The history of women's sports shows that currently female athletes and their sports have become a huge part

FIGURE 1.3   *AAGPBL members performing calisthenics*

of athletics. Yet many feel that this advancement of women's sports and female athletes would not have taken place had it not been for the efforts made in the courts and through protests, marches, community campaigns, and other challenges.

Why Study Race, Gender, Media, and Sports?

The goal of this chapter, as well as this book, is to focus on the broader surface issues related to sports and how sports have become part of the social and cultural worlds that Americans live in today. Later in the book, we will move away from the broad topics and discussion of history, theory, and research, and unpack practical findings as they relate to race, gender, media, and sports. With a unique perspective, knowledge in these areas will enable us to move further into understanding why so many Americans place such importance on sports and look up to our culture's elite athletes.

Sports are an important part of our social lives and have meaning that goes far beyond the competition. People interested in studying sports in society are mostly concerned with (1) research that increases the understanding of the culture and society in which sports exist, (2) the values created around sports, (3) the role media play in the development, maintenance, and/or change in how we view female athletes, athletes of color, and athletes who participate in sports considered masculine or feminine.

Overview of Modern Sporting History

Baseball

According to historical records, the first baseball team began in the United States in 1723. Other historical records report that "base ball," as it was called then, started in New York City in 1823 and was regularly played on Saturdays on the outskirts of New York City (in what is now Greenwich Village) in 1823. The New York Knickerbockers were the first official ball club formed in 1845. At this time in American society, base ball functioned more as a social club for the upper-middle-class residents living in New York City. In fact, in the early turn of the century, the sport of base ball required a runner to ring a bell while shouting, "Tally one point, sir." For the run to count, the runner had to make the proclamation. Base ball, which then changed to "baseball," rose to popularity with working-class fans after the American Civil War (Smith, 2018). For approximately ten years (between the 1850s and 1860s), the formation of working-class teams was rising all across the United States, attracting fans and gaining popularity among working-class people. Toward the beginning of the 1870s, a new professional, all-white baseball team was organized, supported financially by a group of investors in Ohio. The Cincinnati Red Stockings were then moved from Ohio to Boston, Massachusetts, and became the Boston Red Socks (Smith, 2018).

The early 1890s also saw the start of one black baseball team. At the beginning of the 20th century, records show that black ballclubs were independent, as were the white ball clubs. Each racial group stayed segregated and competed within its group until 1920, when Rube Foster created the Negro National League (NNL), which ultimately led to the formation of the Negro League World Series.

The formation of the NNL ultimately led to the organization of the National Baseball Commission, a group whose mission was to regulate and govern the sport of baseball. This commission later morphed into what we now know as "Major League Baseball" (MLB; Smith, 2018). It was fall of 1903 when the first "World's Series" began with the Boston baseball team from the American League (AL) reigning victorious over the Pittsburgh National League. With the threat of another world war, many players were at risk of being drafted in the armed forces. Major professional baseball players such as Lou Gehrig (who died prematurely), Joe DiMaggio (who rose to fame when he made 56 hits in consecutive games), and Ted Williams (famous for having a batting record of over .400) helped propel baseball into the American culture. The early 1900s were notorious years for baseball, particularly when Stan Musial was noted to have led the St. Louis Cardinals to three World Series titles during this time in American history. Because many players were drafted to serve in World War II, and because of the popularity of baseball in American culture, the AAGPBL was formed specifically to provide the sport to Americans who looked to baseball for entertainment and as a way to pass time while husbands, sons, and fathers were at war.

Basketball

Basketball, a sport credited as "the brainchild of Dr. James Naismith," was created in the early 1890s. It started in college, and its growth developed into "professional teams and leagues, with the National Basketball Association emerging around 1950" (Wood, 2010).

It has been reported that Naismith liked to play a game where the point was to knock a duck off of a rock by throwing a large rock. According to reports, the challenge for Naismith was creating a sport and finding a small space for that sport that would provide youth with opportunities to learn specific skills during cold winter months. He first started the game with the use of a soccer ball and two baskets at the end of the small space; this was the first recorded game of basketball (Kingston, 2018).

Football

History tells us that American Football, a sport that was known to exist in a variety of forms, may extend back to the early 1870s when college players from Princeton and Rutgers played a sport that resembled soccer but used rules associated with soccer played in England. We also learn from historical records that the sport of football that we are most familiar with in the 21st century began in the 1881. We learn from archives that Walter Camp, coach of the Yale football team, is responsible for establishing policies that mandate that when an offensive team fails to gain five yards after three downs they will be forced to surrender the ball on 4th down. We also learn that it is Walter Camp who "established the norm of a seven-man line, a quarterback, two halfbacks, and a fullback" (Professional Football Researchers Association, 2010).

In 1823, William Web Ellis is said to have started the sport known as rugby football. Mr. Ellis was reported to have picked up a rugby football and then simply ran with it. Initially, football in America closely resembled rugby football. Similar to rugby, a ball was placed on the ground and kicked by foot toward a goal or over a line. This type of football originated in Britain; eventually, the sport found popularity in America, and it was the end of the 19th century when the game became popular in the United States (Davis, 2010; MacCambridge, 2005; Perrin, 1987). According to historical accounts, football started at the beginning of the 20th century in colleges. With the formation of the National Football League (NFL) in 1920, football quickly emerged as another American pastime and popular sport. Interestingly, football was more popular in American Midwestern industrial towns until the late 1950s, when professional football and the NFL entered the scene. The NFL is now ultimately the dominant league in American culture (Davis, 2010; Fox, 1998; MacCambridge, 2005; Perrin, 1987).

Ice Hockey

Ice hockey's history began in 1810 in Canada. The sport of ice hockey that we are most familiar with in America today entered American culture somewhere around the 1800s and became known as the National Hockey League (NHL). According to Gidén and Houda (2010), ice hockey is believed to have evolved from simple stick-and-ball games played in the 18th and 19th centuries in the United Kingdom and elsewhere. The game is popular in Russia, Europe, the United States, and Canada. In fact, ice hockey has officially been recognized as the national winter sport in Canada. Even though ice hockey is known to have been formed and developed in Canada, attributes and features of the original game have been maintained and kept to the current day. For fans and professional players, the highest accolade in the sport is "the Stanley Cup," a competition that recognizes the all-time best team in ice hockey. The Stanley Cup first appeared in ice hockey as early as 1893 and eventually became the championship trophy of the NHL. In the early 1900s, the Canadian rules were adopted by the Ligue Internationale de Hockey sur Glace, the precursor of the International Ice Hockey Federation, and the sport was played for the first time in the Olympics in the 1920 Summer Olympics.

Motor Car Racing

Motor racing, according to historical texts, is a sport whose origin is difficult to trace. According to modern sports history, motor racing "began more with motorized bicycles or tricycles than cars, though not by many years" (Smith, 2018). It was toward the end of the 19th century, according to the history of sports, that racing cars led to the development of race car tracks. It was in the early 1900s when the Indianapolis Motor Speedway was built, and it was then that other types of motor racing evolved (i.e., Formula One and NASCAR) (Smith, 2018).

Soccer

Football (a term widely known in Europe), or soccer (the familiar name in the United States), is often considered the world's favorite sport. The governing body for soccer was formed in 1904, now "known as the Federation Internationale de Football Association, or FIFA" (Smith, 2018).

Tennis

The oldest of sports as we know them in today's time is tennis. According to historical records, tennis dates back as far as the 1500s (http://www.thepeoplehistory.com/sports.html). Tennis evolved from England in 1877, the period when the first Wimbledon Championships were performed. Tennis's governing body, known as the International Tennis Federation, was founded in 1913 and is made up of 13 national tennis associations.

The Olympics

The Olympics, according to history, grew out of an ancient Greek tradition held in the early 1800s (Smith, 2018). In 1896, the Olympic Games eventually merged with the administration of the International Olympic Committee. Historical records show that the "Olympics have been held every four years, missing only 1916, 1940, and 1944 due to world wars" (Smith, 2018). The original Olympic Games, interestingly, only accepted male athletes to compete. It was four years later in the Paris Olympics in 1900 when women were added to the games.

In its early onset, the Winter Olympics initially were held with the Summer Olympics. Then, in 1924, in Chamonix France, a decision was made to combine both the Winter and Summer Olympics which also happened to be the same year as the Paris Summer Games (Smith, 2018). The Summer and Winter Games were later separated in 1994 when the Winter Olympics were held in Lillehammer, Norway. The Summer Olympic Games followed in Atlanta, Georgia in 1996. Originally, the Winter Olympics had nine sports events, yet as of this writing, the Winter Olympics have held up to 15 sporting competitions.

Golf

Golf is another sport like motor racing whose origins are widely disputed by various historians. Some historians trace the game of golf back to different European stick-and-ball games that ran rampant throughout history (http://www.thepeoplehistory.com/sports.html). Sometime in the 15th century, golf emerged in Scotland and then spread in popularity across areas controlled by the British Empire in the early 19th century. As with other sports, golf also has a governing body. The governing body of golf is known as the Professional Golfers Association of America (PGA). Formed in 1916, the PGA has over 41 sections worldwide and is known as the world's largest working sports organization (Smith, 2018).

Boxing

Boxing dates back to Ancient Greece. From historical literature, we learn that the sport "originated sometime in 1867 when the Marquess of Queensbury published a code of rules" (Smith, 2018). From what is known, we find that these rules that started in 1867 are still used in the sport today. In 1921, the National Boxing Association merged forces with the World Boxing Association (WBA), and as a result, four sports organizations emerged, and they are as follows: "the WBA, the International Boxing Federation, the World Boxing Organization and the World Boxing Council" (Smith, 2018).

Cricket

Cricket, another sport whose origins are not quite as clear as the other sports at best started to appear in our culture sometime in the 1770s. The first known match was played between two countries. It was 1877 when a cricket match was played between Australia and England. The governing body of cricket known as the International Cricket Council was later founded in 1909. At that time, the council was known as the Imperial Cricket Council, which included only "three countries, England, South Africa, and Australia. Currently, the International Cricket Council consists of 10 full members" (Smith, 2018).

Background of Major Sporting Leagues

Professional sports teams have been defined as "athletic organizations comprising talented, expert players hired by club owners whose revenues originally derived from admission fees charged to spectators seeing games in enclosed ballparks or indoor arenas" (Riess, 2017).

Sports teams by definition are usually members of a league that is in charge of scheduling competitions and a championship season. According to sports history records, professional baseball teams emerged in the East and Midwest in the 1860s (Riess, 2017).

MLB is known to have set the precedent for the professionalization of football, basketball, and hockey (Riess, 2017).

Professional team sports gained considerable popularity after World War II (Riess, 2017). Records show that professional leagues were faced with conflicts dealing with issues such as franchise relocations and nationwide expansion. Other conflicts during this time found them facing problems related to player salaries and racial integration. Research also suggests that the NFL became the most successful professional sports organization because of its success in securing national television contracts and beating MLB as the American pastime in the 1970s. While the NFL, PGA, MLB, NHL, National Basketball Association (NBA), and other leagues have all become lucrative, the rise of "free agency" has also increased. Currently, many American professional team athletes are extremely well paid, averaging more than $2 million a year.

Major League Baseball

The first known professional baseball league was established in 1871. Known as the 10-team National Association of Professional Baseball Players, the league initially consisted of baseball clubs that were housed in the East and Midwest. Although, initially, the league struggled through its first five seasons because of low entry fees (i.e., franchises were required to pay just $10 to join), teams arranged their own schedules. Furthermore, teams were of uneven quality, and players, who earned between $1,300 and $1,600 per year, often left their teams ("revolve") for clubs offering more lucrative salaries (Reiss, 2017).

New competing leagues appeared in the late 1880s. The National Association's main rival was the American Association (AA), which was established in 1882. The difference between leagues was primarily that the AA catered to a working-class audience. Unlike the National Association, the AA held their games on Sunday, charged $0.25 admissions, and sold liquor at the stadiums. Eventually, increasing operating costs led the AA to join forces with the National League (NL, and the two leagues merged in 1892.

In 1901, the AL was created as a new major league in baseball. In 1903, the AL merged with the NL, which is what we have come to know in current times as the World Series. The World Series during this time was heavily reported on in daily newspapers, specialized sports weeklies, and general interest periodicals. Baseball also became a prominent topic in juvenile literature and popular music. Star players were renowned heroes, idolized for their prowess (like Ty Cobb) and their exemplary character (Christy Mathewson). The game was so popular that owners rebuilt stadiums, changing them from the wood stadiums that were constructed for $30,000 to $60,000. Five of these wood stadiums burned down in 1894, which allowed for the construction of larger, more modern stadiums for the time. In 1909, the first fire-resistant major league ballpark was built, Philadelphia's $500,000 Shibe Park, followed by nine more stadiums that were built from 1909 through 1916. Capacities averaged about 25,000, although the Polo Grounds in New York seated 54,000. They had idiosyncratic dimensions, often reflecting the available space in congested industrial cities. The "classic" ballpark era culminated in 1923 with the $2.5 million, 63,000-seat Yankee Stadium, the first MLB site not known as a park, field, or grounds.

MLB did very well in the interwar years, despite the impact of the "fixed" 1919 World Series, and remained the preeminent professional sport into the 1940s. The nature of the game on the field changed from finesse to a power game because of slugger Babe Ruth, who hit 714 home runs. He was the era's preeminent sports hero and a model of consumption, freely spending his $80,000 salary. In the interwar era, nearly all top athletes aspired to play MLB, especially for the New York Yankees, who won 11 pennants and eight World Series in the span of a few years. The Yankees and the St. Louis Cardinals flourished by establishing extensive farm systems to produce new talent.

In the 1920s, our culture experienced a Great Depression, which ultimately undermined the success that baseball enjoyed in the early days. The Depression produced financial losses for baseball teams and players. Public demand for sports as entertainment was the one thing that allowed baseball to avoid the financial destruction that most businesses experienced during the Great Depression. To address the public's demand, MLB adopted marketing innovations, such as holding night games, an annual all-star game, and radio broadcast of games by 1940. MLB regained its profitability by the mid-1930s.

Professional baseball during the 1930s was also racially segregated. The only acknowledged African American players up to 1930 were the Walker brothers, who played for Toledo (AA) in 1884. Blacks were excluded from organized professional baseball in 1899 by an unwritten understanding, which limited them to traveling with all-black sports clubs. The NNL was created in 1920 by black entrepreneurs to take advantage of the potential market among the growing African American inner-city population. The league lasted until 1931, failing because of founder Rube Foster's mental illness and the economic impact of the Depression. A new NNL began in 1933, largely created by inner-city policy bankers. The NNL became a profitable and leading community institution. The Homestead Grays became the league's top team, with a roster that included Satchel Paige, Josh Gibson, and Buck Leonard, who would have been MLB stars if white.

Pressure for integration grew during World War II from black and white journalists and liberal politicians, pointing to the heroic accomplishments of black participants in the war and the participation of Olympic champion Jesse Owens in 1936 and heavyweight boxing champion Joe Louis. However, intense dislike of a racially integrated baseball was noted, because many white people viewed the integration of blacks and whites in baseball as a sign of a more significant desire to have racial integration in American society. The big step moving baseball to integrate players was taken by Dodgers president Branch Rickey, who signed Jackie Robinson on October 23, 1945, because he believed it was the right thing to do. That decision would help the Dodgers win a pennant, and from a financial perspective, winning the pennant was great for business. Although Jackie Robinson was not the star of, say, the Kansas City Monarchs, he was, without a doubt, an outstanding all-around athlete and a college-educated veteran who lived in integrated Los Angeles. Robinson did, however, have the background needed to cope with life in the MLB. Despite the racism he encountered, in 1947, Robinson was named rookie of the year and ultimately led the team to the World Series.

Figure 1.4 is a photo of Jackie Robinson taken during his first season. Despite the fact that Robinson's presence caused racial tensions among fans and teammates, the Dodgers's manager and owner publicly supported Jackie Robinson and reportedly stated, "I'm the manager of this team, and I say he plays."

In fact, the integration of black and white baseball players in the MLB was probably the single most colossal development in American sports history. Jackie Robinson's presence not only affected American society and culture but also his success in a predominantly all-white baseball league opened the door for other blacks to become interested in playing the sport. The interesting thing was that the integration of black players was extremely slow. Yes, African Americans such as Willie Mays and Hank Aaron dominated the league, but their entrance into the league did not happen until 1951 and 1954, respectively. Progress was even slower in the AL. The last team to recruit black players was the Boston Red Sox in 1959. By 1965, records show that 20% of MLB players were black or Latino, and 38% of the All-Stars were men of color. Conversely, in 2016, the MLB reports having only 9% African American MLB players compared to 70% in the NFL, 74.4% in the NBA, and 5% in the NHL. Professional baseball was extremely popular after World War II, with attendance doubling to an

FIGURE 1.4   *Jackie Robinson*

average of 16,027. Minor leagues alone numbered a record 52. However, television coverage soon saturated broadcast markets, which together with television's popularity as free entertainment led to many minor leagues going out of business and MLB franchises losing money in the early 1950s. Some argue that media emphasized these players were giving young boys of color role models to emulate. By the time the other sports entered our culture, media had switched the emphasis to the superstars of football and basketball, resulting in a lack of role models from baseball who could encourage and inspire young boys to play baseball.

The formation of a players' union in 1954, the Major League Baseball Players Association (MLBPA), had a huge effect on the MLB. In 1965, the union hired an economist from the United Steelworkers of America as its director who ran the MLBPA like a traditional trade union with a strike in 1972. In 1981, was the first strike since 1972. At the heart of this strike was the idea that the MLB owners demanded compensation for loss free agents to other teams. From the players perspective, this ruling would devalue the purpose and significance of being a free agent. Months after the strike began, it ended with the players agreeing to restrict free agency to players with six or more years of major league service. As a result of the settlement, it was said that the owners enjoyed a "limited victory" on the free agent compensation issue.

Then, in 1985, MLB experienced another strike, but this time it was recorded as an "in-season strike." Unlike the strike in 1972, games that were missed during the season were made up at the end of the season. The reason for this strike was a disagreement about pension funds and the salary cap. While the strike of 1985 was not known to affect the season, owners were extremely unhappy with the negotiation and resolution.

A less widely known strike in the MLB happened in 1990 when the disagreement was about revenue sharing, free agency and salaries. It is believed that one reason that this strike was not widely publicized is because the major impact of the strike was its effect on spring training. And even though negotiations delayed opening day of baseball season by a week, the entire 162-game season was played without interruption.

The strike in the MLB that resonates with fans and sports journalists is the event that took place from 1994 to 1995. The 1994 season ended before it could even begin. And unlike the prior strikes in MLB history, the season never restarted. That is, an entire season had to be canceled because of conflicts and labor disputes. This was the first time in American sports history that any strike of this magnitude was known to occur. For zealous professional baseball fans, not having a World Series was devastating and to show their disdain, many fans never returned to watch their favorite sports teams play. It wasn't until April of 1995, one month after the regular season was to start, that MLB returned. But, in lieu of having 162 games, there was a 144-game schedule, due to the delayed start.

Another noteworthy detail about the 1994–1995 strike as the cancellation of the World Series as mentioned in the previous paragraph. The cancellation of the World Series was a huge public relations disaster for both sides. However, one positive result of the strike is the fact that the protest and union action resulted in a dramatic change in player compensation, and as a result, MLB has not seen another strike since 1995. In Chapter 15 of this text, we will talk about the power of athlete's activism and unpack the role that it plays in times of unrest and injustice.

The average professional baseball player salary in the early 1950s was approximate $11,000; it reached $19,000 in 1967 and $52,300 in 1976 (Riess, 2017). After the strike, the professional baseball salary skyrocketed, surpassing $1 million in 1993. Today, the average MLB player salary is $4.17 million (Riess, 2017). The MLBPA succeeded because membership was unified against a divided ownership. Presently, the baseball player union is known as the strongest union ever in the United States.

The worth and cost of MLB teams have dramatically escalated since the 1950s because of higher ticket prices and increased TV revenues. The Yankees, for example, have risen in worth from $11.2 million in 1964, to $635 million in 2001, and to $3.2 billion today (Riess, 2017).

Professional Football and the National Football League

Professional football emerged among working-class athletic clubs in the steel manufacturing areas of Pennsylvania and Ohio, which took winning seriously and hired top players for big games. The first known professional football player was William "Pudge" Heffelfinger, an All-American lineman at Yale University. Heffelfinger received $500 in 1892 to play for the Allegheny Athletic Association against the Pittsburgh Athletic Club. The first professional football teams were located in Pittsburgh and surrounding communities, drawing close to 3,000 spectators.

In 1902, the first professional football league, known as the Ohio League was formed. Due to a gambling scandal in 1906 involving teams from Massillon and Canton, the Ohio League disbanded. An interesting tidbit of historical research revealed an unknown fact and that is that a journalist known as David Barry established a professional football league among working-class athletic clubs in the steel-manufacturing areas of Pennsylvania. Barry's 1902 professional football league consisted of two teams; the Philadelphia Phillies and the Pittsburgh Pirates (Reiss, 2017). According to Reiss (2017), Barry's "National Football League" lasted exactly one year.

In 1910, eight years after the Ohio League football shutdown, Canton, Ohio returned to the football league, winning four league championships in 1915, 1916, 1917, and 1919. The leader off the winning Canton football team was former All-American and Olympic star Jim Thorpe (Reiss, 2017). The Canton team later claimed the title of "Professional Football Champions of the World" in 1916 (Reiss, 2017).

In 1920, owners of professional teams, as we mentioned previously, many of which were affiliated with an industrial organization, met in Canton, Ohio, to form a league. It was in 1920 when the American Professional Football Association was formed and later renamed the NFL in 1922. Thorpe was the initial president, replaced in 1921 by sportswriter Joe Carr. The 14 teams of 1920 were charged a $100 membership fee (side note: historical records show not one team paid the fee). The league was not well organized at the time and teams were responsible for making their schedules.

In 1925, the Chicago Bears signed Harold "Red" Grange. His agent, C. C. "Cash and Carry" Pyle, signed a contract for Grange to immediately join the Bears and then play a 19-game exhibition series. Grange drew large crowds, including about 70,000 to New York's Polo Grounds. Grange's presence added considerable prestige to the NFL. It was in the mid- to late 1920s that we began to see more collegians considering professional football as a career. It is interesting to learn that in this era, 80% of the professional players had no college background. Grange was reported to have earned about $250,000 for the season.

A small number of African Americans played in the early NFL, most notably All-American end Paul Robeson (Riess, 2017). In 1933, an increase in racism, along with the Depression and the opposition of white players, fans, and owners, forced black football players out of the league for over a decade. The Depression hurt the NFL, which had just eight teams in 1932. Green Bay, an original NFL franchise, was the only small town still in the league, with 19 others having dropped out. The league that year streamlined footballs to make them easier to pass and increase scoring, and staged its first postseason championship game. One year later, the College All-Star Game began with the NFL's champion playing a select group of college seniors at Chicago's Soldier Field. Another important process in sports during this era was the introduction of the college draft in 1936 to improve rosters of weaker teams. By 1940, when the T formation was widely used, the league was drawing nearly 20,000 attendees per game.

FIGURE 1.5A   *Woody Strode*

FIGURE 1.5B   *Kenny Washington*

The NFL struggled during World War II. Despite its struggles, there were three events that marked the change in the NFL. First was the start of the All-American Football Conference (AAFC), whose eight owners had previously tried unsuccessfully to get NFL franchises. The AAFC included franchises in San Francisco, Los Angeles, and Miami, making it a truly national league, accessible only by air travel. The NFL responded by moving the Cleveland Rams to Los Angeles, where it was pressured to integrate the team. The command was issued by the Los Angeles Coliseum Commission, which operated the Coliseum. The Los Angeles Rams added former University of California, Los Angeles All-American Kenny Washington and his college teammate Woody Strode to their team roster. Figures 1.5A and 1.5B are pictures of Woody Strode and Kenny Washington. The significance of these two players is the fact that they were the first blacks to play football for the league in 1946. The Cleveland Browns of the AAFC subsequently signed Marion Motley, featured in Figure 1.6B, who helped lead the team to four AAFC championships. Bill Willis, featured in Figure 1.6A, made history and a significant milestone when he became the first black man to start in football. The AAFC ended in 1950 when Cleveland, Baltimore, and San Francisco joined the NFL. Like the MLB, NFL integration proceeded slowly, but by 1955, the Washington Redskins were the only team that had not signed a black player. Owner George Preston Marshall did not hire an African American until 1962, when he signed Bobby Mitchell, only after pressure from Attorney General Robert F. Kennedy and Secretary of the Interior Stewart Udall, who threatened to evict the team from the new, publicly owned stadium.

Football teams in the 1950s and 1960s, according to research, often were restrained by quotas on the number of black players they could have (Riess, 2017). Black players were under-recruited and underpaid, and they were "stacked" (we will define this term in Chapter 3). Black football players were often recruited to play in "speed positions"—positions that excluded them from the more "intelligent" roles, such as middle linebacker or quarterback. As of current practices, this has changed, but change has been slow and uneven. As of 2014, for example, nine of 32 NFL quarterbacks were black. According to Stahl (2017), "the Jacksonville Jaguars' Shahid Khan, a Pakistani-American and the Buffalo Bills' Kim Pegula and her husband, Asian-Americans are currently the only people of color who are majority owners of NFL franchises." None of the principal owners in the NFL are black—a problem that is not specific to football. According to a 2013 study, the only owner of a major league professional team is Michael Jordan who is principal owner of the Charlotte Bobcats (Stahl, 2017). We will come back to this topic and issue in Chapter 12 of this text when we discuss disparities in team ownership.

FIGURE 1.6A   *Bill Willis*

FIGURE 1.6B   *Marion Motley*

Professional football's biggest crisis was the rise of the American Football League (AFL) in 1960. This league was organized by wealthy businessmen previously unable to buy an NFL franchise. They placed six of eight teams in non-NFL cities, with hopes that these teams would survive until the NFL agreed to let them join. The NFL took up the challenge by expanding into Minneapolis-St. Paul to preempt a vacant site and into Dallas to compete with an AFL franchise there. The leagues ultimately merged in 1966 to form one 24-team league. The merger helped to cut costs, a move that was facilitated by congressional actions to circumvent antitrust implications. The league was, however, allowed to keep its separate conferences, with the winners playing in a championship game that they called the "Super Bowl." The event became the preeminent single sporting contest in the United States, with viewership surpassing ratings of all other television programs. Since then, the NFL has fought off other rivals wanting to enter the U.S. sports culture.

The NFL Players Association (NFLPA) was founded in 1956. In 1968, a collective bargaining agreement was signed and provided minimum salaries and a pension to all players in the league. Football players tried to unionize, but the courts overturned several contracts that the union had agreed to because it was in an unequal bargaining position and could not negotiate a fair contract.

In 1982, NFLPA executive director Ed Garvey led a 57-day strike that saw marginal success in the collective bargaining agreement. When the agreement ended in 1987, the then executive director, Gene Upshaw (1983, 2008), led a strike over the free agency policy, and owners retaliated with replacement players. This was met with some success, even though fans complained that the quality of the games was subpar. Once the players returned to the football field, they sought to settle the salary and free agency issue in the courts. At the time, it was ruled only that owners would be exempted from the antitrust law. The union reorganized itself into a professional organization, and individual players presented a new antitrust case against the NFL's Plan B, a plan that gave teams a right of first refusal for players seeking free agency (Riess, 2017). After the antitrust case against the NFL, the owners eventually settled by granting free agency. The players then accepted a "hard" salary cap based on 64% of total team revenues. Then in 1993, the NFLPA reorganized and rebranded itself as a labor union. It was then that the NFLPA entered a new contract and "a new collective bargaining agreement" (Riess, 2017). In 2011, following a brief summer strike, a new 10-year agreement made it possible for football players to receive 47% of all revenue. However, a limit was placed on rookie salaries. The agreement also stated that the league would provide $50 million for medical research.

In addition to the medical research fund, owners pledged approximately $1 billion for the retirement of professional football players. Today, the NFL has 32 teams located throughout the United States in nearly all the leading television markets, reflecting the major role of its national television contract in producing huge profits.

Perhaps the NFL's greatest current problem is the number of players who suffered and suffer from concussions and other head blows leading to chronic traumatic encephalopathy and, ultimately, memory loss, depression, dementia, and even suicide. As of 2015, 199 players have been diagnosed with concussions. In 2010, the NFL introduced rules to promote safer play. Rules that were considered to promote safer play included a ban on the use of helmets against defenseless players, stopping the clock and play when a helmet came off a player's head, and moving the kickoff to the 35-yard line to reduce the number of kickoff returns. Retired and approximately 4,500 former players, along with their families, sued the NFL in 2011 for damages. The NFL settled the lawsuit for $765 million in 2013, but the plaintiffs filed an appeal in 2016.

The National Hockey League

At the turn of the century, historical records show us that ice hockey was a popular sport in Canada, but only in a few locations here in America in the late 19th century. Jack "Doc" Gibson founded the Portage Lakers (Michigan) in 1904 now known as the first professional hockey team. One year later, Gibson established the first professional hockey association, the International Hockey League. In 1904, our culture saw hockey teams appear in the Upper Peninsula of Michigan (Calumet, Houghton, and Sault Ste. Marie), Pittsburgh, and Sault Ste. Marie (Ontario).

Six years later, in 1909, the National Hockey Association (NHA) was founded by railroad mogul Michael J. O'Brien and his son Ambrose. In 1911, Frank and Lester Patrick established the Pacific Coast Hockey League. Lester Patrick then expanded the hockey league, placing teams in Portland (1914), Seattle (1915), and Spokane (1916). Before the 1917–1918 season, Montreal, Ottawa, and Quebec quit the NHA to form the NHL.

According to American history records, by 1926, there were four Canadian and six U.S. teams, including the "Bruins, Chicago Black Hawks, Detroit Cougars (the future Red Wings), New York Rangers, New York Americans, and Pittsburgh Pirates" (Riess, 2017), whose owners were associated with their city's sports arenas. The new teams paid a $15,000 fee to join the NHL, and they played a 44-game season and relied mostly on gate receipts for revenue, which mainly went to the home team. The "Original Six" hockey franchises were "the Boston Bruins, Chicago Blackhawks, Detroit Red Wings, Montreal Canadians, New York Rangers and Toronto Maple Leafs" (Riess, 2017). With the advent of mass media, the NHL games were broadcast over radio and on CBS-TV from 1956 through 1960. By the 1960s, several cities were enticing NHL franchises to their cities to promote their cities. As a result, the NHL added six new teams in 1961 and then six more U.S. teams between 1970 and 1974.

In the early 1970s, the NHL took a very proactive role in promoting the sport internationally. The NHL was perceived as the defender of the free world in competitions against the Soviet Union, beginning with the 1971 Summit Series in which the NHL All-Stars topped the Soviets by a narrow 4-3-1 margin. NHL hockey players and owners were by nature conservative, and a player's union was not formed until late 1967. Under the leadership of Alan Eagleson, the National Hockey League Players' Association was created. Eagleson tried to maintain a close, conciliatory relationship with the league owners, but players wanted a more aggressive leader. Players felt that their salaries and risky, dangerous working conditions were significantly far behind the salaries and working conditions that players involved in other team sports received. In 1991, Eagleson retired and was replaced by Detroit lawyer and player agent Bob Goodenow. As a top decision maker, Goodenow did what players wanted Eagleson to do: he pursued an aggressive agenda on behalf of the players. One year later, the union chose to strike over salaries and marketing rights for players' images on merchandise. The collective bargaining agreement ended in 2003, and with that closure, the NHL union, as well as the owners, were also ready for a change. Players' salaries averaged $1.5 million, and owners began blaming players for the league's financial pains. The dispute ended with the owners introducing a salary cap and pulling back on rising wages. The average NHL salary is currently $2.62 million.

Professional Basketball and the Rise of the National Basketball League

Basketball was invented in 1891 (first game on December 21, 1891) by Dr. James Naismith at the YMCA College in Springfield, Massachusetts. It was Dr. Naismith's desire to create a sport that was physically challenging to play indoors during the winter. By 1898, the six-team National League of Professional Basketball was formed in metropolitan Philadelphia, and it lasted six years. Players earned about $5 per game. Scores during the games were very low, and the sport was so physical that some owners were forced to install steel metal cages around the courts.

In 1937, the 13-team National Basketball League was established, like the early NFL, by small businessmen, local boosters, and industrial firms in small and midsized Midwestern cities who played in high schools and other small arenas. Players were mostly college graduates who worked for the corporate sponsors. In 1926, the Harlem Globetrotters, an all-black basketball team, entered the scene. From what is known about their history, we learn that they "began as the Savoy Big Five, one of the premier attractions of the Savoy Ballroom which opened in November 1927" (Smith, 2018). They were originally billed as a "basketball team of African-American players that played exhibitions before dances" (Mertz, 2000; Robinson, 2006).

Historical accounts tell us that Abe Saperstein, "a leading figure in black basketball and baseball in the 1920s, 30s, 40s, and 50s, primarily before those sports were racially integrated, soon became involved with the team as its manager and promoter" (Davis, 2005). Saperstein (portrayed in Figure 1.7) is also credited with introducing "the three-point shot, which went on to become a

FIGURE 1.7   *1950 World Series Harlem Globetrotters with owner Abe Saperstein (right) and team secretary W. S. Welch (left)*

mainstay of modern basketball today" (Davis, 2005; Mertz, 2000; Robinson, 2006). In 1926, the Harlem Globetrotters began playing basketball in Chicago, Illinois and were called the "Savory Big Five," named after the Savoy Ballroom where games were played). In late 1927, Saperstein changed the name from the "Savoy Big Five" to "the Harlem Globetrotters" because all the players were African-American and it was common knowledge that Harlem was predominantly African-American neighborhood (Robinson, 2006).

Why Harlem? It was stated that Saperstein considered Harlem to be the "center of African-American culture at the time" (Davis, 2005). It was also assumed that there was a certain mystique that came with a team from "out-of-town" (Davis, 2005). Fun fact: research shows that it took almost four decades after the team originated before they played in Harlem in 1968 (Davis, 2005; Mertz, 2000; Robinson, 2006).

History tells us that the Globetrotters were persistent competitors in the "World Professional Basketball Tournament, winning the championship in 1940" (Mertz, 2000; Robinson, 2006). Then, in 1948, the Globetrotters played the Lakers, and it was this game that put the Globetrotters in the national news headlines. This sporting event became historic in that it was the first time that an all-black basketball team defeated one of the "best white basketball teams in the country, the Minneapolis Lakers (now known as the Los Angeles Lakers)" (Mertz, 2000; Robinson, 2006). Not until 1941 did the Harlem Globetrotters start taking their basketball talents and making them comedy routines. It was a player known as "Goose" whose comedic talents took the team into the entertainment realm of the game. Reece "Goose" Tatum, who joined the Globetrotters in 1941, fused basketball skills with comedy, and these two factors propelled the team into a world of celebrity and fame that made them known more for entertainment than sports. In 1950, research shows that NBA teams started recruiting and seeking African American players. Then a Harlem Globetrotters player known as Chuck Cooper became the first black player to be drafted in the NBA by Boston (Mertz, 2000; Robinson, 2006).

The early NBA game was not as heavily attended or as popular as the top college games. In the early days, the NBA had to rely on doubleheaders that featured the Harlem Globetrotters just so that they could attract fans. One possible explanation for the decrease in attendance were the 1951 National Collegiate Athletic Association (NCAA) betting scandals. The scandals severely wounded attendance at the college games, and fans began giving more attention to professional games. The NBA also began to receive more publicity through national television coverage.

In 1954, it was decided that one way to make the game more fan friendly was to increase scoring. The 24-second shot clock was also introduced to prevent teams from stalling. Another fan-friendly strategy was to institute new penalties to stop excessive fouling. The fouling team was penalized after the seventh violation by allowing the opposing team to take a foul shot, plus a second foul shot if they made the first, or three chances to make two if fouled.

By the late 1950s, the NBA integrated by adding several superstar black players to their roster. The players included Bill Russell of the Boston Celtics, Elgin Baylor of the Minneapolis Lakers, Wilt Chamberlain of the Philadelphia Warriors, and Oscar Robertson with the Cincinnati Royals. The quality of play and the athleticism of players in the NBA during this time also increased.

The American Basketball Association (ABA), organized in 1967 by advertising executives, emerged and became a huge rival for the 10 cities in which the NBA teams were housed. The ABA's owners thought that interest in professional basketball spread beyond the NBA's 10 cities. They believed that their 11-team league had many more attractive players, such as Julius "Dr. J" Erving, and that those players would also attract fans.

The rise of the ABA provided an opportunity for the National Basketball Players Association (NBPA) to fight the NBA's monopolistic control. The NBPA's first accomplished action happened in 1964 when players at the All-Star Game refused to participate unless the owners agreed to concrete concessions. As a result, a pension plan was created for players in 1965. Two years later, the NBPA was able to secure raises for the players, primarily because they threatened to strike. By 1970, players also received a minimum salary, medical insurance, severance pay, first-class air travel, and accommodations at five-star hotels. In 1975, average salaries jumped from $18,000 in 1965 to $110,000.

In 1978, the NBA signed a 4-year, $74 million contract with CBS (Riess, 2014). By the early '80s, the NBA consisted of more than 75% players of African American descent. This statistic led some of the NBA owners to be highly concerned that their white fans would be intimidated and alienated by the predominance of black players and fans. However, despite this concern, fans flocked to the games, and the NBA became more popular than ever. Some historians believe the instant popularity was incited by the rivalry between Larry Bird's Celtics and "Magic" Johnson's Lakers (Riess, 2017).

The era of prosperity can also be attributed in large measure to Commissioner David Stern, who took over when 17 of 23 teams were losing money. Stern promoted and negotiated greater television coverage and convinced the NBPA to accept a salary cap. Stern was also able to convince the owners to accept a revenue-sharing system with players so that they could maintain equality among teams. In addition, Stern created marketing and promotions campaigns that emphasized superstars of the league. An example of this strategy is the legendary icon Michael Jordan. Jordan is said to have "led the Chicago Bulls to six NBA titles between 1991 and 1998" (Riess, 2014). As a result of these strategies and others involving expansion to international countries, NBA revenue rose 500% during Stern's tenure. The average NBA player made $4.58 million.

The most successful women's pro sport team is in basketball. The first league started in 1997 and consisted of the eight teams of the Women's National Basketball League (WNBA; Heath, 2006; Sandomir, 2003). Teams were affiliated, at that time, with local NBA teams. As of this writing, there are 12 WNBA teams. The professional women's basketball games have been televised on ESPN since the league began in 1997.

Soccer in the United States

Founded in 1996, Major League Soccer is seeing massive profits playing in soccer-specific stadiums. Research shows that there are 20 teams whose average value is approximately $153 million.

Scholarly Study of Sport History

Anyone interested in the scholarly study of sports history should begin by reviewing the literature in Steven Riess's *A Companion to American Sports History* (2017), which includes chapters on baseball, football, basketball, race, ethnicity, social class, business, media, stadiums, and biographies.

Twenty years ago, Stephen Hardy urged historians to examine the special nature of the industry of sport and study the game form along with the types of sporting organizations they created—namely, teams that played in cartelized associations. Historians have given considerable attention to racism in professional sports. Much of the scholarly work in this area focuses primarily on African Americans in sports. Some scholars have examined the business of blacks in baseball, while others seek to understand the role of sports in fulfilling the entertainment motives and needs of growing black communities. Other scholars study the profitability of black sport, focusing specifically on the late 1930s and early 1940s (i.e., Neil Lanctot). Those interested in the history of baseball should review Jules Tygiel's (1983) classic book, *Baseball's Baseball's Great Experiment: Jackie Robinson and His Legacy*.

In this book, Tygiel (1983) elucidates the role of journalists and civil rights activists, the effect of World War II, and the appearance of Negro Leaguers in the maturation of the sport. Tygiel (1983) also centers his work on the actions of Dodger president Branch Rickey in breaking the color line, as well as the courage of Jackie Robinson in combating prejudice. Tygiel's (1983) book is important in understanding the history of baseball because it provides a record of the slow process by which MLB teams integrated, even after the great success of early black pioneers. Historians Adrian Burgos (2007) and Samuel Regalado (2013) have also written about similar baseball players who are known in history books as baseball's pioneers. Burgos (2014) and Regalado (2013) chronicle the entrance of Latino ballplayers who encountered bigotry in a foreign land, exacerbated for many who carried the double burden as black and Latino. Little to no attention has been given to women professional athletes and their leagues. As we will discuss later in this book, women athletes and their accomplishments barely made a dent in the American sports media world.

Primary Sources for More on the History of Team Sports

While this chapter does not begin to do justice to the history of team sports in America, those interested in studying the history of professional team sports can find published collections of primary sources, beginning with four edited volumes of the series Sports in America: A Documentary History, including George B. Kirsch's *Sports in War, Revival and Expansion* 1860, 1880; Gerald R. Gems's *Sports Organized*, 1880–1900; Steven A. Riess's *Sports in the Progressive Era*, 1900–1920; and Douglas O. Baldwin's *Sports in the Depression*, 1930–1940. A superb collection of documents on baseball can be found in Dean A. Sullivan's four-volume *A Documentary History of Baseball*. For documents in black sports history, see David K. Wiggins and Patrick B. Miller, eds., *The Unlevel Playing Field: A Documentary History of the African American Experience in Sport*.

Digitized Internet sources are invaluable for historians and scholars interested in major professional team sports. The textbook author used many of those sources to gather the basic historical review for this chapter. For example, baseball-reference.com is an excellent and definitive source of data on the statistical accomplishments of major league players, including advanced sabermetrics and salary data. There is much information on current and former major league and minor league teams. Similar sources exist for pro football, hockey, and basketball. Websites maintained by individuals include considerable and valuable primary data, including Doug Pappas, longtime Society for American Baseball Research Business of Baseball committee chairman, who collected data on the baseball business.

The Psychology of Sport

Sports psychologists study behaviors regarding attributes that exist inside individuals. The psychology of sports centers on motivations, perceptions, self-esteem, self-confidence, attitudes, values, affects, cognitions, and behaviors. The psychology of sports deals with the communication of certain ideals and the social influences on how these attributes affect individuals. Sports psychologists ask questions, such as, "How does the media affect individual athlete's cognitions, behaviors, perceptions, and self-esteem?" They focus on the culture that exists outside and around groups, and on how people use sports to give meaning to their lives.

Research in this book will focus on the social meanings of sports that may be associated with age, social class, gender, race, able-bodies, sexuality, and media. Research and information will focus on the experiences and problems of groups of individuals and the issues that affect persons of color; male and female athletes; lesbian, gay, bisexual, transgender, queer (LGBTQ) individuals;

and adolescents. We will review the organization of media and the relationships between media and athletes and sports. Hopefully, after finishing this book on race, gender, sports, and media, readers will be prepared to engage in the following behaviors:

Think critically about the relationship between sports and media so that you can evaluate and understand the issues and controversies associated with the interactive role that media and sports play in bringing about ideals, attitudes, and behaviors toward athletes and the sports they participate in. See the role that media play in creating social constructions of reality that have both positive and negative effects on Americans. Understand media's role in shaping our ideals and the understanding of sports that leads you to view particular athletes and sporting events/activities in a particular manner.

Why Sports Is Important in American Culture

Sports, as we have learned, have become deeply embedded in our American culture. Superstar, home run, and slam dunks are all clichés or phrases with meanings that are often used both in sports and in our day-to-day conversations. Language, norms, behaviors, opinions, values, and other elements of culture all have some influence on how we participate, spectate, or perceive sports in American culture. We know that "halls of fame" or other versions of ways to honor our athletes can be found in all major sports at the professional, college, and high school levels. Museums and other halls exist, as we know, to worship sports, worship the athletes who excelled in their sport, and help us record and chronicle the actions of sports heroes. Sports stars are lifted to role model status in terms of how they are perceived by young, impressionable teens in our society (Adair, 2015; Dadigan, 2016; Ireland, 2016; Ziemer, 2000). The role model status happens whether the athlete wants to be one or not. A national study examined kids' perceptions of athletes' behavior both on and off the field. The study not on revealed that young kids report learning lessons about sports and life from watching and emulating behaviors of famous athletes (Adair; 2015; Ziemer, 2000). At higher educational institutions, we know that athletics is a multimillion-dollar-a-year enterprise and a major profit-generating institution. For example, it is widely known that every university or college that makes it to the NCAA Basketball Tournament receives a half-million dollars per game.

Higher educational institutions and athletes are unrelentingly intertwined. Athletics, especially those successful programs, can gain national recognition for higher educational institutions. Most athletic directors and presidents are closely involved in the hiring of coaches. As we will discuss throughout this textbook, we will soon discover that sports have an important and intense relationship in our culture. Sports are related to many cultural elements, which include education, extracurricular and leisure-time activities, social status, social mobility, sexuality, race, and gender issues.

Significance of Sports in Society

Media invests much of its resources in sports coverage. For example, newspapers will devote at least a quarter of its pages to sports. Within many major newspapers, sports staffs are often very large and may be as heavily staffed as news staffs are at other papers. Businesses spend a lot of their profits on sports, spending that includes financial contributions, advertising, promotions, and buying ownership of some professional teams. Many companies might even sponsor professional and college sports teams. For example, consider the major college football games; corporate companies underwrite many of these events. Many if not most of the football bowl games are named after corporate sponsors.

Major cities spend millions of dollars on sports stadiums for the exclusive use of major league teams. They may even use the promise of building bigger and better stadiums to lure teams to their cities. Later in this text, we devote a chapter to the discussion of the effect of professional teams and their movement from city to city. We will unpack the claim that these promises and arrangements are beneficial to the local economy by adding jobs and encouraging tourists to visit the city.

The History of the "National Anthem" and Sports

If we carefully study the ritual of standing and singing during the national anthem, we would learn that "The Star-Spangled Banner" is not a required ritual or act for many other public gatherings in America (Bologna, 2018). For example, in the entertainment industry, the anthem is not played nor are we asked to stand and fix our eyes on the flag when we attend movies, go to musical concerts, ballet and other dance performances, award shows, Broadway shows, key note lectures or other venues related to entertainment. Since sports is often associated with entertainment, why is that the national anthem is performed during sporting events and few, if any other, entertainment events?

The "Star-Spangled Banner" was inspired by victory in war. It was the result of the mere sight of the flag still waving at sunrise. The song was declared America's national anthem in 1889 when President Woodrow Wilson signed the executive order. "On July 27, 1889, Secretary of the Navy Benjamin F. Tracy signed General Order #374, making 'The Star-Spangled Banner' the official tune to be played at the raising of t; he flag" (Bologna, 2018; Little, 2017). It was reported that during WWI, a bomb had exploded in Chicago, (the city in which a championship baseball game was held), killing four people and injuring at least twelve others (Little 2017).

Then one day after the event in Chicago happened, it was during the World Series, when an impromptu recital of the song happened during the seventh inning. It was the World Series game between the Chicago Cubs and the Boston Red Sox. What was interesting to learn was the fact that they used the national anthem to get the fans to "wake up," yawn, and stretch. It was a smaller-than-usual crowd that day of the Championship game. But something happened that changed everything. It was during the seventh-inning when the U.S. Naval band started playing the anthem. While fans were already standing during the seventh inning for their "afternoon yawn" and were already standing when the orchestra started playing, a member of the armed services was standing at attention with his eyes set on the flag at the top of the lofty pole in right field. Players and fans alike turned to the flag and placed their hands over hearts and began to sing. When the song was over, the presumed tired and bored fans were said to have "erupted in thunderous applause" (Little 2017). At the time, the New York Times reported that it "marked the highest point of the day's enthusiasm" (Little, 2017). The song would be played at each of the Series' remaining games, to increasingly rapturous response. We were at war, and the song inspired the crowd for a hopeful victory.

Red Sox owner Harry Frazee planned something he said was "special" when the series shifted to Boston. Frazee, "hired a band to play 'The Star-Spangled Banner' before all three games at Fenway Park" (Landers, 2017). It was stated that the more the band played, the more the crowds kept loving it. And that is how the tradition of performing the anthem before every game was born. The now controversial anthem (we will discuss this later in the text) is believed to be a song that celebrates our First Amendment rights with lyrics that force us to remember that our country is based on freedoms. The "Star-Spangled Banner" and its history with sports is focused on victory and the fact that others fought for our freedoms during World War I and World War II.

Currently in 2019, a major controversy has erupted over whether or not players are allowed to sit or kneel during the national anthem. Some Americans, including our current President, find kneeling offensive, claiming it is disrespectful to those who serve in the U.S. military; while others believe that the protest is why we celebrate living in American; the U.S. and our right to free speech should guarantee players to have the ability to protest in whatever manner they choose.

Although the national anthem first started in 1918 during baseball games and was played consistently after that event, playing the anthem before the start of baseball season was the American standard. Once American entered into World War II, the National Anthem began being played before the start of the National Football League also included the playing of the anthem before games. According to an article titled, "*The history of singing the national anthem before NFL games*," written by Kight (2017), we learn that in 1945, Elmer Layden, the then-commissioner of the NFL, went on record saying "The playing of the national anthem should be as much a part of every game as the kickoff. We must not drop it simply because the war is over. We should never forget what it stands for."

Interesting, though, is the historical data that shows from 1945 to 2008, NFL players would stay in their locker rooms during the national anthem, before the start of games. And, it was not until 2009 when "NFL players began standing on the field for the national anthem before the start of primetime games" (Kight, 2017). In 2015, Senators John McCain and Jeff Flake released a report revealing that the Department of Defense had spent $6.8 million between 2012 and 2015 on what the senators called "paid patriotism" events before professional sports games, including American flag displays, honoring of military members, reenlistment ceremonies, etc. The DoD justified the money paid to 50 professional sports teams by calling it part of their recruiting strategy. However, many teams had these ceremonies without compensation from the military, and there was nothing found in the contracts that mandated that players stand during the anthem.

Today, the national anthem is performed before the beginning of all special occasions (i.e., graduation ceremonies). Many feel that the mere repetition of the national anthem played before every game and event actually oversaturates and lessens its impact and patriotic effect (Steinberg, 2006). Currently, the national anthem is performed before "all MLS, NBA, NFL, MLB, and NHL games (when there is at least one American team playing), as well as in a pre-race ceremony portion of every NASCAR race" (Steinberg, 2016). For international sporting competitions, such as the Olympics, we find anthems from every participating country performed after athletes who come from those country win medals. Interestingly, the NHL requires a performance of both Canadian and American anthems to be played before games. In MLB, it is also common now for American and Canadian anthems to be performed before all games that involve the only Canadian MLB team.

Perhaps the win-win solution might be saving the national anthem for American events that honor war veterans. Events and holidays such as the fourth of July, Veteran's Day, the presidential inauguration, and Memorial Day, coupled with frequent published media stories designed to educate and publish the history of the anthem, may perhaps encourage Americans to switch their focus from sports to the meaning and purpose of the song, and the role it should play in our lives (Steinberg, 2016). Historical archives tell us that the words/lyrics in "The Star-Spangled Banner" were written by Francis Scott Key, who wrote the first verse after being held by the British. Mr. Key, according to history, looked out over the fort he was being held in thinking he would see the opponents flag flying high in the sky, but instead saw the red, white, and blue banner proudly flying. It was at this point that the writer of the song realized that the Americans won the war and were brave (Alchin, 2014).

In his article, published on the Undefeated website, author Martenzie Johnson (2016) wrote the following with respect to the origin of the national anthem and the meaning of the lyrics. "After witnessing 25 hours of combat—And the rocket's red glare!/The bombs bursting in air!—Key assumed the Americans had lost, but was then elated to see the Stars and Stripes still flying the next morning at Fort McHenry." We also find from our research that the song's author had an extensive history with slaves. According to historical records, Key was frequently advocating the idea to send freed blacks (not his slaves) back on boats to Africa (Johnson, 2016). Key was known to be very proslavery, antiblack, and an "anti-abolitionist." In fact, if we conduct research, we would learn that

Francis Ford Key actually owned hundreds of slaves while he was writing the four verses to the "Star-Spangled Banner." He owned slaves while writing the national anthem, at one point referred to blacks as "a distinct and inferior race of people."

America honors war. Our country honors sports. Moreover, and more importantly, our country values winning and competition. It seems that any song that is deemed a national anthem should be one that "symbolizes" and honors all people and the rights and freedoms of all. As we can tell from the brief history of the national anthem and its purpose, we find that it clearly was not written to honor veterans. Perhaps our national anthem might be "I am proud to be an American where at least I know I am free." According to research (several historical publications on the subject), "The Star-Spangled Banner" is not a patriotic song that reflects the rights and liberties of all U.S. citizens, their cultural, religions, and lifestyles, nor is it a song that affirms and honors the rights and liberties that this country holds sacred.

Sports and the Media

Sports generates identifiable target audiences that can be sold to advertisers seeking consumers with specific needs, desires, and wants for products and services. Sports media offer advertisers a means of meeting consumer needs by attracting worldwide attention (i.e., the Super Bowl). Sports media can also offer a means by which sports and athletes can be presented in certain ways by creating brand images that ultimately link the sport and athlete with products, values, and lifestyles related to American culture.

Importantly, media is a male-dominated industry. Thus masculine culture (i.e., hegemony) is not only evident in sports media but also deeply embedded in media corporations. It can be argued that masculinity is deeply embedded in sports media and the institution of sports; it is possible that the interplay of these two forces reaffirms the legitimacy of masculinized values, attitudes, and opinions.

Sports coverage consists of exaggerations overcoming injuries, heroic achievements, socially constructed rivalries, and or crimes or events that media deem important. Media strive to create and maintain "celebrity" of athletes and teams, and will create villains and heroes for the sake of perpetuating beliefs about athletes and their identities. Research suggests that most people accept distorted images and coverages, and often will not challenge traditional stereotypes presented in media. Thus it is important to study media to determine why and how images and messages found in sports media shape the lives of the American people. Media and mediated ideas have become ever present in the lives of American people. This is why it is important to study the relationship between sports and the media. The media represent sports to us through images and messages that usually reaffirm our stereotypes and promote ideas of masculinity, femininity, and restrictive gender roles. Later in the book, we will explore the way new media, such as social media, video games, and virtual sports, may complement messages found in traditional sports media.

Controversies in Sport

Research in the area of race, gender, media, and sports provides evidence that there are areas that are in need of change, particularly regarding the way media represent groups and the emphasis given to some sports over others. Media gatekeepers and decision makers often avoid making changes for fear that the changes will jeopardize profits. For example, when asked why newspapers do not feature female athletes on the front pages, we often hear "women athletes, and their sport just doesn't sell papers." This example shows how editors, producers, and journalists often prefer approaches that are aligned with their presuppositions, allow them to blame stereotypes and the creation of stereotypes on weaknesses and failures of individuals or groups, and enable them to oppose and reject the need for change, particularly regarding increased coverage of female athletes.

Listed next are just a few of the controversies in sports centered around race, age, politics, sexual orientation, and gender:

- Most sports programs and sports media are organized around the values, interests, attitudes, opinions, and experiences of men.

- Cases of exclusion in sports media and sports organizations are related to gender, sexuality, skin color, ethnicity, able-body, age and weight, and physical attractiveness of female athletes.

- Differences in social class and wealth are highlighted by wealthy people being able to engage in sports that lower-income people are not afforded access to.

- Skin color and race often influence the type and frequency of media coverage and define athletic ability, leadership, and other talents.

- The emphasis of the role of LGBTQ individuals playing alongside heterosexuals and fair treatment by team players and sports media.

- Should transgender athletes experience different treatment than hetereosexual athletes? Should athletes identifying as transgender be able to fully participate in a sport?

- Are there differences in how athletes living with physical and mental challenges are presented in media?

- Disparities in the diversity of owners of professional teams is disconcerting. Why and what can be done to close the gap?

- Are their media disparities in sports coverage between able-bodied athletes and those dealing or living with mental and/or physical challenges? It is believed that media must do a better job covering and emphasizing Paralympic Games (aka "Special Olympics").

- American culture values and places excessive meaning in to the body in sports and also pay closer attention to the athlete's body and body image, particularly if the athlete is female.

- Uncovering the real problem with kneeling during the National Anthem and the role that professional athletes should play in societal conflict. In other words, should athletes be prohibited from using their voice to speak out about injustices or share their faith?

- Several disagreements among the role that politics, religion, and conflicts in customs and traditions should in American culture are also controversial topics in sports.

On the Need for Equitable Coverage

In terms of asking for equitable coverage, we need to define what is meant by this concept. One way we define equitable coverage is by stating that equity does not mean we want an equal number of images and articles on male and female sports and their athletes. When we talk of equitable coverage, we talk about achieving equity through news coverage and representations of female athletes as powerful and talented—basically asking reporters to cover them in the same way they do male athletes (see Fink & Kensicki, 2002).

When referring to equitable coverage in the media, we are focused on equivalent frequency and presentation of all types of athletes and all sports in mainstream media and other venues that garner large audiences. For coverage to be equitable, we should find the number of female athletes who participate in masculine sports, such as basketball, wrestling, boxing, soccer, or rugby, to be covered in major media at the same frequency as those stories about male athletes participating in the same competitive sports. We should also have mediated stories and mass coverage of female *and* male athletes who participate in feminine sports, such as gymnastics, synchronized swimming, cheerleading, and dance (see Kane, 1996). In addition to equity in the number of times a story appears that focuses on male and female athletes and the sports they participate in, we must also consider equity in the way the stories are covered. Research shows that not only are women's sports placed in the background or appear as afterthoughts in media but also disparities in the quality of the stories are apparent and often trivialized (Grappendorf, Henderson, Sanders, & Peel, 2007).

We know from research that in terms of women's sports and athletes, data confirms that most media coverage of female athletes and their sports includes information that relates to the marginalization, objectification, or the sexualization of female athletes (Eastman & Billings, 2000; Frisby, 2017a; Frisby, 2017b; Grappendorf et al., 2007; Messner, Duncan, & Jensen, 1993). As researchers continue to investigate disparities in coverage, we know that much work still needs to be done. With respect to athletes living with physical and mental disabilities, women, athletes of color, various sports that are deemed gender inappropriate, and other marginalized groups, many positive steps have been made but more need to be taken before we can say with confidence that all athletes and all sports are receiving equitable coverage. Sports media and the journalists who write stories for these media must begin considering the notion that when we speak of wanting more "equitable sports coverage," we are referring to equality in terms of writing, producing, and publishing information about athletes and their sports—information that is factual and that takes the same perspective regardless of gender or race. When journalists make equity in coverage a priority, they will soon realize that this simply means that we must begin to write from a human-interest perspective.

Conclusion

Acknowledgment of the lack of focus on sports media must be the first action that media professionals work on to correct disparities among athletes. For sports media to move forward, journalists need to focus their efforts on increasing the frequency of images of female athletes who appear on their covers. Efforts should also be taken to increase the representation and portrayals of female athletes in their designated uniform in lieu of scantily clad apparel. Positive images of female athletes in uniforms and active shots of their performance during their sport can be used to change current perceptions that women, and namely female athletes, must be sexualized and objectified, as well as attractive, to gain attention from the media (Frisby, 2017).

A recent study conducted by Daniels (2012) suggests that images of female athletes play a significant role in the way girls think about women's athletics, female athletes, and themselves. "Researchers interested in sports journalism and mass media should study the facts that are responsible for the resistance in our culture and in sports journalism to improve the depiction of female athletes as the athletes that they are, as well as the overall coverage of female sports" (Frisby, 2017).

QUESTIONS FOR REFLECTION AND DISCUSSION

Use the following questions as a guide for your discussion about the history of sports in American culture.

1. How do you think media portray athletes? Male athletes? Female athletes? Are portrayals positive? Negative? Neutral/objective? Explain.

2. Some argue that professional female athletes receive less coverage than their male counterparts. Do you agree or disagree? Why or why not? What about major international sporting events, such as the Olympic Games? What do you think about the coverage in these instances?

3. If sports journalism attracted more female journalists, would that facilitate a more equitable and balanced coverage? Why or why not?

4. How would the "average" American describe an athlete? Male? Female?

5. How many of your favorite sports are masculine sports? Feminine sports? Which gender had a higher proportion of athletes? Explain your own personal findings.

6. Whose beliefs and ideas about sports and athletes come to be accepted as the "right" and correct ideas?

7. How can sports media create equitable coverage and include those marginalized sports and athletes? Write a news or magazine article that promotes a sport that is excluded and a group of athletes who receive minimal media coverage.

8. How can sports media gatekeepers and decision makers revise decisions they make about the sports that should be represented in media?

9. Which group(s) do media emphasize, and do you think it is based on social class? Why or why not?

10. What ideas do media communicate about natural, ideal, and deviant bodies in sports and athletes? Give examples.

11. How are athletes and their bodies represented in sports media? Moreover, how do those representations influence the self-esteem of the reader, self-confidence, stereotypes toward body image, and our own identities?

12. How are bodies in sports media portrayed regarding gender, skin color, ethnicity, age, and ability? Review examples of athletes and the news stories of coverage related to the athlete's body (e.g., Serena Williams).

13. What notions of beauty and physical attractiveness are presented in sports media, and what do these ideas tell us about our American culture and the emphasis on youth, health, beauty, and culture?

14. Can a law like Title IX create gender equity? Why or why not? What about sports such as dance and cheerleading?

15. Why are some sports activities and not others selected and emphasized in sports media?

16. How do sports media affect your ideas about bodies, masculinity and femininity, social class, race, ability, achievement, and aggression and violence, particularly regarding athletes?

17. Do male athletes objectify themselves in female media to sell products? Why do you think women are depicted more in sexual ways than male athletes? Does the status quo make it all right? Why or why not?

18. How can sports journalists use knowledge about stereotypes, racism, sexism, and ageism to communicate positive understanding and act as change agents in the controversies associated with sports?

19. How do journalists use their experiences and knowledge about sports in news stories?

SUGGESTED ACTIVITIES

1. Make a list of female athletes who have been portrayed in media in their uniforms and describe them using similar attributes that are used to describe male athletes.

2. Flip through the pages of a magazine targeted toward women. Compare it to a magazine targeted toward men. Is there a difference in how the women are portrayed in the publications? Replicate this process using sports magazines this time. Is there much difference in how female athletes are portrayed in the publications? Now replicate the aforementioned using printed news stories? Are the stories similar? How are female athletes portrayed? How are male athletes portrayed? How are black male athletes portrayed?

3. Who are the most influential and celebrated athletes in sports media today? What cues can you find in the media that make them important? What cues or ideas are found in the stories that support the idea that this is a celebrated athlete?

4. Do a comparison of sports websites such as ESPN and Sports Illustrated. Analyze the landing/home pages. How are these sports sites using words, images, and photographs of athletes to reach and appeal to the reader?

5. Compare and contrast the way female athletes are presented in a variety of media. How do the portrayals vary? Do you see different manifestations or versions of the differences in attributes and stereotypes? What similarities do you see in how athletes are portrayed? How are male athletes portrayed?

6. Provide examples of media coverage of male athletes participating in feminine sports, such as gymnastics. Did you find many news stories related to gender-appropriate sports and the athletes who participate in those sports? What do you think about your findings?

7. List your sports heroes. What qualities attract you to them?

DIGITAL AND ONLINE RESOURCES

1. baseball-reference.com
2. basketball-reference.com
3. chroniclingamerica.loc.gov
4. football-reference.com
5. hockey-reference.com
6. "Sports in America," https://usa.usembassy.de/sports.htm
7. "History of Sports in the United States," https://en.wikipedia.org/wiki/History_of_sports_in_the_United_States
8. History of Sports, www.historyofsports.info/sports_in_usa.html
9. "The Bizarre History of American Sport," https://www.si.com/vault/1962/01/08/590449/the-bizarre-history-of-american-sport
10. *Encyclopedia of Sports in America*: A History from Foot Races to Extreme Sports, https://www.abc-clio.com/ABC-CLIOCorporate/product.aspx?pc=B6271C

SUPPLEMENTAL READINGS

Acosta, R. V., & Carpenter, L. J. (2008). *Women in intercollegiate sport: A longitudinal, national study thirty-one-year update 1977–2008.* Retrieved from http://webpages.charter.net/womeninsport/2008%20Summary%20Final.pdf

Bellamy, R. V., & Walker, J. R. (2008). *Center field shot: A history of baseball on television.* Lincoln, NE: University of Nebraska Press.

Billings, A. C., & Eastman, S. T. (2002). Gender, ethnicity, and nationality: Formation of identity in NBC's 2000 Olympic coverage. *International Review for the Sociology of Sport, 37*(3), 349–368.

Billings, A. C., & Eastman, S. (2003). Framing identities: Gender, ethnic, and national parity in network announcing of the 2002 Winter Olympics. *Journal of Communication, 53*(4), 569–586.

Billings, A. C., Halone, K. K., & Denham, B. E. (2002). "Man, that was a pretty shot": An analysis of gendered broadcast commentary surrounding the 2000 men's and women's NCAA final four basketball championships. *Mass Communication and Society, 5*(3), 295–315.

Bissell, K., & Holt, A. (2006). *Who's got game? Gender bias in coverage of the 2004 Olympic Games on the web.* Paper presented at the annual meeting of the International Communication Association, New York, NY. Retrieved from http://www.allacademic.com/meta/p14267_index.html

Burk, R. F. (2002). *Much more than a game: Players, owners and American baseball since 1921.* Chapel Hill, NC: University of North Carolina Press.

Chernoff, H., & Lehmann E. L. (1954). The use of maximum likelihood estimates in 2 tests for goodness-of-fit. *The Annals of Mathematical Statistics, 50*, 579–586.

Coenen, C. R. (2005). *From sandlots to the Super Bowl: The National Football League, 1920–1967.* Knoxville, TN: University of Tennessee Press.

ComScore Network. (2005, June 2). *The score: Sports sites score.* iMedia. Retrieved from http://www.imediaconnection.com/content/6027.asp

Creapeau, R. (2014). *NFL Football: A history of America's new national pastime.* Urbana, IL: University of Illinois.

Cunningham, G. B. (2003). Media coverage of women's sport: A new look at an old problem. *Physical Educator, 60*(2), 43–50.

Cunningham, G., Sagas, M., Satore, M., Amsden, M., & Schellhas, A. (2004). Gender representation in the NCAA News: Is the glass half empty or half full? *Sex Roles, 50*(5/6), 861–870.

Danielson, M. N. (1997). *HomeTeam: Professional sports and the American metropolis.* Princeton, NJ: Princeton University Press.

Davies, R. O. (2012). *Sports in American life: A history.* West Sussex, UK: Wiley-Blackwell.

Duncan, M., & Messner, M. (2000). *Gender stereotyping in televised sports: 1989, 1993, and 1999.* Los Angeles, CA: Amateur Athletic Foundation of Los Angeles.

Duncan, M., Messner, M., & Williams, L. (1991). *Coverage of women's sports in four daily newspapers.* Los Angeles, CA: Amateur Athletic Foundation.

Eastman, S. T., & Billings, A. C. (1999). Gender parity in the Olympics: Hyping women athletes, favoring men athletes. *Journal of Sport and Social Issues, 23*(2), 140–170.

Eastman, S. T., & Billings, A. C. (2000). Sportscasting and sports reporting. *Journal of Sport & Social Issues, 24*(2), 192–213.

Eastman, S. T., & Billings, A. C. (2001). Biased voices in sports: Racial and gender stereotyping in college basketball announcing. *Howard Journal of Communication, 14*(4), 183–202.

Entman, R. M. (1993). Framing: Toward clarification of a fractured paradigm. *Journal of Communication, 43*(4), 51–58.

Fetter, H. D. (2003). *Taking on the Yankees. Winning and losing in the business of baseball, 1903–2003.* New York, NY: Norton.

Fink, J. S. (1998). Female athletes and the media: Strides and stalemates. *Journal of Physical Education, Recreation, and Dance, 69,* 37–45.

Fink, J., & Kensicki, L. (2002). An imperceptible difference: Visual and textual constructions of femininity in *Sports Illustrated* and *Sports Illustrated for Women. Mass Communication and Society, 5*(3), 317–339.

Goffman, E. (1974). *Frame analysis: An essay on the organization of experience.* New York, NY: Harper & Row.

Higgs, C. T., & Weiller, K. H. (1994). Gender bias and the 1992 Summer Olympic Games: An analysis of television coverage. *Journal of Sport and Social Issues, 18*(3), 234–249.

Huffman, S., Tuggle, C. A., & Rosengard, D. (2004). How campus media cover sports: The gender-equity issue, one generation later. *Mass Communication and Society, 7*(4), 475–489.

Jones. D. (2004). Half the story? Olympic women on ABC news online. *Media International Australia, 110*(1), 132–146.

Kane, M. J. (1996). Media coverage of the post title IX female athlete: A feminist analysis of sport, gender, and power. *Duke Journal of Gender Law and Policy, 3*(1), 95–127.

Krippendorff, K. (2004). *Content analysis: An introduction to its methodology* (2nd ed.). Thousand Oaks, CA: Sage.

Landis, J. R., & Koch, G. G. (1977). The measurement of observer agreement for categorical data. *Biometrics, 33*(1),159–174.

Lee, J., & Choi, Y. (2003). *Is there gender equality in online media? The photo analysis of the 2002 Salt Lake Winter Olympics and the 2002 Busan Asian Games coverage.* Paper presented at the annual meeting of the International Communication Association, Marriott Hotel, San Diego, CA. Retrieved from http://www.allacademic.com/meta/p111735_index.html

Levine, P. (1985). *Albert Spalding and the promise of American sport.* New York, NY: Oxford University Press.

Lombard, M., Snyder-Duch, J., & Bracken, C. (2002). Content analysis in mass communication: Assessment and reporting of intercoder reliability. *Human Communication Research, 28*(4), 587–604.

MacCambridge, M. (2004). *America's game: The epic story of how pro football captured a nation.* New York, NY: Random House.

Malec, M. A. (1994). Gender (in)equity in the NCAA news? *Journal of Sport and Social Issues, 18*(6), 376–378.

Martin, C. R. (2004). *Framed! Labor and the corporate media.* Ithaca, NY: ILR.

Mathews, M., & Reuss, C. (1985). *The minimal image of women in Time and Newsweek, 1940–1980.* Paper presented at the Association for Education in Journalism and Mass Communication annual meeting, Memphis State University, Memphis, TN.

Messner, M. A., Duncan, M. C., & Cooky, C. (2003). Silence, sports bras, and wrestling porn: Women in televised sports news and highlight shows. *Journal of Sport and Social Issues, 27*(1), 38–51.

Messner, M., Duncan, M., & Jensen, K. (1993). Separating the men from the girls: The gendered language of televised sports. *Gender & Society, 7*(1), 121–137.

Messner, M. A., Duncan, M. C., & Wachs, F. L. (1996). The gender of audience building: Televised coverage of women's and men's NCAA basketball. *Sociological Inquiry, 66,* 422–439.

Miller, J. (1990). *The baseball business: Pursuing pennants and profits in Baltimore.* Chapel Hill, NC: University of North Carolina Press.

Nathan, D. A. (2003). *Saying it's so: A cultural history of the Black Sox scandal.* Urbana, IL: University of Illinois Press.

Oriard, M. (2007). *Brand NFL: Making and selling America's favorite sport.* Chapel Hill, NC: University of North Carolina Press.

Peterson, R. W. (1990). *Cages into jump shots: Pro basketball's early years.* New York, NY: Oxford University Press.

Rader, B. G. (2008). *Baseball: A history of America's game* (3rd ed.). Urbana, IL: University of Illinois Press.

Rader, B. G. (2009). *American sports: From the age of folk games to the age of televised sports*, 6th ed. Englewood Cliffs, NJ: Prentice Hall.

Real, M. (2006). Sports online: The newest player in media sport. In A. A. Raney & J. Bryant (Eds.), *Handbook of sports and media* (pp. 171–184). Mahwah, NJ: Lawrence Erlbaum Associates.

Riess, S. A. (1989). *City games: The evolution of American urban society and the rise of sport.* Urbana, IL: University of Illinois Press.

Riess, S. A. (1999). *Touching base: Professional baseball and American culture in the progressive era*, Rev. ed. Urbana: University of Illinois Press.

Riess, S. A. (2014). *A companion to American sports history.* Chichester, West Sussex, UK: Wiley-Blackwell.

Riffe, D., Lacy, S., & Fico, F. G. (1998). *Analyzing media messages: Using quantitative content analysis in research.* Mahwah, NJ: Lawrence Erlbaum.

Ross, J. A. (2015). *Joining the clubs: The business of the National Hockey League to 1945.* Syracuse, NY: Syracuse University Press.

Rowe, D. (1999). *Sport, culture, and the media: The unruly trinity.* Philadelphia, PA: Open University Press.

Sagas, M., Cunningham, G. B., Wigley, B. J., & Ashley, F. B. (2000). Internet coverage of university softball and baseball websites: The inequity continues. *Sociology of Sport Journal, 17*(2), 198–212.

Schiavone, M. (2015). *Sports and labor in the United States.* Albany, NY: State University of New York Press.

Seymour, H., & Seymour, D. (1960–1989). *Baseball: The People's Game.* Three vols. New York, NY: Oxford University Press.

Shifflett, B., & Revelle, R. (1994). Gender equity in sports and media coverage: A review of the news? *Journal of Sport and Social Issues, 18*(2), 144–150.

Surdam, D. G. (2012). *The rise of the National Basketball Association.* Urbana, IL: University of Illinois Press.

Surdam, D. G. (2013). *Run to glory and profits: The economic rise of the NFL during the 1950s.* Lincoln, NE: University of Nebraska Press.

Surdam, D. G. (2015). *The big leagues go to Washington: Congress and sports anti-trust.* Urbana, IL: University of Illinois Press.

Tuchman, G. (1978). Introduction: The symbolic annihilation of women by the mass media. In Tuchman, G., Daniels, A. K., & Benét, J. (Eds.), *Hearth and home: Images of women in the mass media* (pp. 3–38). Oxford University Press: New York.

Tuggle, C. A., Huffman, S., & Rosengard, D. (2002). A descriptive analysis of NBC's coverage of the 2000 Summer Olympics. *Mass Communication and Society, 3*(3), 361–375.

Tuggle, C. A., & Owen, A. (1999). A descriptive analysis of NBC's coverage of the Centennial Olympics. *Journal of Sport and Social Issues, 23*(2), 171–182.

Tygiel, J. (1983). *Baseball's great experiment: Jackie Robinson and his legacy.* New York, NY: Oxford University Press.

White, G. E. (1998). *Creating the national pastime: Baseball transforms itself, 1903–1953.* Princeton, NJ: Princeton University Press.

CREDITS

2

Theory and Research About Race, Gender, Media, and Sports

LEARNING OBJECTIVES

After reading this chapter, students should be able to:

- identify and explain mass media research as it relates to sports media, race, gender, and age;
- recognize and discuss the mainstream theoretical and research approaches to sports media research;
- recognize and discuss qualitative and quantitative data collection approaches to mass media research; and
- use media literacy skills to understand and evaluate the media's presence and influence in your life.

Introduction

This chapter summarizes the popular mass communication theories and approaches used by mass media researchers that help explain the effects of exposure to sports messages about race, gender, and age on audiences and sports fans.

Research in sports and media is designed to answer questions that go beyond the experiences encountered by one or a few persons. Media researchers design research studies on media and people that will offer data and information through the use of methods developed by other researchers. The information shared in this chapter will help you connect theory and research with the focus on expanding your knowledge of the sports journalism industry and the effects of mediated messages about athletics and the athletes who participate in them. The main idea is to have you begin to examine the media critically to see if the appropriate messages, ideas, themes, and information are being published or produced.

Theories Used in Sports and Media Research

In the late 1940s, Harold Lasswell developed a model that described the act of communication by identifying who said what, what was said, in what media was it said, to who was the message directed, and with what effect was the message perceived. Lasswell's model of communication has been considered "one of the earliest and most influential communication models" (Shoemaker, Tankard, & Lasorsa, 2004). Lasswell, a renowned political scientist and theorist in communication studies, viewed the mass media as prominent suppliers of propaganda and other messages designed to influence people's behaviors and attitudes (Shoemaker et al., 2004). During this time, mass media would allow propaganda-type messages to reach millions of people at a time, and mass communication researchers such as Lasswell feared that the spreading of lies otherwise known as propaganda to support political agendas would be harmful and even dangerous. The magic bullet or hypodermic needle approach proposed by Lasswell suggested that lies contained in propaganda affected everyone in the same way at the same time.

The War of the Worlds

The fear among Americans that mass media messages have the power to affect everyone negatively in the same way at the same time helped formulate what is known as the direct effects model of mass media and communications on society. Stemming from Lasswell's "magic bullet theory," the direct effects theoretical model assumed that audiences passively accept mass media messages. One effect of this passive acceptance of mass media messages would be predictable reactions to the message. A clear illustration of how consumers respond to mass media messages made history during a 1938 radio broadcast. It was Halloween morning in 1938 when Orson Welles informed listeners of the radio show known as *The Mercury Theatre on the Air* that they would hear a broadcast adaptation of *The War of the Worlds. The War of the Worlds* was, at the time, a 40-year-old novel that Welles adapted into a radio broadcast series. The adaptation consisted of a series of fake news bulletins that were broadcast as if they were part of a normal radio show. The fake news bulletins were produced so that when listeners tuned in to the show, they would believe that the story was "real" and that the news about an alien invasion was taking place during the show; hence, the reason for the show to be interrupted. Some listeners misunderstood, while others had tuned in late and did not hear the disclaimer that aired just before the show began. Many listeners then became so enthralled in the story and the realism of Welles's adaptation of the novel that they believed they were listening to an actual news story (see Figure 2.1). Proving the theory of direct effects of mass media messages, *The War of the Worlds* radio broadcast showed that listeners who were not aware that they were consuming fake news messages assumed that the messages were authentic and as a result responded

FIGURE 2.1   *Orson Welles, arms upraised, directing a rehearsal of CBS Radio's* The Mercury Theatre on the Air *(1938)*

accordingly. Soon after the broadcast, listeners made fearful calls to the police for help. Newspapers, radio stations, and journalists were convinced that the radio broadcast had caused a nationwide hysteria. In fewer than 12 hours, the broadcast and Welles's face and name appeared on the "front pages of newspapers coast-to-coast, along with headlines about the mass panic his CBS broadcast had allegedly inspired" (Holmsten & Lubertozzi, 2001.

Marshall McLuhan's Influence on Media Studies

In the 1960s, Marshall McLuhan developed a theoretical approach that at the time represented a new and innovative way to study attitudes toward media. "The medium is the message" is a phrase that McLuhan, an English professor, became widely recognized, as it asserts that media are influential in manipulating human behavior and cultural norms (Stille, 2000). McLuhan, author of two books in the early 1960s, illustrated how media technology changed both individual behavior and cultural norms. For example, it was a phrase in the book titled *Understanding Media* that propelled McLuhan in the field of media effects. In the book, McLuhan coined the phrase "the medium is the message." For mass communication researchers interested in media effects, McLuhan's phrase began to represent a fresh, new perspective on attitudes toward media. The central point of the McLuhan phrase is the notion that media is instrumental in shaping human and cultural attitudes, behaviors, and experiences. McLuhan's work had significant influence on the development of theory in the world of media effects and studies in that he created a new way for the mass communication scholars and researchers to analyze the media's influence.

Agenda-Setting Theory

The limited effects perspectives of Lasswell and McLuhan led to the idea that messages generated in the media serve to reinforce attitudes rather than to change them. For some mass communication researchers, this direct-effect type logic seemed to underestimate the effect that the media have on culture. Together, these researchers began to investigate possible outcomes of exposure to media. A derivative of this thought process is the agenda-setting theory. Agenda setting argues that mass media have the ability and the power to determine the issues that concern the public. The theory is a contrast to the direct effects model in that the theory posits that it presumes "the issues that receive the most attention in and from the media are the issues that become important in the public sphere" (Valkenburg, Peter, & Walther, 2016). In other words, the issues that receive media attention and hype are the issues that the public discusses and debates, and is most concerned with. Thus the media, according to this perspective, have the power to influence the public perception of issues that are or are not important. So when the media "fails to address a particular issue, it becomes marginalized in the minds of the public" (Hanson, 2009).

Those specializing in agenda-setting research analyze the salience, or relative importance, of an issue and then investigate the attributes that make the issue become important (Dearing & Rogers, 1996). The salience of an issue, according to research, ultimately determines where the message is placed within the public agenda. Agenda-setting research studies the promotion of an issue in the mass media and ultimately how it appears in its final form as a law or policy (Dearing & Rogers, 1996). McCombs and Shaw tested these notions in 1972 and compared the frequency of media news stories about different issues found in the 1968 presidential election with the perceptions that voters had on the importance assigned to the various issues. The researchers found a significant correlation (0.97) between the frequency of coverage and undecided voters' perceptions of how important the issues were.

The initial agenda-setting theory is a simple idea that centers on the media's agenda and the public's perception of issue salience. When media critics argue that media have agendas (i.e., partisan media), they are often relying on the presuppositions set forth by agenda-setting theory.

Media effects scholars' argue that it is actually the that media determines the issues that consumers should think about. For example, agenda-setting theory is used to help understand and explain trends in our culture, such as the rise of trends in health food and gluten. By promoting gluten-free ideas through strategic messages, ads, commercials, public relations campaigns, and various media outlets, the mass media were able to move the idea of consumption of gluten into the public arena. After exposure to many messages about the health effects of gluten consumption, we saw evidence of this issue moving from the personal health issue to a public health issue. More recently, coverage of violence and shootings and the involvement of athletes has been a prominent feature in news stories, and in later chapters, we will investigate the role that exposure to these stories has had on the public discourse and athletes of color. We will consider this theoretical perspective in later chapters when evaluating what happens when media ignore some groups and emphasize others.

Uses and Gratifications Theory

Uses and gratifications theory attempts to provide a paradigm to help explain the role that media play in people's everyday lives. Mass media scholars are most interested in how people use media and the gratifications obtained by the consumption of particular media. Uses and gratifications theory proposes that people use the media to satisfy specific gratifications or needs. For example, a person who is a fan of and frequently watches a program such as *The Bachelorette* simultaneously tweets about it on Twitter. According to the theory, this viewer might be gratifying his or her entertainment and surveillance media uses. Another example of uses and gratifications of media use is the study of the motives and use of social media. Research in social media informs us that many people use social media for entertainment, for surveillance, to communicate with people who share similar attitudes and values, or to demonstrate their independence and self-expression. Uses and gratifications is a paradigm that explores how people "actively and deliberately seek out media to fulfill certain needs or goals" (Katz, Blumler, & Gurevitch 1973). In a study of Twitter use, Saunders, Alhabash, and Frisby (2011) found that "compared to Whites, Black Twitter users significantly spent more time on Twitter, reported having more followers, a higher intensity of use, and also a higher likelihood of using Twitter to communicate with offline friends" (Saunders et al., 2011. The researchers also found that regarding uses and gratifications of using Twitter, "both Black and White participants were equally motivated to use Twitter for self-expressive purposes" (Saunders et al., 2011. Media use gratifies an individual's need, and, according to the uses and gratifications paradigm, it is the need that motivates and determines how media will be used. When researchers determine consumers' motivations behind their media use, we can understand, predict, and explain various factors that motivate social groups' media choices (Papacharissi, 2009).

With respect to how the uses and gratifications theory might be used in sports research, we might, for example, want to determine motives for consumption of specific sports media and its related messages. Scholars using this theory might also explore consequences associated with the consistent use of particular sports media. In the case of the Super Bowl and Twitter, individuals might, according to this paradigm, use social media as a way to stay informed about the achievements of an athlete, to determine the outcome of a game/competition, or even to vent frustrations with referee calls and/or penalties. Or some consumers may rely on sports media to serve their needs to interact with others. Through the uses and gratifications theory research, scholars have identified common reasons that people provide for their reasons to consume specific media. Those common reasons or gratifications as they are often referred to in media theory classes are consumption, relaxation, social interaction, entertainment, arousal, escape, and other interpersonal and social needs. Many mass media communication scholars believe that when we examine a person's reasons for using media, then we gain a better picture and deeper understanding of why some media are more popular than others. We also gain knowledge of specific benefits that certain media offer to individuals.

Symbolic Interactionism

Symbolic interactionism is a sociological theory that tests the idea that an individual's sense of self and self-concept stems from the process of social relationships and interactions. In other words, the way we interact with others is based primarily on the meaning we have for the person. Thus the theory of symbolic interactionism examines the hypothesis that media construct symbols and then explains the shared cultural meanings instrumental in the development of our social identity and self-concept. This theoretical framework helps "mass media researchers better understand the field of sports media and journalism because of the critical role the media plays in creating and propagating shared symbols." In short, we use socially constructed meanings and symbols in our environment to help us decide who to interact with and how we should interact with people, and to determine, at times erroneously, the meaning of a person's words or behaviors (Blumer, 1969). Symbolic interactionism theory consists of three core dogmas: meaning, language, and thought (Blumer, 1969). These core assumptions lay the groundwork for people to determine who they are and how they will socialize into a larger community (Griffin, 1997). Because of the media's power, research shows that it has a significant influence on the construction of symbols. By using symbolic interactionist theory, mass media researchers are now able to explore the various ways media can influence how our society uses and shares certain symbols. Symbolic interactionists then investigate shared symbols to understand better how these shared cultural symbols affect an individual's attitude, behaviors, and opinions (Jansson-Boyd, 2010).

Advertising is a perfect example to help explain how symbolic interactionism might be applied in mass communication research. Scholars may use this theory to study how media create and use cultural symbols to influence individuals. Consider this: Through their use of appeals and images, advertisers can create ad slogans and messages that transfer meaning and images to certain products. The messages offered in a commercial, for example, might create a shared cultural meaning that makes the message and the product more desirable to consumers. When we see an athlete or individual driving a BMW, what thoughts come to mind? Often, one thinks that luxury vehicles, such as BMWs or Mercedes, mean that a person is rich, successful, or influential. This message may be "shared" because of the perception or idea that BMWs or Mercedes are expensive cars, and one must be rich to own that type of car. Ownership of luxury automobiles is symbolic of a person's membership in a particular socioeconomic class. Other shared symbols disseminated through the media are flags (e.g., the meaning of the Confederate flag), religious images and symbols, music, housing, and even the celebrities we endorse. All these symbols "gain shared symbolic meanings through their representation in the media" (Blumer, 1969). Shared meaning and symbolism are the essence of the theory of symbolic interactionism.

Spiral of Silence

The spiral of silence theory, proposed in 1974 by the German political scientist Elisabeth Noelle-Neumann, states, "People who hold a minority opinion often silence themselves to prevent social isolation" (Noelle-Neumann, 1984). The fear of loneliness consequently leads a person to keep his or her opposing views silent instead of voicing thoughts that may go against popular belief. Media, in this regard, play an essential role in shaping prevailing opinions and ideas. Media also influence public perception about the things people find and perceive to be majority opinions about an issue. What topics do people notice and understand to be prevailing opinions? Figure 2.2 shows the process of the spiral of silence theory and helps visually explain how members of a minority group stay silent based on their perceptions of the majority group.

Spiral of silence is a theory that, related to agenda setting, is used to predict, explain, and understand the role mass media play in the formation, expression, and preservation of opinions. Exposure

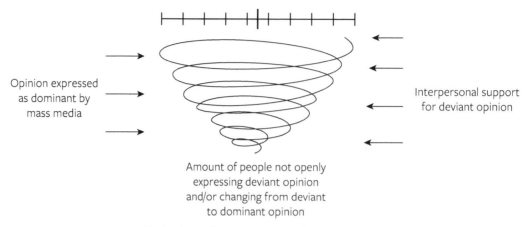

Opinion expressed
as dominant by
mass media

Interpersonal support
for deviant opinion

Amount of people not openly
expressing deviant opinion
and/or changing from deviant
to dominant opinion

Elisabeth Noelle-Neumann's Spiral of Silence

FIGURE 2.2   *Spiral of Silence Theory, Noelle-Neumann (1974)*

to mass media gives people the illusion that consensus is increasing. As a result, social pressure to adopt the dominant position also grows, which then reduces the minority voice to silence, while the "perceived" popular opinion appears to align with the perceptions of the majority opinion. Noelle-Neumann noticed this when some Germans disagreed with Adolf Hitler's policies during the 1930s and '40s (Rossen, 2016). Noelle-Neumann observed that before and after World War II, the individuals who opposed Hitler's policies were also the same people who tended to keep their opposing thoughts and opinions silent for fear of isolation. She theorized that the fear of isolation and the stigma that would be ultimately associated with one's outspoken opinions would result in "the spiral of silence."

Recently, a 2011 Pew report showed substantial evidence for the existence of spiral of silence processes on social media. The research found (1) compared to in-person conversation, people were less likely to discuss specific topics in social media; (2) people on Facebook were more willing to join in online discussion if they felt that their Facebook followers supported them, and they were less likely to share their opinions to offline friends if they found their Facebook or Twitter friends not on their side; and (3) Facebook and Twitter users were less likely to share their opinions in face-to-face settings than others. In conclusion, in the online discussion, the influence of spiral of silence was not as significant as in the face-to-face settings. The spiral of silence studies in chatrooms showed that the difference between people's willingness to speak in different opinion climates was moderate at best.

In a related study, Gearhart and Zhang (2015) conducted an experiment that examined the spiral of silence theory in a social media environment. Through an experimental manipulation, the "researchers presented respondents with a hypothetical scenario (i.e., friendly or hostile) concerning gay bullying, an issue suited for investigation due to its moral components" (Gearhart & Zhang, 2015). Data obtained found that a person's willingness to self-censor was a significant predictor of response strategies used online. Using an empirical test, Gearhart and Zhang obtained data showing that people who encounter content that is aligned with their opinions will speak out on social media, while content that might be perceived as disagreeable may result in postings that stifle the expression of their opinions. In other words, data obtained in this experiment supports the spiral of silence theory in a social media environment. Regarding gay athletes, some research suggests that only a small percentage of the group will publicly identify themselves as gay because of the stigma that certain parts of our culture have about sexual orientation. We might also see a sort of "spiral of silence" with respect to LGBTQ athletes. Research using the spiral of silence might survey LGBTQ individuals and their perceptions of majority opinion concerning sexual orientation. It is possible that research in this area might find that those individuals who think or feel that a majority of Americans do not like or accept them might also be more likely to stay in the closet, so to speak (a term that we will discuss in Chapter 6 of this text).

Cultivation Theory

Emerging from sociology and anthropology, cultivation theory focuses primarily on group differences based on the frequency of exposure to mass media messages. Gerbner (1970) made a significant departure from earlier, more traditional theories of mass media effects. In fact, the main difference between this theory and others previously discussed is that cultivation theory assumes individuals are passive in their search and use and absorption of mass media messages. Cultivation theorists study the effects of television primarily because they argue that televisions are a prominent fixture in the individual's daily life. For these theorists, the TV is almost another member of the family, a source of information that tells the most stories about the most people (African Americans, LGBTQ, Latinas, the upper class, the poor, etc.). Under this theory, individuals who watch an inordinate amount of television may develop ideas about the real world, along with a mental picture of reality that does not align with events in real life. According to cultivation theory, heavy television viewing has long-term effects that eventually affect the attitudes and behaviors of viewers. The theory suggests that heavy viewers of television, particularly news media, are thought to be 'cultivating' attitudes that "force them to believe that the world created by television is an accurate depiction of the real world" (Gerbner & Gross, 1976).

Cultivation theory is used in different research studies. Some scholars use the theory to study differences in perception between heavy and light users of media, while others might use it to determine how stereotypes are formed and maintained. To use this theory in research and ascertain the effects of cultivation, researchers first must ascertain data and content found in media outlets that an individual normally watches. The media content is then analyzed to determine the various types of messages appearing in that media. Researchers then must identify other variables and attributes that are involved, such as an individual's geographic culture and living environment, additional media consumption and selective exposures, and the influence of friends and family. For example, parents might have strict or relaxed influences on their children's exposure to TV and the content that they watch. Socialization, therefore, may be a factor that influences the way children consume messages in media. If an individual's parents have significant influence in his or her life, then the social messages that he or she receives from them may compete with messages received from television.

Related to cultivation theory are two theories known as social cognition theory and social learning theory (SLT). These two closely related media effects paradigms use information obtained from the media based on exposure and easy retrieval from memory to determine how the information consumed from exposure may be disproportionately represented regarding the frequency of events, people, or things. In other words, when exposed to media, factors such as distinctiveness, novelty affective valence, and frequency and recency of the exposure work together to influence cognitive structures, which, based on these factors, have significantly impacted their thoughts, ideas, and behaviors simply from exposure to messages on television. Thus media portrayals of athletes of color, women, LGBTQ athletes, social class, and sports, just to name a few, may be correlated with the frequency of exposure to events prominently displayed in the media. This type of analysis provides a way to examine in closer detail some of the potential effects of mass media on consumer cognitions, affect, and behavior.

Social Cognitive Theory

Bandura developed social cognitive theory (SCT) from his SLT. Bandura named it the "social cognitive theory" to reflect the emphasis on internal mental variables. As opposed to social learning theory (SLT), the SCT is used to "explain how consumption of media messages is related to observations of others" (Bandura, 2008). According to this theory, when people observe a person in media performing a particular behavior and there are consequences associated with the behavior, they will not only remember the behavior but also ultimately use the learned behavior to help guide their subsequent behaviors. This theory also purports that observational learning may encourage consumers to change learned behaviors. What is most important is whether or not the model performing the behavior is rewarded or punished for the behavior. The SCT allows the assignment of agency, or causality, to both the communication of mass media and the internal cognitive thought and perceptive processes of individuals (Bandura, 1977).

Figure 2.3 shows the process and continuous interaction between behaviors (i.e., a skill), our thoughts or cognitions (i,e, involves thoughts, perceptions, self-efficacy, motives and personality) and the social context or environment (i.e., the situation, role models and relationships). The social context plays a crucial role in that learning happens primarily in a social context. Bandura's social cognitive learning theory examines the interaction among thoughts, behaviors and the social environment because a key component in this theory is the importance of observational learning, imitation and modeling. While the theory does not suggest that these three components are equally weighted in the role they play in observational learning, it does assert that the factor that is most important at the time, (i.e., an individual's beliefs or thoughts, the social context and behavior) will determine the extent to which people will learn new knowledge and skills. Here's a media example that will make this more clear; Advertisers often select and rely on endorsers that will appeal and persuade a particular target market to be interested in a product, service, or an idea. Individuals exposed to the message may take time to reflect on the message the role model's message. a lesson to the class, students reflect on what the teacher is saying. This is where the social context and environment comes in to play; the endorser has an opportunity to influence the consumer's cognition or beliefs, and this is an example of the cognitive factor. Consumers who idolize certain endorsers

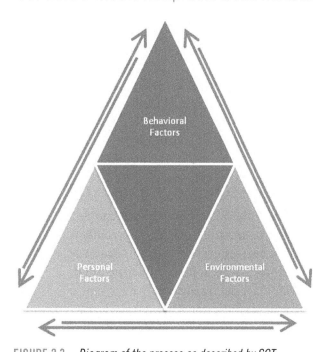

Bandura's Triadic Reciprocal Determinism

Behavioral Factors

Personal Factors

Environmental Factors

FIGURE 2.3   *Diagram of the process as described by SCT*

(like athletes) will attend to the message and ultimately the cognition and environment will ultimately influence behavior. In 1961, Bandura conducted an experiment which is now known as the "Bobo Doll study." Children watched the video that depicted an adult woman being aggressive by hitting the doll and shouting mean words at the doll and were later allowed to go into a large playroom. Without any cues or aided instructions, the children who were allowed to enter the playroom with the Bobo doll instantly began imitating the woman and starting aggressively hitting the dolling and shouting aggressive words, using similar language observed by the woman in the video.

The SCT model broke away from previous models of behavioralism and operant, or instrumental, conditioning. One issue related to cognitive models tends to put causation of behaviors in a unidirectional frame. In other words, the cognitive frameworks conceptualized human behavior as being a dependent variable of the environment. Bandura disagreed with the notion that human behavior is ultimately controlled by the environment. He believed, and his theories reflected, that humans have the capacity for self-directed agency, or to guide their behavior.

SLT, similar to SCT, suggests that people learn from exposure to media through a process of selective exposure; selective perception; involvement, participation, and reinforcement; and modeling. One way to consider these two theories is to understand that SLT considers what we think and believe but that the emphasis is on behavior and what we learn after exposure. To some extent, it measures the relationship between our thoughts and our behaviors while also considering the role that media play in the relationship. Bandura stated in 1989 that the further development of the SLT determines that learning will most likely occur if there is a close comparison and identification between the observer and the model. Identification also determines if the observer has a sense of self-efficacy. Self-efficacy functions as an important set of determinants of human motivation, affect, and action, and operates a motivational, cognitive, and affective intervening process. A useful part of this theory is that the conceptual framework can be used to analyze the effect of media on behavior. Figure 2.4 shows how social learning might relate to aggression after exposure to media messages. For example, messages obtained through

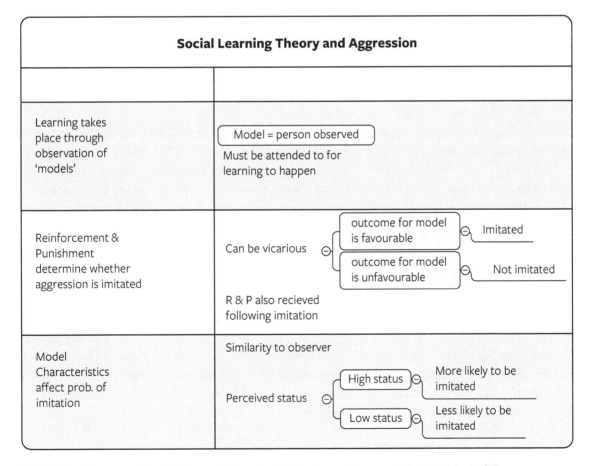

FIGURE 2.4   *The process by which the social learning of behaviors, such as aggression, occur in the SLT*

the media are considered a symbolic communication. Symbolic communication leads to observational learning, described by Bandura, that ultimately influences behavior. This theory might be used to explain why some children are vulnerable to the influence of celebrity athletes and others they look up to in the media.

Symbolic Annihilation

Gerbner (1972), the theorist who gave us cultivation theory, is also responsible for offering the theory of symbolic annihilation. Symbolic annihilation is used to "describe and explain the absence of representation, or underrepresentation, of some groups of people in the media, often based on their race, sex, sexual orientation, socio-economic status, etc." (Tuchman, 1978). From a sports journalism perspective, symbolic annihilation might be used to help scholars understand how sports media maintain inequalities in types of sports or based on an athlete's gender. This term is usually applied to describe how the media promotes stereotypes and denies specific identities. In 1979, Tuchman took the theory of symbolic annihilation and separated it into three phases: absence, trivialization, and condemnation.

Language use in the media is one way that media contribute to the trivialization and condemnation of racial groups, such as African Americans, in popular media venues. For example, sports reporters may describe an African American quarterback as being a natural athlete, whereas a Caucasian quarterback is often described as possessing cognitive skills and leadership abilities. In this example, trivialization happens when an athlete of color's accomplishments are reduced to natural talents or physical features, yet a white athlete's athletic accomplishments are because he can solve problems and think strategically.

Symbolic annihilation is a theory appropriate for use in the sports journalism area in that the research focuses on the media and the messages that make certain groups invisible through the intentional lack of representation of the marginalized groups in all forms of media ranging from advertising, movies, news media, songs, television, sports coverage, social media discussions and posts, radio, magazines, digital media, and visual art.

According to Gerbner and Gross (1976), "Representation in the fictional world signifies social existence; absence means symbolic annihilation" (p. 182). The basic idea conveyed in this quote is that "groups that are valued in our culture tend to be shown frequently and positively in the media, and viewers or readers come to learn more about these groups' purported characteristics and their implied value to the culture simply because of their heavily featured exposure in the media" (Gerbner & Gross, 1976). But when other groups (e.g., Native Americans) are not valued and included in the same media and in the same culture where the valued group is presented, then there arises the simple idea that media have cast them aside and do not have storylines that feature them; thus, people "assume" that this group is devalued or considered to be an "out-group."

The absence of a particular group in the media sends a subtle message that the "out-group" is not worthy of attention, and members of the "in-group," or valued group, learn how they should or should not act when confronted with a member of the "out-group" (Gerbner & Gross, 1976). For example, some proponents of the theory argue that this theoretical process might explain the controversy over the naming of athletic teams using Native American names (e.g., Washington Redskins). A plethora of research shows that exposure is highly influential in shaping people's beliefs, attitudes, and behaviors (Paik & Comstock, 1994; Shrum, Wyler, & O'Guinn, 1998). According to Gerbner and Gross (1976), the basic postulate is this: those who are heavily exposed to news media tend to be most influenced by and fearful of the things that they see, hear, and read. Data obtained using this theoretical framework leads to the conclusion that media exposure that lacks representation will also affect what people do not see, hear, and read (Akers, 1973; Bandura, 1977, 2008). For example, SLT (Akers, 1973; Bandura, 1977, 1989) argues that people and, in particular, "young children, acquire their beliefs, attitudes, and propensity to engage in behaviors directly based on first-hand experiences they have with others who exhibit particular behaviors through media exposure" (Bushman & Huesmann, 2006). Accordingly, SLT, people, despite age, ethnicity, and background, tend to learn and gather information about the world around them and the people in their world and in our American culture by simply exposing themselves to media. The research methods most aligned with this theory are surveys, experiments, and longitudinal panel studies.

Framing Theory

For some mass media researchers, media have the power to form or manipulate thoughts and beliefs (Tuchman, 1978). Other researchers believe media control and guide people's thoughts solely by purposively selecting, publishing, and/or broadcasting certain coverage and in the way they portray events. Entman (1993) uses framing theory to posit that journalists may occasionally follow the "rules for objective reporting, yet may inadvertently rely on frames based on their biases and opinions" (Entman, 1993). Journalists, Entman (1993) believes, use frames in their news stories, and one effect of framing news stories may be that exposure to the content will ultimately stop people from making a balanced and "objective" evaluation of the story, group, or individual and the situation surrounding the newsworthy event. Entman (1993) explains the concept of framing and why it is problematic. According to framing theory, stories that are framed in biased content not only include a journalist's own personal biases but also passively allows readers to understand their mediated messages in ways that may encourage, maintain, enhance, or even create stereotypes and misperceptions (Entman, 1993).

According to Scheufele (1999), "Media and individual frames have to be considered when reading a news story" (p. 106). When readers consume the main storyline of a news story, the way they process the headline cognitively is what helps them attach meaning to the events and focus of the story (Scheufele, 1999; Scheufele & Tewksbury, 2000). Scheufele (1999) goes on to explain that "viewing media or news frames as necessary to turn meaningless and nonrecognizable happenings into the discernible event" is what leads a story toward "being framed" (p. 106). We can use research and conclusions made from data obtained in studies to determine that framing frequently happens when a "phrase, image or statement insinuates a specific interpretation of an issue presented in media" (Frisby, 2016). A study conducted by Frisby in 2016 used framing theory and found that frames are used in news stories to link previous knowledge held by readers to recent events, and the associations made between old news and new news are used to help solidify beliefs the individual may have about the person, event, and context by which the event occurs. Frames are used to link topics to certain beliefs that carry with them explanations and implications of a problem. The theory of framing aids the study of sports media and effects of exposure to frames in sports news in that one of the strengths of framing is that the theory can be used to explain, predict, and understand common themes found in media messages and news stories about sports and athletes.

Framing theory argues that images and inclusion of words found in mass media tend to provide a context or meaning for the information presented in the media content. This theoretical framework analyzes journalists in the stories they write and collects data that shows how exposure to frames is used to determine what and how people think about information in the news story (Gamson, 1992; Gamson, & Modigliani, 1989). Framing explores the context in which information published or broadcast in media outlets is conveyed and how this content might be used to shape individual assumptions and perceptions about the information. Framing theory also investigates how and when messages in media and the information given might be taken out of context. Research that uses framing as a framework suggests that often media messages that people perceive to be "out of context" might also be perceived as meaningless (de Vreese, 2005; Gamson & Modigliani, 1989). In addition, framing researchers argue that information presented within a frame might also be influenced by context and associations (de Vreese, 2005; Gamson, 1992; Gamson & Modigliani, 1989; Scheufele, 1999; Scheufele & Tewskbury, 2000). When exposed to media messages, consumers may respond in such a way that they make conclusions or form attributions about an issue or about a person. The opinions are formed through frames published in a news story, an advertising message, intangible ideas or political events, along with and how they consume the circumstances surrounding the event(s) presented in the news coverage.

We know from data obtained in studies that employ framing theory that people are exposed to a plethora of frames in a single day, and when those frames present conflicting information, the conflicts with prior information and current information will likely result in situations where people will experience a cognitive experience widely known as cognitive dissonance. Cognitive dissonance, research tells us, causes a reduction and neutralization of framing effects. The overall result? Audience members exposed to conflicting messages rely on internal frames (heuristics) that are developed through symbolic interactionism and socialization—processes that take place over one's lifetime. This reliance on internal frames happens because frames serve as mental cues and reference points that determine a person's future attributions, conclusions, and judgments. We also know that individuals who are stressed and under time pressures can enhance conclusions and judgments made based on frames used in a story (Salovey & Wegener, 2003; Salovey & Williams-Piehota, 2004; Scheufele, 1999).

Frames set expectations. Framing works because media allow people to put cues from their environments in a particular context (Entman, 1993; Ko & Kim, 2010; Williams-Piehota, Schnieder, Pizarro, Mowad, & Salovey, 2003). Vague frames often lack context, and according to this theoretical framework, frames that are vague or confusing may actually encourage individuals to interpret media stories based on their internal expectations. In a research study, Dorfman, Wallack, and Woodruff (2005) provide information regarding two very different types of frames: conceptual and news frames. Conceptual and news frames help researchers using this theory understand how to create and produce messages that "determine what needs to be changed and how to create change through the power of language" (Ko & Kim, 2010).

From a journalism practitioner perspective, framing theory has significant implications. Frames, for one, can be used to help journalists determine which points of the story need to be emphasized and the details that need to be explicated and understood from those story details that should be left out or de-emphasized. Because frames are sometimes used by journalists who simply rely on their own biases and experiences, research shows that frames are usually implicit rather than explicit (Hellsten, Dawson, & Leydesdorff, 2010). Research also shows that news frames are effective simply because they are known to be cognitive and occur within an individual's mind. Because of this, frames help us interpret and organize meaning and symbols, often referred to as frames, that are found in the environment, in our culture, and in the world around us. News frames rely on heuristic mental cues that come from family and friends, or even situations that are often not personally experienced but observed in the media (consider the SLT). News frames also rely on and are formulated based on our exposure to the news, entertainment media, family, peers, in-group identities and associations, and group memberships. From a mass media perspective, news frames aid in journalism by providing a context that helps people interpret the meaning in stories. According to Entman (1993), news frames tell us in important ways what we should and should not consider important, what is and what is not important (Entman, 1993).

Episodic and Thematic News Frames

News media use frames, as we mentioned, to organize and present information so that the reader is able to frame the event, the person, the conflict, and the facts, and integrate the story with information already stored in memory (Entman, 1993). Episodic news frames are those news frames that have information contained in the story that is often "rich with meaning in lieu of fact" (Gross, 2008). When readers are exposed to episodic news frames, they are confronted with opportunities to interact and engage with a story in such a way that they feel that they have been afforded an opportunity to solve problems or accept consequences of their behavior (Dorfman et al., 2005). According to Dorfman et al. (2005), news media must go to extreme efforts to frame events that are effectively and accurately involved in the context of the issue. These efforts include specifically providing facts from credible sources and ensuring that the facts are understandable and visible to the audience. According to Dorfman et al. (2005), when stories provide objective data and information, this is referred to as a thematic frame. Thematic stories, according to the literature, rely on credible and reliable sources and other objective information, as well as information that involves sources and quotes that stem from sources other than personal accounts. Thematic frames offer background, consequences, and other cues that provide context. In a study on the effects of thematic frames, Iyengar (1991) found that viewers exposed to stories that contain thematic frames tend to show stronger, long-lasting effects from exposure to the thematic frame (see also Frisby, 2016, for similar implications of framing theory in news stories). In fact, individuals exposed to thematic frames often place blame for the issue on society and public policy (Iyengar, 1991).

In terms of effects of exposure to episodic frames (i.e., news stories that emphasize meaning in lieu of fact), people are most likely to blame individuals or groups for their situation. For example, in an experimental study investigating the effects of exposure to thematic and episodic frames, Iyengar (1991) found that when exposed to *episodic* frames in news stories about homelessness and poverty people were much more likely to blame homelessness and poverty on the individual. Participants who were confronted with episodic news stories were afforded opportunities to interact and engage with the news story in such a way that they were found to attribute homelessness and poverty to an individual's laziness or education. (Dorfman et al., 2005; Gross, 2008; Iyengar, 1991). Interestingly, participants in this study who were confronted with thematic news stories (i.e., objective data and facts) about high rates of unemployment or poverty, evidence showed that they were more likely to attribute the causes of homelessness and unemployment to governmental policies and other factors that they felt were beyond the victim's control (Iyengar, 1991).

Schema Theory

Stereotypes are known as schemas for people perceived as belonging to a particular group. Stereotypes or schemas serve as structures in our minds and help people to simplify complex issues, experiences, people, or things in our environment. Schemas help us to process incoming stimuli quickly based on the identification and presence of a few similar and relevant characteristics that the perceiver can recognize. People have schemas about objects, events, and people. Schemas help people organize and categorize events, experiences, people, and other things we encounter on a day-to-day basis. Because of schemas, people can make judgments about their surroundings without having to exert mental effort.

Schemas help people organize and categorize not only their knowledge of events but also their expectations. Schemas tell us the attributes and characteristics that objects, events, and people possess and lead us to expect certain things once those attributes or characteristics have been encountered. For example, when you meet an individual you are unfamiliar with who belongs to a particular group, whether the group is based on gender, race, sexuality, social class, or others, the schema that you have in your mind about that group will tell you the behaviors, features, and traits that you should expect to encounter should you engage in conversation with that person.

The expectations that are associated with schemas are defined as "priming." When we encounter an event, object, or person, the related concepts that are in our brains are primed, and the result of that priming is that we are much more likely to expect and respond to them than we would an object, event, or person who is unfamiliar and who has no related concepts in our minds. This means that schemas are created through consistent and frequent repeat exposures. Schemas and primes that are presented to us often and consistently are thought to become easily accessible, and as a result, they tend to change our interpretation of things and integrate the object, event, or person into a schema that is congruent with prior beliefs and knowledge.

Queer Theory

Research in sports studies is beginning to use a queer theory framework. Scholars who use queer theory as a framework study sexual identity, which we will discuss in Chapter 3 of the text. Scholars using the queer theory typically analyze the manner in which "sexual identity is created by cultural norms during different historical eras" (Fisher, Knust, & Johnson, 2013). Sykes (1998) conducted a study using queer theory to gather the life stories of six female physical education teachers, three of whom identified as homosexual and the other three who identified as heterosexual. The Sykes (1998) study showed how these teachers, based on their sexual orientation, accepted or resisted the lesbian label/stereotype (e.g., not being "out" in the open about their sexual identity). Sykes also applied queer theory as a way to explain and understand the "heteronormative status of physical education" (Sykes, 1998; Van Ingen, 2003; Weed, 1996). In her research, Sykes (2013) found that the field of physical education encourages individuals who are LGBTQ to stay in the closet so that they will not disrupt the heteronormative environment that is most evident in high schools and their physical education curricula (Roper, 2013; Sykes, 2013). Using queer theory, Sykes was able to use data that allowed her to identify the silence and the awkward moments that participants feel while being inside the "closet" (Roper, 2013; Sykes, 2014). Sykes (2010) also documented the pressure that lesbians have when engaged in what is termed "heteronormative talk" when they are outside of "the closet." Sykes's results challenge our culture's desire to place one in a hetero or homo category, which is actually one of the main purposes of queer theory (Sykes, 1998). The Sykes (1998) study also supports the data and research obtained using the spiral of silence theory.

Using Media Research to Test Theory and Obtain Information About Media Effects

Research on Media Effects in Sports

This section of the chapter is designed to guide you through the process of research so that you can get a sense of how research involving gender, race, age, and sports in media have been discovered and executed. Some of the basic questions we ask when we research sports media are "who," "why," "how," "what," "when," "where," and "which." Who is typically involved in an investigation of the producer of the audience's message? Why seek evidence that examines and explains the causation for events (often answered through experiments)? How do we explore how processes work? For example, work in cognition and attitudes delineates the process of how schemas and priming work. "What" questions are used with quantitative data about particular experiences and phenomena. Content analysis and other survey methods help researchers answer questions that are most interested in, for example, "what is the extent to which themes related to objectification of female athletes will appear in sports stories?" "When" research questions take into account the timing of certain events. Scholars who are interested in addressing when questions will often look at cultural events in our history and determine the effects of those events in sports (e.g., Title IX and the emergence of female sports). "Which" questions seek to determine variables or elements that have a significant effect on dependent variables and those that do not. Which sport receives the most coverage and value from media and how? And, lastly, the "where" questions seek out the location of events to perhaps explain the cultural phenomenon. This research question is often employed by critical cultural scholars and other cross-cultural media researchers interested in looking at environmental surroundings and other pressures that are endemic to the individual to explain why something happened.

Antisocial and Prosocial Effects of Media Content

Many scholars are often focused on investigating the antisocial effects of viewing television. Violence and other antisocial behaviors happen to be two of the most researched topics in mass media and mass communication studies. Comstock, Chaffee, and Katzman (1978) conducted a study that found that many empirical research studies that focus on antisocial effects tend to outnumber research found in all other media effects areas by four to one. Paik and Comstock (1994) analyzed 217 studies conducted between the years 1959 and 1990. The researchers obtained data that showed and supported the notion that media effects scholars tend to center their studies around antisocial effects of media exposure—an area of research focus that has been apparent for more than 20 years.

This focus on antisocial effects of exposure to mass media has been evident in scholarly work that dates as far back as the 1920s. It was this era that motivated scholars and media critics to believe that exposure to media content was an influential source of information, effects on attitudes, and behavior for children. Building on this research, Klapper (1960) conducted a summary of information that was known during this time about how exposure to mass media affects social interactions. Klapper was led to conclude that media reinforces existing attitudes and predispositions.

It was during the 1960s when scholars began showing concern about the antisocial effect of the media. Studies seem to turn to research centered on understanding how people are affected by media, paying particular attention to the effects of consistent exposure to content on broadcast television. Several seminal research studies were conducted that showed that individuals who consumed television content frequently were much more likely to learn (summarized in Comstock & Paik, 1991) aggressive behavior because of their viewing of violent media content than were those individuals who were least likely to watch violent television content (Wimmer & Dominick, 2011). Studies during this time also showed that television content was more likely to prime attitudes and that priming was a more probable effect of exposure than was a cathartic (or cleansing) effect obtained from watching violent content on television (Comstock & Paik, 1991). In 1965, Senate subcommittees were asked to examine the relationship between viewing aggression and violence on television and delinquent behavior among teens. Experimental research in the area of violence and aggression proves a significant cause and effect of exposure to content. Data obtained shows a significant positive relationship between exposure to crime and violence on television and antisocial behaviors. This effect is greatest among adolescent viewers. Findings in this research area ultimately led to the creation of the National Commission on the Causes and Prevention of Violence. In a report published by this commission, an idea was presented, and studies shown, to support the notion that television violence teaches viewers—and demonstrates how—to engage in violence. The report then concluded with recommendations on how media might be used to reduce the effect of television violence.

Prosocial effects of television have also been investigated. One example of this research on the prosocial effects of exposure to media was when studies showed the positive effects of watching *Sesame Street*. The research found that exposure to *Sesame Street* was instrumental in preparing toddlers for public school. The study, however, also showed that exposure to the show was not helpful in closing the knowledge gap that existed between advantaged and disadvantaged children (Minton, 1975).

Approaches to Mass Media Research: Research Methods and Techniques That Rely on Theory

Mass media effects scholars use most of the research methods discussed in this chapter: content analysis, laboratory experiments, surveys, field experiments, observations, and panels. This next section will explain five popular research methods used in social science research that aids scholars with testing theories.

The Experimental Method

Experiments are often used to determine the cause and effect of exposure to media messages. Scholars using experiments as a research method are mostly interested in the effect of the media. The idea is to randomly assign and expose one group of subjects to a manipulated media content stimulus while a control group sees a different type of content or no content at all. The experimental research approach relies on independent and dependent variables. The independent variable is a variable that can be controlled or manipulated; a common independent variable might be the race of the athlete. A dependent variable, a variable that is known or speculated to be influenced by the independent variable, such as behavior or attitudes toward an athlete, is measured immediately after exposure. Outcome behavioral variables might be measured by using either a pencil-and-paper test known as a communications or conceptual test. For example, one group of participants might view a short segment from a television show depicting a chase, two fistfights, two shootings, and a knifing involving an athlete of color. Participants in another group might view a 3.5-minute segment depicting a similar event, but the athlete would be a representative from the majority group. Then the control group might watch a segment of similar length that shows athletes of all backgrounds competing in athletic events together—which would be considered a prosocial, positive message. After viewing, the participants would go into another room to measure their responses to the segments. We would then measure the effect of the exposures on participants' responses and reactions to the target. Experimental studies that examine the effect of media exposure on attitudes toward athletes of color and female athletes might use the same approach.

The Survey Approach

A common research method found in many studies is the use of questionnaires that incorporate measures of media exposure and familiarity with the sport and athlete, along with measures of individual difference variables, such as bias, implicit bias, prejudice, discrimination, and other cognitive variables. Also included in many surveys are measures of demographic and sociographic variables simply because it is possible that these variables may mediate or moderate exposure to specific media. Results are usually expressed as a series of correlations.

Field Experiments

Researchers interested in field experiments and sports might use unedited feature-length films about athletes. Feature-length films might be of athletes from different ethnicities and perhaps both genders. Participants in this bogus learning experiment would be told that they have a good chance to meet and greet the "stars" of the film they watched. Results of this type of field study might be used to show that participants who saw film clips that were in line with their previously held notions of the target group and ethnicity of the athlete engage in more negative interactions and behaviors than those participants who were exposed to content that was much more positive.

Panel/Longitudinal Studies

Primarily because of the extreme length of time and the expense involved in conducting panel studies, some scholars will rely on this research method to examine the long-term effects of media exposure. Researchers using this method typically interview some participants and administer surveys to them over a length of time. Measures of media exposures, personalities, and other behavioral measures would be administered to the participants at different periods in their lives. The results may support or disconfirm the hypothesis that attitudes and stereotypes about athletes in later life are caused in part by media exposure during early years.

Agenda Setting and Content Analysis

The standard study using the agenda-setting theory might include a survey, an experiment, or a panel. However, one frequently used method is known as content analysis. When researchers use content analysis to study media, they are seeking to define and analyze themes, patterns, and frames frequently used in the mass media. In terms of agenda-setting research, scholars rely on surveys or questionnaires that obtain data from participants on the level of exposure to certain media and the level of importance of the media content. It is presumed that individuals who see the same story in different media begin to think the topic is important and therefore results in this area often attempt to show the media's ability to set an agenda for consumers just based on the frequency of presentation.

What is content analysis? This research technique is based on measuring the frequency of something in a representative sampling of mass media. Researchers using this technique want to learn something about media by examining what they write or produce. Content analysis might also be used to compare and contrast different variables, such as gender or race, to determine differences in how media treat members of those groups. Several research methodologies have been used to establish the media agenda. The most common method groups media coverage into broad themes and then measures the amount of time or space devoted to each story. Ideally, content analytic techniques use traditional media: television, radio, newspaper, and magazines. Unfortunately, including all media in content analysis can be extremely difficult and challenging for researchers to handle. Thus most studies typically use content analysis to examine one or two media, usually television and the daily newspaper.

Concerning research on sports media, content analysis of print and broadcast media show that journalists are not immune to biases. That is, journalists are also consumers of media and therefore have both gender and racial biases (Frisby, 2016). Research continues to show that women are objectified and even marginalized in the media (Billings, Halone, & Denham, 2002). Studies also show that, in terms of sports media, athletes are stereotyped based on race by journalists (Banet-Weiser, 1999; Frisby, 2016). Marginalized depictions, according to research, affect our perceptions and images of athletics. Frisby (2016) used a content analysis to determine if news stories were found to depict and marginalize athletes based on their race. In the work, Frisby (2016) found that white male athletes tend to receive more positive attention from sports media, and they receive more salient coverage than black male athletes. Data in the Frisby study (2016) further showed that, currently, sports coverage of athletes is not the same quantitatively or qualitatively for black male athletes. Black male athletes were most often portrayed in news stories as criminals and perpetrators of domestic/sexual violence and were shown to be moral failures (Frisby, 2016).

In another content analysis focused on the use of microaggressions on female athletes in the United States, data show that media set an agenda that sends messages concerning appropriate roles for women. Research supports this notion and shows that in most media, women are expected to fit into roles that our culture has for females. We find that women are held to very restrictive ideas in terms of how to act and behave, even when they participate in physical competition (Ho & Kaskan, 2016). Allen and Frisby (2017) created a content analysis seeking information on how often and in what context microaggressions were used in reporting on female Olympic athletes during the 2012 and 2016 Summer Olympic Games. Data obtained in the Allen and Frisby study show that, currently, print media in sports news rely on several microaggression themes in their stories ($p < 0.001$). The content analysis showed significant microaggressions relating to second-class citizenship, racist and sexist language, jokes relating to racism and sexism, and stories that focused predominately on a female athletes' bodies, shape, and appearance in the news articles about female sports figures. Further, data showed significant relationships between female athletes' participation in a masculine or feminine sport and the frequency of microaggressions, ethnicity of the athlete and types of jokes and language found in printed news stories, and the increase in microaggressions printed in accounts for the 2016 Summer Olympic games.

New technology has now created challenges for mass communication researchers, especially when it comes to measuring media effects. For example, innovations in satellite and cable television, blogs, social media, and other outlets provided by the Internet have greatly affected the depth and acquisition of information available to people in today's media culture.

Measuring the Media and Public Agendas

Agenda setting uses various research methods to in order to answer research questions, tests hypotheses, and collect data. One methodology frequently employed in agenda-setting studies involves asking respondents to respond to open-ended questions, such as, "What do you feel is the most important issue related to sports and athletes?" Or, "What is the most important issue related to athletics in your community?" A second research method used in this theory often asks respondents to review a list of social issues and then rate the perceived importance of the issues found in the list. The third research method is a variation of the aforementioned research approach. This methodology provides a list of issues, but unlike the previous method, participants are asked to list the issues in rank order of importance. The fourth research method involves a paired-comparisons analysis. Issues on the list generated by the researchers are paired with other issues. Participants are then asked to consider each pair of issues and then to identify the most critical issue. Responses are tabulated, and the issues are presented by showing what respondents identified as most important to least important.

As with all types of research, each research method discussed in this chapter has advantages and disadvantages. Open-ended items in any research study allow respondents to have their own individual freedom of thought in responding and providing their opinions about issues. However, critics of the open-ended method believe that this method tends to favor people who are skilled at verbalizing their thoughts. Compared to the open-ended measures, closed-ended rankings and rating techniques used in survey measures often ensure that all respondents are given the same common list and vocabulary. One interesting caveat of these methods is that researchers assume that participants in the study are consciously aware of the issues that have been preselected. Researchers also restrict participants from expressing a personal point of view. The paired-comparisons method has an advantage over the other methods in that it provides interval data. Interval data allows researchers to conduct more sophisticated statistical techniques. The main disadvantage of the paired-comparison method is the time it takes to complete this type of study. Researchers find that it takes significantly more time to complete a paired-comparison study than the time involved with the other research methods.

Three essential methods are often used in data collection that relies on agenda-setting theory: (1) length of time involved in the media agenda under investigation, (2) the discrepancy in time between when the agenda was observed and the observation of the consumer's perception of the media agenda, and (3) the total length of time for the observation of the audience agenda measurement. Currently, agenda-setting researchers are seeking ways to incorporate more detailed longitudinal analysis measures into the agenda-setting research method.

For some agenda-setting scholars and researchers, experiments are employed to test causation and causal directions. Experiments as a research method are also used to measure the effect of frequent exposure to different message frames. For example, researchers manipulate the frame employed in a news story. In a hypothetical story about athletes, sports, and agenda setting, researchers might create a story in which an athlete is stereotyped and create another story in which the athlete goes against culturally accepted stereotypes. Next, researchers would measure the reactions that readers reported after exposure to the news stories. Data revealing that the frame emphasizing the most positive reactions might also show higher increased liking for the athlete compared to the news frames that contained stereotypes and less positive frames.

Cultivation of Social Reality

How does media influence our perceptions of the real world? Cultivation theory assumes that repeated exposures to media themes and media portrayals actually influence perceptions that align with the media portrayals that were consumed. In effect, as mentioned in a previous section of this chapter, cultivation of social reality presumes that one learns from the media environment. When we study cultivation, we are seeking to determine what people learn from media exposure and how that information then transforms into information that is widely applied to other circumstances and most likely that it is applied incorrectly to the real world. As with agenda-setting, academic scholars sometimes question the accuracy or meaning of cultivation research and its findings (Wurtzel & Lometti, 1984), yet many critics have attempted to replicate or rely on the methodology themselves.

Potter (1988) found a relationship between the extent to which we identify with characters we see on television and the informational motives and needs of a viewer. In fact, data obtained found that identification with characters in television might have significant effects of cultivation. In other words, Potter (1988) asserts that consumers respond in different ways to television content. As we learn from uses and gratifications theory, people have and are motivated to use and consume media for a variety of different reasons, and it is that information that cultivation theorists use to determine the strength of the cultivation effect. Currently, cultivation analysis is a popular theory to research and gains a plethora of attention from media scholars. Cultivation researchers use the theory to analyze attitudes toward issues such as health and fitness, cosmetic surgery (Nabi, 2009), gun control, and mental health (Diefenbach & West, 2007) based on the level of media exposure.

Cultivation Analysis Research Methods

Cultivation analysis research relies on two steps when performing an analysis of the effect of attitude cultivation. First, objective facts and other descriptions of the media must be obtained to identify common themes and messages in the media. According to Wimmer and Dominick (1997), the common themes and messages are used in the research to assist scholars in identifying specific issues, policies, and social topics. The successful identification of the themes, messages, and depictions occurs by using a set of questions that determine a cultivation effect. Each survey question looks like a multiple-choice question, where the answer is poised between two or more distractor items. These distractor items are aligned with the idea that is presented in media, while another is more in line with actual statistics found in the real world.

Condry (1989) believes that cultivation tends to rely on the extent to which respondents make attributions about the world around them or if they are making judgments about the world compared to themselves. Sparks and Ogles (1990) also demonstrated a cultivation effect when data observed in their study showed that individuals who report high media use perceived a higher fear of crime as well as higher chances of being victimized when compared to individuals who report lower media consumption. Similar findings to support cultivation analysis were obtained in a study conducted by Shanahan, Morgan, and Stenbjerre (1997). Data obtained in the Shanahan et al. (1997) study proves that heavy consumption of television is related to a general state of fear and perceptions that the world is violent. Yet the researchers also found that this cultivation effect was not related to "viewers' perceptions of specific sources of environmental threats" (Shanahan et al., 1997).

For cultivation researchers to survey people about television exposure, participants are often divided into two groups: heavy and light viewers. Next, researchers will compare the two groups' answers to the question to determine whether massive exposure to TV viewing is associated with fear of the real world. In these types of studies, we must rely on correlations between the participant's total exposure to television viewing and index scores that reflect the correct number of answers to the comparison questions. Often reported "is the overall percentage of heavy viewers minus the percentage of light viewers who gave the correct answers" (Morgan & Shanahan, 1997). For example, if 80% of heavy viewers state that the correct answer to the question is the answer that depicts the message found on television while 72% of light viewers are able to detect the correct real-world statistic, then the cultivation index would show the cultivation differential is approximately 8%. Laboratory experiments often employ the same general research method but with one caveat: Experimental research often manipulates the participant's exposure to television content by showing the experimental group one or more TV programs.

One essential criterion when researching cultivation effects focuses on measurement of cultivation. It has been documented that decisions centered on how one measures cultivation can affect the findings. For example, Potter and Chang (1990) used five different measurement techniques to determine cultivation effects: (1) obtain a measure of participants' total TV viewing exposure, (2) identify their exposure to different TV genres, (3) control for total exposure and compare the exposure to program types, (4) create an index for viewing by dividing time spent by the type of program, and (5) weight an index by multiplying hours viewed per week by the index calculated in step 3 (also see Hetsron & Tukachimski, 2006). Data collected using the techniques found in the Potter and Chang (1990) study shows that "total viewing time is not a strong predictor of cultivation scores."

Potter (1991a) demonstrated that the cutting point that distinguishes heavy viewers from light viewers is a crucial procedure in the research methodology that media scholars use, and their use of creating the two groups can and will ultimately influence the results of the cultivation analysis. Potter's research is used to explain why cultivation effects are small in magnitude. Research might find minimal effects because when researchers divide viewers into heavy and light groups, the process may negate individual differences among viewers. Diefenbach and West (2001) provide another insight into possible ways of gathering data and support for cultivation. In their study of the cultivation of media, the researchers were unable to determine that a relationship exists between heavy consumption of TV and viewer estimates of murder and burglary rates.

Audience Characteristics

To know as much as they can about the people affected most by exposure to media messages, researchers often conduct media audience research. This research relies on survey data that answers questions about their activities, interests, opinions, media preferences and exposures, needs, desires, and, to some extent, things they dislike. This research method produces data that allows scholars to obtain a profile of the audience and the media that they expose themselves to on a regular basis.

Uses and Gratifications

Using survey research, this method can show how consumers use media in their daily lives and why. Although researchers have yet to create an exhaustive list of uses and gratifications, preliminary results taken from studies employing this theory provide insights into some general trends (Wimmer & Dominick, 2011. Primary uses and gratifications are often found to be (1) information, (2) surveillance, (3) entertainment, (4) escape, and (5) pastime. The primary media use currently seems to be for the purposes of getting information. A Pew Research Center survey (2013) confirmed this and found that "more than 80% of their respondents reported using the Internet to find information on a specific topic" (for more on the survey, see Anderson & Rainie, 2012).

A recent study conducted by Nielsen Market Research (2007) revealed that about 75% of participants report using the Internet specifically for informational needs, with most participants stating that they look for detailed information on products or services. Thus, effectively consumed, research tells us that the appropriate media can entertain and inform in positive ways and not just in antisocial ways. However, because research shows that many children in our culture do not receive instructions on how to use media or even how to interpret media messages, exposure to mediated messages may actually have a negative effect on their attitudes toward issues such as safe sex, health and fitness, body image, attractiveness, obesity, cyberbullying, aggression and violence, low self-esteem, depression, alcohol and substance abuse, and other public health problems.

Qualitative and Quantitative Research

Data collected in research studies in the form of tables, numbers, facts, figures, and other information is typically used to describe and document what occurs in a situation or as a result of an experience.

Data collected is used to discuss trends found in the media to explain or understand social events, people, groups, patterns, beliefs, images, and relationships.

Data is often collected through qualitative or quantitative research approaches. A qualitative approach is defined as collecting information about people or events and analyzing that information through descriptive or interpretive procedures. Information obtained through qualitative research is presented in the forms of feelings or open-ended questions that allow individuals to explain and describe an event or situation by telling researchers what they feel, say, believe, and do.

Qualitative Research Methods

Queer research reveals one challenge to the validity and reliability of the findings: It is possible that not all persons who are "out" or identify with the LGBTQ group will want the public to know they identify as LGBTQ (Roper, 2013). This "spiral of silence" also makes it extremely difficult for qualitative researchers to solicit participants for interviews and focus groups. One possible explanation for the popularity of qualitative research methods over quantitative research is that qualitative research uses simplistic methods to solicit participants. Qualitative researchers often obtain participants through snowball sampling methods—a sample procedure that relies on a referral network where the researcher has an "in" with participants through personal and professional contacts. Then the participant is asked to refer other interested people who fit the criteria for the study. The snowball sampling method affords persons who identify as LGBTQ to have a voice and to be included in the research while still maintaining their privacy, confidentiality, and pride regarding their identity. Listed next are a few of the qualitative research methods, along with a brief definition of each:

Focus groups involve a group discussion section with, on average, six to 12 individuals who are assembled to discuss a specific topic so that they might produce new insights about media. A professional moderator is used to guide the discussion. It takes a greatly skilled moderator to lead a focus group effectively. Moderators help achieve the main goal of focus group discussions: to get new ideas and gain a better and deeper understanding of media consumers.

Fieldwork is another qualitative research method that allows media researchers to learn from the experiences of people through direct observation. Media audience researchers are attempting to capture the real-life experiences of people, and this research method makes it easy to capture media use, exposure, and effects.

Use of secondary research sources, such as the data collected from the Census Bureau, the National Archives and Records Administration, and the Current Population Survey, is also a qualitative research method. Media scholars also rely on market research sources such as the Nielsen Retail Index, the Consumer Mail Panel, the Audit Bureau of Circulations, and the Pew Research Center, among many others.

The Internet also provides qualitative research sources. It has changed the way we approach research in a qualitative study. Search engines now provide researchers with access to ginormous amounts of data, at little to no cost. Of particular value regarding qualitative research are online social communities, such as Google Plus, Facebook, Twitter, Instagram, Pinterest, and Snapchat. Social media allows scholars to identify the spread of issues, topics, and audience reactions that not only let researchers know where people go on the Internet but also tells them what people do when they are there and tracks other places people go and how long they visit the pages. By tracking retweets or number of shares, media researchers can identify the topics and issues that engage consumers and certain social groups.

Quantitative Research

A quantitative research approach collects information about a person, place, or thing and translates the individual's thoughts, feelings, attitudes, and behaviors into numbers that can be analyzed using statistical procedures and tests. The numbers obtained are often presented in tables or in figures that show the numerical differences and similarities between or among groups. This type of research approach is used when researchers would like to see the "big picture" or are interested in general patterns, causation (experiments), relationships between variables, and comparisons between groups.

Quantitative Research Methods

There are a few common methods to collect quantitative numerical data. Listed next are a few of the methods used in studies specializing in quantitative research.

Surveys are the most common method used in sports media research. A survey is a method used to collect information from a sample of people by using a questionnaire. Surveys are employed to collect information in direct response to the study's research questions. Surveys can be conducted in person, by e-mail on the Internet, or by phone.

A survey might also seek to discover if a media message is communicating what the media/journalists wanted to communicate. This research method is called a communication test, and these are performed to prevent conflict and misinformed media messages. This type of research should be performed to test objectivity and facts, especially regarding the perpetuation of stereotypes. Communication tests allow sports researchers and journalists to prevent sending out stories that communicate ideas and opinions that are completely wrong. Keep in mind our discussion of schemas and priming: People's selective perceptions and schemas encourage them to see what they want to see, so communication tests help identify ways audiences might perceive a story—whether intended or unintended by the journalist. This research method, perhaps, could be used to determine "fake news" from "real news," for example.

Recall studies document media that consumers are exposed to and then record the elements of the message that mixed with the readers' or viewers' thoughts and reactions. This research method is helpful when seeking questions related to elements of a story or ad that resonates more with people. This method would work well with the uses and gratifications theoretical perspective in that the researcher could focus on the individual's motivation to be exposed to the media. It is possible that people remember parts of a sports story that they want to remember, even if certain facts were not mentioned or included. It is possible that exposure to, motivation to be exposed, and memory may all interact to create ideas and experiences in our minds. Regardless, this research method requires that we review schemas, stereotypes, and other cognitions, and determine their role in elements of stories that are recalled freely and without aid.

Thought listing or cognitive response analysis is a quantitative research method that measures thoughts and ideas that exposure to a news story generates in the minds of the reader/viewer. Cognitive responses are collected by having individuals read a story or watch a story, and when finished, they are asked to write down thoughts that occurred while reading or watching the news story. The responses are then analyzed by counting the number of thoughts or by scoring the ratio of favorable to unfavorable thoughts. Some researchers like to determine how many times the individual had a thought that was related to some aspect of his or herself.

Attitude change studies rely on experimental approaches that measure attitudes after exposure to media content. The studies may enlist surveys, or they may incorporate lab or field experiments. Attitude tests are premised on exposure to a particular media message and often include some pre-and postexposure measurement so that researchers might be able to determine the change related to exposure to the mediated message.

Regarding social groups, some media scholars might employ quantitative research methods that allow them to identify feelings and emotions elicited by particular news stories. For example, in testing a particular news story involving athletes of color and drugs, researchers might expose the story to a representative sample of athletes of color and measure how they respond to the story and the imagery used in the story. In today's turbulent media culture, particularly regarding racial conflicts, journalists may want to take more time to conduct resonance tests and ask readers, "How do you feel about this story?" "How do you feel the story represents athletes of color?" And, "Does this ad match your own experiences with [social group]?"

A content analysis is one of the most important and commonly used techniques in research concerning media. Researchers using this method want to learn something about media by examining what they write or produce. A content analysis might also be used to compare and contrast different variables, such as gender or race, to determine differences in how media treat members of those groups.

Sports media researchers and scholars are typically interested in asking one or more of the following questions:

- How are athletes and sports represented in media coverage? And how does that portrayal affect behaviors and attitudes?

- Why do we have gender-appropriate categorized sports? What cultural factors have led to the segregation of specific sports based on gender? How do genderfluid and nonbinary individuals fit into sports if sports are split solely between men and women?

- Who has power in sports? What role do owners play in professional teams? Does social class influence the ethnicity and background of owners of professional sports organizations? How is the power used in the institution of a sport?

- What happens to athletes or teams who resist civil rights issues in our culture? Who decides what athletes can and cannot protest, and what can they protest that will gain the most support? Is protesting by athletes ethical, unethical, or something they should just avoid during their careers?

- What changes are needed in the world of sports journalism and media coverage to effectively bring equitable coverage to marginalized athletes and sports?

Research That Results in Media Literacy

Media literacy teaches people to apply critical thinking skills when exposed to media messages. Media scholars are finding that media literacy is a key and much-needed 21st-century skill. According to the website, Media Literacy Now, a focus on media literacy involves critically analyzing messages regarding the health and well-being of our children. These activists also believe that media literacy and a focus on children is important because they affect future participation in the civic and economic lives of our culture.

Media literacy is concerned with developing a critical understanding of mass media. Workshops in media literacy teach techniques used by media and the effect and influences of the techniques on consumer attitudes and behaviors. More specifically, media literacy also aims to enhance potential journalists and other students' abilities to create media products that are objective, equitable, and fair. According to a Kaiser Foundation (2005) study, children spend over 40 hours a week consuming media. This statistic mandates the need to make sure media scholars and others teach students and adults to analyze messages in media content so that they can know and appreciate messages that media want them to learn from exposure to the content. The key with media literacy training is to be sure that people learn how to unlearn or not integrate messages considered to be antisocial or wrong. "Knowing how to 'read' messages in the media is called media literacy" (Worsnop, 2003). Media literacy means taking a second look at the content and the source of the message that is produced and published in mass media.

Media literacy involves expanding the basic idea of "literacy" (the ability to read and write) to helping people learn, understand, explain, and negotiate symbols and meanings in a culture that is composed of powerful symbols, images, and words (Aufderheide, 1993). Media literate individuals should be able to decode, evaluate, analyze, and produce both print and broadcast, as well as social media, successfully and accurately. As a media literate individual, you learn how to ask the right questions. Questions such as who created and produced the message? Why did they create and produce the message? How and why did they choose what to include and what to leave out of the message? How do you think the author intended to influence you? (Aufderheide, 1993).

Media Literate Americans

For Americans to become media literate, they must learn to

- identify the influences of media messages and how those messages may be used to manipulate them;
- identify media forms, contents, and outcomes, realizing that media provide multiple interpretations of content. Media literate people can also explain how media influences people by way of examining ideas, images, and words used in media content and their social and cultural consequences;
- critically evaluate media messages so that research can uncover the covert messages and values found in media messages;
- understand media messages in ways that do not damage our self-esteem;
- identify appropriate media used to communicate with media audiences. Specifically, they look for media to deliver specific messages and outcomes to receptive audience members. They also recognize that media has individual, social, and ethical consequences; and
- media literacy is the most efficient means of specifically challenging individuals to understand the constructed nature of media representations and how images and messages might influence their own beliefs about themselves and others.

The main goal of this book and the information contained in it is to challenge readers to think, elaborate on, and recognize images and messages embedded in sports media content that eventually spill over into American culture. The main idea behind the notion of media literacy is the discussion and application of research and the presentation of statistics concerning the representation of images of athletes. Chapters in this textbook will encourage readers to expand their thoughts and should help the media effects scholars understand how Americans, especially sports fans, may perceive what they view in different types of media; this is the heart of media literacy. We must keep in mind that research tells us that by "mid-adolescence, teens have watched many thousands of hours of television—more time than they spend with teachers in school" (see more from the Kaiser Foundation, 2005). Now in 2018, we must add to that statistic the number of hours teens spend surfing the Internet, on social media, interacting and playing video games, shopping, going to movies, texting or using cell phone/smartphones and related mobile applications, and many other extracurricular activities.

Conclusion

Theories and research in sports help media scholars understand that games are more than reflections or mirrors of society. Research helps us to discover how sports media provide meaning; how they help us to understand and explain individual relationships, and the role that media play in informing us of those relationships; and how relationships are created, maintained, or changed.

Experiments and surveys are popular research methods used to study the effect of media on individual behavior. The more elaborate research methods used in many field experiments and panel studies are infrequently used in published studies. Laboratory experiments are used to expose causal relationships and tend to show a stronger positive relationship between media exposure and the effect on antisocial behavior than the other research methods. Learning about the ways that research and theory help us predict, explain, and understand sports media and their mediated messages is part of the process of helping us engage in critical thinking skills as well as enhance our media literacy abilities. When we begin to start critically examining the media, asking questions, using theory, and researching to answer the questions, then we can become aware of the role media play in creating values and ideas about sports, athletes, and events in our culture. It is hoped that this chapter will lead you to become a more informed participant in the journalism, sports psychology, sociology of sport, and mass communication industries.

The direct effects model of media studies has since been discredited because it assumes that media audiences passively consume and subconsciously accept media messages. This theory and associated research methods often attempt to prove that there are predictable reactions in response to exposure to mediated messages.

Reliable theories in media effect often do not credit the media with this much influence and power. For example, agenda-setting theory, a theory used to replace the direct effects theory, allows the presupposition that media consumers are much more active regarding media content, especially about selectivity and exposure to media content.

Other theories used in mass media research focus on the additional attributes and characteristics of the influence and effects of media exposure. For example, the spiral of silence theory investigates how one's perception of majority opinion affects an individual's feeling of confidence in sharing his or her opinion.

USING THE INTERNET

Listed next are websites that provide information about media effects research:

1. www.pewinternet.org. The Pew Research Center's Internet & American Life Project is an academic publication that includes research on the "effects of the internet on children, families, communities, the workplace, schools, health care, and civic/political life" (Levin & Arafeh; Levin, Richardson, & Arafeh, 2002). The Pew Research Center is a good reference for those interested in current data on Internet use and gratification.

2. http://www.aber.ac.uk/media/Documents/short/cultiv.html. The site contains a helpful overview of cultivation analysis and its methods.

3. http://zimmer.csufresno.edu/~johnca/spch100/7-4-uses.htm. This site contains an extended discussion of the uses and gratifications approach.

QUESTIONS FOR REFLECTION AND DISCUSSION

1. In terms of how media affect our culture, what are your thoughts about media effects? What theory are you using to predict, explain, and understand the effects of media? What theory would you use to determine the effects of media on society?

2. Consider the argument concerning media and violence and aggression. This also affects political issues concerning gun control. To what extent do you feel that media exacerbate violence in its content?

3. Define and operationalize episodic and thematic frames. Can you provide an example of current news stories in sports that demonstrate the use of an episodic frame? Thematic frame? What cues were used to help you determine one from the other?

4. How do you make sense of discussion and arguments about media effects regarding violence? How do you make sense of the media's role in creating and maintaining stereotypes?

5. Think of a time when you had to review something or rewatch a movie or a show, reread a book, or even reevaluate a news story. What happened when you had to go back and reread or rewatch the content? Did that "second look" at the content result in a modification of your initial reaction? Why or why not?

6. With the advent of social media, many users are finding that more individuals are comfortable posting hateful narratives and replies to posts. What variables might play a role in this new "freedom of speech"?

7. Why is media literacy important?

8. Part of becoming media literate involves taking an informed stand on why the media are important. Why do you think media are important? What new ideas will you use to help you to stay current with press coverage of media developments in the sports journalism industry?

SUGGESTED ACTIVITIES

1. Media theories have a variety of uses and applications. Research one of the following topics and its effect on culture. Next, take one of the five topics listed below and apply at least two of the research methodologies discussed in this chapter. Then write a one-page essay about the topic and the research method you've selected.

   Media bias
   Internet habits
   Television's effect on attention span
   Advertising and self-image
   Racial stereotyping in film

2. Many of the mass media research and theories discussed in this chapter were developed more than 50 years ago. Distinguish how each of these theories can be used today in the sports media and journalism research program agenda. Do you think these theories are still relevant to modern mass media? Why?

3. Find a show that attempts to motivate its viewers to think about and discuss race relations, racial and ethnic identity, and experiences of two racial groups. The purpose of this activity is to determine what perceptions you and others take away from the show. Does it perpetuate or help reduce stereotyping? What does the show say about people's feelings regarding interracial dating? Questions you must address to obtain the media literacy skills are as follows: (1) What do I see? (2) What do I think it means? (3) How did the meaning that I got from the image(s) and portrayal(s) get that way? (4) To what extent is the portrayal or issue appropriate, a good thing, or handled efficiently? (5) What does the representation or issue tell me about some aspects of our media system or our society? (6) Why do I say that or feel this way?

4. Find a news story you've recently read or viewed regarding how it might prime stereotypes of a social group's achievements or athletic success in sports media. Identify the "cues" or frames in the story that might be congruent with a person's schema. What are the implications of framing, stereotypes, and schemas for sports journalists? What ideas do you have that might suggest ways sports journalists can limit the extent to which they "inadvertently" cue and prime specific stereotypes? Rewrite the news story you found in a way that you can change the content so that it gets the desired message across without triggering a stereotype or schema.

5. Find a magazine cover or image of an athlete. How might the image prime our stereotypes of the social group to which the person belongs? Next, redesign the ad or magazine cover to get the desired message across without having to stereotype the individual. For example, a stereotyped image might be that of a picture of a female athlete in her full athletic gear and uniform on the cover of a magazine.

6. Next, identify a medium that you would like to analyze. For example, you can use a comic book. Obtain comic books of the same subject. Seek comic books for a year or 5 years. Then you might want to count the number of female comic book characters of color, or maybe even from the LGBTQ group. Count each time you see a figure in a frame on the page. Determine the percentages of the images you found. Next, you want to discover patterns in your data: Are there interesting differences in the types of female comic book characters you found? If so, what are they? Why do you think this occurred? Discuss the problems you faced in doing your content analysis and how you dealt with those problems. Now write a press release to the media about your findings. Be sure that you discuss the issues you investigated, your method, your results, and your conclusion.

7. Construct a survey instrument designed to either execute a communication or resonance test. You are interested in determining stereotypes found in news stories about athletes and how your respondents react to the message.

8. Construct a survey that assesses how much time respondents spend exposed to various media. When and why do they partake of different media? Note: This is a sample of doing a study focused on uses and gratifications.

9. Collect several different news stories about an event or topic in the news. Be sure to gather stories from a number of varied sources. Can you identify differences in how the stories are framed? What themes or differences, if any, were you able to detect?

3

Gender, Sex, and Racial Identity in Sports

LEARNING OBJECTIVES

After completing this chapter, students should be able to:

- critically consider social issues related to gender, race, and sexual identity that shape our world;

- define identity regarding gender, race, and sexuality through the lens of sports;

- recognize the role that sports play in identifying a sense of empowerment and oppression of masculine and feminine sports and identities;

- understand the role that sports have in enhancing self-esteem and well-being for athletes;

- learn the potential that identity has in challenging gender norms and providing opportunities for athletes to lead and act as change agents in the sports industry; and

- discuss the intersectionality of gender, race, and sexual identity in sports studies, focusing on media coverage of athletes—particularly athletes who are often marginalized in American sports.

Introduction

Sports participation has become a fixture in the lives of many Americans. From an early age, many people are engaged in or connected to various sporting activities in some fashion. Sports participation intersects race, gender, and ethnic boundaries. We know that our racial or gender identity influences the level of involvement and participation in particular sports. Particularly, some sports have strong ethnic labels associated with them, which may make participation in a specific sport a self-defining activity (Harrison, Lee, & Belcher, 1999). This self-defining role, according to research, has been called "athletic identity" (Brewer, Van Raalte, & Linder, 1993). Research on athletic identity shows that identity has historical roots, especially when it comes to athletes who identify as African American. The integration of African Americans in American athletic competitions was deemed a catalyst for a significant amount of research focused on race and sport. Historical research on sports and race or ethnicity of athletes often relied on genetic, biological, and anthropometric assumptions—those assumptions have produced unreliable explanations. However, overrepresentation of African American athletes, especially those found in a limited number of sporting events, led scholars to examine African American athlete's self-conceptualization and identity. In other words, because of the country's history regarding race relations, it was hypothesized that participation in sports might create essential meanings for athletes of color.

Sports provide people with a physical means to differentiate themselves from others. The relationship between sports and identity is most visible in events such as the Olympic Games, volleyball, or World Cup soccer. When Jackie Robinson broke the racial barriers in baseball, Americans began to understand the influential nature of sports, especially regarding the role it plays in dividing us or unifying us as a nation. The next sections in this chapter will survey the concepts of gender, sex, and race identities, and their effect on sports and media coverage of these identities.

Masculine and Feminine Identity and Sports

Customarily, sport in American culture has been described as a "masculine" activity. Masculine identity, therefore, has also influenced the field of sports in American culture for years. According to Wachs (2003), "Like many other public environments, sports historically have been associated with masculinity" (p. 178). This cultural ideology of masculinity also related to identity and how it significantly affects athletes and their perceptions concerning opportunities to be encouraged to participate in sports. Our society's definition of the sports that are the most appropriate for boys and girls and men and women are very much considered to be tangible cultural artifacts of the effect that masculine identity has on our ideas of what it means to be boys or girls, men or women. All of these ideologies can not only influence athletes' self-confidence and esteem but also these identity ideologies can be communicated in the media.

In Chapter 2, we defined and discussed the development of stereotypes. One of the most widely held presumptions in American culture that appears to be directly related to gender and sports is the idea that there are certain sports deemed to be more "appropriate" and "inappropriate" for females and males. In this chapter, we hope to show that media tend to cover females participating in gender-inappropriate sports more negatively than they do female athletes participating in gender appropriate sports, such as ice-skating and gymnastics. Media scholars and sports media researchers continue to discover that sports that tend to include and emphasize skills related to beauty and grace, such as gymnastics, dance, and figure skating, are often regarded as "feminine." The literature further shows that the sports that rely heavily on violence, aggression, and physical contact, such as football, boxing, and combat sports are often associated with "masculinity" (Koivula, 2001). These cultural beliefs regarding femininity and masculinity are not created by what we do, but what society and, in particular, media think we should (or should not) do.

Defining Gender

Identity is an important topic in sports research. An in-depth review of the literature shows that scholars who study sports often recognize that athletes' identities are intersected with other aspects of their identities, such as gender, ethnicity, sexual orientation, social class, and religiosity (Crenshaw, 1991; Krane & Barber, 2005; Ryba & Wright, 2005; Sasaki & Kim, 2011). According to the American Psychological Association (2007, 2011, 2015), gender identity is described as "the psychological sense of being male or female." One's psychological sense of being "male" or "female" is socialized and developed within the context of culture. In fact, Bornstein (2012) identified 15 areas where our identities intersect. The areas listed in his work include "class, race, age, ability status, mental health, religion, family/children, politics, appearance, language, habitat/ecology, citizenship, sexuality, and humanity" (Bornstein, 2012).

Culture provides norms and opinions about how we should and are expected to act, dress, look, interact, and respond. These norms and opinions work together to contribute to gender identity. For many Americans, sex and gender are easily confused. We often forget that biological or assigned sex is about "biology, anatomy, and chromosomes" (Andersen & Hysock, 2009;

Scheper-Hughes, 1987). On the other hand, research informs us to consider gender as a type of label that is based on a culture's expectations, morals, values, and guidelines about how men and women are supposed to act (Begley, 2009; Eliot, 2009).

Yet confusion in how the words sex and gender are often used is commonplace in our culture in that sex and gender are often assumed to be one and the same with parallel characteristics. This assumption in using the terms interchangeably is incorrect. According to the American Psychological Association website on gender identity (2011), sex "refers to a person's biological status" and can be identified by "sex chromosomes, gonads, internal reproductive organs, and external genitalia," while gender refers to "the attitudes, feelings, and behaviors that a given culture associates with a person's biological sex" (American Psychological Association 2011, 2015).

In our gendered culture, people are typically classified into two categories: male or female. In American customs, it is assumed that a baby who is born with a penis is labeled a male, and thus he will be "masculine." And continuing with this illustration, babies born with vaginas are categorized as female and thus determined to be "feminine." Sex and gender, although different constructs as defined earlier, are inextricably intertwined in American culture and often construed to be the accepted sex and gender labels. Integrating sex and gender constructs is a sociological process that is particularly endorsed in cultures such as the United States, where males are frequently found to hold an unbalanced share of wealth, influence, control, and power.

Defining Gender Identity

Gender identity refers to how a person feels on the inside and how those feelings are demonstrated and expressed in their actions (Powell & Butterfield, 2003). For example, the way we dress, the accessories we wear, and our appearance, along with the way we act, are all the ways in which we express our gender identities. When asked which gender they identify with, most people will say that they are either male or female. Some might say that on the inside they feel like a "masculine female" or a "feminine male." Some people may say that they do not identify as male or female. On their website, Planned Parenthood informs us that for the most part, "some people's assigned sex and gender identity are pretty much the same, or, are in line with each other." According to information on the web page, when one's sex and gender identities are aligned, they are referred to as "*cisgender*" (Planned Parenthood, 2018).

Regarding women and sports, we learned in Chapter 1 of this text, and from historical research in sports, that female athletes were afforded fewer opportunities to play at the professional level in sports. Until current times, it was even a complicated, complex challenge just to get fans to want to watch, let alone pay to watch, women play aggressive, physical "masculine" sports. However, they would pay to watch those sporting events that our culture considered to be more "ladylike." Feminine sports considered to be ladylike were those sporting activities by which women competed alone (e.g., figure skating, golf). Other sports that were deemed more "ladylike" were sports that would have nets that separated teams, including sports such as tennis and volleyball. According to Coakley (2009), in the new millennium, sports fans tend to be more willing to pay to watch women play sports. Research shows that the most popular spectator sports—that is, the sports that fans are willing to pay for—are "tennis, figure skating, gymnastics, and golf—all of which are consistent with traditional notions of femininity" (Coakley, 2009, p. 248).

After the introduction of Title IX, sports in American experienced a rise in the number of women participating in sports. The increase in female athletic participation, some argue, caused many fans and even top executives in the sporting industry to conclude that some sports are more appropriate for males while other sports are more suitable for women. In other words, in more recent times, sports fans have come to view some sports as "gender neutral" (Hardin & Greer, 2009). For example, Hardin and Greer (2009) reported that here in the United States, sports such as "soccer, tennis, and swimming are viewed as gender neutral and much more acceptable for both males and females" (p. 21). One important caveat must be noted; the gender-neutral label for some sports varies based on the geographical location. For example, as we will learn in later chapters in this text, in many Middle Eastern and other cultures, soccer, swimming, or track and field are not acceptable activities for girls or women to participate in (Walter & Du Randt, 2011).

Without regard to sexual orientation, many athletes who participate in gender-inappropriate sports are often ridiculed and subjected to violence and hate crimes. These responses are frequently derived from a culture's ideals regarding what it means to be male or female. Therefore, men who engage in feminine sports (e.g., gymnastics) and women who participate in masculine sports (e.g., basketball, boxing) are oftentimes treated as if they are nonexistent or even disparaged by fans and media. For example, Kian and Hardin (2009) investigated how the gender of sports journalists affects their stories and coverage of athletes and sports. In other words, the major point of the investigation was to learn how the sex of a sports journalist affects the way he or she frames an athlete in the sport of basketball. Data obtained in the study showed that the gender of the journalist significantly influenced how male and female sports journalists covered and framed stories about men and women basketball players (Kian & Hardin, 2009). Moreover, the researchers used the data obtained to show that female sports writers frequently "include female athletes more in their coverage and are less likely to reinforce traditional gender stereotypes of female athletes than male sports writers" (Kian & Hardin, 2009). From this study, we might conclude that our culture's hegemonic, homophobic stereotypes about appropriate behaviors for men and women are sustained and reinforced in sports media. Frisby (2017b) conducted a study that measured gender differences on the cover of sports magazines.

In her work, for example, Frisby (2017a) found little to no improvement in how female athletes are portrayed and no improvement regarding sexualization and objectification, particularly when compared to male athletes. We find that female athletes are continually held to cultural norms that suggest that they display the appropriate "feminine" behaviors and that they must do so in order to garner media attention and avoid being labeled as homosexual. In this same way, we see that male athletes are always presented in media as masculine, engaging in appropriate masculine behaviors, and, more interestingly, they are often and more frequently presented as being heterosexual (Coakley, 2009; Frisby, 2017a; 2017b; Knight & Guiliano, 2003). One suggested remedy for these strict general roles for appropriate male and female behaviors might be to consciously attempt to bridge the gender inequity gap that currently exists in the sports media professional industry. Lapchick, Milkovich, and O'Keefe (2012) have recommended the following: (1) make conscious and deliberate efforts to recruit sports journalists from "diverse backgrounds and institutions," (2) create policies that will "encourage diversity in hiring practices," (3) foster an environment that communicates a passion for inclusion in the sports media newsroom, and (4) "encourage mentoring practices that help young media professionals exercise their skills and network themselves in professional settings" (Lapchick, Milkovich, & O'Keefe, 2012).

Some gay men could possibly experience frustration in intersectionality of identities and the homophobia that is a traditional component of sports that our culture consider masculine (e.g., football). We will discuss a few nationally recognized media stories related to this, but what we must realize is the pressure that these athletes might feel when they have to "consistently hide their true identity from their teammates, coaches, and the public" (Roper, 2014, p. 15). Intense pressures and internal conflicts may arise simply because of the cultural norms and other perceptions obtained from media exposure. Media may communicate an unspoken message that a majority of Americans will disagree and dislike them because of their sexual orientation. Again, the spiral of silence theory could be used here to test what happens when male athletes reveal their sexual identity and orientation as gay. Research in this area might be used to obtain documentation and data that will either confirm or disconfirm the idea that our culture tends to be hypercritical and less accepting of gay men (Knight & Guiliano, 2001). Some research has found support that our culture is more accepting and less hypercritical of female athletes who identify as lesbian (Knight & Giuliano, 2001.

What Is Queer Theory?

Feminist theorists dislike and oppose the binary definitions assigned to gender and sexual orientation. The main presupposition behind queer theory is the idea that it explores "the processes through which sexual identity is, and has been, constituted in contemporary and past societies" (Edgar & Sedgwick, 2002, p. 321). Scholars using the queer theory typically apply this theory in order to explain, predict, and understand how sexual identity is created by societal and cultural norms during different eras.

Defining Gender Roles

Gender roles tell individuals how they are supposed to and are expected to act, speak, dress, feel, and conduct themselves based on their assigned gender. For example, societal norms tell us that girls (and women) are expected to behave and dress in typically feminine ways. Girls and women are supposed to be "polite, accommodating, and nurturing while boys and men are to be strong, masculine, aggressive, and bold" (AnoushkaBhardwaj, 2017). Every culture, society, and racial and ethnic group have gender role expectations.

Effects of Gender Roles and the Associated Stereotypes

A *stereotype* is a "widely accepted judgment or bias about a person or group—even though the stereotype may be overly simplified and not always accurate" (Hinton, 2017). Stereotypes centered on gender also cause, and are related to, the unequal and unfair treatment of women solely based on their membership in a gender-related group. This is called *sexism*.

Research on the topic of gender tells us that there are four basic kinds of gender stereotypes (Miller, Lurye, Zosuls, & Ruble, 2009).

- *The first type of gender stereotype is referred to as a stereotype regarding personality traits*. This stereotype deals with the expectation that women are often expected to be "supportive, verbal, and impassioned while men are usually expected to be self-confident, masculine, unemotional, and aggressive" (Williams & Best, 1990).
- *Domestic behaviors* are stereotypes that tell us that women are mainly responsible for having and caring for children, preparing meals, and cleaning the house. Men, according to domestic behavior stereotypes, are expected to protect their families financially and physically, take care of finances, participate in contact sports, and do home repairs.
- *Stereotypes related to occupations and careers* assume that jobs like those of teachers and nurses are and should be performed by women. In terms of prescriptions for men, this stereotype implies that careers in engineering and service jobs, such as policeman and sheriff, doctor, lawyer, and pilot are careers that are just for men.
- *The fourth and last stereotype is physical appearance.* The physical appearance stereotype in American culture mandates that women should be thin, forever young, and graceful. This stereotype in our culture communicates the idea that compared to women, men are

expected to be muscular, tall, handsome, and debonair. This stereotype in our culture carries with it the expectation that men and women are also expected to dress and appear in ways that are appropriate and related to their gender (men wear the pants in the family, and women should wear dresses, appear youthful, and apply makeup, particularly lipstick).

Related Stereotypical Gender Behaviors

- ***Hyperfemininity*** is defined as the "exaggeration of stereotyped behavior that's believed to be feminine" (Matschiner & Murnen, 1999). ***Hyperfeminine*** individuals often exaggerate specific behaviors they think are feminine. Common behaviors that are perceived as expressing femininity are actions such as being passive, innocent, sexually inexperienced, forgiving, easygoing, sexually playful, or flirtatious, refined, nurturing, and accepting (Planned Parenthood 2018).
- ***According to a report commissioned by Planned Parenthood (2017), hypermasculinity*** is the "exaggeration of stereotyped behavior that is believed to be masculine" (Hollender, 2016; Planned Parenthood Report, 2017). ***Hypermasculine*** individuals exaggerate qualities they feel are masculine. Consistent with the personality trait stereotype, hypermasculine individuals think they are supposed to be extremely competitive, particularly with other men. They believe that they should and are expected to "dominate women through behaviors like being aggressive, worldly, more sexually experienced, insensitive, physically imposing, ambitious, and demanding" (Planned Parenthood, 2018). Figure 3.1 is an illustration of the conundrum in our country between what it means to be a boy or girl, man or woman. Behaviors and actions that help men to "be a man" or "to man up" are said and felt by boys from a very young age. We hear these phrases in media, in advertisements from our peers, and, perhaps, from our moms and dads and other family members.

FIGURE 3.1   *To be a man or a woman*

We see these gender-related stereotypical behaviors in many aspects of sports journalism and in media messages written about female and male athletes. Female athletes who participate in masculine sports, such as basketball, for example, are often the focus of stories that downplay their accomplishments and skills as athletes. Pictures like those of Dominique Canty, an American professional women's basketball player, most recently with the Washington Mystics, shown in Figure 3.2 are clear examples of ways that we would like to see female athletes who play masculine sports portrayed; however, these images and others often unintentionally help maintain stereotypes that the women

FIGURE 3.2   *Dominique Canty of the Chicago Sky (at time of photo)*

athletes who participate in the sport have masculine-like behaviors and physical attributes. For example, an article found in a sports section of a newspaper tells readers that Britney Griner and other WNBA players have to participate in makeup and wardrobe sessions.

For the WNBA, these sessions are the league's way of making sure that the athlete's femininity is protected, and at the same time, they can reduce the idea that all women in the WNBA are lesbian. This type of practice reinforces the more traditional gender roles. The WNBA and their sessions on makeup and grooming, however, could also alienate women who identify with and have more masculine characteristics, as well as those female athletes who participate in the more masculine, aggressive sports. According to Ho and Kaskan (2016), adherence to gender roles in mediated stories not only perpetuates sexism but also may cause fans to have negative responses and attitudes toward female athletics and their given sport.

Sexual Identity

Similar to gender, sexual identity is made up of two categories: "heterosexual" or "homosexual." However, according to the American Psychological Association (2011, 2015), sexual identity is a process that takes place along a continuum or spectrum that spans from "exclusive homosexuality" to "exclusive heterosexuality" (American Psychological Association, 201). This sexual identity continuum is often known as the lesbian, gay, bisexual, transgender sexual and orientation concept (American Psychological Association, 2011). Basically, according to the American Psychological Association's (2011) definition, sexual orientation and one's sexual identity are considered now to be more dynamic and fluid than they used to be. Aligning with the previous discussion on queer theory, the use of the term "queer" applies to individuals who desire to define their sexual identity as a "process that is in a constant state of unrest. Probably the best description of an individual who identifies as "queer" might be someone who sees him or herself as even being perhaps gender neutral (Gamson, 2000).

What Is Sexual Orientation?

Research on sexual orientation tells us that this is a concept that informs us about physical attraction and the person one is most attracted to and desires to engage in a relationship with. Sexual orientation includes gay, lesbian, straight, bisexual, and asexual (Wood & Schaurer, 2017). Information posted on the Planned Parenthood website (2018) defines sexual orientation as those feelings directed at people you are attracted to and desire romantic relationships with.

Closer examination of Figure 3.3 shows a diagram of possible sexual orientations (homosexuality, heterosexuality, bisexuality, gynephilia, and androphilia. In other words, the Venn diagram shows four basic possible combinations of the relationship between the "gender that you are" and the "gender that you are attracted to." While the terms identified in the diagram "gynephilia" and "androphilia" are not common, nor were they defined in this chapter, the diagram was included

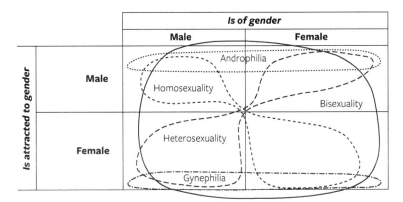

FIGURE 3.3   *Venn diagram of various relationships of gender expression, orientation, and identity*

here to help illustrate and differentiate the distinction between what we are most familiar with—the distinction between homosexual and heterosexual orientations. For example, if you are a female, and you are attracted to both males and females, then according to the figure and our culture's definition of orientation, your orientation would be bisexual. In sum, we are basically referring to the relationship to one's gender and the object of one's affection when we identify one's sexual orientation.

Sexual Orientation Is Different From Gender and Gender Identity

According to the article "Coming Out While Still in the Game," Wood and Schauer (2017), define sexual orientation as something that an individual feels drawn to romantically, emotionally, and sexually. It must be carefully noted that sexual orientation should not be confused with sexual identity. **Sexual orientation is a different construct than sexual identity** in that the latter is about who you are—male, female, gender neutral, etc. Sexual orientation is about who a person feels drawn to and wants to be with romantically, emotionally, and sexually. Transgender is related to feeling that your biologically "assigned sex is different from the gender that one identifies with" (Wood & Schauer, 2017). Transgendered people are not gay, lesbian, or bisexual (Wood & Schauer, 2017).

Planned Parenthood, a nonprofit organization specializing in spreading vital information about health, sex, and reproductive health care, provides an all-encompassing glossary of terms used to help us understand sexual orientation. The list that follows was obtained from the Planned Parenthood. org web page on sexual orientation.

- Individuals attracted to another gender, as identified in Figure 3.3, are often identified, and will identify themselves, as being straight or heterosexual.
- Individuals who are oriented to and are attracted to others in the same gender are identified as and often self-identify with the term "homosexual." It should be noted that gay women may prefer the term lesbian (Planned Parenthood, 2018).
- Those individuals oriented and attracted to both men and women are identified, and typically self-identify, as bisexual.
- Attractions that span across many different gender identities (male, female, transgender, genderqueer, intersex, etc.) are often considered pansexual or queer.
- According to the definitions on the Planned Parenthood website, people who identify as "unsure about their sexual orientation may say that they are questioning or curious."
- "People who report no sexual attraction to either sex will often identify as asexual" (Planned Parenthood, 2018).
- Abstinence or going through moments in time when one does not want to or have any interest in sex is not to be confused with being asexual. Restraining from sex is often referred to as "being celibate" (Planned Parenthood, 2018). According to the Planned Parenthood website, celibacy is "a choice you make, and asexuality is a sexual identity—who you naturally are."

As with many of these labels, we must acknowledge those people who do not ascribe to them and would argue that the labels do not describe or apply to them. There are individuals in our culture who do not ascribe to any labels that may be used to describe them. The point of this section is to provide background on identity and how it is used in sports. Where you stand on the issue of the use of labels is up to you.

Identifying as LGBTQ

LGBTQ stands for lesbian, gay, bisexual, transgender, and queer/questioning.

Although researchers try to ascertain data that tell us how many people identify as LGBTQ, we are finding that it is very difficult to get an accurate number. The difficulty in obtaining data and accurate numbers is due to many people being unsure about their orientation or often reporting no sexual attraction, gender identity, or sexual identity. As mentioned in the previous section,

- gender identity is who you are and feel you are on the inside and how you express those feelings in your behavior, language, feelings, and dress;
- sexual orientation is the romantic or sexual feelings and attraction you have toward others; and
- sexual identity is how you label yourself (e.g., using labels such as queer, gay, lesbian, straight, or bisexual).

Sometimes, all of these identity labels are similar for one person. For instance, a cisgendered woman may be attracted to women, identify as a lesbian, and have sexual relationships with only women. But in some cases, gender identity, sexual orientation, and sexual identity do not always line up. For example, a man who has feelings for other men may not act on those feelings. There are those people who may engage in same-gender sexual behaviors and orientation but will not identify as bisexual, lesbian, or gay. When we truly understand our culture, we can understand the reasons for these situations. As we know, in some cases, coming out as LGBTQ can provoke bullying, fear, and discrimination, making it uncomfortable for people to want to "come out."

Lately, professional athletes who have retired have "come out" publicly to talk about and announce their sexuality and sexual orientation. Retired NBA center John Amaechi wrote a book in 2007 about his sexuality. At the same time that the Supreme Court was debating the issue of same-sex marriage in 2013, we noticed many athletes started to feel comfortable coming out about their sexuality. In fact, many of the athletes were not at the end of their professional careers but were either in their prime or just beginning. Some of the players who came out during this time were soccer player Robbie Rogers, NBA center Jason Collins, and WNBA player Brittney Griner. Then in 2014, before entering the NFL draft, Michael Sam publicly came out. While some athletes may have experienced a few negative comments, it was noted that all of these athletes reported being welcomed with overwhelming praise and support.

Olympians and Beyond

Olympic athletes have also started publicly coming out about their sexuality. Olympic freeskier Gus Kenworthy came out about his sexuality in 2014, just after winning a silver medal in the Sochi 2014 Olympic Winter Games. Mr. Kenworthy came out by sending a tweet that simply stated, "I am gay." In an interview, Kenworthy was quoted as saying, "Hiding everything away is so painful. You're constantly lying and constantly feeling like you're deceitful." The Olympic athlete went on to say in another related article published in the Huffington Post in 2015, "I'm just at that point where I'm ready to open up and let everyone see me, for me and I hope everyone accepts it" (Grenoble, 2015). Kenworthy is an Olympic medalist and an elite athlete competing in an action sport typically categorized as a masculine sport.

In 2016, it was reported that the Summer Olympics held in Rio had the highest number of publicly out LGBT athletes. *Outsports* and Olympic and LGBTQ historians identified at least 55 out athletes who competed along with three coaches. (Rosen, 2016). According to reports, the Summer Olympics in Rio included "44 lesbian or bi women, 11 gay men, yet no outed transgender Olympians."

Interestingly, the data collected showed no record of publicly out male athletes from the United States, "yet there were a record 11 publicly out male athletes from other countries" (Rosen, 2016). Statistics also showed that there were no openly transgender athletes competing in the Summer Olympics in Rio in 2016.

Here is a current list of LGBTQ athletes who came out and participated in the 2016 Summer Olympics held in Rio. This list was obtained from an online article compiled and written by *Outsports* (2016).

1. Nicola Adams (Great Britain, boxing)
2. Seimone Augustus (USA, basketball)
3. Tom Bosworth (Great Britain, race walk)
4. Rachele Bruni (Italy, swimming)
5. Anne Buijs (Netherlands, volleyball)
6. Tameka Butt (Australia, soccer)
7. Isadora Cerullo (Brazil, rugby)
8. Tom Daley (Great Britain, diving)
9. Carlien Dirkse van den Heuvel (Netherlands, field hockey)
10. Lisa Dahlkvist (Sweden, soccer)
11. Elena Delle Donne (USA, basketball)
12. Katie Duncan (New Zealand, soccer)
13. Nilla Fischer (Sweden, soccer)
14. Amini Fonua (Tonga, swimming)
15. Larissa França (Brazil, beach volleyball)
16. Edward Gal (Netherlands, equestrian)
17. Kelly Griffin (USA, rugby)
18. Brittney Griner (USA, basketball)
19. Carl Hester (Great Britain, equestrian)
20. Michelle Heyman (Australia, soccer)
21. Mélanie Henique (France, swimming)
22. Jen Kish (Canada, rugby)
23. Valentina Kogan (Argentina, handball)
24. Stephanie Labbé (Canada, soccer)
25. Alexandra Lacrabère (France, handball)
26. Hedvig Lindahl (Sweden, soccer)
27. Ari-Pekka Liukkonen (Finland, swimming)
28. Robbie Manson (New Zealand, rowing)
29. Hans Peter Minderhoud (Netherlands, equestrian)
30. Ian Matos (Brazil, diving)
31. Angel McCoughtry (USA, basketball)
32. Eefje Muskens (Netherlands, badminton)
33. Nadine Müller (Germany, discus)

34. Marie-Eve Nault (Canada, soccer)
35. Ashley Nee (USA, kayak white-water slalom)
36. Meghan O'Leary (USA, rowing)
37. Maartje Paumen (Netherlands, field hockey)
38. Fiona Pennie (Britain, canoe)
39. Mayssa Pessoa (Brazil, handball)
40. Jillion Potter (USA, rugby)
41. Megan Rapinoe (USA, soccer)
42. Helen Richardson-Walsh (Great Britain, field hockey)
43. Kate Richardson-Walsh (Great Britain, field hockey)
44. Tessie Savelkouls (Netherlands, judo)
45. Caroline Seger (Sweden, soccer)
46. Caster Semenya (South Africa, track and field)
47. Rafaela Silva (Brazil, judo)
48. Martina Strutz (Germany, pole vault)
49. Susannah Townsend (Great Britain, field hockey)
50. Sunette Stella Viljoen (South Africa, javelin)
51. Julia Vasconcelos (Brazil, taekwondo). Julia confirmed to Claudia Custodio (@Cau__ on Twitter) with ESPN Brazil that she is a lesbian.
52. Marleen van Iersel (Netherlands, beach volleyball)
53. Linda Villumsen (New Zealand, cycling)
54. Jeffrey Wammes (Netherlands, gymnastics)
55. Spencer Wilton (Great Britain, equestrian)
56. Kirsty Yallop (New Zealand, soccer)

Coming Out Before the Draft

In February of 2014, Missouri defensive lineman Michael Sam came out nationally during an interview with ESPN. In the interview, football fans heard Michael Sam say, "I am an openly, proud gay man." It was also noted several times in sports media that most, if not all, of Sam's Missouri football teammates, coaches, and friends were well aware of his sexual orientation as early as August of 2013 (Connelly, 2014). Sam was drafted in the seventh round by the St. Louis Rams. Sam's draft to the Rams made him the first active openly gay player in the NFL. Soon after making the team, the Rams cut him, and Sam later spent time training with the Dallas Cowboy's practice team until they, too, cut him from the roster.

Robbie Rogers, a midfielder for the Los Angeles Galaxy, made headlines in 2013 when he publicly announced that he was gay. At the time of his coming out, Rogers felt that sports in America were finally ready to accept athletes with differing sexual and gender identities and orientations. Shortly after that, NBA center Jason Collins came out as gay. It was then that many felt that American sports were finally breaking more barriers and ready to accept professional athletes who publicly announced their sexual orientation. Many started to feel that Americans were accepting of these athletes who want to live their lives free from hiding their sexual attractions and who may suffer from anxieties that relate to the idea that they are not being true to themselves.

Multiple WNBA players have come out over the last 10 years. This coming out seems to have set an example for young women who may aspire to participate in sports. Yet some believe that the increase in WNBA players announcing their sexual orientation may have created image problems for the league. That is, some feel that this coming out trend in the WNBA is supporting, and maybe even perpetuating, the stereotype that the WNBA players are all lesbian. We must keep in mind that basketball in our culture is considered to be a masculine sport, and if behaviors by women relate to our ideals of what it means to be masculine, then our minds will store this information in mental nodes that are connected. And the few male athletes who are supposed to be masculine yet have come out publicly have also met resistance. For instance, Jason Collins retired from the NBA. Michael Sam was never afforded an opportunity to play even one "down" in a single regular season of the NFL.

Why is it that more athletes have not "come out" at the professional level? Some argue that it is not because of a lack of support from fans and coaches, but it is primarily related to homophobia in our Western culture. *Homophobia* is a concept that is often associated with our culture, and now it is connected to the sports world. We often hear of homophobia in sports media coverage when it comes to the image of a locker room. It is during sports broadcasts of the locker room where we learn that athletes who do not identify with heterosexual lifestyles are frequently made fun of and bullied, and are victims of homophobic slurs. In fact, it is common to hear homophobic slurs thrown around casually in locker rooms.

Since this chapter is on gender, sexual, and racial identity, we must talk about the cultural norm that drives our notions of what is masculine or feminine. The stereotype that we have in this culture is that the "typical" gay man is more effeminate and is not as masculine as a heterosexual man and, therefore, is weaker than straight men. This notion may be perhaps the most significant hurdle male athletes who are struggling with coming out have to overcome. While the stereotype that men should engage in masculine sports and gay men have no place in sports that are deemed masculine has no basis in fact, it is a stereotype and norm that permeates our culture.

From infancy, we are socialized in this culture to believe that the norm for being a man and what it means to be masculine translates to a larger notion that "boys/men don't cry." So what would being gay mean in American society? This presupposition is so ingrained in American culture that there seems to be a disconnect between our ideas as to what is masculine and feminine and homophobic. But the ideas themselves must create confusion in gay athletes—a confusion that tells them that they have to deny their sexual orientation and fake their gender identity so they will not appear "soft" and that they conform to our cultural norms when it comes to defining what it means to be a man. A perfect illustration of this in sports media is how the New York Giants receiver Odell Beckham Jr. was made fun of and media stories focused on how opposing team players would direct homophobic slurs at him simply because he "acted" and behaved differently than the stereotypical tough male football player. The behaviors that Beckham displayed are those that we discussed earlier—behaviors that are mostly aligned with gender identity. Beckham is often the victim of negative media stories because he dyes his hair; wears fashionable, trendy clothing; and likes to dance—sometimes shirt-less—with male friends in videos. Beckham posts these visuals frequently on Instagram. Is it possible that Beckham knows he is serving, or wants to serve, as a change agent to make us uncomfortable about our gender-specific notions? Perhaps the idea of media is to produce stories that challenge the idea many Americans may have, such as if an athlete is not acting a specific way, that does not mean that he or she is gay, weak, less than, or to be ridiculed because of that behavior. The very fact that Odell Beckham Jr. dances and enjoys times out with his male friends and happens to wear skinny jeans does not, nor should it, diminish his talents as an athlete. Perhaps sports media should offer and produce more shows that show younger athletes from the millennial generation who are not constrained by strict notions of what it means to be masculine or feminine.

Today's generation of young adults and their tolerance toward sexual identity is an important and significant moment for LGBTQ rights in America *and* sports and sports journalism. Hate crimes and acts of discrimination are alive and active, particularly toward LGBTQ people. In 2016, there were a record number of deaths in this group alone. In fact, 49 people died at the hands of a gunman who decided to shoot people attending a gay nightclub in Orlando, Florida. This news event served, and continues to serve, as a reminder of the hate and discrimination many groups have suffered and continue to suffer, especially if those groups do not prescribe to cultural norms and expectations. But just as we recognize the negative events, we must also recognize the positive strides happening for LGBTQ individuals. Gay marriage is *legal*, and public opinion polls are starting to show that American's attitudes toward individuals who identify as LGBTQ are becoming more favorable. And in sports, there are many opportunities to effect change. While some athletes who have tried to achieve change have met resistance and ended their professional careers prematurely, there is still power in numbers.

We hope that it is sooner rather than later that athletes in other major league sports reveal their sexuality. However, each professional league's culture regarding acceptance of LGBTQ athletes is different; some leagues may be more accepting than others. Many scholars and supporters firmly believe that the more players who chose to come out publicly, regardless of league and where they are in their careers, the easier it will become for other athletes in other leagues to follow.

Summary: Differences in Sex, Gender, and Gender Identity

- Sex is a label assigned by a doctor at birth based on the genitals and chromosomes. A baby's sex is put on a birth certificate.

- Gender is a much more complicated concept. According to information obtained on the Planned Parenthood website, the concept of gender is a "social and legal status that has a set of expectations from society about behaviors, characteristics, and thoughts" (Planned Parenthood, 2017) Cultures have different standards about the way that people should behave based on their gender. Instead of being about body parts, gender in American culture is more about how you're expected to act because of your sex.

- Recall that gender identity is how a person feels on the inside and how those feelings are expressed. We express gender through our clothing, behavior, and personal appearance.

Racial Identity in Sports

Defining Whiteness as Racial Identity

"Whiteness" is a term that describes the thought associated with people who are racially identified as white. Whiteness, as with gender, is a socially constructed concept. In other words, the meaning of whiteness and the label we associate with a person's skin color is determined by our culture and society. Labels such as whiteness also shape a person's worldview and lived experiences—two more characteristics that are not inherent in individuals or groups but are determined by our American culture and society.

Research tells us that there are "three primary elements of whiteness contributing to whites having power and privilege" (Bush, 2011; McIntosh, 1993). These features serve both as benefits and obstacles to whites (Bush, 2011; Johnson, 2006; McIntosh, 1993). The first is the power to define and establish social norms. This is related to a society's ability to establish social rules that serve as a benefit and an obstacle in that whites often come to understand what is deemed appropriate living standards and ultimately will devalue anything or anyone that deviates from it (Bush, 2011; Johnson, 2006). The second element in terms of defining whiteness is the idea that power and privilege are structural advantages. In the United States, the advantage of whiteness refers to the disparate level of control and influence that whites have. This "institutionalization of white privilege means whites are afforded benefits far less accessible to racial minorities as a result of policies, laws, and customary behaviors in society" (Edwards, 2008, p. 10). Peggy McIntosh (1998), in a paper titled "White Privilege: Unpacking the Invisible Backpack," identifies privileges or benefits that whites receive. Some of the benefits McIntosh mentions in this seminal work are benefits such as "being able to be with people of your own race most of the time, finding food at the grocery store that is familiar with your own ethnic cuisine, and going shopping without being followed or finding your race widely represented in the media and educational resources" (for more refer to McIntosh, 1988, 1989, 1993, 1997, 1998). Most significantly, when we talk about white privilege, we must also mention the fact that whites can choose to not "see" race. Whites in American culture are positioned in such a way that privileges are received whether they want them or not. Most whites, according to work in this area, tend to avoid or deny their privileges and are not open to understanding how their privileges and avoidance of this issue contribute to the injustices and inequalities in our American culture (Johnson, 2006, pp. 25–27).

The final element involved in whiteness is what has been termed "white transparency": Transparency is when whites prefer not to think about norms, behaviors, experiences, or perspectives that are white specific. This is one way to avoid understanding how whites may contribute to injustices. Among college students, Bush (2011) found that "whites reported significantly less often than Blacks that they think about their racial identity and significantly more that they never do" (Bush, 2011, p. 56).

Implications

1. Power and privilege are benefits whites have but are often unaware of them.
2. We learn from the literature that whites develop a sense of racial identity through learning. We learn from social psychology research that racial identity for the majority of white individuals is developed through observation of those closest to them, reflection of the behaviors they observe, and interactions with others from different cultural backgrounds.

African American Identity and Sport

We know from research opinions, feelings, and beliefs about who race operates in our culture in powerful ways. The study of race as a biological and genetic variable has had an ominous reputation (Wiggins, 1997). In America today, for example, we classify people as African American, yet physical features (e.g., skin tone, nose, eye color) may cause them to be classified as European. This is a common example of how the lines are blurred between races. According to LaVeist (1996), our use of the word "race" is a social construct, rather than a biological one. According to LaVeist (1996), being African American has more to do with shared experiences than shared genetic material.

Even though scholars can recognize problems when we assign individuals to racial categories, using race as a label is still the "most widely used method of classification in America" (Hewstone, Hantzi, & Johnston, 1991; Lillie-Blanton & LaVeist, 1996). In their work, Hewstone et al. (1991)

assert that use of race as a prominent classification in our culture is largely influenced by our social surroundings, culture, customs, beliefs, and political associations. These influences ultimately affect our self-concepts and our ideas about ourselves and others (Haslam, Oakes, Reynolds, & Turner, 1999).

Being an African American presumes a hodgepodge of meanings in the minds of both African Americans and nonAfrican Americans. Take just a moment to think of and then list all of the adjectives and images that come to mind when you hear the words "African American." Whenever people take a moment to reflect on the images and ideas that come to mind when asked, "What are you?," we often find that the most common words to describe African Americans are "athlete" or "entertainer" (Entman, 2007). The significance of this belief is the idea that being black or being an African American in this culture either directly or indirectly comes with an association with athletic ability and sports.

The Role of Stereotypes in Racial Identity Development

As mentioned previously in this chapter, we know that stereotypes are defined as "beliefs about the characteristics, attributes, and behaviors of members of certain groups" (Hilton & von Hippel, 1996, p. 240). Unlike racism that deals with discriminatory behavior against different groups and prejudice that deals with the feelings we have toward a specific group, stereotypes are the "pictures in our heads" (Lippmann, 1922) and are oftentimes used as shortcuts in our minds that help us to make decisions and come to conclusions easily and quickly. Stereotypes rely on traits associated with a group, and through those trait associations, judgments are made about the commonalities within a particular group. It is well documented that stereotypes significantly influence the way we perceive and think about other people. Figure 3.4 shows the intricate relationship among stereotypes, prejudice, and discrimination. Stereotypes also influence the behaviors we associate with others. In our culture, being identified as an African American often evokes many stereotypes, some negative—depending on who is being asked to identify the stereotype. This is why we discuss stereotypes as they relate to athletes. Once we gain a basic knowledge of the stereotypes, it becomes easy to understand why we find few ardent and zealous identifications with positive stereotypes for people of color.

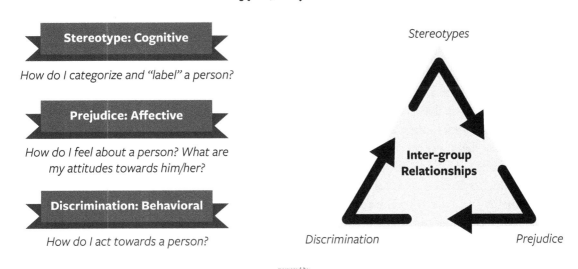

FIGURE 3.4   *Relationship among stereotypes, racism, and prejudice.*

African American athletes, however, often have superior stereotypes associated with their athletic abilities and accomplishments. This stereotype, according to Wiggins (1997) is pervasive in American culture. Even Stone, Perry, and Darley (1997) document the ever-present notion that invades our culture: the idea that African American athletes are naturally gifted with athletic superiority. It has been a widely held belief for centuries that African Americans are biologically different, and because of a unique muscle fiber, they are naturally gifted to excel in athletic competition. While the study is over 20 years old, Stone et al. (1997) provided empirical evidence that supports this myth. In the study, the researchers asked participants to listen to a radio broadcast of a basketball game. Participants were then asked to rate their perceptions of both the African American and European athletes (Stone et al., 1997). Data clearly showed that participants in this study felt that the African American basketball players in the game had displayed more athletic prowess and talents. They also stated that the white basketball players were more intelligent and hustled more than the African American basketball players (Stone et al., 1997).

Empirical evidence over the years shows that these racial stereotypes are omnipresent and are salient. Studies further show the influence that these stereotypes have on perceived performance by athletes (Steele, 1997; Steele & Aronson, 1995) and athletic performance (Stone, Lynch, Sjomeling, & Darley, 1999). That is, white athletes are naturally more intelligent and Black athletes are naturally more athletic. Research in social and cognitive psychology teaches us that stereotypes are the basis of establishing one's group identity. In the case of ethnic or racial identity, this means that we can infer that the influence of the development of skills in certain sports *and* the development of athletic skills plays a vital role in the development of African American racial identity.

Black Masculinity and Identity

Overemphasis and media coverage of African American athletes in specific sports, such as football, basketball, and track and field, can significantly change and confound the perceptions Black youth may have when exposed to Blacks in sports. This statement relates directly to the data evidence in the Frisby (2016) study. Frisby (2016) found that African American male athletes receive significantly more negative media coverage than white male athletes. Furthermore, research demonstrated in the content analysis of media coverage that white male athletes tend to receive significantly more media coverage that is deemed positive than African American athletes. Discrepancies in positive and negative stories based on the color of the athlete's skin show that these disparities appear most often in a certain type or category of news story. Black male athletes were the focus more often in news stories that were about crime and domestic and sexual violence. In the same content analytic study, Frisby (2016) also found that sports media tend to write more news stories about African American athletes who misbehave as opposed to publishing news stories about those African American athletes who give back to their communities and are known to do positive things for humankind.

It is possible that these media stories about Black athletes may significantly affect a young black boy's aspirations to play professional sports. We know from a plethora of research that children of color are influenced, and their ideas are mainly shaped, although not entirely, by television and other forms of media (Frisby, 2016). Thus one important and significant implication for sports reporters and journalists is to make a point of highlighting different aspects of African American male athletes that go beyond their criminal activity and athletic prowess. More reporting on African American athletes must also be conducted to determine their influence on young adolescent black boys and men (Frisby, 2016)—stories that focus on athletes and role models who are able to perform or performed well in the classroom as well as on the field or court. In her article, "Delay of Game," Frisby (2016) suggests that sports reporters should start producing media content that focuses on positive stories involving former African American male student-athletes. Media coverage could highlight Black athletes who attended college, achieved academic and athletic success, were engaged campus leaders within and beyond athletics, graduated in 4–6 years, and took divergent postcollege pathways (e.g., they enrolled in graduate school in lieu of participating in the professional league's "draft"). Frisby (2016) argues that positive stories will advance a more accurate and complete understanding of African Americans. Positive and accurate media coverage might also help provide realistic depictions of African American men and athletes, *and* showcase the diversity that exists within the group. An overemphasis of depictions of African Americans that challenge present-day stereotypes might preclude or even change the perpetuation of negative stereotypes of African American males and male athletes.

The perceptions young black boys may obtain from consistently seeing black male athletes participating in football, basketball, and track and field may relate to their ideas that those are the only relevant sports in which they can excel. Consider this: The more frequent exposure to particular stimuli, according to schema theory discussed in Chapter 2, the more likely that heuristic or schema will be easily accessible (Johnson et al., 1995).

The Role of Intersectionality in the Gendered Realities of Athletes

Athletes today have to navigate identities, including ethnicity or race, social class, gender and sexual orientation, religion, and physical characteristics, such as skin tone, level of attractiveness, and able-bodiedness. What happens when these identities intersect? As noted previously in this chapter, the intersection of these identities may cause some people in our culture to experience what is referred to as white privilege, while others may experience pressures, barriers to economic success, and other factors that may prevent them from reaching their maximum potential (McIntosh, 1988, 1989, 1993, 1997).

For example, a female who happens to be:
Caucasian, lower-class, heterosexual, Jewish, American, and living with physical challenges may have different experiences and media reactions while participating in sports than a woman who may have fewer intersecting identities (Holliday & Hassard, 2001). For instance, Beal (1970) published a report that stated that African American women are frequently caught in an experience known as "double jeopardy." Double jeopardy, according to Beal (1970), is a term that means that their two minority identities, being a woman and being African American, tend to cause many more frustrations and stressors than other minority identities might encounter.

Consider next a female who happens to be:
Latina, lesbian, agnostic, middle class, educated, and attractive, and may experience a different reality while participating in sports. The harsh reality for many of us in this culture is that (a) female athletes with intersections of multiple identities have been and continue to be marginalized, and (b) female athlete's gender differences are magnified by another minority identity (sexual preference, social class, etc.). As we noted in the history chapter, women in American culture have always had less power than men in this patriarchal society. And empirical data in sports media shows that in sports, women in American culture have less power in media, and patriarchy is demonstrated in that women are also not well represented or frequently portrayed positively in sports media.

As a student interested in gender, sex, race, and sports media, you must begin to start a critical analysis of images and other messages in the media and then purpose to use your talents to identify cases of stereotyping based on gender, race, and or sex in media content. As research shows, news coverage, magazines, TV, film, and the Internet contain overwhelming portrayals of misinformed stereotypes relating to gender, race, and sex. When we consider schema theory, be aware that some stereotypes and negative images are hard for others to see because of their biases. Be the change agent and hold discussions about the stereotypes in media. Use your voice and knowledge to help others see stereotypes in media and to understand how those stereotypes cause others harm and hurt. Create media content that showcases people's inner qualities, qualities that accurately express who they are, irrespective of what society tells us that the gender stereotypes and expectations should be.

When you see media coverage that includes sexist or racist comments or jokes, challenge them. As we know from history and excessive media coverage, the influence of covert stereotyping extends much further than sports and athletics. According to Kaskan and Ho (2014), gender identity, and traditional gender roles offered in frequent media content sends the message to women, young and old, that athleticism for females is unattractive. Other common messages in media give one the impression that for female athletes, physical appearance is more important than the athletic skill(s). We even find hidden messages that unintentionally communicate that a female athlete's ability is genetically secondary to the talent and ability of men. One consequence of exposure to media's presentation of gender roles and athletes may be evidenced in a female athlete's self-esteem. It is possible that continuous exposure to and consumption of these types of hidden messages may actually affect athletes perception of their body image and, ultimately, their physical health. These unintended consequences may actually be more severe for women who have little to no interest in athletics or sporting extracurricular activities. For example, research in health communication shows that some women even avoid lifting weights and engaging in strength training for fear that they will become "bulky" and unattractive, even though weight training exercise has been found to strengthen bones and ward off osteoporosis, diabetes, heart disease, and depression.

Research on gender and media reveals that sports coverage shows sexism toward female athletes. Instead of framing female athletes as sexual objects, sports media should offer coverage that praises a female athlete for her ability to juggle athletics with her expected gender role as mother or girlfriend—the socially suitable, fundamental, and acceptable gender roles for women. Sexism in sports media manifests for female athletes in a myriad of ways—if we consider the earlier discussion of gender roles ascribed to females, we find those female athletes are most appealing when they can be idealized in the two roles men find most relatable: sex objects and caregivers. Thus it can be concluded that sports media, which are primarily owned and dominated by men, are perhaps the reason that media still struggle to understand women outside of the stereotypes of their gender identity.

Mass Media and Perpetuation of Identity Values in Sport

Mass media is designed to reach specific audiences. For example, messages through broadcast media—namely, television—have a profound effect on viewers. Research suggests that heavy users of television often interpret some media messages as fact (Gerbner, 1972). This interpretation can lead to a distortion of reality, especially when research using cultivation and agenda-setting theories continue to show how media have the ability to shape viewer perceptions. We find a powerful influence on how media shape perceptions, especially when we conduct research on the negative portrayals of athletes of color. We also find evidence of this influence when research discovers associations between exposure to portrayals based on race or gender and stereotyped beliefs that consumers hold about both.

Koivula (1995) argues that media scholars must examine the effect of mass media on our attitudes. Socialization is a by-product of exposure to messages found in sport-related media. That is, socialization is defined as a "process through which media viewers learn beliefs, values, knowledge, and skills about our society" (Koivula, 1995; 2001). Television's passive presence has the potential to allow stereotypes to be reflected in the images and messages found in content that is frequently and repeatedly consumed by viewers. According to Rada and Wulfemeyer (2002) bias can veer itself in many different directions: from what we hear (e.g., spoken commentary broadcast by on-air announcers) to what we see (e.g., production of sports that are broadcast). Research suggests that these two forms drive misconceptions and misperceptions of gender and race within a sport.

We know that women have struggled with gaining equality throughout history. From obtaining the right to vote to the right to work, women continue to fight issues related to sexual and domestic violence and sexual objectification to name a few. These struggles can also be found in sports. The sports industry has historically been characterized as a patriarchy, a man's world where women should know their place—if they have one at all. The advent of Title IX in 1972 made it possible for women who desired to participate in sports to become part of the male-dominated world of athletics. Title IX stated that "in the United States no one might be (a) prohibited from, or (b) refused benefits that come from, or (c) be in any way discriminated against a program or activity which is supported by the federal government" (Lipka, 2006; Lipka & Wolverton, 2007). While evidence shows that female athletes are currently more active in participating in sports than they have been in the past, research still reports that the media tend to objectify them sexually, downgrade and devalue their athletic skills, and perpetuate stereotypes about female athletes. Research has documented over the last 17 years that in terms of coverage, women's sports receive strikingly less coverage than men's (Messner, 2002; . With the increase of female athletes since 1972, evidence continues to show this disparity in coverage (Koivula, 1995; 2001).

When media and journalists cover women's sports, research shows that female athletes are described in the story in either a sexual way or in a more traditionally tied gender role (Rada & Wulfemeyer, 2002). Research demonstrates the frequency by which media is often found praising male athletes for their athletic ability but seems to only appreciate female athletes for their physical attractiveness and ability to manage roles as a mother, wife, or girlfriend. An example of this pattern found in sports media is *Sports Illustrated* (Allen & Frisby, 2017; Frisby, 2017a; 2017b).

Research shows that adjectives and other descriptions centered on a sports skill are frequently absent in stories that involve female athletes (Rada & Wuhfemeyer, 2002. Instead, Rada and Wuhfemeyer (2002 obtained data that found sports media tend to make references to female athletes that revolve around an "aesthetic judgment" (e.g., graceful), or they tend to make note of the athlete's femininity or lack of femininity (Koivula, 1995). Frequent media messages consumed in various media regarding women may lead to learned beliefs and prejudices that ultimately become deeply embedded in our society. We are confident that one massive effect of this consumption is that the stereotypes will ultimately halt any progress that can be made in terms of women participating in sport. Female athletes still find themselves being held to a strict gender role that relates to personality traits, domestic behaviors, and physical appearances. We also notice that female athletes are often ascribed by media and audiences to belonging to stereotypes that were created centuries ago but are still being reinforced in our culture and our sports media.

Like women, African Americans as a group struggle when it comes to equitable treatment by media and by society as a whole. African American men are overrepresented in most major prof-it-generating sports, such as football and basketball. Even though we find that African American athletes may have reached equal status regarding playing for college and professional teams, we still see discrepancies in the way sports media cover them and their sport (Frisby, 2016; Rada & Wulfemeyer, 2002). Sports commentators have been observed describing African American athletes with phrases or language that refers to their power or physique. Sports media often have been found using descriptors that appear to be positive and complimentary, yet the words may be limiting and demeaning. For example, research suggests that when sports reporters are writing about or discussing quarterbacks, they often refer to white quarterbacks using language that focuses on intelligence while describing a black quarterback's physical strength and prowess. While on the surface, the focus on the black quarterback's strength could be interpreted as a compliment, research on this topic suggests that the actual connotation of these descriptors is that white athletes are smarter or have more leadership qualities than black athletes. As Rada and Wulfemeyer (2002) explain, a sports journalist's compliments are not valid compliments. In fact, these scholars argue that compliments used to discuss African American athletes are often very different than the compliments these same commentators used to discuss white athletes (Rada & Wulfemeyr, 2002). In their study, Rada and Wulfemeyer (2002) found that African American players often receive a greater number of negative comments than white players do, particularly when the comments are related to a player's intellect. The research question that is of most interest to many scholars is this: Do sports media reinforce a stereotype that African American males are more physically superior than they are smart?

African American male athletes are often described as having toned muscular physiques. Descriptions of African American male athletes obtained in sports media discovered that the emphasis on the physical tends to reinforce stereotyped images of black men as muscular and toned rather than intellectual (Rada & Wulfemeyer, 2002). Researchers have obtained data that show white athletes are commonly described by the media based on their intellect.

If we think about gender and race in the sports world, many Americans may struggle with the thought that women athletes experience microaggressions on a daily basis. In fact, the author experienced, first hand, the reaction some have when research is presented that shows when compared to men, microaggressions were up by 40% for female athletes. While inclusion in the new millennium includes opportunities for women to participate in sports, inclusion has not expanded into how female athletes are portrayed in sports media. The frequency and numerous depictions of sexual and demeaning media stories about female athletes found in today's media show that inclusivity in sports media is seriously lagging (Allen & Frisby, 2017). The Summer Olympics of 2016 in Rio de Janeiro revealed many NBC commentators treating and referring to female Olympians in negative ways, using microaggressions in their coverage. Even though many viewers are able to acknowledge perceptions of gender bias within a sport, as we can conclude from Allen and Frisby (2017), we also know that very little is being done to combat the disparities and biases in sports. Some Americans seem to find it more difficult to recognize racial bias that may lurk around in the sports media. Sports commentators' who make racist or stereotypical comments expect many viewers to accept their statements as "normal" and acceptable (e.g., references to a black athlete's natural athletic prowess and a white athlete's intelligence), never thinking that what they are hearing is a microaggression, a subtle form of racial discrimination. More viewers must put into practice a concept we discussed in Chapter 1—media literacy. Media literacy requires that consumers take personal responsibility to evaluate sports media and its coverage through the looking glass of racism, sexism, and lookism. We must begin to accept that sports media often praise whites for intelligence while praising African American athletes for what they think are natural skills, power, and physique. We must be open to the idea that this disparate treatment in sports coverage is rooted in a long-term system filled with inherent racial biases. Future training should be held by media personnel, especially broadcast commentators. Currently, there seems to be a trend that shows many of the national sports commentators are ex-players—players who actually lack any sort of formal training in communications. With proper training, sports journalists might be made aware of the disparities, might learn how to describe plays and other athletic performances more efficiently, and might respond appropriately in the stressful live sports atmosphere. Moreover, adequate training might enable commentators to keep racist and sexist comments in check (Lopez, 2018). It might. Additional research is also much needed to determine the long-term effects of the framing and frequency of sports stories on the sports viewers' beliefs and attitudes toward race and gender. Perhaps the more Americans read results about these portrayals, the higher the chance that bias toward groups of athletes might be reduced or even dispelled altogether.

Studies on gender and sports media find that messages in sports media often reinforce perceptions of "violent masculinity." Violent masculinity occurs when media praise and glorify athletes who continue to play while injured. Through the use of language found to describe war and conflict, research shows that sports commentary sends messages that violence and aggression are an exciting and rewarding behavior. Research further indicates that sports broadcasts tend to focus heavily on violence in professional sports, and the focus is demonstrated when they replay and overanalyze footage of injuries, accidents, and fights. The studies in this area conclude that a focus on rivalry, conflict, and competition reinforces the idea and social norm that tells us that violence and aggression are normal and natural expressions of masculine identity.

INTERNET AND VIDEO RESOURCES ON IDENTITY (GENDER AND SPORTS FACT SHEET)

The teaching resources listed in the sections below are part of a fact sheet distributed by Sociologists for Women in Society (Chawansky, 2011). The fact sheet was prepared by Megan Chawansky, PhD, Department of Education, University of Bath (United Kingdom) (see https://socwomen.org/wp-content/uploads/2018/03/fact_02-2011-sport.pdf).

- *A Hero for Daisy*. 1999. 40 minutes (DVD). Distributed by 50 Eggs Productions. Viewers will learn the story of Chris Ernst, an Olympic athlete and Title IX activist. The video depicts the athlete's journey to ensure Title IX compliance as she competed and represented the Yale women's rowing team in 1976.

- *Girl Wrestler*. 2004. 53 minutes (DVD). Distributed by Women Make Movies. This video chronicles 13-year-old Tara Neal and her athletic quest to compete in the sport of wrestling. Viewers will see the obstacles she had to endure, including regulations in the state of Texas that prevented her from competing with boys once she entered high school.

- *Murderball.* 2005. 88 minutes (DVD). Distributed by THINKFilm. Watching this video shows viewers how masculinity, race, and disability intersect.

- *Playing Unfair: The Media Image of the Female Athlete.* 2002. 30 minutes (DVD). Distributed by the Media Education Foundation. This exploratory video shows a comprehensive examination of the cultural and historical ways that female athletes have been treated and portrayed in media. It also addresses the increased choice/impetus for female athletes to pose nude or in a sexually provocative manner.

- *100% Woman.* 2004. 59 minutes (DVD). Distributed by Films Media Group. This documentary follows Michelle Dumaresq, a competitive downhill mountain biker, as she tries to find space and her place in the international women's mountain biking community as an athlete who is transgendered. This is a compelling production that allows for discussions around issues of access, gender, and women's sports.

Gender and Sports Teaching Resources: Suggested Websites

- Black Women in Sports Foundation: nonprofit website dedicated to involving Black girls and women in all facets of sport (http://www.blackwomeninsport.org)
- Muslim Women in Sports blog: blog maintained by Sertaç Sehlikoglu Karakas that contains a variety of news stories and clips on Muslim women athletes from around the world (http://muslimwomeninsports.blogspot.com/)
- The National Association for Girls and Women in Sport (NAGWS): contains various resources on the experiences of girls and women in sport (https://eric.ed.gov/?id=EJ867682) and National Girls and Women in Sports Day (http://ngwsd.org).
- The Tucker Center: University of Minnesota's center for research on girls and women in sport and physical activity (http://www.cehd.umn.edu/tuckercenter/) and the blog (https://tuckercenter.wordpress.com).
- Title IX blog: features academic and popular commentary on Title IX (http://title-ix.blogspot.com/)
- Women's Sports Foundation: excellent resource for research and activities emerging from a nonprofit dedicated to advancing the lives of girls and women through sport and physical activity (http://www.womenssportsfoundation.org/)
- Women Win: global organization interested in helping to empower girls and women through sports (http://www.womenwin.org/)

QUESTIONS FOR REFLECTION AND DISCUSSION

1. What's your gender type? Do you conform to the societal expectations attached to your biological sex or do you challenge those expectations? Are you a gender conformist or a gender change agent? How male or female are you? (You might even want to take the Bem Sex Role Inventory to see how "male" or "female" you are in your behavior and feelings. Go to www.mindgarden.com).

2. How might legislation regarding sexual orientation be reformed in sports to better address the issues as they relate to transgendered individuals?

3. In which areas of sports would you say women, LGBTQ, African Americans, and transgendered people have come closest to inclusion and full assimilation? Alternatively, which areas in sports need the most attention, particularly from sports media?

4. Explain and analyze the concepts of sex and gender, and the differences between the two.

5. What movements for gender equality in sports have been emphasized over the past few years? What changes have been made regarding gender equality in sports, equal coverage, and equal emphasis on sport and gender? What changes can be made in the sports journalism industry to change disparities in coverage? How serious are these issues?

6. What connotations do the terms *homosexual, gay, transsexual, transgendered, lesbian, bisexual,* and *queer* suggest in our present culture? Consider the term *cisgender*, which relates to a person whose sense of identity and gender corresponds with his or her birth sex. In current society's conflict with labels, what forces do you think created a need for this new gender identity?

7. Regarding equality in sports, what do you think is the most important issue facing LGBTQ athletes? What would you say warrants the attention of sports journalists regarding inequality or equality issues as they relate to LGBTQ persons?

8. Why do you think we rely on stereotypes? Can you think of the ways that stereotypes have positive outcomes for athletes from different groups? Defend your response. What are some ways that stereotypes can negatively influence athletes from different groups?

9. How has reading this chapter shaped the way you see, experience, and respond to white privilege and what it means to be white?

SUGGESTED ACTIVITIES

1. Make your autobiographical lists of privilege. Identify instances when you may have experienced privileges as they relate to
   - Sexual orientation
   - Class
   - Region
   - Religion
   - Gender
   - Gender identity
   - Employment
   - Physical ability
   - Handedness
   - Language
   - Neighborhoods
   - Nation of origin
   - Families' languages of origin
   - Ethnicity

2. Identify words or phrases that express the qualities or attributes you define as masculine. Identify the values you associate with those words. Next, suggest words or phrases that express the qualities or attributes you define as feminine. Write out the values that you associate with those words or phrases that you consider feminine. Write responses to and discuss the following:
   a. What do I consider to be masculine? What values did I assign to the words and phrases and why?
   b. What do I consider to be feminine? What values did I assign to the words and phrases and why?
   c. What are the things that I consider to be gender neutral? What values do I assign to gender-neutral things in our culture?
   d. Are there new constructs in our culture that are challenging the notion of masculinity and femininity? If so, what are they? If not, identify ways that people can begin to challenge our cultural notions concerning what it means to be a man or woman, boy or girl.
   e. Were you surprised by your thoughts? Why or why not? What surprised you the most?

3. Select an advertisement, photograph, news story or any mediated message that expresses the idea of gender and sexual identity discussed in this chapter. Prepare a brief written (or oral) reflection on the image you found. Then prepare a revised and better-produced media message, and write a brief reflection on the elements that you found problematic.

4. Watch televised sports shows and channels for seven days. Identify the constructs of gender that are displayed in sports media. Note how male and female athletes are portrayed in news, advertisements, and panel discussions. What are common identities found in the media focused on athletes? Prepare a brief report to share with your instructor and with the class.

5. As a future sports journalist, list and explain the concerns you may have in covering gender, sex, and race in sports. What areas might challenge your beliefs? If none, explain experiences in your upbringing that have caused you to feel this way about yourself.

6. Identify three or four groups in your community that are representative of the identities discussed in this chapter. What considerations should be made when interviewing them? From this list, prepare interview questions that you will use to report or publish a story on the particular identity? In other words, how would you cover a transgendered athlete in a way that educates the public and yet encourages awareness of and change in the issues that prevent individuals who identify with this group from competing in professional sports? Who do you know who has "come out"? Perhaps you can interview him or her and others to write a story that educates readers/viewers on the consequences of coming out for professional athletes. The goal of this activity would be to encourage other athletes who are feeling burdened with coming out and are fearful of the backlash.

7. Clip five news articles from the sports section that focus on individual athletes. Analyze the stories according to issues related to gender, sex, and racial identity. Focus on the sources as well. Whom did the sports journalist use as sources? What types of frames or words/heuristics are used in the story to communicate our culture's norms and expectations of what it means to be male or female? Is membership to a particular gender, sexual orientation, or race being emphasized? Is separation of the group emphasized or downplayed?

8. Clip 10 news articles from the sports section on a team or individual athlete. Five articles should focus on male sports and athletes and five on female sports and athletes. Record whether each article addresses the athlete's occupation/sport, age, gender, race, religion, ethnic group membership, physical ability, political affiliation, personal or professional background, lifestyle, marital status, children, and other issues related to family relationships. Where was this information provided in the story? Was it relevant to the story? Why or why not? Did you find differences in the amount of information shared for men versus the women? Now, write a press release or news story that shares the results of your investigative report.

9. Review the Center for the Study of White American Culture, http://www.euroamerican.org. This site provides visitors with resources to engage in self-discovery and awareness of what it means to be white. Here visitors can take quizzes about whiteness and are offered opportunities to read papers that educate and inform them about whiteness and how it fits into a multicultural society, such as the United States. This site also provides valuable objectives and recommendations for ways that cultures and societies can build functional multicultural values. After exploring the site and reading all of the resources, write a thought paper based on your experiences engaging in content on this site.

4

Issues of Race, Ethnicity, and Sports

LEARNING OBJECTIVES

After completing this chapter, students should be able to:

- define race and ethnicity, and know the difference between the two social constructs;
- distinguish the role that ethnic identity plays in participation sports;
- identify the role of sports in ethnic relationships;
- discuss the issue of race and sports, with special attention to the participation of athletes in various sports;
- understand and define "stacking" in sports and the basic explanations for the over- and underrepresentation of races/ethnicities in sports;
- appreciate the three body types and describe body types regarding somatotype theory;
- realize the differences in nature or nurture influences in the disproportionately overrepresented and underrepresented groups in major sports;
- identify biological explanations about why people from different racial/ethnic backgrounds have certain physical or mental attributes that suit them for specific positions;
- be familiar with the sports that members from various ethnic groups participate in and do not participate in; and
- be aware of issues and controversies related to race and sports.

Introduction

Defining Race

Race is a social construct that "categorizes people based on visual differences that are used to indicate invisible differences" (Wolf & Le Guin, 2003, p. 2). However, a significant problem with the categorizations is that they are vague and reflect social rather than physical differences. Race is distinct from ethnicity in that race involves an "assumption of a biological basis in differences" (Clair & Denis, 2015). Matthew Clair and Jeffrey S. Dennis (2015) described race as "distinguished by perceived common physical characteristics, which are thought to be fixed, whereas ethnicities are defined by perceived common ancestry, history, and cultural practices, which are seen as more fluid and self-asserted rather than assigned by others" (p. 7). Some scholars might categorize individuals into one of four distinct races—typically white or Caucasian, black or African American, Asian, and Latino/a—while ignoring or downplaying biological differences that exist within racial groups (Andreasen, 2000; Smedley & Smedley, 2005).

It was at the turn of the century when American sociologist W. E. B. Du Bois was concerned that the social construct known as race was often used by scholars as a biological explanation. Du Bois felt that race is a social construct that is more aligned with "social and cultural differences between different groups of people" (Gannon, 2016). Du Bois was one of the first to denounce the simple notion that "white" and "black" should be used to describe and delineate discrete racial groups. For Du Bois, black and white distinctions overlook and even ignore the depth and breadth of the differences in people and in diversity in our culture (Gannon, 2016). For some current-day scholars, race as a social construct needs to be phased out. For many sociological scholars, the race construct interferes with scientific understanding of diversity in human genetics.

Ethnicity, many scholars believe, is a better construct that reflects cultural differences. To these contemporary scholars, ethnicity is used to describe a group of people who share a historical and cultural heritage (along with a sense of group identity). Members of the American society share a cultural identity, and this cultural identity is known as our ethnicity.

Defining Ethnicity

Ethnicity refers to groups who share a common identity-based ancestry, language, or culture. Ethnicity is often based on religions, beliefs, and customs. The issue of race in American sports often centers on the idea that was discussed in Chapter 3 of this text: the notion that blacks are physically superior but intellectually inferior to whites. And as discussed in Chapter 3, we know that in sports such as basketball and football, physical prowess has transformed in American culture to be the main feature that defines the African American community.

Beliefs about African Americans and physical prowess are inversely related to intelligence. In fact, anti-intellectualism is a stereotype that permeates our culture, especially for African American athletes (Beamon, 2009; Buffington & Farley, 2008; Clair & Denis, 2015; Edwards, 2003: Entine, 2000). Research seeking to analyze the differences between black and white athletes often centers on identifying and providing quantitative data to support the idea that there are physical differences between blacks and whites. Often results tend to find that African American athletes are more physically suited than white athletes for sports that rely on speed and agility. This stereotyped idea leads some people in our culture to conclude that African Americans evolved differently than Caucasians and the differences resulted in unique physiological traits that are common among a group of people. Therefore, it is assumed that these unique physiological traits can only be found in African American athletes, and these traits are solely responsible for the speed and strength that only African American athletes seem to get naturally.

Consequently, the dominance of African Americans in sports tends to focus on arguments related to their physical differences in lieu of other characteristics or attributes that may explain and help us understand why some sports have more African Americans than others. The implications of research in this area tend to reinforce stereotypes that result in perceptions that African Americans are supernaturally gifted in terms of physical competencies. Studies often avoid or trivialize other factors, such as enthusiasm, mental power, motivation, dedication, commitment, and hard work, and fail to aim an eye toward how a combination of these variables may affect the success of all athletes.

Sports and Ethnic Identity

Through participation in sports, we learn that our racial and ethnic identities have the ability to tell us who we are and what we aspire to become. Participation in sports help define values that matter to us, and involvement in sports also helps to distinguish athletes from other Americans. Sports media tend to facilitate these ideas of differences in ethnicity and athletic performance through broadcast media, traditional print media, photojournalism, and digital media, as well as interactive media that all work together to encourage consumers to identify and connect with people who are different than themselves while at the same time allowing consumers to identify and see themselves as part of a group or as part of the outgroup. Opportunities that allow minorities to play, watch, interact, and engage with sports have proven over time to be especially important. We find that participation, interaction, viewership, and engagement are variables that not only affect athletic performance but also work in tandem to offer minority athletes a foundation that incites pride and celebration.

The style of play may also prove to be meaningful regarding ethnic identity. For some scholars, the glitz, gaudiness, glamour, innovation, originality, and panache often associated with African American culture have been identified as attributes that have changed sports in our culture today. How? The link with blackness is often observed in celebrations after significant plays, dancing in the end zone, and other behaviors that are often aligned with a concept known as "urban blackness." Changes in how sports are played have also caused those who make decisions about what is published and produced in the news to write stories that affirm whiteness. We find this to be true especially when those controlling the news and what is in or out are white. Currently in American sports, we find that not only do sports teams depend on an athlete's ethnicity to attract fans and sell products but also for-profit corporations are finding flamboyancy lucrative in terms of increases in earnings.

For instance, in the world of golf, Tiger Woods exemplifies how ethnic identity operates in sports. In several media interviews, Woods could be heard stating his preference to be identified and accepted as Cablinasian. Woods defined a "Cablinasian" as an ethnicity that captures his Asian and African American heritage. In an effort to show support for Woods's identity request, Nike created an advertising campaign showing kids from a wide variety of minority groups. In the ad, the children are confidently stating, "I'm Tiger Woods." From a strategic communications perspective, the message that we were to take away from this ad campaign is that Tiger Woods is an example of the multicultural heritage that many Americans share. The message was also set to convey both African American and Asian American athletic excellence, along with a strong source of ethnic pride. Media coverage of the campaign, however, frequently represented Tiger Woods in frames that aligned with stereotypical understandings of black athletes. When coverage was positive, however, media coverage expanded on the Cablinasian aspects, but, interestingly, when Woods was the subject of negative news coverage (e.g., his multiple affairs and the golf club and car incident), we found typical stereotypes associated with the idea that African American athletes are criminals. The black athlete as criminal, particularly in terms of Tiger Woods, became more commonplace in news coverage of that specific time period.

Sports and Ethnic Relations

While many sports commentators and fans have viewed sports in America as a unifying factor and a perfect example of multiculturalism, sport is a much more complex construct regarding ethnic relations. Over time, participation in sports is used to encourage a healthy competitive inner force, discipline, machismo, and willpower. In time, it was believed that athletes would come to appreciate sports, especially their chosen sport, as an opportunity to alleviate misconceptions and prejudices. An example of these misperceptions and prejudices was demonstrated in the movie *Remember the Titans*. Disney released the film, which starred Denzel Washington as Coach Herman Boone, Will Patton as Coach Bill Yoast, and Wood Harris as Julius Campbell, in 2000. *Remember the Titans*, based on the true story of the 1971 Titans' high school football team, serves as a perfect illustration of discrimination between the Caucasian and African American students who learn to overcome racial differences and unite as a team.

The main idea of the film was to show how athletes coming from two very different racial groups could unite and win a championship series. Coach Boone, the head coach, integrated the players and told them to learn each other's cultures and ways.

As depicted in the movie, we know that participation in a sport involves issues with social status and struggles with social class. And in addition to the social struggles, we know that sports participation often comes with resistance to women, minorities, and those with differences in sexual orientation. Current-day controversies, for instance, over sports teams and their use of Native American mascots, images, team names, and symbols is yet another example of ways our culture struggles with ethnic identity. As we will discuss later in this chapter, the topic of mascots that represent characteristics of Native American culture tends to reinforce notions and themes of history involving the surrender of American territory, white privilege, and ethnocentrism. Over the past 35 years, a multiethnic coalition, led by indigenous people, has challenged mascots as objects or symbols used in sports culture, arguing that their use is an example of misappropriation, misuse, and misunderstanding of Native American culture and history. Opponents protest and continue to petition educational organizations and professional teams to change their names or stop the use of mascots that rely on indigenous cultural artifacts and symbols. While some insist that mascots actually pay homage to Native Americans and their culture, critics assert that mascots actually denigrate Native Americans by perpetuating historical patterns of discrimination and dispossession of American land. Moreover, supporters of the use of Native American mascots argue that these objects serve as a symbol of honor, while opponents emphasize that these mascots remind us of our history and racism.

Race, Intelligence, and Physical Superiority in Sports

The belief that African American athletes are intellectually inferior to white athletes is a stereotype that can be traced, as we highlighted in Chapter 1 and previously in this chapter, back to Jackie Robinson's entrance into major league baseball. As discussed in Chapter 3, we know that a focus on physical differences based on race has been deeply rooted in American sports history and most certainly in the history of sports journalism. An example of the focus on physical differences in race is evidenced in comments made by former CBS sportscaster Jimmy "the Greek" Snyder. Recall that in January of 1988, Snyder made a comment that conveyed the idea that African Americans are much better athletes than whites. But he went on to say that the only reason for their athletic superiority is because of their genetic heredity. Snyder, along with many others, presumed that African American athletes were born with muscle fibers that caused them to have bigger thighs and greater muscularity than white athletes. Snyder went on to argue that because of "breeding" and the selling of slaves, the physical nature of the breeding of blacks resulted in giving blacks a special edge and an athletic advantage. Because of Snyder's comments on air, he was fired within 48 hours after the broadcast. The reason? It was believed that Snyder was a racist and that his quotes about genetic superiority and dominance in sports by African American athletes perpetuated a negative bias against successful African American athletes. It was also believed that his comments perpetuated an idea that the only way African Americans could be successful in sports was linked to physical capabilities that were not owing to any act of their own but because of heredity (Seligman, 1988).

Seligman (1988) conducted an analysis of Jimmy "the Greek" Snyder's comments and found tones of prejudicial assertions that he made that were really more against whites. From Seligman's work we learn another perspective and interpretation of Snyder's comments. Seligman believed that

Snyder seemed to label white athletes as lazy. Seligman further went on to argue that the message Snyder intended to communicate was the idea that white athletes are simply "not willing to put in the amount of practice time necessary to excel." Seligman also noted that Snyder seemed to praise the plethora of African American athletes who are dedicated to training hard and working hard to become better at their sports. In light of the extensive research and literature that has been published over the years comparing white and black athletes, we may be left to conclude that Snyder's comments were miscommunicated and misunderstood. It can be speculated that Snyder may have misconstrued the information regarding the differences between black and white athletes, and the explanations for their athletic accomplishments. In an analysis of this incident, Seligman (1988) argues that Jimmy the Greek's error in judgment and in what he said may be that he simply stated the thing that "millions of Americans know, which is that the races have different physiques on average" (p. 123).

Demographics and Domination of Sports

African Americans, according to sports history, were segregated into black leagues, and the fact that they currently dominate in basketball and football shows the overrepresentation that some sports have in terms of ethnic participation. While African Americans currently comprise 13.2% of the total U.S. population, only one sports league is made up of a diversity of players and that is Major League Soccer (MLS). MLS, according to demographic sports data, shows more diversity in its sport, particularly when measured across white, African American, Asian, Latino, or other racial groups. Research shows close to half of the players in the MLS are white (48%), with Latinos comprising 25% of the players, African Americans making up 10%, and close to 17% of the athletes identify themselves as "other" (Edelstein, 2017). The "other" category may a result of, for example, Cuban players who used to identify as black but now identify with other cultures or groups, such as Afro-Latina, Blatina, etc.

In every other major sports league, demographic data show that at least half of the players participating in the sport come from a single race or ethnicity. Research shows that more than three-quarters of all NBA and WNBA players are African American and that over half of players in the MLB league are white. (Research has not investigated the NHL, which is almost entirely white.) According to data in a story about race and ethnicity in sport, the Huffington Post reported that African American male athletes are only 6% of the U.S. population, yet they make up close to 75% of the players in the NFL (Goodman, 2016). Back when Jackie Robinson was the only black in a white league, we knew that to be an anomaly. Compare and contrast that to the present day—there is a complete role reversal. After World War II, African American athletes started coming from segregated black leagues to join predominately white leagues. This is one explanation for why blacks have become "disproportionately represented in basketball, football, track and field, boxing, and to a lesser extent in baseball" (Lapchick & Mathews, 2001; 2002). This over- and underrepresentation of racial groups in the demographics of sports still, to this day, continues to encourage debate and interest in understanding why African American athletes dominate some sports and do not participate in others.

While African Americans tend to be overrepresented in sports such as football, basketball, track and field, and boxing, we must ask the question that begins to provide some understanding as to why people of color are underrepresented in sports such as surfing, swimming, equestrian, golf, tennis, figure skating, lacrosse, and soccer, to name a few (Lapchick, Little, & Mathew, 2008). One hypothesis offered that may explain the lack of diversity in these sports centers on beliefs that we hold in our culture about success (winning and losing).

Reasons for Demographic Disparities in Sports: The Three Somatotypes

In today's scholarly environment, as we discussed in Chapter 1, race is now more of a sociological construct than it is a biological construct. Because of shared symbolism and experiences, many sociologists prefer the construct of "ethnicity." Regardless of the construct, the idea that African American athletes may demonstrate superiority in certain sports might be linked to environmental influences (i.e., nature vs. nurture). For some scholars, a lack of opportunities resulting from discrimination in the broader American culture may have passively encouraged blacks to pursue certain sports at which resources in the environment may help them to become successful. Inner-city youth may then learn how to play basketball using anything round and practice throwing it in a dilapidated hoop. To be a successful playing football when resources are low, all one needs is the field to run and an object to serve as a ball. These and many other examples are used to support the idea that success regarding athletic performance is predominantly mediated by one's environment and enhanced practice or playtime that allows individuals to work on skills rather than possessing some inherent genetic abilities.

According to the somatotype theory, individuals are born with a genetic body type based on body composition and skeletal frame. "Most human bodies are unique combinations of the three body types: ectomorph, mesomorph, and endomorph" (Carter, 1970, p. 536). Somatotyping is helpful in sports in which the body shape could influence the resulting performance. The somatotyping system was developed by W. H. Sheldon in 1940 and is used to describe the body build of an individual. Figure 4.1 shows the differences in these three body types.

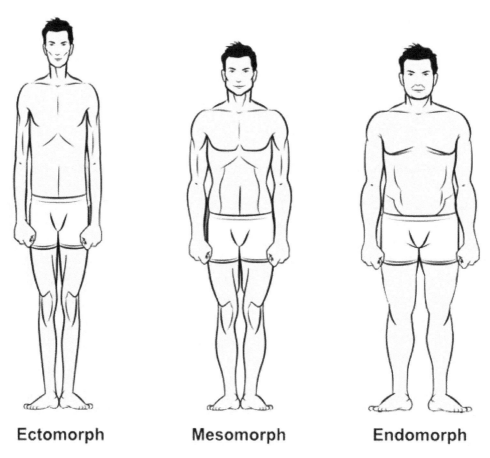

Ectomorph　　　**Mesomorph**　　　**Endomorph**

FIGURE 4.1　*Examples of different body types*

Sheldon evaluated the degree to which a body type was present. Using a scale from 1 to 7, where 1 is the minimum and 7 is the maximum, Sheldon identified certain somatotypes and physiological capabilities that are associated with certain types of body frames (Carter, 1970). Athletes are said to be part endomorph, part mesomorph, and part ectomorph. According to somatotype theory, height is not taken into the classification of the body frame.

Somatotypes and Sports

It is clear that some body types or somatotypes lend themselves well for participation in a specific sport (Carter, 1970). Carter's early work (1970) on somatotypes in sports find that, for example, swimmers tend to fare on the lower end of the endomorphic scale than say bodybuilders, wrestlers, and football players. Somatotypes in sports also shows that basketball players often fit the ectomorphic body type than any of the other athletic groups. Weightlifters, according to somatotype theory, frequently fit the body image known as the mesomorph. Even though there is a range of variability in

> ## DISCUSSION QUESTION
>
> Do you know what body type you are? Take the body test!
>
> Listed here is the body scale. Find out which one of the three basic body types you have.
>
> The three basic human body types have been identified as the "endomorph, characterized by a dominance of body fat; the mesomorph, characterized by a well-developed musculature; and the ectomorph, identified by a lack of much fat or muscle tissue" (Carter, 1970). According to information on bodybuilding.com, author King (2017) describes each of the three body types. An ectomorph body type is described as a body build that naturally looks smaller and thinner, while the endomorph body appears overweight and often appears heavier than he or she really is, especially if they are muscular and well-toned (King, 2017). The mesomorph, perhaps considered the "ideal" type, looks "well proportioned." Even if a mesomorph appears to look a little heavier, because everything is in proportion with the individual, the goal is often to look like a mesomorph even if you are not.
>
> Take the test found on www.bodybuilding.com to find out your body type: https://www.bodybuilding.com/fun/becker3.htm.

athletes and body types, face validity of the presuppositions of the theory, along with the descriptors, almost always support the idea that an athlete's body type naturally fits the skills and athletic abilities associated with certain sports. For example, it just seems to make sense that wrestlers, bodybuilders, weight lifters, and football players would align most closely with the mesomorph body type. These sports require muscle, body tone, and strength. It also goes with our culture's idea that this body type, one that is incredibly muscular and bulky, would naturally fit into those sports that require muscular strength. For basketball players to be successful in their sport, somatotype theory suggests that they should be extremely tall and lean (low endo/high ecto, etc.). And we know as we mentioned earlier in this text, according to theory, athletes interested in ballet or swimming need to be lean but strong. Therefore, the theory on body type suggests that successful swimmers tend to have bodies that are muscular and toned (little to no fat) yet also tall and lean (high meso and low endo). The takeaway from this information is to understand that the body typology, as established by Sheldon and researched later by Carter (1970), supports the idea that our body type does not depend on our biological race.

In a study focused on explaining and providing a theory to help us understand why long-distance runners from Kenya tend to dominate that sporting event, Moore (1990) explored and investigated the Kenyan culture and environment. Moore's research revealed several factors found accountable for understanding and explaining why Kenyans are successful in distance running. The factors that Moore (1990) found were (a) residing in a geographical area that has an altitude of 7,000 feet, (b) food and lifestyle (for example, Kenyans consume a diet high in complex carbohydrates), (c) the culture considers running as their one and only means of transportation, and (d) Kenya is known as a liberal and very tolerant culture that reinforces competition, dominance, and defeat. Moore's research shows that, over time, physical environment and resources aid in the biological traits exhibited in Kenyan athletic skills. When running is the primary means of transportation, it makes sense when explaining why they have been so successful in distance running. Moore (1990) also found that cultural norms and influences have played a huge role in explaining and understanding their athletic performance in long-distance running. Culture may also be responsible for attitudes about running and the desire and motivation to achieve success on the international sports docket. The argument that centers on a biological advantage that Kenyans have over other groups of athletes coming from different parts of the world has support from several studies that frequently demonstrate that adaptation to physical surroundings (nurture) creates athletes from Kenya who are (a) able to perform at a higher percentage of their V02 Max (e.g., 89% vs. 81%, Noakes, Myburgh & Schall, 1990), which is due to atmosphere and geographic factors, and (b) physical traits such as quadriceps that have greater muscles that allow for a greater supply of blood, smaller muscle fibers, and more enzymes that build muscle and burn fat. The presence of enzymes also ensures that the body can get by without glycogen and protein (Burfoot, 1992; Burfoot James, Foster, Self, Wilkins, & Phillips, 1990; Saltin, 1971). Taken together, these factors have been used to explain why Kenyans appear to have a high resistance to fatigue when participating in distance running when compared to other groups who do experience fatigue when engaged in a sport of high-intensity aerobic activity.

Why Is Marathon Running a White Sport?

In this section, we specifically take a moment to discuss cross-country running and distance running/marathon training. Research over time continues to show that this sporting event used to be and currently is predominantly and incessantly white. Despite the lack of fees, expenses related to equipment, and access to a track, we find a continued lack of representation of people of color. With less than 5% of the minority population found to participate in the sport, we find that several factors may be used to explain this stereotypical association of whites with running and the lack of minorities participating in cross-country or long-distance running. Some of the factors are related to issues of safety and areas for potential athletes to run distances (e.g., think of the inhabitants of Kenya compared to residents of New York, etc.). Issues with hair and discrimination or policies related to hair may also be of issue. For example, Middle Eastern athletes may be expected to don a hijab, which covers the hair. Ballet dancers and cheerleaders are expected to put their hair in ponytails or buns. What happens if you desire to dance in a ballet, but your hair, depending upon the length, is not conducive to being put braids? What happens when you are a person of color who happens to wear your hair in a natural style such as an afro? Later in this chapter, we will discuss the issue of black female athletes' hair and why it continues to be a contributor to low participation in swimming. Although we know swimming is a sport that is also predominately and persistently white, we use black women and the issue of hair to enhance the suggestion that there are factors that may help to explain why some sports, such as running and swimming, may attract few people of color.

Linking Genetic Attributes to Specific Athletic Abilities

Perhaps it should be argued that the success of many black athletes is related to their physical environment and access to resources. This argument is related to the nature versus nurture philosophy of human behavior. The basic presupposition could be explained by the lack of resources and access to opportunities that are linked to institutional racism and discrimination. Comparatively speaking, success in sports must have appeared much more achievable than mainstream jobs. Success in the sport of running can be explained by resources needed to succeed in sports. Perhaps blacks found that the extraordinary amount of energy and hours needed to devote to sports to become proficient was much more likely than corporate jobs, and, therefore, they came to dominate sports for which they had resources available within their environment. If we consider the resources needed to run in track and field or to play football and/or basketball, we begin to understand that participation in these sports requires little to no resources outside of the individual. For example, we might find low-income children playing basketball with an old, beat-up, rusted basket found in an abandoned lot. Or, in the case of football, we might find children playing with any kind of ball but using an open area to tackle and run for touchdowns. And the examples can continue with boxing and track and field. Other sports, which we will discuss in detail, require access to a club (e.g., golf, tennis, sailing), expensive equipment, and time with one-on-one trainers/coaches (e.g., golf, tennis, swimming).

Nature Versus Nurture

A study was conducted over 27 years ago that has since become a seminal study in the area of sports and differences in athletic performance (reported in Coakley, 2007). Since then, studies consistently show that most sports journalists will acknowledge systematic differences in basketball performance between blacks and whites (Billings, 2003; Billings, 2004). A plethora of research in this area continues to prove that sportswriters will and often recognize and report on an African American's athletic performances that deal with individuals' ability to jump, their speed, and their reaction time, yet they tend to avoid or ignore any references to other influences on their performance. It is believed that Carlton's work makes a critical point: When we observe differences in athletic performance, we must consider the fact that those differences might be directly related to culture and access to resources (e.g., Kenyan runners). The differences in how inner city (e.g., African American) and suburban (e.g., white) children learn to play the game may also affect athletic performance. Carlton's main thesis supports the statement made in the previous section: Urban children, those living in low-income neighborhoods, will learn how to play sports, such as basketball, on overcrowded playgrounds, while rural youth have opportunities to hone their athletic abilities that may often require memberships and other criteria for entrance.

Extending this explanation on how cultural and environmental factors can oust falsehoods about inborn, biological differences in racial and sports capabilities is the story of the Philadelphia Department of Recreation swim team (see Hoose, 1990). For years, fictional accounts have been told that assert black athletes lack the buoyancy to swim. This "myth" is couched in the idea that the lack of buoyancy is related to the increased muscle mass and bone density that blacks are often born with. Therefore, over time, the idea was inferred that black athletes avoid swimming as a sport and were often told that swimming is a sport that would hinder their success instead of enhancing it. (Recall earlier in the chapter that we discussed that athletes' potential to succeed has been used to encourage and even discourage them from participating in sports). When reflecting on environment and resources, we made the point that resources needed to play certain sports are limited in that the only equipment needed is space. Thus, regarding swimming facilities, it should be noted that finding a vast amount of swimming pools in African American neighborhoods is not only rare, but we can say confidently that pools in predominately black neighborhoods are relatively scarce. And if we consider our history in this culture, there was a time when whites were extremely reluctant and even unwilling to share neighborhood swimming pools with blacks.

Swimming, track and field, and volleyball are known as "Olympic sports" because of the financial profits these sports are known to achieve. Consequently, for these reasons, we know that African Americans exhibit little to no interest in regard to swimming as a sport or excelling in that sport.

The idea that African Americans are not interested in swimming as a sport may be used to explain the media hype and emphasis in 2016 when an African American female swimmer took home a gold medal. The 2016 Summer Olympics in Rio was when Simone Manuel made Olympic history as the first African American woman to compete in the swimming competition and not only compete but also win the Olympic gold medal in freestyle swimming.

If we believe in the argument that the reason African Americans tend to dominate sports such as basketball and football is based on environment and not inherent biological advantages, then we must accept the argument that white athletes also tend to dominate sports based on their environment and cultural influences.

Because of economic advantages and social reinforcement, it is possible that children are encouraged to seek out different sports that are in line with their social status and the number of resources available in their environment. As presented earlier in this chapter, the environmental argument supposes that a viable biological predisposition, motivation to practice for long periods of time, and access to resources starting at an early age are all positively and significantly related to honing skills and acquiring the optimal physiological tools for performing with the cream of the crop, or, as the industry describes this group, the "elite level." For example, to play tennis, one needs a racquet, balls, and access to a court. To swim, children need access to a swimming pool. To compete in gymnastics, they must have the ability to enroll in classes and have a coach, along with access to a gym and funds to buy costumes and leotards; these are all resources needed to succeed in this sport. Regarding hockey, children need to be able to afford the equipment and the uniform, and must have access to an ice rink. Contrast those resources with equipment needed to play football, basketball, or baseball. In these sports, all that is needed is some form of ball, empty fields that can be marked with makeshift goals or baskets made from trash cans, etc. When considering resources and access to resources, it becomes plain to see that representation in sports and physical achievement may be more related to nurture and access to resources than biological or physiological superiority. From this perspective, skin color is only important in this instance because it focuses on the affiliation with one's cultural background—a culture that is known to support or oppose athletic achievement.

Arab American Athletes

This section of the text explores Arab American representation in sports. Dr. Jack Shaheen, a scholar in mass communication, maintains that Arab Americans are the "most maligned group" in America and that Muslims and Arabs are often depicted as terrorists (Shaheen, 2008). Shaheen's (2008) work centers primarily on depictions of Arab Americans in Hollywood. Few, if any scholars, have published work on Arab Americans in sports. Research revealed that in terms of participation in athletics, Arab Americans are deeply involved in U.S. sports and are typically found playing soccer and/or basketball (Nahhas, 2016). For example, research that followed Arab Americans revealed those who have actively contributed to or are still active in adding their culture and lifestyle to American sports. The contribution of Arab American athletes is very significant and varied. In a news article titled "Here Are Some of the Greatest Muslim-American Athletes" While the majority of the population of the Arab world is Muslim, most Arab Americans, self-identify with Christian religion (Arab American Institute, 2016). While it is common for many Americans to confuse the terms Arab, Middle Eastern, and Muslim, let's provide a brief distinction among the terms.

An Arab-American is someone who identifies closely with the ethnicity and culture of the countries or territories in western Asia and Africa where Arabic is the official language of the state A Middle Easterner is often from the region of the world that lies largely between the Mediterranean in the west and the Indian subcontinent in the east. The association most closely aligned with this ethnic group is the idea that it is known for large reservoirs of oil. While roots of Muslim culture are often traced to the Middle East, we learn that the reason for this misperception is due to the fact that the religion known as Islam was said to originate in the Middle East. A Muslim American is an individual who professes the Islam faith, prays five times a day, fasts during Ramadan, gives charity to the needy, and makes the pilgrimage to Mecca at least once during their lifetime (Arab American Institute, 2016).

In 2015, our 44th president made a statement proclaiming that "Muslim Americans are some of our greatest sports heroes (Smith, 2015). Inspired by controversy, sports journalist Allan Smith (2015) compiled a list of the top athletes who happen to identify as Muslim and the list included sports legends like Muhammad Ali, Kareen Abdul Jabbar, Husain Abdullah, and many more.

In another related news story, we learn of Justin Abdelkader, an ice hockey forward playing for the Detroit Red Wings in the NHL. Abdelkader's ethnic origin is Arabia. His paternal grandparents came to the United States from Jordan when Abdelkader was 19 (Barnas, 2009; Thabet, 2013). Research also revealed other Arab American professional athletes who are active in the NBA. Alaa Abdelnaby is currently a basketball announcer for a CBS-affiliate television station in Philadelphia. Abdelnaby played college basketball with Duke and later was drafted and played 5 years with the Portland Trail Blazers (Blackistone, 2011). One of the first internationally born professional basketball players who is of Arab descent is Lebanese-born retired professional basketball player Rony Seikaly (Blackistone, 2011).

The NFL boasts the highest number of professional Arab American athletes. For example, Oday Aboushi is a current NFL athlete of Palestinian descent who plays with the New York Jets; retired NFL player Doug Flutie is of Arab descent, as his father is Lebanese; Drew Haddad, recently retired from the NFL where he played for a combined total of 5 years with the Buffalo Bills and the Indianapolis Colts, and retired in 2005 after a season with the San Diego Chargers; and NFL retired quarterback Gibran Hamdan, identified as having Palestinian and Pakistani descent, played over 5 years.

A complete list of current and former Arab American athletes can be found on Wikipedia and the Arab American Institute's website, (2016). However, it is clear that this ethnic subculture is active and trying to dismantle negative stereotypes that plague the group. We found Arab Americans who participate as race car drivers, played college and professional football, who are professional baseball and basketball players, have participated in the Olympic games, and found success in track and field. All in all, Arab Americans are active in the professional sports world here in the United States. For example, we found the following athletes who participate in various American sports:

Dina Al-Sabah, professional figure competitor (Wilkins, 2003); Sarah Attar, track and field athlete (Saudi Arabian father) (Culpepper, 2016); Ahmed Kaddour, professional boxer from the NBC show *The Contender* (Lebanese) (Boxing News, 2018); Sam Khalifa, MLB baseball player (Brownfield, 2013); Joe Lahoud , a Lebanese professional MLB player with the Boston Red Sox, (Nowlin 2018) and Faryd Mondragón, born in Cali of Lebanese descent is an MLS player for Philadelphia Union (Niblock, 2010). For more information on Arab American athletes, refer to "Sports and the Middle East" published by the Middle East Institute and "Arab Americans as Athletes, published online 2016 at https://www.arabamerica.com/heritage-month-arab-americans-athletes/.

Asian American Athletes

In the United States, Asian American athletes tend to be frequently represented as having body types that are physically and athletically inferior to other minority athletes. This stereotype has led to a devaluing of and an unfair practice that results in prejudging potential athletes in the recruitment process of Asian American athletes in professional sports. Why are only a few Asian Americans participating in football, basketball, track and field, tennis, and soccer, for example? We know from watching the Olympics that Asians can be found in other parts of the world participating in sports such as swimming and gymnastics, but in terms of American culture, the lack of representation of this group in other sports is fairly shocking. Support for this statement can be found in an overwhelming number of research studies that prove that Asian American athletes were and currently are underrepresented in a majority of professional sports (a point duly noted by many sources; see Carrington & McDonald, 2001; Franks, 2000). Research currently shows that in 2016, Asian Americans consisted of approximately 6% of the population (U.S. Census Bureau, 2016), yet we find that in terms of sport, Asian American athletes only represent approximately 2% of the players in the NFL, 1.9% of the players in the MLB, and less than 1% of the players in the NBA and NHL. Case in point: Kailer Yamamoto, a Japanese-American NHL player who "made his NHL debut on October 4, 2017 against Calgary" (Wilkins, 2018). A list of NHL players who are known to have East Asian and/or Southeast Asian ancestral ties shows that, as of this writing, Yamamoto is currently the only Asian American currently playing in the National Hockey League. (refer to https://icehockey.fandom.com/wiki/List_of_Ice_Hockey_Players_of_Asian_Descent). Basketball is another professional sport that has been identified as the one professional sport with the lowest number of Asian American athletes actively participating (Roos, 2017). Jeremy Lin, a professional player with the Brooklyn Nets. Linn who identifies as Chinese American, caught basketball fans and sports journalists by surprise. In fact, a term known as "Linsanity" was created in 2012 simply because most American basketball fans were not used to seeing a tall Chinese American professional basketball player (Roos, 2017). In fact, Asian American scholars and athletes alike credit Jeremy Lin's presence in a professional basketball as one that challenged traditional stereotypes while also providing a role model and showing young Asian Americans that that a tall, Taiwanese-American man can play basketball in the NBA (Roos, 2017).

Disparities regarding Asian participation in sports is often explained by "genetic differences." It is genetic differences in Asian athletes that causes them to be slower than "their American, African, or European rivals." The idea that there are genetic differences in Asian athletes is a notion that has been widely accepted. In fact, *The People's Daily*, an Asian newspaper, wrote that Asian athletes are more "suited" for those sports that require "agility and technique," such as table tennis, badminton, and gymnastics (Yardley, 2004). According to information presented in the newspaper, it was stated that Asians have "congenital shortcomings" and "genetic differences" that put them at a disadvantage when competing against "black and white athletes."

In the past two decades or so, our culture has seen a slightly higher representation of Asian athletes of mixed racial heritage. The difference is quite substantial when we compare athletes of mixed racial heritage to those of full Asian racial heritage who participate in sports. The athletes who best fit this description are Tiger Woods, Hines Ward, and Roman Gabriel, who are all of mixed racial Asian heritage.

Latinx Athletes

The year 2016 was record-breaking in the sporting world for Latinos. Latino athletes rewrote the history books regarding race and sports and changed the perception of sports fans.

Here are some of the highlights of Latino athletes found in sports media coverage in 2016:

According to an article written by Salgado (2016) titled "The Top Ten Latino Sports Moments of 2016" on the Pan American World website, Auston Matthews made history as the first Latino to be drafted first overall in the NHL Entry Draft (https://www.nbcnews.com/storyline/2016-year-in-review/top-ten-latino-sports-moments-2016-n698676). Matthews, born to a Mexican mother, was drafted as the top pick in the entry draft back in June (Lomax, 2008; Salgado, 2016; Shropshire, Briley, Ezra, Fields, Hawkins, Iber, & Smith, 2008). With that selection, the Toronto Maple Leafs made history in two ways. Not only was Matthews their first number-one pick since 1985 but also Matthews is the first NHL player of Hispanic descent to be drafted as the number-one pick. According to a 2016 story on NBC, Matthews outperformed Raffi Torres when he became known as the highest ever Latino draft pick (fifth overall, 2000). Scott Gomez holds a similar honor, as he has been billed as the first Latino draft pick in NHL history (27th overall, 1998) (Salgado, 2016).

Hispanic Players and the 2016 World Series

The 2016 MBL Series was a memorable year for many reasons, according to NBC news. It was October of 2016 when the Chicago Cubs won their first championship in 108 years. But 2016 also allowed sports fans to become aware of some of professional baseball's top Latino players. The Chicago Cubs included pitchers on their rosters like Jake Arrieta, Aroldis Chapman, Hector Rondon, and Pedro Strop. The Cubs also listed infielder Javier Báez, catchers Willson Contreras and Miguel Montero, and outfielders Jorge Soler and Albert Almora on their side. The Cleveland Indians at the time included designated hitter Carlos Santana; infielders Francisco Lindor, José Ramírez, and Erik Gonzalez, catchers Roberto Perez and Yan Gomes; and pitchers Danny Salazar and Dan Otero on their rosters (Salgado, 2016).

Latin America Was Also Well Represented at the 2016 Summer Olympics

From a media perspective, the coverage of Latin Americans at the 31st Olympiad in Rio de Janeiro, Brazil, from 20 countries helped to showcase Latin America. Brazil's soccer team won gold, and the men's field hockey team from Argentina won a gold medal in their respective event. Colombia's Oscar Figueroa won a gold medal, while Luis Javier Mosquera won a silver medal in weight lifting; Cuba's Ismael Borrero and Mijaín López earned gold medals in wrestling; and Julio César De La Cruz, Robeisy Ramirez, and Arlen Lopez all won gold medals in boxing. The Dominican Republic had an athlete, Luisito Pié, win the bronze in tae kwon do. Mexico took home five medals in swimming and diving, tae kwon do, boxing, and the modern pentathlon. Venezuela's Yulimar Rojas, Yoel Finol, and Stefany Hernandez also earned medals, while Monica Puig won the first gold medal, making Olympic history for Puerto Rico. "Bolivia, Chile, Costa Rica, Ecuador, El Salvador, Guatemala, Nicaragua, Panama, Paraguay, Peru, and Uruguay were also given an adequate amount of media attention in the sport of track and field" (Salgado, 2016).

José Quintana and Julio Teherán Make Baseball History

In 1998, Latino baseball player Édgar Rentería was the first Colombian national to be selected as an MLB All-Star while playing for the Florida Marlins. Then 18 years later, in 2016, two Latino pitchers were the first Colombians to participate in baseball's midsummer classic. It was history in the making when José Quintana of the Chicago White Sox and Julio Teherán of the Atlanta Braves were honored by the MLB, sports fans, and media when they were both named to the MLB All-Stars (Salgado, 2016).

Monica Puig Earned Puerto Rico Its First-Ever Olympic Gold Medal

Monica Puig, of Puerto Rico, won a gold medal in women's singles. In its Olympic history, Puerto Rico has participated in 18 Olympiads and had less than 10 medals to show for its participation.

Interestingly, none of the medals were gold, and six of the eight medals received came from boxing. Further analysis showed that of the eight medals, six were bronze. All of this makes Puig's performance in the 2016 Summer Olympics historical and record-breaking as a Latina and an American female athlete.

Laurie Hernandez Wins Gold in USA Gymnastics

Gymnast Laurie Hernandez's athletic prowess on the vault, balance beam, and floor exercise helped to propel the United States to a total of 13 medals—eight of which were gold—and Hernandez added two (gold and silver) to her own collection.

Representation of Latino Athletes in Other Sports

Baseball is the most visible sport, particularly from a media perspective, where Latinos have been known to prosper. Latinos ranging from Sammy Sosa to Roberto Clemente to Manny Ramirez have become a major force in the MLB. On closer inspection of the NBA's, NFL's, and NHL's athletes and rosters, we find that the representation of Latino athletes has, as of this writing, not yet reached the level or numbers found in the MLB, which begs some important questions: Why the disparity between baseball and other professional major sports? What policy changes must be made in sports such as basketball, football, swimming, and hockey to increase inclusion in these and other sports within the Latino community? Answers to these and many other questions may be observed in the Latino ethnic culture and their access to resources. Is it possible that the availability or lack of availability of certain sports in their communities may explain differences in which sports Latino/as are actively involved with? It is possible that influencers and environmental tools, such as access to role models, media attention, coaches, trainers, and exposure to the sport, which creates access policies that address specific socioeconomic problems, might actually encourage young aspiring Latino children to consider participation outside of baseball?

The relationship between Latino baseball players and the media seems to have always been one of negative portrayal and conflict. While sports media argue that language presents massive barriers to reporting, some feel that media have improved and are now working to understand the players. History tells us that early on, sports media were unwilling to attempt to communicate with Latino players by having translators present, and this led to conflict in the media-player relationship.

Latinos have also experienced discrimination in sports media through blatant disregard for the pronunciations of their names. Before players assimilated into American culture and society, it was documented that baseball officials and media used to change Latino players' names to sound more American. Roberto Clemente was, for instance, nicknamed Bob by officials and sports announcers. Despite the conflicts and problems with sports media that Latino baseball players experienced, changing demographics of America and, in particular, baseball fans are now demanding that the MLB embrace Latino culture and its language. Many teams are also incorporating the Spanish language into its communications, marketing, and social media. Some professional sports teams, such as the St. Louis Cardinals, have started using Spanish-speaking radio, set up Spanish-only Twitter accounts for fans and players to interact, and have planned Latino nights to reach out to and engage with fans of Latin descent.

As we frequently mentioned, in terms of sports, we understand that basketball is considered an urban, inner-city sport dominated by African Americans. Therefore, it should be no surprise that the NBA is considered to be a league filled with a predominant presence of African American players.

This stereotype seems to be frequently enforced in media messages and content, particularly when they pay more attention to those players who are perceived to be rebels and defy or disobey what Caucasian Americans consider to be proper, respectable, and normal behaviors. And regarding the NFL, the kicker position holds a disproportionate number of Latino players. Stacking, a term that will be discussed later in this chapter, is evident in the NFL not only with African Americans but also with Latinos.

Of special note, though, are professional players, such as Tony Gonzalez. Over his 16-year career as a tight end with the Kansas City Chiefs and the Atlanta Falcons, Gonzalez was a six-time pro bowler holding several career receiving records. Aside from his on-the-field accomplishments, Gonzalez, we learn from news media, is an athlete who is known to be very active in the Kansas City community and internationally as well. To better understand Spanish language, media reported that Gonzalez spent the summers of 2004 and 2005 studying Spanish in San Miguel De Allende, Mexico, and in Costa Rica. We also learn from researching news articles that Gonzalez promoted participation and encouraged involvement in the NFL while in Rio de Janeiro, Brazil, in 2003, encouraging more Brazilians to take up the sport of football. To increase awareness and introduce children to sports, Gonzalez formed the Gonzalez Foundation in 1998, which supports the Shadow Buddies program. Gonzalez also uses funds from his foundation to support the Boys and Girls Clubs. As previously stated, Gonzalez is well known in the Kansas City, Missouri, community for his philanthropic campaigns and contribution. He spends much of his time making contributions to any effort that is focused on erasing the discrimination that has victimized Latinos in U.S. sports.

Native American Athletes

Native Americans with a few notable exceptions have had very limited participation in sports in American culture. Sports teams with nicknames such as the Redskins, the Warriors, the Chiefs, the Savages, etc., still tend to be controversial and elicit heated arguments regarding the ethical considerations of the names. The chants and tomahawks are perceived by many indigenous people as poking fun at and mocking their culture—a culture that is filled with rituals and chants that are sacred. When Americans engage in these behaviors without a knowledge of their meaning, it is understandable why many Native Americans feel that chants, war paint, and use of tomahawks present the perception that we are engaging in a mockery of their culture—a mockery that contributes to the enhancement of stereotypes and prejudice. As it stands, the lack of Native Americans in media and a lack of frequent positive presentations of the culture result in a trivialization and devaluing of the group (Gerbner, 1972). Currently, it seems as if media stories about Native Americans as mascots in sports are moving away from arguments on the right or wrongs related to the use and naming of Indian mascots and away from this group's past accomplishments.

FIGURE 4.2 *Billy Mills crossing the finish line at 1964 Tokyo Games*

NATIVE AMERICAN ATHLETES IN AMERICAN SPORTS

A generation of indigenous athletes in the new millennium is starting to turn attention back to Native Americans. The most notable athlete of Native American ancestry, is Billy Mills. Mills, an Oglala-Lakota-Sioux American Indian made history in 1964, and as of the time of this writing in 2018, is famous for becoming the first Native American athlete to ever win an Olympic gold medal for the 10,000 meters footrace (Ballard, 2008). Figure 4.2 is a classic photograph of Mills' participation in the 1964 Olympics when came from behind and won a gold medal in the 10k race (Ballard, 2008). As of the writing of this chapter, Mills is still the only Native American to ever win a gold medal in the 10k event (Ballard, 2008). Thanks to the hard work of many successful Native Americans who attained successes on the court, on the field, and on the ice, we were able to gather a list of Native American athletes in American sport:

I'm sitting in a Starbucks in Rapid City, South Dakota. Across from me, my girlfriend is studying Lakota language flash cards in preparation for her upcoming semester at Oglala Lakota College. We should be at a friend's house watching the Denver Broncos play the New England Patriots in the American Football Conference Championship. But, as you know, time is subject to change. And, for professional sports, times are definitely changing.

The conversation about Native Americans in sports is slowly turning away from the use of Indian mascots and also focusing less on past accomplishments. A new generation of indigenous athletes from all across Turtle Island is bringing attention back to Native Americans on the court, on the field, and on the ice. Still, we can't have a conversation about Native Americans in sports without first mentioning the legends:

"The Greatest Athlete," Jim Thorpe (Sac and Fox), not only won two gold medals during the 1912 Olympics but played professional football, baseball, and basketball.

In 1964, Billy Mills (Oglala Lakota) became the second Native American to win Olympic gold, as well as the only American to win the gold medal for the 10,000-meter run.

During a 16-year career in Major League Baseball, Charles Albert "Chief" Bender (Chippewa) developed the slider pitch, pitched a no-hitter, and pitched in five World Series.

Ellison "Tarzan" Brown (Narragansett) won the Boston Marathon in 1936 and 1939, while also competing in the 1936 Olympics in Berlin.

NFL Hall of Famer "Injun Joe" Kapp quarterbacked with the Minnesota Vikings and the Chicago Bears, as well as the British Columbia Lions (CFL). He is the only athlete ever to have played in the Super Bowl (1970), Grey Cup (1963), and Rose Bowl (1959).

Today, the legacy continues. 2013 was one of the biggest years yet for professional and collegiate Native American athletes. In 2013, Major League Baseball and the National Football League saw five Native Americans among its best teams:

NFL quarterback Sam Bradford (Cherokee) played for the St. Louis Rams (out much of the season with a torn ACL)

Kyle Lohse (Nomlaki) pitched for the Milwaukee Brewers

Joba Chamberlain (Winnebago) pitched for the New York Yankees

Jacoby Ellsbury (Navajo, now with the Yankees) and Shane Victorino (Native Hawaiian) played for the Boston Red Sox

Did I mention that Ellsbury, Victorino, and Lohse each have at least one World Series ring? And that, in 2013, Ellsbury and Victorino both earned their second World Series Championship with the Red Sox? Jacoby Ellsbury is known to us as a supporter of the Navajo Relief Fund (NRF), a program of National Relief Charities. In 2010, he launched a charity wine named ZinfaldEllsbury and donated a portion of the proceeds to NRF and two other charities. At the press conference we attended, Jacoby talked about his grandmother weaving rugs and shearing sheep in 120 degrees with no air conditioning. He appreciates the hardworking lifestyle but has concerns and Jacoby Ellsbury realizes that children of the reservation can draw hope from seeing someone of Navajo descent playing in the majors—hope that also carries over into school.

Sisters, Jude and Shoni Schimmel (Umatilla), were launched into the national spotlight as they helped carry the Louisville Cardinals from the number five seed to the title game of the 2013 NCAA Women's Basketball Tournament. Despite their loss to the UConn Huskies in the championship game, the Schimmel sisters finished the 2013 NCAA Women's Season as the pride of Native Americans everywhere.

Finally, four-time PGA Tour Winner, Notah Begay III (Navajo), continues to fight Type 2 diabetes in Indian country with the Notah Begay III Foundation. Partnering with Nike's N7, Johns Hopkins Center for American Indian Health, and the W.K. Kellogg Foundation; Begay is taking a holistic approach to reducing the rates of diabetes among Native Americans through sports, research, and community-based programs.

Soon our attention will turn toward the upcoming Super Bowl XLVIII. While Sam Bradford and the Rams didn't make it to this year's Super Bowl, and the Denver Broncos and Seattle Seahawks currently have no Native athletes on their rosters, I remain comforted by this thought: If 2013 proved anything about Native American athletes, it is that their legacy isn't static but changing with the times, the players, and the nations they represent. (Bentley, 2014).

Equity Issues in Race and Sports

Discussions of race and sports have always been topics that are intertwined in discussions about American culture and sports. To some extent, American media tend to write and publish more stories on African Americans (see Frisby, 2016; 2017a; 2017b). African American athletes are often over- or underrepresented, varying by sport. Black men made up 57% of college football teams and 64% of men's basketball teams in 2013 while only being 2.8% of full-time undergraduate students (Harper, 2006; Harper, 2009; Harper, 2009b). In other regulated sports, white people predominate the players.

One area that has received more attention over the past few years is equity in sports, despite the interest in issues and controversies relating to ethnicity and athletic achievement. As previously stated in this chapter, African American athletes tend to be overrepresented in college and professional sports such as basketball, boxing, football, and track. African American female athletes are "disproportionally represented as well in basketball and track" (Anthony, 2000; Hunter, 1996). The WNBA has been reported to have a "disproportionly large representation of African American females" (Lapchick, 2018). However, this disproportionality in select sports for African American athletes causes further thought about the underrepresentation of African American athletes in other sports, such as bowling, badminton, lacrosse, skiing, figure skating, softball, and volleyball.

Another related equity issue concerns the question of who holds power and control in sports. Even though African Americans are known to dominate sports, the domination is as players, particularly in those sports described as "revenue-producing sports." But if we turn the discussion to the topic of ownership, we quickly learn that people of color are undoubtedly underrepresented in positions of ownership, management, and coaching. Currently, whites have a majority of the control regarding ownership of professional teams, management, and coaching. Recent research on diversity and inclusion at the college level shows that colleges also fail in terms of hiring black coaches and administrators (Lapchick & Matthews, 2001; Lapchick & Matthews, 2002). This issue has recently received greater attention among college athletic administrators and suggestions have been presented for how demographics regarding power and control might be changed (e.g., Lapchick, 2018).

Stacking

Equity in sports has another more recent issue, one that has become known as "stacking." Stacking has been defined as "the likelihood of white and black players being disproportionately represented in certain playing positions such as pitcher and outfielder in baseball or quarterback and cornerback in football" (Berghorn, Yetman, & Hanna, 1988; Entine, 2000; Jones, Leonard II, Schmitt, Randall, & Tolone, 1987). Various ideas have been provided on stacking, and the data shows that Caucasians are more likely to hold positions of leadership, while African Americans tend to hold positions that are more peripheral roles, such as assistant (Berghorn et al., 1988). Historically, regarding stacking in basketball, the center and guard positions have been noted as being disproportionately held by whites, while positions such as a forward used to be identified as a position normally held by African Americans.

Some explanations have been offered that help us interpret and understand the stacking phenomenon. Coupled with stereotypical notions and opinions about cognitive and physical capabilities that may be race-related (e.g., Eitzen & Sanford, 1975; Hoberman, 1997; Williams & Youssef, 1975), the belief that whites are more suitable for positions requiring greater cognitive skills, such as decision making and thinking, while African Americans are better suited for positions requiring physical prowess, has been the dominant idea motivating player positions and based on ideas related to genetics and biological differences, as discussed earlier in this chapter. White and African American players are often placed in positions that match these assumptions and stereotypes held by people in control and with power (i.e., coaches, owners). To support this hypothesis, future empirical research is needed that can test the effects of having African American athletes proportionately distributed across a variety of playing positions and then determine the role that early exposure has on player position. This research could also show the opposite and that is that once African Americans move up the ladder of athletic success, their achievements often lead to being "stacked" or disproportionately placed into specific playing positions.

Some argue that stacking is no longer an issue because African American athletes have become dominant in three major professional sports. However, others have gone on record to argue against this assertion. For example, research on diversity in the NFL shows that although 65% of the players are of African American descent, they are still disproportionately found serving in offensive positions, such as running back and wide receivers. And, regarding defense, research shows that African Americans are also disproportionately found on defense as cornerbacks and as safeties. Concerning professional baseball, stacking is prevalent and is supported by data that shows that 15% of African American players tend to be put in positions covering the outfield.

FIGURE 4.3 *Illustration of what is meant by "sports stacking"*

This work further shows that although they are overrepresented in the outfield, African American baseball players are underrepresented in positions of catcher, center, pitcher, and third baseman. In Figure 4.3 we find various images of sports in which stacking is common—from swimming to basketball, soccer, and field hockey—sports where positions are typically held by a dominant ethnic group.

Although stacking is interesting and complex, it also provides insights into the level of covert and even overt racism in sports. We also see how, in standard practices that are very similar to prejudicial biases, the practice of stacking has practical implications for players. Research on stacking shows that "players who occupy 75 percent of positions typically held by African American players also enjoyed careers that were shorter than 75 percent of those positions that were typically held by whites" (for more on this, refer to Best, 1987). Moreover, research suggests that the average career life for African Americans in the NFL is approximately 3 years, while it is approximately 4 years for whites, an idea that will be discussed at length later in this book.

The second consequence of stacking is posted playing career opportunities as coaches and managers. Later in the book, we will go into further detail about power and control in sports, but now we just want to introduce the implications of stacking regarding longevity and long-term career goals for black athletes. Several research studies on this topic suggest that those individuals, such as coaches and managers, who are in control of recruiting players in baseball (Scully, 1974; Leonard II, Ostrosky, & Huchendorf, 1990), in football (Massengale & Farrington, 1977), and in basketball

(Chu & Segrave, 1981) typically come from positions where they served as central players. While this hypothesis is correlational, the idea here is that owners and administrators tend to engage in the practice of hiring coaches who were perceived as playing or played in roles that were central and directly related to win/loss outcomes of games.

In basketball, it is the guards who run offensive plays. In football, it is the quarterback who makes decisions and is credited with successful plays. By examining these positions and their roles in the sport they play, we begin to obtain a better understanding of the stacking process and how it affects drafts and success in sports. This is why central players are found to become more easily promoted into leadership roles than the players who served in the peripheral positions. As stated previously, central positions are held by white players and, therefore, when they retire, they find that they end up in a hiring pool for teams looking for head coaches. While this perspective may explain some of the diversity in coaching positions, it does actually attempt to explain why we find disproportionate numbers in terms of the ethnicity of managers, owners, and coaches in sports.

The last question that we raise on equity in sports explores an area that rarely garners attention: What about the racial demographics of sporting fans? Who are the people who attend athletic events? What are the racial demographics by sports type? A significant increase in player salaries is directly related to revenue generated from ticket sales. Higher player salaries are ultimately created because of rising ticket demands—which increases revenue—ultimately providing resources to attract and recruit top athletes' revenues (Delemeester, 2008). We know that the owners of teams have changed the way games are played. Venues in this day and time now have skyboxes and other types of luxury viewing areas for sports fans and donors. These viewing areas are only available for and affordable to high social class individuals. Because race and income are related in America, social class can be argued as a factor that changes the appearance of audiences at sporting events. For example, social class and affordability of season tickets often result in predominantly white fans who watch and follow predominantly black athletes in competition against one another.

Then there is the case of Donald Sterling. In April of 2014, Sterling, the owner of the NBA's Los Angeles Clippers, was recorded telling his girlfriend to stop posting pictures on Instagram of herself with black people. He also told her to stop bringing black people to his basketball games. All this was captured on an audio recording posted by TMZ (Goyette, 2014). In the recording, Sterling is overheard demanding that she cease "broadcasting" the fact that she associates with black people. Sterling can be overheard on the recording saying to his then-girlfriend, "You can sleep with [black people]. You can bring them in; you can do whatever you want. The little I ask you is not to promote it on that … and not to bring them to my games." At one point on the tape, Sterling asks the girlfriend to identify the benefit that she might obtain from associating with black people. And it doesn't stop there. Sterling is recorded calling his then-girlfriend "stupid" when she asks why the race of the people she associates with matters. Sterling becomes enraged and doesn't answer her question. She then asks him to tell her if his thoughts would have been different had she appeared in the photo with Larry Bird? He remains silent.

When it comes to race, the comments by Don Sterling are not the most troubling racial incidents in his career as the Clippers's owner. Another troubling event occurred in 2006 when he was named in a legal housing discrimination lawsuit that alleged that Sterling refused to rent apartments to black families in Beverly Hills and other Los Angeles neighborhoods. The lawsuit alleged that Sterling had once said, "Black tenants smell and attract vermin."

Research shows a strong relationship between the fact that more than 75% of NBA players are black and that the league also has a larger share of minority fans than any of the other major sports leagues. Then in September 2014, Atlanta Hawks co-owner Bruce Levenson wrote an inflammatory e-mail saying that the team's white fans might be afraid of its black fans. In retrospect, Levenson says he wrote that e-mail in an attempt "to bridge Atlanta's racial sports divide" (Associated Press, 2014). According to news stories about the e-mail, Levenson went on record saying that he sent the e-mail because he was very concerned about low attendance at the games and that he was simply expressing a need to attract suburban whites to the NBA games. Levenson later held a press conference where he stated that he ultimately understood that his e-mail made it appear that he believed white fans were more important.

As previously noted, the NFL is known to be dominated by black players when compared to white players.

> *There are very few Asians or Hispanics in the NFL, though Pacific Islanders—especially Samoans—seem to be well represented for their small population.*
>
> *This does not match the NFL fan base. Seventy-seven percent of the fans are white, 15 percent are black, and 8 percent are Hispanic. Moreover, it is an older audience, with 37 percent of NFL fans over 55.*
>
> *Perhaps these older white fans started following football when the demographics were not so skewed. Younger generations of whites don't seem as enthralled by the mostly black league. Only 20 percent of NFL fans are in the 18–34 age bracket. That number slips to 9 percent for viewers 17 and younger.*
>
> *The website Caste Football is dedicated to race and sports and makes a compelling case that many white athletes are excluded from college and pro football simply because of their race. But even if this were not the case, why should whites—or other non-blacks—follow a mostly black league? Blacks don't follow hockey; only three percent of NHL fans are black.*
>
> *"The National Basketball Association (NBA) has already felt a ratings slip due to demographics. The league composition fluctuates around about 75 percent black. Consequently, there are more black NBA fans (45 percent) than white (40 percent)."*
>
> (Bradley, 2016)

An online survey conducted by ESPN shows that 73% of fans gave a very high rating to the sports world regarding equal opportunities. Compare that number to the 19% of sports fans participating in the survey who gave high ratings for equal opportunities to people of color to the corporate world. The survey also revealed 72% of the respondents felt that sports do more to unify people across racial lines. Few respondents perceived that sports would, or is a factor known to, divide race relations. However, when responses were broken down by ethnicity and race, African Americans reported being more skeptical than white sports fans about the level of progress in equity that is experienced in the sports world (Fogarty, 2011; Muede, 2017). Data revealed that among African Americans, 36%—compared with 65% of whites—believe that sports actually do help African American athletes to succeed (Fogarty, 2011; Muede, 2017). Perhaps respondents were using their perceptions of stacking in sports, seeing this process as a limiting one rather than an opportunity.

Researchers conducting the ESPN survey found that most African-Americans (71%) believe that there are fewer opportunities than whites to become owners of professional sports franchises (Fogarty, 2011). Data show that 72% of all athletic directors at major Division I universities are white. Sixty-four percent of all MLB managers and 62% of all head coaches in the NFL are white. Further data show that 58% of all head coaches at major Division I schools are white. Despite this evidence, a majority of white sports fans still believe that African-Americans have equal opportunities in sport (Fogarty, 2011).

Michael Jordan, the owner of the Charlotte Bobcats, is the only black owner of a professional sports team. According to the University of Central Florida's Institute for Diversity and Ethics in Sports, "Jordan bought the team from another African American, Robert Johnson." According to historical records, Jordan and Johnson are the only two men who constitute majority owners of a sports team in the history of sports. Research shows that 47% of white sports fans surveyed do feel that African Americans have fewer opportunities to own teams. Forty-four percent stated that African Americans have the same opportunities to own teams as whites do but that they just do not acquire them for whatever reason. The online survey consisted of 1,822 sports fans (1,213 whites, 435 African Americans) and was conducted December 15–21 by Hart Research Associates, commissioned by ESPN.

Sports fans participating in the ESPN survey seemed to be divided on their views about whether the NFL needed a rule for hiring head coaches. The fans are referring to the Rooney Rule. Pictured in Figure 4.4 is Dan Rooney, the man credited with the development of the NFL's Rooney Rule. The Rooney Rule requires the NFL to consider minority candidates for head coaching and senior football operations positions. Of the 473 African American fans surveyed, 57% believe the rule is not only necessary but also that it will be needed in future years (Fogarty, 2011). Compare that percentage to the 20% of the surveyed white fans who did not see a need for this rule in the coming years (Fogarty, 2011). "Twenty-three percent of polled white fans stated that the Rooney Rule was unnecessary and not needed to begin with" (Fogarty, 2011). It was useless in their opinion. However, this was an interesting statistic in that only 7% of African American sporting fans expressed the idea that the Rooney Rule was unnecessary (Fogarty, 2011). This is just more data proving the racial divide that is inherent in sports.

In summary, racial and ethnic stacking in sports teams involves those sports and sports teams that are overrepresented with racially or ethnically mixed players from certain backgrounds and other nonrevenue sports that are underrepresented regarding race and ethnicity in players and diverse players holding certain positions.

Summary of examples of stacking in sports:

- Major league baseball is known to have black players most heavily concentrated in outfield positions. Black MLB players are seldom in central, key positions like the catcher, pitcher, or any other infield except first base.

- Major league football and college football: Blacks are likely to play safety, cornerback, and end on defense and running back, and pass receiver on offense, yet white football players are found to be stacked or overrepresented in positions of quarterback and guard on offense, and middle linebacker on defense.

- Basketball in the '50s and '60s saw African American players overrepresented as forwards, while whites played primarily in positions as centers/guards. According to

FIGURE 4.4   *Dan Rooney, chairman of the Pittsburgh Steelers, credited with spearheading a requirement that NFL teams with head coach and general manager vacancies interview at least one minority candidate, which has become known as the "Rooney Rule"*

historical research, it was during the early '80s when we began to see this pattern disappearing among male athletes. Research suggests that this pattern can still be observed among female basketball players at times.

- Women's intercollegiate volleyball: African American female volleyball players are often spikers, while whites are often in positions of "set and bump."
- Soccer: Black West Indians and Black Africans are stacked or found to be overrepresented in the central position known as "forward" in soccer. This stacking also occurs with black players in forward positions in Britain, while white soccer players are found in positions of goalie and midfielder.

Other Controversial Issues in Race and Sports

Playing Opportunities

Perhaps the area in sports that has afforded minorities with the most opportunities is the position played. As conveyed in Chapter 1, historically, sports have provided a means for individuals who tend to be on the lower end of the socioeconomic ladder to achieve recognition and wealth, especially when financial success and advancement in other areas in corporate America were difficult to attain. Whether impediments and barricades are due to an individual's lack of experience, lack of understanding, level of expertise, or even his or her prejudices and discrimination practices, sports offered talented youth opportunities to show skills and abilities in terms of sports and competition. Although sports have similar discriminatory practices that can be found in the larger American culture, we still find a large number of people of color being allowed to participate in mainstream professional sports. A brief historical overview of African Americans' assimilation and integration into sports shows that it was in 1947 when Jackie Robinson was nationally recognized as the first African American to play in the mainstream in an all-white professional league.

When we review data to ascertain playing opportunities for different racial and ethnic groups, we find that African Americans make up approximately "77% of NBA players, 65% of NFL players, and 15% of MLB players" (see Lapchick & Matthews, 2002; Lapchick, 2018). Further investigation into playing opportunities shows that African American males make up approximately 60% of basketball players and 51% of football players on NCAA Division 1 teams (Lapchick & Mathews, 2002; Lapchick, 2018). Lapchick and Mathews (2002) obtained data that show, regarding playing opportunities in the NCAA Division 1 category, female athletes make up approximately 35% of basketball players.

When we examine playing opportunities for African Americans in other sports, research typically finds that participation in sports such as lacrosse, golf, swimming, volleyball, and skiing by athletes of color decreases dramatically. Except for Tiger Woods, many of us may find it extremely hard to name a well-known African American golfer. Extending this to tennis, we may also find it challenging to think of players other than Venus and Serena Williams. These two sisters are prominent professional tennis players who happen to be African American females, yet we might find it extremely challenging if and when we are asked to name other living African American professional tennis players. Arthur Ashe was noted as the first African American male tennis player who won three Grand Slam titles in the '70s. Ashe was also credited as being the first African American male tennis player who was a part of the United States Davis Cup team. Ashe passed away from HIV in 1993.

We know that in other sports, such as soccer, hockey, tennis, equestrian, golf, swimming, lacrosse, skiing, and skating, few African Americans are observed as active participants or as fans of these sports. These dramatically different disparities between African American and white athletes participating in sports such as lacrosse and equestrian are not arbitrary, unintentional events. Previously in this chapter, we discussed access to resources and the role that environment plays in involvement with certain sports (e.g., basketball and football). We also noted that admittance into exclusive training facilities, access to expensive equipment, and individualized coaching, while not necessary variables needed during an individual's early developmental years, are often resources that are not easily accessible to people of color. Then again, Caucasian athletes, research shows, often lean more toward individual sports than team sports.

Interestingly, we learn that access to individual sports is highly contingent on resources and is strongly aligned with expenses that are often relatively high and outside the affordability limits for other social classes (we will discuss social class in a later chapter of this text). Therefore, it can be hypothesized that finances and even social status are partially responsible for disparities in participation in sports by race and ethnicity, as well as discrimination. It might also be that role models and culture work together to play a much greater and significant role in influencing the sports people select and become involved in. Culture and role models may serve as filters for involvement in particular sports activities.

The Role of Media in Race and Ethnicity in Sports

Thoughts and presuppositions about the ideas of race and ethnicity in our contemporary culture and society tend to be shaped by messages and images found in sports media. When we consider the social construction of symbols and the meanings that are associated with those symbols, we must recognize the role and influence that media have on our ideas about race and ethnicity and sports. The media, according to Entmann (1993), are a pivotal force when it comes to creating frames or metaphors that appeal to a desired or anticipated readership or viewing audience. According to Hall (1995, 1997), the media are vehicles known to constantly shift meanings we have that may be related to race and ethnicity, and to provide dominant ideas about race and ethnicity. This shift can be seen in the way that the media celebrate and honor successful African American athletes such as LeBron James, Stephen Curry, and Michael Jordan. Framing research shows that sports media also use their sphere of influence to confirm and reinforce racist stereotypes (Entmann, 1993). Research on media and race over the years shows that stereotypes about race have been embedded in messages and news coverage found in mass media for years. According to research, these images can be easily ascertained and interpreted to show stereotypes such as the "the benign and happy slave figure," "the black brute who rapes white women," or "the promiscuous black woman" (Wilson, Gutierrez, & Chao, 2012, pp. 36–37).

Sports media play an important role in the creation and expression of symbols and meaning given to symbols, particularly those related to race and ethnicity (Bruce, 2004). Boyle and Haynes (2000) and Rowe (2003), three prominent sports scholars, argue that television coverage and media hype afforded to male sports has increased during the past few decades. Emphasis on professional male sports is most evident in the popularity of male athletes, such as LeBron James, Michael Jordan, Stephen Curry, and others who serve as role models, who are a continued source of empowerment for many young black viewers and consumers of media. Like other scholars in this area, Davis and Harris (1998) found significant evidence that supports the idea that sports media frequently portray racial and ethnic minorities in stereotypical ways. As a result of the frequent portrayals, research is left to conclude that through exposure to stories about athletes in popular sports media, our ideas and stereotypes are being reinforced, and the media content also works to confirm racial and ethnic inequalities that can be observed in society at large. Bruce (2004) urges sports commentators, who often work under pressure, to meet deadlines and perform perfectly on live broadcasts. For Bruce

(2004) the solution is simple: They must first realize that many times under the intense pressure to meet a deadline, the stress may often unconsciously cause them to draw on their own previously held biases and ideologies simply because they do not have enough time to think about or respond objectively and rationally to events that occur on the playing field.

James Rada of Ithaca College conducted a frequently cited study on NFL broadcaster comments. In his seminal research titled, *Color Blind-Sided: Racial Bias in Network Television's Coverage of Professional Football Games*, Rada (1996; Rada 2000) found that broadcasters tend to describe individual athletes in ways that highlight leadership and intelligence-related attributes for white football players, yet when reporting on African American football players, broadcasters tend to discuss their physical qualities and appearances. In Rada & Wulfmeyer's (2005) follow-up study to the aforementioned research, *Color Coded: Racial Descriptors in Television Coverage of Intercollegiate Sports*, Rada and Wulfmeyer (2005) analyzed sports journalists' comments obtained from college football and basketball games. Rada and his team of researchers obtained data that, once again, showed that sports commentators make positive comments about the intellect of white players. That was not found for African American players. In other words, comments about intellect were not equally distributed for white and black football players. Rada's study also found evidence that shows that negative comments were made most frequently by sports broadcasters when discussing an African American football player's intellect. When analyzing comments about white football players' intellect, Rada's data shows that white athletes receive an unbalanced frequency of positive comments with respect to their performance, yet sports commentators made African American football players the focus of negative comments about their performance, particularly if the athlete was in a leadership position such as quarterback. And when the athletes were the subject of human interest stories, African American athletes were the focus of the negative stories. In a content analysis conducted in 2016, Frisby found support for the finding: When sports journalists covered a story about an African American athlete, the focus of the story was primarily negative and centered on the suggested stereotype that African American male athletes tend to be violent and criminal.

In another related research project, Billings (2004) designed a research study that investigated how sports broadcast media described quarterbacks in the NFL in the year 2002. We know from historical research that in 2002, African American quarterbacks were beginning to infiltrate the position. For example, quarterbacks such as Donovan McNabb and Michael Vick were making their appearance in leadership in the NFL. In *Depicting the Quarterback in Black and White: A Content Analysis of College and Professional Broadcast Commentary*, Billings (2004) found that many descriptors of the football players made by sports announcers were equally distributed. However, differences were found when the researchers controlled for comments related to physical skill. Similar to the findings obtained in the Rada (2000) study, Billings (2004) found that when African American quarterbacks made game-changing plays and were successful on the field, sports broadcasters frequently attributed their success to physical, biological talents and skills that, as research shows, are frequently associated with African American athletes.

The power of media exposure is a frequent focus in sports media effects research (refer to Chapter 2 in this book). Sports viewing has become a culture-wide ritual (e.g., Super Bowl parties) that can be hypothesized based on theories, such as cultivation, symbolic annihilation, and others, that frequent and long-term exposure to media content may result in years and even decades of having racial and ethnic stereotypes passively being placed in the American psyche and perhaps ingrained in heuristics related to what it means to be a black athlete and white athlete, and the sports that different races and ethnicities that athletes compete in. Even though research has yet to measure long-term effects, it would be wrong for us to assume that the effects of exposure to these stereotypes are not real.

A central point that helps explain the various ways that sports media create and portray ideas and themes about minority groups is to examine the categories and classification practices used to produce stories and media content. Sports media have the capacity and capability to focus on and frequently present certain racial and ethnic group themes more prominently than they do others. In doing so media have opportunities to construct social realities that perpetuate racial and ethnic stereotypes that consumers actually use to organize and understand events and experiences that happen in the world around them (Hall, 1995). As discussed in Chapter 2, certain theories are used to help us predict, explain, and understand the media's role in the social construction of reality. Scholars interested in this topic often rely on schema theory and its presuppositions that help us begin to see how media use categories related to race and ethnicity in their stories.

George Cunningham and Trevor Bopp (2010) conducted a study in 2010 titled *Race Ideology Perpetuated: Media Representations of Newly Hired Football Coaches*. In this study Cunningham and Bopp (2010), along with a team of researchers, analyzed press releases that were used to inform media of all new hires involving assistant coaches. Data obtained in this study showed that in terms of white coaches, the press releases were significantly more likely to describe white coaches as intelligent, great strategists, and decision-makers than they were black coaches. Moreover, data revealed that press releases about new black assistant coaches were more likely to focus on "recruiting skills and relationships with players" (Cunningham & Bopp, 2010). Results obtained in this and many other studies show us that news frames involving race/ethnicity and coaching hires maintain the stereotype discussed previously in this chapter that denotes the idea that hiring a black (or minority) assistant coach is equivalent to the "bridesmaid who will never be a bride" (Frisby & Engstrom, 2006).

The Rooney Rule, named after Dan Rooney, was created in the NFL as a reactive strategy and process to address the hiring and firing of coaches. The Rooney Rule was conceptualized in reaction to the firings of two head coaches, Tony Dungy of the Tampa Bay Buccaneers and Dennis Green of the Minnesota Vikings, in 2002. Uproar and confusion concerning Dungy's firing were primarily associated with the head coach's winning record with the Buccaneers. Green, many believe strongly, had just experienced what was known to be his first losing season in 10 years in the NFL. The Rooney policy was created so teams would be required to include minority candidates in a recruiting pool for head coaching and senior football positions. The Rooney Rule is often described in sports as an "example of affirmative action, although there is no quota or preference given to minorities in the hiring of candidates" (DuBois, 2016; DuBois, 2017). Established in 2003, several variations of the Rooney Rule are, as of this writing, currently being used in other industries. After the induction of the Rooney Rule in 2003, research revealed increases in the hiring of African American head coaches in the NFL. Mike Tomlin, for example, was then hired as head coach for the Pittsburgh Steelers. In 2006, we continued to find an increase in the overall percentage of African American coaches (22%, up from 6%). This increase is directly related to the institution of the Rooney Rule in 2002.

To illustrate the increase, *Business Insider* created a list in 2017 that shows that the "number of African American head coaches in the NFL is on the rise" (Gaines & Nudelman, 2017). Of the 11 minority coaches hired since the start of the Rooney Rule, six are still, at the time of this writing, serving as head coaches in the NFL. The NFL has 32 teams with positions that range from head coach to offensive and defensive coordinators. According to a brief overview of positions in the NFL, we learn that 96 "prestigious" positions are available. Currently, research shows that African Americans hold five of those positions as head coaches, four as offensive coordinators, and eight as defensive coordinators. Desronvil (2016) published an online article titled "NFL African-American Head Coaches Win. Hire Them" that delineates African American head coaches from 2006 to present day. The head coaches of color identified in the article are Todd Bowles (New York Jets), Jim

Caldwell (Detroit Lions), Hue Jackson (Cleveland Browns), Marvin Lewis (Cincinnati Bengals), and Mike Tomlin (Pittsburgh Steelers) (Desronvil, 2016). Successes of African American head coaches such as Mike Tomlin, David Shaw, and Kevin Sumlin have started to change stereotypes regarding blacks and their ability to lead a team to victory. However, we must note that a few sports media and sports analysts have insinuated in news stories that Kevin Sumlin's success is closely associated with and attributed to a talented quarterback (i.e., Johnny Manziel).

There comes a point when we must realize that research results on race, ethnicity, stacking, and stereotypes in sports are not simply a biased research process in which the studies are conducted and designed by researchers seeking to support their opinions and beliefs. Content analysis research, while an extremely rigorous research method consisting of extensive hours searching for and coding thousands of news stories, images, and broadcaster comments, is important in this area because this method can analyze the absence or presence of words, images, themes, ideas, and meanings in media. This research method allows investigators to make inferences about race, ethnicity, and stacking that is objective and will systematically identify messages in sports media. To establish validity and consistency in the coding of variables in a study, scholars often employ three to five coders for inter-rater reliability. Intercoder reliability aids in ensuring that we measure what we intend to measure, and more importantly, that more than one person saw the variable and interpreted the meaning and theme of the variable according to the principle researcher's operationalizations (definitions).

Conclusion

This chapter on race and ethnicity of athletes illustrates that all athletes should be considered extremely talented. This chapter also highlights issues related to race and ethnicity in America and the stereotypes and myths upon which these concepts were founded. We also discussed the areas where improvements are needed with respect to race and ethnicity within and outside sports media. It is possible that if sports and sports media take the lead in implementing these changes, then our society may become more united.

We discussed overrepresentation of African Americans in major American sports and provided research that supports the idea that "stacking" or overrepresentation in certain sports cannot be the result of biological predispositions that cause African American athletes to excel, but success in sports is more likely because of resources found in the environment, nurture instead of nature, and an aspiring athlete's access to resources. As previously discussed, for years, scholars have debated the idea that race as a biological concept is a mute argument simply because variability in genetics is obvious when we look within and between ethnic groups. In essence, research has yet to prove that genetic predisposition causes athletic prowess and natural abilities. We know that people come in all shapes and sizes. We know that within and between ethnic groups there are intersections in skin tone, abilities, and capabilities. And when we talk of intellectual capacity, we must also realize that this same argument is just as compelling. In other words, we cannot believe that biological differences in race exist but not intellectual superiority.

Biological explanations, if you recall, refer to the idea that individuals with different racial and ethnic backgrounds are born with innate physical or mental attributes that make it easy for them to succeed in specific sports positions (e.g., speed agility and quickness are biological gifts given to African Americans, while whites are given biological gifts of intelligence, dependability, and leadership). We must be mindful that those sports media who strongly support the biological explanation for athletic talent, skill, and ability are basing their perceptions, whether they are aware of it or not, on stereotypes. Scientific evidence as of this writing has not been found to support the biological explanation for the demographic disproportionality of African Americans and their participation in sports. America was founded on the idea that all Americans are equal and should be given an equal opportunity to succeed.

For example, do African Americans excel at sports that involve playing with balls? While we might quickly respond positively to this question, we must also keep in mind that sports such as tennis and soccer also include balls, yet African Americans are not found as active participants in those sports as they are in other sports, such as football and basketball. As some scholars ask, if Kane's (1971) research is correct and African Americans are born with longer arms, then why the lack of active participation by this group in the high jump or javelin? If African American athletes are gifted with longer arms, then why are there fewer athletes of color participating in the shot put or as pitchers? If muscle fibers are different for African American athletes and result in making them faster and known for speed, then we need explanations for why more athletes of color are not active participants in cycling, skiing, and speed skating. These are all known as speed sports, yet we note an underrepresentation of athletes of color in each of them

QUESTIONS FOR REFLECTION AND DISCUSSION

1. Are sports institutions free of prejudice and discrimination—the kind found in other aspects of society? Why or why not? Do you agree that sport is one of the few ways that individuals from lower social classes find their way to financial success and accomplishment? In other words, is sport the only way underrepresented groups succeed?

2. Does participation in sports help to address and change prejudicial attitudes *and* improve relations in teams among athletes from different racial and ethnic backgrounds? In other words, do you believe that African American and other ethnic athletes have the propensity to change the way society views black men in general? Why or why not? Support your response.

3. Given the disparities in sports by race and ethnicity, do you think it is possible to have fair and equal participation in nonrevenue-generating sports? Why or why not? How can media encourage different groups to participate in sports such as hockey, tennis, swimming, volleyball, golf, skiing, equestrian, lacrosse, dance, figure skating, soccer, cycling, and snowboarding, to name a few?

4. Do you think that, given the massive popularity of social media and consumer-engaged media, our thinking of race, ethnicity, and athletic superiority, along with stacking, will change? Why or why not?

5. Imagine 20 years from now. Do you think the disparities in sports will change by having some minority groups overrepresented in the minor sports, such as hockey, tennis, swimming, volleyball, golf, skiing, equestrian, lacrosse, dance, figure skating, soccer, cycling, and snowboarding, to name a few?

6. The pressure to interview minorities as head coaches is challenging, particularly for those sports that have little to no participation by athletes from different ethnicities. Can this be corrected? Why or why not? What role does the media play in encouraging minorities to participate either as fans or as athletes in these nonrevenue-generating sports? Explain your answer.

7. What are some race and ethnical stereotypes that exist about athletes or sports?

8. Why is using a team name such as the Fighting Sioux or the Redskins a problem? How should media cover team names to balance coverage and present more positive Native American media stories?

9. How has race affected participation in sports? How does race in sports mirror societal views of various ethnic and racial groups?

10. How can sports media challenge the views of race and ethnicity, and help transform racial and ethical relations?

EXERCISES

1. Take the quiz on Project Implicit https://implicit.harvard.edu/implicit/demo/. This is a series of association tests that are completed online. They are intended to show unconscious preferences across a variety of status categories.

2. Consider how journalism, sociology, communication, psychology, and other disciplines may have historically constructed race: How do you believe these areas may construct and interpret race differently? How has the construction of race and ethnicity been controversial in media? How have the themes of race and ethnicity in sports media been used as a means to construct race and add to discrepancies in how we view race and ethnicity? Provide current examples.

3. Write about your very first encounter when you became aware of your race or ethnicity.

4. Let's pretend you are a media producer and creator of a potential hit series that centers on sports. For this role play, you are to write a scene that contains dialogue between at least two different voices. Think of shows such as *All in the Family* or *This Is Us*. One character should be cast as the bigot or racist. This character has unconsciously (or consciously) consumed all the various stereotypes and ideas that are portrayed and consumed about different racial/ethnic groups. Let this character verbally share all stereotypes he or she knows about certain ethnic groups and sports. Note: The person doing this voice does *not* have to believe what he or she is scripted to say. In fact, he or she may find the words and statements offensive. The person may be ashamed to even have the words in his or her head (review material on heuristics and schemas presented in Chapter 2 of this book). The point of the activity is to illustrate that the ideas and themes we are exposed to in the media are "housed" in our minds, even if we do not believe or approve of the ideas (e.g., the "N" word).

   The second character should be cast as the voice of reason. As in *All in the Family*, Michael Stivic served as the voice that was used to show that Archie Bunker's "stereotyping and bigotry" was wrong. In your script, this character's purpose is to challenge and question statements, assumptions, and stereotypes made by the first character. When you are done, write a reflection on your scene. Be sure to provide context (i.e., the frame) for the setting. You should also provide a synopsis of the show. In your reflection statement, be sure to provide ideas as to where these characters "came from." In other words, how did you imagine these characters and their relationship? Take a closer look at the themes outlined in the first and second characters. Who did you learn these ideas from? Where did you learn these ideas? Which character was easier to script and why? Use your reflection to discuss how stereotypes are learned and unlearned.

5. Work in small groups to write definitions for the following terms: race, racism, prejudice, bias, privilege, ethnicity, discrimination, stereotyping, inequality, injustice, indifference, and ignorance. How do each of these terms differ in denotation and connotation from "racism"? Discuss which of these terms seem best to apply to help make sense of sports media's coverage of different athletes.

6. Similar to the first activity, this one involves having you cast a fictitious film or television show involving athletes. Unlike the first exercise, in this one, you will provide pictures or photos of the cast. Be sure to include pictures of individuals who represent different races, ethnicities, ages, and sexual identities (*print out the photos of all the individuals you would do a screen test with for the role). All individuals are in the running for the following roles: the hero (athlete/coach/owner), the hero's family and friends, the hero's/central character's love interest, the central character's neighbor/friend. Who is the antagonist or the central character's enemy (a racial group, media, etc.)? Why is the enemy upset with the main character? Who are the others involved in your film or show? Be sure to write out roles and their motivation for their character(s).

How did you decide which individuals would be cast for the role in your show? How did factors such as race/ethnicity, social class, religion, skin tone, gender, sexual orientation, and age affect your casting decisions? Explain the variables of the script, the show's theme, and the intersectionality of these themes that affected your decision. To what extent do you think your casting decisions will affect cultural meanings conveyed in your final production? How? In your honest opinion, in what ways is casting for this show relevant to a discussion of race, ethnicity, and sport (part of this exercise was found on the website Critical media project's (2017) website. The website provides resources for students and teachers that help to encourage students to enhance their critical thinking and problem solving skills. Many of the examples on this site offer class activities and real-world media illustrations from most every aspect of journalism (i.e., broadcast, print and digital reporting, magazine, photojournalism, and strategic communication).

7. When children play sports, they bring with them ideas about themselves and their ability to play the particular sport. Where do these ideas come from? Watch 6- to 8-year-old children playing on a playground during recess. Record their activities. What do you see and hear? Use this activity to help you apply the concept of stacking and influence of media and sports heroes on a child's perception of self and athletic ability.

ADDITIONAL RESOURCES

Greenfield Community College, http://www.intergroupresources.com/rc/race-and-racism-curriculum.pdf. This online resources offers definitions of concepts related to race and sports as well as ideas for classroom-led discussions and multi-media resources that might be used to help elucidate many of the ideas expressed in this chapter. Also on the site are links to White Privilege checklists, research, databases and Internet sites.

Gregory Jay, "Who Invented White People," a talk on the occasion of Martin Luther King Jr. Day, 1998, http://uuwhiteness.us/wp-content/uploads/2017/06/READING_-Who-Invented-White-People.pdf, https://www.montgomeryschoolsmd.org/uploadedFiles/schools/senecavalleyhs/academics/staffdev/race-links.pdf

History of Race in Science, http://www.racesci.org/. This informative site is sponsored by the Program in Science, Technology, and Society at the Massachusetts Institute of Technology. It includes a comprehensive bibliography, links to recent articles in the media on race and science, and links to sites on health, genetics, eugenics, ethnic study, and racism.

Index of Native American Electronic Text Resources on the Internet, http://www.hanksville.org/NAresources/indices/NAetext.html. Part of the WWW Virtual Library, this index includes images, speeches, articles, and other Native American–related resources.

Search Latino.com, http://www.searchlatino.com. Search Latino provides links to sites about Latinos in the arts, technology, education, music, politics, and other fields. Shelby Steele "I'm Black, You're White, Who's Innocent?" and "I think the racial struggle in America has always been primarily a struggle for innocence … Both races instinctively understand that to lose innocence is to lose power."

The Arab American Institute, http://www.aaiusa.org/. A rich website devoted to the Arab American community and the challenges and issues they face in contemporary American society. This website primarily provides policy and civic research support but includes a section on publications that contains many articles and essays on Arab/American relations. A link to an educational packet on current discussions in the Arab American community, the Middle East, and Islam, and includes many articles from Arab American Institute staff writers.

Resources

Many of these resources are adapted from the Bedford/St. Martin's reference website: www.bedfordstmartins.com/rereadingamerica

Allen Johnson on White Privilege, http://www.csuchico.edu/pub/inside/archive/02_02_28/allen_johnson.html

Digital History: Mexican American Voices, http://www.digitalhistory.uh.edu/mexican_voices/mexican_voices.cfm Sponsored by the University of Houston, this site includes texts by Mexican Americans and others writing about Mexican Americans. Contemporary texts are included at the bottom of the page.

Eric Lui, "Notes of a Native Speaker" "I never asked to be white. I am not literally white ... But like so many other Asian Americans of the second generation, I find myself now the bearer of a strange new status: white, but acclamation."

Ethnic Studies, http://207.44.246.88/cgi-bin/netoh/page.cgi?g=Science%2FSocial_Sciences%2FEthnic_Studies%2Findex.html&d=1 The Internet Open Highway Project presents this directory of links to information for ethnic studies, encompassing countries across the globe.

Exploring the Japanese American Internment, http://www.jainternment.org Produced by the National Asian American Telecommunications Association, this site offers video clips about the history and present-day impact of Japanese American internment during World War II.

Greenfield Community College—Links to White Privilege: Databases & Internet Site, http://www.gcc.mass.edu/library/pathfinders/WPInternet.htm

Gregory Jay, "Who Invented White People," http://www.uwm.edu/~gjay/Whiteness/Whitenesstalk.html A talk on the occasion of Martin Luther King Jr. Day, 1998.

History of Race in Science, http://www.racesci.org/ This informative site is sponsored by the Program in Science, Technology & Society at the Massachusetts Institute of Technology. It includes a comprehensive bibliography; links to recent articles in the media on race and science; and links to sites on health, genetics, eugenics, ethnic study, and racism.

Index of Native American Electronic Text Resources on the Internet, http://www.hanksville.org/NAresources/indices/NAetext.html Part of the WWW Virtual Library, this index includes images, speeches, articles, and other Native American-related resources.

Jack Hitts, "Mighty White of You: Racial Preferences color America's oldest skull and bones" *Harper's Magazine*, July 2005, "The story of the Ancient European One is this kind of story, toggling back and forth between the world of fiction and (possibly) non-fiction, authored by a few curious facts and the collective anxiety of the majority."

Naomi Shihab Nye, "To Any Would-Be Terrorists," http://www.arches.uga.edu/~godlas/shihabnye.html "Because I feel a little closer to you than many Americans could possibly feel, or ever want to feel, I insist that you listen to me. … I am humble in my country's pain, and I am furious."

Native Americans, http://www.americanwest.com/pages/indians.htm This site includes information on leaders of the past, organizations and government sources for Native Americans, photographs and images from the past, and links to other useful Native American sites.

Nova: The Mystery of the First Americans, http://www.pbs.org/wgbh/nova/first/race.html

On Raising Bilingual and Multilingual Children, http://www.imdiversity.com/villages/asian/Article_Detail
.asp?Article_ID=2404 This page, part of the Asian-American Village page of IMDiversity.com, gives
thorough information on raising bilingual children, as well as a list of related readings and resources.

The Other Race Card: Rush Limbaugh and the Politics of White Resentment by Tim Wise, http://www
.counterpunch.org/wise10032003.html Article on Rush Limbaugh's comments.

Paul L. Wachtel, "Talking About Racism: How Our Dialogue Gets Short-Circuited," http://jonsenglishsite
.info/Class%20Docs%205/4_TalkingAboutRacism.pdf "The real crime of which white America is now
most guilty is not racism. It is indifference. Understanding the difference between the two is a crucial
step in liberating ourselves from the sterile and unproductive impasse that has characterized the dialogue on race relations in recent years."

Reginald McKnight, "Confessions of a Wannabe Negro" "I can't say when I first noticed my blackness … I do,
however, remember the very day I noticed that my blackness made me different."

Racial Bias from Another Perspective: Limbaugh, the United States and South Africa by Heather Gray,
http://www.commondreams.org/scriptfiles/views03/1006-09.htm

Rush Limbaugh 'Very Uncomfortable' With Trump's NFL Comments, https://www.thedailybeast.com/
rush-limbaugh-very-uncomfortable-with-trumps-nfl-comments

The Center for the Study of White American Culture, http://www.euroamerican.org This site is not a
white supremacist site; rather, it is a place for "cultural exploration and self-discovery among white
Americans." Click here for a racial awareness quiz, a series of papers on whiteness and its role in a
multicultural society, and objectives for creating a society based on multiracial values.

The Martin Luther King Jr. Papers Project, http://www.stanford.edu/group/king Developed by the King
Center for Nonviolent Social Change, this site contains a collection of historical information about
Martin Luther King and the civil rights movement, as well as some of King's writings, speeches, and ser-
mons, such as the "I Have a Dream."

The *New York Times:* "How Race Is Lived in America," http://www.nytimes.com/library/national/race
The *New York Times* won a 2001 Pulitzer Prize for national reporting for its series, "How Race Is Lived in
America." This page offers more than a dozen articles on the current state of race relations in many parts
of the country.

The United Nations Declaration on Race and Racial Prejudice, http://www.hri.ca/uninfo/treaties/19.shtml

The United Nations declaration against racial prejudice lays out a universal conception of human rights,
http://www.un-documents.net/a18r1904.htm

Viewing Race, http://www.viewingrace.org/ The National Video Resources organization was founded by
the Rockefeller Foundation in 1990. Their Viewing Race project is a database of independent films, articles, discussion and media resources on the subject of race and diversity to combat racism and promote
tolerance.

Whites Swim in Racial Privilege by Tim Wise, http://www.alternet.org/story/15223/

Discussion of white privilege-particularly in relationship to the U of M affirmative action policies,
https://www.mediaed.org/discussion-guides/Tim-Wise-on-White-Privilege-Discussion-Guide.pdf

CREDITS

5

Media Portrayals of Athletes of Color

After completing this chapter, students should be able to:

- demonstrate a balanced awareness of the issues and debates involving African American athletes, women, and sports;

- think critically about sports and how they are portrayed in American culture;

- discuss issues related to behaviors and reactions to athletes of color; and

- understand why gender and racial equality in sports journalism are important and needed.

Introduction

The fact that sports are a major part of American culture can certainly be supported by the hundreds of thousands of fans who get caught up in events such as the "Super Bowl," the "World Series," "March Madness," and the "World Cup." One might also find support for this statement simply through an examination of some resources and media time spent on sports-related events. However, it was not too long ago that athletes of color and women were not allowed to contribute or participate in this important product of our American culture. For decades, athletes of color were prohibited from participating in the professional sports leagues of white America. And before Title IX, only 32,000 females participated in collegiate athletics (Olmstead, 2016). Since 1972, with the inception of Title IX, the popularity of women's athletics has been on the rise (Cahn, 1994; Grau, Roselli, & Taylor, 2007; Hardin, Lynn, & Waseldorf, 2005; Kennedy, 2010).

In the world of sports, barriers and walls with respect to race/ethnicity, gender, and sexual orientation are still serving as obstacles when it comes to addressing stereotypes and the exclusion of women and athletes of color in sports media. Research shows that obstacles still seem to preclude athletes of color and female athletes from appearing proportionally in news coverage and media messages found in traditional mainstream media speaking in particular about sports media (Daniels, 2009; Duncan, 1990; Hardin, Chance, Dodd, & Hardin, 2002; Kane, 1996; Koivula, 1999; Lapchik & Mathews, 1999; Leath & Lumpkin, 1992; Leath & Williams, 1991; Mesnner, 2002; Perdersen & Whisenant, 2003; Primm, Preuhs, & Hewitt, 2007). Despite the fact that here in the United States sports are intertwined in the fabric of our culture, we find that sports media seem to overlook and even (intentionally) ignore the presence of female athletes and athletes of color. We found evidence of this lack of attention when we conducted studies that attempted to ascertain how often women and athletes of color appear in headlines and major news stories. Inclusion of women and athletes of color is significant and important, and that is the main idea that the information in this chapter wishes to convey.

Research on the stereotypes and portrayals of athletes of color in sport settings shows that white athletes are portrayed as achieving success because of controllable factors, such as a strong work ethic or intelligence, while African American athletes are frequently portrayed as being successful because of innate, uncontrollable factors, such as natural talent or physiological or biological advantage (Billings, 2003; Billings, 2004; Billings & Eastman, 2002; Birrell, 1989; Brown, Jackson, Brown, Sellers, Keiper, & Manuel, 2003; Denham, Billings, & Halone, 2002; Eastman & Billings, 2001; Wonsek, 1992). Also, Wonsek (1992) obtained data that further supported the notion that white athletes are often portrayed in sports media as having natural leadership abilities. This stereotype with regard to white athletes was discussed in detail in Chapter 4.

Regarding media representations, Van Dijk (1993) found evidence that the portrayals of ethnic minorities, which often depict people of color as criminals or deviant people, serve as enforcement of stereotypes and maintenance of racial hierarchies that exist in American culture. In a 1996 research study, Sabo, Jensen, Tate, Duncan, and Leggett (1995) investigated racial hierarchies reported on in international athletic events. Sabo et al. (1996) were unable to uncover evidence that could show media bias against African American athletes. However, the researchers found significant relationships between media bias and portrayals of Asian and Latina/o athletes. In fact, Asian and Latino/athletes were often found in portrayals that were biased and further supported specific stereotypes held by each group. Other studies focusing on media portrayals in television coverage during the Olympic Games found more support for the suggestion that white American male athletes receive the most frequent broadcast coverage and are often portrayed more positively when compared to black athletes (Billings, 2003; Billings, 2004; Billings & Angelini, 2007; Billings & Eastman, 2002; Billings & Eastman, 2003; Birrell, 1989; Brown et al., 2003; Denham et al., 2002; Eastman & Billings, 2001).

Billings and Eastman (2003), for instance, found that the media frequently attributed an international athletes' success to his or her experience, while attributing American athletes' success to his or her composure and courage. Billings and Angelini (2007) also found empirical support for the hypothesis that suggests that the ability to concentrate and commit is the explanation for the success of white American athletes. International athletes, the research found, were frequently described as having more experience, which ultimately led to their successes. Moreover, media tended to provide explanations for American athletes' failures by stating that the athletes lacked concentration. They would then attribute international athletes' losses or failures by mentioning their lack of athletic strength or ability. It is believed that these representations send messages to viewers that American athletes are more physically superior than those from other countries (Billings & Angelini, 2007). To prove this, a study on individuals' perceptions of factors contributing to a baseball player's success supported the effect that these types of representations had on consumers. Survey respondents in this study considered speed and physique to be more important and relevant for African American athletes, whereas access to facilities and coaches was more important for white athletes. Respondents reported believing that a mix of speed, physique, and access to resources were important factors for Latino/a athletes (Gonzalez, Jackson, & Regoli, 2006). This finding provides support for the hypothesis that stereotypical depictions found in sports media influence the ways people in this society view athletes of color. The data from this study further reinforces how stereotypes are created and sustained in American culture.

Stereotypical Coverage of African American Male Athletes

Media's role in constructing and influencing our and beliefs about male athletes has been of significance to many researchers (Whisenant & Pedersen, 2004). In their work, Whisenant and Pedersen (2004) argue that the "media's words and images have a major impact on societal processes and institutions" (p. 55). These researchers further argue that the "influence of the media is projected not only by what is being said but also what is not being reported through the absence of coverage" (Whisenant & Pedersen, 2004, p. 55). Fujioka (2005) supported their argument when he stated that "negative minority images have been prevalent in the mainstream media" (p. 451). It may be concluded, then, that exposure to negative portrayals of African Americans may lead those who frequently expose themselves to sports media and messages contained in the media to begin to create negative stereotypes about African Americans (Frisby, 2016; Fujioka, 2005; Rada, 1996). Sports media have been known to publish and broadcast messages that encourage certain stereotypes of African American men (Fujioka, 2005; Rada, 1996), stereotypes such as those we have discussed at length in this text (naturally gifted to be successful athletes, etc.).

According to Fujioka (2005), sports journalists rarely produce news stories about African American male athletes who are active participants in their communities. Very seldom do we find stories in mainstream national media that focus on philanthropic activities that African American athletes are involved in. For example, Walter Payton, a running back for the Chicago Bears from 1975 to 1987, created a foundation that plays a role in helping those in his community who are less fortunate. The Walter and Connie Payton Foundation also provides opportunities to help members of underserved populations live with dignity and pride. So we ask, how many national news stories and/or headlines educated consumers in our culture about this phenomenal organization? Few, if any national media news stories were located that focused on African American athletes who serve as positive role models (see Frisby, 2016, for research data). Instead, we find a proliferation of news stories about black athletes who are accused of crimes, domestic and sexual violence, drunk driving, bankruptcy, and other negative, antisocial messages. Research shows that very few stories in media focus on the positive contributions that athletes of color have and are making. And, within this same regard, we find that little if any research has been conducted that examines differences in the coverage of black and white male athletes (Frisby, 2016). As stated previously, research continues to show that sports media tend to show that stereotypes of black athletes are mostly the same—that is, in terms of athletic abilities and the idea that they are naturally gifted in terms of speed and agility. And as information in Chapter 4 of this textbook provided, we know from stereotypes of white athletes that they are typically depicted as being more dedicated and intelligent (Denham, Billings, & Halone, 2002; Rada, 1996; Rainville & McCormick, 2007).

In the last 100 years, participation in sports by African Americans and women has significantly increased. Even though African American athletes have increased their participation in several intercollegiate and professional teams, we find that these athletes continue to be subjected to differential treatment and frequent stereotyped themes and ideas in media produced stories about their sports (Rada & Wulfemeyer, 2005). Sports commentators, according to research, frequently describe African American athletes in terms of their strength and/or body size, shape, and frame, using adjectives that they feel (see Rada and Wulfemeyer, 2005) are meant to be complimentary. But as Rada and Wulfemeyer (2005) explain, these so-called athletic compliments often are used to reinforce racial biases and stereotypes. According to Rada and Wulfemeyer (2005), in terms of sports media and descriptions, their research obtained evidence that African American athletes, when compared to Caucasian athletes, tend to receive a greater number of negative comments, particularly when descriptors were made regarding on-field performance. An earlier study in this area conducted by

Eastman and Billings (2001) also provided evidence of how sports media reinforce stereotypes. In this same study, the researchers obtained data that supports the idea that sports journalists and their news stories actually perpetuate stereotypes about African Americans, particularly when they use words such as "very fast" or "very strong." While any one individual story may not seem to be a big deal, when black men disproportionately show up in the media as criminals or narrowly defined "types" of sports heroes, this gives us a distorted image of them. Wenner (1995) believes that the sports media's narrow view of African American male athletes is extremely troubling because it takes away the "star role" and ultimately limits the way we think about the athlete. In fact, Wenner (1995) goes on to write, "Confronted by media to focus on black men as athletes, we miss out on seeing the diversity of everyday successes by African American men" (p. 228). In sum, the literature on sports coverage of African Americans shows that, in terms of space in news media, African Americans consistently receive less coverage than their Caucasian counterparts.

Young African American boys often have aspirations to play professional sports, and their motivations are shaped largely, although not entirely, by their consumption of images found in media—namely, television and other popular forms of social media. Thus, in her work on media effects, Frisby (2016) indicated that sports reporters and journalists should turn their focus to other aspects and possible lead stories regarding African American male athletes. We know that media themes of African American men tend to fall into one of three categories: entertainer, athlete, or criminal. Frisby (2016) found evidence that confirms Entman's (1992) findings when data showed then that when compared to white athletes, news stories about the criminal activity or violence committed by blacks were more prevalent than stories involving white athletes. The implication is simple: sports media and sports journalists must move beyond looking for stories that are about a black athlete's criminal activity and athletic physique and prowess.

Frisby (2016) believes that media should frequently cover stories that show African American athletes engaged in prosocial behaviors as well as portrayals of their successes in athletics. The researcher goes on to say that sports reporting must publish and broadcast stories that depict African American athletes who performed well in the classroom *and* found success on the field or court. For example, media could focus on stories that involve former male student-athletes of color who graduated from 4-year colleges, achieved academic and athletic success during their college years, were active leaders on campus—showing that the leadership extended within and beyond athletics—and perhaps found careers outside of professional sports (e.g., enrolled in medical or graduate school, began full-time jobs in their fields of study). Positive coverage of African American athletes, such as the examples provided earlier, could not only advance society but also increase the frequency of these stories and give individuals a better and more complete understanding and realistic depiction of African American men. Stories that go beyond crime and athleticism of black male athletes might also have the potential to preclude the continued perpetuation of negative stereotypes.

Sports media might highlight the personal stories of success and strategies that African American athletes used to balance academics with athletics. Stories might cover the role that athletic departments play in encouraging the balance of academics with the time needed to be successful in a sport. Sports journalists might also start to focus on and commit to writing stories about African American male athlete's postcollege aspirations and goals. An increase in stories of this nature might be used to convey the idea that not all college athletes of color aspire to have careers in professional basketball and football. This might mean that vulnerable and impressionable youth who are exposed to and ultimately consume these messages may become encouraged to seek out other opportunities rather than following "role models" that fit into one of Entman's (1992) categories/labels.

The argument that success for athletes of color is based on a natural, innate athleticism is often associated with what is currently categorized as a racist theory. Racist theories propose that African American athletes, as we discussed in previous chapters, possess physiological and biological qualities that contribute to their exceptional ability to go fast and have superior skills related to jumping and reflexes (Carlston, 1983, p. 89). These stereotyped assertions are in direct opposition to media accounts and stereotypes used to describe the white athlete (Coakley, 2009; Staples & Jones, 1985). But why are the faces we see in popular media constant, obvious, overt, and ruthless attacks targeted toward African American athletes? Are African American athletes more acclimated to moral failures, criminal activity, or violation of the laws and rules of the sports league? A research study conducted more than 20 years ago by Sabo, Curry-Jansen, Tate, Carlisle-Duncan, and Leggett (1995) purported that stereotyping of African American athletes is not as overt as we might think it is. For these researchers, racial stereotyping in media messages by sports journalists is covert and systematic (Sabo & Jansen, 1992). Seminal work conducted by Rainville and McCormick just 18 years earlier in 1977 obtained data that shows that sports announcers tend to create stellar reputations for white athletes while simultaneously creating antisocial and negative reputations for athletes of color. In a content analytic study of broadcast commentators for basketball and football, journalist Derrick Jackson (1989) also showed sports broadcasters were more likely to describe African American players with descriptors related to their physical prowess and natural abilities while demeaning those African American players' intellectual capabilities.

Black Athletes and Crime: Fact or Fiction?

It is possible to speculate that when black athletes commit any crime it will automatically make the news. Why? Perhaps it is the biases of sports reporters and editors that leads them to write stories that fit in with our cultural expectations and beliefs. Perhaps white athletes do commit crimes at the same rate as black athletes, but their crimes go largely unnoticed and unreported. It's possible.

Do sports media tend to focus more on alleged criminal and antisocial behaviors of African American athletes? A simple review of news stories found on the cover pages of sports media will often show that when it comes to reporting about black athletes, the media love those stories that lean more toward criminal activity and alleged acts of sexual and domestic violence. For example, in 2009, Plaxico Burress, a New York Giants football player, served a prison sentence for carrying an illegal firearm. A quick search of a news database yields many more stories of black athletes involved in crimes. For example, Jovan Belcher of the Kansas City Chiefs murdered his girlfriend and then committed suicide. Several stories covering this one event would completely overshadow positive news stories about black athletes, even if they were published. Therefore, we can conclude based on the research that in terms of athletes and stories of crime, sports media tend to focus on the more than 29 professional NFL athletes who have been arrested since the 2013 Super Bowl (Frisby, 2016; Leal, Gertz, Piquero, & Piquero, 2016; Luther, 2014).

Contrary to popular belief, if one conducted an extensive review of police data, it would prove that professional athletes are arrested at a rate that is less than half of that of the general population with respect to assault charges and domestic violence. In other words, pro athletes are not found to be more violent than the general population, and according to statistics, they are markedly less inclined to be involved in violent behavior. NFL players, according to a story published in the *Boston Globe* in 2013 and recent research, engage in criminal activities at a much lesser rate than the general population (perhaps not unexpectedly given their relatively high incomes). If we hold gender constant, the data further show that professional athletes commit even fewer crimes than the entire male population in the United States. When we consider the consistent image that sports media create when it comes to NFL players (e.g., they are aggressive, violent, and wild partiers), research once again shows that over 624 of males in the population have been arrested for drunk driving since 2000 (Blumstein & Benedict, 2012). According to the *Boston Globe* article "The Myth About Crime and Pro Athletes," the arrest rates for drunk driving for professional football players is over half of that for all young men between the ages of 20 to 29 (Benedict, 2004; Benedict & Yaeger, 1998; Blumstein & Benedict, 2012; Keane, 2013; Pomeroy, 2014; Space Coast Daily, 2014). Over the last twenty-plus years, studies investigating the relationship between violence and professional football players consistently find that the rate of violence toward women in professional football is no worse than the frequency of domestic violence in the general public (Blumstein & Benedict, 2012).

In 1999, using a sample size consisting of 342 African American football players, researchers discovered that of the 342 players, 77 or 28% were arrested for crimes involving domestic and sexual violence (Blumstein & Benedict, 2012). However, when the researchers compared the rate for African American professional players, they discovered that the rate of similar crimes in the general public was nearly double the rate observed in the NFL and African American athletes (general population rate obtained was 47%). Thus, we can conclude based on the empirical evidence from the Blumstein and Benedict (1999, 2012) studies that African American professional football players are having to confront social stereotypes that suggest that they are more violent and are guilty of violence toward and that violence in the NFL is more prevalent than in our larger, general American population. To conclude, based on the empirical evidence, we can safely conclude that NFL players have lower crime and arrest rates than the general population, including sexual assault, homicide/suicide, domestic violence, DUI, and drugs (Blumstein & Benedict, 2012). In fact, when you look at the aggregate rates of all players versus the general population, their arrest rates *are less than half* of the average non-NFL player.

Are sports media and sports journalists biased in terms of how they frame stories concerning African American male professional athletes? Are the frequently published news accounts of violent and aggressive behavior demonstrated by black athletes to be explained by examining the racism of the sports journalists? What is the effect of exposure to these frequently published stories associating criminal activity with African American athletes? In a study supported by the National Science Foundation, the National Opinion Research Center collected data that shows that 56% of Caucasian Americans believe African Americans are more violent than whites (Lapchick & Matthews, 1999). This aligns well with a study that shows that in terms of media portrayals, African American men are often depicted as "brutes." The brute stereotype characterizes black men as primitive, temperamental, uncontrollable, violent, and sexually powerful (Smiley & Fakunle, 2016). Therefore, if we compare Lombardo's (1978) research with the results of the Lapchick and Matthew's (1999) study, we can speculate that sports media have a tendency to create a portrait of white athletes that makes them appear friendlier and like law-abiding citizens, while African American athletes are scary, violent, and antisocial. The survey conducted by Lapchick and Matthews (1999) analyzed 1,600 daily newspapers published in the United States and showed that in terms of who is writing and producing the story that fewer than half-a-dozen editors were African Americans. That is, tabulated results in the Lapchick and Matthews (1999) research show that when a news story was published by a newspaper that employed an African American sports editor, it was often the case that the journalist and editors and their newspaper was located in cities or towns that did not have professional sports teams. In other words, even when a newspaper employed an African American sports editor and/or a sports journalist, the effect was negated and not evident in published news coverage because the reporters were not able to observe, visit, or report a story on sports, particularly if there are not community ties with and to a team. Careful analysis leads us to conclude that in terms of sports journalists working in today's media, we have a case where there are more male Caucasians writing for papers that have a predominately white readership. And furthermore, it is possible that the white readers of traditional sports news media may acquire their preconceived notions about African American athletes as black men from the perceptions held by white sports reporters.

Scholars have long been interested in understanding and explaining how sports media actually shape individual attitudes and beliefs about athletes. Greater interest is now being paid to the role that media play in creating opinions and ideas in our society about athletes (Whisenant & Pedersen, 2004). In fact, Whisenant and Pedersen (2004) believe that the media's "words and images have a major impact on societal processes and institutions … the influence of the media is projected not only by what is being said, but also what is not being reported through the absence of coverage" (Whisenant & Pedersen, 2004, p. 55). According to media scholar Fujioka (2005), "Negative minority images have been prevalent in the mainstream media" (p. 451).

Entman has spent years investigating how media shape images of black males. Entman's prolific work in this area shows three common media depictions of black men in media. They are either presented as consummate entertainers, criminals, or athletes. Therefore, when a black athlete is covered in the media and receives publicity committing a crime (even if it is just alleged), research shows that this media coverage will probably morph into a negative image for all black men in our culture. Therefore, according to Entman (1992), when black athletes are in news stories involving crime, they stand accused and ultimately blend into our cultures existing negative stereotypes that all black men are violent, irresponsible, and mean (Entman, 1992; Entman & Rojecki, 2000). Entman and Gross's (2008) research found that African American male athletes and black entertainers often receive more publicity for allegedly committing a crime than they do for their positive contributions to society. Some research studies have concluded that local news programs often misrepresent African American athletes as primary perpetrators of crime. Research on sports media has consistently proven over the course of 20 years that stories involving athletes of color often involve the perpetuation of African American male stereotypes (Fujioka, 2005; Rada, 1996). Research conducted on coverage of male athletes in broadcast news stories has, over the years, shown that the stereotypes of white and black male athletes have remained unchanged—that is, white athletes are thought to be more intelligent and have incredible cognitive and mental skills. while African American athletes tend to dominate the sports work in terms of their natural athletic abilities (Denham, Billings, & Halone, 2002; Rada, 1996; Rainville & McCormick, 2007).

In Chapter 4, we discussed the controversial disparities in how African American athletes are usually described when compared to white athletes. We noted that these representations and statements might communicate an idea that African American athletes are naturally given gifts of great athleticism and that white athletes attain greatness through hard work, discipline, and intelligence. A vast body of literature in the area of sports media shows that media such as television, radio, magazines, newspapers, and social media not only create ideas and stereotypes *but* also shape and influence the way Americans think, feel, and respond to stereotypes. Research conducted by Cynthia Frisby (2016), a professor of strategic communication at the University of Missouri School of Journalism, shows that media consistently rely on racial stereotyping in their news stories. Frisby has conducted a sequence of studies where data reveal that news media tend to perseverate on stories that focus on the criminal and violent behaviors of black athletes while publishing more stories about white athletes that are significantly more positive.

Curious about the frequency by which sports media focus on criminal actions of the African American athlete compared to white athletes, Frisby (2016) sought to examine the content of 155 sports news stories featuring male athletes. Coding for specific news frames and themes commonly used in these news stories about male athletes, Frisby (2016) found that many of the stories included frames/themes related to crime, domestic violence, training/hard work, moral success or failures of the athlete, a violation of rules held by the league, accomplishments, and philanthropic organizations the athlete may be involved in, along with stories about their lifestyles and/or romantic relationship status. Data in the study found sports journalists covered news stories about white athletes at a much higher frequency (43%) than stories published about African American athletes (39%). In terms of the ethnicity of the athlete when the news story involved a crime, data show that 66% of the crime stories involved African American athletes, while only 22% involved white athletes. Furthermore, Frisby's data revealed that over 70% of the news stories that were about domestic violence were primarily written about African American athletes. Compare that percentage with the fact that Frisby (2016) found evidence proving that only 17% of the news stories in sports media involved white athletes. Finally, Frisby's (2016) data show that of all the news stories obtained, 53% of them involved African American athletes. That is, over half of the stories were written with negative undertones compared to less than 30% of similar stories that were written about white athletes. As one can tell, the difference in frequency of the stories is significant and clearly shows a problem with how African American male athletes are treated in media, particularly when compared to white male athletes. Frisby concludes the study with a statement of the implications. These data, Frisby argues, clearly help illustrate and delineate the idea that stereotypes in sports media are real and do exist. To reduce and possibly eradicate racial and ethnic stereotyping, sports journalists and reporters alike must change their way of thinking and begin to reflect on how their own biases concerning stereotypes that deal with race, ethnicity, natural ability versus intelligence, as well as gender and ethnic differences of athletes, may actually contribute to the perpetuation of stereotypes in their published works. In other words, what relationship do one's own biases have on whether an athlete is perceived as a criminal versus the hero? Taken together, research in this area shows that negative media coverage actually legitimizes inequalities in power and social status in the sports world. Not only does it legitimize inequalities but also disparities regarding how athletes are treated in the media are just as likely to impede and undermine hope and inspirations that African American athletes may have.

Frisby's seminal work on the various ways in which media portray male athletes is one of few studies providing quantitative empirical evidence supporting the inequality of coverage in sports media with regard to covering different types of athletes and the sports they participate in. Frisby (2016) stated that she hopes her work will become an important resource for future sports journalists interested in understanding how media portray and cover athletes from different ethnic backgrounds. Images produced by the media, along with the influences that these images have and can produce, warrant further study in that we know that nonverbal communication of images and visuals has a direct relationship with, and can significantly affect, thoughts, opinions, and behaviors of those who consume the messages found in sports media. Up to this point, this chapter has focused on a variety of ways that sports media perpetuate negative impressions of athletes of color. We touched on possible reasons for the perpetuation of negative stereotypes and disparities in treatment that African American and white athletes experience in current sports media.

Scholars interested in the effects of distorted racial portrayals of athletes use one main theory to guide their study: cognitive accessibility theory, which we discussed in Chapter 1. It is a theory that suggests that people use mental cues or heuristics (shortcuts) to make judgments. Using this theoretical perspective, scholars can determine outcomes of exposures to news imagery of a majority of African American athletes and determine if the imagery primes or activates the black athlete criminal stereotype when making judgments regarding race and crime. Based on Entman's research (2000), it seems plausible to assume that, with respect to the imagery used in media stories, that two of the three microaggression images discussed above would be located in mass media. Thus exposure to a majority of negative news stories containing African American male athletes may activate other ideas or heuristics, such as "fear of black men" and "black men create most crime."

Coverage of African American Female Athletes in the Media

Research tells us that disproportionate and skewed portrayals of African American men are certainly problematic, but we also have evidence that shows that coverage in sports media of female athletes and athletes of color is even more problematic (Kane, 1996). Kane and a team of research scholars (Kane 1996) conducted an extensive content analysis of *Sports Illustrated* magazine covers. In the study, Kane, along with other media researchers, found that African American women were depicted on the covers in only 5 of 1,835 all the *Sports Illustrated* magazine covers. Another study conducted 5 years before the Kane (1996) study analyzed the magazine covers published between 1954 and 1987. Data in this study showed that when compared to male athletes, female athletes were depicted on only 6% of covers during this 33-year-old time period (Lumpkin & Williams, 1991). In addition, we find that when the feature articles are about African American female athletes, images of these athletes on the cover were extremely rare (Leath & Lumpkin, 1992; Lumpkin & Williams, 1991). Frisby (2017b) collected recent data that continues to show that diversity in terms of who appears on the cover of major sports magazines is currently still disparate, with depictions of various women of color and female athletes in uniform appearing in very few covers. If we elaborate extensively on these findings, we might be led to conclude that female athletes of color are being marginalized by sports media as are African American male athletes. Implications of data obtained suggest that our culture's dominant ideas and standards of what it means to be beautiful and female in our culture are heavily applied to female athletes. Research over time seems to force us to realize that our American culture favors a heterosexual, white ideal body over other bodies and skin tones. As we will soon learn, research from various sources and disciplines continues to show that our culture believes that the image of beauty is white, thin, and beautiful (Aulette & Wittner, 2012).

Media Treatment of Serena Williams

Serena Williams has seen her share of unfair treatment. For example, in October 2014, Ms. Williams found herself embroiled in the media spotlight when the Russian Tennis Federation president Shamil Tarpischev criticized Serena Williams' body image and her physical appearance. Tarpischev, when talking about Ms. William's looks, insinuated that the celebrated tennis player looked more like a man. The Women's Tennis Association (WTA) made sure Tarpischev apologized and issued a fine of $25,000. The WTA also disqualified him from working in an organizational WTA capacity for the year 2015. The media fascination with Serena William's body has followed her throughout her career. It is a well-known fact that all women in this culture are subject to unattainable standards of beauty and femininity, but femininity is racially coded, and it is often associated with white women. In the book titled *The Beauty Myth*, Wolf (2002) argues that the beauty standard is constructed mainly by advertisers who want women to buy products designed to make them more beautiful. Wolf (2002) also argues that women of color are constantly reminded through advertising and idealized images that femininity is *not* appropriate for blacks.

The greatest female tennis player, Serena Williams, is one of a few African American female athletes who happen to dominate in their sport. Since 2002, Ms. Williams has ranked in the top three of talented female tennis players. However, American sports fans have not been known to completely embrace the concept that Serena Williams is a champion. Scholars and communication researchers believe that racism and sexism have played a huge role in American's response to Serena. In our

Western world, strong, independent, confident women are often depicted negatively (e.g., bitches, angry black women). For Serena, it is believed that when we intersect race, gender, and sport, we find that her recognition as a top athlete in a white sport suddenly becomes problematic.

Serena Williams is a tried-and-true expert in the field of tennis, and she continues to achieve. Her body and physique are the result of years of training. But for women, having a physique that is muscular and toned works more as a distractor, which undermines their achievements and turns the focus on their looks. This is an example of sexism in the most dangerous form. When pundits and sports journalists frame their statements as a joke, they often align it with a criticism that Ms. Williams and other athletes of color are unable to "take a joke." That is, sports journalists will often trivialize their statements and describe Ms. Williams and other athletes of color as individuals who are humorless. These types of "jokes" in media are furtive and shrewd. When sports journalists such as Tarpischev's and others feel inclined to write off their statements as jokes, this cognitive rationale is known as a "microaggression." Women are often the brunt of jokes involving microaggressions. When Tarpischev called Serena and her sister men, he also insinuated that they are scary to look at. This type of "insult" asserts that blacks, by being black, are scary, intimidating, and threatening.

In December 2016, Serena Williams conducted an interview on ESPN's *The Undefeated In-Depth*. During the interview, Ms. Williams talked about sexism in tennis in general, especially when it came to her being defined as "the greatest athlete ever."

Here's what she had to say: "I think, if I were a man, I would've been in that conversation a long, long time ago. Like six, seven years ago. Eight years ago. I thought being a woman is a whole new set of problems from a society that you have to deal with, as well—and being black. So it's a lot to deal with." During a post-Wimbledon semifinal press conference, Serena was asked how she felt when she was labeled "one of the greatest female athletes of all time." She replied, "I prefer the word 'one of the greatest athletes of all time.'"

Negative media coverage, as well as verbal attacks, are not new experiences for Serena Williams. In fact, in many interviews with sports media, Ms. Williams has stated that she has experienced a plethora of attacks in the mass media as well as social media. Scholars and experts in racism in America believe that the many attacks that Serena experiences may possibly stem from her "status" and appearance in a sport that is uncommon for an African American. Serena Williams is a strong, African American female playing and competing for resources (i.e., prize money) in a predominately white sport. Yes, Serena Williams has experienced media coverage that is known to be racialized, sexualized, and dehumanizing. A review of the sports commentary about Serena Williams encourages us to ponder the question, how do microaggressions leak into the media, especially when journalists are supposed to be objective, fair, and accurate? If there is complimentary commentary about Ms. Williams, we might even go so far as to assume that the compliments are centered on the stereotypes that we mentioned in a previous section of this chapter and that is that her tennis skills are ingrained and owing to a simple explanation: Serena is simply a product of natural physical gifts that only athletes of color are given.

It is June 2015, and moments before Serena won the French Open, news media rushed to cover a story that compared one of the best female tennis players, Ms. Williams, to an animal. In this same story, the journalist compared her to a man and claimed that she was "frightening and horrifyingly unattractive." If we are objective reporters, then we must recognize that an accurate description of Serena Williams is that she is a dark-skinned black woman who happens to be very muscular. We might further mention that hard work and dedication produced an athlete who is very accomplished, talented, and skilled.

Before the June 2015 incident, we learned of another news story published in 2006. In this story, Dr. Peter Larkins is interviewed and says that he was making an attempt to compliment Ms. Williams, but instead what he did was offer his medical expertise and opinion in explaining her athletic talents. In the article, Larkins was recorded saying that based on his medical expertise in female tennis player's body types, he believed that Serena's talents were simply due to her African American race. In the article, he explained Ms. Williams' competitor's loss by saying, "It is the African-American race. They just have this huge gluteal strength. … Jennifer Capriati was clearly out of shape and overweight." In an online article published in January 2017, Desmond-Harris (2017) wrote, "With Serena, that's her physique and genetics." This sentiment has been expressed and published in several studies (Author, 2002; Cock, 2004; Frisby, 2017c; Lee & Eagleman, 2013. In fact, according to Sue (2010), quotes and comments like those made by Dr. Larkins, is a prime example of a microaggression that simply associates a female athlete's win to the weakness exhibited by the opponent. In other words, Sue (2010) would argue that in many cases, sports media frequently make comparisons of the winner to the loser's weaknesses rather than simply writing a story solely focused on the winner's abilities and accomplishments.

Comments made by sports journalists and commentators about Serena Williams's body type seem directly related to values upheld in American culture—that is, our culture values and upholds cultural norms related to body image, physical attractiveness, and gender roles. We know that journalists and sports commentators do not exist in a bubble and are not immune to influences and biases in our culture. We know that journalists have their own attitudes, opinions, and behavior. Keeping those things in mind, we must consider and elaborate on the idea that negative comments about Ms. Williams and her body frame and image are not isolated to or made only by white male sports commentators and journalists. In fact, no one is immune to the effects of America's values concerning beauty, physical attractiveness, and body shape. People of all backgrounds may view athletes using a similar lens. Take for instance Jason Whitlock. Jason Whitlock, a black sportswriter, published an article that criticized Serena Williams in his Fox Sports column published in 2009. In the article, Mr. Whitlocke not only attacked Ms. Williams but also when describing her gluteus maximus, he described as her "oversized backpack." In the article found online, Mr. Whitlock went on to say, "I am not fundamentally opposed to junk in the trunk, although my preference is a stuffed onion over an oozing pumpkin" (Whitlock, 2015). "Generally, I'm all for chunky sports stars … but tennis requires a mobility Serena cannot hope to achieve while lugging around breasts that are registered to vote in a different U.S. state from the rest of her" (also quoted in Frisby, 2017c; Whitlock, 2015).

Even a close friend of Serena's joined the bandwagon. It was summer 2012 when Serena's friend Danish tennis player Caroline Wozniacki was photographed holding a sign believed to mock Serena's body. In the photograph, readers saw Ms. Wozniacki with her top and the back of her tennis skirt stuffed with towels. And while the mockery was said to be a joke, Serena responded by saying it was in bad taste. Serena went on to say, "I don't think she meant anything racist by it." But was it just a bad joke?

Currently, the sports industry has a few visible athletes of color who have reached positions of high status, income, and power in the United States. That is, in today's culture, we see Latinos, Asians, and Native Americans, who typically rank lower than whites on many measures of living conditions and opportunities, actually succeeding financially. Regarding media treatment, athletes of color are often victims of images that stereotype, produce emotions such as fear and anger, and create perceptions that result in misunderstanding and rejection. For example, in May 2017, LeBron James, basketball player for the Cleveland Cavaliers of the NBA, was the victim of an alleged hate crime. Despite his high status and reputation, someone felt the need to spray paint the N-word on

James's front gate. Why? Some believe that it is because LeBron James has been one of many athletes of color to speak out on social issues from Trayvon Martin, to wearing an "I Can't Breathe" shirt in remembrance of Eric Garner, to speaking up about Tamir Rice and making a public stand with friends and fellow athletes, Dwyane Wade, Carmelo Anthony, and Chris Paul at the 2016 ESPYS, where they spoke about racism and police brutality while calling on athletes to spark positive change in their respective communities.

According to Fox News in St. Louis, James is reported as saying, "Being black in America is tough," further illustrating the idea that athletes of color are still unable to fully enjoy their lives and other benefits in our culture. When James was asked about the hate crime at his house, he was reported as saying, "No matter how much money you have, no matter how famous you are, no matter how many people admire you, being black in America is tough" (McKirdy, 2017).

LeBron James is not the first athlete of color to be victimized. African Americans and, to a lesser extent, Hispanics, report being victims of violent offenses at much higher rates than whites and non-Hispanics (see Wheelock & Uggen, 2005). In fact, when it comes to higher rates of violent attacks and victimization (including homicide, rape, robbery, and aggravated assault), African Americans have been victims in higher proportions than whites (U.S. Department of Justice, 2014). And again, a documented fact to address stereotypes is research that shows African American crime rates were reported to be well below the crime level rate found for whites between 2001 and 2003 (for statistics refer to Blumstein & Benedict, 2012).

Racial Prejudices in Sport Media

Evidence on prejudices depicted in televised sports shows that these programs actually reinforce stereotypes (see Rada, 1996; Rada & Wulfmeyer, 2000). The early 1990s found many sports professionals faced with having to tackle and confront racial issues in sports. Many sports reporters have had to do this with little to no training or even warning. How do they handle diversity in sports and associated news stories with little to no training? Suddenly, we find Tom Brokaw hosting a special on NBC about African American male athletes. Shortly after that, CNN and ESPN jump on the bandwagon, and they too produced documentaries on black athletes. In addition to the increased focus on professional sports journalists' sudden interest in diversity in sports, we then started seeing an increase in academic research studies that were focused on representations of athletes of color in televised athletic events (see, for example, Jackson, 1989; Rada, 1996; Rada & Wulfemeyer, 2000; Rainville & McCormick, 1977). In 1995, a team of researchers, Sabo, Jansen, Tate, Duncan, and Leggett, examined seven televised international sports events that were aired on several different networks. After examining a total of 161 athletes from 31 competitions, the data showed that race, ethnicity, and nationality were treated differently by each of the sporting events. The research team also found data suggesting that African American athletes were presented more positively and not negatively as research found in the past. Yet the researchers did find that Asian athletes were often portrayed by cultural stereotypes. Furthermore, the data showed that Hispanic athletes in the televised broadcasts were also frequently described in terms of their physical characteristics. An interesting finding in this study was the data that showed minorities were underrepresented as commentators and interviewers.

In their study, Sabo and his team of researchers (1995) found support for the fact that sports media, in an attempt to make a conscious effort to appear objective, will often show signs that they genuinely want to treat athletes fair, irrespective of their race or ethnicity. To find support for this hypothesis, Sabo, Jansen, Tate, Duncan, and Leggett (1995) analyzed commentary for the opening and closing ceremonies of the Olympics and found evidence that showed equal depictions and focuses on racial and cultural diversity (Sabo et al., 1995). The researchers found that many images showed racially mixed groups of athletes participating in the opening ceremonies. Research noted that another production offered a similar image of "unity among races through a broadcast sequence of shots showing an Asian sprinter, athletes engaged in hugs, a Black track, and field athlete, an athlete of color kissing a medal, a White female gymnast, and a Russian weightlifter" (Sabo et al., 1995).

The content analysis that Sabo and his team of researchers designed (1995) further produced unique and challenging findings that showed that sports producers made efforts to select athletes to be interviewed on air. The researchers found that sports producers seemed to make a conscious effort to interview athletes from a cross-section of races and ethnic groups. Interestingly, a case of ethnocentrism or nationalist bias was perhaps more evident in the data in that what was displayed was the idea that American sports media were more bias toward American athletes, and the bias resulted in interviews with more American athletes when compared to foreign athletes.

Sabo et al. (1995) also found that, unlike prior studies, black athletes were not described in terms of their physical gifts. The researchers found support for the idea that sports broadcasters seldom used physical descriptors when discussing African American athletes. However, their data did show that when compared to their Asian, Hispanic, or white athletic counterparts, sports journalists were twice as likely to describe Asian athletes using physical descriptors when compared to black athletes (80% vs. 39%). Regarding how sports media depicted African American athletes, the researchers found that sports commentators were least likely to offer and air negative comments about black athletes (for more see Sabo, Jansen, Tate, Duncan, & Leggett, 2005). Data analyses did not show significant differences in the frequency of positive evaluations by race and ethnicity—again, a finding that counters data obtained in previous research (Sabo et al., 2005). However, unlike prior research reported throughout this text, the study data showed that "African American athletes were significantly less likely than Asian and white athletes to receive negative evaluations from commentators" (Sabo et al., 2005).

Several findings in sports media research show data provide empirical support for the notion that Asian athletes are often depicted in ways that draw on stereotypical descriptions. The descriptions often paint the group as passive, submissive conformists who also happen to be hard workers and fanatically focused on obtaining success (Sabo et al., 1995). Sabo et al. (1995) found that sports journalists tend to be less constrained when reporting on and describing the performances of Asian athletes. For example, when describing a weight-lifting competition among Asian athletes, Sabo et al. (1995) found that the event was advertised and described as "the serenity, the calm, that is the East. The mystique of the Orient with its mysterious inner strength." Basically, this description of the sporting event was framed and supports stereotypical portrayals of the Asian culture. The study also found other statements that portrayed Asian athletes as model minorities who hard workers, conformists, and individuals who are extremely self-disciplined (Sabo et al., 2005).

Interestingly, Sabo et al. (2005) discovered that when compared to African American athletes, Asian American athletes were significantly more likely to be described in physical terms. Sabo et al. (2005) obtained data that revealed that sports commentators frequently referred to Asian athletes in terms of their physical size (e.g., "she's slight at 103 pounds," "look at the quadriceps, how they seem so overdeveloped and bowed," "she's a slight athlete, only about 100 pounds") and were also significantly more willing to talk about the emotions and personalities of Asian athletes (refer to Sabo et al., 2005).

In terms of Hispanic athletes, Sabo et al. (1995) found that media also appeared to make a conscious effort to describe Latino athletes in a positive and more favorable light. Interestingly, the data show that in all the broadcasts, Latino/a athletes were likely to be recipients of the commentator's lavish songs of praise. For example, praise was frequently expressed when the Cuban men's gymnastics team was excelling in the race. Data show that commentators repeatedly bemoaned the poor performance of the U.S. men's team while overemphasizing the performance of the Cuban team.

Yet despite the fact that minorities are actively visible in a wide variety of sports, media research shows that white athletes hold the greatest visibility in terms of sports broadcasts. Sabo et al. (1995) analyzed comments made by sports announcers as well as the interviews they held with athletes. Despite the overwhelming number of athletes of color, data revealed that whites accounted for a very large share of network interviews and other appearances (Sabo et al., 1995). Specifically, they found that out of 368 network interviews, white athletes accounted for 92% of those appearances. Black commentators made up the remaining 8% (Sabo et al., 1995). Data further revealed other ethnic minorities (e.g., Hispanic, Asian, Pacific Islanders, and Native Americans, to name a few) were not identified in the sample nor was data available to use in the content analysis. Findings in other studies on sport and ethnicity also seem to support the notion that the athlete's race and ethnicity influences who commentators choose to interview. Data also suggests that sports commentators are biased in choosing to interview specific athletes and very specific sporting competitions (for details on the study, refer to Sabo et al., 1995).

Sports, the Middle East, and Media

Biases, prejudices, and discriminatory acts against Arab Americans have become part of our everyday life. Since September 11, 2001, and the terrorist acts leveled against the towers in New York City and the Pentagon in Washington, DC, we find that any efforts to understand Middle Eastern culture and communities have become cloudy, to say the least. We find that Americans typically tend to lump all Arabs together and view them as "the other group." Since 9/11, we find that negative images of Arab Americans persist, and individuals from this group are often incorrectly blamed for violent acts or they are racially profiled, particularly when trying to board an airplane. News reports of acts of political violence are one source of these sentiments.

To curtail negative images of Middle Easterners in the news, the Society of Professional Journalists, in conjunction with the Poynter Institute, issued guidelines that suggest policies for journalists to follow when reporting on this ethnic group that encourage a more neutral or objective approach, especially when journalists find themselves covering alleged acts of terrorism and other mediated messages that may put this group of people in a negative light.

We would be amiss if we did not discuss the portrayal of Middle Easterners in media—namely, entertainment media. From movies to shows, it is hard to find instances in which Middle Easterners are not portrayed negatively. Shaheen (1984) has spent years investigating images of Middle Easterners in entertainment media and came to the conclusion that the prevalent images found most in American media are those that include the wealthy "sheik," the uncontrollable and crazy villain and killer, the polygamist, and misogynists, and the list goes on. Shaheen's research also shows that there is a consistent image of Middle Easterners that implies ties to Islam, and ultimately an illusionary correlation is made that associates Islam with violence and acts of terrorism. And not to forget portrayals of Middle Eastern women, Shaheen found that most Middle Eastern women are depicted frequently as belly dancers and harem girls.

Soccer

Sports in the Middle East centers on soccer. In fact, we find that in the culture and lives of people living in the Middle East, soccer is by far the most popular sport. Soccer is by far the region's most popular sport. Other sports are popular as well. Wrestling in the Middle East is rooted deeply in the custom and norms for people living in Iran. For example, Moroccan runners Saïd Aouita and Hicham El Guerrouj introduced track and field as a sport to the region of Maghreb. As a point of illustration, Maghreb includes the countries Algeria, Morocco, Tunisia, Libya, and Mauritania.

Bahrain, an Arab country situated in the Persian Gulf, hosted its very first FIA Formula One World Championship in 2004. This sporting event was noted as being the first event ever to take place in the Middle East. Closer inspection of media coverage of Middle Eastern athletes reveals two diabolically conflicting dichotomies: One viewpoint views sport as an activity designed to bring different groups together. This perspective is also rooted in the desire to unite people and bridge the gaps based on social class, ethnicity, and racial divides. The second conflicting dichotomy involves the idea that sport is merely a reflection of the larger society. From this perspective, athletes have a particular type of influence on the social order (Bale & Cronin, 2002; Carrington, 1986). Research shows that in terms of Jewish and Arab athletes, they are rarely allowed or given opportunities to communicate and interact with one another. In fact, further research shows that Jewish and Arab athletes are not allowed to develop friendships.

International sports media frequently portray the success of the Arab athlete as if it was contingent on Palestine. In other words, Palestinian athletes in the Middle Eastern culture must continually prove themselves. Some athletes, for example, are often forced and expected to adopt the Jewish culture and the Hebrew language (Adler, 2016; Baskin, 1991; Bowker, 1997; Hauptman, 2001). In fact, in an online article by Aburaiya, Avraham, and Wolsfeld (1998), when Arab athletes express discourse in media about their Jewish heritage, and use media to bring issues to the public "they are scolded and silenced." The online resource goes on to say that "silencing practices are effective in making the Palestinian players highly cautious and largely prevent[s] them from voicing the opinions and adversities of Israeli-Arab relationships in public" (Aburaiya, Avraham, & Wolsfeld, 1998)

> "… while sport certainly has the potential of bringing the Jewish majority and the Arab minority in Israel closer together, in most cases this potential remains unfulfilled. Arab soccer players are largely unable to bring any real issues and concerns to public debate, as their political speech is heavily criticized, especially when it is not in line with the ideal picture of coexistence."
>
> (Aburaiya, Avraham, & Wolsfeld, 1998)

Cultural research also shows that these athletes are mandated by their cultural norms to withhold any signs of cultural uniqueness. In fact, athletes are not allowed to create national identities for themselves that differs from the identity of the country of Palestine. And, lastly, Palestinian athletes are not allowed to have political aspirations and opinions (Bale & Cronin, 2002).

Football

In a commercial for Cellcom, an Israeli cell phone provider, we can see depictions of smiling Israeli soldiers playing soccer at the barrier that separates Israel from the West Bank. The soldiers appear to be playing a version of football in which they kick the ball to the opposing team (Egarter, 2017). As the opposing team attempts to return the ball, we hear a voice say as the images appear, "What, after all, do we all want? A little fun" (Egarter, 2017). The minute it aired, protests and angry consumers lambasted the Nike ad because of the eerie depiction of earlier years when there were weekly protests taking place in the villages of Bil'in and Ni'lin.

Several Middle Eastern films show the intersectionality of race/ethnicity, social class, and gender. One film portrays a Jewish team (including a few Arab players) struggling in a poor "development town." The town consists predominately of Mizrachi residents who wish to engage in a sports competition with the powerful and wealthy elites of the country. Another film depicts the members of a Middle Eastern women's football team who confront their culture's long-held prejudices. According to Jewish and Palestinian culture, women are not allowed to play or participate in a "man's game." The film was directed by a woman and illustrates the struggles that women face in patriarchal cultures. Viewing the film, we take away the message that for women in this culture, the sport of football gives them hope and a sense of personal autonomy. We also learn that many Israeli female footballers share these sentiments.

Arab Women Athletes

As with female athletes in America, research shows that sports media pay little to no attention to female athletes in the Middle East. Just as female athletes in American sports media are rarely featured, we find the same patterns in international sports media. A quick glance at published stories from international sports media shows that the sources cited as well as stories about the accomplishments of athletes tend to put the media spotlight on Middle Eastern male athletes.

The Global Media Monitoring Project conducted a report in 2005 that sought to compare news stories focused on men and women living in the Middle East. The research covered 78 countries, including the Middle East, and found that of all stories published, only 21% of the sources interviewed in the story were female. In other words, similar to the content analysis of male and female athletes in the news in America, the project reported that fewer women were mentioned in news stories or portrayed in the news. Despite an increase of Middle Eastern women in sports, the earlier project found that, compared to 1995, only 17% of all stories in sports media were focused on women. The researchers found that 10 years later, the results remained dreadful. In fact, the researchers involved in this project found data that shows that for every story about Middle Eastern female athletes, five stories were published about Middle Eastern male athletes. The following profound quote concluded the report: "The world we see in the news is a world in which women are virtually invisible" (al-Ariqi, 2009).

Snow Skiing in the Middle East

The first Emirati figure skater, Zahira Lari (see Figure 5.1), had to fight obstacles, jump over hurdles, and face conflicts put in front of her by the United Arab Emirates. Not only is Ms. Lari breaking the norms in her country about gender roles but also she contradicts the typical stereotypes held in American culture about Middle Eastern women. In fact, the American socially constructed idea of female Middle Easterners is that they typically dress in *I Dream of Jeannie* attire, are demure, understated, and submissive. In fact, many perceptions of Middle Eastern women are held that suggest that they are not allowed to have any rights or to express their opinions. However, Ms. Lalri's participation in sports is as a woman who is confident, strong, and independent. We see her as a Middle Eastern female athlete who expresses her opinion and confidence who is shattering not only the gender norms within her country but also disrupting the Western perception of Arab women. In fact, one example of Ms. Lari's impact can be found in a recent Nike commercial. The campaign titled "What Will They Say About You?" features successful female professional athletes from various parts of the Middle East. Nike's main motive for producing the commercial was to "highlight the stories of amazing athletes to encourage and inspire others" (Egarter, 2017).

As a side note, Nike's desire to create an ad that uses the power of sports in America to address stereotypes and make positive changes in our culture is one perfect example of how advertisers, marketers, strategic communication practitioners, and sports journalists can start effecting changes in not only the sports world but also in American culture.

In the 2016 Summer Olympics, some social media users took to Twitter and other social media to express their criticisms and disdain for the Nike commercial. The main theme of the complaints was that the ad and the women were shown wearing too little and showing too much skin. The popular hashtag. #Olympics_Women_Don't_Represent_Us was created to demonstrate that many were opposed to women participating in the Olympic Games, period. The hashtag garnered over one million

FIGURE 5.1   *Zahra Lari, a figure skater, wears the hijab*

tweets where social media users would also learn of an Egyptian beach volleyball team that was being mocked and humiliated. The volleyball team members found themselves on the defensive side of Arab social media because of their uniform: a long-sleeved T-shirt and leggings. Despite a large show of support for the uniform, there were a few users who seemed determined to post negative commentary about women in sport, no matter how they acted or dressed.

In February of 2017, Nike released a commercial online that portrayed female Arab athletes engaged in boxing, running, ice-skating, and fencing. The online commercial caused quite a controversy in Middle Eastern countries because of the idea that it portrayed Arab women leading traditional lives. The commercial starts with a woman who appears nervous as she gazes at the street just outside of her front door. She adjusts her hijab, a veil that covers the hair and chest, and symbolizes the Muslim culture's standard of modesty, before she sets out on what appears to be a morning jog. An off-screen female narrator speaking with a Saudi accent says, "What will they say about you? Maybe they'll say you exceeded all expectations." Social media analytics showed that not less than 48 hours later, the YouTube video had been shared more than 75,000 times and viewed close to 400,000 times (Aswad, 2017). But not all comments or replies to the video were positive. Some Arab women were upset in that they felt that the ad was not a true representation of them. One woman said, "We do not wear a hijab and go running in the streets. Shame on Nike" (comments were shared on Nike.com).

The online commercial featuring Arab female athletes was filmed, according to Nike.com, in the "older, rundown suburbs of the glitzy Gulf Arab emirate of Dubai" (Aswad, 2017). The commercial's creative strategy was to depict the everyday struggles women from this culture face. Interestingly, the ad showed the struggles and friction that some of the women appearing in the ad face from other women from similar ethnic backgrounds (personal communication, Nike, June 2017).

For Middle Eastern women, exercising in public is a rare occurrence. In fact, it is even rarer to find a women-only gym in the Middle East. Health clubs that are for women only are not just few and far between; if there is one to be found, it will not be fully equipped for women to learn a variety of sports. And we learned that women-only gyms are "often more expensive than gyms for

FIGURE 5.2   *Israeli Female basketball team*

men" (Aswad, 2017). Take the following as an example. In American culture, physical education is offered for all boys and girls. However, in Saudi Arabia, girls are prohibited from engaging in physical education in public schools, even though young girls may attend all-girl public schools. And as of this writing, the author of the book found that female gyms are presently illegal in the kingdom because female athleticism is deemed un-Islamic (Aswad, 2017). Figure 5.2 shows Israeli female professional basketball players, post-game celebration.

Here in the United States, Muslim female athletes have found success by participating in a variety of sports. Some of the sports that Muslim female athletes participate in include tennis, association football, fencing, volleyball, and basketball. In fact, it was during the broadcast of the 2016 Summer Olympics that viewers met 14 Muslim women participating in the Summer Games. In fact, Muslim women were shown winning medals and participating in a vast range of sporting competitions. This depiction of Muslim women's participation in sports leaves one to speculate that their increased participation may signal that women in that culture are becoming more empowered. Some would say that the increase in participation in sports by Muslim women may be greatly influenced by our Western culture. In the Summer 2004 Olympics, Afghan sprinter Robina Muqimyar was praised by American media for wearing her burqa while training. Why did American sports media focus on this athlete and her burqa? Some may speculate that from our worldview, the burqa seems constraining, hot, and may hinder athletic performance. Scholar Mahfoud Amara helps us understand the type of media coverage that occurs when we apply our standards of clothing and rituals to others. Similar to ethnocentrism, "orientalism" is the idea that our culture is superior to those of the Middle Eastern culture (Said, 1978; Sardar, 1999). That is, media content often shows portrayals of Middle Eastern women in the context of family or religion and not in sports or other professional positions. As a result, when we are confronted with images that go against the expected portrayals, American media will then reflect our dominant Western ideology. This is the basic premise of orientalism and was also evident in the commentary made by sports broadcasters when talking about Muqimyar.

Another application of Orientalism to the field of athletics and its intersectionality with gender may center on beauty and the beauty bias as it applies to female athletes. Researchers would quite possibly investigate how the health and beauty manufacturers use narratives of gender to define and socially construct the ideal female body. As we discussed in chapter 3 of this textbook, we know that there are certain body types that are more popular and attractive, according to our culture's standards. Health and beauty manufacturers, according to the theory of orientalism, would shape their discourse and narratives to be aligned with our cultural discourse of femininity, attractiveness, popularity, and image.

Just as female athletes in America are the objects of criticism when they do not conform to our culture's ideals, Muslim female athletes are also the objects of criticism, especially when they fail to meet the American culture's norms, ideals, and way of life. In fact, it was not until the year, 1996 when Middle Eastern athletes were even allowed to participate in the Olympic Games (Syed, 2012). Even in the Olympics, a debate continues at the time of this writing about whether Muslims should be engaged in head covering for religious purposes. At the heart of the debate is whether the hijab, which is a religious symbol in the Muslim culture, should be considered a religious symbol in our culture. For some, the hijab appears to be out of place or inappropriate in the American culture's athletic environment. Samie and Sehlikoglu (2012) believe that media coverage of hijabi athletes at the 2012 Summer Olympics portrayed them as "strange, incompetent, and out of place" (Samie, 2013; Shergold, 2012; Shirazi, 2001). Researchers also discovered that media attention afforded to Muslim athletes was disproportionate and showed a very low female-to-male athlete ratio (Synovitz, 2012). In fact, we witnessed orientalism and the sports media's "othering" when Muslims were expected to participate in the 2012 Olympics in London.

In an article published by the *New York Times*, we learned that "observance of Ramadan posed challenges to Muslim athletes." Ramadan, which typically takes place in the months of June or July, depending on the moon, placed Muslim Olympians during the 2012 Olympic Games in a predicament: to honor the Ramadan holiday and fast for a certain period. Ramadan is the time of the year in which Muslims are not allowed to eat, drink, swear, insult, or engage in limited sexual relations. From the Muslim religious perspective, Ramadan is also considered a "charitable month" in which Muslims as a community work together to help the poor and the needy. So how do Muslim athletes negotiate participating in the Summer Games with honoring the holy month of Ramadan? The answer is, it depends. Research tells us that Muslims are allowed to engage in an 18-hour fast or a pre-morning fast, or they may plan to postpone Ramadan for a month. We found that many of the Muslim athletes often observe Ramadan and fasting a month after the Olympic Games. But we also learned after researching this ritual that some Muslim athletes may choose to opt out of the fast entirely, and as many Protestants do with the Bible, they will apply various interpretations of the Koran. Thus in answering the question of how Muslim athletes negotiate sports and Ramadan, the bottom line is that it is completely a matter of personal choice (Borden, 2012).

Muslim female athletes have been vocal as of late, expressing their concern that sports media frequently pay attention to their clothing and not their athletic successes or achievements. If we consider the theory of "orientalism" and "othering," we can speculate that the reason for the attention on their clothing choices is directly related to our Western culture's ideals regarding appropriate uniforms for female athletes. For example, Turkish tae kwon do athlete Kübra Dağlı was posted the following statement on social media, "They don't speak of my success, but of my headscarf. I don't want this. Our success should be discussed."

Saudi Arabian All-Female Basketball Team

It is a well-known fact that Saudi Arabia has ultraconservative and restrictive gender policies. Many civil and human rights organizations hoped that the International Olympic Committee (IOC) would "punish" the kingdom for its gender discrimination; after all, in 1970, the IOC barred South Africa from participating in the Olympics because of the country's policy regarding racial discrimination. Many felt that if the IOC could take action against apartheid for its race-based acts, then, surely, they would do the same for Saudi Arabia in 2012. In a surprising move, the Saudi government stated that two female Saudi athletes would be allowed to participate in the 2012 Summer Olympics. Sarah Attar and Wojdan Ali Seraj Abdulrahim Shaherkani competed in the 800-meter race and in judo, respectively. The two women were allowed to compete because the IOC cited a clause in their policy that provides opportunities for athletes to compete "when their participation is deemed important for reasons of equality" (Nafjan, 2012).

Saudi Arabia as a culture has what is known to be a hostile view toward women participating in any type of sport. In fact, in Saudi Arabia, females do not have permission to enter health clubs or to watch or observe sports in a stadium. In Saudi Arabia, as we mentioned earlier, women and girls are not permitted to partake in physical education courses or activities in schools. The only means by which a woman living in Saudi Arabia can participate in a sport or even practice a competitive sport is if she attends an expensive private school and/or goes to college. Recall from a previous section of this chapter that health clubs and colleges are prohibited for women and are also prohibited from publicizing their activities.

In 2003, nine years before the first two Saudi women competed in the Summer Olympics, the first public women's basketball team was organized. The team's founder, Lina Almaeena, also cofounded the "first women's sports organization, Jeddah United" (Nafjan, 2012). Starting with just six women, the organization known as Jeddah United has grown to include over 300 men and women from across the kingdom. And as expected, when anything addresses change, we find that Jedda United has not been without critics. In fact, research revealed that conservative Saudis feel that the organization is "corrupting young girls' morals" (Nafjan, 2012).

Saudi conservatives, such as Sheikh Abdulrahman Al Shathri, an Islamic cleric and public notary, wrote a book to justify the restrictions placed on female athletics in their culture (Nafjan, 2012). In the book *Girls' Sports and Scouting in Schools and Universities*, which is now in its third edition, offers reasons why women and girls should not participate in sports whatsoever (Nafjan, 2012). From his perspective, any girl or women wanting to participate in sports will lose their attractiveness and appear more masculine (Nafjan, 2012). The book describes in detail all the reasons why physical education is a bad idea for girls. Al Shathri believes participation in sports tends to orient women to achieve a more masculine physique (Nafjan, 2012).

In the book published in 2010, Shathri does find activities that he feels are more conducive to Saudi women; he is a major advocate of household chores, such as vacuuming, and feels that this is the best alternative to physical education. He supports his beliefs with documented evidence he obtained from medical journals that provide evidence showing housekeeping burns calories just like sports. According to Shathri, participation in sports corrupts Saudi women and leads to behaviors, such as "lesbianism, disruption of the menstrual cycle, hymen tearing, loss of femininity, and Westernization" (Nafjan, 2012). He also believes that participation of Saudi women in international competitions requires them to appear uncovered in front of men—a behavior that is frowned upon in the culture.

Latino Athletes

Research on portrayals of Latino athletes in mainstream American sports media also shows massive gaps in depictions of Latinos. News stories featuring everyday culture and behaviors associated with Latinos can be placed in one of two categories: portrayals as problem people or as partygoers always looking for celebrations. The first category, problem people, is operationalized around portrayals that depict Latinos as undocumented migrant workers, landscapers, and drug dealers who are unable to speak English and cannot adjust to our culture's way of living. The second category is the idea that media typically show Latinos as a group of people who frequently and colorfully celebrate many holidays. For example, Puerto Ricans celebrate Puerto Rican Independence Day; then there is Miami's Calle Ocho Festival or the widely popular and celebrated holiday known as the Cinco de Mayo Fiesta. We find that most media messages and news coverage of these celebrations will often show colorful folkloric costumes and Latinos engaged in singing and dancing to music from their homeland.

Latinos undoubtedly have greater visibility in American media today than in years past. The 1960s found media making huge concerted efforts to improve portrayals of Latinos. Currently, we find blockbuster movies and popular television programs that include Latino characters among the cast. In addition, we find a few mediated messages and themes that are built around Latino athlete or stars. In terms of news anchors, currently, we can find Latinos seated at the desk of many international and national network news programs (e.g., Soledad O'Brien).

Before we go on, we must take a moment to define the term Latino. For purposes of this chapter, Latino/a refers to individuals/athletes who are from Latin countries, such as Mexico, Cuba, Venezuela, Portugal, Brazil, Puerto Rico, and the Dominican Republic (Salinas & Lozano, 2017). Research on the origin of the term *Latinx* shows that it emerged in American culture in the early part of the 21st century (Salinas & Lozana, 2017). The term officially appeared in American Spanish dictionaries in 2004 (Pastrana, Battle, & Harris, 2016) and is commonly used more by community activists and in higher education contexts because, it is believed that these are the environments where those who seek to advocate for individuals who advocate intersectionality by combining the identity politics of race and gender (Salinas & Lozano, 2017). While the term Latinx has gained traction and appears more frequently in news stories, it has not been without its share of controversy. The major complaint, according to research, is that the term is disrespectful to the Spanish language. The alternative to Latinx has been Latin@ where the @ symbol is a combination of the "a" and the "o." While this alternative first surfaced in the mid-1990s, this term was also accused of adhering to our culture's view that gender is a binary concept.

In terms of whether journalists should use Latina, Latino, Latinx, Latin@ or Hispanic, a consistent tip is to simply as the person you are interviewing or reporting on what term they most prefer and identify with. In an online article written by Wolfe (2018), the differences in definition of Hispanic (and Latino/a) is primarily contingent upon the source you use. "Some say that 'Hispanic' refers to race" but research revealed that there are distinctions between the two terms, as Hispanic and Latino are often used to define regions of origin, not their race. According to the U.S. Census Bureau (2018), *Hispanic* is a term used to describe "any person, regardless of race, creed, or color, whose origins are of Mexico, Puerto Rico, Cuba, Central or South America—or of some other Hispanic origin." Areas conquered by the Spaniards were considered part of a region originally called Hispania, which is where the term *Hispanic* likely derived. In conclusion, for many those who identify as an Hispanic or Latino will often express their personal preferences, just as some African Americans may prefer to be described as a brown person, person of color, or Black (Taylor, Lopez, Martinez, & Velasco, 2012). What we do know, however, is that those individuals who identify closely with the

Hispanic/Latino demographic often prefer to identify themselves based on their country of origin (Taylor, Lopez, Martinez, & Velasco, 2012).

In baseball, Latinos make up the largest minority group, as we mentioned in Chapter 2. In fact, we found that many Latinos athletes have become stars in the MLB. As of this writing, Latinos are starting to participate in sports outside of baseball, including hockey, football, and basketball.

Stereotypical Portrayals of Major League Baseball Players

Several researchers have argued to change stereotypical portrayals of MLB athletes, some of which date back to the 1880s (Baldassaro, 2005). Such studies have discussed stereotypical depictions of black, Italian American, Latino, and Asian baseball players (Baldassaro, 2005; Iyer, 1988; Mayeda, 1999). In Nowatzki's (2002) study focused on baseball and race at the turn of the 19th century. In this historical study, he found that newspapers often placed derogatory words, such as colored, coon, clown, negro, dusky, mulatto, Spanish" (p. 85) in front of black baseball player Moses Fleetwood Walker's name in the 1880s. Although it was acceptable for Italian Americans to play in the MLB because of their white skin color, Baldassaro (2005) reports that during the 1920s and 1930s when several players from this group entered the league, the media often used derogatory nicknames for the players, such as "wop," "dago," and "spaghetti bender" (p. 99). Even during this time in our culture, names such as "wop" and "dago" were viewed as offensive. These derogatory nicknames were often accompanied by stereotypical portrayals of Italian athletes. Historical documents show that Italian baseball players were commonly photographed in front of a heaping plate of pasta. Records further show that frequent references were made to the Italian athlete eating spaghetti to highlight his ethnic group membership as an Italian American (Baldassaro, 2005).

As increasing numbers of Latino players entered the MLB in the 1950s and 1960s, the U.S. media also stereotyped these players (Regalado, 2002). For example, Regalado found that Latino players were given Americanized nicknames by the U.S. press, such as "Chico" (p. 21), which was one of the most popular nicknames used for Spanish-speaking players. Dominican-born Jesus Alou's name was protested by a group of ministers in San Francisco who opposed his name because it was "the one given to our Lord" (Regalado, 2002, p. 21). Regalado (2002) also reported that the U.S. media and international Latino players have historically had a rocky relationship because of the reporters deeply held stereotypes about these players, the language barrier, and the reporters' lack of understanding of Hispanic culture. Most recently, researchers have shown that reporters also use stereotypes to describe Asian MLB players in the U.S. media. A study of articles from the *Los Angeles Times*, the *New York Times*, and *Sports Illustrated* covering Japanese MLB players Hideo Nomo and Hideki Irabu discovered that sports reporters often describe their performances in stereotypical ways (Mayeda, 1999).

Asian American Athletes

Stereotypes presenting Asians as model minorities are regularly found in sports media's coverage of Asian athletes. The model minority theory "suggests that Asian Americans conform to the norms of society, do well in school and careers, are hard-working and self-sufficient" (Wong, Lai, Nagasawa, & Lin, 1998, p. 100). Wong et al. (1998) stated that the stereotype of the "model minority" is unfounded and untrue, and gives a false impression that diversity is nonexistent in the Asian American culture. The model minority theory and the idea that Asians are an economic threat originally appeared in media coverage about an Asian athlete who signed a 4-year contract with the New York Yankees for $12.8 million (Mayeda, 1999). Nakamura (2005) conducted a study of Japanese player Ichiro Suzuki and found that the U.S. media stereotyped Ichiro as the "other," or as being different from all other MLB players because of his Japanese background. In his published work, Gray (1995) suggests that the ways media and popular culture present different races serve as "cultural signifiers" (p. 13) and help support stereotypes and other notions people in our culture may hold.

Native Americans, Mascots, and the Media's Role in the Controversy

In our culture, an ongoing national debate has taken place concerning whether Native American imagery should be used as mascots, nicknames, and logos for schools and sports teams. Scholars, as well as media critics, conduct studies and research examining the use of the mascots, nicknames, and logos. In fact, some research studies have shown that our culture is divided on the topic: Many sports fans enthusiastically support the use of Native American imagery, while other fans are strongly opposed to the use of this type of imagery. Proponents who support keeping the imagery believe strongly that the use of mascots, nicknames, or logos is our culture's way of honoring Native American people. Supporters feel that the use of these symbols elicits feelings related to our history. Critics, however, are firm believers that these symbols are offensive and degrading because they are items known to be sacred to Native Americans, and the use of these sacred symbols perpetuates stereotypes—stereotypes that are offensive and degrading. While supporters of keeping Native American mascots, images, and logos normally offer up the argument that the images used by the teams are complimentary and that they are not hurtful nor are they intended to cause offense to all Native Americans. Those opposed to the use of Native American images often cite research that delineates the effects that exposure to these images of Natives have on non-native individuals. Research further notes that the sports fans are oftentimes unaware that the use of their images, the paint they put on their faces, and the dances that are performed in tribes are often religious rituals. We find that sports fans who engage in arm signals and other behaviors send the message that they are poking fun at Native Americans. Many times, these behaviors are seen on sports broadcasts, and we often wonder if sports fans who approve of a team name like "the Redskins" actually know the original meaning of it? We find that some fans perform tribal dances or paint their face without having any knowledge about the meaning of the dance or symbol. It would be like a Caucasian person dressing in blackface and then trying to do hip-hop. More times than not, a person seeing that behavior would assume, using heuristics or schemas, that the person is making fun of blacks and their love of hip-hop music.

Most important, however, is the research that shows the negative effect these mascots and nicknames have on Native people. Over time, exposure to these behaviors has been found to have a lasting negative effect on Native American's and even non-Native American's self-esteem and self-perception. Imagine if you are in the group, and you are watching people who look nothing like you perform a dance that looks nothing like the dance you've grown up to know and love? What are the effects of these and many other misconceived, cartoonish, and dehumanizing images? While some news media have taken stances and spoken out against Native American athletic imagery, many have not. *The Oregonian* and the *Minneapolis Star Tribune* have both instituted policies that state that they will no longer cover stories or publish articles about sports teams that continue to use Native American nicknames and imagery (Locklear, 2012). Other news organizations that have not taken steps to implement policies against the use of mascots in sports believe firmly that the media's responsibility is simply to report news and not to try to change society's culture. Do sports media help perpetuate racism when highlighting or showcasing those sports fans who are adorned in Native American athletic symbols, clothing, or imagery? What is the media's responsibility regarding supporting a group that is excluded from news coverage? (refer to Chapter 2, symbolic annihilation).

Let's begin this discussion with a topic most frequently raised in sports media: the desire to change the Washington Redskins to a less offensive name. Interestingly, sports media and media scholars have documented disagreements over what the term Redskins means. There's one train of thought that believes the word "redskins" was coined centuries ago to describe the fact that Indians painted their faces red. Others believe that the name "redskins" dates back to a time in American history when Native Americans were scalped, and their skin was removed from their bodies and hung out to dry. The fact that some people do not find redskins offensive is most likely due to the fact that most people in our Western culture are not aware of its historical roots and its true definition. Perhaps the Washington Redskins have become cultural icons and symbols to those opposed to changing the name. We will now turn to a brief discussion on the origin of the word "redskin."

What Is a "Redskin"?

"Redskin" was a term used by Native Americans to differentiate between two races (i.e., pale face = white man, redskin = Native American). Information obtained from the Smithsonian revealed that the first use of the word redskin in America appeared in 1769 when the Piankashaws were negotiating with Col. John Wilkins. The first use of the word "redskin" was in 1769 during negotiations between the Piankashaws and Col. John Wilkins of the General Army of the United States (Alden, 1982). Ethnophaulisms or labels that refer to one's skin tone, like "redskin" typically reduces an individual down to their group affiliation. Originally, the use of the term "redskin" by Native Americans in the early 18th century, was to be understood by Europeans (Reid, 2018). When Native American speeches were translated, newspapers would print the "redskin" term (Reid, 2018). Just as the word "nigger" is used to demean African Americans, In the United States, the term "redskin" often evokes negative reactions for some due to the fact that the term is frequently associated with the term in conjunction with 19th-century scalp hunting the reward that Europeans received for every skin scalped or obtain from deceased Natives. For some, this association with scalping and other early century practices such as embarking on a hunt for redskins, with a goal of obtaining their scalps is still, to this day, considered demeaning by some Native Americans (Alden, 1982; Reid, 2018).

Native American Mascots, Nicknames, and Logos and the Media's Involvement

For over 30 years in American culture, there have been frequent debates about the use of the word "redskin." The question has also been raised as to whether public schools, colleges, universities, and professional sports organizations and leagues should use images of Native Americans for their teams (Native American mascots, 2008). The debate centers on whether the use of this imagery should be changed to another image that does not reflect a racial group. It is thought that a change would eliminate the negative depictions of Native Americans.

The question has been raised about the media's role in the debate of Native American sports mascots and images. Some argue that mass media may have provoked and promoted racism by continuing to cover the controversy. The media's involvement in the controversy also brings to the table a discussion of whether the media should be involved in the debate concerning Native American athletic imagery in news reports. Time and time again, scholars interested in this topic have published studies and analyzed various ways that Native American imagery has been and continues to be depicted in mass media. As we mentioned previously in Chapter 2 of this text, the framing theory "assumes that people use their expectations of situations to make sense of them and determine their actions in them" (Dunegan, 1993; Folkes, 1988; Yows, 1995) Taking this thought further is the idea that the mass media reinforce the dominant segment of society's existing patterns of attitudes and behavior toward minorities by perpetuating rigid and usually negative portrayals (Martin, 2008;

Mastro, Behm-Morawitz, & Ortiz, 2008; O'Neil, 2009; Ramasubramanian, 2007; 2011).

Many of the images observed in mass media appear to be offensive and degrading to Native people. It is hard to find images that honor the group instead of mocking the Native American culture, traditions, history, and religion. If we are honest, we would find that many of the images and mascots portray stereotyped portrayals of Native American people. For example, consider the mascot known as Chief Noc-A-Homa, the original mascot used for the Atlanta Braves (see Figure 5.3). The chief's name symbolized a "screaming Indian," and, to make matters worse, the chief lived in a teepee and would come out dancing whenever the Braves hit a home run. It should become evident that the portrayal of the "Indian mascot who lives in a teepee" had an air of "ridicule." The stereotype that Native Americans live in teepees was also perpetuated in the ritual associated with baseball. According to Merskin (1998), Native Americans are symbolically annihilated in depictions and portrayals in mainstream

FIGURE 5.3   *Chief Noc-A-Homa taking the mound*

media. As a result of the exclusion of Native Americans in media messages, we find that the group now experiences effects of trivialization and exclusion, including being devalued, marginalized, and forgotten (Merskin, 1998, p. 335). Merskin (1998) goes on to argue that when people can see themselves being portrayed in media, and they see the portrayal as positive, the result of the representation is a positive view of themselves and of the people in the world around them (Merskin, 1998, p. 335).

With respect to journalism and Native American imagery, Jensen (1994) was interested in understanding how journalists felt about the use of imagery. What was discovered was the fact that journalists believe that Americans are just too sensitive and seek out ways to be offended. Many of these journalists did not see any reason for changing the names of team mascots. In fact, Jensen (1994) reported that journalists believe that any policy that seeks to end the use of Native American imagery in sports is simply a "misguided attempt to be politically correct" (Locklear, 2009).

For another perspective on the issue, Beadle (2002) begs the question, "Where will it end? Will the Fighting Irish of Notre Dame have to change its name because it's offensive to Irish people?" (p. 1). In fact, research uncovered the reason some journalists support the use of Native American imagery in sports; it is their belief that journalism is about being objective and devoid of controversy (Locklear, 2009). If one aligns with this argument and rationale, then one believes that the job of a journalist is to publish stories that contain facts and not one's opinions (Bender, Davenport, Drager, & Fedler, 2009, p. 72). In 1992, the president of NBC stated, "Newspapers are supposed to be mirrors and tribunes and records of society, journals, and registers of fact—news pages are not supposed to be edited to bring about social change" (Jensen, 1994, p. 20).

Denny (1999) believes that the "media promotes racism by using offensive team names in newspaper headlines, television news and radio reporting" (p. 1). The rationale for this belief is the idea that the journalistic principle of remaining objective is a difficult standard to hold and a difficult expectation to achieve. "No human can be objective. Family, education, personal interests, religious, and political beliefs all influence how reporters cover stories and what stories they see as newsworthy" (Bender et al., 2009, p. 136). Opponents argue that regarding ethnic groups, there are no other groups

FIGURE 5.4   *Protests against Native American mascots.*

in American culture being portrayed as mascots. It is believed that other ethnic groups would not tolerate such a portrayal and would make public outcries of racism if a team were to take on a group's imagery for use as a mascot. Figure 5.4 is one snapshot of individuals who find mascots named after Native Americans offensive. Many activists make signs and banners in order to express disdain for teams named after their culture or that use symbols or other artifacts representing their customs and heritage. Is it possible that our culture accepts Native American images as mascots because this ethnic group is annihilated and forgotten in our media and culture, and has been banished to reservations? Thus teams using Native American mascots or logos (e.g.., tomahawks) are actually engaging in a standard that "exacerbates a tragic American legacy of government-sanctioned genocide, bigotry, racism, and economic and political deprivation against Native American tribes" (Beadle, 2002, p. 1).

The activist group known as the Native American Journalists Association (NAJA) have deemed Native American athletic imagery as "racist" and "offensive" (Locklear, 2009). In 2002, the NAJA began a campaign urging all news organizations to obstruct the use of mascots and nicknames depicting Native Americans (Locklear, 2009). In 1992, the editor of the *Oregonian* issued a statement that read, "The Oregonian will immediately discontinue using sports teams' names and nicknames that many Americans feel are offensive to members of racial, religious, or ethnic groups. Initially, this will include references to Redskins, Redmen, Indians, and Braves" (Jensen, 1994, p. 18). That news organization believed that those team names were actually perpetuating beliefs and stereotypes that have the potential to damage the dignity and self-esteem and self-respect of many indigenous people in our country (Jensen, 1994, p. 18). A year later, in 1993, the *Minneapolis Star Tribune* followed suit and discontinued using their platform to cover news about teams that relied on Native American mascots and imagery.

Himebaugh (1994) believes that sports journalists can use their venues to make changes in our culture. The scholar goes on to say that journalists can take steps to be purposive in the effort to eliminate stereotypes of Native Americans. Many organizations and journalists firmly believe that journalists need to spend time learning about the culture and the struggles that Natives face. He argues that journalists who believe the images honor the culture should spend time observing the Native American lifestyle in reservations, perhaps spending time trying to understand their customs, rituals, and religion. We find too many instances of media that cover stories about Native Americans who are often framed negatively and that focus on issues such as alcoholism or poverty. When some people are asked to identify what they know about Native American people, the most common answer to the question is that they are alcoholics and/or making money from casinos (Patterson, Welte, Barnes, Tidwell, & Spicer, 2015; personal communication, June 15, 2018). These are again notions that one can speculate are obtained because of frequent exposure to messages in media. However, it is believed that sports media can correct this overreporting of negative news by reporting on the more positive news that happens within that culture as well.

All in all, we know that as of this writing, Native Americans are starting to see significant progress regarding stereotypes of their culture in media. Many organizations and Native American journalists are starting to take actions that will help eliminate the stereotypes in media and increase portrayals and depictions of the group in national mainstream media. A case in point is the organization known as American Indians in Film. The main purpose of this group, which was organized by Sonny Skyhawk, is to "improve the image of Native Americans in motion pictures and television" (Himebaugh, 1994, p. 2).

If we were to summarize the preceding sections on Native American representations in media, we might conclude that indeed American media frequently promote racist thought and bias through stereotypical images and portrayals of Native Americans, particularly in American sports. We find that in terms of portrayals of Native Americans, the media promotes and perpetuates racism toward this group when they agree to use derogatory and offensive imagery in their messages. The use of Native American imagery should remind many of us of the struggles and difficulties that Native Americans have suffered through (refer to Figure 5.5). We should see those images and be reminded of the country that was taken from them and note that the freedoms that they once enjoyed are

FIGURE 5.5 *Washington Redskins: offensive or honorable?*

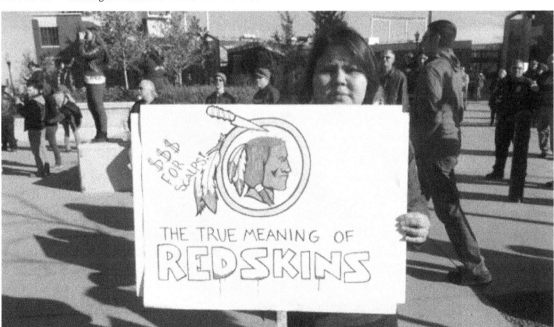

virtually gone. It is possible that the effects of the mascots that appropriate Native American culture and imagery covertly communicate messages to our society that it is "acceptable" to portray and think of Native Americans in a negative manner (Beadle, 2002).

Bender et al. (2015) believe that every time media uses the imagery in stories, it consequently encourages the demeaning and devaluing of Native Americans through their use of descriptive words or phrases, which, taken together, ultimately cast the group in a negative light.

To understand this argument better, we must once again consider both the framing and stereotype theories. Framing theory is used to explain, predict, and understand how people integrate new information into their prior belief systems, and it also helps us make sense of the world. Framing theory helps us understand arguments concerning the use of Native American athletic imagery for sports teams because if we review the news frames and the context by which all stories are written about Native Americans, it can be speculated that the frames would bring out negative ideas and thoughts about the group. Framing theory, when applied to the Native American culture, might also show that American culture will continue to view Native Americans in negative ways and continue to isolate them from positive media coverage and integration into our larger society.

Stereotype theory may also be applied to the discussion of Native American imagery in sports in that it "aids in understanding how the media help perpetuate certain clusters of belief about particular categories of people" (DeFeur & Dennis, 1994, p. 606). Concerning a study on sports and American culture, stereotype theory research concludes that media continuously perpetuate stereotypes of Native Americans through the use of Native American athletic imagery (DeFleur & Dennis, 2012). The use of Native American athletic mascots, nicknames, logos, and imagery is without a doubt a very delicate and emotional issue, and continues to remain controversial (Locklear, 2009).

Conclusion

In this chapter, we have provided research that centers on the way media may unintentionally help shape our attitudes, thoughts, opinions, and behaviors. Scholars in media effects and other disciplines often find evidence of racial and ethnic stereotyping in the way sports media portray male *and* female athletes. In today's modern era of technological advances, we know that people will and are paying attention to the media. Hence, the reason for the popularity of social media, and microblogging sites such as Twitter. So although media technology may continue to advance and evolve, media messages and content published will also need to change. Sports writers, editors, and producers must start addressing the unique differences in athletes and their content to appeal to the preferences of those in the multicultural audience. This means that writers, editors, and producers must engage in activities that allow them to challenge their prejudices and biases and determine how those biases play out in their writing or broadcasts. To sum up the information in this chapter, one might believe that sports media is racially insensitive. However, there are many obstacles we find in sports journalism that may also be responsible for the insensitive coverage.

Regarding stereotypes of athletes in media and their effect on other athletes, we must take a moment to discuss the NFL. In 2013, Richie Incognito allegedly engaged in negative behaviors toward Jonathan Martin by throwing the N-word around very casually in the locker room and cafeteria and using the degrading word on text and voice messages. While the Miami Dolphins suspended Incognito indefinitely for "detrimental conduct," his alleged behavior should be no surprise to anyone. Name-calling, trash-talking, racial and ethnic slurs, hazing and bullying in locker rooms, cafeterias, stadiums, or arenas are part of the sports culture and are often reflected in sports media. Disparaging monikers of athletes in the past and currently might be reflected in the culture of sports and the media. It is this culture of sports and the media that represent the culture that defines and shapes attitudes, and opinions of the greats can be construed unequivocally as ethnic slurs in today's world. This seems to be the message that Bladassaro (2005) seems to suggest in his early work on stereotypes of MLB players in his book *Beyond DiMaggio: Italian Americans in Baseball*). According to Baldassaro (2005), Italian Americans experiences with media in baseball mirrored the general experience of Italian Americans in society.

In a recent study published by the Institute for Diversity and Ethics in Sport, findings show that in terms of better and increased portrayals of minorities and women covering sports in America's news outlets, nothing has changed in over 10 years. According to the report published online by the Institute, the statistics are dismal in that approximately "90 percent of all sports editors are white, and an equal percentage are men" (Waldron, 2013). In the report, we find that of all the assistant editor, columnist, reporter, and copy editor jobs in sports, more than 85% of them are filled by white men (Waldron, 2013). The data obtained in the study that stands out is what happens to these data when ESPN is taken out of the equation. In the report, the researchers conducted a simple analysis to see what the employment numbers would look like if ESPN were taken *out* of the equation. When it comes to diversifying sports, ESPN is the leader in sports journalism according to the Institute's report. The report further shows that of the "12 people of color who are sports editors at media outlets (the largest newspapers and dot-coms, with a circulation of 175,000 or more), four work for ESPN, which employed two of the six African-American sports editors and two of the four Latino sports editors" (Bucholz, 2017). The report found that 11 women are currently serving as sports editors, but of those 11 women, ESPN employs six of them.

ESPN is a sports media with an incredible hiring policy, which can be found on its website (www.espn.com). ESPN is the recipient of numerous awards as a result of its hiring practices. In fact, ESPN has been noted for its diversity among writers, editors, and columnists. Women and minorities can be seen on the channel serving as hosts of sports shows, analysts, announcers, and field reporters.

Given the efforts of ESPN in trying to bridge the employment gap for women and minorities in sports journalism, we must ask the question, why is there a lack of minorities in sports journalism/media? Some argue that the disparity may be related to social and institutional obstacles that exist concerning access to higher educational institutions, academic programs, economics, or cost to attend school, as well as visibility of careers in journalism. A few minorities report negative experiences in their high schools in which they left with the idea that journalism is for writers, and they, in fact, are not good writers. Ultimately, young minorities do not think that a journalism degree will pave the way into the sports media world; they think that the degree will have them placed in rural "areas of dominant influence" or ADIs. Even if minorities want to pursue journalism and sports writing, it has been said that many young people of color do not believe that sports journalism is a job that is accessible to them or even a career that can be pursued. Some scholars and professors would argue that young people of color do not think of journalism as a career simply because the portrayals and depictions of minority reporters writing and talking about the sports are few and far between. The obstacles that stand in the way of diversifying sports journalism for people of color are also obstructing the way to the top for women interested in principle positions in sports journalism. We find that female sports journalists today still face stigmas when reporting on sports, especially when they cover men (Waldron, 2013).

Many obstacles that have stood in our way, as well as the misperceptions that are associated with women and people of color, seem to be slowly fading into the distant past. We owe much of these changes to diversity and inclusion changes, as well as developments that have been put in place by ESPN. ESPN has opened the door of opportunity for minority and female sports reporters by making these individuals, their jobs, and their positions in sports more prominent and highly visible (Waldron, 2013). While there are many other barriers that seem to be blocking both minorities and women from entering the world of sports journalism, we can continue to work in the area and show that despite the fact that these barriers still exist, media outlets must work together to break down the barriers preventing these changes.

QUESTIONS FOR REFLECTION AND DISCUSSION

1. Who are the most influential athletes? Who are the most influential African American, Latino(a), Native American, Middle Eastern, and Asian athletes? What makes them influential? Were some of the influential athletes in certain ethnic groups easier or harder to identify? Why or why not?

2. Flip through the pages of a national newspaper's sports section. Carefully read the stories about the sporting teams or athletes. What type of stories do you find? You may also compare the covers and content of top sporting magazines such as *Sports Illustration*. Are the groups mentioned in this chapter in the news and written stories?

3. Explain and analyze the concepts of portrayals of athletes as criminals, sexual objects, or regarding their attractiveness. Explore these concepts for a week in sports media. For example, look for news stories that highlight an athlete's philanthropic activities. Many athletes have foundations that seek to help vulnerable populations. Did you find news stories that focused on these athletes? Why or why not? Explain your answer and be sure to conclude with implications for sports media professionals.

4. Some people say that Native American mascot and imagery are issues of petty political correctness. What do you think they would say if a team created imagery and behaviors of their ethnicity? How would whites respond if a team of mostly marginalized groups created a mascot called "Whitey" or "Cracker?" What do you think would happen? Would a majority of people take a "well we did it to the Native Americans and now it is our turn" perspective? Why or why not?

5. As you recall, in Chapter 3, we discussed ethnic identity. How do you think sports are related to ethnicity? What role does the media play in aligning identity with sports and assimilation? Explain.

6. Should race or ethnicity matter in the reporting of accomplishments and athletic achievements? How can media do a better role, in particular, in the news stories of crime and athletes?

7. Could sports survive without the media or vice versa? Explain your answer.

8. What are the dilemmas for Middle Eastern women in sports? Review the pro-hijab Nike commercials. Why do you suppose some women opposed the ad while others celebrate their freedoms and appreciate the ad for sending inspirational messages to other women? What strategies might a sports journalist or advertiser use to continue the message set by Nike?

SUGGESTED ACTIVITIES

1. Take out a blank sheet of paper. Draw a picture of a Native American. Now look at your picture and determine where the image came from. Now think of how many friends or people you have come in contact with who are Native American. Make a list of their names. How many people do you know or have on your list? Do they fit the image you drew on the page? Think of the films and television shows you have viewed over the last few years. To what extent did the images come from your media exposure? Using symbolic annihilation as your theoretical foundation, write a short paper that portrays Native Americans and your honest and candid thoughts regarding this marginalized group. What does the controversy about the mascots and the theory of symbolic annihilation tell you about the state of affairs as they relate to Native Americans in today's culture?

2. Take a look at the website www.treatycouncil.org/about.htm. The website was created and is maintained by the International Indian Treaty Council, a nongovernmental organization whose goal is to support Native Americans in their fight against injustices. Spend some time visiting the site and reading the information provided. How effective do you think this website is regarding educating and informing people about Natives? How effective do you think it is in building awareness of Native American people? Does it address stereotypes effectively? How might the sports media incorporate the information provided in their stories?

3. Seek out a news story, old or present day, about the mascot or Native American controversy. Evaluate the story from a media literacy perspective. Also, if we as journalists are supposed to inform and educate, consider the effectiveness of the story and its ability to educate the reader.

4. Read a sports paper for an entire week. Look for stories about African American, Latino, Middle Eastern, Asian, and Pacific Islander athletes. Are there any stories about these athletes in your community? If so, what types of stories are they? Are there stories about prominent Hispanic/Latino athletes? Explain and discuss your findings.

5. Provide a coherent comprehension of the wide-ranging issues and debates that relate to sports and athletes from different races, ethnicity, and sexual identities. What are common themes in the issues as you see them, and how might you use your talents as a sports reporter or consumer of sports media to address these issues?

6. Find an athlete from one of the groups discussed in this book or chapter. Interview him or her and write a news story that might be used to help set the way for better stories about the group and the athlete.

CREDITS

Fig. 5.1: Source: https://www.youtube.com/watch?v=nlizoMDBG4E&t=98s.

Fig. 5.2: Source: https://commons.wikimedia.org/wiki/File:Emekizr.jpg.

Fig. 5.3: Source: https://commons.wikimedia.org/wiki/File:Noc-a-Homa_praying.JPG.

Fig. 5.4: Copyright © 2014 by Fibonacci Blue, (CC BY 2.0) at https://commons.wikimedia.org/wiki/File:NotYourMascot2.jpg.

Fig. 5.5: Source: https://www.bbc.com/news/magazine-30314290.

6

LGBTQ Athletes and Their Contributions to Sports

LEARNING OBJECTIVES

After completing this chapter, students should be able to:

- define and delineate terminology associated with sexual orientation and LGBTQ issues;

- address how people who identify themselves as lesbians, gays, bisexuals, transgender, and queer are represented in the media;

- explain the representations of the LGBTQ community in sports media;

- understand the role advocacy groups play in creating inclusive environments in sports;

- define and explain intersectionality and the complex relationship between race, gender, and sexual orientation.

Introduction

The purpose of this chapter is to understand and appreciate the history and effect that the LGBTQ group has had on the sports industry and sports media. The first athlete to "come out as gay" was Dave Kopay, a former running back for the San Francisco 49ers. Kopay retired from the NFL in 1972 and 3 years later made the choice to come out of the closet and share his sexual orientation in a *Washington Post* article. In the same year, professional tennis was introduced to the first transgender woman to play a professional sport. In 1975, Renée Richards, whom some would describe as a pioneer, filed suit against United States Tennis Association (USTA), which tried to prevent her from playing in the U.S. Open. In 1977, Dr. Richards (she is currently a practicing ophthalmologist) won the lawsuit and later went on to earn an induction into the "National Gay and Lesbian Sports Hall of Fame in 2013" (Bailey, 2015). While these events transpired more than 40 years ago, what makes this worth mention is the fact that before 1975, our culture did not know of any gay, transgender, bisexual, or lesbian athletes—and we know, of course, that there were some, but fear of coming out must have precluded them from making the announcements during this era.

Coming out during the 1970s in the midst of social and cultural upheavals meant that individuals who dared to do so would be ultimately labeled as immoral and filled with sin and would suffer through intense ridicule and discrimination. For example, in 1979, the women's head basketball coach at Penn State, Coach Rene Portland, implemented what is now known as the 25-year antilesbian campaign. Historical records show that the women's basketball coach consistently dismissed any player that she "thought" or perceived to be lesbian. Another example of the climate for individuals identifying as LGBTQ happened from 1976 to 1979. Glenn Burke, retired MLB player for the Los Angeles Dodgers and Oakland Athletics, was dismissed from the team because of his sexual orientation. Burke was "the first and only MLB player to come out of the closet and publicly acknowledge that he was gay during his career" (Stern, K., 2009, p. 78).

In 1981, Billie Jean King initially denied that she was lesbian. However, despite this, she was removed from all of her commercial sponsorships. In the same year, historical records of LGBTQ athletes and sports show that a *New York Post* article "outed" Martina Navratilova—a tennis champion who worried about what the article and outing would do to her career. Coming out publicly and making an acknowledgment that one is an LGBTQ athlete came with a price and led to missed opportunities that extended beyond playing in sports, not to mention lost profits from commercial endorsements. During the '70s and '80s, it is safe to assume that Americans were simply not prepared mentally to accept the notion that athletes might identify their sexual orientation in a way other than the traditional heterosexual orientation.

"Transgender" was not even in the vocabulary during the 1970s or '80s. It was in the late '80s that a few states started to create laws that would prohibit any individual from being discriminated against on the basis of his or her sexual orientation. The state of Wisconsin was the first to enact such a law, and it was the only state with such protections until 1989 when Massachusetts became the second state to prohibit discrimination by sexual orientation.

Times have changed in America since the 1970s and 1980s such that portrayals and representations of the LGBTQ community have greatly increased. In terms of sports, we have seen a rise in the number of LGBTQ athletes who are choosing to come out of the closet (see Chapter 3). As was the case with Michael Sam, we find that even teammates and coaches are becoming more and more supportive of athletes who identify as LGBTQ. Also, media and other Internet sites publish news and positive messages regarding LGBTQ individuals and their inclusion in sports. *Outsports*, an Internet sports media magazine, also serves as an advocate for LGBTQ individuals and seeks a way to allow sports fans to interact with LGBTQ athletes. The NCAA has also started providing programs and resources to school athletic departments that educate their college athletes about this community of individuals. The NCAA sends out educational materials and resources that touch on diversity topics, including defining terms, gender identity, and sexual orientation.

In the new millennium, many heterosexual male athletes are speaking up and speaking out publicly against anti-LGBTQ hate crimes, bias, prejudices, and discriminatory actions. Many heterosexual athletes are currently using their voices to talk about the consequences of bullying, teasing, and violence toward LGBTQ individuals. Heterosexual athletes are also serving as advocates for same-sex marriage and for the inclusion of LGBTQ athletes and coaches who are out on sports teams. For example, Steve Nash and Sean Avery have joined forces to serve as pioneers and advocates "speaking out publicly about their support for LGBTQ people in and out of the sport" (Cunningham, 2015). Other professional sports teams, such as the Boston Red Sox, Chicago Cubs, and San Francisco Giants, have joined forces and shared their talents to prevent LGBTQ youth from committing suicide. The "It Gets Better" YouTube video shows inspirational and uplifting stories, and seeks to positively affect the lives of lesbian, gay, bisexual, transgender, and queer youth.

Definitions and Terminology

Language in media interviews or presentations is an important area of study for a sports journalist. (Most definitions were retrieved from the following sources: Carleton College Physical Education, 2018; Human Rights Campaign, 2018; other definitions obtained from additional sources will be listed after the definition of the term.)

Biological/Anatomical Sex   The Planned Parenthood website defines biological/anatomical sex as those "physical characteristics typically used to assign a person's gender at birth, such as chromosomes, hormones, internal and external genitalia and reproductive organs" (Planned Parenthood, 2018).

Bisexual   An individual who is not only physically attracted to both sexes but also sexually attracted to both men and women.

Coming Out   A term used in America that expresses when an individual acknowledges and makes known to others his or her sexual orientation and gender identity. Coming out also defines the moment when the person begins to acknowledge and accept his or her sexual orientation or gender identity.

Cisgender   An individual whose gender identity matches the sex assigned at birth.

Cross-dresser   A person who likes to wear the clothes of the "opposite" sex. In terms of their sexual orientation and gender identity, cross-dressers are completely satisfied with their assigned sex and gender identity. Cross-dressers simply like to pander to their opposing side, either masculine or feminine. Most cross-dressers do so because they, according to Ryan (2015) "want to dress and represent the gender he/she admires, is excited by, loves. Some believe that for male cross-dressers, dressing like a woman is merely a dramatic is a way for them to understand, learn more about, and get closer to the "experiences of the sex one is profoundly curious about" (Ryan, 2015). Research on this group reveals that even if a cross-dresser fantasizes about being transformed into the gender, they are not interested in or seriously considering making a transformation for the rest of their lives.

Gay   Individuals who are attracted physically and sexually to the same biological sex.

Gender   A socially constructed term that depicts the relationship between one's biological sex and the link to one's self-perceptions of who one is and what it means to be a man, woman, both, or neither (Planned Parenthood, 2018). This is a term that defines how we are expected to act. Recall that socially constructed terms involve a society's/culture's set of expectations about behaviors, characteristics, and thoughts. American culture has definite standards about the way that people should act and think based on gender. Research in this area informs us that when classifying a person's gender, one must rely on noticeable physical features. An example of the tangible cues that we use to classify a person's gender includes behaviors that link the outward appearance with the self-perception of a person's gender identity. As we stated in Chapter 2 of this text, biological sex and gender identity are different constructs in that gender identity is not connected to a person's physical anatomy.

Gender Expression   How people express and communicate gender identity to others. Expression of gender identity is made through the way we act, the way we dress, how we wear our hair, our language and vocal tone and expression, and other nonverbal forms of self-presentation. Gender expression also involves the "looking glass self," which is basically the notion that we behave according to how others view gender. We adjust our expression and behaviors to match the ideas that others have about appropriate mannerisms, appearance, and other characteristics regarding men and women.

Gender Identity   Describes the feelings we have about being a male, female, both, or neither and how you act and express them. "One's gender identity can be the same or different than the sex assigned at birth" (Human Rights Campaign, 2018).

Gender Roles   Vary by culture and are used to describe a culture's expectations about actions, cognitions, effects, and physical characteristics that "should" be consistent with one's assigned sex.

Genderqueer (also see queer)   Can be understood as the merger of two other constructs: gender identity and sexual orientation. Individuals identifying as genderqueer typically do not accept society's gender roles and fixed binary categories of gender; instead, they are known to adopt a more flexible idea of gender identity and sexual orientation.

Hypersexuality   Describes an individual who overstates and is over the top in terms of clothing (or lack of) and his or her emphasis on body parts.

In the Closet   Also referred to as "closeted," it is a term that depicts an LGBTQ person who has not publicly revealed his or her sexual identity, orientation, or gender identity.

Intersex   Someone who is born with various combinations of male and female genitals, and different combinations of X and Y chromosomes. Intersex is often referred to in the medical profession as a disorder of sex development (DSD). People with intersex conditions (DSD) are born with physically mixed or atypical bodies in regard to sexual characteristics (e.g., chromosomes, internal reproductive organs, and genitalia; PEAR Equity Committee, 2014).

Lesbian   Typically applied and used when describing women who are physically and sexually attracted to other women.

Outing   Situations when a person's gender identity is revealed to others without their permission. In American culture, when a person is outed, he or she might experience serious consequences that relate to jobs (e.g., recall the scenario when athletes were excused from participating in teams), personal safety (e.g., hate crimes and bullying), and religious or family situations (e.g., being denounced from a denomination and/or family).

Sex   Identified at birth and based on the genitals and chromosomes we are born with. A person's sex goes on the official birth certificate.

Sexual Orientation   Describes one's romantic and/or sexual attraction toward others.

Transgender   An "individual whose gender identity does not match" his or her biological sex. Some transmen and women identify as female to male (FTM) or male to female (MTF), or don't identify as trans at all (PEAR Equity Committee, 2014).

Transition   "A person's process of developing and assuming a gender expression to match their gender identity," which includes coming out to those around him or her, changing his or her name, and sometimes hormone therapy and/or surgical procedures (PEAR Equity Committee, 2014).

Transsexual   Individuals who may or may not undergo transformational "surgery and hormone therapy to obtain a physical appearance typical of the gender they identify with." The term is mostly considered outdated, although some people do still identify with it (GLBT Resource Center of Michiana, 2018).

*For more on transgender, watch the YouTube video published by Asphodel (2014) titled *The Difference Between Transgender and Transsexual*, https://youtu.be/DkFkrHR7FyQ).

Advocacy Groups for LGBTQ Athletes

The Gay Lesbian Straight Education Network (GLSEN), a national advocacy group whose mission is to make kindergarten through 12th grade schools safe and respectful for LGBTQ youth (GLSEN, 2018). The most fascinating and exciting part of the Changing the Game project is that game changers on the site are not all LGBTQ. This is a project that shows people from all different backgrounds, different ethnicities, and different sexual orientations coming together to provide resources and support for those working in K–12 athletic environments to create a "safe and respectful place for athletes of all sexual orientations and gender identities/expressions" (GLSEN, 2018).

In August of 2011, the NCAA released a set of recommendations and best practices for colleges and universities to include transgender athletes on their sports teams. This resource guides NCAA athletic programs on how to ensure and create an atmosphere in which transgender student-athletes feel respected and given equal opportunities to participate in their sport of choice (NCAA, 2018).

August 5, 2011. This date is significant because it is the day that the NFL passed a policy that will be in effect until 2021. The NFL policy established in 2011 asserts that discrimination against any player on the bases of race, ethnicity, religion, or sexual orientation will not be tolerated (NCAA, 2018).

According to the NFL website, this policy was enacted with the hope that it can open doors to the acceptance of the gay community and, in particular, homosexual NFL players and for more players to feel comfortable in coming out before retirement.

MLB joined forces with three organizations in July 2013 when it strengthened its antidiscrimination policy (www.mlb.com). Bud Selig, then commissioner of MLB and the league's Players Association, along with New York City's attorney general Eric Schneiderman, worked together to enact a policy for LGBTQ athletes. The new policy enhanced the initial one established in 2011 by creating a code of conduct and a focus on training and educational programs. In addition, the enhanced policy written in 2013 provides specific "guidelines for athletes to report and address harassment and discrimination while playing in the MLB" (Green, 2015). The new harassment and discrimination policy put into action a code of conduct that was distributed to every major and minor league player while also creating training and education programs for MLB athletes. The policy spells out specific guidelines for reporting and dealing with harassment and discrimination, according to the Associated Press (AP).

Following the example of the NFL and MLB, the NBA added sexual orientation to its nondiscrimination policy. The policy includes protections based on sexual orientation and is designed for gay male pro basketballers. The 2000s have also seen an increase in activist organizations whose missions are to focus on reducing and even eliminating anti-LGBTQ bullying and other practices in sports. Many of these nonprofit organizations seek to make a concerted effort to include heterosexual athletes so that they can help create an image of sports that is respectful and safe for all LGBTQ athletes who make decisions to come out during their professional careers. These organizations also offer support to those LGBTQ athletes who are receiving widespread media attention. Nonprofit organizations such as "Athlete Ally, founded by Hudson Taylor, the Ben Cohen Stand Up Foundation, and Patrick Burke's You Can Play Project, are just some of the non-profit organizations that are being led by straight male athlete allies" (Cunningham, 2011a, 2011b, 2011c).

Addressing Challenges

Some important challenges need to be highlighted as we talk about the growth of the LGBTQ sports equality movement. For example, when we say we accept an individual who identifies with the LGBTQ, do we mean it?

A current challenge to our culture's acceptance of LGBTQ athletes involves transgender athletes. For example, Caitlyn Jenner (see Figure 6.1), once known to the world as Bruce Jenner, a former gold-medal-winning track and field star, challenged our culture's fixed ideas about the ways males and females are supposed to think, feel, and act. In fact, when Caitlyn Jenner made a national

FIGURE 6.1   *Caitlyn Jenner interviewing for LGBT rights for Human Rights Day, December 10, 2015*

appearance on ABC in 2016, we found people in our culture were captivated by the broadcast—a media event that allowed Americans to understand something that didn't make sense in terms of their view of clear distinctions of gender. A world-record holder in the decathlon at the 1976 Summer Olympics, Bruce Jenner went from athlete to reality TV star in the MTV show *Keeping Up with the Kardashians.* Jenner revealed her identity as a transwoman in 2015 (Pilkington, 2015), when she appeared on the cover of *Vanity Fair.* Jenner's coming out story became a national news sensation when we learned the deep psychological turmoil and struggle that the most beloved male track star of the 1970s identifies as woman and would like to be known as Caitlyn.

To understand the significance of this historical event, we will offer a brief synopsis of Caitlyn's history. In the early 1970s, Bruce Jenner was the popular and well-loved athlete of the decade. Jenner was diagnosed with dyslexia and, as a result, struggled in school at a young age yet was able to excel in sports. A college injury while playing football forced Jenner to turn his interest in athletics to track and field. It was during her college years that Jenner's track coach sparked the desire and passion to train for the Olympics. Then in 1972, during the Olympic trials, Bruce Jenner landed in third place and went on to place 10th in the Munich Games (Biography.com, 2018). In February of 2015, the media began producing stories that suggested that the beloved Olympic athlete known to many as Bruce Jenner was actually transgender. Tabloid media and other national news coverage began showing images of Jenner that depicted gradual changes in Jenner's physical appearance.

Despite speculations, it was two months later, in April 2015, that Jenner appeared in an exclusive TV interview with Diane Sawyer on ABC's *20/20.* During the highly rated broadcast, viewers watched intensely as Caitlyn Jenner described her history identifying with the female sex. Viewers were also introduced to the idea of using appropriate gender-based pronouns, such as "he" when referring to Bruce Jenner, and "she" when referring to Caitlyn. The ABC telecast demonstrated how American viewers received the transition from MTF in delicate stories about when Caitlyn first noticed discrepancies in her sexual orientation and the emotional agony of feeling one way inside and physically appearing as a different gender on the outside. The 2015 broadcast has been used as an example of the role media can play in educating consumers about concepts that are new or complex. Viewers were able to sympathize with Caitlyn when she provided details of her life-long history with her sexual orientation and the emotional experience of talking to her children about the transition (Biography, 2018).

Caitlyn Jenner's transition was challenging for some in our society, but journalists struggled as well. Even for journalists who felt confident writing about transgender people, the stories relating to Bruce Jenner's gender identity were awkward. To make sure journalists reported the story correctly, the National Lesbian and Gay Journalist Association (NLGJA) distributed an open letter to journalists who might be covering Caitlyn Jenner's personal story. In the letter, the association dealt with the idea that newsrooms would have many questions concerning the appropriate way to write and publish stories about transgender individuals. In an attempt to provide resources to help newsrooms prepare and write better stories, they gave advice on how to word descriptions and use pronouns so that coverage would be fair and accurate.

"We are not an advocacy group. Our mission is to ensure fair and accurate coverage of issues that affect the lesbian, gay, bisexual and transgender (LGBTQ) communities" (ACES, 2018). For news editors with questions about their coverage of transgender individuals, the stylebook published by the NLGJA offers detailed guidelines for media professionals to help them with rules regarding when and how to use pronouns and correct terminology. The open letter informs journalists that transgender individuals should first be asked which gender and pronoun they identify with, and then the journalist is to use the name and the gender they identify with and prefer. For some journalists, the issue was more on the use of he/she pronouns. When do we use "he," or when do we use "she" and vice versa? The NLGJA provided journalists with a section of their stylebook that references pronoun usage. The rule is as follows:

"If a source shares a transgender or gender-nonconforming identity, it is best practice to ask for preferred pronouns," according to the NLGJA. The site also warns journalists to avoid assumptions about the individual's transgender status. It even suggests that journalists should avoid the topic of transgender, particularly if it is not germane to the story (refer to ACES, 2018, https://aceseditors.org/news/2015/resources-for-editing-stories-on-transgender-individuals).

Of special note, the NLGJA advised journalists that when they are writing about events before the transition to a different gender, the journalist should avoid mixing pronouns within their story. According to the NLGJA, using different pronouns ("he" or "she") in one story is ultimately confusing to the reader and the only way that a journalist can avoid the confusion is to use the person's first name at the time, use the last name as appropriate, or use a structure that explains the timeline.

If the subject's pronoun preference is not known, the NLGJA suggests one way to make the story more accurate: Avoid pronoun use altogether. According to its stylebook, the absence of a pronoun does not disrupt the flow or accuracy of the story. Note: Refer to the release of the *Vanity Fair* article on Caitlyn Jenner (Pilkington, 2015; Toomey & Machado, 2015). Interested journalists and copy editors can find ways to review their style and provide tips on how to discuss style issues with clients.

This example was provided from the *AP Stylebook* on how to report transgender in news stories:

"Brooklyn Alexander, formerly known as Chandler Alexander, came out as transgender last week. In a statement, Alexander said she had felt this way since childhood. Alexander grew up in Missouri. In middle school, Alexander was described as being very outspoken in class about social issues and public policies, gender rules, friends said. She remains to this day to be extremely outspoken about her beliefs" (The Associated Press Stylebook, 2018).

Sports, Sexism, Female Athletes, and Homophobia

Some sports journalists have written about homophobia in the NCAA and describe it as "the elephant in the room" (Buzinski, 2017), particularly for women's basketball. In a March 2017 story on women college coaches, the *New York Times* ran a story on Dawn Staley, the South Carolina head coach who hired an assistant head coach who happens to be lesbian. The story that ran in the *New York Times* did not go into detail or specifics about the assistant head coach's sexual orientation, which left some to speculate that lesbian basketball athletes are something men in the industry have been aware of and written about for a long time and that we just don't talk about it. And while it is speculated that there may be several lesbian coaches in women's college basketball, only two head coaches have "come out" publicly: woman's head basketball coach at Vanderbilt Stephanie White and La Verne (California) head coach Julie Shaw (Buzinski, 2017).

Homophobia, the intolerance of lesbian, gay, bisexual, intersexed, and transgender people (Adams, Bell, & Griffin, 2007; Spijkerber, 2013), is deeply rooted in the idea that any sexual orientation outside of heterosexuality is immoral and deviant. Homophobia supports negative feelings of prejudice, acts of discrimination and harassment, and hate crimes aimed at any individual who identifies with or is perceived to be nonheterosexual. Homophobia in sports is powerful and often is one cultural notion that prevents individuals from playing certain sports. In fact, research on this barrier in sports reveals that homophobia, both blatant and subtle, is still used as a recruiting tool in many college women's sports. Female head coaches tend to be fired (or overlooked in the collective pool of qualified job candidates) simply because of judgments based on physical features that may be perceived as lesbian or that they may actually be lesbian. For female athletes in a male-dominated world like sports, sexual orientation and fear of being labeled a lesbian, or even fear of being associated with lesbians, led many women to avoid certain sports, such as basketball and, ultimately, de-emphasize their interest and athletic skill(s) to participate in a sport.

Female athletes who are not yet out of the closet may fear being outed, and this fear affects their ability to relate to teammates. The fear is real for many female athletes in that those assumed to be lesbian based on physical attributes or even the female athletes who are lesbians find that contracts are terminated, they are released from participation on teams, or the time allowed to compete or participate in their sport is devalued, reduced, or even diminished (Krane, 1996; Krane, 2001; Krane & Barber, 2005; Krane, Barber, & McClung, 2002; Plymire & Forman, 2000). Female athletes and head coaches are under great pressure to engage in behaviors that express their femininity and heterosexuality. This pressure often serves as a defense mechanism to guard against homophobia from fans and managers and the act of discrimination that often accompanies homophobia. For women athletes, the climate and fear aligned with homophobia mandate that American culture intentionally include women's sports and LGBTQ athletes in advocacy efforts for diversity and inclusion. In 2013, WNBA star Brittney Griner made history and was deemed a trailblazer when she came out of the closet and announced, just before the WNBA's draft, that she identified herself as a lesbian.

To combat negative press and the idea that the WNBA is a sport consisting solely of lesbian players, the organization started offering "makeup" classes. The makeup classes are part of the WNBA's orientation training. The purpose of the classes is to teach the female basketball players how to apply makeup and create feminine hairstyles, as well as to offer fashion tips on what to wear to various events—all designed to increase the perception that these are feminine athletes and to support our culture's norm of what it means to be female and how women should and should not act. Basically, the idea of the two-day orientation training sessions is to teach the women basketball players that they are females first and athletes second. This "makeup" training was implemented in 2012 by the WNBA with help from the WNBA Players Association, which wants players to recognize the importance of dressing professionally and displaying a physically attractive appearance off the court. Therefore, the motivation behind the orientation and makeup sessions is to provide female basketball players with the specific grooming skills needed to present themselves as feminine professionals when they appear in public and are off the court.

To help the athletes "dress the part of being female," fashion experts and hair and makeup stylists provide resources and workshops disseminating a plethora of facts that can be used to help the athletes prepare for media attention. This event is often held just before the WNBA draft, which is nationally televised on ESPN (see WNBPA, 2012). After learning all of the "how-to's and what-not-to-do's in the areas of wardrobe, shoes, accessories, makeup application, hair styling, and even undergarments," the athletes are given an opportunity to apply what they learned (WNBPA, 2012). Female basketball players receive manicures, learn how to apply makeup, and have one-on-one fittings for bras. To ensure that every female basketball player in the WNBA benefits from these workshops, they are each assigned their very own personal stylist. The personal stylist is given the task of preparing their "draft day look" (WNBPA, 2012). The stylists help the athletes understand how to flatter their figures better and improve their appearance. Perhaps this is a way of addressing the elephant in the room and using the workshop to combat the stereotype that the WNBA is "a bunch of lesbians playing basketball."

Reflect on Sports: Gay Female Head Coaches in Basketball

In 2016, the head coach of the WNBA's Indiana Fever, Stephanie White, was recruited and hired to serve as "head coach of Vanderbilt University's women's basketball team" (Buzinski, 2016). Coach White happens to be married to a woman. Together, the couple has three children. As previously mentioned, homophobia has long been a problem in women's basketball, making Coach White's hiring incredibly significant. White is open about her sexual orientation and has been an outspoken advocate for same-sex marriage for several years. This head coach does not hide who she is, which, unlike other coaches, is a rare phenomenon; many of the lesbian coaches feel that they cannot come out publicly and choose to stay "in the closet." Coach White and the media attention given to her recent hire may be used to influence other coaches and fans about their notions concerning gay female head coaches.

At the time the gender equity law, a subsection of Title IX, was enacted in 1972, women were "head coaches of more than 90 percent of women's college teams across two dozen sports" (Longman, 2017). However, as of 2017, the total number of female head coaches has declined to less than 40%. And if we explore the number of female head coaches for men's teams, we would find an even staggering number—only 3% of women coaches are presently serving as head coaches for male sports teams. Disparities in women head coaches, upper management, and leadership at the university level show that "80 percent of college athletic directors are men" (Longman, 2017). If we were to conduct research to determine who is the most successful head coach in women's college basketball, we might be surprised to learn that that person is male. As of 2018, we learned that "Coach Geno Auriemma of Connecticut has won 111 consecutive games and is seeking its fifth consecutive national title—and 12th overall" (Longman, 2017).

Coming Out as a Gay Athlete

Collin Martin, a professional Major League Soccer player, who recently announced that he is gay (Rhodes, 2018). According to the news coverage, Martin is one of two professional soccer players to come out and play as gay. While Robbie Rogers was the first to come out in 2013, Martin is the "only openly gay active player in any major pro sports league in the U.S." (Rhodes, 2018).

In August of 2018, the Chicago Cubs hosted "Out at Wrigley" as a way to show support for the LGBTQ group (Grant, 2018). However, the crowd expressed disdain and could be heard booing because of one player, Daniel Murphy, who has been outspoken about being against the "gay lifestyle." Cub fans were upset that owners signed Murphy knowing his attitude toward LGBTQ individuals. Despite that, the owners, Laura and Tom Ricketts, took time out to visit the LGBTQ fans seated in the stadium and candidly answered questions they had about them signing the player.

In August of 2018, racewalker Anthony Peters came out as gay on social media. In an article written by Peters (2018), he stated, "The responses I got were powerful and accepting." Unlike the response Murphy, an antigay athlete, received, fans and individuals alike took time to reply to Peter's post with comments that, according to him, were "empowering" and "supportive" (Peters, 2018).

The fear of homophobia, losing a job, or loss of playing time for female athletes leads to an environment that fosters a "don't-ask-don't-tell" type of atmosphere. Research on sexual orientation in sports tends to suggest that homophobia and the perception that one will be treated as an outcast is speculated to be the thing that keeps many LGBTQ athletes, coaches, and advocates in the closet. Although in very recent years, our American sports culture has witnessed enthusiastically positive support from fans and the public for those LGBTQ athletes who come out of the closet. College athletes who have chosen to come out of the closet since 2016 are as follows: "former Missouri football player Michael Sam, UMass men's basketball player Derrick Gordon, and Purdue women's basketball player Bree Horrocks, it does appear that gay men and women in sports must also navigate homophobia" (Ryan, 2017).

Interestingly, homophobia in sports offers new situations for these athletes to endure. Take for example stereotypes about female athletes. For some reason, lesbian athletes seem to create a sort of fear with head coaches in that they are often unsure how their fans and public will perceive them and their program. In today's culture, it does appear that when a gay athlete comes out publicly to his team, consider for example Michael Sam's experience coming out to his Missouri teammates and coaches, we witness the idea that neither fans nor consumers of the media messages related to Sam walked away with the perception that if Michael Sam is gay then the entire team must be gay. So why do sports fans assume that the entire WNBA consists of lesbian players? In American sports culture, we can speculate that for female lesbian athletes, it is more of a risk to come out, and if you do, you risk having the entire team becoming "guilty by association." Thus female lesbian athletes not only have to be concerned and fearful of what will happen to them but also worried about how their teammates will be perceived—a phenomenon commonly associated with female athletes in the WNBA. These examples of lesbians show that the stakes involved are much different for gay female athletes when compared to gay male athletes.

Rene Portland, the former Penn State women's head basketball coach, was known to have a "no lesbians" policy for decades. Portland ultimately resigned in 2007 after a former player filed a lawsuit that was settled out of court. Lisa Howe, the women's soccer coach for the University of Tennessee agreed to resign in 2010 after telling her players she and her partner of 8 years were expecting a baby (Yates, 2010). Lisa Howe, coach of the women's soccer team, signed a confidentiality agreement with Belmont University in 2016 that prohibits her from speaking specifically about her parting with the university (maxs, 2010; Yates, 2010). Gay female athletes need straight allies and other lesbian coaches to find the courage to speak out. But a significant, long-lasting culture change that makes lesbian coaches feel safe in coming out must be implemented by top sports administrators, who are typically straight men. And it should be noted that progress is being made.

The University of Minnesota's Tucker Center for Research on Girls and Women in Sport conducted a study in 2016 focused on addressing the number of (or lack of) female head coaches in sports. Researchers found that the number of female head coaches was dependent on the sport. Data obtained in this study conducted in 2016 showed that the sports with the highest percentage of female head coaches for women's teams were field hockey, lacrosse, golf, equestrian, and softball. These sports received the highest accolades for having the most female head coaches in the "American Athletic Conference, the Atlantic Coast Conference, the Big 12, the Big East, the Big Ten, the Pacific-12 and the Southeastern Conferences" (Longman, 2017). In terms of women's basketball, the report revealed that the sport had as many as 53 female head coaches. In other words, out of 86 universities included in the study, women's basketball has the highest percentage of female coaches.

However, that "percentage of female coaches dropped to 61.6 percent from 64 percent in 2015–16. Of the eight head coaches hired in 2016–17, two were men who replaced women" (Longman, 2017). To address these statistics, the Women's Basketball Coaches Association developed a workshop called So You Want to Be a Coach. The workshop is targeted and designed for graduating female basketball players, and the purpose is to raise awareness and encourage them to seek opportunities to serve as head coaches for women's sports.

Intersectionality: Race, Racism, Sexism, and LGBTQ Athletes

Now let's consider examples of intersectionality in sports. An athlete who is gay faces homophobia, and an athlete who is black faces racism. An athlete who is black and gay faces both, and it's common that the athlete will have to deal with "racism inside the LGBT community and homophobia in the black community. Similarly, a disabled lesbian Muslim will have to deal with ableism, homophobia, Islamophobia, racism, and sexism. She might find physical barriers to accessing LGBT venues, but even when she can get into the building, she might still face racism and Islamophobia from the white LGBT community." Having intersectional identities, research shows, often results in the individual feeling that he or she does not fully belong in one of the groups or another. This confusion of feelings might eventually "lead to isolation, depression and other mental health issues" (Equality Network, 2018).

A search on the Internet revealed that the term "intersectionality" was first credited to an American civil rights advocate named Kimberlé Williams Crenshaw. According to research, intersectionality is a term that depicts the overlap among social identities. Some define intersectionality as the various ways that our social identities intersect. Intersectionality purports that our multiple identities intersect to create an entire identity or sense of self that differs from individual identities. When we talk about individual identities, we are talking about identities that relate to "gender, race, social class, ethnicity, nationality, sexual orientation, religion, age, mental disability, physical disability, mental illness, and physical illness" (Institute of Medicine, 2006). From a theoretical perspective, intersectionality argues that traditional operationalizations of social constructs, such as homophobia, sexism, classism, racism, ableism, and xenophobia, are not mutually exclusive. We find that in lieu of acting independently, these social constructs interrelate or intersect to create multiple forms of discrimination. Intersectional identities often come with their own set of oppression, domination, and discrimination.

As previously stated, some female athletes are often viewed negatively as exhibiting traditionally masculine behavior (e.g., women basketball players). Assertive females are often disliked and referred to as "bitches," while assertive male leaders gain respect, for instance. However, could this distaste for assertive females vary by race (Miller, 2016)?

Unlike white women, African American women are often stereotyped as being assertive, confident, and not very feminine. Chapter 7 of this text further explores this issue by discussing how media portray Serena Williams. But for now, we must recognize that sports have the power to magnify and bring to the forefront some of the most significant challenges. Sports in America have the venue to showcase gifted female athletes, many of whom are inspiring role models. Sports media has the potential to bring these gifted players to the forefront and create a positive effect on society by highlighting their captivating stories of successes, failures, challenges, and other related life stories. To illustrate this point, we conducted a search of a few undeniable, brilliant female athletes of color. We found, for example, "Kadeena Cox, Sarah Storey, Ruqsana Begum, Kate Richardson-Walsh and Jessica Ennis-Hill" listed on a website that informs us that "each of these women are all unequivocally phenomenal female athletes" (Moore, 2017). Yet these athletes have each experienced discrimination and negative experiences in terms of some aspect of their identity. We find that each of the earlier listed athletes experienced some form of "phobia" as it related to their sexual orientation, race/ethnicity, ableism, or xenophobia (Moore, 2017).

Intersectionality is a very important concept when we consider the role it plays in helping us understand issues of diversity and inclusion within a sport. Intersectionality is used to offer insights concerning where and how exclusion from a sport can be challenged. Intersectionality also aids in the identification of realistic and practical opportunities for an individual's access to sport. For example, intersectionality can be used to help us understand and relate to the experience of a young African American girl who aspires to be a successful athlete when she grows up but who happens to come from a low socioeconomic background, may identify as a bisexual, lives with a physical challenge, and has a passion for playing basketball. If we want this aspiring young athlete to gain access to a sport she loves and is committed to, it is imperative that we become aware of and recognize and understand all of the obstacles she will face. We must begin to determine how each of the intersecting identities serve as barriers impeding her access to participate in the sport she loves.

According to research on girls and sports, before they turn 14, girls are dropping out of sports at twice the dropout rate of boys. Factors that have been found to encourage this attrition rate include "social stigma, lack of access, safety and lack of positive role models" (Moore, 2017). The barriers affecting attrition are enhanced for girls when gender and race intersect with socioeconomic status and disability. We also find heightened effects to the barriers when it comes to the dress code for a sport, poor or inappropriate coaching, lack of equipment and other resources, discrimination and prejudice limiting access to training centers, and lack of inclusive practices.

Research from Sporting Equals (2017) shows that "Asian and Black females have the lowest participation rates in some sports (34.3% and 33.9%, respectively), compared to White females 40.8%" (Moore, 2017). If we consider the intersectionality of gender and religion, we find that Muslim female athletes are the group with the most minuscule sports participation rate (25.1%), particularly when the rate is compared to those who do not identify with one religion (51.8%) (Moore, 2017). Only when we understand intersectionality among constructs such as gender identity, ethnicity, culture, religion, and social status will we begin to generate strategies that will genuinely lead to broader participation in sport by men and women of all backgrounds.

When we think of issues of intersectionality in the current climate, what comes to mind is Colin Kaepernick's "take a knee" silent protest of police brutality toward young black men in America. Kaepernick, in an attempt to bring awareness to the number of black youth being killed at the hands of white police officers, chose to kneel when the national anthem was performed during the pregame ritual. Yet historical records show that this silent protest is not the first to be held by professional athletes. More than 20 years before the NFL silent take a knee protest focused on racial injustice and patriotism happened in our culture, we learned of an NBA player named Mahmoud Abdul-Rauf, who also found himself in the midst of a media scandal regarding his protest of the national anthem. In fact, Abdul-Rauf was in the midst of a similar controversy when he engaged in a protest that involved sitting during the anthem to protest the treatment of those who followed the religion of Islam. Both Kaepernick and Abdul-Rauf believe the national anthem and the American flag are aligned with our country's history of tyranny and oppression toward people of color. What has happened in both instances is what some have termed a public fiasco and massive public relations challenge for sports promoters. Abdul-Rauf, who protested similarly to Kaepernick, was also blacklisted from the NBA. At the time of this writing, it is presumed that Kaepernick has also been blacklisted from playing in the NFL. Despite similarities between Abdul-Rauf and Kaepernick's method of protest, we find that Abdul-Rauf's strong identification with the religion of Islam specifically added another dimension of cultural controversy. Records show that the intersectionality of gender and religion actually prevented Abdul-Rauf's activist message from spreading. Figure 6.2 is a depiction of Abdul-Rauf's silent protest during the national anthem. Although the athlete was actually standing during the anthem, he still received backlash for engaging in a protest involving the treatment of those who follow the teachings of Islam.

FIGURE 6.2   *Mahmoud Abdul-Rauf*

In the '90s, athletes were not widely known to serve as activists or extremists, or to be interested in politics. Early in 2016, Michael Jordan decided to use his platform to issue an open statement condemning racial injustices that were happening among police officers and the black community. It was then that Jordan announced his $2 million donation to establishments that were interested in addressing our culture's problem with injustices based on race. He was also interested in financially offering support to organizations that focused on social justice. This meant that civic organizations that rose up in 2016, such as Black Lives Matter, found support from high-profile athletes such as Jordan and others who found a platform that allowed them to express themselves more freely without threatening the success of their athletic professional careers. While Kaepernick has retained all of his endorsements, some feel that his activism hurt his professional career. Unlike Kaepernick, Abdul-Rauf was denounced and attacked by national sports media. Kaepernick, on the other hand, has been perceived to garner encouragement, support, and, to some extent, anger and resentment in the media.

In the last two years, we have seen a resurgence of professional athletes using their platforms to raise awareness about racial injustices. For example, NBA professional superstars Dwyane Wade, LeBron James, Carmelo Anthony, and Chris Paul appeared on the stage of the ESPY awards show to not only show their solidarity against racial injustice but also to bring awareness to the sports media and fans of their mission to end gun violence in our society. These superstar athletes had a message they wanted the world to hear. What they shared was something in their hearts and the hearts of many in America: a reaction to the shootings in Florida, Louisiana, Minnesota, and Texas.

In August of 2016, Carmelo Anthony made an Instagram post asking all athletes to take action against social injustices. Chris Paul, Dwyane Wade, and LeBron James wasted no time and immediately responded to the post (see Figure 6.3). It later became known that the athletes started a thread using text messaging. In the message thread, it was later revealed that the focus of the communication was to ascertain how they might be able to use their status and celebrity platforms to get a message across in our culture that racial injustice must end. These athletes were also passionate about using their platforms to encourage other athletes to join the cause. As they began to deliver their messages live on stage, the broadcast messages began circulating on social media platforms around the world that the speech the four athletes were delivering was actually not part of the original script for the

FIGURE 6.3 *Carmelo Anthony, Chris Paul, Dwyane Wade, and LeBron James at the opening of the ESPYs*

night's awards show. Viewers from all over the nation tuned in to hear what the iconic basketball stars had to share. The purpose of the speech, it was later reported in the media, was to showcase the fact that professional sports have enjoyed a tradition of activism, and the athletes wanted to establish the idea that it was the duty of all high-profile athletes to raise the consciousness level of racial injustices (Jones, 2016).

A discussion of intersectionality in sports has to involve a discussion of LGBTQ coaches and athletes of color who not only experience homophobia but also discrimination in the context of racism. This next section will briefly summarize racism and its effects on the experiences and participation of LGBTQ athletes and coaches of color.

As previously mentioned, we know that LGBTQ athletes, as well as athletes and coaches of color, are not afforded the same opportunities or experiences as white LGBTQ athletes and coaches. Athletes of color, we learn, often experience what has been termed a "double tax" of racism and homophobia, while women of color experience the triple tax that relates to racism and homophobia, as well as sexism. The difference between the double tax that exists for male athletes of color and the triple tax that exists for female athletes of color must be addressed in the sports industry. LGBTQ athletes experience several fears, which include fear of being isolated from the team and coaches, fear of being excluded and left out by family and friends, and the fear and reactions that people in our culture have when it comes to intentional and unintentional discriminatory and racist actions demonstrated by a predominantly white LGBTQ community. These fears result in a feeling that many LGBTQ athletes of color experience that may ultimately cause them to feel that staying in the closet and hiding their sexual orientation is a much better fate than coming out. It is possible that many LGBTQ athletes fear being outcasts, and therefore they choose to stay in the closet and hide their sexuality to be accepted in the sports world and in the larger culture and community. Or perhaps they may feel compelled to ignore the implied racism that runs throughout the white LGBTQ community so that they can belong or feel as if they do.

Whites, heterosexuals, LGBTQ, "and advocates, educators, and researchers in sport need to understand the role of intersectionality and how our voices and points of view may unintentionally show our biases and privileges" (Ali Center, 2016). The knowledge taken from this research should be used to inform readers, viewers, and others who are interested in our work. Sports enthusiasts must begin to make intersectionality a priority to ensure that LGBTQ athletes are a part of our dialogues and work at all levels.

Bisexuality and Sports

Advocates of LGBTQ members frequently include the "B" when speaking of LGBTQ individuals and sexuality issues in sports (Women's Sports Foundation, 2018). When it comes to sports media and stories about LGBTQ athletes' efforts to differentiate bisexuality from homophobia, we find these stories are few and far between. In fact, when it comes to finding media coverage that details the experiences of athletes who identify with the LGBTQ sexual identity, along with experiences that are encountered by bisexual athletes and coaches, we find that sports media rarely cover these athletes, share their stories, or pay attention to their treatment and experiences. For example, there was a lawsuit in which bisexual men playing in sports were forced to choose their gender. These bisexual men were told that they were required to distinguish whether they were men or women so that they could prove their eligibility to play in a gay sports league (Association for Lesbian, Gay, Bisexual, and Transgender Issues in Counseling of Alabama, 2016). This legal case is demonstrative of our culture's need to engage in a deeper understanding and appreciation of the complexities involved in sexual orientation. American culture needs to address sexuality and the experiences of LGBTQ coaches—namely, bisexual coaches and athletes. Americans need to understand specifically how bisexual people are different from lesbian, gay, transgender, and queer individuals. Education on sexual orientation must show that in terms of sexuality, our sexuality is not a binary concept. We must address the current policy that forces athletes who are bisexual to identify themselves in terms of gender, sexual orientation, and identity as male or female (Adams & Andersen, 2011). LGBTQ activists in sports, as well as many sports journalists, need to ensure that our messages do not contribute to the invisibility of bisexual athletes but include their messages and experiences by addressing them and their accomplishments in their sports.

Sports journalists need to do more homework on athletes who are transgender, intersex, or bisexual. At the beginning of this chapter, we included the terms that will help to delineate one from the other, but it is clear that many Americans do not understand the meanings. We know that many Americans simply do not understand or are just not aware of the fact that our sexual orientations and gender identities are very different elements of our selves. In other words, we need to be educated on the ways that sexual orientation and gender identity are different for each individual. We know that many Americans were not aware that cross-dressers are not necessarily homosexual and that transgender and intersex individuals are oftentimes not sexually oriented to be lesbian, gay, bisexual, or queer. All of the individuals in this group might identify with being heterosexual.

Sports media, as in the Caitlyn Jenner stories, need to do a careful job of educating the public about these terms. Why? Because we cannot claim to want to advocate effectively for inclusivity and equality if we do not take the time to understand differences in sexual orientation and to listen to individual experiences and inner feelings. Similarly, effective sports journalism demands that transgender and intersex athletes and advocates are included in messages about lesbian, gay, and bisexual athletes. The inclusion of this group of athletes will ultimately help LGBTQ athletes find equality in the sports world and in the freedom to be and express who they are on the inside and out.

Implications

What are the implications for LGBTQ athletes and the attainment of sports equity? Scholars offer the following recommendations. The first concerns the use of the term LGBTQ. This means that sports journalists should only use the term "LGBTQ" if the story is addressing every element of the term (i.e., lesbian, gay, bisexual, transgender, and queer). Second, we must understand that in terms of LGBTQ, equality in sports is not just about embracing our diversity; it's the idea of reflecting on the ways that race, sex, sexual orientation, gender identity, and gender expression intersect and make us who we are. To achieve equality in sports for members of this group, efforts must be made to show conscientious effort and work being done to eliminate racism, homophobia, transphobia, sexism, and other phobias in sports. Next, we must ensure that all athletes, athletes of color, women, LGBTQ, those from various social classes, and others, are included in all aspects of the sports world and sports media. This means we need to make a conscious effort to have individuals from all backgrounds on media/news panels, in our promotional and advertising materials, in our pregame and postgame media interviews, as well as in our scholarly research.

We know that 2014 was a good year for LGBTQ athletes. In that year, we found a resurgence of LGBTQ athletes in the news who were seeking acceptance, equality, and justice. For example, Robbie Rogers signed a contract joining an MLS team, the Los Angeles Galaxy, making him the first active and openly gay athlete in a North American professional team sport. Next, news on the first actively open professional basketball player, Jason Collins, made news in the same year. Then we learned of Michael Sam, the former Missouri college football player who became the first active openly gay player with an NFL team. It was in that same year that Brittney Griner, WNBA player, became Nike's first openly gay athlete featured in advertisements and promotions. Despite these frequent stories of gay athletes, we still find that in American culture, our sports media needs to do more to continue the path to equality.

We still learn of events where many LGBTQ athletes are confronted with challenges when it comes to American's acceptance of them in sports. According to the Gay, Lesbian, and Straight Education Network's 2017 National School Climate Survey, close to 30% of all LGBTQ athletes are often harassed, victims of bullying, or attacked simply because of their sexual orientation or gender expression. Another survey called the "Campus Pride LGBTQ National College Athlete Report" (2012) provides data that shows that close to 40% of LGBTQ athletes report feelings of being harassed simply because of their sexual orientation and identity. Taken together, these two research reports and the statistics noted in them show that many LGBTQ athletes participating in sports today in America still do not feel comfortable with revealing their true sexual orientation identities to coaches and fellow athletes, and especially to the sports media. Why?

Even in this current era, we learn that many LGBTQ athletes continue to experience discrimination based on their sexual orientation. We also know that this group is often marginalized in sports in that we find coaches will demand that LGBTQ athletes keep their identities hidden (Reed, 2014). Research tells us that often times coaches will attempt to "encourage the athlete even try to change their sexual orientation and gender identity" (Reed, 2016). Huffington Post reported a story that detailed experiences where teammates of LGBTQ athletes will often try to "ostracize LGBTQ athletes through name-calling, rumor-spreading, or encouraging others to avoid contact with them" (Longman, 2017; Reed, 2016). This news article also tells readers about instances in which LGBTQ athletes are victims of physical threats and may even have their personal property vandalized. And as discussed earlier in this chapter, we know that a few coaches will not allow an LGBTQ athlete to join their team, and if they are on the team, we find that athletes are given reduced or little playing time (Reed, 2016).

No one wants to be uncomfortable or face their prejudices, hatreds, and biases. This statement may explain why some feel that moving toward equity in sports for those of varying sexual orientations may be a painfully slow process. To reduce racial and sexist biases, individuals have to be confronted; they have to have contact and face-to-face conversations with those from the various groups, and they must be willing to change. Facing challenges is part of life and is a process of growth and change that must happen. This same process is also needed in sports to achieve inclusion and equality. Ultimately, change in any area, and sports in particular, requires a team effort. Achieving inclusivity and equality in sports is going to take a collective effort on the part of many people and organizations, such as colleges and universities, the NCAA, professional leagues, sports fans, and people of color and ethnic groups, as well as heterosexual athletes. Equality in media coverage in sports requires the same collective efforts that we witnessed in the civil rights movement of the '50s and '60s.

Whenever sports media and sports journalists find the opportunities, we must pitch and seek out stories that go against the status quo. For example, media hardly cover stories that inform and educate its readers and viewers on bisexuality and transsexuality. These stories are few and far between in sports media, research, and policy. A lack of adequate media coverage and understanding regarding strategies, desires, and ways to address the issues is still prevalent in today's sports media. Lack of sports news coverage suggests that issues related to LGBTQ athletes can be trivialized or ignored in sports media, resulting in a symbolic annihilation of the group and its important contribution to the sports world. Recall that mass media symbolically annihilate groups by ignoring them, either through a lack of coverage or invisibility in the news. Examples of this annihilation of the LGBTQ group are evident when we peruse the news and sports news as they relate to LGBTQ athletes. And as this chapter shows, representations of LGBTQ athletes were few and far between before 1970 and are even fewer in this current era. We find that in terms of sexual orientation and gender identity, issues of equality and inclusion are viewed differently in sports, particularly when we consider other issues, such as race, gender, or disabilities. We find that the feelings of prejudice are also vastly different. Sports has many different dimensions from team versus individual, elite versus recreational, health and social benefits of participation, and influence of fans and spectators, and each of these brings up its own unique challenges and opportunities related to LGBTQ inclusion and equality.

THE ATHLETE ALLY PLEDGE

"I pledge to lead my athletic community to respect and welcome all persons, regardless of their perceived or actual sexual orientation, gender identity or gender expression.

Beginning right now, I will do my part to promote the best of athletics by making all players feel respected on and off the field" (Athleteally, 2018).

Issues and Controversies

One major issue for LGBTQ athletes might center on language in the locker room. We find that even in instances when an athlete's teammate thinks of him or herself as an advocate and ally, we still find stories of locker-room talk by heterosexual athletes' that include nicknames and other ethnophaulisms that cause some gay athletes to feel very uncomfortable. Research finds that even when teammates are accepting of their LGBTQ teammates, they often are unaware of the consequences of words and even behaviors, and how those might affect a teammate's coming out. Joking around about being homophobic to pretending to be gay, even if in a joking way, causes feelings of insecurity in an LGBTQ person who has perhaps come out and for those who remain in the closet. Take for example when a professional NBA player said in a media interview "no homo." While the athlete was issued a fine by the NBA, he also apologized for the language he used around his teammate. This incident serves a perfect example of the need for educating players on language and the need to create an environment that provides comfort for all players. This needs to happen even before they learn that they may have gay teammates.

The responsibility to educate players about locker-room language not only falls on the players but also on coaches, managers, owners, and, more importantly, sports media who have the opportunity to send messages to a larger audience. These various groups may not realize that it is their responsibility to help build trust, friendship, and inclusivity among their players. What is most needed are consistent trainings and discussions with individual teams to clarify expectations for how to act around teammates in and out of the locker room (Leichenger, 2014; Leichenger, 2018). The NFL Players Association created a policy that includes locker-room behavior, and it calls for harsh punishments and consequences for teams who display unsportsmanlike behaviors in the locker room.

Women's sports provide support for the idea that the need to continue to fight for diversity and inclusion does not stop once access is made for individuals in a particular group. Although much of our focus in America revolves around men's sports, our country has known instances where openly gay female athletes have met success in sports for decades. From female professional athletes such as Billie Jean King, Martina Navratilova, and Brittney Griner, we do often find instances that insinuate that female sports are a much safer space for out lesbian athletes (Tignor, 2013). Megan Rapinoe, an athlete in the National Women's Soccer League's team known as the Seattle Reign FC, came out to the media in 2012 (Leichenger, 2014; Leichenger, 2018). As was the case with Michael Sam, we find that her teammates, family, and friends already knew of her sexual orientation.

While women's sports are perceived to be more open to LGBTQ athletes, the historical sexism and rigid gender roles in the sporting world tend to foster their own culture of homophobia for women athletes (Leichenger, 2014; Leichenger, 2018). Writing in her new book, Brittney Griner, one of the top college basketball players of all time, discusses how failing to meet the expected gender image of a female can cause bullying (Leichenger, 2014; Leichenger, 2018). As mentioned in an earlier section of this chapter, the climate in women's sports is still dangerous, particularly for women coaches to come out. Not only do they feel discriminated against, but it is also thought that they are not getting jobs, and many are being asked to engage in a "don't-ask-don't-tell" type policy. Griner was not allowed to come out about her "sexual orientation while playing basketball for Baylor University because of the school's discriminatory policies toward LGBTQ people" (Leichenger, 2014; Leichenger, 2018).

Brittney Griner and others who are apprehensive about coming out are not basing those feelings on intangible or made-up presuppositions. Kathy Marpe, the former University of San Diego head coach, felt that she had to hide her sexuality for a "25-year career because rumors about her sexuality may cost their program recruits" (Leichenger, 2014; Leichenger, 2018). College coaches frequently position "family values" as a selling point for their programs (Leichenger, 2014; Leichenger, 2018). Colleges that use family values to sell their athletic programs also serve as an example of the subtle bias that remains the greatest obstacle to women's and men's sports alike.

In terms of transgender athletes, we know that transphobia in sports is more overt for this group rather than common covert practices that others in the LGBTQ group undergo. Trans athletes face challenges such as transphobia and other forms of overt discrimination practices that do not stem from a simple misunderstanding but from those individuals who identify as straight. Fallon Fox, a "mixed martial arts transgender fighter pictured in Figure 6.4, has been criticized for what some believe is having an unfair advantage to other female martial arts fighters" (Leichenger, 2014; Leichenger, 2018). That is, many perceive that transgender women have physical characteristics from their male body type that puts them in an unfair advantage when fighting against women.

Next, consider Gabbi Ludwig, a 52-year-old transgender basketball player. Ludwig plays basketball at Mission College in Santa Clara, California (Leichenger, 2014; Leichenger, 2018). Ludwig is 6 foot, 5 inches and weighs 217 pounds, and still hears taunts from fans and comments from people who feel that it is wrong for her to play with and against women. Yet what is not known among the public is that female hormones actually cause one's weight and muscle mass to decline. NCAA policy dictates that transgender

FIGURE 6.4 *Fallon Fox is an American mixed martial artist. She is the first African American openly transgender athlete in mixed martial arts history.*

"athletes wanting to play on a women's team must undergo at least one year of testosterone suppression before becoming eligible" (Leichenger, 2014; Leichenger, 2018).

Kye Allums, portrayed in Figure 6.5, is a basketball player at George Washington University, was placed in the media spotlight for being a transgender man on a women's basketball team (Thomas, 2010). Allums chose to delay the transition process from FTM, even though he identifies strongly as a male. While Allums is not the first transgender athlete to participate in the NCAA, Allums's story raised awareness in our culture in terms of increasing the level of consciousness held toward transgender athletes (Leichenger, 2014; Leichenger, 2018). In 2017, the state of California voted to

FIGURE 6.5 *Allums (50) of the George Washington Colonials battles Shenise Johnson (42).*

enact a law that allows college athletes to decide whether they want to compete as a man or woman based on their gender identity (Leichenger, 2014; Leichenger, 2018). And in fact, "the International Olympic Committee and NCAA have both passed standards for the transitioning of trans athletes" (Leichenger, 2014). Still, these policies have strict guidelines, with some states not having the means for a trans athlete to participate in the sports in which they identify.

As more athletes come out, we find that frequency of coming out creates an open and tolerant atmosphere, and high-profile media coverage helps to enhance the visibility of these athletes. Fostering inclusive environments is needed because LGBTQ athletes need to experience the freedom to be themselves; they need to live freely and be who they are and live the life that aligns with their identity; they need to experience being who they are without fear of harassment and bullying. As we can tell from this chapter, there is much work left to achieve the environment needed for LGBTQ athletes to succeed and feel safe to express who they are.

Conclusion

Participants in sports come from many backgrounds, ethnic heritages, and intersections. As our culture experiences improvements in technology, we hope that these advancements improve issues of diversity and inclusion for LGBTQ athletes. It is no secret that not all Americans support the idea of acceptance and inclusivity of LGBTQ athletes; homophobia, transphobia, sexism, classism, colorism, and racism are strong emotional issues that crop up at various moments in the sporting media. Of all the media coverage of sports that has been produced over the years—that is, those stories that cover racial and ethnic equality and diversity—research still shows that there are fewer stories published in high-profile media that address issues of homophobia, racism, sexism, and sexual orientation in sports. For LGBTQ athletes, the lack of media coverage seems to provide a sort of invisible hurdle or wall making it difficult for these athletes to cross over.

Gay athletes such as Olympic gold medalist Greg Louganis, tennis great Billie Jean King, former football player Michael Sam, and tennis great Martina Navratilova have over the years been covered and appeared in media stories published in mainstream traditional media; however, these depictions in media are rare, particularly when one considers the frequency of the stories in the highest and most popular sports media. Women's sports seem to be far more accepting and welcoming of lesbian athletes than men's sports have been. The WNBA, women's tennis, soccer, golf, and other sports have counted numerous lesbian athletes among their ranks. Compare that with male-dominated popular sports—baseball, football, basketball, soccer, and hockey—which seem to be highly reluctant to accept that there are indeed gay athletes among them. An important point to make a note of is this: Although the news has highlighted male athletes in the mainstream, many men in the sports world who have come out of the closet did so after their careers had ended.

QUESTIONS FOR REFLECTION AND DISCUSSION

1. Who are the most influential LGBTQ athletes from the last five years? Who are the most influential African American, Latino(a), Native American, Middle Eastern, and Asian American athletes? Were some influential LGBTQ athletes in certain ethnic groups easier or harder to identify? Why or why not?

2. What is your state's current law about sexual orientation? What is your university, college, or school's policy on sexual orientation? Review the NCAA and professional policies about sexual orientation. Is there room for improvement? Explain your answer.

3. Why the hesitancy to hire female head coaches who may be gay? As a sports journalist, what would you do to help improve the hesitancy with regard to hiring LGBTQ head coaches?

4. How do portrayals of LGBTQ athletes differ from other groups?

5. Think of popular media vehicles. Consider movies, prime time or even radio shows. Do you see different manifestations of LGBTQ athletes when compared to heterosexual athletes? Are LGBTQ athletes' voices included in the narratives on mainstream media?

6. In which media will you find the highest proportion of stories on LGBTQ athletes? Mainstream or niche media—media created for specialized audiences? Which of these media have a larger reach, and what will it take for stories about LGBTQ athletes to be featured in both media?

7. Do stereotypes vary based on the type of sport an LGBTQ athlete participates in? In other words, professional women basketball players are thought to display masculine behaviors from the way they walk, talk, and dress. Do the stereotypes in the LGBTQ athletic world differ by gender? Why or why? Remember to conduct research to back your thoughts up with examples from recent media.

SUGGESTED ACTIVITIES

1. Select an ad from a popular sports magazine. Now redesign the ad for placement in an LGBTQ magazine. Are there differences in how you would lay out the elements in the ad? Would the message for the product change? Why or why not? Review ads in magazines. *Curve* targets lesbians, and *Instinct* targets gay men. Now review your redesigned ad. Are there differences or similarities in the ad you found in traditional sports media? Are there similarities or differences in the ad you recreated? Write a brief paper summarizing your thoughts, experience with this activity, and conclusions.

2. Locate sports media coverage on transgender and intersexual athletes. How are players represented in the stories? Often media do not help consumers understand the difference in these terms. Write three news stories that you believe will help your readers obtain a better perspective on each of these identities. Then write your pitch to your editor on why these stories need to be published (or broadcast).

3. Examine several news stories about transgender athletes. Do you see certain themes repeated? What are the themes? Do you believe MTF transgender athletes are treated differently than FTM transgender athletes? If so, how? If not, why not? Provide examples from the media to support your research.

4. Look for print news stories about LGBTQ athletes. Now content analyze the stories for hidden frames and themes. How do sports journalists frame the stories? What themes and ideas do they use to help the reader understand and accept the athletes' sexual orientation?

5. Provide a coherent comprehension of the wide-ranging issues and debates that relate to sports and athletes from different races, ethnicities, and sexual identities. What are common themes in the issues as you see them, and how might you use your talents as a sports reporter or consumer of sports media to address these issues?

6. Find an athlete from one of the groups discussed in this book or chapter. Interview him or her and write a news story that might be used to help set the way for better stories about the group and the athlete.

ADDITIONAL RESOURCES

LGBTQ Resources: NCAA Inclusion Initiative Framework, http://www.ncaa.org/about/resources/inclusion/lgbtq-resources

NCAA: Five ways to have an LGBTQ-inclusive athletics department, http://www.ncaa.org/about/resources/inclusion/five-ways-have-lgbtq-inclusive-athletics-department

Advising Lesbian, Gay, Bisexual, Transgender, and Queer Student Athletes, https://www.nacada.ksu.edu/Resources/Clearinghouse/View-Articles/Advising-Lesbian-Gay-Bisexual-Transgender-and-Queer-Student-Athletes.aspx

Resources for Trans Inclusion in Sports, https://www.transathlete.com/documents https://www.campus-pride.org/resources/lgbt-sports-history-timeline/

LGBTQ and Ally Athletes/Issues in Athletics, https://www.unh.edu/safezones/lgbtq-ally-athletes-issues-athletics

CREDITS

Fig. 6.1: Source: https://commons.wikimedia.org/wiki/File:Caitlyn_Jenner.jpeg.

Fig. 6.2: Source: https://www.youtube.com/watch?v=x4i5W0tTLeQ.

Fig. 6.3: Source: http://time.com/4406289/lebron-james-carmelo-anthony-espy-awards-transcript/.

Fig. 6.4: Copyright © 2010 by Hambone Productions, (CC BY-SA 3.0) at https://commons.wikimedia.org/wiki/File:Fallon_Fox.jpg.

Fig. 6.5: Source: https://www.youtube.com/watch?v=WEkjgB1j-8Q.

7

Sexualization of Female Athletes

LEARNING OBJECTIVES

After completing this chapter, students should be able to:

- explore the sexual representation of female athletes;

- think critically about sport and how it is portrayed in American culture;

- discuss the influence that our culture has on gender roles and norms concerning what it means to be a woman;

- provide an overview of the lack of (but improving) athletic opportunities and resources for women and persons of color; and

- understand why gender and racial equality in sports journalism is important and needed.

Introduction

After Title IX was passed in 1972, female athletes were afforded the same opportunities as male athletes in collegiate sports. Equal access included access to equipment, training and practice facilities, and scholarships (Huffman, Tuggle, & Rosengard, 2004). After Title IX was established, American sports also witnessed an unprecedented increase in female participation in competitive sports (Acosta & Carpenter, 2008). Nevertheless, we still find disparities in the number of active female athletes when compared to the number of actively participating male athletes (Duncan, Messner, & Williams, 1991; Fink & Kensicki, 2002; Tuggle & Owen, 1999). In addition, scholars who have established research agendas on the participation of female athletes and depictions in media show significant and widespread gaps in how media cover male versus female sporting events (Messner, Duncan, & Cooky, 2003). One issue with media coverage of female athletes is that media tend to treat their bodies more as sex objects rather than as powerful and agile. In this chapter, we will discuss media preoccupation with female bodies, provide examples of sexualization in media, define objectification, and discuss how masculinity and femininity play out in the sports world.

An example of how the media focuses on female athletes' bodies instead of their accomplishments can be obtained from news stories covering the women's soccer World Cup competition in 1999. It was then that Brandi Chastain, a professional soccer player, and the women's soccer team won the World Cup for the USA. Chastain's winning goal happened when she scored on a penalty shot, which ultimately became the "winning" play, a defining moment in history for women's soccer. In lieu of the image of the "defining moment" and the penalty shot, one major media in sports, *Sports Illustrated*, published a cover photo of Brandi Chastain taking her jersey off on the soccer field. Although the reason for removing her jersey was to celebrate this historic victory, the media chose to depict her showing off her abs and sports bra. At the time, a female removing her shirt became the topic of conversation, not the team's athletic achievements. Consequently, media hype surrounding Ms. Chastain taking off her jersey eventually influenced cultural norms for women here in America. After the thousands of images capturing the removal of her jersey, we noticed more women entering health and fitness clubs wearing sports bras and shorts, but the most important consequence might be the distraction that fans and readers experienced after exposure to the image. In other words, the image of Ms. Chastain in her sports bra showing her abs took the attention away from the most revered and highest accomplishment in women's soccer—winning the World Cup.

In sports media, we frequently find images of female athletes depicted in what some term "nonathlete" roles, such as being mothers, balancing life and training, sharing their favorite recipes, and/or participating in softer stories that involve relationships with family and friends (Daniels & Lavoi, 2013). For example, Fink and Kensicki (2002) conducted a content analysis of images found on the covers of *Sports Illustrated* and the now out-of-circulation magazine *Sports Illustrated for Women*. In the study, the researchers analyzed several photos of female athletes from 1997 to 1999. Data analysis revealed that a majority of the photographs depicted female athletes in their homes and other settings related to family life ("55% compared to 23% of similar photographs of male athletes"). Moreover, Fink and Kensicki (2002) also found evidence that close to a third of the photos were of female athletes performing in their sport of choice ("34% compared to 66% of similar photographs of all male athletes"). Furthermore, analysis of the photos showed that only 5% of all the photographs were considered pornographic or sexually suggestive. In terms of a sports magazine geared toward women, Fink and Kensicki (2002) found that *Sports Illustrated for Women* actually published more images of female athletes competing in their sport (56%) compared to fewer than 25% of those images that portrayed female athletes in nonsport settings. In their study, Fink and Kensicki (2002) also reported that just 2% of cover photos for *Sports Illustrated for Women* were of female athletes in pornographic or sexually suggestive poses. We must note that this study took place right after a highly broadcasted performance of U.S. female athletes in the 1996 Atlanta Olympics.

Sexualization in Sports Media

Throughout history, women in this country have struggled to gain equality with men when it comes to representations in sports media. It is no different in the world of sports and sports journalism. Time after time, research continues to provide data showing that female athletes, and the sports they participate in, receive dramatically less coverage than male athletes. The difference in coverage is even greater when we consider that female athletes constitute a majority of all participants in American sports (Koivula, 1999; Salwen & Wood, 1994). We find that when sports media offer commentary on women's sports, female athletes are often sexualized or trivialized (treated in a demeaning way). For example, during a women's road race, broadcast sports commentators could be heard frequently referring to the female athletes as "girls." Biographical sketches of the athletes show that sports broadcasters obviously were not aware of or ignored or chose to ignore the idea that the top successful female athletes representing the United States were women and not girls. The female road race athletes were at the time Shelley Olds, age 32; Evelyn Stevens, age 28; and Kristin

Armstrong, age 42, and not "girls" as they referred to them. *Merriam-Webster's* (2018) defines the noun "girl" as a "female child, from birth to full growth." Another definition of girl provided in MerriamWebster.com (2018) is "a young, immature woman, especially formerly, an unmarried one." The very fact that adult women over the ages of 25, at the top of their professional careers and sport, who were living full lives with countless accomplishments all while competing, were referred to as "girls" in sports coverage is bewildering and perplexing, to say the least. When adult women are called "girls," this serves as one perfect example of the demeaning commentary female athletes typically receive in sports media.

Another typical example of the sexual manner in which media comment on female athletes happens to be one of the most talked about issues: whether the women's beach volleyball competitors should have to wear bikinis.

The problem with sexual references in sports media rests in the fact that many of our incredible female athletes work hard and accomplish much, yet the media coverage becomes nearly all about their uniforms, consisting of bikinis, instead of the commitment, effort, and intense training that these female athletes commit to play volleyball. Take, for instance, the headline NBC ran when reporting on women's volleyball that read, "Olympic Beach Volleyball: Great Bodies, Bikinis and More." If NBC published a headline that was not focused on bodies and uniforms of the female athletes, perhaps the headline would have read, "World-class Athletes to Represent the United States in Olympic Games."

Sports media is often guilty of praising male athletes for their athletic ability while praising female athletes for their physical attractiveness. A perfect example of this can be found in the magazine *Sports Illustrated*, which is considered the premier sports magazine in America. This sports media vehicle has also made a name for itself because of its infamous inclusion of female athletes who are often portrayed as sexual objects.

Frisby (2017a), following the Fink and Kensicki (2002) study, sought to analyze the content found on the covers of *Sports Illustrated*. The researcher's data show that female athletes receive strikingly less media coverage than male athletes. This finding supports previous research that shows that even when statistics reveal that female athletes make up a large majority of the athletes participating in sports today, news coverage of the female athlete and her sport is sparse (see Koivula, 1999). Although a plethora of scholarly research confirms and documents the presence of narrow and limiting images of women in mainstream media, Frisby's (2017a) data provides more support for the idea that there are few, if any, galvanizing and encouraging images of female athletes—namely, images of those highly accomplished, award-winning, medal-winning female athletes competing in today's sports industry. In other words, it is a challenge to find images and stories covering female athletes in today's high-profile sports media environment. It might be presumed that since the passage of Title IX and the significant increase in female athletes in the professional sports industry that an increase in media coverage of female athletes would follow suit. Yet, as of 2018, we find little improvement in the frequency of stories about female athletes in major sports media. As depicted in Figure 7.1, we see a visual representation of the data obtained in the Frisby (2017a, 2017b) studies. Data support the idea that female athletes appearing on the covers of popular high-profile sports magazines is negligible. Specifically, depictions of female athletes are trifling in terms of frequency of news coverage and depictions, particularly when their coverage and depictions are compared to the coverage and depictions of male athletes and their sports (e.g., Daddario, 1998; Duncan, 1990; Kane, 1996; Messner, Duncan, & Cooky, 2003; Pedersen, 2002; Pedersen, Whisenant, & Pedersen, 2004; Pedersen, Whisenant, & Schneider, 2003; Vincent, Imwold, Johnson, & Massey, 2003).

FIGURE 7.1   *Representations of female athletes on the covers of sports media*

Exclusion and Trivialization of Female Athletes

In sports media research, two major themes are found regarding coverage, depictions, and portrayals of females in sports: exclusion and trivialization. Research in this area shows that sports media frequently exclude female athletes by not featuring them in news coverage and front page or lead stories, particularly stories of their successes, achievements, and commitment to their sport (Fink & Kesincki, 2002; Kane, 1996; Messner, Duncan, & Cooky, 2003; Pedersen & Whisenant, 2005; Vincent et al., 2003). Furthermore, when sports journalists do cover women's sports, we find stories that trivialize, demean, or objectify female athletes by comparing their abilities to male athletes (e.g., "the female Michael Jordan" when referring to Simone Biles, a gymnast), "minimizing their accomplishments, or describing them as sex objects" (see Frisby, 2015). Research shows that in terms of sports media, journalists tend to write and publish more stories about the personal lives of female athletes than they do about male athletes.

The male-dominated sports media, according to literature published in this area, tend to trivialize female athletic events, particularly in broadcast when they refer to women's sports and related news as "in other news." These three words are metacommunication type language that is used to signal that the next reports are not as important as the stories that preceded them. News reports that center on female athletes have been found to trivialize them and frame the narrative about females' physical appearance and attractiveness rather than report on their strength, athletic accomplishments, and abilities. When discussing female athletes, it always seems that sports media imply that there is a "yes, but" to a female athlete's athleticism, as if it's a secondary attribute. "They're women athletes, but...." There is an illusory correlation that female athletes must be young and attractive. Contrast that image with older or less stereotypically "attractive" female athletes and we find that this group tends to receive little to no media attention. Dedication to sports must be moderated by humble and womanly character traits, or the female athlete is seen as manly, overaggressive, unattractive, or "butch." Examples of this sexist media coverage of women can be found in media stories about female athletes.

When we narrow the focus to female athletes of color, we also find evidence that sports journalists have been known to describe female athletes of color by associating them with animals or savages. Stories have been published that characterize the tennis professionals Serena and Venus Williams as "savage" or "animallike," along with a range of other animalistic adjectives (Desmond-Harris, 2017). In her online article for Vox, Desmond-Harris (2017) writes of instances in which fans and sports journalists berate Serena Williams. The author writes, "The racism that underlies the characterizations of her as hypersexual, aggressive, and animalistic also means that when she dares to express frustration, she's stamped with the infamous 'angry black woman' stereotype" (Desmond-Harris, 2017). The Caucasian female athlete, as preferred by sports media, is often an attractive, highly feminized young woman who happens to have a talent for her sport.

One visible sign of gender roles and stereotyping of sports in American culture lies in the classification of sports as "women's" and "men's." We also learned in previous chapters that certain sports in our culture are even perceived as masculine or feminine sports. American male athletes might be branded as "effeminate" if they compete in sports such as ice-skating, cheerleading, gymnastics, and other activities that rely on grace and elegance. We also know that in the United States, female athletes are often encouraged to participate in the more feminine "appropriate sports," such as cheerleading, softball, gymnastics and ice-skating, sports where traits and behaviors perceived as "female" are demonstrated. These sports, it can be speculated, demonstrate the more accepted norms of behavior that our society has come to accept: we expect women to be "ladylike." We reject sports and behaviors that have women exhibiting strictly prescribed gender roles that tell us what it is like to be a man. We learned in earlier chapters that the U.S. culture encourages masculine behavior that is aggressive, physical, and violent. Therefore, those sports that involve physical contact, such as football, basketball, rugby, boxing, and wrestling, use behaviors that mesh sports' relationship with American culture's notion of masculinity. The consequence of this cultural relationship is most evident when women and girls participate in masculine, violent, highly physical contact sports. In many of these instances, we find that the female athletes are often described negatively, such as being "unattractive," "masculine," or "unfeminine" (Kelinske, Mayer, & Chen, 2001). In a society where women play rugby and play football, sports in our culture still retain many traditions, gender disparities, and inequalities. In the article "Are Sports Media and

Journalists Sexist?" Aimee Lewis (2014) examined six sports in which differences between men and women were found to exist. In her article for the BBC, Lewis discusses why those distinctions continue in sports today (Lewis, 2014). She identifies disparities within certain sports based on whether the athlete is a male or female. For example, in gymnastics, female athletes participate in four events (vault, uneven bars, balance beam, and floor), while male gymnasts compete in six events (floor, pommel horse, rings, vault, parallel bars, and high bar). As Lewis (2014) points out in her article, we find that closer examination of the events shows that men and women gymnasts only share two events; the vault and floor exercise (note: male gymnasts do not use music during the floor event).

According to research on sports media, we learn that female athletes are frequently trivialized and marginalized in the media (Billings, Halone, & Denham, 2002), and athletes are stereotyped based on race (Banet-Weiser, 1999). We learn from published research on the frequency of stories that white males are afforded more media attention and salient coverage than women and athletes of color (Banet-Weiser, 1999; Billings et al., 2002; Frisby, 2016), while female athletes are "famous" or depicted in media coverage for more nonsports/nonathletic behaviors (Billings et al., 2002).

An extensive boost regarding sports participation rates has also been identified among female athletes. Despite the increased opportunities for female athletes, media coverage of them still lags significantly behind that of male athletes. And regarding quality coverage, that too is sorely lacking. There is no doubt that the condition of an athlete's body is important to performance in most sports (e.g., this leads some athletes to use performance-enhancing drugs, which is a problem!). However, when female athletes are sexualized in sports news coverage, this trivializes their power and fails to emphasize what makes these women succeed in their sports. Depictions that lower the status of women as objects to be looked at has been the subject of research and women in sports. These depictions, which lower the status of women or girls and ultimately cause them to be viewed as inanimate objects, void of emotion, feelings, and intelligence, and valued only for their sexual accessibility to men, are known as sexual objectification.

Sports media frequently target and attract American male viewers with the frequent sexualization of female athletes. This reliance on sexualization and objectification of female athletes incites a fundamental attribution error that may communicate that objectification ultimately leads males to trivialize female sports and may eventually result in male viewers' reduced enthusiasm in or involvement with women's sports (Messner, Duncan, & Jensen, 2010). Trivialization of female sports is repeatedly found in commentaries and broadcasts when sports journalists use phrases such as "in other news" to reinforce "already-existing negative attitudes or ambivalence about women's sports and women athletes" (Messner et al., 2010, p. 129). Thus we learn that sports media has the ability to distract men from the real essence of women's athletics by turning female athletes into sexual objects. Furthermore, by focusing solely on a female athlete's sex appeal and demeaning her athletic accomplishments, sports media effectively perpetuates stereotypes of what it means to be female, attractive, and, perhaps, athletic. Thus it can be argued that because of media portrayals of female athletes, male sports fans may be unintentionally discouraged from supporting and attending women's sporting events. Despite the targeting of male sports fans through sexual objectification of female athletes (e.g., *Sports Illustrated* swimsuit edition), sports media may not be aware of the fact that their messages and images may actually reinforce harmful stereotypes and at the same time fail to encourage men to become dedicated female sports fans. To explain this in more detail, we turn now to a theory that helps us predict, understand, and provide a framework for sexual objectification.

Research on Sexualization of Women in Sports

The number of female athletes actively participating in sports increased drastically in 1972, after the passage of Title IX (Acosta & Carpenter, 2008). A careful survey of research conducted over the last 15 years demonstrates disparate coverage of female athletes in sports media when compared to the coverage of male athletes (Duncan, Messner, & Williams, 1991; Fink & Kensicki, 2002; Fink, 2015; Frisby, 2017b; Tuggle & Owen, 1999). Scholars believe that the disparities in news coverage between men's and women's sports has more to do with the fact that sports media and American culture tend to see female athletes as sexual beings and not as athletes (Fink, 2015; Gray, 2016; Messner, Duncan, & Cooky, 2003). Some theorists suggest that American culture has two mutually exclusive views of women: they are either attractive or masculine. A female athlete who happens to be toned and muscular is often placed in the masculine category because, it is believed, women cannot be attractive and athletic. We find evidence to support this as sports media write and publish stories praising female athletes for their beauty rather than reporting on their strength, athletic prowess, and proficiencies (Halbert, 1997; Krane, 2001).

An exemplary event that showcases exactly how sports media sexualize and trivialize female athletes can be found in media coverage of the 1999 women's soccer World Cup competition. During the final competition for the renowned World Cup, Brandi Chastain scored a goal on a penalty shot. That score turned into a historic and defining play in women's soccer. To celebrate the team's victory, Chastain fell to her knees, pulled off her jersey, and waved her jersey and arms in the air while showing her sports bra and abs. Instead of reporting on the victory, major sports media chose to report on and hype the image of Ms. Chastain in her sports bra. In fact, a high-profile and popular sports magazine, *Sports Illustrated*, made the decision to put the photo of Chastain removing her jersey on the cover of their magazine. While the women's soccer team received excessive coverage and media hype at the time, the coverage was not about the historic win by the U.S. team; instead, media chose to focus on the fact that a female athlete removed her jersey on the playing field. The media hype was not about the women's soccer team winning the World Cup. Scholars such as Frisby (2017a; 2017b) believe the metacommunication about the female athlete appearing in her sports bra and showing her well-defined abs sends messages with sexual overtones that subtly communicate the idea that the image of her sports bra and abs was much more newsworthy than winning the World Cup. Some argue tsdahat the hype surrounding Chastain and her sports bra may have distracted sports fans from the team's triumph in winning the World Cup.

More than 20 years of research and analysis of portrayals of women in popular culture documents the idea that women are frequently trivialized, sexualized, and objectified. Frisby and other researchers in this area hope that research will begin to find evidence that sports media have started changing portrayals of female athletes. Researchers hope that findings and implications from data collected over the years will allow sports media and journalists to understand the importance of emphasizing female athletes' accomplishments and begin publishing more empowering images of and better news stories about female athletes. Given the plethora of research showing vast differences in the way female athletes appear in sports media when compared to male athletes, many activists and scholars anticipate the day when we find media showing increased attention to the female athlete's accomplishments (e.g., Kane, 1996; Messner, Duncan, & Cooky 2003; Pedersen & Whisenant, 2005; Vincent, Imwold, Johnson, & Massey, 2003).

In a recent investigation comparing depictions of athletes on sports magazine covers, Frisby (2017b) was interested in learning if there has been a shift in how sports media depict female athletes on the covers of magazines. After analyzing covers of two prominent sports magazines, Frisby found that, as of 2018, portrayals of female athletes have yet to show improvement. In fact, Frisby

(2017b) found that changes have not been made in how female athletes appear on magazine covers since 2002. Implications taken from the Frisby (2017b) study can be used to support arguments concerning how media use empowering images of women—namely, of female athletes. We find that even in the current day and time, female athletes continue to receive minimal coverage or positive empowering depictions when compared to the way sports media cover male athletes and their sports (e.g., Kane, 1996; Messner, Duncan, & Cooky, 2003; Pedersen & Whisenant, 2003; Vincent, Imwold, Johnson, & Massey, 2003).

When female athletes are on the covers of sports magazines, the depictions are typically of them in nonathlete roles (Frisby 2017b). Building on the data obtained in the Fink and Kensicki (2002) research, Frisby (2017b replicated their study and analyzed the covers of sports magazines. Frisby (2017a; 2017b) obtained data, consistent with Fink and Kensicki (2002), that showed when female athletes appeared on the covers of sports magazines, they were either sexualized or posed in non-athletic contexts, while photographs of male athletes showed them active in their team uniforms and sports settings.

Coverage of African American Female Athletes in the Media

In sports media, we find even more disparate and disproportionate depictions of female athletes of color (Kane, 1996). Research conducted on magazine covers between the years 1954 and 1987 shows that African American female athletes were found on only five of the 1,835 covers (Lumpkin & Williams, 1991). Serena Williams is a current example of the female athlete of color most frequently found on covers. However, is Serena Williams the only female athlete of color deemed worthy enough for the cover of *Sports Illustrated*? Research also shows disparities in the feature articles published in popular sports magazines. Feature articles about African American female athletes, studies show, were also uncommon (Leath & Lumpkin, 1992; Lumpkin & Williams, 1991). It can be argued that women of color are also marginalized by our culture's dominant ideals and norms governing gender roles. One cultural value that exists is a bias toward a heterosexual, white, idealized, and physically attractive body over other body types. American culture has a deeply rooted value of the ideal body type; the culture considers the ideal body to be thin and beautiful (see Chapter 4 on body types), according to research published by Aulette and Wittner, 2009.

Objectification Theory

Objectification theory, according to Fredrickson and Roberts (1997), postulates that a woman's value comes from her body and physical appearance. If we apply this theory and its argument to help us explain, predict, and understand depictions and representations of female athletes, we find consistency in their objectification with depictions of women in music videos. Previous content analyses found evidence that supports the idea that women in American culture are cherished when they engage in self-objectification—showing the body in the most sexually alluring ways (Andsager & Roe, 1999; Seidman, 1992; Vincent, 1989). For example, Sommers-Flanagan, Sommers-Flanagan, and Davis (1993) research collected data that showed that in terms of music videos, female artists depicted were significantly more likely to engage in sexually alluring and arousing behaviors than male artists. The behaviors demonstrated by the women in music videos include licking their lips seductively, pelvic thrusting, and stroking their bodies. In terms of attire, Seidman (1992) conducted a content analysis of music videos and discovered that, compared to male artists, female artists were likely to be scantily clad and shown to wear sexually provocative attire.

Exposing one's body is one way to express sexual objectification. Exposing body parts or wearing scantily clad clothing (Aubrey, Henson, Hopper, & Smith, 2009) is the most frequent way sexual objectification is communicated. While does not depict skin, research using eye-tracking devices shows that the male eye usually starts at the chest area and spends most of the time gazing at the midriff area. Another example of a similar pose in sports is the cover of 2015's *Sports Illustrated* annual swimsuit edition. On the cover is the image of model Hannah Davis. The model is posed in a way that makes it appear as if she is pulling down her bikini bottom to within a millimeter of her pubic area. Outrage was expressed by those who felt the image was rather pornographic and the fact that the model is shown drawing attention to her private area, an area that only romantic partners or gynecologists should be familiar with, shows a clear example of sports culture's acceptance of objectification. Not only did Ms. Davis support her appearance on the cover but also many supporters posted comments on social media stating that this is natural and supports our culture's marketing idea that "sex sells stuff." Heat analysis of the image shows the path a viewer's eye takes when looking at the image; the eye starts at the top left-hand corner of a page and ends up leaving out at the bottom right-hand corner of the page. A quick scan of the image leaves no surprise where one's eyes will land.

The cover of the 2015 issue of the magazine is as previously stated the most blatant and clear example of objectification and sexualization of women in media. Of course, *Sports Illustrated*'s annual swimsuit cover is not without controversy. It is almost as if they are relying solely on the "sex sells" myth of advertising. The argument in this section of the chapter is not that we should avoid beauty and physical attractiveness. We are not saying it is wrong to celebrate a beautiful woman, a toned body, or both, especially when some women work very hard to achieve and maintain their physical looks. Yes, the idea of "if I have it, I should flaunt it" is fine, but keep in mind theories we have used to understand the effects of exposure to constant images like these. Theories such as framing, agenda setting, schema theory, objectification, and sexualization all work together to suggest that constant exposure to these images may result in a trivialization of a female athlete's talents and athletic prowess. Hannah Davis's image overpowers and sucks the life right out of the fact that this edition of *Sports Illustrated* includes the portrayal of a plus-size model. Robyn Lawley, who self-reports that she wears a size 12, appears in the sports magazine in a bikini of her choice and design. The question that we hope is raised is this: Did we see media hype about this image? Why or why not? Why was she not on the cover? If media were to hype the image of a plus-sized model on a cover, would it be framed positively or negatively? Why do you suppose *Sports Illustrated* did not emphasize that there was a "plus-size model inside *Sports Illustrated*?" Why was there no mention of the article with a headline that read, "Plus-Size Models Give *Sports Illustrated*'s Swimsuit Edition More Curves?"

Art designers and directors know that the position of her Hannah Davis's hands in her cover photo encourages a reader to attend to nothing else in the photo but the area between her legs. Heat analysis would show that few readers, both men and women, were least likely to stare more at Hannah Davis's eyes or even her breasts than at her "private area." Some scholars argue that implicit in this cover is an invitation to picture her naked. Is there anything left to the imagination? From a visual communication perspective, we know that headlines and images work together to help us understand a message and form conclusions. Consider this headline, which was found on the cover of the racy magazine: "Hannah Davis Goes Down South." This headline appeared just above her right arm. Accidental placement? It is impossible not to see this as an intentional strategy that involved reducing this woman (and ultimately most women) to sexual objects. Often the point of objectification is to gain prolonged gazes from men; the male gaze. This statement raises another question to ponder: Why do we rarely see men, and even male athletes, scantily dressed with their arms and hands pointed at their genitals?

Objectification in Sports

Examples of objectification of female athletes in sports can be found in images of Danica Patrick. Ms. Patrick is an athlete who succeeded in a predominantly male sport. In the 2012 GoDaddy commercial Danica Patrick, a is shown in a scantily-clad, skimpy dress and camera angles involved several close-up shots that encouraged focus on various parts of her body, a classic example of objectification (Frisby, 2015). This type of portrayal makes her athletic accomplishments pale in comparison. Take, for instance, women's beach volleyball. This sport has been known for being objectified for its "sexiness" and its "uniforms."

Examples of sexual objectification can be found in the numerous close-up shots of female volleyball players and their backsides in scantily clad uniforms compared to volleyball uniforms that the male athletes wear (see Figure 7.1). Fredrickson and Roberts (1997) argue that sexual objectification requires the portrayal and representation of a woman. In fact, for it to be considered sexual objectification, there must be a "collection of body parts" (Fredrickson & Roberts, 1997, p. 174). The collection of body parts takes the focus away from the woman as a whole—the total person. In other words, images that emphasize breasts, the gluteus maximus, thighs, etc., will neglect showing or even emphasizing the woman's face, contrasted with a visual portrayal of a woman as a total person. To clearly identify and classify objectification, you must evaluate images based on the extent to which women are shown segmented into various parts of their bodies (i.e., cleavage/chest, butt, legs, stomach).

Research has offered many explanations for why media tend to objectify female athletes. One hypothesis centers on our culture's patriarchal hierarchy in that objectification of women and athletes is viewed as an attempt to limit their power. Through the objectification of women (including athletes), media are able to reinforce our cultural ideals concerning what is feminine and what is masculine. Taking this thought a little further, we can then begin to understand why sports media objectify women, and the explanation is simple: American sports are considered masculine activities (Pederson, 2002). In a masculine society like the United States, masculine beliefs often give privilege to males. The mass media and sport are considered the two most prominent social institutions in our culture, and within that relationship, the relationship between athletics and masculinity has made gender a very pertinent issue. Sports media then may encourage this masculine value as one of importance simply because of their extensive coverage of male-dominated sporting events. This media coverage may then strengthen the idea that female athletes are in many ways considered inferior. In other words, extensive coverage of male-dominated sports like football and basketball may lead people to believe female athletes have no place in sports—ultimately supporting notions of male power and control. This serves as one reason why sports media tend to underrepresent, stereotype, trivialize, marginalize, and sexualize female athletes in their coverage; it is simply a way in which the idea of what is masculine and what is feminine is maintained. This may explain why mass media places an emphasis on a female's sexuality and physical appearance; it is simply a means to not only divert attention away from that the threat to what we consider to be masculine but also it may serve as a means to reaffirm the sexual difference between males and females (Raney & Bryant, 2006).

Some might argue that female athletes allow themselves to be objectified or sexualized and do not understand this part of the debate. However, it can also be argued that females who allow themselves to be sexualized in the media or who choose to be represented in this manner may do so because of the pressure to be attractive and feminine. That is, female athletes may be under pressure to engage in behaviors that show that they are both attractive and heterosexual. Because of such pressure, not only from society but also from the mass media to uphold masculine ideals, those female athletes participating in aggressive, more masculine sports, such as basketball, soccer, softball, sports that are viewed in society as less feminine, may especially feel this pressure to allow themselves to be portrayed sexually in the media so as to avoid being labeled a lesbian and thereby potentially maximize their social and career status (Harrison & Fredrickson, 2003).

Gender-Appropriate Sports

Research shows that female athletes who participate in sports that are considered, by American standards, "gender-appropriate" sports, such as gymnastics, synchronized swimming, and tennis, are often depicted in sports news stories with very limited views about their athleticism. Research on our culture's perception of which sports are better suited for women than men tend to be published and receive more coverage in print and electronic media. Data obtained from several studies provides evidence supporting the fact that female athletes who compete in gender-appropriate sports receive more press and news coverage than the female athletes who participate in masculine or "gender-inappropriate" sports, such as boxing, hockey, rugby, wrestling, and basketball (Tuggle & Owen, 1999; Vincent Imwold, Johnson, & Massey, 2003). The Emmy-award-winning documentary *Media Coverage and Female Athletes* presents evidence-based research that shows that although a vast majority of athletes actively participating in sports are women, we find documented evidence that women's sports and female athletes receive less than 4% of all sports and media coverage. The documentary also shows evidence that supports prior research proving that male athletes are less likely to appear in sexually provocative poses than are female athletes (Tucker Center for Research on Girls & Women in Sport, 2014).

Empirical research on how female athletes competing in sports are treated in sports media obtained data that shows that when female athletes compete in sports that our culture deems "sex appropriate," media devote more time and space, and give these athletes much more coverage in terms of length of stories and number of features than the coverage devoted to female athletes competing in sports such as bodybuilding or wrestling (see studies from Jones, Murrell, & Jackson, 1999; Salwen & Wood, 1994). According to a story found on the Bleacher Report, the reason for gender disparity in sports is consumer interest drives content, and the consumer interest is not there for women's sports. For some consumers, it is perceived that women's sports aren't at the same level or quality of men's sports and that is what makes it less entertaining, less fascinating, and worthy of watching (Macdonald, 2014).

Hardin, Shen, and Yu (2008) using framing theory (see Chapter 2 in this book), found that sport in the U.S. culture is entrenched in the idea that it is the domain of men and that the acceptance of this value is now a view of sports that is taken for granted as the status quo. Hardin et al. researched the sex typing of sports to see how media use visual priming through sports images. The results of their study found that media tend to prime viewers to accept stereotypical or nonstereotypical presentations of athletes. In other words, their research reinforces the idea that traditional gender stereotypes persist in influencing the way individuals categorize sports.

In defining what constitutes gender-appropriate sports, we learn that those sports "emphasize grace, balance, style, poise, glitz and glamour. Sports that fit these attributes are sports like figure skating, synchronized swimming, and gymnastics (Pedersen, 2002; Tuggle & Owen, 1999; Vincent et al., 2003). Taking this further, we wonder why male gymnasts are not featured in sports media. The converse is true for male gymnasts; it is a gender-inappropriate sport for males. The interesting point about male gymnasts is the fact that the amount of strength and training it takes to participate in events like "the rings" is phenomenal. The idea that male gymnasts receive little or no coverage is an inverse relationship of the effects of what happens when athletes participate in gender-inappropriate sporting events.

The sport that has seen the highest increase among female athletes is soccer. Research also shows that the sports that have the highest rate of female athletes are collegiate team sports, such as volleyball, softball, tennis, track and field, swimming, and basketball—sports that are not typically known as gender-appropriate or feminine sports (Acosta & Carpenter, 2008). Yet to support the disparity in media coverage of female athletes participating in team and gender-inappropriate sports, we find that female athletes and their athletic abilities and performances are often ostracized or disregarded and maybe even overlooked by sports media (Pedersen, 2002; Vincent et al., 2003). In fact, Vescey (2007) found little to no coverage of the U.S. women's soccer team when they competed in the World Cup competition. The lack of coverage of this event was first evident 8 years earlier in the way the media covered the U.S. women's soccer team's World Cup win.

In a study on media reactions and responses to the types of sports and sports journalists' coverage of female athletes, Allen and Frisby (2017) found a significant relationship between masculinity/femininity of the sport and frequency of negative statements made about female athletes in printed news stories. Allen and Frisby (2017) found that media clearly wrote fewer stories about female athletes who participate in sports known to be more feminine, leading her to conclude that higher frequency levels of negative themes in news stories about female athletes are related to whether the sport is considered in our Western culture to be masculine or even if the sport is identified as gender neutral. Based on the data, we can conclude that when female athletes compete in sports that our culture deems masculine or gender neutral, the athletes are significantly more likely to be victims of negative publicity and coverage than those female athletes who compete in gender-appropriate sports. Empirical evidence shows that when female athletes participate in masculine sports, they are often targeted by news stories regarding their body image, physical "masculine" appearances, and musculature.

Acknowledgment of the lack of focus in sports media is one way that sports journalists can begin to address the disparities in coverage. In fact, the sports media must acknowledge their use of inappropriate images of female athletes when compared to male athletes. "Media scholars, editors, journalists, strategic communications practitioners and others interested in this topic must advocate for change in how stories are reported about athletes" (Frisby, 2017a). For example, sports media can begin to increase the number of female athletes photographed in their uniforms and competing "in action" and in their sport. These types of images published at the same frequency as the sexualized and objectified images of female athletes might actually change individual, and even our culture's, perceptions of what it means to be thin, beautiful, muscular, and athletic.

Girls and Young Women and Self-Esteem

Daniels (2012) conducted a study on girls and self-esteem and found that images of female athletes play a significant role in how young girls see and feel about themselves. Data also shows that images of female athletes—namely, positive portrayals of female sports and athletics, can play a valuable role in encouraging them to consider participating in sports. Sports media need to understand that it is incredibly important for them and us to continue working in this area so that we might learn the effects of long-term exposure to and consumption of sexualized depictions of female athletes. Research in this area might be used to show if, over time, exposure to sexualized images of famous athletes and entertainers might actually result in the tendency for young girls "to self-objectify themselves, have lower self-esteem and focus too much on their physical appearance" (Frisby, 2017a; Frisby, 2017b). The discipline of sports journalism should encourage the systematic process of obtaining facts and conducting research that uncovers those elements that may be used to explain why our culture resists changes in terms of what is masculine and feminine in sports. It is imperative for the sports media to want to be passionate about improving the way female athletes are shown in media. Sports journalists must also want to be sure that all sports receive similar coverage. For example, for every story about female gymnasts, we need to ensure that stories are published about their male counterpart—the male gymnast. In fact, journalists may want to do a story on how media treat female athletes and the consequences experienced in our culture when female athletes are treated unfairly in the media.

Making Progress

This chapter shows that there are far fewer stories about athletes of color and women than there are of white male athletes. Research presented in this chapter also reports how sports media treat female athletes who participate in gender-appropriate sports versus females who participate in gender-inappropriate sports. In addition, this chapter presents research that shows that in terms of media coverage, we find that male athletes frequently and consistently tend to gain more visibility in sports news when compared to female athletes and female athletes of color. Data obtained in several studies show that female athletes receive little visibility in sports news coverage when they participate in team sports. Female athletes who appear in the news are often participants in individual sports as opposed to team sports.

Information and research discussed in this chapter also highlight the strong tendency to idolize white male athletes, focusing on them more as heroes and social celebrities. Thus we have learned that male athletes tend to be found more extensively in stories published in sports media than stories about female athletes, but we also find that when female athletes are featured in news stories, the coverage tends to be unrelated to their sport and athletic abilities but centers on their lifestyle, marital status, attractiveness, and other "soft news" issues. We also determined that sport is a world that is totally dominated by men. We know that in sports journalism there are very few female sports reporters, which may explain why there are fewer stories and less media coverage focused predominately on female athletes. With this idea, we should not be surprised that news stories and coverage are loaded with the presence of American culture that respects and honors males and masculinity. Disparities between male and female sports reporters result in the tendency for news coverage to support and perpetuate traditional stereotypes in our culture. But as future media professionals and strategic communicators, you have the opportunity to change sports coverage. See the checklist of recommendations at the end of this chapter for ways that you can improve the coverage of sports.

On a positive note, it is worth noting that, regarding equality of coverage and positive portrayals of female athletes, media are trying to present better portrayals of female athletes. Take, for example, *ESPN Magazine*'s "Body Issue" (see ESPN, 2018, http://espn.go.com/espn/bodyissue). The "Body Issue" depicts photos of naked female *and* male athletes. The issue also depicts female athletes with body types ranging from mesomorph, endomorph, and ectomorph, that also includes Paralympians. What is most significant about this issue and the images portrayed in it is that the athletes are shown in generally active, gender-neutral poses. The ESPN "Body Issue" praises women athletes for their athleticism and not their attractiveness. The magazine also emphasizes the hard work and dedication that athletes devote to staying fit and toned.

Another positive example of media representation of women athletes can be found in the Always commercial for its "Like a Girl" campaign, released in the summer of 2014. The Always "Like a Girl" commercial urges girls to transform the cultural ideal that acting "like a girl" is a weakness and seeing that phrase as positive and portraying the strength of being a girl. Research shows that the effects of this campaign have been largely positive and significant, with "76% of women and 59 percent of men ages 16 to 24 reporting that the message and campaign have changed their perception of the phrase 'like a girl'" (Nudd, 2015).

Nike's "Voices" ad, released in recognition of the 40th anniversary of Title IX, is yet another example of how strategic communication practitioners are using their skills to create positive portrayals of female athletes. In the ad, female athletes such as Lisa Leslie, Marlen Esparza, and Joan Benoit-Samuelson, who competed in the Olympics, talk about their personal experiences with gender-based discrimination in their professional sports careers. The video also shows a wide range of young girls who we hope would never have to endure the gender-based discrimination that these female Olympians faced.

Women as Olympians

As mentioned several times in this chapter, we know that an increase of women participating in sports is at an all-time high. Fink (2015) collected data that shows that in terms of participation by males and females in the London 2012 and Rio 2016 Olympics, female athletes represented 45% of all Olympic athletes. Despite the increase in participation, in this culture, female athletes are expected to act as "women first and athletes second" (see Trolan, 2013). However, physical talents and expertise have through the centuries been linked to masculinity. Today, we view female athletes as "anomalies in the sports world" (see Gray, 2016). Although female athletes who win medals do so because of their incredible talents and training, sports reporters and other media practitioners often credit a female athlete's accomplishments to men (Gray, 2016). For example, one sports commentator commented that a female Olympic swimmer "swims like a man" (Gray, 2016). Studies over time have shown that in our culture, an individual's thoughts, feelings, and perceptions of the stigmatizations that may result because of participation in a sport may likely create insecurities related to body images, homophobia, harassment, racial insults, attacks, and insults aimed at his or her level of attractiveness (Dworkin, 2001; Krane, 2001; Krane, Chio, Baird, Aimar, & Kauer, 2004).

Microaggressions and Female Athletes

Microaggressions "are the brief and commonplace daily verbal, behavioral, environmental indignities, whether intentional or unintentional, that communicate hostile, derogatory, or negative racial, gender, sexual orientation, and religious slights and insults to the target person or group" (Sue, 2010, p. 5). Research shows that microaggressions are easily acknowledged in sports media covering women's sports. In fact, some argue that sports media aid in the perpetuation of a "dismissive, hostile and sexualized environment for female athletes at all levels" (Ho & Kaskan, 2016; Kaskan & Ho & 2014). The identifying characteristic of athletes is gender and not their "strength, dedication or performance" (Ho & Kaskan 2016).

Ho and Kaskan (2016) took the microaggression themes in the research published by Sue (2010) and created seven microaggression categories: "sexual objectification, second-hand citizenship, use of racists/sexist language, restrictive gender roles, sexist/humor jokes, a focus on traditional feminine appearance and a focus on physical shape and body image" (Frisby, 2017c; Ho & Kaskan, 2016). The seven categories were created because the researchers believed that they allowed for more precise analysis and examination of the ways that female athletes are covered in published stories found in sports media (Ho & Kaskan, 2016). Scholars believe that that white individuals rely on microaggressions because they may not be conscious of the bias in their comments. In other words, people who rely on microaggressions may not recognize the implicit biases they hold and ultimately reveal those hidden biases in their statements and behaviors (Constantine & Ladany, 2000; Constantine, Smith, Redinton, & Owens, 2008). In other words, microaggressions are those statements or behaviors that occur automatically, without elaborate thought or planning. Sue, Bucceri, Lin, Nadal, & Torino, (2007) believe that these microaggressions are so frequent in human behavior that we often dismiss the comments and statements or interpret them as being harmless jokes (Sue, Bucceri, Lin, Nadal, & Torino, 2007).

According to Sue, Capodiluo, and Holder (2008), "microaggressions are revealed in three distinct forms—microassault, microinsult, and microinvalidation" (p. 330). A microassault is an "explicit racial derogation characterized primarily by a verbal or nonverbal attack meant to hurt the intended victim through name-calling, avoidant behavior, or purposeful discriminatory actions" (Sue et al., 2008, p. 331). Examples can be found when an individual describes another person as "colored" or "Oriental," "girl," "lady," and other adjectives that reduce a person down to their group membership and its associated stereotype.

A microinsult, according to Sue, Capodilupo, and Holder (2008), can be identified in a comment or message that appears to be rude or insensitive. Sue, Capodilupo, and Holder (2008) further describe a microinsult as a message or statement that is meant to humiliate or put down an individual's ethnic heritage or identity. A microinsult can be visibly observed when an individual engages in a shrewd or humiliating brush-off or insult. These microinsults are often not noticeable or recognizable to the communicator, but they relay a clandestine message that is rude, offensive, and upsetting to the target of the message (Sue, 2010). Scholars studying microinsults find that an analysis of the context is an important part of understanding the meaning of the insult. In fact, research proves that microinsults can occur in metacommunications and often convey the idea that minorities are trivial and unworthy.

Microaggressions "are characterized by communications that exclude, negate, or nullify the psychological thoughts, feelings, or experiential reality of women or people of color" (Sue, Capodilupo, & Holder, 2008) A case in point is when a white person says to a person of color, "I don't see color," or "We are all human beings," the metacommunication behind this statement is to abrogate their negative experiences as people of color living in America (Sue, Capodilupo, & Holder, 2008).

Kaskan and Ho (2016) found that female athletes are frequent targets of microaggressions. According to these researchers, microaggressions are consequences of frequent objectification and assumptions that they are second-rate citizens when compared to men. We also find that microaggressions tell women to act in accordance with their ascribed gender roles. Daniels (2012) conducted a study that found that, compared to male athletes, female athletes are not highly regarded because of their portrayals in media that show them engaging in sexualized and objectified poses.

Often framed as a joke, we find, for example, intellectuals and sports journalists who reprimand Serena Williams, a top-performing female athlete of color, through descriptions of her that insinuate she is an individual who is humorless, does not recognize that racial "jokes" are funny, and takes things too seriously. All these accounts are leveled against the top tennis player simply because she refuses to giggle and even laugh at jokes that are clearly "racial" but perceived by the majority to be funny.

Sexist and racist jokes stated by sports announcers, commentators, and reporters are often imperceptible. This statement finds support in a published sports story found in national media in October 2014. Let us take a brief review of the series of events: Shamil Tarpishchev, the Russian Tennis Federation president, very critical of Serena Williams, stated that this athlete appeared to look like a man. While the descriptor may have been forgotten as easily as it was stated, many scholars immediately recognized this as one perfect example of microaggressions leveled against female athletes in sports media. Scholars studying and analyzing the frequency of microaggressions often count the frequency of these types of statements that are published in sports news and note the inferences that are made with respect to the athlete's race and body shape. Researchers will then analyze the number of times that the perpetrator stated that their racist or sexist comment was either taken out of context or was meant to be funny. Saying someone looks like a man is meant to be a joke? Or stating that an African American athlete resembles an ape is to be taken lightly or perceived as funny?

In addition to racist jokes, if we conducted a pseudo search for female athletes participating in male sports, the search would return a plethora of YouTube videos that are aimed at the WNBA. Once more, we find that the literature on the use of microaggressions supports this type of meta-communication behavior that is often aimed at female athletes. The type of microaggression that relates to this behavior is noted in the literature and can be identified by an individual's "jokes like those made about female basketball players are often directed at individuals who belong to another race or gender" (Frisby, 2017c, p. 3). In accordance with microaggression theory, we know that those individuals who rely on jokes use these jokes to express their subtle hostility and prejudices. Humor helps, or so they think, to reduce the sting. Basically, jokes that are perceived to be racist or sexist are often a type of microaggression that is leveled at another's expense. These jokes, we find, are also a way to allow the "joke teller" to indirectly and covertly express his or her resentment toward people of different minority groups and his or her anger toward people of color. Microaggressions found in the form of a joke also serve as covert strategies that allow people in the majority group (whites) to keep minorities and marginalized group members in their role as second-class citizens in American culture.

While many Americans are not conscious of their use of and reliance on microaggressions, we find that one reason for this insensitivity may be due to cultural norms, values, and pressures for one to hide feelings of anger and hostility, especially in today's American culture of political correctness. In fact, we find that when a white individual is confronted about his or her racist or sexist statements, the frequent rebuttal from him or her is, "Oh, I was just kidding! They shouldn't be so sensitive? [Insert name] cannot even take a joke?" Keep in mind what researchers found when Serena Williams refused to laugh at racist jokes about her.

Another factor that plays into the categorization of a microaggression is the focus on restrictive gender roles that mandate the acceptable behaviors that men and women should engage in (Sue, 2010). This microaggression can be evident in sports media stories where an overemphasis of femininity is closely linked to perceived "feminine" sports that were mentioned in a previous section of this chapter. We know from research that sports media (as well as fans) often downplay the performance and other attributes of a female athlete when the athlete participates in sports that our culture considers to be masculine.

Restrictive Gender Roles

In a recent study on the frequency of microaggressions used in sports media, Frisby (2017c) found that when sports journalists wrote about the two top tennis players of the year (2016) they often reported on Serena's musculature, her body shape and size, her blackness, and the clothing she wore while competing at Wimbledon. In fact, the news should have been something along the lines of Angelique Kerber wins Wimbledon, but instead, data show the story that most sports media found newsworthy was centered on Serena Williams. Why?

Another recent Frisby (2017c) study found a significant relationship between online commentators and journalists and their frequent "jokes" and racial insults about Serena Williams. Frisby (2017c) found words in stories referring to the elite tennis player as either a "gorilla" or "manly" while making fun of her "skimpy outfits." Some sports reporters even referred to the most accomplished black female tennis player as a "savage beast" (Frisby, 2017c). In fact, in collecting articles for a content analysis of microaggressions of female athletes, Frisby (2017c) found a story that clearly illustrates the use of microinsults and microaggressions. In a story that was reportedly a positive, complimentary story about Serena Williams, Dr. Peter Larkins shared his thoughts about the tennis player's body shape and size. In the article, Dr. Larkins compared her shape and fitness with other female tennis players. He was quoted as saying, "It is the African-American race. They just have this huge gluteal strength.… Jennifer Capriati was clearly out of shape and overweight. With Serena, that's her physique and genetics" (Desmond-Harris, 2015).

Physical Shape and Appearance of Female Athletes

Sports fans and sports media have a peculiar attraction when it comes to the size and shape of a female athlete's body. We find that stories published by sports journalists and coverage of females in sports media have a direct relationship with America's expectations and cultural norms concerning body image, body type, and level of female physical attractiveness, as well as ethnicity. We must realize that journalists in all specialized areas, especially those working in sports, are not inoculated from the influences that American culture has on our preoccupation with beauty, idealized images of women, and our culture's preoccupation with physically attractive and idealized images of women. These norms have significant effects on our attitudes, opinions, and behaviors.

The effect of our culture's preoccupation with attractiveness and ideal body images does not pertain to whites only. Research on this topic reveals that black male commentators and journalists also make these types of microaggressive sexist comments when it comes to female athletes. Consider the sports journalist, Jason Whitlock. Whitlock criticized Serena Williams in his 2009 online Fox Sports column. In the column, Whitlock a journalist of color, described top professional tennis player, Serena Williams, as having a gluteus maximus that was the equivalent of an "oversized backpack." In the article, Whitlock takes this analogy a bit further by stating, "I am not fundamentally opposed to junk in the trunk, although my preference is a stuffed onion over

FIVE FEMALE JOURNALISTS AND HARASSMENT IN SPORTS REPORTING

Suzy Kolber

When the veteran ESPN sideline reporter interviewed Joe Namath during a nationally televised football game in 2003, the result was cringe-worthy. Ms. Kolber asked questions about football, but the seemingly inebriated Mr. Namath responded with an awkward pass. "I want to kiss you," he slurred, preceded by a half-hearted lean-in. To her credit, Ms. Kolber took it in stride. But nearly 10 years after the incident, the iconic quarterback is still something of an Internet punchline. And unfortunately for Ms. Kolber, it's difficult to hear her name without thinking of a drunken Mr. Namath making her—and millions of viewers—feel extremely uncomfortable.

Erin Andrews

Googling "Erin Andrews harassment" returns at least six separate incidents. The most serious occurred when Ms. Andrews, a Fox Sports broadcaster, was filmed in her hotel room through a peephole. Her stalker was eventually convicted in 2010 and given a 27-month prison sentence. Ms. Andrews has also been harassed on the job. Most recently, the hip-hop artist 50 Cent gave her an awkward kiss as she was reporting from a NASCAR event. (Ms. Andrews later tried to defuse the situation and said, "It was my fault!" in an interview.) In an incident from several years ago, a college football player approached Ms. Andrews from behind and gyrated his body, much to the delight of onlooking spectators.

Ines Sainz

The case of Ms. Sainz, a Mexican TV journalist, sparked debate about work-appropriate conduct for female reporters. In 2010, Ms. Sainz was harassed by players and coaches at a New York Jets practice. According to reports, she was subjected to catcalls and ogling in the Jets' locker room, and while on the field, a

(Continued)

Matt Lundy, "Five Female Sports Reporters and the Disrespect They Faced," *The Globe and Mail.* Copyright © 2013 by The Globe and Mail, Inc. Reprinted with permission.

continued ...

coach hurled passes in her direction so that players could get close to her. (The Jets' owner made an apology to Ms. Sainz, which she accepted.) Not everyone was quick to defend her, including female reporters. Jemele Hill, an ESPN.com columnist, said she had "a hard time feeling sympathetic" for someone whose conduct "insults some women" in sports reporting. Ms. Hill referenced an episode from a Super Bowl media day, when Ms. Sainz "went around touching players' biceps as part of what she called a 'strongest arm' competition." Then there are Ms. Sainz's fashion choices. "A quick Google search turns up numerous images of Sainz standing on a football field in clothing that seems better suited for a nightclub," Ms. Hill wrote. Regardless, Ms. Hill noted that Ms. Sainz never deserved to be harassed, no matter how she dresses.

Karen Thomson

Don Cherry's comments were inspired by an interaction between the Chicago Blackhawks' Duncan Keith and Karen Thomson, a sportscaster with TEAM 1040 in Vancouver. Ms. Thomson asked him about a slash he committed on the Canucks' Daniel Sedin. Mr. Keith said he didn't take a swipe at the opposing player, then added: "I think he [Sedin] scored a nice goal, and that's what the ref saw. Maybe we should get you as a ref maybe, hey?" Ms. Thomson responded in jest, saying she couldn't skate, to which Mr. Keith responded: "First female referee—you can't play probably either, right, but you're thinking the game, like you know it?" Ms. Thomson initially joked about the event on Twitter, then added: "Hockey is an emotional game and things are often said in the heat of the moment. I think this is what happened last night. I've moved on."

Lisa Olson

Ms. Olson was reporting on the New England Patriots in 1990 when she was sexually harassed in the locker room. During the incident, Ms. Olson said a group of naked players crowded around her to make lewd gestures in an aggressive manner. She described their actions as a "premeditated mind rape." The Patriots went on the offensive, saying that the Boston Herald should never have assigned a female reporter in the first place. Ms. Olson settled a lawsuit against the Patriots, but the ensuing torment—including abusive phone calls, death threats and slashed tires—was enough to derail her efforts to report on two other Boston teams. The Herald eventually transferred her to Australia.

an oozing pumpkin" (quoted in Frisby, 2017c, p. 266). Another article obtained in the Frisby (2017c) content analysis included the following quote, "Generally, I'm all for chunky sports stars … but tennis requires a mobility Serena cannot hope to achieve while lugging around breasts that are registered to vote in a different US state from the rest of her" (Frisby, 2017c, p. 266).

Reflect on Sports: Women in the Locker Room

Listed in the box are five rare incidents that help to illustrate the type of harassment that females working in the world of sports journalism experience in the context of doing their jobs.

Women Working in Sports Journalism

The question concerning the appropriateness of male or female reporters in locker rooms is a topic that is often in the news and in headlines. In October 2015, an NFL Network postgame interview accidentally showed televised images of several Cincinnati Bengals players who were nude. While the interview was brief and approximately one minute, several undressed football players were in the camera's eye throughout the live broadcast. Bengals offensive tackle Andrew Whitworth and other teammates could be seen coming in and out of the showers and/ or changing clothes. Although the interviewer was a male sports reporter, what would have happened had the interviewer been a female sports reporter? What consequences and other controversies might have ensued if a female sports reporter had been in the midst of nude male athletes?

The issue in broadcast sports journalism has more to do with when the interviews should take place as opposed to where. There is a "camera-on policy" for 10 minutes after the game. However, some players feel that these media interviews take place too soon after the game. Players are still coming off the thrill of a win or the agony of defeat. Is that a situation where sports media can enter the locker room but with their cameras off? To do the job of covering a team on a daily basis—namely, to interview players—male and female sports journalists must go into the locker room. This is an especially valid argument, particularly on game day; the only access to players after a game is inside the locker room. And while male and female sports journalists may not want to go into a locker room (they are often smelly, hot, and cluttered), under the current NFL media policy, players and reporters have little choice. The quick solution might be to wait a little longer so that all players have a chance to change clothes or make the players available immediately after the game in a place other than the locker room. For example, the players could be brought to a spot outside of the locker room or a different room entirely. Maybe even in the hallway of the building. Either way, the interviews can take place outside of the locker room and may provide an atmosphere that is much more comfortable for the players and both male and female sports reporters.

Female sports reporters in the early 1970s could not interview go into the locker room to interview male athletes. This policy even included pre- and postgame interviews. No women were allowed. Period. It was in 1978 when sports reporter Melissa Ludtke who worked for *Sports Illustrated* took the New York Yankees to court. Ludtke sued the team for not allowing her to do her job and interview the players in the locker room. She wanted to, within the scope of her work for the sports magazine, interview Yankee players during the 1977 World Series. A federal judge made a decision that banning female reporters from entering the locker room was a violation of the 14th Amendment. However, even though this ruling changed the policy banning women from entering locker rooms, we know that the law cannot change our culture's attitudes, thoughts, and expectations of what women can and cannot do. We still find in today's era that many of our female journalists are met by male sports professionals, be it players or staff, with anger, hostility, and trepidation as a journalist/reporter. Unfortunately, we still have instances where male athletes have dropped their towels to taunt the female reporter during interviews in the locker room.

To make locker rooms better environments for both male and female sports reporters, some have offered the idea of identifying a location that is outside of the locker room. The idea is to find a more neutral, gender-free atmosphere for all postgame interviews. The idea is that the players will then have some "down time" after the game and have opportunities to shower, collect themselves, and mentally prepare for questions about their game performance and the win/loss. However, some female reporters in favor of locker-room access believe that this would remove the ability to capture the raw emotion players exude immediately after a game is completed.

Inequality Across the Board

In 2014, it was found that men, especially Caucasian men, greatly outnumber women in the sports journalism industry. Female reporters are often criticized about their wardrobes and physiques, and not about their knowledge or reporting. In a report by the Institute for Diversity and Ethics in Sport, evidence was collected that showed improvements in the number of women of color sports journalists. While this finding was encouraging, the report still found evidence that suggested that the number of female sports columnists and editors was still dismal. Data collected on the sports media venues where female sports journalists can be found showed yet another dismal fact: The majority of female columnists and editors work primarily at ESPN, which, as we have already established, makes a huge effort in the areas of diversity and inclusion. Without the diversity and inclusion efforts documented by ESPN, the figures of women in sports would look much worse. Data on gender distribution in sports newsrooms report that as of 2017, "90 percent of sports editors are white and 90 percent are male" (Mccreary, 2018; Phillips, 2018). For those interested in more revealing statistics on the gender disparities in sports, go to the article published in the *New York Daily News* (Phillips, 2018).

Harassment of Female Sports Reporters

For more confirmation of the way our culture treats female sports reporters we do not have to go far. A search of the Internet produces evidence of the sexism in titles of websites such as "Top 15 Hottest Sideline Reporters in Sports." This headline alone does absolutely nothing in terms of framing the profession of sports reporting as a serious job (Ava, 2016). And as if harassment by other media in sports was not an issue, many female sports journalists find themselves confronting harassment from fans, athletes, and fellow male sports reporters. An event that helps illustrate this harassment took place during the World Cup held in South Africa in 2010. This was the year that Spain was playing in its first game against Switzerland. South Africa ended up losing the game 0–1. In a strange twist, the Spanish media, as well as postings found on social media, cast blame for the loss on female sports reporter, Sara Carbonero. Ms. Carbonero happened to be the reporter who was on the field at the time reporting on the match. Ironically, the female sports reporter's mere presence on the field was enough evidence for fans and Spanish media to blame her for the loss. It was believed that her presence on the field was a distraction for Spain's goalie. Other remarks also blamed Ms. Carbonero for a lack of professionalism and even attacked her credibility as a journalist. Many expressed the idea that Sara Carbonero was not a credible or "real" sports journalist because she was too beautiful. Once again, we see examples of how a woman's physical attractiveness is seen as a hindrance to her career.

Social Media and Raw Critics and Commentary

Social media is now a risky vehicle for fans to make unedited commentary and attack women interested in or working in sports journalism. In fact, sports are one area where we see the consequences of women working in male-dominated fields. Admittedly, while males can be subjected to insults, we find that social media is a convenient vehicle by which women sports reporters find themselves the targets of many malicious attacks. The Pew Research Center conducted a study in 2014 that showed that, when compared to men, women are much more likely to be targets of online sexual harassment and stalking.

What are the solutions to these disappointing statistics for women interested in sports reporting? Listed next are a few suggested solutions for improving these problems:

Sports media must become more proactive, just like ESPN has, when it comes to targeted hires of women and people of color. Thus sports media must include writing roles and being more flexible with working conditions, hours, and schedules. Along these same lines, we find that higher education institutions, such as colleges and universities, must educate inspiring sports journalists about the need to work together with sports media to produce news stories that show sports journalism in a positive manner, especially when trying to engage and encourage young women to take courses in sports journalism.

Create and produce content that shows how male sports fans treat women. Using facts, experts, and other objective data, media messages that educate readers on biases held by male reporters and fans may help to raise awareness of the treatment and equity issues. Recall, for example, a video of male sports fans reading "real comments about women sports reporters to their face" (#morethan-mean, Just Not Sports, 2016). This video shows the public's fascination with this disparity in that millions of people have watched the video online. The creators behind the #morethanmean video have a podcast dedicated to sports culture. They interviewed a mix of people, including friends and family, and asked them to read mean and often harassing tweets while in the presence of two popular female sports journalists, Sarah Spain and Julie DiCaro. The video has sparked a conversation about the line between harmless online trolling and online harassment. In fact, many other female sports reporters have sounded off on social media, saying they've also been subjected to similar online hateful speech.

Conclusion

A 1994 book written by Mariah Nelson titled *The Stronger Women Get, the More Men Love Football* shows the harassment and other offensive acts leveled at women in sports. While the book is now 23 years old, if we fast forward to news coverage of female athletes in 2017, we find very similar instances and events still taking place in sports media. We now have several female athletes who are becoming central to conversations among sports media and fans. And now women sportswriters are starting to become a part of our cultural conversations in all sports. ESPN as we mentioned in this chapter several times, is doing a great job putting female sports reporters in prominent positions. ESPN's show *Around the Horn* made history in 2016 when it featured four female sports journalists analyzing sports without men.

We know that female athletes endure intense training and are offered phenomenal opportunities to compete in the sports world. Yet, despite the rise of female athletes in sports, research continues to find that they are still fighting barriers in our culture because of our society's expectations regarding hegemonic femininity. Hegemonic femininity is a concept that communicates the idea that women can be successful as long as they are attractive, composed, and thin. We also find that outside of sports media, mass media in our pop culture environment in 2018 are also quick to validate that as well. We find that when female athletes are framed through our culture's hegemonic femininity expectations, it becomes difficult for female athletes to overcome microaggressions. Microaggressions, as we mentioned, prevent hard-working and skilled athletes from receiving the recognition that they deserve. We find that especially in terms of female Olympians who by all measures of success should relish the idea that they reached the highest level in sports, yet microaggressions committed by sports media actually take the spotlight away from them and may even present them as paling in comparison to male athletes.

The most controversial issue surrounding professional sports today is particularly centered on the issue of access. Locker rooms are typically open access to sports journalists before or after practices and games. However, in this chapter, we briefly discussed how this particular work environment becomes awkward for female reporters and the athletes themselves.

We also know that from the athletes' perspective, many simply want to "leave the office" when their workday ends, and for them, the workday ends after the game. Therefore, it should come as no surprise that immediately after practices and games, they head to the locker room, strip down, and hit the showers. The athletes' locker room is often housed in a part of a large complex that includes training rooms, lounges, and other areas that sports media are not ordinarily given access to enter. And while most nudity takes place off camera when reporters are in the locker room, we still see images of shirtless, disheveled, or sweaty athletes who find themselves facing several microphones and cameras, with reporters asking for comments immediately after a game. These visions of male athletes are enduring in sports coverage today.

We know that in our culture, female athletes participate in sports where a reporter's access to the locker room is not considered controversial. Take for instance the USTA. The USTA bans all media from entering locker rooms for men and women. The National Women's Soccer League does not have a league-wide policy that prohibits reporters' presence in the locker room. In fact, their manual says only that each team's media relations staff is in charge of determining who enters the locker room postgame. The manual goes on to inform the media that their media relation's staff will coordinate player interviews with the head coach, and, together, they will determine who gets access and when. In another illustration of how certain teams deal with the locker-room issue, we find that although the MLS allows media in locker rooms, they regulate the use of live broadcasts or photographs in female locker rooms. In fact, broadcasts and pictures of sports journalists in the female athletes' locker room may not happen at all.

Scholars suggest that if one feels strongly about the appearance of female reporters in men's locker rooms or male reporters in women's locker rooms, then we must advocate that media should be prohibited from interviewing and entering the locker room. Pundits suggest media follow the same protocol that is followed when covering Olympic games. Very seldom do we see reporters in locker rooms during Olympic competitions. But still, this suggestion begs the following questions: Does the saying "boys will always be boys" make it okay to make allowances for this type of male behavior? The locker room is, as an NFL executive stated on ESPN, "a widely held supported fortress of male dominance" (www.espn.com).

As this chapter shows, disparities in sports and media treatment of female athletes is not limited to media coverage. We find disparities and somber numbers in terms of the number of women sports reporters, producers, editors, and others in the sports journalism industry. Research in 2014 investigated the number of bylines written by female sports reporters, and data in the study showed that female bylines hovered around 3% (Morrison, 2014). And, finally, we know that in 2018, the number of female sports journalists showed an increase in the number of women of color sports journalists, but, overall, representation by women in roles as columnists and editors is dismal at best. And, as mentioned, we must conclude the chapter with the statistic that shows that, in terms of where female sports journalists are employed, ESPN, a major traditional sports medium, has made diversity and inclusion an important mission. For example, Lapchick's (2018) most recent research shows that of the 44 women working in sports journalism, ESPN was found to employ 38 of the 44 females in sports. In other words, ESPN employs 86% of women working in the sports journalism industry. Moreover, Lapchick's (2018) research uncovered statistics showing that of the 44 female sports journalists, four identified closely with African-American ethnicity (9%), one was Latina (i.e., .2%) and two identified as Asian (5%). All seven women of color are, at the time of this writing, currently working for ESPN (Lapchick, 2018). This means that if ESPN were taken out of the equation and women employed with this sports media were removed, "the overall percentage of female columnists would drop from 19 percent to 3 percent" (Lapchick, 2018).

We also learned from research that ESPN continues to work on diversifying the newsroom and sports profession. Despite the fact that today's statistics on employment in sports communication and journalism show that more than 90% of sports editors are white and 90% are male, what we really need is for more sports news organizations to be willing to make changes and become fit for balance and equity in terms of diversity in the newsroom and diversity in the sports we cover.

QUESTIONS FOR REFLECTION AND DISCUSSION

1. Do female athletes have to objectify themselves to sell magazines? Why or why not? Do male athletes objectify themselves in female media to sell products? Why do you think women are depicted more in sexual ways than male athletes? Does the status quo make it everything right? Why or why not?

2. Some argue that female sports reporters do not know the masculine sports as well as men do. What do you think? Do you agree? Why or why not?

3. What hurdles do you think exist for women who are sideline reporters? What are the hurdles, and how do women in sports overcome these obstacles?

4. Should women sports reporters have to justify their presence in the locker room? Why or why not?

5. Are there disparities in the way female and male sideline reporters interview athletes? Defend and support your answer?

6. Is there a credibility gap between male and female sports reporters? Why or why not. Support your answer.

7. Are women viewed as token sports reporters without much expertise? Why or why not? Provide a rationale to support your answer.

8. What do you think takes for a female sports journalist to prove she is knowledgeable about sports? What must she do to gain access to areas for interviews like male reporters? What will it take for a former female basketball player to get a job as a color analyst on college and professional basketball broadcasts?

9. Pretend you are a sports journalist, and your "beat" is football and basketball. What must you do as a female reporter do "deem yourself" credible? Defend and support your answer.

SUGGESTED ACTIVITIES

1. Conduct a content analysis on how female sports reporters are treated. What themes or incidents did you find? Discuss using research and other citations to support your findings.

2. Locate sports media coverage and bylines in sports media written by male and female reporters. Is there a difference in the way they write and frame their stories? If so, how? If not, what similarities did you find? Did you see certain themes repeated by men and women? What are the themes?

3. Look for print news stories about LGBTQ athletes. Now content analyze the story for hidden frames/themes. How do sports journalists frame the story? What themes and ideas do they use to help the reader understand and accept the athlete's sexual orientation?

4. Collect stories from print sports media for a month. Are there differences in the way male and female reporters cover sports, especially regarding the athleticism of female athletes? Provide your data and support your conclusions. (PhysOrg.com, 2009).

5. Interview either a local or national female sports journalist. What aspects does she love about her job? What does she dislike most? What changes would this sports journalist like to see take place for female reporters to be treated civilly without harassment and like male reporters? How does she feel about locker-room access?

CREDITS

Fig. 7.1: Sports Illustrated. Copyright © 2017 by WarnerMedia.

8

Hegemonic Masculinity in Sports

LEARNING OBJECTIVES

After completing this chapter, students should be able to:

- define and understand the concept of hegemony. The chapter will introduce readers to how our understanding of sports in American culture is a process of socialization; explain the sports industry's process to maintain control, power, and leadership by white males; and examine sports fans' acceptance of that power and influence;

- demonstrate a clear understanding of gender-appropriate sports and their relationship to hegemonic masculinity;

- explain how hegemonic masculinity can be maintained in American culture as long as sports fans and individuals in our culture are satisfied with their lives and are zealous about living the status quo because they have no compelling reason to change the masculine hierarchy;

- think critically about stereotypes related to certain male sports;

- recognize the effect of media on gender-appropriate sports and the creation of masculinity; and

- explore strategies for combating hegemonic masculinity in sports.

Introduction

Hegemonic masculinity has a perspective frequently used in studies centered on the media's preoccupation with men and masculinity, particularly with regard to sports. To say that sports media is preoccupied with presenting and worshiping male athletes is a statement that has been supported throughout this textbook. Research over the decades continues to show that media has constructed symbols, narratives, and images that taken together tell Americans which sports (e.g., football) are masculine and that the sports that are, are aligned with sports fans' values, social lives, and notions about what it means to be female or male. Because sports media are a part of our everyday lives, we must consider the role that media play in the construction of hegemonic masculinity in sports. Hegemonic masculinity is a concept that helps us explain and comprehend how sports media select images. It is also a concept that helps explain the role that inclusivity and diversity play in terms of leadership and management in sports and editorial practices in sports journalism. In this chapter, we will begin to understand the influence that hegemonic masculinity has on sports media, news coverage, and ultimately on the fans who consume and are frequently exposed to messages in sports media.

Over the last 50 years at least, we learn that media scholars who study sports in America have identified a strong relationship between masculinity and the depiction and representation among sports considered to be masculine (see Chapter 7). Sociologists and scholars of sports have obtained data that reveals sports media are more likely to use hegemony in their mediated messages and sports news coverage. The concept of hegemonic masculinity is also used to help further our culture's acceptance of violent and aggressive contact sports, as well as the homophobia that we find frequently covered in highly visible and popular sports media. For example, American football is known to have an inordinate number of players who get concussions from playing in the sport. Scholars have found that hegemonic masculinity and attributes such as indifference, toughness, risk taking, and aggression have become normalized in today's cultural environment. Players and fans have come to accept these behaviors as simply "part of the game." Our society favors the idea that if a male athlete is not able to play through a concussion, the male risks being blamed for a team's loss or labeled effeminate.

As discussed in Chapter 3, gender is used to categorize, label, and distinguish males from females (Blinde & Taub, 1992; Koivula, 1995, 2001; Kolnes, 1995; Ross & Shinew, 2008). Gender as part of our social construct is divided into bipolar constructs: male and female. In fact, if we seriously consider this classification and our culture's preoccupation with assigning one of the two labels to athletes, we would be remiss if we did not mention how sports are segregated in American culture. We have men's tennis and women's tennis, for example. Then we have sporting events that are classified as "coed" or "mixed." As we consider interpretations of our gender identity, discussed earlier in the text, we can see how these dichotomous labels for gender in the very sports that we participate in can become problematic. We also see how the intersectionality of an individual's race, ethnic background, gender identity, sexual orientation, and socioeconomic status might also interfere with the mutually exclusive segregation of sports based on two categories of gender: male and female.

Hegemonic masculinity in American culture is also the idea that we have norms and expectations that center on how men should act and treat women. In reality, hegemony's function in our culture is one that justifies the social norm that allows men to dominate, control, and maintain sole power over women in all aspects of life. The control that men have over women in American culture is manifested in many civilizations involving the human race. While hegemony emphasizes male dominance and the manly male over a male who behaves in a feminine way, or what our culture considers to be feminine behaviors, we know that in America, male dominance is clearly evident in images, narratives, discourse, and mediated messages produced and published in the mass media. We even see signs and symbolic images of hegemony in corporations, conglomerates, and, to some extent, our democratic government laws and practices.

One common misconception when one thinks of hegemonic masculinity is that it is thought to describe violent, aggressive, and bad behavior expressed by men or young boys. Another misunderstanding of the term is when it is used to describe what is often termed the "alpha male." For those unfamiliar with the term, alpha male is used to describes men who are aggressive and physically violent. Cultural ideals of hegemonic masculinity do not always conform to the personalities of actual men or the realities of everyday achievements of men.

Trujillo's 1991 work took the concept of hegemonic masculinity and separated it into five subcategories that were believed to identify the circumstances and environments when hegemonic masculinity is most likely to occur. The five situations that influence this concept in American culture, according to Trujilo (1991) are "(l) when power is discussed in terms of physical force and control (particularly in the representation of the female body); (2) when masculinity is defined through occupational achievement in an industrial, capitalistic society; (3) when hegemony is discussed in terms of familial patriarchy; (4) when the masculinity is 'symbolized by the adventurers and risk-taking men of yesteryear as well as the images of present-day outdoorsman,' and finally (5) when heterosexually is centered on the representation of the phallus" (Trujillo, 1991, pp. 291–292).

Hegemonic masculinity has been characterized as being predominately related to "white, heterosexual, and middle-class men with an ideal physique" (Paloian, 2018). The standard body type for females, as we discussed in Chapter 7 of this text, is one that fits the ectomorph very thin and lean yet toned body type. Men, however, in American culture are expected to have endomorphic body types that are toned and muscular, especially biceps and well-defined abdominal muscles (Dworkin, 2001; Krane et al., 2004). Frisby (2017c) obtained data that show female athletes do not fit the ectomorphic, thin, and lean body image. Athletes such as Serena Williams and mixed martial arts fighter Gina Carano tend to receive more microaggressions (negative commentary) and experience more challenges in their professional careers. Female athletes, Frisby (2017c) found, grapple with having to meet our culture's expectation of having a thin, lean body type, and yet their body type leans more toward the masculine image that consists of large, toned muscles, including having large biceps and quadriceps (Dworkin, 2001). Meanwhile, we also learned in Chapter 7 that men who have more "feminine" body shapes and participate in sports that are perceived to be more "feminine" sports, such as figure skating, dancing, and cheerleading, are just as likely to encounter backlash from the media and sports fans (Anderson, 2005).

History of Hegemonic Masculinity

Hegemonic masculinity, developed by Connell (1987), shows how masculinity varies across time and culture. It legitimizes male dominance in American culture. The concept also provides a rationalization for our society's treatment of women and female athletes as sex objects and second-class citizens (Connell, 2005). The idea of a hierarchical patriarchal society allows scholars to explain the how and why of male dominance, particularly in the sports world. Scholars who center their careers on the study of hegemonic masculinity in American culture analyze and apply the concept to offer up information that explains how and why males are dominant over women in certain situations and why male dominance exists in existence in cultures where men dominate women and even men who are thought to be "feminine" (Connell & Messerschmidt, 2005; Carrigan, Connell, & Lee, 1985).

Masculine norms in American culture often emphasize certain values, such as aggression, toughness, autonomy, and risk taking (Connell, 1987, 1995). In the United States, a hegemonic masculine character most frequently depicted in mass media and in sports typically resembles white, middle-class, breadwinning men who are also "strong, competent, in control, competitive, assertive (if not aggressive), rational/instrumental, and oriented toward the public" (Grindstaff & West, 2011).

In a culture where women are viewed primarily as objects for the sexualized male gaze and male pleasure (refer to Chapter 7), and where gender is understood in binary terms such as male versus female (refer to Chapter 3), we also note that in American culture, men are treated differently, particularly in terms of how they are perceived as sexual objects. In addition, in American culture, gay men are often linked to our culture's ideals of femininity and what it means to act and be female (Grindstaff & West, 2011). Because gay males are linked to femininity, they are often labeled as sissies, wimps, fags, etc. These ethnophaulisms are defined as "ethnic, gender, or racial slurs typically caricaturing some identifiable (often physical) feature of the group being disparaged" (Kimmel, 1994; Kimmel, 1996; Kimmel, 2010).

"Marginalization" is a term found in Connell's (1995) work that describes the relationships and intersectionality of race, class, and gender in our culture. This intersectionality is important to discuss in the context of hegemonic masculinity because it provides a broader context for us to understand how the term relates to marginalization and dominance in the sports world and sports media. To illustrate this relationship we find in Connell's (1995) work, we use the example of African American celebrity athletes and how race and white male dominance are intertwined. Connell's (1995) discourse is on how sports media (and popular national pop media) may depict some African American athletes in a way that it appears that they exemplify hegemonic masculinity, yet what is left out of the story that shows their fame and wealth is that these athletes do not enjoy the same benefits of wealth and power as white male athletes. In other words, for African American athletes, hegemonic masculinity does not "trickle down" to give them the same social authority as white men have (Conner, 1995). If we add social class into the mix, we continue to find differences in hegemonic masculinity. In fact, working-class, blue-collar men across all ethnic and racial categories may express hegemonic masculinity in their subculture, but once this group is in the broader context of American culture, we find that even they experience backlash and discrimination. In other words, research shows us that working-class males are also marginalized within our culture and are also second class to those people who have all the privileges of wealth and political power (Fine & West, 1998; Messner, 1992; Willis, 1977).

One argument, which has been published by multiple researchers, is that female athletes also face dilemmas in American culture. Female athletes are not only expected to succeed in their sports but also to maintain hegemonic femininity. This, according to research, is an expectation that can quickly turn into a tricky balance for female athletes to create and sustain (Dworkin, 2001; Krane, 2001, Krane et al., 2004; Mennesson, 2000; Ross & Shinew, 2008). This tricky balance between athletic success and maintenance of hegemonic femininity is described in most sociology research and literature as the "female/athlete paradox" (Kolnes, 1995; Krane et al., 2004; Meân & Kassing, 2008). In his article, Krane (2001) argues, "Sportswomen tread a fine line of acceptable femininity … engaging in athletic activities is empowering, yet maintaining an acceptable feminine demeanor is disempowering" (p. 116). This discourse supports the idea stated at the beginning of this chapter that hegemony and masculinity continue in our culture because we continue to uphold traditional expectations about how female athletes should look, act, and respond. Hegemonic masculinity and our culture's acceptance are also demonstrated in the way we respond to femininity and, in particular, how femininity is frequently maintained by sports media and sports fans' various and widely held attitudes toward female athletes (Hardin, Chance, Dodd, & Hardin, 2002; Krane, 2001). Research suggests that female athletes are challenged with the task of learning to balance hegemonic femininity and athletics (Paloian, 2018).

Masculine and Feminine Sports

Published research has been conducted to provide insights into how Americans classify sports into those that are appropriate for men and for women. Koivula (1995) surveyed participants to determine how we categorize a variety of sports based on gender roles. The participants employed in the study were asked to rate certain sports by whether the sport was "female or male appropriate." The results revealed that participants perceived most sports to be categorized as gender neutral. Those gender-neutral sports included cycling, jogging, and tennis. Koivula (1995) also found evidence that suggested that "30% of the sports were thought to be more masculine" (see Koivula, 1995, p. 387). The more masculine sports included football, weight lifting, and boxing. Participants in this study reported that the "fewest amount (about 10%) of sports that were considered feminine sports were dance, figure skating, and synchronized swimming" (see Koivula, 1995, p. 389). As discussed in the previous chapter, classifying sports in this way has massive influences on a male's and female's choice about the sports type(s) they might be interested in. This understanding may also be used to explain the level of commitment exhibited by men and women, and the role that gender plays in influencing that commitment. For example, women who have at some point showed interest in what could be perceived as a masculine sport may have less commitment to the sport than a man. A possible explanation for the Koivula (1995) finding is that the perception of gender-appropriate sports may encourage people to avoid those sports that might be perceived as inappropriate (e.g., male synchronized swimming). Participation in gender-inappropriate sports might lead athletes to believe that they will be victimized because of our culture's ideas, negative thoughts, feelings, and stigmatizations concerning the incongruity between one's gender and participation in what we consider to be more gender-appropriate sports. It is also a possibility that perceptions of gender-inappropriate athletic participation may result in athletes having anxieties that relate to body image insecurities, homophobic bullying, and intense fears about their nonconformity (Dworkin, 2001; Krane et al., 2004). Taken together, the data obtained from Koivula (1995), (Dworkin, 2001), and Krane et al. (2004) leads us to speculate that one reason female athletes do not participate in gender-appropriate or even gender-inappropriate sports is that there may be a much greater risk for them when it comes to being disillusioned, quitting, or having no interest in the more appropriate "feminine" sports (Halbert, 1997; Koivula, 1995).

Research on gender-appropriate athletic events also reveals that sports perceived to be graceful, nonaggressive, nonviolent, and aesthetically pleasing are those that are frequently associated as the sports that are most appropriate for women yet completely unsuitable for male athletes. Even in today's culture in 2018, we find that physical attractiveness and beauty are particularly important attributes in the world of female and feminine sports. If we apply the theory of hegemonic masculinity to this statement, we might be able to understand why; physical appearance and beauty are most evident in women's sports because of the congruence held in America and in sports media related to gender-role stereotypes (what it means to be a woman and how women are supposed to act) and our idea of femininity (how we express our gender role and gender identity). Typical examples of feminine sports for females are dance, cheerleading, and figure skating. Why these sports? One explanation for this, particularly when we consider gender expression, gender identity, and how those concepts intersect with hegemonic masculinity in sports, is that these sports are typically considered feminine because of the idea that competition in these sports involves emotion, grace, beauty, and other very expressive attributes that are only supposed to be performed by women. It is hypothesized that these graceful movements in our American culture are frequently used to emphasize an athlete's feminine physique (Koivula, 2001). Interestingly, these types of athletic events are usually individualistic rather than team oriented.

Cultural scholars point out that individualistic sports are often perceived as feminine or gender neutral, while those sports that are mostly team oriented are viewed as masculine. They use this idea to explain why women basketball players, volleyball players, and soccer players (all sports that males play as well) tend to receive microaggressions and other negative commentaries (see Frisby, 2017b). The common thread among these sports is that they are considered contact sports, and in the United States, contact sports are deemed to be more male appropriate. When a sport is individualistic, frequently involving opposing athletes to be separated from one another (e.g., a team sport like swimming) and involves individual athletes competing in individual lanes despite the fact that they compete in the same swimming pool, this is often aligned with American masculine values and supports an individualistic culture. Masculine sports focus more on competition, strength, and aggression, and less on being pleasing aesthetically or graceful. Examples of sports that emphasize strength and aggression are football, wrestling, ice hockey, and bodybuilding. These are sports that often require male athletes to overpower and defeat their opponents. Masculine sports are often those that also require athletes to lift extraordinarily heavy weights or use their large muscles to subdue heavy competition or objects. The major component of masculine sports is that athletes must use their bodies to defeat their opponents (Alley & Hicks, 2005; Dworkin, 2001; Ross & Shinew, 2007).

Men and women participating in "gender-inappropriate" sports in today's culture continue to experience negative consequences in the media and from fans. Negative consequences such as being labeled as a deviant or strange, or being given nicknames that relate more to LGBTQ people, are often associated with athletes who compete in gender-inappropriate sports (Blinde & Taub, 1992; Halbert, 1997; Kolnes, 1995). If we apply the idea of hegemonic masculinity, we might be able to explain these negative consequences and reactions from the media and fans in this way: female athletes who participate in "masculine" sports (e.g., boxing or football) may be seen in American culture as women who are actively challenging the "boundaries of femininity" (Halbert, 1997, p. 11).

If we want to consider the challenge that female athletes who participate in male sports face, we must turn to the sport of boxing. As we know, boxing is a sport that is characterized by its hostility, aggression, brutality, and violence; it is considered the most masculine of all sports. Female boxers, as a result of this perception of the sport, are thought to be gender deviants (Halbert, 1997). This gender-deviant characterization is exactly the thing that makes Ronda Rousey and the many female boxers legendary. While they are displaying raw aggression, a trait that is supposed to be associated with men, they are also addressing stereotyped notions. In 2017, we found an interesting occurrence: Fans are taking female boxers seriously, and yet the athletes are able to leave their femininity intact and undistorted.

In America sports, fans are often less familiar and infrequently exposed to images or media messages about female athletes who display masculine qualities such as large muscular strength and well-toned biceps, quadriceps, and abdominal muscles. We also find few, if any, stories about female athletes who use their bodies to defeat and subdue opponents. If sports media coverage of female boxers follows the same pattern as coverage of other female athletes, we would expect that media stories would frame these athletes as abnormal, odd, aberrant, manlike, and going against God's nature and our expectations of how women are supposed to act (Dworkin, 2001; Krane, 2001; Krane et al., 2004). To support this hypothesis, recall that in her study, Frisby (2017c) found that when writing stories about Serena Williams, many sports commentators often employ microaggressions related to her ethnicity, musculature, and competitiveness. But in terms of female boxers, contrary to expectations in America about their participation in the sport, we have yet to find one story that focused on the deviant nature of female boxers.

Male-Appropriate Sports

Historically in American culture, sports have been a masculine (and segregated) institution. As mentioned in Chapter 7 of the text, despite the increases in participation by female athletes, the world of sports is still an institution that is largely structured, ordered, and led by and/or for men. Masculine sports such as those mentioned in this chapter are aligned with socially sanctioned behaviors such as physical violence, aggression, and power (Messner, 1992, 2002). In fact, in his work, Messner (1992) discusses how, since the 19th century, sports in our culture have been organized to reinforce male dominance. According to Messner (1992), sports have served our culture for more than 100 years to support hegemonic masculinity and male power and control, and that is why it still exists despite increases of female athletes and increases in women's sporting events.

When we consider the fact that men dominate football, we must also note how female athletes are excluded from this and other sports that are publicly supported and considered to be extremely masculine. The sport of American football is at the core of the concept of hegemonic masculinity.

The sport-masculinity bond in American culture also excludes women on a symbolic level. It is exclusive in that the bond seems to say that "real" men are strong and aggressive, and that "real" women cannot or ought to not be aggressive. This theory might also be used to explain the sexualization and objectification of female athletes, and why many perceive strong female athletes to be "masculine" or at least not truly feminine (refer to Chapter 7).

Cheerleading

Cheerleading sets the stage in American culture for individuals to exercise their gender identities and femininities and masculinities. When we consider cheerleading in America, especially using images found currently in sports media, we often think that cheerleading is a female sport. However, what is not commonly known (especially for the author of this text) is that cheerleading began as an all-male activity. Somehow, and in some manner, cheerleading in America has become a predominantly female sport. If you were to conduct an "on-the-street" type interview and ask Americans to describe a typical "cheerleader," we might find common themes that describe an individual who is physically attractive and popular (Adams & Bettis, 2003; Anderson, 2005; Grindstaff & West, 2006; Grindstaff & West, 2011; Hanson, 1995). In fact, many media images of the cheerleader often depict young, pretty, popular girls who, in some instances, are mean to their fellow classmates. And if we take the idea of cheerleading and apply it to cultural customs in America, we find that cheerleading means that one must engage a cognitive heuristic script that involves behaviors associated with being female, such as enthusiasm, positivity, encouragement, sex appeal, and other physically expressive behaviors. According to Connell (1987), these traits are called "emphasized femininity." As depicted in Figure 8.1, we find that the common depictions of cheerleaders in sports media are

FIGURE 8.1   *The all-male cheerleading team. Cheerleading is a sport that requires athleticism and physical fitness. In our culture, male cheerleaders challenge notions of masculinity. Why?*

those of women who have their hair in ponytails; wear hair bows, ribbons, and short skirts; and express other behaviors that emphasize femininity.

Cheerleading used to be an auxiliary sport, but today, it is a sport that has national (and increasingly international) appeal. It is currently a sport that involves competitions and summer training camps. Compared to earlier times when cheerleading involved jumps, splits, and dance routines, currently, it includes high-level stunts that involve cartwheels, handstands, somersaults, flips, and tumbling. In addition to dance, cheerleading now involves building pyramids and amazing acrobatic performances. In fact, over the last 40 or 50 years, cheerleading has endured some significant changes, which involve intense physicality and the idea that young men are starting to gravitate toward the sport. In 2018, we find more male cheerleaders, particular those who engage in the competitive arena.

Cheerleading in today's culture involves athleticism and physical prowess and fitness. Yet the visibility of male cheerleaders is absent in sports media. Hegemonic masculinity might also help to explain the lack of visibility of male cheerleaders in media images and stories. Given our culture's expectation that men should participate in masculine sports and other activities that highlight their strength and power, it is no surprise, or should be of no surprise, that symbolic importance of cheerleading sporting events is invisible in the media. Perhaps if more sports media covered male cheerleaders (in the same way they should cover male gymnasts), we might find that with the increased visibility of male cheerleaders (gymnasts), along with the intense upper-body training they dedicate themselves to, cheerleading could gain legitimacy, particularly in the eyes of the public and sports fans. This change in perception of cheerleading seems to be more evident in Western culture in myriad ways. Research on cheerleading in American culture shows, for example, "colleges and universities that have both coed and all-girl cheer squads, the coed squad typically supports men's sports, while the all-female squad supports women's sports" (Grindstaff & West, 2011). The coed cheerleading squads typically perform during the male athletic events because of the large crowds and popularity of football and basketball, which are often popular male sports. Although the number of male cheerleaders is less than 10% of cheerleaders overall (see Adams & Bettis, 2003), we do find that white male cheerleaders are well represented on major cheerleading squads.

Coed cheerleading is increasingly more athletic and prestigious than it was 50 or more years ago. Why? Some argue that perceptions may have turned positive because male cheerleaders bring a strength to the sport that allows squads to engage in more dramatic acrobatics and pyramids. Male cheerleaders, as we have noticed, have the ability to "build higher and stronger" pyramids and "do the cooler stuff that girls just sometimes can't do" (Grindstaff & West, 2011). Why do fans feel that cheerleading squads are more credible when men are included? Some scholars argue that it is the presence of strong, muscular, and physically fit men who can hold a female cheerleader in the palm of his hand that is a concept that undermines the predominance of female cheerleaders.

Observation of behaviors displayed by male and female cheerleaders show that when squads perform on the sidelines of sports events, male cheerleaders frequently do not engage in the higher levels of emotional expressiveness as their female teammates. That is, "male cheerleaders are often held to lower standards of emotional expressiveness" (Grindstaff & West, 2011). We find that male cheerleaders smile less and do not move as frequently as female cheerleaders. We also find that male cheerleaders are often not observed using pom poms. Moreover, research revealed that some schools release male cheerleaders from participating on the sidelines, and they are only required to participate in cheerleading competitions (Grindstaff & West, 2011). Coaches continue to face difficulties in recruiting and retaining boys and men into cheerleading. Scholars contend that this difficulty is due to its feminine stigma.

Pervasive images of masculinity published in sports media often support our cultural pre-suppositions that communicate the idea that real men are physically strong, aggressive, and in control, according to Harry Brod (1987). An example of this depiction can be found in a 2018 commercial for Hefty trash bags featuring John Cena. In the ad, Cena is surrounded by three women. His well-toned and large biceps and chest are evident in the camera. He is seen describing the trash bags as "Hefty's strong, tough," and then over the intercom we hear, "Your husbands are waiting." One of the women responds, "I don't have a husband," and another agrees and says, "Me either." While Cena does not say that these are features that represent masculinity, it's through the close alignment of the image of Cena's body and weight lifting physique coupled with the words he uses to describe the Hefty bags that we get the idea that if something is physically strong, it is attractive and appealing. In his article, Brod (1987) argues that their insecurities about their musculature lead some men in our culture to hold on tight to preserving their gender expression and masculinity. In fact, in terms of the intersectionality of gender and social class, we learn that working-class, blue-collar males have less access to the resources that may invoke or validate their masculinity (e.g., corporate authority and power, economic wealth and power) and seek to find validation of their masculinity through weight lifting and enhancing their physical bodies (Brod, 1987). Brod (1987) writes that economic power, workplace authority, and the physical body all work together to provide the working-class male with "a concrete means of achieving and asserting manhood" (p. 14).

Femininity and Adornment

Research on female athletes shows that when asked to list accessories and hairstyles that female athletes choose for athletic performances, male athletes stated that ponytails, headbands, and bows are the most likely hairstyles chosen by female athletes when preparing to compete in a sports activity. The ponytail may be relatively innocent and inoffensive; it is a very good illustration of our culture's inflexible standards of beauty, and it also clearly shows a focus on white images and ideas of what it means to be feminine. For example, given the nature of African American hair texture, many young women who try out for cheerleading squads find themselves in a quandary, particularly when their coaches require ponytails. Oftentimes, the effort it takes to wear a ponytail requires resources and money (e.g., hair weaves or extensions, hair relaxers, and other processes not normal for a Caucasian woman or young girl). We know that athletes rely on ponytails and headbands to keep hair from getting in their eyes or in their faces. But if we observe even the images on headbands for female athletes to wear to the gym or in sporting competitions, we always find pictures of white, blonde women. This is clearly a demonstration of how our culture has continued to accept these images, and it also supports hegemonic masculinity because no one challenges the cheer coach or the manufacturers of hair bows, headbands, or scrunchies to include photographs of black women. We find in our culture that the ponytail is a symbol that expresses our expectations of how young girls and women are to express their femininity. Even in dance, ballet dancers are expected to have their hair in a bun (similar to a ponytail but woven into what looks like a bun). If we are honest as a culture, we must start seeing that the ponytail is a symbol that expresses a hairstyle trend that occurs in a culture where white individuals dominate. We must realize that in American culture, we have an ideology that says long hair is for (young) women (older women are expected to sport shorter hairstyles) and that men are to have shorter hair. Currently, we do have instances of the "man bun," but if we peruse comments online about the male bun, we find that many Americans are still not comfortable with men who don long hair simply because it challenges our society's value that tells us that the length of one's hair is actually one way that we separate women from men and enforce the gender dichotomy (Little & McGivern, 2011; Ready, 2001)

Taken together, information presented in this section on female adornment and expectations of women athletes putting their hair in ponytails, we are left asking an important question: Should athletes of color who may have different hairstyles (e.g., short, twisted, braided, natural) be required to find a way to force their hair into a ponytail despite the length and texture? As mentioned in Chapter 4, research confirms that close to 40% of African American women in the United States will report that they refrain from physical activity because of issues with maintaining their hair and other concerns associated with daily hair maintenance. The intersectionality of race/ethnicity and sports now makes the discussion of hair and its effect on gender and sports and hegemony crucial in that the notion of hair can help answer the question: Why do some Africa-American women choose not to swim? Or play tennis? Or dance? Are there some young girls of color who either quit cheerleading or are dissuaded from trying out because of their perception that their hair will not fit in a ponytail? And the list of questions on sports can go on. As of the time of this writing, the author found that for some African American women, issues and concerns about their hair are factors that prohibit them from participating in sports. Although not central to this chapter, but to illustrate the point, we must consider African American female fan reaction to Gabby Douglas, the first gold medalist gymnast in the Olympics in 2012. In lieu of writing tweets praising this rare accomplishment, many black women took to social media to ridicule and attack her "nappy hair." Then in 2016, even with Simone Biles's appearance on the Olympic gymnastics team, Douglas was once again the victim of social media harassment based on the appearance of her hair. This is why we must start candid and honest discussions about the motivation behind these attacks that surely had a negative effect on Douglas's sense of self and athletic accomplishment. Hair is important in American culture, and the significance of hair is a concept that is not often brought to the forefront in sports media.

Representations of Hegemonic Masculinities in the Media

Sports media is influential and plays a vital role in their depictions and representations of athletic women. Through the use of idealized images and perpetuating notions of our culture's passivity with respect to how female athletes are treated, we find that sports media must take some responsibility in the role they have in reinforcing strict and restrictive gender roles and stereotypes. Sports media must start evaluating all the ways they communicate hegemonic masculinity. Sports media must also analyze their mediated messages, narratives, and discourses, which can be traced back over the years. Just as research has shown, it is hoped that sports media starts seeing patterns of male superiority and female inferiority frequently evident in their coverage (Buysse & Embser-Herbert, 2004). Highly visible sports media often depict male athletes as superior and muscular in their stories when they emphasize the male athletes' accomplishments. Female athletic inferiority, as studies have shown over the last 30 years, is frequently framed in ways that demean and trivialize women's accomplishments. Typical sports coverage of female athletes emphasizes in subtle, covert ways that female athletes are and must be females first. In sports media, female athletes are rarely seen as athletes first and foremost. In fact, stories about female athletes rarely make the first page in the sports section of a newspaper, and they are rarely the lead story in a broadcast. Although sports coverage of female athletes and their sports has increased, research shows that coverage is often second to male athletes and male-dominated sports. Secondhand coverage of female athletes and their sports seems to express a hegemonic masculine hierarchy—one that says women are not to surpass men in sporting competitions. Buysse and Embser-Herbert's (2004) work on the patterns of male superiority and female inferiority can be applied to an event that occurred in 2015 involving John McEnroe. McEnroe is a male tennis celebrity athlete who, during an interview, stated with confidence that he was sure he could beat either Williams sister (Serena or Venus) in a game of "mixed" singles. The McEnroe news story illustrates current male hegemony in sports because implicit in his statement was the idea that men were better than women. This is male hegemony at its best in that it clearly helps elucidate the air of superiority and dominance in American sports.

Buysse and Embser-Herbert (2004) published research that illustrates how media portray a bias for male athletes and sports through their analysis of photographic media coverage. Their research included analysis of "media coverage (from six of the most prestigious athletic conferences) of female and male sports teams of many different types of sports" (Flanagin, 2010). Sports included in their analysis were selected based on previously published research. The sports they included in their study were gender appropriate. Data obtained in the study found that female athletes were often reported as being more passive in news coverage when compared to male athletes. Furthermore, Buysse and Embser-Herbert (2004) found that participants reported thinking that female athletes were least likely to be portrayed competing in their sports environment/context. In depictions of the athletes in sports media, the researchers expected to obtain data that showed that female gymnasts would likely be found in stories about gymnastics when compared to male athletes (Buysse & Embser-Herbert, 2004). However, data obtained in the Buysse and Embser-Herbert (2004) study provided empirical evidence showing that gymnastics, a sport that is typically perceived to be gender inappropriate for men, frequently covered male gymnasts more than female gymnasts. The researchers concluded that female athletes, even those who participate in gender-appropriate sports, will not likely be found in sports media, especially when they compared stories to those focused on male athletes. According to the research, the feminine traits and attributes that were frequently found in stories published in sports media were those that centered on female athletes' sexual attraction and appeal, their adornment or fashion sense, and, interestingly, their inaction or negative performance in sporting events.

Another example of hegemonic masculinity in the media happened in August 2016. In a televised interview, a reporter said to Andy Murray, "You're the first person to ever win two Olympic tennis gold medals, that's an extraordinary feat, isn't it?" (Malloy, 2016). However, Andy Murray was quick to correct the sports reporter, John Inverdale, after the BBC presenter forgot about the Olympic gold medals won by the Williams sisters (Malloy, 2016). Murray responded, "Well to defend the singles title, I think Venus and Serena have won about four each … it's obviously not an easy thing to do, and I had to fight unbelievably hard to get it tonight as well" (Malloy, 2016). Many scholars, fans, and Twitter responses accused the sports reporter interviewing Murry of "forgetting the existence of female athletes and 'everyday sexism.'" Why would he ignore or "forget" the Olympic achievements of two of tennis's greatest female athletes, Serena and Venus Williams? What reason might the journalist offer to explain his oversight? Racism? Sexism? Or a bit of both (Malloy, 2016)? Murray acknowledged that he had won two medals but had to point out to the sports reporter that the Williams sisters had each won four. For background on the sports reporter, his bias or ability to forget female athletes' achievements is not a new story. It was reported that this reporter has a history when it comes to female tennis players. In 2013, he created an uproar after saying on BBC's Radio 5 that a French star tennis player had to be a "dogged" player because she was "never going to be a looker" (Domonoske, 2016).

One principal source of our society's social construction of hegemonic masculinity can be found in character roles frequently portrayed in our American movies. Pundits and feminists believe that the movie industry supplies our culture with a never-ending diet that passively includes consumption of violent male images. In an article titled "Hegemonic Masculinity in Media Content," these overly masculine images are also found in the music video industry. Add to the movie industry and music video industry the widespread practice of advertisers who often stress differences between men and women. Whether the depictions are covert or overt, we know that many of the images and roles found in popular media, let alone sports media, frequently reaffirm how women differ from men (e.g.., women are from Venus, men are from Mars). And we must not forget how our culture defines the traditional male role as breadwinner and protector. Also, the pursuit of "being ripped," "being cut," or "being muscular" is now one of the main vehicles used by some men in our culture to express their masculinity. In 2018, we find that to be a man in our culture seems to come with the desire that he must develop large, well-toned muscles—the desire to be "built" or "cut" is not for its practical use, but young boys and men seem to associate this desire to be physically fit, musculature man with getting women. In other words, physical fitness and muscles are the only way that he can become physically attractive to women, or so our culture implies. To confirm or disconfirm this idea, one just needs to conduct a review of the literature on body esteem expressed by men. What motivates weight lifters to have big muscles? Again, introspection and candid discussion of the lack of focus by scholars to conduct experiments on how men respond to idealized images of "ripped" men in media may ultimately lead to progress and understanding the answer to this question.

In sports media, and to a large extent media in popular culture, we find frequent depictions of violent and aggressive males. Research also supports this idea. We find that sports magazines with a predominantly male audience, along with popular televised sporting events with male viewers, are frequently cluttered with millions of dollars' worth of advertisements that represent confident, ripped, and aggressive male models. Lately, from an advertising perspective, we find increases in the number of ads targeting men. We find ads for products that aid in the process of developing muscles and physical strengths. Many of the products in today's cluttered advertising environment include ads for sexual enhancers, supplements, weight training machines geared toward increasing biceps and abs, and supplements that promise to enhance muscle size.

Effects of Masculinity on Male Athletes

Advertisers often use peripheral cues to make products appear manly and in a highly masculine context. Just as in the Hefty trash bag commercial, we find frequent images in ads that are framed through the use of images of the rough and rugged outdoors. We find that in advertising, images of the rugged, outdoorsy male communicate an idea that masculinity must be adventurous, aggressive, and violent. These characteristics ultimately provide men with a standard of what is perceived as "real manhood,"—a standard that they later use to judge themselves.

As mentioned in the chapter on gender identity and expression, we find that men and male athletes who are not aggressive tend to express emotion (i.e., boys don't cry or wear pink) and appear timid, lacking power or control, and often are put in social contexts that cause them to be bullied or called names such as "pansy" or "queer" by coaches and teammates. As described previously, mediated communications and images in media overtly send messages that tell Americans that being a man means you have to be aggressive, calm, and cool in intense instances (e.g., think of Danny in *Grease*). We also find messages that suggest that the "true man" is strictly heterosexual. And we find that, in America, sports reinforce the hegemonic masculinity found in a broader context and sports media, and they are a vehicle used to reinforce and reproduce ideas of masculinity and femininity (Hatty, 2000). Hatty (2000) argues that through depictions and news coverage, media may alleviate fears of feminization among middle-class men. The media, according to Hatty (2000), alleviates fears through their use of visual cues employed in ads and messages that ultimately create what Messner, Dunbar, and Hunt (2000) call the "televised sports manhood formula."

"Homophobia is crucial to the definition of masculinity," according to Leach (1994). Leach suggested that masculinity does not allow men in this culture to have any emotional or sexual attachments. As a result, we find that fear of gay men reveals and reinforces "oppressive hetero-sexual themes, such as male competition for [women]" (Leach, 1994, p. 37). Since women have become more independent over the last century, heterosexual men in America appear to have become even more focused on their physical attractiveness and overall physique (for more on this, see Hoberman, 1997; Hoberman, 2005). To illustrate how this preoccupation with male physique has become more intense in today's climate, Hatty (2000) analyzed depictions of the male body in media. Findings show that for men in the current climate, media seem to communicate that to be idealized and attractive, a man has to have large shoulders; large, muscular, well-defined, and toned biceps; a strapping, strong chest; a burly back, complete with well-toned muscles; and a very narrow waist. As many of us know, it takes an inordinate amount of willpower, focus, and determination to build this type of physique. Men who spend time at the gym and focus on their muscular develop-ment may appear to be preoccupied with their looks as a way to protect their sense of masculinity. Perhaps the effort it takes to build muscle and gain that buff look serves as a way for some men to define their self-concepts and prove their self-esteem (Kimmel 1996; Kimmel, 2010). For Luciano (2001), the increase in women who are opting to join the workforce and gaining some positions in leadership may force men to realize that they are no longer the ones who are in charge of "bringing home the bacon." In fact, women in today's American culture and economy are slowing becoming the breadwinners and heads of household. This, too, challenges the notion of hegemonic masculinity in that women are challenging the idea that men are the breadwinners. The traditional role of man as the breadwinner that was once used in this country to attract a spouse is no longer a magnet for (some) women in the new millennium. Consequently, large numbers of men whose egos were built around their yearly salaries are now looking to regain their attraction by appearing somewhat hypermasculine around women. In short, when women entered the workplace, reducing the idea that men were the only ones who could earn a salary, all of a sudden, the men started looking to regain their attractiveness through their musculature.

Capraro (2000) used research to highlight many of the issues that are created when men focus much of their lives on their performance and achievements. Capraro (2000) offered up a concept known as "gender-role strain." Gender-role strain, according to Capraro's (2002) article, is the "tension between the actual self and the gendered, idealized self" (p. 35). Gender-role strain is most likely to occur when men try to meet the expectations others have of them. Similar to the looking-glass self, we find that men tend to learn how to perform in their gender role, which is buried deep in the principles of hegemonic masculinity. Yet Capraro and Capraro's (2002) research is innovative in that it is one of a few studies that focus on male emotions and the effects of constraining those emotions. Research in this study found that when men perform masculine roles, many of them experience a certain type of stress, strain, and even some role conflict (Capraro, 2000). From health research and medical journals, we know that with the feelings of stress and strain come feelings of inadequacy and depression. Certified psychologists and psychotherapists often say that when men who experience these stressors are not afforded opportunities to express those emotions, the constraint may precipitate mental health challenges, antisocial behaviors, chemical and drug abuse, dependency on alcohol, and, in some cases, behaviors leading to suicide. After reading literature on hegemonic masculinity coupled with the understanding of what masculinity means (emotionless men), we find that men in our culture who engage in "manly" activities are aware the value that is placed on manly man type behaviors such as drinking copious amounts of alcohol (frat parties and drinking on college campuses). We also find that a covert sign of our culture's emphasis on masculine activities that include drinking games and getting drunk involves the sense of power that one achieves if and when one survives the risk-taking behaviors. This is a type of control and power that delineates the real men from those who otherwise lack it. Again, this is a cultural example of hegemonic masculinity and challenges associated with this concept in America and in sports.

Acceptance of Violence, Hegemony, and Sports

Hegemonic masculinity establishes and reinforces authority, power, and control that only men in our culture are able to have (Young & Atkinson, 2008, p. 172). As mentioned in the introduction of this chapter, we find images of hegemonic masculinity in sports media by way of their reliance on images that denote courage, power, dominance, emotional detachment, aggression, and violence (Young & Atkinson, 2008). That is the overall purpose for writing this text: We must examine research that presents the various ways that our sports media actually use their voices to encourage ideas of masculinity, femininity, gender expression, and many other factors and begin having discussions about this topic. Each chapter of this book points us back to one overarching problem and controversy in our culture, in sports, and, in particular, in our sports media; Everything in our culture is often filtered in ways that pits an "us versus them" mentality (i.e., gender, sexual orientation, race/ethnicity, social status, and/or religion)

In terms of hegemonic masculinity and violence, we find a study conducted by White and Young (1999), who obtained data that show that within competitive sports, there is a significant number of violent acts that are used to support the dogmas associated with masculinity and what it means to be a man. Research continues to confirm the idea that masculinity is celebrated and revered in sports media and is used to reaffirm and support the idea that men should be tough and strong (Boyle & Haynes, 2009, p. 135). Supporting the idea that sports media revere male athletes and lift them up to be heroes and role models in our culture, we find that evidence in the frequency that media seem to devote their attention, time, and space to male sports and those athletes who support the images our culture has concerning what masculinity is and how it is depicted (Boyle & Haynes, 2009, p. 135).

The sports media tend to "normalize" violence within sport through depictions (Trujillo, 1991). It's as if violence in sports is not only acceptable but also what sports fans want. We find that images used in sports media often imply that violence is and can be desirable (Trujillo, 1991). Many of the images and stories we find in the media show men committing acts of violence who are at the same time role models whom one should aspire to become (Young & Smith, 1989). The media is not the only vehicle known to encourage problematic ideals of masculine behavior. Others in the world of sports who are also known to encourage masculinity and masculine behavior are fans, players, managers, and owners. Basically, everyone involved in and interested in sports can be found supporting the inclusion of violence in sports. In fact, some might argue that out of the sporting context, violence is wrong and unethical, but if the same violent behavior is performed in sports, we find that fans are often tolerant and even accepting of the violence. The more violence is displayed in the sport, the more we find that sports media will frequently and consistently sensationalize the violence as a way to make a profit. In a study supporting this idea, Miedzian (1992) found evidence suggesting that owners encourage players to be violent. According to Miedzian (1992), violence in sports is vital, as it serves as the main vehicle that elicits spectator applause.

It has been claimed that violence is a mechanism in American sports used to reinforce "masculine assertiveness and confidence" (Kaufman, 1999, p. 3). Messner (1990) argues violence in sports is an "occupational imperative" that comes with certain practical consequences when violent behaviors are not performed in the sport. Other researchers agree, and they argue that male athletes who do not exhibit violent behaviors are at risk of being demeaned or devalued, or they will experience harsh backlash and punishment by fans. Sometimes the backlash can come from coaches and teammates if the male athlete does not act violently in the sport (Pappas, McKenry, & Catlett, 2004, p. 295). According to research on this topic, coaches are often guilty of encouraging violence not only to provide entertainment but also to increase fan involvement. Some scholars believe that violent sports are accepted in our culture because they work as a catalyst that allows players and fans to release anger and hostility. In fact, many perceive that the violence in sports is cathartic. That is, the perception is that violent sports are simply just structured activities that allow athletes to express their aggressive and hostile energy in an acceptable, harmless manner (see Miedzian, 1992, p. 183). The pressure to be violent has physiological effects. When we regard the physiological effects of hegemony that acts of violence encourage, we must consider the internalization of the violence. To what extent does participation in a violent sport "cause" male athletes to internalize violence? It is possible that athletes who "internalize" feelings of violence and aggression are possibly giving in to the demands of hegemonic masculinity and other values that pressure men to be dominant, violent, aggressive, and in control (Kaufman, 1999, p. 1).

A theory proposed almost 80 years ago known as frustration-aggression theory is not frequently used in mass communication or social psychology, but it is useful in an explanation of the effects of internalized violence. In fact, it was in 1939 when Dollard, Doob, Miller, Mowrer, and Sears proposed a theory focused on ways to predict, explain, and understand aggression and violence that is acceptable in some situations, such as sports, but unacceptable in other situations. In other words, what happens when one who is paid to act violently gets frustrated outside of the sports context, and he or she finds that his or her success is blocked? What happens when a male's need to show his masculinity in terms of power, control, and domination is prevented from "winning"? We find that an individual's frustrations can build on an innate drive to be aggressive and the likely response is violence (Cashmore, 2002). Interestingly, we find that any individual can be vulnerable to feelings of frustration and limits in how to express the frustration, but in the way that frustration-aggression theory is structured, we find that two conditions must be met: The aggressive behavior must be observable, and the frustration must lead to the aggressive behavior. However, how does one measure the existence of frustration (Dollard et al., 1939, p. 1)? Despite its infrequent use, the theory is a great way to analyze the effects of violence in sports and the effects on athletes who participate in violent sports.

Violence in the Sport of Mixed Martial Arts

In a sport that is extremely male driven, it should come as no surprise that athletes interviewed in the media often are very vocal about their opinions regarding male dominance and the fact that violence is rampant in the world of mixed martial arts (MMA). In recent sports news, we learned of an event involving Miguel Torres, a celebrated MMA fighter. In the article, Torres was quoted as saying, "If a rape van were called a surprise van more women wouldn't mind going for rides in them. Everyone likes surprises" (Bastone, 2011). The then Ultimate Fighting Championship (UFC) president fired Torres for making that comment, which was inadvertently made at the same time that comments about violence were raised at that year's UFC conference. During the conference, it was reported that discussions surrounding the use of violence in the sport was extremely controversial, and the fact that Torres made a comment linking rape with surprises was the impetus for his firing. In another recent sports news article about violence in the MMA, we learned of Rashad

FIGURE 8.2   *The Ring Card "Girl"*

Evans, a former light heavyweight UFC champ, who chose to ridicule his future opponent, Phil Davis. In an attempt to "sound manly," Evans was quoted as saying, "I'm going to put my hands on you worse than that dude on those kids at Penn State" (Castillo, 2011). This comment was a subtle jab at former Penn State assistant football coach Jerry Sandusky, who at the time faced 40 counts related to the sexual assault of children. This was obviously a statement that should not have been made or considered a quote (Graham, 2011).

Hegemonic masculinity requires male athletes to punish and stigmatize other male athletes who exhibit so-called feminine behaviors. Therefore, we can say with confidence that hegemonic masculinity supports demeaning and degrading girls and women. We also find that hegemonic masculinity confirms our culture's expectation of female athletes to engage in what we know as feminine behaviors (Connell & Messerschmidt, 2005).

The UFC is the MMA's most prominent organization. In the UFC, hegemonic masculinity was clearly evident at one point because of its lack of female fighters. Years ago, women participating in the UFC were only there to serve as ring card "girls." Figure 8.2 is an illustration of a ring card "girl," the common name given to women who are in the boxing ring between rounds of combat sports such as boxing, kickboxing, or MMA. The woman then carries a sign displaying the upcoming round number. Figure 8.2 is an example of how women are used as objects of display in this particular sport. Because they are often shown in poses that emphasize their feminine features, the theory of objectification becomes evident (Aubrey, Henson, Hopper, & Smith, 2009; Fredrickson & Roberts, 1997; Harrison & Fredrickson, 2003) Images such as this give us a clear example of how female athletes are sexualized objects presented alongside male fighters. Again, illustrating the subtle application of many of the dogmas enveloped in our culture's focus on hegemonic masculinity.

As of the current writing, MMA has approximately 28 female athletes participating in the sport. The list that follows the contains names of the best athletes in sports who make their living engaging in competition that considers crushing opponents and knocking them out as a victory. Although MMA is still primarily a male sport, athletes such as Ronda Rousey, Miesha Tate, and Gina Carano are making strides in this sport by proving that they can hold their own in the ring, even if pitted against a male MMA athlete. Interestingly, some scholars believe that even though these female athletes are physically attractive, they are drawing in new fans through their athletic prowess. Sports media is starting to show coverage of these athletes. Male journalists are finding that these MMA athletes are fighting as tough as they can and are knockout gorgeous outside of the ring. It is a little surprising, but welcomed, that the sports news stories, so far, emphasize their wins, their losses, and other athletic achievements. Here is a list of the active professional female MMA fighters as of this writing:

- Ronda Rousey
- Miesha Tate
- Gina Carano
- Holly Holm
- Cat Zingano
- Cristiane Justino
- Paige VanZant
- Sarah Kaufman
- Rose Namajunas
- Carla Esparza
- Jessica Eye
- Joanna Jedrzejczyk
- Michelle Waterson
- Erin Toughill

- Tecia Torres
- Marloes Coenen
- Joanne Calderwood
- Jessica Penne
- Julia Budd
- Alexis Davis
- Kaitlin Young
- Karolina Kowalkiewicz
- Sara McMann
- Felice Herrig
- Julie Kedzie
- Leslie Smith
- Megumi Fujii
- Charmaine Tweet

These women of MMA are as tough as they are hard working. This list of the top female MMA fighters ranks the greatest female MMA fighters "from best to worst based on the votes received by MMA fans" (Ranker, 2018). Of interest is that the rules of voting on the fighters were that fans had to vote on the fighting skills of the female athletes and not on attractiveness.

Boxing

A documentary called *T-Rex* follows middleweight boxer Claressa Shields, a young athlete who comes from Flint, Michigan. She was also an Olympian in the 2012 Olympic Games held in London, England. Some reviews feel that the documentary does a great job of showing the problem in boxing. Shields is sitting with two Team USA representatives and her coach, Jason Crutchfield, in a nondescript lobby. In the documentary, she has returned home after winning four decisive victories and, more importantly, having won the first American gold medal in women's boxing. During the video, the Olympic Team's public relations consultant, Julie Goldsticker, describes why sponsors are attracted to certain people like Michael Phelps, Ryan Lochte, and Gabby Douglas. She then turns to Clarissa Shields to say, "I would love for you to stop saying that you like beating people up and making them cry" (Cooper & Canepari, 2016). This comment illustrates the subtle backlash female athletes experience when their thoughts, behaviors, and words are deemed gender inappropriate. This is a constant problem in boxing for female athletes. Shields, according to our culture's standards, should not enjoy fighting, nor should she participate in the sport solely to gain financial success and freedom as a boxer. Boxing is a violent male-dominated sport. If Claressa Shields was a man exhibiting and communicating that same bloodlust for combat, would she be valued and honored?

Consider this for a moment: Why does our culture deem it acceptable for male boxers to tout violent acts used in boxing to win, yet when a female boxer publicly admits that she actually enjoys and loves being aggressive, she is criticized, corrected, and cast out? Why was Shield's behavior on the video considered unfathomable, unconscionable, or even wrong? As we stated earlier in this chapter, our cultural norms and values tell us that it is inappropriate for a woman to like violence or engage in aggressive behaviors simply because it is believed that these kinds of emotions are

FIGURE 8.3   *Claressa Shields*

frequently attributed to men. The public relations firm for Claressa Shields had no idea how to position her and sell her to sponsors. They admitted that. They were not sure how to sell her to sponsors even knowing that Shields was featured in a highly visible media outlet: the *New York Times*. Shields had many national media features: She was, in addition to the *New York Times*, featured in the *New Yorker*, appeared on NPR, and highlighted in many more major sports media appearances. Professional publicists said that they could sell her. The documentary depicts her childhood living in Flint, Michigan. The documentary is a narrative that is filled with social class issues of being disadvantaged and living through abuse and sexual violence, yet she goes on to win Olympic gold. This is the "American Dream," yet they had no idea how to sell her. Shields received many comments that informed her that the way she talks about boxing is too rough and too tough for a girl. She is quoted as saying, "I do enjoy hitting people, or I wouldn't be a boxer. I'm not gonna pretend that isn't part of it or part of me" (Team USA, 2018). Figure 8.3 shows Shields in the boxing ring in June 2018 fighting competitor Hanna Gabriels for the championship.

One issue for women's boxing is that, unlike ESPN, sports' largest media broadcaster journalism venues, such as HBO and Showtime, have expressed reluctance in broadcasting women's fights and/or making them pay-per-view. Showtime has not aired a women's boxing match since 2001; HBO and PBC have never shown a women's boxing match. In 2010, the International Boxing Association introduced skirts to help "distinguish" the female fighters from the men, as if the fans are so ambivalent that they cannot tell the difference. The Polish national boxing coach went so far as to tell BBC Sport that the skirts were mandatory. He is quoted in a *New York Times* article saying, "By wearing skirts, in my opinion, it gives a good impression, a womanly impression. Wearing shorts is not a good way for women boxers to dress" (Richcreek, 2016). Another disparity in how media and others respond to gender-appropriate sports can be found at the 2012 London Olympic Games. At the 2012 Games, where skirts were optional, all the women's matches, "including the gold-medal finals, were fought in the afternoon while men fought in prime time; the women fought on consecutive days with only one rest day, while the men fought every other day to include rest" (Richcreek, 2016).

Women's boxing has never been an easy sell. The first female boxer dates back to 1722 when Elizabeth Wilkinson challenged Hannah Hyfield to a boxing match through an ad she placed in the *London Journal*. Boxing needs to recognize that there is money to be made from female fighters in MMA. In 2011, UFC president Dana White reversed the decision that barred female boxers from participating in the sport. "White now calls the decision to open up a women's division one of the smartest and most bankable decisions he's ever made; earlier this year, his company sold for $4 billion" (Richcreek, 2016).

Weight Lifting

In American culture, we know that young girls, when compared to boys, are less likely to be encouraged to participate in weight lifting. Yet if we survey the average woman in America, we would find that many, if not most, women will be able to express their level of understanding about the benefits that weight lifting provides. In this chapter, we have learned how American culture relegates muscularity to men, a value that may have prevented women from being interested and participating in other sports. Perhaps women at early ages are precluded from learning, expressing interest, and/or practicing weight lifting. Data collected in several studies on perceptions of weight lifting show gender differences in participating in weight lifting among college students. In fact, one study showed that college women, when compared to college males, report using weight training equipment and lifting weights less frequently. The data speaks for itself. Obser-

FIGURE 8.4   *Musculature of a female bodybuilder*

vations of people working out in fitness clubs and local gyms will show fewer women in the free weights section. We also find support from empirical studies that find women report feeling less comfortable than men in a gym. Uncomfortable feelings are further enhanced when women are asked to rate their level of comfort when using weight machines and free weights.

Research on the lack of women who are interested in and participate in weight lifting, and their thoughts and concerns should cause reason for pause. We find that women tend to be more concerned that they will appear to be incompetent while lifting weights, but not only that, many women feel that weight lifting will result in large manly muscles. Again, we find that women's concerns about participating in this particular sport stem from the idea in our culture that weight lifting, like some other sports, is more appropriate for men. Weight lifting in American culture is a sport that is related to masculinity. Figure 8.4 illustrates the musculature of a female bodybuilder. The idea that muscles on women are unattractive is one in which the woman displayed in Figure 8.4 is trying to change. Women like her are overcoming obstacles and challenging our culture's perception of women and bodybuilding.

Women are not inoculated to the effects of our culture's preoccupation with and emphasis on hegemonic masculinity. We find that deeply embedded in the reason women are not interested in weight lifting is the idea that women must be held to a different standard and should be physically strong or fit but also physically weak and vulnerable. The idea that women should be weak and vulnerable may have possibly caused some women to avoid weight lifting. A fear of becoming too muscular and "big" has been known to cause many women in our culture to avoid lifting weights. Similarly, the fear of a backlash for challenging our culture's expectations of what it means to be female may explain why women may not be found lifting weights in the weight room of a gym or fitness center. Despite the universal benefits of weight lifting and the prescription of weight lifting to both male and female athletes, women making the choice to avoid lifting weights should lead us to consider why being thinner and less muscular is a negative for men and male athletes but ideal for women and female athletes. A small, thin man who has too much body fat runs counter to what we in American believe is the idealized image for masculinity.

Fear of Being "Too" Masculine

Just as women have fears about becoming too manly if they lift weights, the converse is true for men. We find that men report having similar feelings of discomfort when they do not meet our culture's expectations of how masculine men are supposed to look when physically fit. Hegemonic masculinity, we now understand, affects individuals differently. We would be remiss to skip over a discussion of how the intersectionality of race, ethnicity, social class, sexual orientation, and age affects how athletes' response to restrictions in sports. Despite the fact that (some) female athletes shy away from sports that force them to deviate from what it means to be feminine, we know male athletes fear or shy away from activities not because they will be viewed more according to femininity but because they are afraid that they will appear unmanly by our culture's standards based on the expectations of the male physique. Why do men have this perception? Research still has to uncover it. Interestingly, we learned that some women may avoid certain sports because of a fear that they will look too manly, but men, on the other hand, do not express a fear of appearing feminine if they participate in a sport; they fear not having muscles, abs, "guns," and a thin waist. Perhaps men who participate in these studies are afraid to vocalize or admit this, yet we find an inverse relationship between men and women and their fears concerning participation in sports. We might also speculate that perhaps men are not concerned about appearing feminine if they participate in female sports because of their sense of control to do what they want. Their need to exhibit masculinity is achieved in other more broader venues, or they have a confidence and a certainty that sports media will preserve their masculinity by framing their athletic achievements in a way that supports hegemonic masculinity.

Female athletes, according to research, are physically unable to develop "oversized muscles" (Krane et al., 2004). Women have a fear of oversized muscles because of a subconscious perception that oversized muscles violate our culture's gender norms. There is even a perception that oversized muscles are part of the stereotype that there is a relationship between one's athleticism and sexual orientation (Halbert, 1997). As of late, our culture's desire to associate female athletes with lesbianism has been demonstrated frequently. Some researchers believe one reason for this is that some female athletes may express their gender identity in the form of musculature and behaviors that one may perceive to be too manly (Halbert, 1997, p. 11). Perception of a female athlete's sexual orientation is often based on her physical build. In fact, we know from research that those who are muscular are more likely to be called lesbian, or "dyke," or "butch" (Blinde & Taub, 1992, p. 529). For some female athletes, Dworkin's (2001) study helps explain how ethnicity affects females who come from a variety of ethnic backgrounds. We also find that a difference in social class and how social class is perceived affects how we view our bodies and the need to exercise. By relying on female participants, Dworkin (2001) found that women reported knowing that engaging in cardiovascular exercise is good for burning fat, but they were also able to acknowledge that cardiovascular exercise helps them stay lean. Women in the study thought that cardio will help them avoid turning their lean stature into manly man muscles that are large and overstated. Dworkin (2001) found that for many women, an increase in muscle size, whether the increase is related to muscle or fat, is unattractive and extremely masculine. Most women expressed increased muscle mass and weight lifting as masculine, which they tried to avoid. Dworkin found that the women in his study believed that weight lifting and weight work are activities that build bulk and make one more "masculine." He also reported that women believe cardiovascular activity is more feminine compared to weight lifting. The fact that the women in the Dworkin study perceived differences between weight lifting and cardiovascular exercises helps to illustrate an important conclusion in terms of how gender-appropriate sports, body ideals, and other expectations are perceived in our culture.

In a study conducted by Krane, Waldron, Michaelenok, and Stiles-Shipley (2001), we find that "women who had to wear revealing uniforms, such as bathing suits or leotards," exhibited more apprehension than women who were fully clothed (p. 319). The researchers also reported that women in the study expressed another directed fear that others will call them fat or too big for the bathing suit or leotard (Krane et al., 2001, p. 320). Of particular interest was the finding that this fear has a cause and effect. The fear results in many women engaging in unhealthy diets that restrict caloric intake, binge eating, or anorexia, and, in rarer cases, excessive exercising (see Krane et al., 2001). For the women in this study, increases in muscle mass contradict our cultures expectation that women must have an ideal body.

Reflect on Sports: Women and Race Cars

Danica Patrick's weight has been an off-and-on controversy since 2005. The problem is that the controversy centers on the idea that Patrick drove a car that was assumed to be at least 30 pounds lighter than the cars driven by men, most of her competition. Many male NASCAR drivers feel that the lighter weight gives Patrick an unfair advantage that allows her and her team to put weight in other areas; this redistribution of weight is a procedure that, male racers believe, set Patrick up for positive outcomes.

While some posts found in social media insinuated that weight might actually aid in the success of a driver, officials in NASCAR quickly dismissed the idea that the redistribution of weight is the only reason Danica Patrick won the Daytona 500. Research on the acceptable weight for cars revealed that cars that suit the acceptable average weight for a driver is 180 pounds. If a driver weighs more than 180 pounds, the rule states that the car they drive cannot weigh more than 3,300 pounds. A driver who weighs less than 180 pounds but not less than 170 pounds must add pounds to their car, which will cause them to level the track by making the same weight as the acceptable 180-pound average weight. Thus the same rule applies to drivers who weigh significantly less than the 180-pound average weight. Therefore, Patrick, who weighs somewhere between 100 and 110 pounds, had to add weight to ensure that her car meets the NASCAR requirement established for a 180-pound driver. Follow the math that a NASCAR car must be adapted to a 180-pound driver, on average. The weight rule is not strictly for female race drivers. Sports news media reported that Mark Martin weighs approximately 130 pounds, which makes him the lightest male driver competing in NASCAR (Pockrass, 2013).

If we read the NASCAR rulebook, fans would find that "drivers who weigh less than 180 pounds have to add 10 pounds to their car for every 10 pounds down to 140. Therefore, the maximum penalty would be 40 pounds" (Newton, 2013). Drivers argue that Patrick should be forced to add at least 80 pounds in extra weight to her car to be eligible to drive in the sporting competition. In 2005, drivers went on record to state their feelings about Danica Patrick's weight and car. Drivers felt that Patrick's added weight, which was only 40 pounds extra, gave her an unfair advantage in the Indianapolis 500. Conflict and mayhem among the drivers were reported when they threatened to skip the competition unless the racing car field was equal and fair. Gordon felt that if all cars weighed the same and there were no adjustments made for a driver's height and weight, Patrick would have lost the race (Newton, 2013).

At an auto performance show in 2014, Richard Petty made an appearance and held a brief on-air interview. Petty, who holds NASCAR's all-time win record with 200 victories, engaged in what some have called "a war of words" with Patrick and her team co-owner, Tony Stewart (Bonkowski, 2014). Richard Petty, in a broadcast interview, was recorded saying that Danica Patrick would be able to win the Sprint Cup only if "everybody else stayed home" (Bonkowski, 2014).

Danica Patrick's biography highlights her accomplishments in the car-racing sports arena. Patrick is the fourth woman to compete in an Indy race series, "the first woman to lead an Indy race, and the first woman to come in fourth" (Jones, 2008). Patrick was awarded "Rookie of the Year" for both the 2005 Indy 500 and the 2005 IndyCar Series season. She also won the Indy Japan 300 and became the first woman to ever win an Indy race.

Do male NASCAR drivers dislike women drivers? When a woman driver becomes popular, do the male drivers spin some controversy about her (e.g., Patrick's body weight giving her an advantage) because they are truly concerned about her well-being or for other reasons related to the idea that race car driving is for men?

To manage the challenges associated with the desire to compete in gender-inappropriate sports, female athletes most often have to create very strong coping strategies and mechanisms that will allow them to appreciate their achievements. Sports psychologists find that positive coping mechanisms create strong, intense feelings of self-acceptance, pride, and empowerment that may not be obtainable in other parts of our culture (Ross & Shinew, 2008).

Women Leaders in Masculine Sports

Evidence showing an unequal distribution in terms of female athletes who hold leadership positions in higher education suggests that female athletes are significantly and substantially underrepresented in sports as a whole and, in particular, in sports with all-male athletes (Acosta & Carpenter, 2012). In fact, as of the writing of this chapter, we learned that of all the head coaches in male sports, less than 3% are women. The same data reported in a study by Acosta and Carpenter in 2012 showed that the 3% of women serving as head coaches in male sports pales in comparison to the more than 50% of men in head coach positions in, yes, women sports; it is a true disparity that continues to show hegemonic masculinity in the world of women's sports. And it should be no surprise that in the same study, the researchers found that close to 97% of all head coaching jobs are given to men (Acosta & Carpenter, 2012). Thus we are led to conclude that female athletes are fairly nonexistent in leadership positions in men's sports and are underrepresented as leaders in women's sports. Few studies have been found or published that center on identifying the factors that are driving the disparate statistics. Basically, the research question that should be addressed is, what are the issues that influence an underrepresentation of female athletes as leaders in women's sports? Few studies actually examine the influence and isolate the factors that may explain why so few leadership positions are given to women in sports considered to be masculine. We could also explore the various elements in American culture that contribute to the lack of women leaders in the male sporting world.

Sport is such a powerful cultural force, an institution that perfectly aligns with expressions of differences in sexual orientation and male dominance and supremacy. We also learned that sports in American culture can be used to illustrate control and superiority in terms of race/ethnic athletic participation. If we were to apply the idea of hegemony to ethnicity and race, we might find evidence that supports a hegemonic ethnicity in sports. If we apply hegemony to sexual orientation, we would see dominance in that realm and would find evidence supporting hegemonic sexuality. We know from research that people of color, because of their media exposure, most frequently idolize athletes and are more likely to pursue athletic careers (refer to Chapters 4 and 5). Yet we also know from research that white men with economic wealth are afforded an endless set of career options and opportunities that might advance their careers into upper management positions. We also learn from research that white males have a choice when it comes to forgoing a professional sports career after college and deciding to enter the professional career world (for more on white men and resources, refer to Messner 1992).

Descriptive as well as quantitative evaluative research reveals that in our culture, the most widely accepted way for gender roles to be learned and supported, particularly in terms of hegemonic masculinity, is through sports—participation and/or observation. Participation and observation of sports in this culture show how hegemonic masculinity is a concept that remains accepted and tolerated. We also learn how ideas, such as male superiority, restrictions regarding gender roles and associated behaviors, and other prescribed norms regarding what is masculine and what is feminine are allowed to survive even in today's changing society (Whisenant, Pedersen, & Obenour, 2002). Even though Title IX, which passed in 1972, caused a growth spurt in terms of the number of women who chose to participate in sports, we also know that Title IX has not increased the representation of women as leaders in sport (Acosta & Carpenter, 2012; Cunningham & Sagas, 2008; Sartore & Cunningham, 2007; Sartore & Sagas, 2007). The disparities found in the number of leadership and/or upper management positions that are given to female athletes causes a real dilemma for those female athletes who wish to pursue a job in sports long after their sports careers have ended. If sports media did a better job of covering and writing stories that illustrate the realities concerning the amount of time and dedication that female athletes devote to sports, perhaps the context allowing them to be considered viable candidates for head coaching and other leadership positions may start to be bountiful. As it stands currently, we can conclude that because of the lack of coverage in sports media and the symbolic annihilation of female athletes by sports media, many women may get the idea after exposure to stories about other female athletes that there are several barriers to sports, making entry difficult and much harder for them than for male athletes. Exposure to media coverage currently found in sports media may also result in uncertainty for women regarding what they should do with the economic capital gained while playing professional sports (Cooper, Hunt, & O'Bryant, 2007; Kamphoff & Gill, 2008).

Several theoretical, empirical, and anecdotal explanations have been offered in sports literature to explain why female athletes are underrepresented in leadership positions (Cunningham & Sagas, 2008; Sartore & Cunningham, 2007; Walker, Bopp, & Sagas, 2011). The relationship between traditional gender ideas concerning masculinity state that men are better able to handle leadership positions because they are tough, strong, confident and know how to lead others (refer to West & Zimmerman, 1987). We can hypothesize that because of the attributes linked to femininity (emotional expressiveness, subdued, subservient, etc.) and the depictions of female athletes within sports media tend to create an idea that female athletes are the best choice in terms of top candidates for leadership positions (e.g., Burton, Barr, Fink, & Bruening, 2009).

Combating Dominant Masculinities

Actions that need to be explored include changes and enhancements in the following areas:

Public Policy

Our government controls the extent to which violence is presented in media content, particularly those mediated messages centered on violence that are consumed by young males. One idea is to provide stricter regulations regarding advertising and promotions and types of violent images and materials that can be published or broadcast in media that are primarily consumed by young audiences. We need to enact policies that govern gender rules followed in sports and that should ensure that sporting institutions and organizations of all types are more egalitarian in terms of the treatment of all people, regardless of gender.

More Published Scholarly Research

Additional research is needed in the area of hegemonic masculinity. Research should expand on the studies in sports and investigate the extent to which hegemonic masculinity is evident in other media content, such as nonfiction books and movies and stories about "regular, everyday men" found in media and trending news stories. For Katz (2011), research in this area is very important and much needed, given our culture's acceptance and tolerance of what is masculine. Katz (2011) believes that research expanding into other media found in pop culture is likely to reveal different depictions and representations of men and masculinity. Research that explores other areas or environments that are similar to sports, but differ in terms of context, is also much needed. In other words, we need research that can help us identify other places, institutions, or contexts in our society that encourage boys to display violent, aggressive behavior and allow them to bully other boys. Are there other subcultures that allow boys to make fun of boys who act more feminine than other boys? Currently, we notice trends in public schools that punish and offer harsh consequences for cyberbullying and other acts of aggression by children who put others down or make fun of others. But we also must be reminded of statistics that show young boys can identify sexual and domestic violence and can often articulate what it means to be a manly man. How does this happen? Obviously, there are other areas in our culture where these messages are being heard, read, and observed in. We need more attempts to teach media literacy, along with many more research findings that may be used to recommend and to design intervention tools.

Encouraging media educators to develop curricula that will challenge and inspire future college students interested in becoming tomorrow's sports reporters, sportswriters, and sportscasters that show them how to avoid using gendered, male-biased, or sexist language. Courses might also teach how the inclusion of symbols in this culture may unintentionally spread a message that supports our culture's implied expectations of what it means to be a man or a woman. Perhaps curricula in this area might be used to encourage future sports journalists to strive to "de-masculinize" sports and the male-dominated culture currently visible in the institution of sport.

Media Making Self-Evaluations and Improvements

We need all people working in sports as journalists, sportswriters and sportscasters, producers, and directors to start recognizing their personal biases and the ways that they may have unintentionally used sexist language or written stories that include microaggressions aimed at female athletes who do not fit our society's ideals as to what is feminine from what is not feminine. We desperately need our sports media to use their voices to empower local, national, regional, and international media associations to encourage our government to formulate policies and rules regarding media production and content. These rules might, for example, force media to begin to de-emphasize the objectification of women and help them stop production of media images and messages that actually perpetuate the concept of hegemonic masculinity in our culture.

Conclusion

American cultural norms and values suggest to us that the sports world is primarily male dominated. In this chapter, we learned that sports and athletes are frequently described by masculine attributes, such as strength, control, superiority, violence, hostility, competition, subordination, and anger. We also discussed the fact that despite the start of Title IX in 1972, we still find discrimination of athletes in terms of admission, access, and treatment in sports and in the sports media (Lopiano, 2000). We discussed research that shows that female athletes, over 46 years after the passing of Title IX, are still facing barriers that limit their pursuit of dreams that involve participating and achieving in athletics and professional sports. One major challenge facing female athletes has to be succumbing to long-standing, traditional gender roles established years and years ago. If women in today's culture continue to challenge hegemonic masculinity, we might find that traditional gender roles will change as our culture shows more acceptance of females who may not display all the attributes of femininity. In fact, it is possible that the challenge for women may actually force fans and others in American culture to become more accepting of female athletes who show interest in male-dominated sports such as wrestling, boxing, weight lifting, and race car driving.

What is seen as the norm for women is conformity toward the notion of being "ladylike." This is reflected in sports media beliefs and practices. Frisby (2017b) found that media present softer news stories and often trivialize a female athlete's athletic accomplishments when compared to male athletes. Understanding the paradox that female athletes experience is a definite step in the right direction. It can lead many in our culture to confront the socially constructed gender roles and prescribed norms that drive our behavior. It will force us to recognize the dichotomy and dual nature that Americans have when it comes to what is masculine and what is feminine. A continued increase in female athletes in sports will give us as Americans an opportunity to reevaluate the consequences that our notions of masculinity and femininity have had. And, perhaps, a challenge of these notions will lead us to develop new ideals and roles for behaviors that can be considered gender-appropriate behaviors. Perhaps, as we learned in the chapter on sexual orientation, the idea of gender needs to dissipate. That is, with the inclusion of bisexual, transgender, and queer athletes, the idea that there is a male and female sport may need to be revisited. As Ross and Shinew (2008) state, "While dualistic notions of gender have been shown to constrain sports participation for girls and women, they are developing ways to persist and succeed within sport" (p. 53).

According to research, we learned in this chapter that when female athletes are given opportunities to participate in sports they desire and like, they are apt to "feel more powerful and in control over their lives" (Paloian, 2018). Research has revealed that behaviors such as eating disorders and problems with perceived body image are more likely to be encouraged when female athletes are in "high-risk" sports. High-risk sports are those in which body size and body frame/type are emphasized. The high-risk sports include running, gymnastics, and swimming (Krane, Choi, Baird, Aimar, & Kauer, 2004; Smolak, Murnen, & Ruble, 2000).

It seems we have more women who consistently challenge our Western traditional gender-role beliefs. Female athletes who challenge our beliefs do so when they participate in a variety of sports. The challenge comes when female athletes win, succeed, and overcome tremendous obstacles to reach a higher elite status in their sport. These challenges by highly accomplished women give us many opportunities to challenge ourselves. Theberge (1985) wrote that this liberation may also free some female athletes from the idea that male athletes are dominant and superior. For those athletes who participate in gender-inappropriate sports, navigating through conundrums in terms of gender and athletic participation may be challenging, but it requires female athletes to face the challenge and deal with various internal and external conflicts and pressures—a skill that media and many sports fans need to see depicted to believe that female athletes would make great leaders in any sport, men's or women's sports to be exact. As female athletes continue to work through the struggles, they face regarding our culture's strict reliance on traditional gender roles, they will find that they can also be change agents and begin to redefine what it means to be an accomplished female athlete in America today. Learning how to persevere seems to be a necessary process when there is a desire to redefine hegemonic femininity.

Addressing Challenges

The first stop in addressing challenges highlighted in this chapter is for sports communication professionals to become aware of their use of faulty images of all athletes. Advocates and agents for change come in many forms, including sports editors, journalists, writers, producers, advertisers, public relations, promoters, and others interested in sports and media. It takes a team and a concerted effort by those who are passionate and interested in this topic to advocate for a change in media content and messages, especially for popular media targeted at and consumed primarily by adolescent boys and girls. Showing more and frequent images of women athletes in their team or sports uniform, for example, may possibly change the sexualization and objectification of women in our media. These images and frequent features or depictions may also address the idea that the overly thin standard portrayal of females currently dominating our media is not, in fact, the ideal body type.

We are also aware that part of the problem that leads to many media faux pas in images of women may be related to the inexperience of the sports reporter. Sports journalists who may be unfamiliar with sports and never watched a women's sporting event or attended a male or female sports competition may subconsciously perpetuate their own thoughts and ideas about men and women who participate in sports. We often assume that journalists are inoculated and protected from the influence of media exposure and images found in media content. However, if we address our personal feelings about women, men, and our ideas as to where we obtained our thoughts and beliefs about what is masculine and what is feminine, we will find that many sports journalists simply employ the thoughts and conclusions they obtained from the numerous stories they have been exposed to over time. In other words, if you are a journalist, how did the stories that frequently portray female athletes as wives, mothers, attractive, sexual beings who know how to manage a household and train for a sport lead you to think about women athletes?

To be a change agent in the sports world, sports media must challenge the stereotypes, biases, and microaggressions that have been published to the present day in sports news stories. Microaggressions and stereotypes that are unchallenged become the gender stereotypes that we accept in this culture. Sports media must be committed and determined to break their routines and the status quo that is currently depicted in sports media by changing the narrative and discourse about female athletes to one that emphasizes their athletic accomplishments, feats, and training schedules. It is possible that if a majority of the news outlets were to commit to this change in reporting, Americans might begin to see a tremendous effect in the way we respond to female athletes. If sports media specifically set out to make it a goal to feature female athletes' issues on front pages and as lead stories, perhaps this placement will move women's sports from the back of our minds to the forefront. Only then will we find hope that our culture and the sports world will begin seeing changes in how Americans view female athletes and how we treat them in everyday life.

Allen and Frisby (2017) conducted a study that found that microaggressions in sports news stories were worse in 2016 with respect to coverage of the Summer Olympics when compared to news stories found in sports media about the 2012 Summer Olympics. This increase in negative news stories about female athletes shows that in terms of making changes in sports media with respect to the procedures and processes used to report sports news, much work is still needed. Consider this for example: In terms of sports news reporting on female athletes in the Summer Olympics in 2016, Allen and Frisby (2017) found that there were significantly more stories that demeaned, trivialized, and focused on the attractiveness and muscularity of female athletes than ever before in the history of female sports and athletes. This statistic literally demands change in sports media.

A recent study conducted by Daniels (2012) suggests that images of female athletes play a significant role in how young girls think of female athletes and participation in women's athletics. In fact, Daniels (2012) found that young girls use images of female athletes to tell them how to think of themselves. This shows the importance of research that investigates and can add to what we already know about the effects of long-term exposure to and consumption of the frequent depictions of female athletes as sexualized objects. Is it possible that long-term exposure causes young girls to self-objectify? Moreover, does exposure to idealized, sexualized images of female athletes affect a young girl's self-esteem, resulting in a social comparison that makes them jealous, envious, or disappointed in their own bodies? We need research that attempts to investigate why in lieu of improvements in how sports media cover female athletes we find an increase in negative stories and images about female athletes' sexuality and attractiveness (McCarthy, 2012).

This chapter shows that there are relatively few female sports reporters, so there should be no surprise that news stories and media coverage are loaded with the presence of male norms and values. The disparity found in the gender of today's sports reporters clearly exemplifies the need we have for change. As future media professionals and strategic communicators, you have the opportunity to change the future of sports coverage. See the checklist of recommendations at the end of this chapter for ways that you can improve sports coverage.

On a positive note, it is worth noting that, regarding equality of coverage and positive portrayals of female athletes, some media are trying to do a better job in terms of how to depict female and to some extent male athletes. Take, for example, *ESPN Magazine*'s "Body Issue" (ESPN, 2018). The "Body Issue" depicts photos not only of women but also of naked male athletes. The magazine includes images of athletes of all body types and sizes, which includes Paraplegic Olympians. What is most significant about this issue is that the athletes are shown in generally active, gender-neutral poses. The *ESPN Magazine* "Body Issue" praises women athletes for their athleticism and not their attractiveness. The issue also emphasizes the hard work and dedication that athletes devote to staying fit and toned.

Another positive example of media representation of women athletes can be found in the Always "Like a Girl" campaign, released in the summer of 2014. The "Like a Girl" commercial urges girls and women to redefine the phrase from one of weakness to one of strength. Research shows that the effects of this campaign have been largely positive, with 76% of women and 59% of men ages 16 to 24 reporting that the message and campaign have changed their perception of the phrase (Nudd, 2015).

Nike's "Voices" ad, released in recognition of the 40th anniversary of Title IX, is yet another example of how strategic communication practitioners are using their skills to create positive portrayals of female athletes. In the "Voices" ad, female celebrity athletes such as Lisa Leslie and Marlen Esparza can be viewed discussing their personal experiences facing discrimination in sports and to some extent in their personal lives based on their gender. These Olympians are shown in the ad alongside a diverse group of young girls who, according to the role models, should never have to face the same type of gender-based discrimination.

Gender stereotyping, as this chapter highlights, seems to be prevalent in sports. However, it is important to note that media has the power to change the way periodicals, magazines, and television ads depict gender and different races. As my research shows, often the race of an athlete is framed in such a way that the athlete of color is presented as irresponsible, a drug user, and violent. The responsibility to create equality in media coverage of athletes of color and female athletes rests with sports announcers, sports media, newscasters, sportswriters and editors, players, and fans across all races. We must begin talking intelligently about race, gender, racism, media, sports, and athleticism. As the saying goes in sports, "Practice makes perfect." So too will practice make perfect regarding media and sports—the more practice everyone involved has at meaningfully talking about gender, race, and stereotyping within sports media, the more equality in sports coverage will improve.

QUESTIONS FOR REFLECTION AND DISCUSSION

1. In your own words, describe the concept of hegemonic masculinity and various ways you feel you have succumbed to our culture's concept of this value.

2. How are male athletes portrayed in sports media? Female athletes? Now consider your own thoughts and ideas about female and male athletes and what they should and should not do. Where did you obtain these thoughts and ideas?

3. Describe the research that found a lack of women serving in positions as head coaches in men's collegiate basketball. What factors do you attribute to this finding? Do you think that one reason for the disparity of women leaders in men's sports may be explained by a lack of interest by female athletes? Why or why not? A lack of social acceptance? Why or why not? What role do you believe sports media play in explaining disparities in leadership in sports by gender? Explain in detail your answer. Where would we find female role models in men's basketball?

4. List and describe your favorite female athletes. Why are they your favorites, and how did they become your favorite female athletes?

5. Some people feel that there is a major difference in the perceived value of women's and men's basketball. They even go on to think that men's basketball is a different sport from women's basketball. Do you agree that these are two different sports? Why or why not? Use research and/or published information to support your thoughts.

6. Consider media portrayals of a woman who serves as head coach of a men's team. What are the challenges that a woman may face leading a team filled with all men?

7. List the advantages and disadvantages that may be found when a female athlete is the head coach of a men's team. How would a woman coach influence a coaching staff that is primarily male? What would her influence be with the players? Would all these relationships differ if the head coach is a female? Explain your answer.

8. Have you viewed a women's boxing match? Why or why not? Have you attended a women's boxing match? Why or why not?

9. Explain what you know about working with a female head coach. Do you know any female head coaches? How and where did you meet her? Who are the female head coaches that you are most familiar with? What sports are they coaching? Are the head coaches with sports that are more aligned with what our culture considers to be masculine and/or feminine sports? What role does the media play in enhancing your knowledge of the female head coach?

10. Do you think we will see increases in women holding positions of head coaches in men's sports? Why or why not? What do you think might help influence how sports fans and the larger culture of Americans learn to accept, recruit, and promote female athletes and women coaching in men's sports? Explain.

SUGGESTED ACTIVITIES

1. Thinking about the concept of hegemonic masculinity, take a moment to identify other events, institutions, and places in American culture where boys are allowed to put down, bully, and compete violently with other boys. Where are those places? If there are none, elaborate on why you think the sports world is the only place where bullying and violence are acceptable.

2. What behaviors do you notice that men use to show masculine superiority over one another? How do they show their superiority over females? Does this display of superiority change in sports? Explain how these behaviors change in different situations.

3. How can sporting institutions become egalitarian along gender lines and change the current climate of hegemonic masculinity?

4. Watch several popular action films and analyze the content and message themes in the movies to determine if the movie creates, enhances, supports, or tries to break down the idea of masculinity. Do men cry in the film? Be sure to identify the themes and frequency that the themes were observed when making your observations.

5. Interview several women at a gym or a fitness center. Ask them to comment on their ideas and perceptions about weight lifting. What common themes appeared?

6. Attend or watch on YouTube a fitness and weight lifting competition. What did you observe? Were there cases of hegemonic masculinity in the competitions? What about female weight lifters? What observations did you make when comparing female weight lifters to male weight lifters?

7. Interview several female athletes from various sports at your school. Ask questions about what attracted them to the sport, including their long-term and short-term goals. Look for aspirations for coaching.

8. Test and challenge the notion that female athletes fear looking masculine and avoid leadership positions. Then write a summary or pitch for an ESPN or CNN special on women athletes in a male athlete world.

9. Watch the documentary *T-Rex*. How will Claressa Shield's story encourage other girls to compete in sports? Write a paper that details how you would promote Claressa and other female boxers.

10. Watch *Tough Guise* (https://www.youtube.com/watch?v=3exzMPT4nGI). In the video, Katz argues that violence in American culture, particularly the violence that occurred in the tragic school shootings in Littleton, Colorado, Jonesboro, Arkansas, and Virginia Tech, needs to be understood as part of an ongoing crisis in masculinity. Using racially diverse subject matter and examples, write a paper evaluating your participation in the culture of masculinity, making certain that you include citations from the video documentary. Why do boys behave in this way? Why are 90% of reported cases of violence committed by boys and men?

ADDITIONAL RESOURCES

Top 10 Sexiest Female Bodybuilders You Probably Haven't Seen Before, https://spotmegirl.com/10-female-bodybuilders/

"Like A Girl" Campaign, https://www.dandad.org/en/d-ad-always-like-a-girl-campaign-case-study-insights/ https://www.huffingtonpost.com/2015/02/02/always-super-bowl-ad_n_6598328.html https://www.campaignlive.co.uk/article/case-study-always-likeagirl/1366870

Nike "Voices" Ad, https://www.youtube.com/watch?v=rK9lLqASGDY

The Masculine Hegemony in Sports: Is Golf for Aladies@?, http://www.acrwebsite.org/volumes/8545/volumes/v29/NA-29

Masculine Hegemony in March Madness?: A Textual Analysis of the Gendered Language Used by Newspaper and Online Sportswriters Covering NCAA Women's and Men's Basketball Tournaments, https://fsu.digital.flvc.org/islandora/object/fsu:254144/datastream/PDF/view

Hegemonic Masculinity in Sport, http://citeseerx.ist.psu.edu/viewdoc/download?doi=10.1.1.877.4878&rep=rep1&type=pdf

Hegemonic Masculinity: Rethinking the Concept, https://doi.org/10.1177/0891243205278639

Toward Sport Reform: Hegemonic Masculinity and Reconceptualizing Competition, https://pennstate.pure.elsevier.com/en/publications/toward-sport-reform-hegemonic-masculinity-and-reconceptualizing-c

CREDITS

9

Violence in Sports

After completing this chapter, students should be able to:

- define and understand the concept of violence and sports violence;

- list and delineate the four types of violence in sports;

- differentiate between in-game and off-the-field violence;

- discuss how media frame violence and sports in media coverage;

- understand the interrelationship between domestic violence and sports;

- describe legal consent and intent in violence and sports;

- learn ways that athletes, coaches, and administrators can break the cycle of violence used in sporting events; and

- provide readers with research, information, and theories to use when discussing sports and violence.

Introduction

Sports violence is defined as "excessive physical force and aggressive behaviors that cause harm or has the potential to cause harm to another" (Coakley, 2009, p. 196). An example of violence in sports can be found during a team practice for the Oakland Raiders of the NFL. On August 24, 2003, linebacker Bill Romanowski punched 27-year-old teammate Marcus Williams in the face. Romanowski's crushing blow broke Williams' eye socket, caused brain damage, and ended his NFL career. Romanowski's actions are the very definition of violence in sport: his behavior caused harm, occurred outside of sports rules, and was isolated from the expected amount of violence that is aligned with his sport. Although you could argue that Romanowski intended to intimidate his competition by punching Williams in the face, his violent act did not provide him with a direct advantage to gaining yardage, tackling, or scoring—the three most aggressive aims embedded in the world of football.

Researchers have identified two forms of aggression in sports: instrumental aggression and reactive aggression (Leonard, 1988). According to Leonard (1998), instrumental aggression lacks emotion and is often related to a task. Reaction aggression, Leonard (1988) argues, involves an aggressive emotional reaction where exerting harm on another is the main goal (Leonard, 1988). In specific American sporting events, we know that violence is most prevalent in team sports where physical contact is associated with the sport. For example, sports that involve extensive reactive aggression plays and behaviors are football, rugby, soccer, and hockey. We also know that violence in these sports is performed primarily by the players on the team, but coaches, parents, and even fans today contribute to and encourage violence in American sports (Leonard, 1988). In fact, some scholars question whether sports fans encourage the amount of violence in a sport or if they simply mirror or reflect the violence observed in a sport.

To understand violence in sports, researchers rely on three major theories that seek to explain the behaviors (Leonard, 1988; Terry & Jackson, 1985). The first theory known as the biological theory proposed by Lorenz (1963) views violent aggression in sports as an innate human behavior. If we agree with this perspective, we would believe that violence in sports is an acceptable behavior for athletes to release frustrations and anger. Recall the frustration-aggression model discussed in Chapter 8, where we learned that catharsis of pent-up hostile feelings is a benefit for players who participate in violent, physical contact sports. According to biological theory, aggression is caused by frustration and is viewed as situational. The second theory, psychological theory, sees aggression and frustration as the main reactions that occur when an individual's goals, needs, and desires are blocked (Leonard, 1988). Research tells us that for athletes, frustration is often created because of four factors: (1) questionable calls by officials, (2) failure of the athlete to execute an important play, (3) injuries that interfere with the athlete's optimum performance, and, lastly, (4) banter from fans, or even verbal insults from coaches or teammates (Abdal-Haqq, 1989). The third and final theory used to help explain the use of violence in sports is social learning theory. Social learning theory maintains that violence is a learned behavior that happens when athletes observe role models and try to imitate the behavior. Observation of behaviors performed by those we look up to must also include rewards or punishments. When celebrity athletes involved in highly violent sports are observed winning, earning six-digit figures, etc., the theory helps us understand the effects of these observations on young vulnerable boys and girls. If young boys and girls who are keenly aware of masculine and feminine gender roles also observe athletes as sports heroes and as role models, then social learning theory predicts that they will ultimately learn to imitate their behaviors. We also know that other influences in one's environment may also encourage, inspire, and confirm violent play. These important social influencers include coaches, teammates, parents, siblings, and peers, to name a few.

Positive and negative reinforcement of behaviors may take the form of rewards, such as media hype, praise, trophies, starting position, and respect from friends and family. Vicarious reinforcement may come from seeing professional players honored and wealthy. Because professional athletes are paid huge salaries, it is possible that for some vulnerable youth, the salary may reinforce the athlete's violent acts within a game. Athletes who are not perceived as individuals who express a particular degree of aggressiveness may also be observed receiving negative reinforcement for their lack of aggression. These athletes may receive negative reinforcement in the form of criticisms from the coach or family members, reduced or no lack of playing time, and/or experiencing persecution from sports fans, coaches, and others. The theories that we summarized earlier, theories concerning the biological nature of, psychological influences for, and social learning of violence in sports, provide scholars with a solid foundation for sports psychologists to conduct interventions that may reduce or prohibit excessive aggression, particularly among young athletes.

The Four Categories of Violence in Sports

According to information provided by the Sports Conflict Institute website, violence in sports has been placed into four categories: forceful physical contact, imposed penalties and sanctions,

FIGURE 9.1   *Body contact in football.*

violence that breaks public laws, and, lastly, violent criminal actions (Coakley, 2001; Kerr, 1993; Kerr, 2002; Sports Conflict Institute, 2018; Tenenbaum, Stewart, Singer, & Duda, 1997; Young, 2000). The first form of violence that we refer to as *forceful physical contact* has been identified in the literature as those physical practices that are commonly found in specific sports. For example, sports that rely on a form of physical contact while competing would be wrestling, martial arts, football, lacrosse, boxing, ice hockey, and rugby, to name a few. Depicted in Figure 9.1 is an example of full-contact in a sport like football where aggressive contact is an expected part of the game.

Imposed penalties and sanctions refer to the physical violent behaviors in sports that are often accepted by the athletes and coaches of the sport, but the aggressive behavior is known to violate rules of the game. An example of this type of violence in sports would be found in soccer or basketball when a player aggressively uses an elbow or a knee to put another player on the opposing team in a vulnerable state. *Imposed penalties and sanctions* represent a category of violence in sports where the guilty players pay a fine for the violent behavior during a game but do not receive intense reprimands or repercussions for their violent "in-game" behavior. Illustrations of this type of violence includes intentional attempts to injure a player or coach by another player or coach, threats of physical harm or actual physical harm sustained by players or coaches by fans or those engaging in the spectating of sports, or threats and acts of violence performed by fans or spectators on opposing fans or other spectators. In this category of violence, a player typically causes bodily injury to another athlete, but the violent behavior, although out of the scope of the game, is considered to be acceptable for athletes and many fans of the sport. Therefore, when a basketball player elbows an opponent who is attempting to rebound, this would be an "imposed sanction" or foul for an athlete but is often considered by some to be essential to the game of basketball.

FOUR DIFFERENT LEVELS OF VIOLENCE IN SPORTS

Violence in sports consists of overly aggressive physical acts that occur in all types of contact sports and go beyond normal play, placing the welfare and safety of players at risk. High levels of testosterone in athletes and the animal behavior that drives them to establish territory could also lead to violent behavior.

These violent acts may range from a simple elbow jab to a brutal attack on another player, but as the level of aggression grows, the danger to the players grows, as well. This video by uhcagent on YouTube shows all aspects of violence in sports. It's graphic and shows bad sportsmanship for the players and fans.

Some experts have identified four different levels of violence in sports, each of which increases in intensity of aggression and violence toward other players.

1. Forceful Physical Contact

The first type of sports violence is body contact, which is often accepted as a normal part of many contact sports, such as tackles in football and body checks in hockey. Players know that body contact is a part of these sports, and everyone expects that this type of body contact will occur. Even though body contact sometimes leads to injuries and can be quite brutal, athletes are expected to initiate body contact in these sports to play the game successfully.

2. Imposed Penalties and Sanctions

The next type of sports violence is borderline violence. These acts are not normal parts of a contact sport; rather, they are illegal tactics that players often use to play "dirty" or to get back at an opponent for a perceived slight. Borderline violence might include the outbreak of a fistfight in hockey or a sharp elbow throw while playing soccer.

These moves are not technically allowed, but players often use them to intimidate their opponents. These actions have become an expected part of contact sports. The concern about this type of violence is regarding the effect it may have on children watching the sport and observing the violence played over and over by the "media." The children may copy this activity or just become desensitized to violence.

3. Violence that Breaks Laws

The third type of sports violence is quasicriminal violence, which includes actions that violate the formal rules of the game. These

Violence that breaks laws is a category of violence that describes the practices of athletes that not only violate formal rules of the sport and game but also are considered flagrant fouls that endanger a player's health and body. An example of this type of violence in sports is when a player punches the opponent in the head during a soccer game. Or when there is a late hit or punch from one football player to another.

The last category of violence is also referred to as *criminal violence*. This type of violence includes behaviors that are clearly and without a doubt outside of the law. This is violence that takes place after a game or competition, or it may be an assault during a game that gives the appearance that the aggression was "premeditated." The violence is often severe enough that a player is seriously injured, killed, or paralyzed as a result of the act. For example, we have seen many cases where players were intentionally hit over the head during an ice hockey game and the act was so blatant that charges or indictments are passed along, and the attack is handled in a state or federal court. According to research, this type of criminal violence is defined as "an intense violent act that causes severe physical harm or even death of the opponent" (Anderson & Huesmann, 2003; Young, 2000. For an act to fit this category, the assault would have to be unquestionably outside of what our culture considers to be the "norm" of the roughest type of violence in sports. As a result of engaging in this type of behavior, an athlete faces criminal charges in the courts.

Sports violence, as defined in the introduction, is the use of violence that exceeds the level of violence our society deems acceptable. In the case of sports violence, we are referring to violent acts that exceed the competitive arena and may be related to the outside world. Violence in sports places the welfare and safety of players, family members, and friends at risk. Some sports psychologists hypothesize that testosterone levels in male athletes, along with an animal like predisposition to mark one's territory may also influence the extent to which penchant or inclination to engage in violent behavior may be much more likely. These violent acts range from an elbow jab to perhaps a cruel, vicious attack on another player. As the level of aggression exhibited by a player grows, the danger to the competing athlete increases as well. In the next section of this chapter, we will go into greater detail about the four categories of sports violence.

Violent acts that are not in accordance with the mandated rules of a sport but are condoned by fans and athletes because the violence is perceived to be a valid and necessary element of the sport's activity is most frequently observed in American sports. The behaviors that our culture consider to be "borderline" or those that fans are most ambivalent toward are those violent acts that involve intentional fouls in the penalty zone of football or a fight after a play in ice hockey. These violent acts, although they are not aligned with the rules on violence, are not in danger of lawsuits but often are punished with penalties that are enforced and carried out by those close to the sport, individuals such as sports leaders and administrators, referees, and umpires. As depicted in Figures 9.2 and 9.3, sports like boxing involve violence that is perceived to be a valid and necessary component of the sport. Remember in 1997 when Mike Tyson bit his opponent's ear? This would be an example of quasicriminal violence. This violent act was reviewed by the Nevada Boxing Commission. In line with the punishments that are associated with an aggressive act deemed borderline violence, the Nevada Boxing Commission banned Tyson for his violent behavior. There are other very firm and strict infractions that come with harsher penalties and can be demonstrated when the violence inflicted on an athlete results in a critical injury. Punishment in cases of quasicriminal violence happens infrequently.

violations can lead to game penalties, such as suspensions and even expulsions. Cheap shots and flagrant fouls can potentially hurt other athletes, and so game officials will punish players who take such actions.

4. Criminal Violence

The final level of sports violence involves criminal violent behavior, which clearly not only violates the rules of a game but also violates the law. No athlete should sanction such behavior, and it is clearly outside the norm of even the roughest contact sport. An example of a criminal act might be a premeditated assault on a player using a hockey stick as a weapon.

Fueled by Fans

Sports violence is often heightened not only by the players themselves but also by the crowd. Depending on various characteristics of the crowd, the intensity of sports violence can increase quickly. Larger crowds at serious or important sporting events, particularly where the spectators tend to consume alcohol, can fuel the level of sports violence that occurs during a particular sporting event.

While some fans and commentators seem to see sports violence as inevitable, the opposite contingent claims that aggressive sports play need not always lead to gratuitous violence that crosses the line between the permissible and impermissible. The difficulty can be in balancing the athlete's passion for success and the fan's drive for a competitive, exciting game with the need to protect our athletes from potentially serious harm.

FIGURE 9.2 *Portrait of professional wrestlers fighting in boxing ring: men hitting bloody opponent in face, tackling him to floor*

FIGURE 9.3   *Portrait of professional wrestlers fighting in boxing ring: men hitting bloody opponent in face, tackling him to floor.*

Roller derby is a sport that is primarily played by amateurs and is composed of all-female teams (Moffett, 2013). As illustrated in Figure 9.4, borderline violence is involved when the team's blocker has to use body contact, changing positions, and other game play strategies and tactics in order to help score while at the same time to deterring the opposing team from scoring.

Aggressive acts that extend outside the formal rules of a game are so incredibly widespread in today's American culture that sports leagues feel pressure to engage actively in administering punishments and penalties. Equipment needed to participate in some sports, such as a stick or a ball, are generally rather innocuous articles, but they can be used to cause extreme physical harm. In our culture today, sports fans and even those involved in public policy and the law believe that the equipment and behavior associated with a game are necessary and significant parts of the sport. Both amateur and professional leagues have formulated policies that penalize players for extreme violent acts. Often, the punishments take the form of high-priced fines and short- or long-term suspensions. To illustrate this point, let's look at the sanctions upheld in the sport of hockey—a sport with a host of penalties for violators. The rules of hockey show a

FIGURE 9.4   *Example of borderline violence in roller derby.*

FIGURE 9.5   *Play, skate, action, goal, player, ice hockey.*

wide variety of sanctions and punishments for acts initiated by any of their athletes. Figure 9.5 is one example of the physical abuse, contact, and player-on-player hits and collisions. The sanctions enforced when the player exhibits behaviors known as "boarding, butt-ending, charging, clipping, cross-checking, elbowing, fighting, high-sticking, holding, hooking, kneeing, roughing, slashing, spearing, and tripping" (see Libby, O'Brien, Kingsley, & Champion, 2018).

In baseball, pitches thrown at a batter with the intent of hitting his head result in the pitcher's dismissal from the game. Managers of the team are also at risk of being removed from a game for confrontations with the referee or umpire. In football, there are infractions when players engage in behaviors identified as "roughing the kicker," "unnecessary roughness," and "holding." For football fans and teams, when a player engages in a high or late tackle, it causes outrage among fans. In basketball, the punishment for quasicriminal violence is known as a "flagrant foul." A flagrant foul is called when the athlete uses excessive or violent contact toward an opponent, and the behavior is said to likely cause injury to the opponent. In some instances, a flagrant foul performed by a player may be perceived as unintentional or it may be intentional. A foul against the opposing player that is viewed as intentional is also known as an "intentional foul" in the NBA. While many of the acts discussed here, roughing the kicker, flagrant fouls, and others, may result in criminal charges or civil lawsuits, they are rare cases in today's courts simply because the violent and aggressive acts occur during the game and during a sporting event that is expected to have some violence. Therefore, if similar violent acts happen outside a sports venue, then we find the player will often be charged with a criminal offense.

Finally, *criminal violence* is behavior considered so aggressive that the only way to address the violence is to address the behavior in court. The reason for the legal component involved in this type of violence is because the act and violence are not sanctioned behaviors by the sports league.

Despite the fact that many sports lawyers and scholars specializing in law work hard to delineate legitimate from illegitimate sports violence, social psychologists and sociologists are not interested in the demarcation of the differences in violence. Rather, social psychologists, psychologists, and psychotherapists are most interested in understanding the causes of sports-related violence and determining if engaging in sporting events that involve violent plays is actually cathartic.

Most sports sociologists, however, challenge the notion that violence in sports is cathartic. For some, social learning theory clearly predicts and explains the violence in sports. Young children learn violence from observing behaviors. This perspective has been confirmed over and over in studies that obtained data that reveal exact differences that vary from one culture to the next in terms of socially acceptable levels of violence in sports. Disparities in a culture's sports-related violence strongly suggest that they are not the result of some innate human force. In our culture, we consider brutal body contact and physical aggression to be masculine. Earlier chapters in this book show that conformity to the gender code certifies an athlete's masculinity. However, female athletes exhibiting similar behaviors are shunned and targets of ridicule and shame.

Illegitimate Sports Violence

When does an injury from a legitimate sports play transform into intentional and excessive use of force that causes harm and injury? When does the violence displayed during a sporting event become a criminal liability? A brief review of criminal law books provides instances involving a few major cases in hockey. The legal cases related to violence in hockey seem to set standards for prosecuting athletes in other sports for violence. There is a thin, unclear line drawn between what is within the rules or outside the rules when it comes to what is acceptable or unacceptable violence in sport.

In-Game Violent Behavior

In-game violence is violence that occurs during the sporting game. Violent tactics in sports games are those behaviors that cause harm to opposing players. Included in this type of violent behavior are the fights that break out between players during a game. An example of in-game violence is one from the 2004 NHL season. Vancouver Canucks player Todd Bertuzzi, at 6 feet, 3 inches and 245 pounds, approached 6 feet, 1 inch and 210 pounds Steve Moore of the Colorado Avalanche from behind. Bertuzzi grabbed Moore's jersey with one hand then punched him with the other hand, ultimately knocking Moore unconscious. Bertuzzi then shoved the unconscious Moore into the ice as he was falling. As a result of Bertuzzi's assault, Moore suffered a broken neck, spinal ligament injuries, a concussion, and facial cuts and bruises. Why? It was obvious that the violence Bertuzzi exhibited were not necessary and as a result drew heavy attention from the media. For some fans and proponents of hockey, Bertuzzi's act of violence was justified in that it could be perceived that it was part of some unwritten code in hockey that says players have a right to monitor "dirty hits" by retaliating with even more vicious hits.

Like hockey, other sports have innate violence. In football, for example, blocking and especially tackling are behaviors that are often done aggressively *and* violently. One violent aspect of the game of hockey is the physical contact that comes from body checking, which is using the shoulder or hip to knock an opposing player against the ice or boards. This is, as all hockey fans know, the sport's most extreme form of violence. Interestingly, we find that the actual fighting between players seems to be accepted as part of the game. Rugby and boxing both have aspects of violence as well. For example, boxing is a sport that is violent in that it consists exclusively of punching in such a way that the winner has an opportunity to knock the other person unconscious. In other words, we watch boxers cause enough physical harm to their opponents that they knock them out and that "knock out" is rewarded and considered the winning punch.

On-Field/Off-Field Violent Behavior

Experimental research is inconclusive in determining whether violent behavior exhibited by players during a sport actually leads to violence outside of the sport in the athlete's personal and social life. It seems reasonable to believe that athletes who are habituated in applying physical violence in sports will naturally use violence in their personal lives, particularly when they are up against difficulties, frustrations, or even the perceived threat of loss—all circumstances that happen in and out of one's sporting event. The athlete who self-identifies with all things masculine, may, when challenged, struggle with responding to the challenger with physical violence. We do find that athletes who return physical violence may actually be performing learned behaviors observed in cultural and environmental environments. In other words, social and environmental influences in an athlete's life may have been well established or observed via social learning theory outside of his or her sport. In other words, participation in violent sports may not serve as the leading trigger for violence. The violence may be due to innate, biological predispositions or the athlete's upbringing. From a biological perspective for understanding violent behavior, it can be speculated that innate predispositions to violence may have led an athlete to participate in a violent sport. We know that often young boys from lower classes are known to adopt a specific sport so that they are allowed to demonstrate their masculinity. As we discussed in Chapter 7, in American culture, one way for a young boy to demonstrate his hegemonic masculinity is to be in an environment that will allow him to respond violently when his "masculinity" or potential manhood is in jeopardy. Sports with high levels of physical contact provide that much-needed environment. Therefore, any challenge to a young boy's manhood may provoke a violent behavior reaction, whether in sports or out of sports, simply because if he does not respond aggressively or violently, he will be the focus of harsh criticism. As we mentioned in Chapter 7, when boys and men do not respond to violence leveled against them, others in their environment or peer group may find the lack of a violent reaction unmanly. This, in turn, may affect the young male's self-esteem in a negative way. Young boys may feel that they have to fight back so that they can save face; otherwise, they will become victims of teasing and bullying.

Alcohol and drugs have also been suggested as influences that may add to the problem of violence. Athletes who are under the influence of alcohol and drugs lose control of their skills or talents and may be more likely to commit violent acts. Violence toward women is a sensitive topic for many, particularly for male athletes. Statistics obtained on the website for the National Coalition Against Violent Athletes (2018; http://www.ncava.org) show that student-athletes who identify as male comprise close to 3% of college students. Despite the small proportion of male athletes as students on college campuses, research shows that male student-athletes are involved in sexual assaults that account for "19% and 35% of all domestic assaults on college campuses today" (NCAVA, 2018). According to this three-year study, we learn that college athletes have been found to commit "one in three college sexual assaults" (NCAVA, 2018).

Regarding the general U.S. population and conviction rates of violence, we find a conviction rate of 80% for sexual assaults, while the rate for athletes is only 38%, that is according to data provided in a report published by the National Coalition Against Violent Athletes. Critics who question the validity of the study believe that the size of the sample was too small to detect differences. Reviews of the report further find another limitation on the design of the study. Reviewers of the study also believe that the researchers did not control for the use of alcohol and tobacco nor did they conduct a pretest to determine baseline measures of the male athlete's attitudes toward women (Crossett, 1999).

Using cultivation theory (see Chapter 2), we might expect a significant relationship between media coverage of athletes arrested for violent behavior and the frequency in which NFL athletes are arrested. As you recall, heavy users of TV are known to think the world is mean compared to those viewers who watch little to no television. Research tells us that of all the athletes involved in sports, professional NBA players are found to be guilty of committing more crimes than any other professional league player (Kim & Parlow, 2009; Mandell, 2014; Snopes, 2017; Tracy, 2014). Research further shows that NFL athletes commit crimes at lower rates than the general population. In his work on crime rates, Morris found that roughly 2,000 DUIs are recorded per 100,000 regular folks compared to a rate of about 550 for the NFL. One study on crime showed that out of all the crimes committed by professional athletes, 3.8% of those crimes are committed by professional basketball players and not athletes involved in highly physical contact sports (Bureau of Justice Statistics, 2008; Morris, 2014; Snyder, Cooper, & Mulako-Wangota, 2018). And, we also find that out of all the crimes and domestic violent acts in a year, only 2.3% of all the crimes are committed by professional football players (Bureau of Justice Statistics, 2018).

The O. J. Simpson criminal case in 1994 and the Ray Rice case of 2014 have led many scholars to begin holding important discussions centered on the idea that football players are perpetrators of domestic and sexual violence because of the level of violence in the sport. However, we know that, over the last five years, football players are not the only athletes who allegedly engage in domestic or sexually violent acts (Bureau of Justice Statistics, 2018). We know that a more significant percentage of NBA athletes committed crimes than other athletes.

Framing of Violence and Athletes by Media

We know from data conducted by the Poynter Institute and the Pew Research Center that the area of sports journalism is dominated by Caucasian male writers who write primarily for Caucasian American audiences. Research shows that a majority of Caucasian news readers hold prejudiced views of African American men (Entman, 2007). Recent research demonstrates that when domestic or sexual violent acts involve football or basketball players, and, when the violent acts are committed by African American male athletes, media tend to give these situations more attention, and as a result, these events receive a greater number of stories and media hype than violent acts committed by Caucasian male athletes (Frisby, 2016).

Billings, Halone, and Denham (2002) have argued for more than 15 years that athletes are stereotyped based on race in sports media. Banet-Weiser (1999) argues that one consequence of having athletes frequently stereotyped in media is the effect that the stereotyped depictions have on consumers' ideas about athletes of color. In a recent study, Frisby (2016) obtained data that shows that sports media pay more attention to crimes and bad behaviors exhibited by African American male athletes than they do behaviors exhibited by Caucasian male athletes. Also, data collected in Frisby's (2016) content analysis revealed that, currently, sports media's coverage of African American athletes is not equivalent in the number of stories and the content and focus of the stories. In other words, data obtained in the study show that, more often than not, African American athletes tend to receive more coverage when the story is about crime, violence than do White male athletes (Frisby, 2016).

Frisby (2016) found evidence revealing that sports media tend to publish news stories that blame the black male athlete for his failings, such as being a criminal or violent. Based on the evidence in this study, we can assume that sports journalists use news frames that may lead readers to form assumptions about black men. In other words, frames that lack facts and quotes from experts may block readers from coming to a balanced and "objective" assessment of the African American athlete (Iyengar, 1991). Since African American men dominate many sports that are considered violent contact sports, when they become involved in violent behavior, it appears that sports media uses the violence to excite and sensationalize the event—resulting in profits for the sports media vehicle. Interestingly, Frisby found that African American athletes often donate millions of dollars to schools, charities, and youth foundations. Where are the news stories about these athletes of color and their positive contributions to our society? Male athletes of color, however, appear in the headlines, receive the most negative coverage, and have their images damaged in the public, which is quite unfair (Frisby, 2016). Journalists need to keep in mind that police officers, dentists, judges, lawyers, politicians, and men from all aspects of American culture (regardless of race) have the potential to engage in domestic and sexual violence. Table 9.1 presents data obtained in Frisby's study on sports media's framing of black and white athletes. The table shows that of all the stories written about crime and domestic/sexual violence, black athletes appeared in news coverage more often than other athletes. Yet in terms of highlighting the athlete's accomplishments, morals, abilities and athletic skills, and personal lifestyles (all positive stories), white athletes were found to be the focus of those stories when compared to black athletes.

Much more research is required before we can make any definitive conclusions about the relationship between violence and sports. We as consumers of media need to keep in mind that in lieu of relying on stories in the news or media hype about the events, and before we jump to conclusions about which sport or race commits the most violent acts, we must seek solid data as to the rates of occurrence so that we can make objective comparisons for other groups of people. Other influential factors should also be taken into account. Influential factors such as the extent to which the individual relies on and uses drugs and alcohol. Drugs and alcohol are important influencers, especially since they may be the leading contributors to violence by athletes and not the athlete's participation in an aggressive, highly physical sports. Sports journalists need to address the role they play in adding to sensationalistic news and the effect these stories may have on society. Most importantly, journalists need to engage in career development sessions that will offer them an opportunity to take appropriate steps to prevent making illusionary correlations between violence and sport (Mullin, 2016).

TABLE 9.1   *Thematic Frames and Type of Story by Race of Athlete*

Type of Media Coverage	White	Black	Other	Totals
Crime	6 (22.2%)	18 (66.7%)	3 (11.1%)	27 (100%)
Domestic/sexual violence	3 (17.6%)	12 (70.6%)	2 (11.8%)	17 (100%)
Training/work ethic/dedication	6 (42.9%)	5 (35.7%)	3 (21.4%)	14 (100%)
Morally successful	10 (83.3%)	1 (8.3%)	1 (8.3%)	12 (100%)
Violating the rules/laws of the league	8 (47.1%)	6 (35.3%)	3 (17.6%)	17 (100%)
Accomplishments	20 (58.8%)	8 (23.6%)	6 (17.6%)	34 (100%)
Personal lifestyle	9 (42.9%)	7 (33.3%)	5 (23.8%)	21 (100%)
Abilities/athletic skills	6 (46.2%)	3 (23.1%)	4 (30.8%)	13 (100%)
Totals	68 (43.9%)	60 (38.7%)	27 (17.4%)	155 (100%)

$X^2 = 63.1$, df = 11, p <0.0001

Source for data: Frisby (2016)

Domestic/Sexual Violence

Protestors found a CoverGirl ad on social media sites and had it photoshopped to show the model with a black eye. The social media campaign, intended for female NFL fans, was edited by protestors to express disdain for the way that the NFL handled the Ray Rice domestic violence controversy. As shown in Figure 9.6 shows, CoverGirl initiated an ad campaign that featured a picture of a woman with a black and blue eye proclaiming it's time to "Get Your Game Face On."

In February 2014, activists started posting the edited version of the ad (Figure 9.6) to Twitter and Facebook. Fans and sports activists were posting tweets and comments seeking Commissioner Roger Goodell's resignation. Many fans and social media users encouraged others to join the effort and boycott the NFL.

In March 2014, Ray Rice, a former football running back for the Baltimore Ravens, was arrested and subsequently arraigned for aggravated assault. Rice was indicted on charges of assaulting his then-fiancée, and currently his wife in an elevator. *TMZ*, a celebrity news show, released a video of the encounter. This video then created a media frenzy and generated a prominent controversy for the NFL. Shortly after the release of the video, the NFL enacted a new policy regarding how they handle domestic violence cases. The Ravens terminated Rice's contract in September 2014. An additional video was released, and Rice was subsequently suspended indefinitely by the league after this footage was made public.

FIGURE 9.6 *Photoshopped CoverGirl "Get Your Game Face On" ad.*

Rice appealed his termination and suspension in federal court and was later reinstated. Since this event in 2014, the NFL has been under intense scrutiny by fans for its handling of the case. It seems that the NFL was aware of the video long before *TMZ* released it, yet they suspended Rice for a mere two games. For many, a two-game suspension was a punishment that did not equal the crime. Since the 2014 Rice elevator incident, the NFL has created a rule that says an athlete must endure a six-game unpaid ban. This suspension, according to the policy, is for any football player found to violate this policy.

In 2010, St. Louis Rams running back Steve Jackson was charged with hitting his nine-month pregnant, then girlfriend. According to reports, Jackson drove her to the hospital but ordered her to say that she slipped and fell while taking a shower. We learned that a week and a half later, the baby was born. Four months later, the couple separated because Jackson continued to make violent threats toward her.

Boxing champion Floyd Mayweather Jr. plead guilty in 2010 to the crime of domestic violence. Another male athlete Tito Ortiz committed domestic violence against his girlfriend, Ms. Jenna Jameson, who later decided to drop the charge. The greatest message not being told in sports media today is the one that emphasizes that many athletes who use violent behavior during a sporting event do not act violently in their personal lives or take work-related frustrations home. If a majority of male athletes were engaged in violent acts off the field, data obtained from court records and news media would confirm the statistics.

Another notable case of an alleged sexual assault involved a one-time incident between boxer Mike Tyson and a young woman. It was alleged that Tyson raped and violently attacked a young woman. Although Tyson was convicted and served time in jail, as in most cases, the female victim had her reputation and integrity ruined. Typically, the perpetrator justifies his behavior by arguing that the victim was "asking for it." Even though Tyson did not go on record and call his victim a slut or claim she asked for it, he did claim innocence and was reported becoming so mad and frustrated that he blurted out "I just hate her. Now I do want to rape her" (Associated Press, 2006; *The Guardian*, 2018). Similar court cases involving athletes and domestic or sexual violence include players Kobe Bryant and Ben Roethlisberger. While Tyson and Roethlisberger both admitted to engaging in consensual sex with the women, both athletes firmly denied that they forced themselves on the women.

In a 2014 news article, we learned of several athletes in the NFL who have been charged with domestic violence. In 2016, Oscar Pistorius was sentenced of 13 years in prison for murdering his then live-in girlfriend. From Chad Ochocinco who has since changed his name back to Chad Johnson to Johnny Manziel to Tito Ortiz to Jose Canseco to Manny Ramirez to Floyd Mayweather Jr. we find that professional athletes are frequently charged with crimes related to domestic violence. From professional players in the NFL, NBA, boxing, and figure skating, sports media are frequently reporting on the increasing number of domestic violence incidents committed by athletes.

For a more exhaustive list of NFL players and their alleged domestic/sexual violence assaults, see a list posted on *USA Today*'s website (*USA Today*, 2018). Listed on the USA Sports online website are arrests, charges, and citations of NFL players for violent crimes. According to the site, "Most all of the players belonged to an NFL roster at the time of the incident." The data was obtained from media reports and public records, and conceived and created by a sports journalist, Brent Schrotenboer.

The Collective Bargaining Agreement

Collective bargaining agreements are used by sports leagues to govern players accused and convicted of violence off the field. The policies were created after years of meetings and negotiations between commissioners, union leaders, and team owners. Of all the national leagues in America, as of this writing, the NFL is the only league to have created a policy regulating domestic and sexual violence. The NBA, NHL, and MLB have categorized domestic violence with broader clauses in their collective bargaining agreement, which seems to cloud the rules regarding the severity of the punishment.

Vague Policies/Vague Punishments

Of the many NFL players who have been arrested for acts of violence, the case involving Jovan Belcher of the Kansas City Chiefs is one that illustrates the consequences of a league's vague punishments and policies. In 2012, Jovan Belcher made headlines when he murdered the mother of his daughter and then turned the gun on himself. At his mother's request, Belcher's body was exhumed to determine if his behavior was due to chronic traumatic encephalopathy. In fact, in one section of the court case, it was mentioned that Belcher was showing signs of cognitive impairment months before the murder-suicide. It was determined that the team allowed, actually required, Belcher to continue to play despite his very visible signs of neurological impairments.

Research shows that the harshest punishment for athletes involved in violent acts was a one-game suspension (Katsaros & University of New Haven Foundation, 2004; Nagel, Southall, & O'Toole, 2004; Rainey, 1994; Rainey & Duggan, 1998) This type of flexible discipline is not just found in the NFL. The NHL rarely uses suspensions for domestic violence acts committed by their players. However, in 2008, there was one exception. In 2008, hockey player Sean Avery received an indefinite suspension for describing his girlfriend using harsh and derogatory words in a sports media interview. The NFL alleged that the athlete's behavior was "detrimental" and "against the welfare" of the NHL (Mandell, 2014).

Just like the NFL and NHL, the MLB has similar vague language and weak disciplinary measures. In most cases, the punishments are up to the wisdom of the commissioner of the league. According to the code of conduct for players, an expert must assess cases of sexual abuse or domestic violence. Consider the case of Mets player Francisco Rodriguez. News stories report that Rodriguez hit a man, his girlfriend's father, in the midst of a heated argument. The penalty for striking the man? The Mets gave Rodriguez a two-game suspension, along with putting him on the team's "disqualified" players list. We learn from news accounts that Rodriguez was allowed to return to the team to play in the season that followed his violent act and court case. However, Rodriguez was traded in 2012 and arrested and charged with domestic abuse. And, according to a story written by Mandell (2014) published in *USA Today*, the charges against Rodriguez were dropped because the victim, along with a witness of the crime, left the country, making it difficult for them to testify. As a result, Rodriguez faced no disciplinary action from the MLB (Mandell, 2014).

In terms of a strict policy against domestic violence, the NBA has as of this writing not published or executed policies for athletes to abide by in terms of sexual and domestic violence. Yet unlike other major professional leagues, the NBA does have policies established that determine what they consider to be unlawful behavior and violent misconduct (Mandell, 2014). Reports in news stories reveal that several NBA players, such as Matt Barnes and DeAndre Liggins, have been charged in domestic violence cases even though they "have yet to be disciplined by the NBA after the charges were dropped" (Mandell, 2014). In 2013, Jared Sullinger was suspended for a game by the Celtics after being charged in a domestic violence incident. While his charges were later dropped, as in the Barnes and Liggins's cases, Sullinger was the only one to experience a one-game suspension.

Changing Disciplinary Actions

Activists against suspensions or discipline for athletes charged with domestic violence believe that because, in most cases, there were no convictions in many of the allegations, punishing athletes makes it tricky for leagues to determine the level of punishment. How does a coach or commissioner process what is found in police reports? Which one should deem the accuser or the alleged perpetrator more credible? In cases where the charges are dropped, how do commissioners stay objective when reading "he said/she said" recollections of the events? On the other hand, why is it that players who have allegedly hit, choked, and kicked women are still able to play when credible evidence obtained supports the victims?

Legal Consent and Intention

It was in 1901 when American football addressed the use of violence at a governmental level. Early records obtained in 1901 showed that six football players died while playing on the field. Back then, sports media made football the villain and condemned the sport for excessive violence that resulted in death. It was the sports media that first demanded that the football league write policies and rules regarding excessive force in the sport. In 1905, Theodore Roosevelt, the president at the time, who happened to be a boxer during his years at Harvard University, advised college administrators to create rules that would protect athletes who played football. To ensure that colleges instituted rules and policies, President Roosevelt informed colleges that all football games would stop if rules regarding violence used in the sport were not changed or implemented.

If an individual hit a person in the face so hard that it knocks him or her unconscious, the individual is at risk of being charged with aggravated assault. In some instances, this violent act results in the person spending time in jail. But what if the knockout punch takes place in a sporting competition such as boxing? From a theoretical perspective, framing theory might help us to understand, explain, and predict how our perceptions of one violent event might change based on the frame or context of a situation. We know that the sport of boxing involves extreme violence because the winner is chosen based on the one who hurt the other the most. But other physical contact sports, unlike boxing, require the use of bats and hard balls, objects that we know if used alone can injure and kill. In 2014, Phillip Hughes, a left-handed batsman who was playing cricket, was hit in the neck by a bouncer during a game, causing a vertebral artery dissection that led to a subarachnoid hemorrhage. Hughes, having never regained consciousness, died two days later. Although he died as a result of playing cricket, neither a legal case nor an indictment was administered. Hughes was the unfortunate victim of an accident that occurred during the game; it was not an intentional show of malice or force by the opponent.

When we think of cases like Hughes and other athletes who are injured or die as a result of the violence in sport, we must stop to consider other instances when tragedy happens within the course of an event. For example, patients agree to let surgeons operate and create incisions, we go to dentists to have teeth pulled, and some of us even consent to cosmetic surgeries. When considering the deaths of athletes that occur while they are "working," we must keep in mind that many if not all athletes actually consent to the risks that come with the game. In other words, they are aware of the element of harm that may come with the terms of their jobs.

In 2005, Aaron O'Neal, a 19-year-old, University of Missouri red-shirt freshmen, collapsed during a summer workout in late July. Two hours after his collapse O'Neal was pronounced dead. O'Neal and Hughes are not the only players who have died as a result of participating in their sport.

Athletes in the NFL and college have met tragic endings as a result of travels on the team bus, acts of suicide, homicides, accidents, and drownings. As in the O'Neal case, some players die from illnesses and injuries sustained during a game. Depositions obtained from the lawsuit later revealed that O'Neal joined the Missouri football team with a pre-existing blood disorder (Day, 2009). At the heart of the lawsuit was the claim that MU coaches and trainers did not take sufficient precautions necessary to work with an athlete who has been diagnosed with a blood condition known as "sickle-cell anemia" (Day, 2009).

National Football League

American courts have continually tried to determine differences in violent acts that are intrinsic to a sport from those violent acts that if performed outside of the sport would be illegal. Intention to harm another is often the legal criteria used in court to determine fault. To decide if serious harm was done to an individual, the courts look to see if the type of attack is written in the rule books for the sport. That is, they look to see if the violence is prohibited by the sport when the violent act occurred (e.g., was the violent act performed during a time-out, when the play was suspended or over). Prosecution is, therefore, determined based on the answers to all these questions.

James Butler, a boxer also known as "the Harlem Hammer," approached his opponent after losing the match. He purportedly approached the opponent to congratulate him. Instead, Butler struck the opponent in the jaw. This attack occurred after the match ended. The opponent passed out and was unable to engage in daily life activities for nine months. As a result of his behavior, Mr. Butler was sentenced to four months in jail. Three years later, in 2004, Butler pled guilty to voluntary manslaughter and arson in the death of a freelance sportswriter. (Butler is currently serving a 29-year sentence for killing the sportswriter.)

As mentioned earlier, families of players such as Aaron O'Neal and others who have preexisting health conditions that may have contributed to their deaths during training or a sporting event find themselves taking out wrongful death suits to set a precedent that colleges and leagues must be held liable for monitoring the physical and mental health conditions of all its players. The NFL reached a $765 million settlement with former players in 2013. The wrongful death suits involved physical conditions ranging from concussions and brain damage, to sickle cell anemia, to heat stroke, to dehydration. The point of the settlements is to set a precedent showing that colleges and professional leagues can be held liable for previously unknown health risks to which players were not aware of.

Many pundits feel strongly that the sports leagues should take personal responsibility and regulate the level of violence in sports on and off the field. In 1980, the Sports Violence Act of 1980 was proposed and suggested that athletes involved in violent criminal acts should serve up to one year in prison. The act also suggests that athletes who knowingly use excessive force during their sport should also serve time in prison. However, the Sports Violence Act failed to gain enough votes. Then in 1983, a newer version of the proposed act was also unsuccessful in creating a court in the sports world to hear cases involving excessive violence.

A frequent example of consent and in-game violence effects are concussions. Here in the United States, there are over three million reported cases of sports-related concussions each year (Langlois, Rutland-Brown, & Wald, 2006). The sports where concussions are most often reported are those in which the player has physical contact with equipment (Guskiewicz, Weaver, Padua, & Garrett, 2000). Medical research shows us that concussions happen most frequently in sports that are competitive and highly physical and violent. In fact, according to a recent study, football accounts for more than 60% of all concussions in sports (Department of Health and Human Services, 2013; Powell & Barber-Foss, 1999). Male athletes are most susceptible to concussions from playing football, and for female athletes, concussions are most likely to occur from playing soccer (Buzzini & Guskiewicz, 2003).

Mass Media and Images of Masculinity and Violence

Mass media also contribute to our culture's acceptance of violence in sports. Mass media exposes sports fans to extensive content containing sports-related violence in traditional and innovative media such as social media images and discussions, television, magazines, newspapers, and radio. Exposure to this type of content provides numerous opportunities for children to imitate violent behavior. Mass media seems to glamorize players, especially those athletes who are the most controversial and aggressive. Sports commentary often associates excitement and reward with violent behaviors.

Masculine Social Norms

Masculine social norms in our culture that are imposed upon men and boys seem to contribute to the American way of life and its culture of violence. As is the case with hegemonic masculinity, we find that our culture has come to accept violent acts both within a sport and in nonsport contexts (Boeringer, 1999; Brewer & Howarth, 2012; Fine, 1987). Research in this area demonstrates that male athletes who participate in highly aggressive contact sports are much more likely to conform to our culture's norms of masculinity than male athletes who do not participate in aggressive contact sports (Gage, 2008). America's norm of we must "win at all costs" is particularly found in sports, and the mentality is reinforced in sports teams. The hypothesis is that the more we praise aggressive acts in sports, the more we will find strong, positive opinions supporting aggression and violence in sports. Scholars also suggest that this association results in a strong adherence to masculine social norms. Not only that, but acceptance of violence in sports also tends to produce a culture of violence (Coulomb-Cabagno & Rascle, 2006).

Jock culture is a term in which scholars define as a culture that relies on aggressive, violent behaviors coupled with heavy alcohol consumption (Sonderlund et al., 2014). Jock culture, it has been suggested, reinforces violence, aggression, and masculinity through its norm that says real men should engage and be able to handle excessive drinking. Recall that excessive intake of alcohol has been a predicted moderator for increased aggression and violence for athletes off the court or in their personal lives (Koss, 1993). If we leave alcohol out of the equation, we still find that sexual violence may likely be related to the athlete's sense of entitlement, especially for those with successful careers. Some scholars believe that the entitlement felt by an athlete may influence the athlete's expectations of how women should act (Bouffard, 2010; Steinfeldt, Vaughan, LaFollette, & Steinfeldt, 2012).

Engagement in Violence and Aggression

Research over the years has found a close relationship between the type of sport that an athlete participates in and violent behavior (Gage, 2008; Guilbert, 2006; McCauley et al., 2014; Messner, 2002; Pappas, McKenry, & Catlett, 2004). For example, football players are expected to exhibit violent behavior because of the nature of their sport. The acts that are deemed natural to the sport are, but not limited to blocking, tacking, and hitting opposing players (Guilbert, 2006; Steinfeldt et al., 2012). The more aggression the athlete's sport is, research suggests, the more likely they are to engage in aggressive acts in nonathletic contexts. Research also suggests that those male sports fans who are violent in their personal lives are often drawn to violent, high-contact sports because, recall, in sports, we are actually allowed to condone, encourage, and even replicate/imitate similar behaviors.

Research on hypermasculinity further shows that men who play violent sports are more likely to display overactive masculine-like behaviors (Gage, 2008). That is, evidence suggests that high-contact sports lead to hypermasculine behaviors, causing the male athlete to believe that gender inequality is acceptable. Some studies have discovered that male athletes who play aggressive contact sports are more likely to support gender inequality than those male athletes who participate in sports such as swimming and tennis (Gage, 2008; McCauley et al., 2014). In fact, this finding was also replicated with hockey players. Pappas et. al, (2004) found that hockey players who are violent in their personal lives also believe that violence is a "logical continuation" of the violence that is encouraged when they are playing hockey (Pappas et al., 2004).

Fans and Spectators: Public Acceptance of Violent Sports

Research on spectator violence reveals that the central issue is whether fans incite player violence or reflect it (DeBenedette, 1987; DeBenedette, 1989; DeBenedette, 1990). The evidence, however, has been relatively inconclusive. Basking in the reflected glory of a team can lead to fans viewing the opposing team as enemies. This cognitive perception process also creates an "us" versus "them" or an in-group/out-group mentality.

Often during a competition, we find sports fans becoming violent in the stands among each other. Figure 9.7 is one example of a "stadium fight" between angry Green Bay Packer's Fans and North Carolina Panther Fans.

It is not uncommon for fans to exhibit anger and to respond negatively toward sports officials and even athletes. In fact, it has been stated that the most violent sports fans are soccer fans. We also know that spectators watching noncontact sports events are seldom found engaging in violent acts. In other words, violence directed at opposing team fans, referees, or ushers is a rare find at a

FIGURE 9.7   *Fans attending an NFL game between the Green Bay Packers and the Carolina Panthers.*

noncontact sport. However, fans who attend contact sports are not only vocal, loud, and emotional but also frequently engage in violent acts. We know from information found in sports law that "a large number of fans have died during pre- and post-game soccer celebrations" (Davidson, 2017).

Violence in terms of pre- and postgame celebrations is considered the most dangerous type of crowd violence, especially when it takes place after a major win. In fact, colleges with intense rivalries (Missouri vs. Nebraska or Missouri vs. Kansas) have had to create laws regarding property damage, particularly after these major victories when students invade the field or court and tear down the goalposts after football victories, or they throw objects on the court to show their loyalty and pride for their university. As a result, colleges have banned alcohol sales and use heavy police and security personnel to prevent fans from rushing onto the field or court when games end.

In fact, sports fan violence is on the rise and has gotten worse. Recall the time when a San Francisco Giants fan was beaten up outside of Dodger stadium. Then there were the riots in Vancouver when the Canucks lost the Stanley Cup to the Boston Bruins. Then there are those weekly fights in the stands at NFL games. With all the reports of fans' violent celebrations, we must come to the realization that there seems to be the idea that fans do more than just celebrate their home teams. In April 2017, Chicago White Sox played the Detroit Tigers and lost. It was Chicago's home opener. Not only were the players angry about the loss, but the fans were too. A fight broke out between Sox fans and Tiger fans, and involved people tumbling down the bleachers while still fighting.

In 2014, the NFL saw at least two major fights between fans. Immediately after a San Francisco 49rs game against the Arizona Cardinals, several fans fell down the concrete stadium stairs in Arizona. It was reported that men and women in red jerseys were throwing punches, choking, and knocking the opposing team fans around. It was reported that the steps were splattered with blood (see Babb & Rich, 2016). Then on the same day, different city, different state, the Washington Redskins were playing the Philadelphia Eagles in Philadelphia, and fans were hitting each other, sending some fans flying over several chairs. Figure 9.8 illustrates an earlier image of the night when Ron Artest, who has changed his name to Metta World Peace has now changed his name to The Panda's Friend (McDonald, 2014). And like World Peace, he wants to continue being known as "a friendly guy" (McDonald, 2014). The Panda's Friend, number 91 of the Indiana Pacers, started a fight in 2004 that involved his opponent, Ben Wallace, number 3 of the Detroit Pistons. Not only did the fight include other players from the Indiana Pacers but also fans in and out of the stands.

For better or worse, violence is an accepted, even expected, part of many sports. If blame were to be assigned for the perpetuation of violent sports such as boxing and football, we could blame mass media for its role in reinforcing violence through their messages and for emphasizing attendance at violent sporting events. Fans could be blamed for reinforcing violence not only through their attendance at violent sporting events but also through their violent behaviors at those events. Television networks could be blamed for broadcasting violent sporting events. Despite the potentially negative social value that ultimate fighting brings to society, fighters now enjoy celebrity status, showing that the public's appetite for ultimate fighting's violence extends beyond the ring. It is also worth noting that the UFC has cages installed around the ring not only to keep the fighters within the designated boundary but also to keep violent fans from entering the ring. Governing bodies could be blamed for not changing the violent nature of games under their jurisdiction.

Domestic Violence and Halloween Costumes

Obviously, violent sports are supported and reinforced by a wide range of people and groups. Why then should we be concerned with the sporting world and its violent games? Here is a recent situation that should challenge our thoughts about violence in media and particularly in sports. In October 2014, an Instagram photo with the caption "Greatest Costume Ever" surfaced showing a child wearing the jersey of former NFL player Ray Rice. Figure 9.8 shows the child dragging a doll on the sidewalk, meant to be Rice's wife, Janay Rice. The 9-year-old child could not purchase the costume by himself. This means that an adult not only purchased the costume but also thought it was the greatest costume ever. And to make matters worse, the Ray Rice costume was the number-one seller in 2014. This statistic makes us wonder why the issue of domestic violence is funny or even great. Images of Ray Rice as a Halloween costume have drawn massive attention on social media as well as criticisms. In one photo, a man wearing a No. 27 Ravens jersey (Rice's jersey) is seen dragging a blowup doll by the leg. This particular image garnered thousands of retweets and comments from those who found the costume "hysterical." In yet another real-life image posted on social media, a Caucasian man made up to appear in blackface can be seen wearing a Ravens' jersey. In the photo, the black-faced white man is posing next to a woman with a black eye. A quick reflection of these images leads us to a sad conclusion: our reflection has to involve thinking that someone's suffering was perceived to be funny and used as a source of entertainment by so many! Perhaps the popularity of making fun of domestic violence becomes funny the more we are exposed to the images in the media, and it becomes easier it is to detach from the reality of it.

FIGURE 9.8   *Ray Rice Halloween costume*

Then there is another instance that happened in Steubenville, Ohio. In 2013, two promising high school football players were indicted and found guilty for a group rape that had been posted on social media. What makes this an even sadder story is the fact that hundreds of text messages and cell phone pictures were uploaded to social media, yet not one person called and reported the crime to authorities. The social media posts provided much of the evidence because the young 16-year-old girl had no recollection of the event. Members of the football team were said to have recorded the assault while doing nothing to protect the girl or stop the attack.

What can be done to break this effect of violence? How can athletes, coaches, and administrators, scholars, sports psychologists, and others minimize, if not eliminate, violence in sports? To accomplish this task, it will take a concerted effort for us to consider what our role is in reducing violence. Next, we must ask how committed we are to reducing the violence. It seems reasonable to speculate that it would be hard for a hockey fan to enthusiastically support a reduction in the violence in the game.

Winning by "Any Means Necessary"

Given the philosophy of win at all costs that exists in some sporting circles, it should come as no surprise when coaches teach and encourage aggressive or violent tactics. They are, as it stands, simply acting toward others in a way that others act toward them. Unfortunately, this win-at-all-cost philosophy often leads to and reinforces the type of unethical, aggressive behaviors that impact negatively and destructively on the development and well-being of young athletes and our culture. Coaches who value sportsmanship and compassion will teach their players to play safely and within the rules of the game, whereas coaches who emphasize strategic reasoning will often teach their players violent tactics that are outside the rules.

Nucci and Young-Shim (2005) offer one suggestion that they believe will preclude aggressive tendencies in young athletes. These scholars recommend that coaches not be promoted or fired based solely on a win-loss record (Nucci & Young-Shim, 2005). If coaches act under the egoistic ethical decision-making model, then they would seek out the actions that bring them pleasure or those that would help them reduce the painful consequences. If getting fired is a painful consequence of losing, coaches, we can speculate, will go to extreme measures to win. When having to choose between losing or winning through the teaching of violent tactics, the latter may cause less pain and more pleasure for a coach since getting fired could be a painful consequence of losing.

External influences, those that are out of our control, seem to make it extremely difficult to lessen or eradicate violence in sport. We might argue that it is solely the glorification of winning and its accompanying rewards that result in violent behavior. We might also say that lenient or weak rules regarding violence exhibited by an athlete may also unintentionally send a message that violence is acceptable in our culture. Materialistic rewards such as money, trophies, and prizes, along with nonmaterialistic rewards, such as praise, recognition, and adulation, motivate athletes to win. Some people might argue that the removal of strong extrinsic motivators would reduce the occurrences of violence in sport

Another view of violence in games is one that centers on an internal locus or physiological response theory. Pappas, McKenry, and Catlett (2004) argue that frustration may actually stir aggressive behavior in athletes, which may partially explain sports aggression. Athletes who experience frustration that accompanies the failure to achieve a goal, make a home run, or score the winning basket may increase the likelihood of aggressive acts. For example, playing poorly in an important game such as the Super Bowl, the NCAA March Madness Championship, the Stanley and Piston Cups, and other important crowd-pleasers, such as a rivalry game in college, the playoffs, and tournaments. These contests alone may elicit a particular response from an athlete, and if he or she performs poorly, that may cause him or her to react violently not only in the game but also at home, in the bar, etc. Therefore, it can be concluded that this reaction may have had nothing to do with the extrinsic rewards that come from competition but with a frustrated athlete who is also highly competitive.

Reflect on Sports: Fan Violence

Peripheral violence in sport is "violence that is related to a sporting event but is not directly part of the game itself and does not involve fighting among players" (Course Hero, 2018). Peripheral violence can occur in any sport and with any demographic. From youth leagues to professional leagues, we might find examples of peripheral violence. It should be noted that peripheral violence also includes the fights and violence that happens between players and fans, fans fighting with other fans, postgame rioting, and violent hazing. A violent example of peripheral violence is the riot that ensued outside of the MLB's historic Fenway Park. This violent event happened right after the New York Yankees lost to the Boston Red Sox in the 2004 American League Championship Series. To subdue the crowd outside the ballpark, the Boston police had to resort to using pellet-like guns. The crowd was estimated to be between 60,000 and 80,000. Police were trying to stop riotous fans from overturning cars, starting fires, vandalizing cars and stores, and climbing the "Green Monster" wall. Tragically, one of the projectiles from an officer's gun hit an innocent bystander in the eye and killed her.

Another incident of peripheral violence was the rioting after Togo took the lead in a World Cup soccer qualifier game against Mali. Officials stopped the game after fans at the 70,000-seat, sold-out stadium rushed the field. As the rioters took to the streets, dozens of people were injured as fans set fire to several cars, looted retailers and local shops, and burned down a multistory building housing the local Olympic committee. Acts of peripheral violence are somewhat difficult to rationalize. What theory or form of logical reasoning helps to explain motivations for fighting between players and fans, fans fighting other fans, postgame rioting, etc.? The athlete who goes into the stands to fight a fan who threw a cup of beer at him gains no real game advantage. The same could be said for postgame rioting. Although the rioting might be linked to fans' emotions after a championship, in this situation, there is, once again, no real game-related advantage.

Fans also attack coaches. Tom Gamboa was the Kansas City Royals' first base coach, who, in 2002, was attacked during the MLB season. A 34-year-old male fan and his 15-year-old son charged onto the field and tackled Gamboa. Fortunately, Royals players intervened. Then in April 2005, in Dallas, Texas, the parent of a ninth-grade football player, upset at his son's lack of playing time, shot his son's football coach/athletic director in the chest. Fortunately, the coach survived the attack. Referees are often targets of abuse and vile comments from spectators and athletes. Referees are verbally abused or even threatened when they make a terrible call or don't make a call at all, according to the fan's and athlete's perceptions. It is not uncommon for some referees to need police escorts after highly charged games.

Fans display of unruly behavior, some feel, is strongly associated with alcohol consumption. It is a widely held tradition to have alcohol at tailgate parties and local bars long before game time. This behavior often results in intoxicated fans who enter the sporting environment completely inebriated.

The way an athlete responds to an abusive fan can be indicative of his or her moral values. Players who retaliate are not practicing respect, honor, moral values, beneficence, and altruism; instead, are giving in to an impulse, which allows their emotions to get the best of them. Recall the 2004–2005 NBA season when Ron Artest of the Indiana Pacers went into the stands to attack a fan who tossed a beer at him. Professional leagues and their governing bodies now have extreme punishments for players who strike fans. Artest was fined with a 73-game suspension. Some feel that stiff fines and suspensions will hopefully deter other athletes from undisciplined actions to preserve fans' long support of the game.

Fortunately, researchers have conducted studies analyzing and isolating certain factors that may cause fan violence at sporting events. According to this research, there are at least nine attributes or variables that set the stage for fan violence. While there are nine major factors listed here, readers are encouraged to go to an article written by Madensen and Eck (2008), which offers greater detail of these and other factors. In their article titled "The Problem of Spectator Violence in Stadiums: What This Guide Does and Does Not Cover" written in 2008, we learn of factors that may contribute to and interact with one another, causing problems with spectator violence in sports.

1. Crowd size and the standing or seating patterns of spectators
2. Composition of the crowd regarding age, sex, social class, and racial/ethnic mix
3. Importance and meaning of the event for spectators
4. History of the strength of the relationship between the teams and their fans
5. Crowd-control strategies used at the event (police, attack dogs, surveillance cameras, or other security measures)
6. Alcohol consumption by the spectators
7. Location of the event (neutral site or home site of one of the opponents)
8. Spectators' reasons for attending the event and what they want to happen at the event
9. Importance of the team as a source of identity for spectators (class identity, ethnic or national identity, regional or local identity, or club or gang identity)

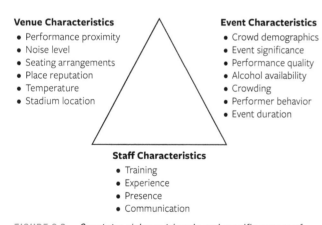

FIGURE 9.9 *Spectator violence triangle and specific causes of spectator violence*

Figure 9.9 is a visual depiction and chart of the relationship among the three variables; the characteristics of venues, attributes and customer service performed by stadium staff and features of the event that includes demographics of the crowd and other aspects of the event that include performance. While some of these factors may be difficult or impossible to change, it is important to understand how each contributes to the likelihood of aggression.

Conclusion

In this chapter, we focused on the relationship between athletes' participation in violent sports and the violence and aggression in certain sports. Social norms regarding masculinity that exist in society and sports seem to encourage attitudes and behaviors consistent with our cultural norms involving hegemonic masculinity (Boeringer, 1999; Brewer & Howarth, 2012; Fine, 1987; Lyndon, Duffy, Smith, & White, 2011; Steinfeldt et al., 2012). In fact, building on the information discussed in Chapter 7, we learn that violence in sports and the acceptance of violence results in the replication of violent acts in nonsports contexts (Steinfeldt et al., 2012). Research also informs us that the aggressive behaviors committed by athletes vary based on the particular type of sport

(Gage, 2008; Messner, 2002). We discussed in this chapter and learned that the sports events that are deemed highly aggressive are most likely to create violent athletes (Guilbert, 2006; Steinfeldt et al., 2012). Finally, information gathered for this chapter shows that athletes are the individuals who are most often found to engage in hostile, aggressive behaviors that include bullying and domestic and sexual violence (Gage, 2008; Koss, 1993; Steinfeldt et al., 2012). Bullying and sexual and domestic violence, we found, are also the types of violence most commonly found in the sports where violence and aggression are deemed to be more socially acceptable (Boeringer, 1999; Lyndon et al., 2011).

However, experimental research on the topic of athletic participation and violent sports is sparse. Most of the research published covers violence exhibited by high school and college athletes, dismissing a very important segment—a segment that many in our culture idolize: professional athletes. Future research is needed to focus on athletes who belong to the NFL, NBA, and MLB, and their perceptions of violence in sports and out of sports contexts. Research in this area would add to a bigger and greater understanding of domestic violence rates in our culture.

QUESTIONS FOR REFLECTION AND DISCUSSION

1. Define sports violence. Using the definition, write out your personal observations of violence in a sporting event and the violence displayed by fans at an event.

2. If evidence exists that proves boxing does increase societal violence, do you think boxing should be made less violent? Explain your answer.

3. Are athletes more prone to committing acts of domestic violence? Why or why not? Share your thoughts and use theory to help support your opinions?

4. As a coach, what would you do if, in your opinion, the referees were making unfair calls? How would you respond if players and referees seemed to be placing your players in danger?

5. Does the probability of athletes engaging in illegal tactics and violent rule-breaking behavior increase as the value of the reward for winning increases?

6. If we removed the rewards associated with victory, would violent incidents be as prevalent in sport? For example, would an athlete be driven to win at all costs if the competition took place out of the public eye, without any external recognition or rewards?

7. As a player, what factors do you believe should be considered when deciding how to deal with violent behaviors performed by the opposing team? What consequences should happen to the team as a whole? What factors would you consider as the coach? As the athletic director?

8. Do you believe an entire team should be punished, even if all team members were not involved? Why or why not?

9. Is fighting in hockey and other sports ethical? Why or why not?

SUGGESTED ACTIVITIES

1. Make a moral argument that supports keeping, as part of boxing, the most violent aspects, such as punching opponents in the face.

2. How can sporting institutions change so that they are less violent and alter their current violent culture? Write a detailed, thoughtful essay on the changes you would propose and why.

3. Go to YouTube and review some of the fan violence discussed in this chapter. Be sure to identify the peripheral violence you noticed and reflect on how the riot or fights might have been avoided?

4. Interview high school or college athletes, both male and female, and get their opinions on violence in sports. Be sure to interview athletes who participate in contact sports and those who do not. Compare and contrast their thoughts about the role of violence in their sport or the lack of violence. Do they agree that fans look for violence in sports?

ADDITIONAL RESOURCES ON SPORTS VIOLENCE

*   "Is Violence in Sports Inevitable" by News.discovery.com
*   "When Winning Is the Only Thing, Can Violence Be Far Away" by Peace.ca
*   "Why Do We Like Violence in Sports" by Liz Collin at Minnesota.cbslocal.com
*   "Violence in Sports Is Inevitable" at http://www.beyondthecheers.com/violence-in-sports-is-inevitable/
*   "Crime and Sports" by Matthew Zadro (lawyer and sports fan) at Offsidesportsblog.com
*   "Sports Injury's, Should We Watch" by Kathy McManus at Libertymutual.com
*   "Has Violence Become a Part of the American Sports Culture" by Kevin Quinn at Academic.marist.edu
*   "Fans Against Violence" by Fansagainstviolence.org
*   "List of Violent Spectator Incidents in Sports" by Wikipedia.org

Videos

*   *Violence in Hockey Cheapshots* by Nukemnow, YouTube
*   *Violence in Sports* by Rachael Beck, YouTube
*   *Parents Behaving Badly* by Curtis Rush, Associated Press

Books

*   *Sports Fan Violence in North America* by Jerry Middleton Lewis
*   *Violence and Sports* by Gilda Berger
*   *Sports Ethics, An Anthology* by Jan Boxill
*   *Rethinking Aggression and Violence in Sport* by John H. Kerr

Apps

*   BEYONDtheCheers by BEYONDthecheers blog, available on iTunes for free
*   192 Sport Title Movies by Blu-ray.com on iTunes

CREDITS

Fig. 9.1: Source: https://pxhere.com/en/photo/600733.

Fig. 9.2: Source: https://pixabay.com/en/boxing-box-boxers-fight-fighting-95606/.

Fig. 9.3: Source: https://commons.wikimedia.org/wiki/File:BoxingNosebleed.jpeg.

Fig. 9.4: Source: https://pxhere.com/en/photo/1127322.

Fig. 9.5: Source: https://pxhere.com/en/photo/1080920.

Fig. 9.6: Source: http://scaredmonkeys.com/2014/09/14/nfls-carolina-panthers-guilted-into-deactivating-de-greg-hardy-who-was-found-guilty-in-july-of-assaulting-threatening-his-ex-girlfriend-nicole-holder/.

Fig. 9.7: Source: https://www.youtube.com/watch?v=pWXdY85zJgE.

Fig. 9.8: Source: https://twitter.com/sjoseph316/status/527110066068283392.

Fig. 9.9: Source: https://popcenter.asu.edu/content/spectator-violence-stadiums-0.

Aging in the Sports World

After completing this chapter, students should be able to:

- articulate age and its effect on sports and why age matters;

- explore physical and emotional aging processes;

- understand the role age plays in eligibility for professional sports;

- learn how sports affect youth and why youth quit sports so young;

- understand major trends and issues involved in youth sports;

- know the physical changes associated with age and sport; and

- understand the issues that athletes struggle with regarding life after sports and retirement.

Introduction

As a field of study, sport communication researchers conduct research on a wide array of topics, from race to sex and gender issues, as well as effects of participation in sport, yet a focus on age receives minimal examination in journals and published literature. From a sports perspective, age is central to participation in many areas. For example, age serves as an indicator by which you participate in certain sports (e.g., pee-wee hoops, senior Olympics). Age is also used in governing rules for age-specific sports. The purpose of this chapter is to introduce readers to the idea that age matters in the study of sports communication.

Age has two characteristics: The first characteristic of age is that it is a continuous classification (i.e., age group or a cohort). The second characteristic involves its dynamic process (i.e., aging is a process that happens across a lifetime). With current news coverage on health care and "the graying of America," advertisers, marketers, financial planners, and the like are starting to focus on the people in our culture aged 55 and older. In a 2016 U.S. Census Bureau report, we find that the U.S. profile of older individuals looks significantly different than it did in 2000. Americans over the age of 65 have grown over the years from 35 million in 2010 to 49.2 million in 2016. As of 2016, the 65 and over age group in the U.S. accounts for 12.4% of the total population (U.S. Census Bureau Report, 2016).

We also learn from the Census Bureau that a significant increase in the number of persons aged 65 or over has risen by a factor of 11 (U.S. Census Bureau, 2018). In 1990, persons aged 65 or over were shown to comprise 1 in every 25 Americans (3.1 million). But in 2016, this same group made up 1 in 8 (33.2 million). According to information obtained on the U.S. Census Bureau's website, over the next 40 years, drastic increases in the age cohort of 65 and older are expected. That is, by the year 2056, the Census Bureau expects that adults aged 65 and older will go from 12.4% of the total population to accounting for more than 25% of the population (U.S. Census Bureau, 2017b). "The cohort of people 85 years and older remains the fastest growing segment of the U.S. population" (U.S. Census Bureau, 2017b). Enhancing our knowledge about age will help us to understand the effect it has on our culture and our behaviors.

Understanding age as a constant classification allows for interesting comparisons and contrasts. Take, for example, the labels that are assigned to various cohorts. We have terms such as "baby boomers," "Generation Xers," and the "millennials," as well as "yuppies," etc. These labels have particular stereotypes or associations as well. For example, the "Me Generation" a term related to baby boomers describes those who were born in the 1980s and '90s. Generation Y is also known millennials, echo boomers, internet generation, iGen, and the net generation (Strauss & Howe, 1991). This group of cohorts has been described as "tolerant, confident, open-minded, and ambitious but also disengaged, narcissistic, distrustful, and anxious" (Walsh, 2018). Millennials, as they are known, are changing American culture and redefining what it means to be a young adult in America. "Gen Me-ers," as some have named the youth and young adult market in this current era, are redefining what it means to be an individual in today's society (Twenge, 2016). Generations and cohorts have certain identifiable attributes simply because of the fact that age cohorts ultimately grow up sharing unique cultural experiences that take place from the time they are born. In terms of one's identity, we know that age plays a vital role in the development of a person's identity.

Age and Its Effect on Sports

Just as in life, age matters in sports as well. Athletic participation in sport by age is a demographic classification by which by an athlete's participation in a sport is well structured and meticulous. For example, to participate in youth sports, athletes must be a certain age by a certain date (Atkinson, 2009). Eligibility for a professional sport requires a certain age to qualify. Participation in Olympic events, such as gymnastics and swimming, for example, have minimum age requirements.

A person's participation in a sport creates another relationship that is worthy of note. With aging comes many related changes that affect the athlete's ability to compete. Aging may influence the athlete's training regimen, tenure in his or her professional sports career, and his or her physical performance. Gatta, Benelli, and Ditroilo (2006) conducted a study using swimmers that reported being between the ages of 50 and 90 years. Data obtained in the study revealed significant changes in the swimmers' performances that related specifically to their speed, stroke frequency, and stroke length (Gatta et al., 2006).

When we investigate minimum age requirements for many of the sports in America, we notice immense variation, which proves to be interesting and thought provoking. Consider, for example, Olympic athletes. The youngest Olympians can be found in diving and gymnastics. Many of the participants are at least 14 years of age. The Olympic sport with the oldest American participants is sailing, and the average age hovers at around 58 years of age. If we use age as a descriptive statistic, many sports might easily be characterized as a sport for "younger" athletes (e.g., gymnastics), while other sports are much more likely to be characterized as a sport for "older" athletes (e.g., golf, sailing, equestrian, and baseball). It seems reasonable to conclude that the differences in sports related to age might be due to the required physical skills and expertise for different sports. The physical nature of the sport may actually explain the obvious variance in ages in sports events.

In 2008, Dara Torres (see Figure 10.1) at age 41, became the oldest swimmer to compete in the Olympics when she raced at the Summer Games in Beijing in 2008. Torres made national and international headlines when she defied age and returned to the sport she loved: swimming. With respect to the Summer Olympic games, Torres represented the United States five times (1984, 1988, 1992, 2000, and 2008). During the 2008 Summer Olympic games, Torres was named the "oldest athlete to earn a place on the U.S. Olympic team" (Atkinson, 2009). After all her hard work and training, Dara Torres earned silver medals in three events: the 50-meter freestyle, the 4 × 100-meter medley relay, and the 4 × 100-meter freestyle relay. Throughout her career, Torres earned 12 Olympic medals and has been identified as one of three women to have received the most Olympic medals in swimming.

In terms of aging, we know that metabolism and muscle fibers decrease. Starting from the time we are born to the moment we enter adulthood, research tells us that muscle fibers increase 20 times in size (Armstrong, Barker, & McManus, 2015. As we enter middle age, medical research tells us to expect a decrease in muscle mass and fibers and increases in glycogen and phosphocreatine. As far as enzymes in our bodies, we know that oxidation enzymes are higher in young children, while anaerobic enzymes are much higher in adults (Armstrong, Barker, & McManus, 2015). Children, according to information obtained, need higher oxidative levels to aid in intense play, while the converse is true for adults. Adults require lower oxidative levels and higher anaerobic levels based on the intensity of their activity. When we age, we also know that blood levels and glycogen depletion increase.

FIGURE 10.1 *American swimmer Dara Torres waves to the crowd after taking silver in the women's 50-meter freestyle event.*

Middle Age to Late Adulthood

As we enter middle age to late adulthood, we start noticing a loss of muscle mass and a slower metabolism. When an adult reaches the age of 30, the average person begins to notice decreases in his or her muscle density and bone mass. Decreases in muscle density happen because of the aging process and ultimately runs the risk of causing osteoporosis. As we age, we also notice changes in body fat. Body fat begins to enter muscles and organs, and the infiltration of body fat inward is most likely to occur when an individual leads a primarily sedentary lifestyle. For women, osteoporosis is expected during the postmenopausal phase when they reach their 50s. Osteoporosis often results in decreased bone mass, a symptom that is also known to increase the risk of disability, broken bones, and, in rare cases, death. According to the website titled Age-Related Issues in Sports Medicine, we learn that sarcopenia is "the loss of muscle tissue and is a normal part of the aging process" (Armstrong, Barker, & McManus, 2015). The normal aging process, along with a sedentary lifestyle, may increase the rate that sarcopenia and slowed metabolism may take place.

Total Joint Replacements and Sport

According to research, we learn that there are more than 500,000 total joint replacement operations performed every year in the United States. Research suggests that, in the United States, approximately 300,000 of those joint replacement procedures are for total knee replacements (Vogel, Carotenuto, & Levine, 2011). People frequently opt to receive a total joint replacement to restore quality of life and to relieve pain. We learn from research that a large proportion of people who elect to have a total joint replacement are those individuals who were active participants in sports. From what is currently known, "it is unclear whether it is safe for these individuals to continue to participate in sports postoperatively" (Armstrong, Barker, & McManus, 2014). Golant, Christoforou, Slover, and Zuckerman (2010) encourage individuals undergoing joint replacements to engage in some sort of postoperative sports participation because being active after surgery is extremely beneficial to a patient's overall health. Individuals living active lifestyles find that they have better balance, cardiovascular health, endurance, coordination, and muscular strength. In addition, individuals who are active in sports after surgery tend to decrease the likelihood of breaking bones or getting bone fractures that happen as the result of injury or falls.

Athletic Training for Senior Athletes

For individuals over the age of 80, it is important that they understand the health benefits of exercise. Medical research shows that for individuals who are over the age of 80, the benefits of physical activity and training continues to increase. Benefits of physical activity for seniors include reduced injuries because of falling, "improvements in strength and endurance, diminished rates of coronary artery disease, and a lower risk of cardiovascular-related mortality" (Armstrong, Barker, A. R., & McManus, 2014; Franklin, Fern, & Voytas, 2004). Older individuals and athletes who continue to engage in sports and physical activities find that they are much more likely to enjoy and participate in a variety of sports activities. The activities that provide the greatest health benefits include playing basketball, lifting weights, cycling, tennis, swimming, running marathons, and golfing. Based on the type of physical activity the older athlete is training for, research suggests that strength training and other physical activity for older individuals should be specially intended to help athletes adapt both metabolically and physiologically (Armstrong, Barker, A. R., & McManus, 2014; Franklin, Fern, & Voytas, 2004).

The American College of Sports Medicine recommends the following training guidelines for senior athletes. The list of training guidelines for athletes and the recommended activities that appear next were obtained from Armstrong, Barker, A. R., and McManus (2014):

- Train 3 to 5 days per week
- Fifty-five to 65% to 90% of maximum heart rate or 40% to 50% to 85% of maximum oxygen uptake reserve
- Engage in 20 to 60 minutes of continuous aerobic activity or experiences that engage large muscle groups. Examples of continuous aerobic activity involving large muscle groups include walking, jogging, running, cycling, rowing, stair climbing, etc.

- Perform strength training: a set of 10 to 15 repetitions for major muscle groups two to three days per week
- Perform flexibility training: stretch major muscle groups at least four times each for a minimum of 2 to 3 days per week

Reflect on Sports: Playing Too Young

Recently retired and even younger players in the NFL show some evidence of brain injury. Medical studies provide documentation of brain injury that is highly visible, especially when the images of the brain are compared to a group of individuals who either have not played football or are without a medical history of having concussions. Researchers examined 42 former professional football players and soccer players on their "short-term memory, mental flexibility, and problem-solving" (Schumacher, Schmidt, Wellmann, & Braumann 2018; Vestberg, Reinebo, Maurex, Ingvar, & Petrovic, 2017). Data obtained in the work shows a significant relationship between those who started playing football before they were 12 years old and physical performance. The athletes who started playing before age 12 were seen to function about 20% worse when compared to the control group. NFL players in the experimental study were separated into two groups: those who played football as young children and those players who did not. Data clearly revealed that the players who reported a history of playing football when they were younger also failed when performing cognitive tests that asked them to recall words from a list that they had been exposed to just minutes before the recall test.

In another study published in *JAMA Neurology*, medical researchers relied on equipment known as positron emission tomography (PET) and magnetic resonance imaging to demonstrate the importance of conducting the PET imaging to aid in monitoring and repairing the brain cells of NFL players and other athletes who participate in violent, aggressive, and highly physical contact sports. Recall from Chapter 9 that information showed that sports such as boxing, football, and soccer give rise to risking injury to the brain. Researchers released the findings obtained in the *JAMA* study just before the Super Bowl so that they could serve as a reminder for young aspiring athletes.

The research released in November of 2016 was added to prior research evidence obtained in the area regarding the effects of violence in sports on athletes (see Chapter 9 of this text). Data obtained in the seminal work conducted at Johns Hopkins Medical Center suggests that athletes participating in highly aggressive, physical contact sports are at risk of developing chronic traumatic encephalopathy (CTE). This work builds on previous studies that show that aggressive, violent sports are related to CTE (Johns Hopkins Medicine, 2016).

CTE has now been associated with memory loss, confusion, a lack of decision making, and early onset dementia. In 2015, a popular movie called *Concussion*, starring Will Smith, hit the theaters to increase awareness about the story of a forensic pathologist named Dr. Bennet Omalu who was embroiled in a battle with the NFL, which at the time wanted to quell all research on CTE brain degeneration in several professional football players being revealed. The NFL, after much pressure, was required to start viewing the issues related to concussions in their players more seriously. However, in 2011, NFL players took their case to court and sued the NFL. The suit alleged that the NFL did not properly inform players of the risk of CTE.

Dr. Omalu closely examined slides of a former Pittsburgh Steeler player Mike Webster's brain. What he eventually noticed was that Webster's brain showed severe damage. As a result of Dr. Omalu's work, Webster's death certificate was changed to show severe brain damage as the reason for his death. Omalu realized that the death was due to the repeated blows to his head over a long period of time. The long-term effects of repeated blows to the head result in a disorder that Dr. Omalu later referred to as CTE. Years later, Dr. Omalu once again found himself conducting an in-depth study of two former NFL football players, Junior Seau and Dave Duerson. These two athletes committed suicide after suffering from brain damage, which later also became diagnosed as CTE. As a result, the NFL currently supports efforts to discuss player health and safety.

Discrimination as a Result of Age and Race in Sports

Denial of an athlete's opportunity to advance and even oversights associated with selection or promotion in the work industry are just a few of the consequences related to discrimination (Hammond, Gillen, & Yen, 2010). Sexism and racism are the two most common areas where discrimination and prejudice are most likely to be found. Disparities in race and gender as we noted in previous chapters are particularly common in certain sports and especially in ownership, coaching, and other high-level leadership in sports institutions.

For professional athletes, discrimination in terms of age may stem from team owners who selectively choose to exclude certain groups of athletes from the draft. Then there may be some acts of discrimination that crop up from some or all of the athlete's teammates. Evidence of this type of discrimination can be observed when we read the biography of Jackie Robinson, the first black MLB player. Mr. Robinson's selection into the major league was wrought with attacks and criticisms from within the team. Players were even known to protest his membership on the team, doing so in front of team managers.

FIGURE 10.2 *Ernestine Shepherd, the oldest female bodybuilding record holder in the world*

Age discrimination in sports is not a new issue or construct. Age discrimination is a topic that rears up often in the professional sports industry. Recall in 2011 when the football team then known as the St. Louis Rams was confronted with continuous discrimination legal suits naming age and gender-related discrimination. Basically, the jest of one case involved a 56-year-old woman named Lory Fabian who was fired in May 2011. In her legal suit, she made claims of ageism in stating that the team had a history of firing middle-aged women. Then, just a few months after this court case, the Rams found themselves back in the courtroom when Todd Hewitt, the equipment manager for the Rams, was let go 10 months short of eligibility for early retirement. In his lawsuit, Hewitt made claims of six other employees on the Rams staff who ranged in age from 50 to 70 who were forced to go into early retirement. These cases lead many to wonder whether the firings are acts of ageism.

As individuals, we develop physically, emotionally, cognitively, and spiritually. Not only do we experience developmental changes from childhood to adolescence to adulthood, but there are also differences in the middle-age life cycle and when one reaches the development phase of old age. Despite America's cultural idea that once we hit 65 years of age we become old or senior citizens, advertisers and marketers are starting to recognize lifestyle differences among people who are 65 and older and showing these differences in their advertisements and promotions. See Figure 10.2 of Ernestine Shepherd.

Ernestine Shepherd, an 82-year-old female bodybuilder, shows us that no one is ever too old to be healthy. Shepherd has been competing as a bodybuilder since celebrating her 56th birthday. Sports advertisers, marketers, and promoters are realizing that with hard work and dedication, older athletes can be used to sell products and services. Shepherd is listed in the *Guinness Book of World Records* as the "World's Oldest Female Bodybuilder."

As highlighted in Chapter 8 of this text, we presented information that showed that in terms of weight lifting and strength training, women have misperceptions about the results of frequent exercise with weights. But contrary to the myths that women hold about weight training, medical research proves that strength training is crucial to a woman's health. Strength training helps to keep muscles, joints, ligaments, tendons, and bones strong. While lifting weights or using weight machines may be challenging, it is also effective in terms of aging (to learn of other athletes over age 65, refer to Orlov, 2016).

The manner in which sports media portray aging athletes has a powerful effect on attitudes and ideas about growing older in American culture. Alex Rotas, a photographer, according to many news stories, has devoted more than 6 years to taking and publishing photographs of older Americans—photographs that she hopes will challenge the assumptions that our country has concerning aging. It seems that in American culture, there is a presupposition that getting older is equated with passivity, helplessness, deterioration, and senility (Phoenix, 2016). Figure 10.3 is a photo of a 97-year-old athlete who decided at 87 years young that he wanted to get in shape and start bodybuilding (Nicholas, 2017). At 97 years of age, Charles Eugster, has in his repertoire a total of 40 gold medals in the sport of rowing (Nicholas, 2017). We also learned that the athlete in Figure 10.3 recently started sprinting, and as of 2017, he now holds "British and World records in his age group for that track event, and is a four-time World Fitness Champion" (Nicholas, 2017).

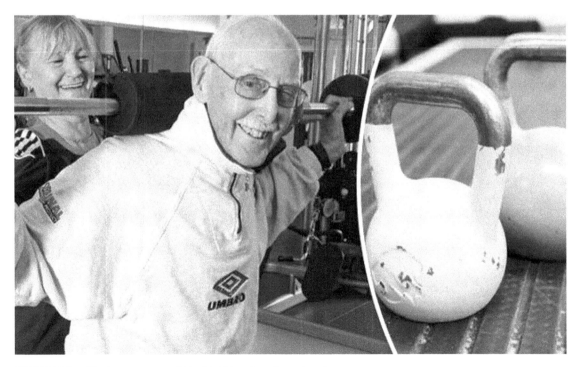

FIGURE 10.3   *Ninety-seven-year-old bodybuilder who refuses to retire.*

Figure 10.4 is an image of Stanisław Kowalski, who, at the time of this writing, is 108 years young (Obrian, 2018). The inspirational male marathon runner became the "oldest person in Europe to run a 100-meter race—smashing the record previously held by a 96-year-old running 32.79 seconds" (Obrian, 2018). In terms of aging and sports, we know that aging affects the depth and height of physical abilities. Yet we find that for adults over the age of 90, regular, consistent exercise allows them to regain muscle loss and reverses other effects of aging. In terms of regular vigorous exercise, it may even reduce the loss of our ability to handle aerobic activities as well as improve the ability of the heart and lungs to send oxygen to the muscles, according to research. In fact, research has shown that regular and frequent exercise has been shown to preclude age-related decline in physical abilities by as much as 50% (McMahan, 2015).

As Figures 10.3 and 10.4 show, older individuals share many positive testimonials attesting to the benefits of exercise on their aging process as well as overall life satisfaction. It is possible that many athletes allow stereotypes like those we discussed in previous chapters to stop them from engaging in rigorous physical exercise. In actuality, based on a preponderance of research on this topic, much of what we believe about getting older and working out is due to our culture's concept of what is considered a young sport and sports that we feel are for older individuals. Why do gymnasts retire after hitting age 20? Why is it that in the tennis world, young tennis players are between the ages of 18 and 24, whereas older tennis players range from 29 to 35? For Atkinson and Herro (2006), stereotypes and misperceptions act as credible contexts for using age to explain a lack of exercise, yet the stereotypes seem to exist solely for one to maintain and perhaps build on negative thoughts about what it means to age and grow older in our culture. The professional sports world is designed to reward the skills that peak for most athletes in their early 20s. Aging athletes suffer the burden of discrimination, which includes pay cuts and job loss, and are often vilified.

FIGURE 10.4   *Competitors in the men's 100-meter final, 85- to 89-year-old age group, at the European Veterans Athletics Championships, Izmir, Turkey, 2014.*

For example, Brett Favre officially retired three times during his long-term football career before finally deciding he would leave the NFL in 2010. After Favre made his first announcement of retirement in 2008, he then began his pattern of making retirement announcements at least once a year. Needless to say, his fans were not pleased at all. In 2008, Favre said he was retiring from the Green Bay Packers. Then the following year he announced his plans to retire from the New York Jets. The last and final announcement Favre made was that he would retire from the Minnesota Vikings. Favre was vilified for leaving Green Bay to become a Viking. The Friday before the Packer-Viking game, the mayor proclaimed the day "Flip-Flop Friday" in honor of Favre's legendary indecisiveness. More than 300 fans gathered at a sports bar to attend the "Funeral 4 Favre." Figure 10.5 shows fans mourning the Brett Favre that "they once knew." Sources reported that the fans organized a funeral procession that originated from Lambeau Field (Youngmisuk, 2009). In a news story published in the *New York Daily News*, we learned that the funeral included "three hearses adorned with black flags bearing No. 4 departed the stadium parking lot Friday afternoon and drove down nearby Brett Favre Pass to circle around the Brett Favre Steakhouse parking lot before making their way to a local Green Bay bar where hundreds gathered for a Funeral 4 Favre" (Youngmisuk, 2009). As you can tell from Figure 10.5, a "dummy" made in Favre's image was laid in a wooden casket wearing a Vikings helmet and a Vikings number four jersey, Wrangler jeans, and flip-flops. According to fans, the mock funeral was held because they felt that his leaving the Packers to join the Vikings was like a "death," and the funeral provided a sense of closure (Youngmisuk, 2009). One fan went on record as saying, "He [Favre] will always be alive in our hearts, but this Brett Favre wearing purple is a different guy altogether. That is the Brett Favre we are going to bury. Actually, we won't bury him, we will let the Packers' defense bury him (today)" (Youngmisuk, 2009).

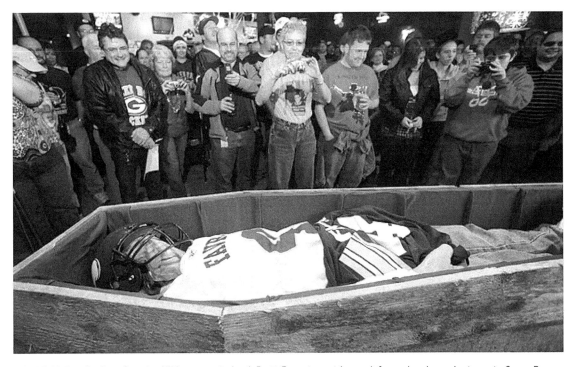

FIGURE 10.5 *Packers fans lay Vikings quarterback Brett Favre to rest in mock funeral as legend returns to Green Bay.*

Eligibility Rules in Professional Sports

Rules in the professional leagues regarding the minimum age of eligibility for participation in professional sports has been a frequent topic of debate and discussion. In the NFL, for example, a court-sanctioned standard says that a player who graduated from high school within one to three years is ineligible to be drafted. This strict age rule says that a player must be out of high school for three years, or he needs to complete for at least three college seasons before he is eligible to engage in a draft to join a professional team (Lupica, 2004). Draftees for the NBA, policies show, must be at least 19 years old and, unlike the NFL, have graduated high school for at least one year. Potential basketball prospects can, however, enter another league known as the G-League for nominal pay if they want to play basketball out of high school. Or the football prospect can opt to play professional ball in Europe.

Initially, the NBA required players is to play for four consecutive years after graduating from high school before they could be eligible for to enter the draft to join a team. However, in 1971, the United States Supreme Court dismissed the rule and requirement allowing high school graduates to enter the NBA. Then in 2005, the NBA modified their eligibility rules and now require draftees to wait at least one year after graduating from high school to enter the draft (Farrell, 2005). MLB rules for eligibility allow players to enter the draft immediately upon graduation from high school. However, if a player decides to attend college, the MLB requires that he stays in school until he turns 21 or reaches his junior year, whichever comes first. Interestingly, players attending a junior college are allowed to enter a draft whenever they want, regardless of age. We will explore this issue in more detail in the next section of this chapter.

There are those who feel that younger athletes should be able to try out for professional teams so that they can earn a decent salary, especially if they come from low-income or poverty-ridden backgrounds. By entering the draft and becoming a professional athlete at an early age, many argue, young athletes can have the resources needed to take care of their families and themselves, especially if they come from low social economic status (SES) backgrounds. According to sports records, athletes who went straight to the NBA after high school are Dwight Howard, LeBron James, DeSagana Diop, and Korleone Young (Bianchi, 2006). Each of these professional athletes not only took advantage of their skills and talents, but they were also able to enjoy financial freedoms that allowed them to live better lives.

The NFL rule regarding age requirement has been in and out of the courts since 2004. However, each time the rule that bars young football players from entering the draft right after high school has survived many legal challenges for more than 14 years. According to spokespeople from the NFL and NCAA, the reason for the NFL's strict rules regarding age and eligibility is primarily to protect athletes from physical injury. It is also said that the age requirement affords time for the young athlete to mature emotionally and to receive a quality education before hitting the hustle and bustle most closely aligned with professional sports. A few critics have stated that they believe that the NFL and NCAA are gaining the greatest profit from student-athletes and their "entertainment value." For many critics, entertainment comes from a passion for college sports and championships such as bowl games and March Madness. There are even those who are vehemently opposed to the fact that college games are televised and generate revenue for the NCAA, yet the student-athletes are not compensated for their "performance" or work. Apparently, out of all the professional sports leagues in America, the NFL is the only league with strict rules prohibiting players with less than three years of experience playing college football from entering the draft. We also learned that the NFL is the only league that requires football players who chose not to attend college to wait three years after graduating from high school (Gehring, 2004; Nieporent, 2004). Research on eligibility revealed that the governing thought that precipitates this rule is the idea that young athletes may sustain injuries while playing in the minor league or college. Participation in the minor leagues does not yield the same salaries as major league sports. Next, consider what happens if an athlete encounters a career-ending injury. If a career-ending injury occurs, the athlete might endure financial distress in that he may be unable to support his family or himself because he doesn't have a degree or other skills to fall back on. Also, one caveat of playing in the minor league is the lack of financial compensation for injury. College athletes, on the other hand, receive no salaries or funds that would allow them to support themselves financially.

Consider the plight of a young, talented athlete who, unfortunately, may not have had access to cognitive resources that others have had. What if the limited resources impede the athlete's ability to succeed in college? But what if the athlete has the expertise and talents needed to play football and to play professionally? Is college a necessary and required path to take to play in the professional leagues? Athletes with little to no interest or drive to attend college often seek out alternatives, especially as a way to build on and showcase their skills and abilities playing ball. New leagues are cropping up in Europe, and they are slowly but surely creating avenues for professional teams to seek out and recruit highly talented athletes. Just as major league organizations can now recruit mature players and those who have successfully honed their skills, European leagues are seeking to recruit talented players who have also honed theirs. In essence, when American professional leagues recruit from the European leagues, they find this is not only efficient but also cost-effective. As a result of these alternative options for recruiting talent, the major leagues not only save time developing the athlete and helping him or her mature, but they do not have to invest funds needed to build the player's future.

Benefits of Going to College

Those who agree with the idea that young athletes should go to college before being drafted feel that the one main advantage is obtaining the much-needed and vital experience of maturation as an amateur athlete. Even if an athlete spends a year or two in school, it is believed that short-term college experiences not only aid in the athlete's educational knowledge but also the ambiance of the college environment leads to his or her growth in public relations, social interactions, and media interviewing opportunities. Experts and academic advisors in sport are firmly convinced that time spent in college not only matures athletes but also their experiences playing their sport and managing their study time and coursework prepares them for the national leagues, and, more importantly, it prepares them for life after sport (Bianchi, 2006). Professors, coaches, and many professionals in the sports world believe that the knowledge gained from college is a necessary and significant component in the transition from teenage years into young adulthood. Scholars argue that college life provides social and educational developments that "may only be experienced while in college" (Bianchi, 2006). These pundits believe that regarding athletic success, development and enhancement of one's skills is something that is going to occur whether the athlete goes to college or has a challenging coach.

Youth Sports

Approximately 45 million children and adolescents participate in some type of organized youth sports in the United States (Merkel, 2013). In fact, data shows that as of 2016, 75% of all families with school-aged children in the United States have "at least one child participating in some organized sport" (Merkel, 2013, p. 151). In a study titled "Youth Sport: Positive and Negative Impact on Young Athletes," Merkel (2013) found higher levels of happiness and health are reported when children are active participants in a sport. In the same study, Merkel (2013) provided statistics demonstrating that children and teenagers who are diagnosed as being overweight often lead sedentary lifestyles. Research shows that when a sport emphasizes fun and at the same time balances the focus on physical fitness, the results are lessons that live on for an individual's lifetime. Studies show that organized youth sports that focus on fun and physical fitness lead to healthy lifestyles for children, which in turn determines their future successes in life (Merkel, 2013).

Research shows that a child should be at least 6 years of age before participating in an organized team sport. By the age of 6, records show that a child will have reached the physical, psychological, and cognitive developmental milestones to begin the practice of learning the basic skills associated with a sport. If physical, psychological, and cognitive developmental stages have not been met, the experience participating in the physical activity can lead to stress and anxiety, eventually leading the child to quit athletics and sports altogether. Introducing young children to a variety of activities, research suggests, is beneficial to children's physical and psychological health.

Surveys of children who like to participate in sports reveal that the main reason they like organized youth sports is because they can have fun (Hansen, Larkin, & Dworkin, 2003). Many children report liking sports, yet it is often the parents who feel that children like to play to win. That couldn't be further from the truth. In fact, to determine how important winning is to young children, the Institution for the Study of Youth Sports sponsored research examining winning versus losing from a child's perspective (Merkel, 2013; Purcell, 2005). Data obtained in the study found that the desire to win games depends on the gender and age of the participant. When asked, children identified three feelings that were more important to them than winning. For a majority of young children, "fairness, participation, and development of skills ranked above winning" (Merkel, 2013). It seems that adults who participate in sports for youth, such as "little league" or "pee-wee" sports, may focus their attention on the wrong thing. In other words, adults working with organized youth sports may be sending the message that winning is the most important part of athletics and sporting events. In fact, the research data obtained states that it is possible that parents and other volunteers working in youth sports may inadvertently communicate that winning outweighs the basic tenets of most, if not all, organized youth sports (Clark, 2013; Merkel, 2013).

Côté and Fraser-Thomas (2007) published a report suggesting that organized sports for young children could potentially meet three major goals. First, youth who participate in sports have more opportunities to be physically active. Physical activity, as we know, leads to overall improved health and reduces or precludes the propensity for obesity. Second, we know that youth sports are vital and much needed in terms of a child's psychosocial development (Wankel & Berger, 1990). Côté and Fraser-Thomas (2007) believe that exposure to youth sports affords young children with the resources necessary to learn about vital skills related to working in teams, discipline, commitment, and dedication (for other research on psychosocial development, refer to Curtis, McTeer, & White, 1999; Evans & Roberts, 1987; Fraser-Thomas, Côté, & Deakin, 2005; Kirk, 2005; Wankel & Mummery, 1990). And the third and final goal that participation in youth sports delivers is an opportunity to enhance skills coordination and motor abilities. It has been suggested that motor skills set the foundation for young athletes as they transition into adulthood. Motor skills in adults make it possible for them to engage in recreational sports (Kirk, 2005; Larson, 2000; MacPhail & Kirk, 2006).

We know from social psychology that young children often feel excessive pressure to win, have low and negative perceptions of their skills and abilities, report feeling left out and unattached to their teams, and think that they are defenseless whenever they are close in proximity to their fellow players and teammates (Wankel & Berger, 1990; Wankel & Mummery, 1990). When children feel pressured to win, research tells us that they leave sports events with extremely low levels of self-esteem or self-confidence (Fraser-Thomas & Côté, 2006; Martens, 1993; Wankel & Kreisel, 1985). After exploring this area, there seems to be a large divide between positive and negative consequences that are linked when young children participate in sports. From a sports psychologist perspective, a way to make participation in sports a more positive experience for children is for all adults involved in youth sports to work together. Together, sports psychologists, parents, coaches, educators, researchers, and other professionals, it is believed, can combine their expertise to assure that our youth have more positive outcomes and reduce the negative experiences and attrition rates in youth sports that occur when youth reach age 15.

SPORTS PROGRAMS AND THEIR INFLUENCE ON YOUNG ATHLETES

"To promote prolonged participation rather than attrition, the developmental model of sports participation stresses how important it is for young children to participate in a wide variety of sports. The model suggests that children need to participate in diverse sports that center on deliberate play activities. Thus, children between the ages of 6 and 12 should try street hockey or driveway basketball because these are the activities that are intrinsically motivating, provide immediate gratification, and designed to maximize enjoyment" (Holt, 2006).

Coach Influence

Several studies on the effects of coaching on youth and their attitudes toward sports found that coaches who were better liked, who create fun practices and team atmospheres, and who focus on team unity have lower attrition rates when compared to coaches who do not provide any of these components (Hine, 2009; Smoll, Smith, Barnett, & Everett, 1993). Unfortunately, several studies have been conducted that highlight the negative influences that coaches have on youth involvement and participation in sport. Coaches who emphasize winning often do not care about their athlete's psychological and physical development. Research continues to obtain evidence that shows that placing emphasis on winning not only results in lowered self-esteem and self-confidence for youth but also goes so far as to say that putting undue pressure on winning takes advantage of young children by manipulating their abilities in lieu of enhancing and teaching proper skills (Gilbert, Gilbert, & Trudel, 2001a, 2001b; Hill & Hansen, 1988; Siegenthaler & Gonzalez, 1997). Thus coaches who focus on winning and do not consider the developmental stages and advancements of youths' psychological and social best interests have higher rates of attrition and burnout among young athletes. In fact, studies have found that youth who drop out and experience burnout after participating in youth sports frequently describe their coaches as being discouraging, unsupportive, and autocratic leaders who are not interested in them as individuals but in winning for their pride. These expressed feelings were the polar opposite for youth who participated in sports under the coaching leadership of democratic, supportive, and positive coaches (Hine, 2009; Horn & Harris, 2002; Pelletier, Fortier, Vallerand, & Briere, 2001; Smoll et al., 1993).

For more on this topic, go to "How to Deal With a Mean Coach" at https://www.wikihow.com/Deal-with-a-Mean-Coach.

Parental and Social Influences

Coaches are not the only source of influence on a youth's sports experiences. Parents and parenting styles, it has been suggested, can also influence a young child's experiences while participating in an organized youth sport (Côté & Fraser-Thomas, 2007; Côté & Hancock, 2016; Fraser-Thomas et al., 2005). Research in this area shows positive interactions, support, and encouragement without parental pressure offer children opportunities to participate and learn a sport in a positive environment. The

FIGURE 10.6   *The bad sports parent.*

FIGURE 10.7   *Supportive sports parents.*

positive learning environment, according to research, is positively correlated with feelings of enjoyment, satisfaction, and confidence for youth. Moreover, research finds that children who participate in a youth sport with the aforementioned listed elements as part of the experience will actually learn to prefer challenges and demonstrate more intrinsic needs and motives to do well than will children who participate in youth sports that are devoid of the positive nurturing qualities (Scanlan and Lewthwaite, 1986). Parents play a huge role in the positive outcomes as well; research shows that if parents provide positive inspiration and encouragement while youth are participating in a sport (see Figure 10.7), then young athletes yield a stronger affinity to sports. And research also finds a decrease in attrition rates of youth while involvement rates in sports increase (Brustad, 1993, 1996; Weitzer, 1989). Parents who are happy, supportive, alert, encouraging, optimistic, and jovial also provide support for youth to stay involved in sports. Figures 10.6 and 10.7 help illustrate the stark contrasts in nonverbal behaviors between supportive parents of young athletes versus parents who lack or do not provide positive and supportive behaviors that encourage youth to stay involved.

Why Youth Quit Sports

The National Alliance for Youth Sports conducted a survey to ascertain why youth drop out of sports. According to the report, close to 70% of American youth said that they quit around the age of 13 because sports was just "not fun anymore" (Miner, 2016). Scholars believe that the "it's not fun anymore" attitude is not a direct reference to fun but is actually a negative, unintended consequence of several cultural and systemic issues. As mentioned previously, coaching style, the practice and game atmosphere, parental style and support, and many other factors may explain why youth drop out of sports. The point was made earlier that playing sports offers youth needed physical activity and an opportunity to experience success, learn how to negotiate loss and failure, and learn how to work on a team.

Trends and Issues With Youth and Participation in Sports

Increasingly, youth in today's culture can be overheard saying that they feel intense pressure to exceed, excel, and find their true passion. Whether adults are aware of it or not, covert messages that tell young children that if they are not the best, then they have failed or if they lose a game, then they are at fault can be extremely harmful to a child's self-esteem and self-concept. Subtle messages like these are often communicated nonverbally, so much so that the child takes the misinterpreted message, reflects similar behaviors demonstrated at home, and ultimately derives the self-concept that he or she is a failure. This self-perception then becomes expressed and reinforced in school where, if we are honest, the atmosphere can be extremely competitive, driven for high scores on standardized tests, and focused on record-setting outcomes, such as the most scholarships and highest grade point average.

For children or youth, participation in a competitive sport may come at a risk. Yes, for some, sports participation may mean that they now have to prioritize their school study, academic commitments, and interests. All of this requires an incessant amount of work and means that they have to deal with pressures that most young children are not expected to endure. Schoolwork, project deadlines, and pressure to succeed can be positive. Just keep in mind that the child's environment in the sports world, in school, and in the home must be a healthy, positive, and supportive one.

The fact that youth quit sports by the age of 13 might not always be due to the sporting environment. From a child development perspective, we know that 13-year-olds endure major psychological and social changes. Many of these changes also involve the desire to find their own identity and sense of self. For some teens, this transition in life also makes them vulnerable to other influences in their environment. Influences in their social environment may actually predispose some teens to quit sports, especially if the environment is perceived to be extremely competitive. The benefits of other more "fun" extracurricular activities may overpower the pressure to compete. Research reported in the *Washington Post* shows that American youth in today's era report getting their first cell phone device by the time they turn 12 years of age. Media research also shows that teenagers are online seven days a week, spending approximately four hours a day on their phones or tablets (Miner, 2016). By age 14, research shows that "girls are dropping out of sports at two times the rate of boys" (Women's Sports Foundation, 2008).

For girls, attrition from sports is most likely due to a large number of factors. Next is a list of the factors posted on the Women's Sports Foundation's website. As of this writing, this is a fairly exhaustive list of factors that influence girls' sports experiences. The list that follows was obtained from the Women's Sports Foundation (2008) and summarizes the reasons for girls to stay in the sport:

DO YOU KNOW THE FACTORS INFLUENCING GIRLS' PARTICIPATION IN SPORTS?

By age 14, girls are dropping out of sports at two times the rate of boys.[1] Through more than 25 years of research, the Women's Sports Foundation has identified key factors which contribute to this alarming statistic. Read on to learn more about how these factors influence girls' sport experiences and why they need to stay in the game.

1. Why they drop out:

Lack of access. Girls have 1.3 million fewer opportunities to play high school sports than boys have. Lack of physical education in schools and limited opportunities to play sports in both high school and college mean girls have to look elsewhere for sports—which may not exist or may cost more money. Often there is an additional lack of access to adequate playing facilities near their homes that makes it more difficult for girls to engage in sports.

Why they need to stay in:

Through sports, girls learn important life skills such as teamwork, leadership, and confidence.

2. Why they drop out:

Safety and transportation issues. Sports require a place to participate—and for many girls, especially in dense urban environments, that means traveling to facilities through unsafe

(Continued)

continued ...

neighborhoods or lacking any means to get to a good facility miles away. And if there isn't a safe option like carpooling with other families, the only option for a girl and her family may be to stay home.

Why they need to stay in:

Girls active in sports during adolescence and young adulthood are 20% less likely to get breast cancer later in life.[2]

3. Why they drop out:

Social stigma. Despite recent progress, discrimination based on the real or perceived sexual orientation and gender identity of female athletes persists. Girls in sports may experience bullying, social isolation, negative performance evaluations, or the loss of their starting position. During socially fragile adolescence, the fear of being tagged "gay" is strong enough to push many girls out of the game.

Why they need to stay in:

Sports are an asset to American families, fostering communication and trust between parents and children.[3]

4. Why they drop out:

Decreased quality of experience. As girls grow up, the quality level of their sports experience may decline. The facilities are not as good as the boys' venues, and the playing times may not be optimal. The availability of quality, trained coaches may be lacking in their community, or these coaches may be more focused on the boys' programs that have more money for training. Equipment, and even uniforms aren't funded for many girls' programs at the same levels as boys so their ability to grow and enjoy the sport is diminished. In short, sports just aren't "fun" anymore.

Why they need to stay in:

More than three-quarters of working women feel that sports participation helps enhance their self-image.[4]

5. Why they drop out:

Cost. School sports budgets are being slashed every day, all across the country. Fewer opportunities within schools mean families must pay to play in private programs while also footing the bill for expensive coaches, equipment, and out-of-pocket travel requirements. This additional expense is just not possible for many families.

Coping in Sport

If you take a moment to Google the words "coping in sport," what results is thousands of research papers. The role of a sports psychologist is to help athletes learn how to negotiate certain demands that come with sporting events, such as competing; losing; having a bad game, or what some call a performance slump; and working with media, especially how to handle negative publicity and media hype. For some athletes, the media's emphasis on a big game or match may affect an athlete's psyche and cause anxiety. For some athletes, social media and fan comments may also affect an athlete's overall sense of self and performance. Some coaches, to avoid the effects of media hype and social media, will take away the athlete's cell phone and ban any access to news, family, and other media that may expose them to messages that could affect their ability to play at their best. Sports psychologists who address these particular important facets of an athletes' life feel not only that they are improving performance for the athlete but also that they are aiding in the athlete's enjoyment of the sport.

Appraisals

Coping processes differ between age groups simply because of child development processes. Younger children have not yet developed cognitive coping strategies. By the time the child reaches middle adolescence, he or she has reached a time in his or her development that includes visualization and positive reasoning. Research shows the level of reasoning is not well developed until mid-adolescence (Reeves, Nicholls, & McKenna, 2009). Athletes who have the cognitive resources that allow them to cope with stress will more than likely have outcomes that are much more positive than athletes who have not learned how to deal with stress cognitively. By the time he or she reaches adulthood, an athlete becomes aware of various coping strategies and also exhibits the skills necessary to apply the right coping strategy to the situation (Seiffge-Krenke, 1995).

Physical Changes Caused by Aging

The aging process seems to relate to a decline in physical capabilities, despite the fact that it seems as mentioned earlier, older Americans are maintaining healthier lifestyles and are in great physical shape. The decline in physical capabilities happens to most adults, but what is not known is why the decline happens. The next section will briefly summarize areas of the human body that decline with age and will attempt to explain the effects on our physical activity.

Heart.   When we age, our maximum heart rate decreases, and we often see an overall slip in our cardiac output. This decline can also limit athletic performance. Medical information tells us that the decline of our heart rate or the reason it slows down is so that it can work more efficiently.

Lungs.   When we age, the rate at which our lungs are able to move oxygen from the air to our bloodstream decreases, which results in less endurance and less overall strength.

Muscles.   A loss of muscle strength and muscle mass is also expected when we age. When we lose muscle mass, we have what is called a fast-twitch in muscle fibers. The faster our muscles twitch, the stronger and more powerful we become. However, when we age, we do not develop new muscle fibers, but we have the ability to increase the bulk of the remaining fibers (Volpi, Nazemi, & Fujita, 2004).

Hormones.   A fairly recent controversy in sports revolves around the role of steroids, testosterone, and other growth hormones. We know that as we age, our hormones decline. Medical research suggests that giving older people human growth hormones may result in an increase in muscle mass, but it does not necessarily affect increases in strength (Mayo Clinic Staff, 2016).

Nervous System.   A decline in the blood flow to the brain is another change to expect in the aging process. Decreases in blood flow to the brain are also related to a decrease in one's reaction time. With the decrease of blood flow also comes a deterioration of one's sense of balance. Aging affects the maximum volume of oxygen (aka VO_2) that our bodies can consume. VO_2 is important to overall physical health because as we age, it provides physicians with an excellent index of how we are aging physiologically and not chronologically (Volpi, Nazemi & Fujita, 2004).

Why they need to stay in:

Girls' involvement with sports is related to higher levels of family satisfaction, in both single-parent and dual-parent families.[5]

6. Why they drop out:

Lack of positive role models. Today's girls are bombarded with images of external beauty, not those of confident, strong female athletic role models. To some girls, fitting within the mold that they are constantly told to stay in is more important than standing out. Peer pressure can be hard for girls at any age; when that pressure isn't offset with strong encouragement to participate in sports and healthy physical activity, the results may lead girls to drop out altogether.

Why they need to stay in:

High school female athletes have more positive body images than non-athletes.[6]

1. Girls drop out at different rates depending on where they live. Sabo, D., & Veliz, P. (2008). *Go Out and Play: Youth Sports in America.* East Meadow, NY: Women's Sports Foundation.
2. Staurowsky, E. J., DeSousa, M. J., Gentner, N., Miller, K. E., Shakib, S., Theberge, N., & Williams, N. (2009). *Her Life Depends on It II: Sport, Physical Activity, and the Health and Well-Being of American Girls and Women.*
3. Sabo & Veliz (2008), *Go Out and Play: Youth Sport in America.*
4. Sabo & Snyder (1993), *Sports and Fitness in the Lives of Working Women.*
5. Sabo & Veliz (2008), *Go Out and Play: Youth Sport in America.*
6. Miller, Sabo, Melnick, Farrell, & Barnes (2000), *Health Risks and the Teen Athlete.*

Age and Sports Injuries

The risk of injury is another important issue for older athletes. "Statistically, older athletes are much more likely to injure themselves than younger athletes who are doing the same sport" (Volpi, Nazemi, & Fujita, 2004). In terms of age, general knowledge obtained in medical journals show that older runners are more physically fit and healthy, irrespective of age. Recall the discussion in an earlier section of this text.

Musculoskeletal Problems

One fact that is unavoidable when it comes to aging is the loss of bone density, which is a major concern for women as they age. Women, according to medical journals, have lower musculoskeletal mass than men and also lose bone much faster than men. While people cannot prevent bone loss entirely, doctors tell us that regular exercise, with an emphasis on weight training, is likely to reduce the rate of bone loss. Nevertheless, research shows that with aging also comes a predisposition to bone fractures.

A decrease in flexibility is another consequence associated with the aging process. This outcome is most noticeable when one has issues with his or her joints, hips, and knees. These injuries can be even more intense during exercise and other high-impact physical activities. Issues with back problems are many times observed in athletes who participate in specific sports. For example, we know that cyclists may experience back troubles because of the placement of the seat. Cyclists who have back pain may improve it by simply lowering the seat on the bike. For swimmers, certain swimming strokes, such as the breaststroke, can affect the back and cause pain whenever there is movement that involves arching the spine. Running uphill can also cause lower back pain when compared to running on a flat surface.

Running

Most common runners' injuries are caused by too much running. Injuries related to running become increasingly evident as one ages. A runner who ages may experience common overexercise injuries, such as stress fractures and back pain. Injury to the knee, shin, and hamstring, along with bursitis, bunions, and calluses, are common leg and foot problems experienced by runners. Runners who run on roads, pavement, and other hard surfaces are more likely to experience stress and injury to the legs, hamstrings, knees, and areas of the foot. Running on soft terrain, such as indoor tracks, grass, dirt, and trails, is highly recommended for older runners.

Deteriorating balance is another result of aging. It is recommended that older runners add exercises that center on balance to the workout routine. Dehydration is also another cause of falling in older runners.

Swimming

Sixty percent of all competitive swimmers suffer from what is known as "swimmer's shoulder." For a swimmer, injuring a shoulder is most often caused by "repeated rubbing of the rotator cuff muscles against the acromion, a bone in the shoulder" (Volpi, Nazemi, & Fujita, 2004). When compared to younger swimmers, the group that is most likely to suffer rotator cuff rupture and rupture of the long bicipital tendon are older swimmers.

Cycling

Older cyclists are more likely to suffer problems with nerves in the upper body. If older cyclists have issues with their nerves in the upper body, doctors most likely attribute this injury to overexercise.

"Other cycling injuries that are common in older people include upper limb fractures (in particular the wrist, forearm, and collar bone), shoulder dislocations, sprains, lacerations, and abrasions" (Purcell, 2016; Volpi, Nazemi, & Fujita, 2004).

To reduce the risk of injury, older cyclists should find their "correct seat height, wear padded gloves, and avoid resting on the hands while riding" (Purcell, 2016; Volpi, Nazemi, & Fujita, 2004). A padded seat actually reduces and prevents other injuries, such as "urethritis, or inflammation of the urethra,

Climbing

Regarding climbing, the weather is one of the main causes of injury for older climbers. Summer temperatures cause dehydration, while cold temperatures or climbing in high altitudes also result in dehydration. Sensitivity to altitudes happens when adults are in areas with heights that are as low as 6,000 feet (1,830 meters). For example, people living in mountain areas are often susceptible to altitude sickness, a sickness that results in "heart palpitations, cough, headache, sleeplessness and difficulty breathing" (Purcell, 2016; Volpi, Nazemi, & Fujita, 2004). Altitude sickness, a common injury for older climbers, can also be fatal.

Golf

Injuries related to golf include problems with one's rotator cuff (shoulder), pain in the neck, lower back pain, or injuries to the elbow (Purcell, 2016). Wrist pain is also a very common injury in older golfers because golf requires a continual extension and twisting of the wrist during the golf swing. Golf-associated injuries can be avoided simply by doing warm-up and stretching exercises before starting the golf game. Golf injuries can also be prevented or treated with muscle-strengthening exercises, particularly of back muscles (Purcell, 2016; Volpi, Nazemi, & Fujita, 2004).

Medical science tells us that compared to younger athletes, older athletes are more likely to have a range of sports injuries (Purcell, 2016; Volpi, Nazemi, & Fujita, 2004). A careful note of consideration is necessary at this point: Although older athletes are more prone to injury, this does not serve as an excuse or provide a reason for not engaging in physical exercise. This does not mean that older Americans should avoid physical activity. Many of the injuries listed earlier can be prevented with appropriate techniques related to strength training, conditioning, warm-up and stretching exercises, and a little common sense. Moderation in physical activity leads to not only an enjoyment of sports and exercise but also produces healthier, more positive, and happier lives.

Life After Sports

Retirement Age for Athletes

Professional athletes in America make millions throughout their careers. Statistics show that many eventually run out of money once their playing days are over (Global Sports Jobs Insight Team, 2018; Saunders, 2018). The average professional athlete's career is over by age 33. For physically demanding sports, such as American football, it's as young as 28 (Global Sports Jobs Insight Team, 2018; Saunders, 2018). Female gymnasts and figure skaters peak in their mid to late teens, their male counterparts in their late teens and early 20s. There's no particular age at which a jockey is at his peak. (See Table 10.1.)

TABLE 10.1

Sport	Average Retirement Age
Badminton Players	35
Boxers	35
Bowlers	31
Cricketers	40
Cyclists	35
Dancers	35
Divers (Saturation, Deep Sea, and Free Swimming)	40
Football Players	35
Golfers	40
Gymnasts	22
Ice Hockey Players	35
Jockeys-Flat Racing National Hunt	45 35
Members of the Reserve Forces	45
Motor Cycle Riders (Motocross or Road Racing)	40
Motor Racing Drivers	40
Rugby League/Union Players	35
Skiers (Downhill)	30
Snooker/Billiards Players	40
Speedway Riders	40
Squash Players	35
Table/Lawn Tennis Players (Including Real Tennis)	35
Trapeze Artists	40
Wrestlers	35

The stereotypical female Olympic gymnast is young, typically early teenage years, short, and well toned. Consider the Summer Olympic Gymnast Team that went to the 2016 games. Simone Biles has been called "the greatest gymnast of all time" (Angyal, 2016; Hunt, 2017). Standing just a few inches shy of 5 feet, this young teenage athlete at the age of 19 exceeded the age at which many of the gymnasts who came before her retired. For instance, in 1986, Olympian gymnast Mary Lou Retton retired at the age of 18 just after winning the gold medal in the individual all-around in the 1984 Olympics. The first American woman to win the all-around in the 2004 Summer Olympics in Atlanta, Carly Patterson, was 16 when she won the gold medal, and she too retired when she was 18 years old. It was reported that Patterson retired from the sport because of back injuries. These early retirements at an average age of 18 or 19 seem to make sense when one considers the physical requirements for a gymnast to compete.

The intense training schedule and intensity for many gymnasts creates a need for rest. This then leads to a desire to retire from the sport so they can stay healthy and in good shape. Unlike for gymnastics, age is irrelevant in the sport of golf. The club professional's ages range from the young to retirement age. For the touring PGA professionals, the average age is quite simple to calculate. According to one study, Berry and Larkey (1999) found that golfers peak in the sport between the ages of 30 and 35 years old. Professional golfers in their early 20s do not see many victories, with a few exceptions (e.g., Tiger Woods).

In a careful review of the professional golfers in 2016, it was determined that the top PGA Tour professional golfers whose ages could be verified were 35 years old or older, results that are consistent with a study conducted in 2013 and with the Berry and Larkey (1999) study.

In tennis, the average retirement age of the current top-10 professional tennis players at the time of this writing is an average of 27 years of age. Today's top-10 professional female tennis players are reporting at an average age of 25.1 years. It was just 10 years ago when the list of the top-10 professional female tennis players included Serena and Venus Williams, Kim Clijsters, and Daniela Hantuchova.

Despite the fact that the list came out a decade ago, as of this writing, each of these women is still actively participating at the elite level in professional tennis (stats obtained from (Garber, 2012).

Statistics show that most professional baseball players reach the professional league at approximately 24 years of age. In 2015 and 2016 the Boston Red Sox had a few outliers in regard to age and retirement. When he was 20, Xander Bogaerts played 18 games, and both he and Mookie Betts essentially became regular starters at the age of 21. Daniel Nava was 27 years old before he was allowed to play his first game in the majors. Research shows that, on average, a player reaching the MLB at a young age will have a longer-lasting career. Career longevity in baseball is closely associated with age and player statistics, so much so that the younger the player, the longer the career.

More often than not, professional athletes, sadly, have no money in their 401(k) programs. No matter how famous or invincible, some professional athletes do not save money so that they are financially stable in the case of a career-ending injury. Few athletes have established trusts for their families that is held for later use. In the next section, we will talk in more detail about retirement and the pro athlete's life after the game. In 1985, Darryl Strawberry was 19 years of age when he signed a professional contract to play in the major leagues with the Mets. At the time, Strawberry's salary was reported to be $7.1 million with a 10% annuity and an annual interest rate of 5.1%. Currently, the annuity listed in his contract yields nearly $2 million and will do so over the next two decades. But Strawberry is unable to receive any of those funds because the Internal Revenue Service (IRS) took over and auctioned it off so that they could recover more $1.5 million in back taxes.

The Reality of Money and Fame

Professional ballplayers often chose to leave the sport for reasons that include retirement, a desire to start a career in acting or in broadcasting, excessive injuries, drug and alcohol abuse, accidents, or gambling problems. Although many professional players, just like entertainers, have huge desires to continue to play because they love the game, they have an extremely difficult time adjusting to retirement or the fact that their careers are ending. Others, owing to lower levels of education and little job experience, cannot think of substitute careers (Rosenberg, 1980a; Rosenberg, 1980b, Rosenberg, 1982). Historically, salaries achieved in professional sports were insufficient, and players were unable to afford a comfortable early retirement. Even in 1980, Rosenberg predicted that the increase in player salaries would be associated with better post-baseball career adjustments. Rosenberg (1980b) also forecast that high salaries would lead other professional athletes to "quit while they are ahead." The reason for this forecast? According to Rosenberg (1980a, Rosenberg, 1980b), when players are offered higher salaries, they are given resources that allow them to retire comfortably even at earlier ages than professional players preceding them in the sport. But some players still retire with a net worth of $0.00. For example, it was reported in 2015 that Terrell Owens, former NFL superstar, is mired in debt. Owens is estimated to have had a salary that was well over $70 million while playing professionally in the NFL. As we mentioned earlier in this chapter, we know that some sports allow players to join the professional leagues when they are barely out of their teens. Then we find that these young players are signed to multimillion-dollar, multiyear contracts. Then if we add endorsements, we find that they may add up to $30 million to their salaries.

The litany of superstars who have gone broke after making millions include Mike Tyson, who spent more than $300 million on cars, jewels, and pet tigers, and purchased multiple homes in less than two or three years. Then in 2003, Tyson was forced to file for bankruptcy. There is also baseball icon Curt Schilling who was reported to have earned a total of $112 million over a span of 20 years. By 2013, it was reported that Schilling became so broke that according to sports news media, he begged the "Baseball Hall of Fame to return his bloody sock from a famous pitching performance against the Yankees so that he could auction it off" (the sock brought in more than $92,000) (Crouch, 2016). Evander Holyfield lost his entire 235-acre Atlanta, Georgia estate valued at approximately $230 million. Holyfield's mansion was described as having "109 rooms and an average monthly electric bill of $17,000" (Callahan, 2015). Reports were also published that alleged Holyfield had to obtain a $550,000 loan to pay for landscaping and that he "owed $200,000 in back taxes, plus alimony and child support for three ex-wives and 11 children" (Callahan, 2015; Crasnick, 2016; Crouch, 2016; Grasso, 2018). NBA icon Jason Caffey earned $35 million over 8 years and was forced to file for bankruptcy in 2007. Caffey, reported to have 10 children by eight women, was arrested in 2007 for nonpayment of child support. Caffey also had to spend time in jail because, at the time, nonpayment of child support carried a "sentence of mandatory jail time" (Callahan, 2015; Crasnick, 2016; Crouch, 2016; Grasso, 2018).

In February 2016, *Sports Illustrated* ran a story stating that approximately "80% of retired NFL players go broke in their first three years out of the League" (Steinberg, 2015). This statistic makes us ponder the question, how does a person who earns an average salary of over a few million dollars a year end up broke and bankrupt? How did a mega athlete like Terrell Owens lose more than $70 million?

It is reported that the "median income in the NFL is roughly $750,000/year," and the "average career span is less than four years" (Steinberg, 2015). According to research, there are four reasons that explain athletes' loss of net worth.

First, athletes lack access to competent financial planning advisors. Athletes are just like other college graduates going to work in the real world in that they are not trained as undergrads in money management, investments, the stock market, the ins and outs of financial planning, or how the IRS and our tax system works. Athletes who enter professional contracts, especially those who do so immediately after high school, often need advisors and people they trust to teach them how to budget, understand the fine print and other legal verbiage found in contracts, and protect themselves legally from deceptive or inexperienced agents. For example, we know that many college athletes are approached on campus by agents and others who offer incentives and financial inducements if the athlete signs with them (e.g., watch the movie *Jerry Maguire*). While there are not many, there are those financial planners who encourage young, naïve players to sign a power of attorney or fiduciary contract that will enable the planner, agent, or advisor to make investments or withdraw money on behalf of the athlete. Many times these transactions occur without prior authorization from the athlete, and, ultimately, this becomes one of the biggest mistakes an athlete can make, and in some cases, it explains why some go bankrupt and lose their millions. Fortunately, the NFL has mandatory seminars after the draft that seek to educate and perhaps protect athletes from bankruptcy and other financial pitfalls. It should be noted that some athletes do not avail themselves of these resources. Reasons for avoiding these protections are unknown and possibly lend themselves to further investigation by scholars and other sports practitioners.

The second reason for athletes' financial problems is divorce. As many people in our culture know, divorce can drain one's funds in legal fees and quickly consume one's assets. Athletes who go through a divorce often end up with half of what they earned playing in their sport. Many athletes, as previously discussed, end up with huge alimony and child support payments.

Forgetting the quick tenure of one's career is the third cause of financial problems. Some research shows that once an athlete is drafted, he or she quickly forgets the career span and the average age of players in their sport. They "forget" that there is a cost of living and because of fluctuations in our economy, their salary will not last forever. In this same regard, we know that some athletes forget that an injury or an accident can stop their career immediately, and then they are left not knowing what to do next. From a quick overview of the athletes who lost most, if not all, of their salaries, we see that spending habits consumed all of the revenue that the athlete assumed would be coming forever (see Evander Holyfield story).

The fourth cause of financial problems for athletes who participate in the NFL, NBA, MLB, and NHL is the "jock tax." The jock tax requires all players with the major leagues to "file taxes in every state that they play in during the fiscal year" (Pro Football News, 2018). As previously mentioned, many professional athletes spend money while they are playing and forget that they need to plan for the future.

Life After the Last Game

Professional athletes train extensively for years. In some instances, like for gymnasts or golfers, we learn that training for their sport consumes a vast majority of their youth. Athletes, like entertainers, must make extensive personal sacrifices to pursue their dreams. We know from reports of gymnasts such as Gabi Douglas, Simone Biles, Mary Lou Retton, and others, that sacrifices also include substantial financial obligations, moving away from family to train with a famous coach in full-time facilities, and a sacrifice of personal or romantic relationships. It is not uncommon for many athletes to think that retirement is nonexistent, or something that is too far off in the future, or something that does not require much thought in the present day. Retirement for some athletes, as well as the average American, is an event that will happen much later in life and comes with the idea that "I will take care of that later." What many forget is that no matter how successful their careers are, their time playing the sport will eventually come to an end. That end may come about because of age, injury, exhaustion, or simply burn out.

The transformation from a full-time college athletic career to a successful professional sporting career to retirement has recently received notable attention in formal academic research. Schwenk, Gorenflow, Dopp, and Hipple (2007) found that one difficulty in making the transition for some athletes is the sudden end of public demand for their athletic superstar performance. Add to that the loss of the athlete's intense love of competition. Few athletes have made their thoughts and related depression public. These athletes are candid about the hit that retirement has on the ego. Some athletes have candidly shared the challenges and hardships that they endured in terms of leaving the spotlight and entering the retirement phase of life. Many celebrated professional athletes who have retired share their stories of aging and retirement with hopes that their testimonies might be used to raise awareness about the depression that happens after athletic retirement (Schwenk, 2000).

For more on depression after professional sports careers end, read "Life After Sports," by Emma Vickers, 2013.

Loss of Identity

Athletic identity is described as the "degree to which an individual identifies with the athlete role and looks to others for acknowledgment of that role" (Brewer, Van Raalte, & Linder, 1993, p. 10). For some athletes, it has been suggested that with retirement comes the loss of a dominant role and a sense of pride that eventually affect their overall self-concept (Lavallee, 2000; Lavallee, 2005; Lavallee, Golby, & Lavallee, 2002; Lavallee, Gordon, & Grove, 2008; Vickers, 2013). Being a professional athlete can be overwhelming in our culture. With the life comes better resources, fame, media attention, and pride, just to name a few emotional benefits. Professional athletes have to move on at some point in their lives. Common struggles that many professional athletes experiences include having to take care of themselves and organizing their own lives instead of relying on an agent or personal assistant (Lavallee, 2000; Lavallee, 2005; Lavallee, Golby, & Lavallee, 2002; Lavallee, Gordon, & Grove, 2008; Vickers, 2013). Some professional athletes find themselves at a crossroads, trying to find something else that they can devote their time and passion to. If we think about it, how does one transition from long strenuous days of training and practice, and the energy of game day and travel to days of literally normal life? According to Lavallee (2000), professional athletes whose identities at the time of retirement are tangled and intertwined with a sport (also known as high-identity athletes) will be more likely to experience higher levels of depression and difficulties adjusting emotionally to retirement.

Potential Biological Factors

Is it possible that the way an athlete responds to retirement may be related to biological factors? Medical research has found a causal link in serotonin levels found in some athletes and depression, and this is said to determine the extent to which an athlete experiences moderate to severe depression when he or she transitions to retirement. The imbalance in serotonin is used to provide some understanding of why some athletes adjust to retirement better than others.

Battling Depression After Sports

Athletes about to enter retirement can avoid the probability of experiencing depression if they engage in the following (the list presented next was obtained from Vickers, 2016):

To be an athlete means that one is mentally tougher, fitter, healthier, and happier than others— or at least that is the public's perception of an athlete. It is this type of perception, standard of perfection, and stereotyping that can make it challenging for athletes to admit that they have issues related to aging and retirement. These adjectives also make it hard for an athlete to seek help from a professional. This means that family, friends, teammates, coaches, and others must maintain a supportive environment so that they are aware of changes in the retired athlete's behavior. Keep in mind that depression is something that is not always evident or transparent (e.g., the highly successful and popular Robin Williams). We also know that for some athletes—namely, male athletes—it is a challenge and often difficult to admit publicly or even privately that something is wrong or that they may be depressed. For many Americans, an admission of depression or other mental health issues is most closely associated with defect and abnormality (although this is a very incorrect view of mental illness). If we take the perception of depression even further and into the professional sporting world, we find that athletes may avoid this discussion simply because they fear public backlash and

LIFE AFTER SPORT: DEPRESSION IN RETIRED ATHLETES

"Reduce exclusive identification with the sporting role and expand self-identity to other pursuits.

Discover interests and competencies for other activities that are outside of their sport (perhaps they should consider coaching or the mentoring of other athletes).

Develop stress management and time management strategies and skills.

Encourage strong relationships with coaches, family, friends, and managers who care about the athletes' sporting success as well as their personal growth. Being supported by significant others to consider other avenues in life will help the athlete keep an open mind and diversify identity.

Take time to consult with a sports psychologist to help identify other adaptation techniques."

(Excerpt from http://believeperform.com/wellbeing/life-after-sport-depression-in-retired-athletes/)

other reactions from sports fans, coaches, family, and friends. Perhaps they feel embarrassed or that they will be judged. Irrespective of their thoughts, the most important message in this section of the chapter is to increase awareness of the role that aging has on an individual and, more importantly, how it affects our professional athletes. We must remember that for many Americans, the transition to retirement is a difficult one, particularly for professionals who have been in the media spotlight for years. If we take this example into other industries, we might begin to understand why some artists, actors, and musicians have cosmetic and plastic surgeries performed to stay young looking.

Discussions about retirement should happen early and often. During these times of discussion and the onset of retirement, it is important and vital for the athlete to have social support and opportunities to communicate feelings. The social support network providing an opportunity to share feelings is important if we want athletes to avoid postretirement depression. Retirement terrifies most people, but it most definitely terrifies entertainers and athletes. The end of one's athletic career can feel like death for an athlete who thrives on fame and fortune. And it is important to note that the longer the athlete's career, the harder retirement seems to be.

Tips on Making the Transition to Retirement Easier

What happens when an elite athlete realizes that this "dream job" isn't happily ever after? What happens when a sudden career-ending injury changes things for an athlete? (e.g., *Remember the Titans* and the car accident.) Research shows that transitioning in this new phase of life can be easy. Players who succeed are resilient, optimistic, and confident. Successful careers in professional sports also demand marketable skills and competencies, as well as formal education (McKenna & Richardson, 2017). For example, professional athletes with college degrees enjoy the transition to retirement much better than those athletes who skipped college to go straight to the professional league. We also learned that players who do not focus exclusively on their playing performance and win/loss records will also make the transition into the retirement phase much easier and will be much happier than those professional athletes who spend their careers focused on winning championships (e.g., Lebron James).

Finally, players who transitioned easily into retirement had a wide range of social networks. A large circle of friends and other social networks allow players to find opportunities and passions that extend far beyond their sport. Social networks that consist of close family and friends are also a vital source of support (McKenna & Richardson, 2017). In fact, many current and former players have reported that if it were not for family and friends, they would have never "survived."

Conclusion

In this chapter, we talked about age as a multidimensional concept. This chapter reviewed and highlighted some interesting findings and research related to sports and age. The neglect of age and sports in mass media coverage, as well as in scholarly journals, however, was also quite apparent. Fortunately, the neglect of research on age now provides ideas and opens a new field of study for aspiring scholars, sports communicators, and sports psychologists. We know that we are all aging. Our sports media professionals are aging. The athletes they report on are aging. And our fans and spectators are aging. We are all getting older each day.

In this chapter, we briefly covered how aging interacts with participation in sports from age of eligibility to retirement to life after sports. We even spent some time discussing the interaction between age and sports and their effect on our bodies. We spent the final pages discussing what happens when professional playing careers come to a close. We learned that ending a sports career and making the transition into retirement is often a challenge for many athletes. Often, retirement comes suddenly, and athletes are thrust into a situation that requires them to reinvest their time, money, and energy into something other than sport. Summarizing retirement and aging in sports, we find that according to research, ending a sports career involves the same level of thought processes as was involved when entering professional elite sports. This is why athletic identity must enter into our discussions and thought processes because of the vital role that identity plays in our developmental process. Athletes who find retirement challenging often have problems because of their sports identity and the way they defined their identity. As discussed, we found that if an athlete is able to expand his or her athletic identity and experiences, then the transition to retirement is likely to be very smooth with little or no feelings of anxiety or depression. Again, we found that athletes who have the most difficulty adjusting are those athletes who have not had the chance or even the desire to do anything outside of playing in a professional sport. Ultimately, for these athletes, the lack of broadening their passions and interests stops them from negotiating a life outside of the sports world (Messner, 1992).

QUESTIONS FOR REFLECTION AND DISCUSSION

1. Think of a teen athlete. How does the sports media portray the teen athlete? What themes or words do you find in sports coverage of teen athletes?

2. Do you see a variance in the age of retirement in different sports? Why or why not? Explain your perceptions and observations. What are the reasons for the differences?

3. Do you agree or disagree with eligibility requirements? Why or why not?

4. Should participation in sports be considered "fun" for children? Why or why not? Who are the real winners and losers of the "it's just fun" logic for youth interested in sports?

5. A new trend in sports involves positive coaching. What does this mean, and how does this affect athletes when they get older and attempt collegiate athletics?

6. We live in a sports world. Consider the statement, "It's like baseball and apple pie … that's American." As a result of the value we place on sports, we find that many individuals are upset when news reports mention contracts and the salaries that head coaches and professional players receive. What are your thoughts? Explain.

7. Do you agree or disagree with the statement, "A child's success in sports is especially important to the parents"? Explain your answer.

8. Both the Williams sisters' father and Tiger Woods's father encouraged their children to specialize in sports. The Williams sisters specialized in tennis, and Tiger Woods specialized in golf, both at early ages. Do you agree with their decisions to have young children specialize at an early age in a sport that was not typical for their ethnic background? Why or why not?

9. Are organized sports programs worth the effort? How do you deal with the "someone must win and someone must lose" philosophy?

SUGGESTED ACTIVITIES

1. Think about the sports you participated in as a youngster. Did you stick with the sport(s)? Why or why not? Refer to the information in this chapter and use it to inform your answer. What role did your parent/legal guardian play in your attitude toward the sport?

2. Review media coverage of professional athletes who retired from their sport in the last three years. Write a paper on the sports that the players participated in and how often the story of the retirement was covered. Were there more stories focused on one athlete, or was the coverage equally distributed? How does the athlete feel about life after retirement?

3. Go to a fitness center, activities center, or senior center. Interview five senior citizens about their attitudes toward aging and physical fitness. See if you observe some of the problems identified in this chapter that have been associated with aging.

4. Write a press release about the upcoming retirement of a very popular athlete. Be sure to include quotes and other valid information that will balance coverage by the media.

5. Gymnasts usually retire from the sport before they turn 20. Why? Write a news story or prepare for a human-interest broadcast that explains this to your readers/viewers.

6. Read the pro leagues' (NFL, NBA, MLB, NHL, etc.) and the NCAA's rules of eligibility. Prepare a series of stories for the sports paper on these rules, and interview experts for both sides of the argument.

7. Research the philosophy of positive coaching. Then interview local head coaches of at least three sports. Find out their philosophies and attitudes toward coaching, their players, and winning. Write a summary paper explaining what you found in your research.

8. Locate several youth sports clubs in your area. Interview the coaches of those youth clubs. Following the same approach as in the previous question, you also want to determine their reward system. Regarding an emphasis on performance, do youth coaches give ribbons or trophies to all players whether they are good or bad, or do they require young athletes to practice and commit just like older athletes? Compare your findings with the information in this chapter.

9. How can youth sports be improved? First, list some of the issues in youth sports and then write elements that you believe (based on research) can be used to improve a child's development based on his or her participation in sports. Next, list some of the major obstacles to your proposed changes.

ADDITIONAL RESOURCES

Physical Activity Resources, https://www.hhs.gov/fitness/resource-center/physical-activity-resources/index.html

Active Aging, http://www.humankinetics.com/activeaging#&sSearchWord=

Go4Life from the National Institute on Aging at NIH, https://go4life.nia.nih.gov

Lifeline, https://www.lifeline24.co.uk/sport-and-fitness-activities/

Fit in the Future: Staying Healthy in an Aging World, https://www.canwelivebetter.bayer.com/society/fit-future-staying-healthy-aging-world?gclid=CjwKCAjworfdBRA7EiwAKX9HeK4LSj3nOrtau1nueUbi-UfL2a180VAnx1cvL1qjmRk3m0xPi3rYz7hoCfjQQAvD_BwE&gclsrc=aw.ds

National Senior Games Association, http://nsga.com

AARP Resources, https://www.aarp.org/caregiving/

Sports and the Able-Body

After reading this chapter, students should be able to:

- become aware of how American culture has a bias toward able-bodies;

- define ableism and realize how sports media helps to create perceptions of unimpaired bodies to be normal and disabled bodies to be inferior;

- provide examples of the various ways that athletes living with disabilities have been depicted in sports media;

- show illustrations of depictions of people living with physical or mental challenges in media and the reactions from sports fans and the larger American culture; and

- learn how to reduce and change ableist language that limits people living with disabilities.

Introduction

In the United States culture, idealized images of beautiful, healthy, able-bodies are everywhere in most media content. In fact, when we think of images of people living with physical challenges, we seldom are exposed to those images. Mass media images, and in particular images in sports media, rarely show people with disabilities, and when they do, the images are often stereotyped or misrepresented depictions of this group. In fact, it is not uncommon to hear jokes about skills or an individual's aptitude without a reference to some type of disability (e.g., retarded). According to the U.S. Census Bureau's statistics (2017a), approximately 19% of 56.7 million Americans live with a physical or mental disability that affects basic day-to-day activities (e.g., housework, driving, walking).

With respect to sports, participating in a sport is vital and serves an important role in the life of an athlete with a disability. In fact, it is no surprise that most sports in our culture are based on able-bodies. Sports for persons living with a disability are often referred to as "para," which is used to denote that the sporting activity is performed by an athlete with a physical and/or intellectual disability.

We know that when sports media tell stories about athletes living with disabilities, they often focus on their disability or difference and not their similarities with other athletes. In fact, when there is an athlete with a disability, most sports journalists and fans have a natural curiosity about how they negotiate their sports in comparison to normal-bodied athletes. Research tells us that over time, the frequent stories that center on their "differences" actually may lead them to start developing athletic identities based on their differences and not their athletic skills and expertise. For athletes living with disabilities, sports have been classified into categories to ensure fair competition. Table 11.1 provides a birds-eye view of the sports played by people with certain physical challenges.

TABLE 11.1 *Various sports played by people with disabilities.*

Paralympic Sports	Special Olympics	Deaf Sports	Other Disability Sports	Extremity Games
Alpine skiing	Alpine skiing	Alpine skiing	Blind cricket	Skateboarding
Archery	Aquatics	Badminton	Blind golf	Wakeboarding
Boccia	Badmitton	Basketball	Electric wheelchair football	Rock Climbing
CyclingEquestrian	Basketball	Beach volleyball	Electric wheelchair hockey	Surfing
Football 5-a-side or Football 7-a-side	Bocce	Bowling	Golf	Moto Cross
Goalball	Bowling	Cross-country skiing	Handcycling	Kayaking
Ice sledge hockey	Cross-country skiing	Curling	Disability Shooting and Hunting	BMX Biking
Judo	Cycling	Cycling	Wheelchair baseball	
Nordi Skiing	Equestrian	Cricket	Wheelchair hockey	
Powerlifting	Figure skating	Football	Wheelchair rugby	
Sailing	Floor hockey	Handball	Wheelchair skateboarding	
Shooting	Football	Ice hockey		
Swimming	Golf	Judo		
Table Tennis	Gymnastics	Karate		
Tennis	Powerlifting	Shooting		
Volleyball	Roller skating	Snowboarding		
Wheelchair basketball	Sailing	Skibob		
Wheelchair curling	Sit Skiing	Swimming		
Wheelchair fencing	Snowboarding	Table tennis		
Wheelchair rugby	Snowshoeing	Tae kwon do		
Wheelchair tennis	Softball	Tennis		
	Short track speed skating	Volleyball		
	Table tennis	Water polo		
	Team handball	Wrestling		
	Tennis			
	Volleyball			

Source: Disabled World. (2018, December 19). Retrieved from https://www.disabled-world.com/

According to research, athletes with mental or physical challenges can receive the same health benefits from exercise and participation in sports as able-bodied athletes. Research shows that athletes living with physical challenges who are also active in sports have reported experiencing fewer physiological problems related to the heart and have better cholesterol levels other nonactive people who are living with challenges. Paraplegic athletes are also less likely to be hospitalized and, according to research, are less susceptible to infections than nonactive paraplegic individuals (Malanga, Filart, & Cheng, 2002).

Sports can, and often do, provide many benefits for individuals who live with challenges, but most noteworthy is that they allow athletes living with physical and mental challenges to be able to integrate into the larger culture and experience opportunities that allow them to have an enhanced and satisfying life. For athletes living with disabilities, participation in sports might span different activities: from those that are strictly recreational, to sports activities that are extremely competitive, to becoming an elite athlete participating in Paralympic sports. In terms of their participation, athletes living with disabilities are often placed into categories based on the level of physical or mental impairment. This classification happens to ensure equitable competition among the athletes. This includes many competitive sports, such as wheelchair basketball, volleyball, cycling, and swimming. In addition, to ensure equality in competition, many sports for athletes with disabilities rely on evaluation systems.

Defining Ableism

Ableism is the discrimination against mentally or physically disabled people. Ableism is as of recent times a preferred term. Instead of referring to people living with physical challenges with terms such as "disability discrimination" or "disability prejudice," a focus on our culture's bias toward able-bodied individuals has been seen as a more appropriate term. As we have learned in previous chapters, racial discrimination is referred to as racism and gender discrimination is called sexism. Racism and sexism were also terms that allow easy expression of the ideas associated with racial and sexual discrimination.

We know that discrimination of individuals living with disabilities can be a complicated and mis-understood concept. For example, we might perceive buildings and lecture halls with steps instead of ramps as institutions that support physically able individuals or ableism. Less obvious perhaps is the notion that ableism also includes assumptions made about what disabled people can and cannot do. Although we know that young people living with physical challenges undergo the same insecurities and preoccupations as nondisabled peers: friends, romantic relationships, finding passion, and making money. Most people who identify with this group tend to be excluded or segregated from integration into every day social activities and relationships that able-bodied individuals can easily engage in (Carlon, Shields, Dodd, & Taylor, 2013; Shields & Synnot, 2014; Shields & Synnot, 2016). Therefore, individuals living with physical and mental challenges often experience feelings related to loneliness, alienation, and feeling like second-class citizens (Ali, 2018; American Psychiatric Association, 2013; George, 2014; National Institute of Mental Health, 2016; New, 2016). Alienation and isolation are not the main reasons that people living with individual differences may be outcast, but it is possible that it is the way that able-bodied individuals in our culture react to and treat them because of their impairment. In ableist societies like the United States, we know that the overall norm is to treat those in its culture with visible differences contrarily, even though people living with physical and mental impairments are no longer physically segregated from the able-bodied majority (e.g., special education classes). In the United States culture, there is still a form of segregation and discrimination leveled toward the disabled athlete, but in more subtle ways (Goggin & Newell, 2005).

Background and History of Disability Sport in America

We mentioned in the introduction that according to the Census Bureau (2017a), there were approximately 16% of the population living with some type of impairment. The term "disability sport," according to the World Health Organization (2012), is used to describe an organized, physically competitive activity aimed at people living with physical and/or mental challenges. As mentioned in the introduction of this chapter, any sport organized for people without disabilities is often referred to as a mainstream, able-bodied sport (Nixon, 2007). Although we have seen attitudes toward athletes with disabilities and disability sports change over the last 30 years, we are slowly seeing American culture accept people in this group. Shapiro, Pitts, and Hums (2012) stated in a recent publication that America is presently seeing a shift from sport and disability to the idea of disability sport.

Being labeled as a disabled athlete in the United States often leads to different emotions. Some athletes report being revered, while others say they experience pity, mockery, or bullying. In ancient Greece, from 500 BC to AD, literature tells us that children were murdered if it was even thought that they had some sort of disability. Early Christians, commanded to be compassionate to everyone, also mocked, tormented, threw stones, and bullied persons with mental illness, as these individuals were, at the time, thought to have impairments because of a sin in their lives and as a result were murdered simply because of the perception of mental or physical impairment. Historical records further show deaf people living in the 15th and 16th centuries were idolized and considered be godly and superior, particularly when they were compared to individuals who were able to hear. Not until the emergence of public policies focused on civil welfare did our culture start treating disabled people with dignity. This was also the time in our culture when segregated institutions and establishments such as special education programs and housing for mentally and physically challenged individuals began to surface (Barnes, 1997).

American culture's obsession with bodily perfection or idealized images, Stone (1995) suggests, is onerous not only to people living with disabilities but also to the able-bodied. Our culture's obsession with ableism alienates everyone, both able- and disabled-body individuals. Stone (1995) further states that American culture often views disability as a condition to be avoided. Norms in our western culture also encourage the denial of visible differences while striving to attain an ideal body.

In 1996, a law known as the Disability Discrimination Act (DDA) was passed to address and reduce discriminatory acts that many individuals living with disabilities were reporting. According to the DDA, people who are living with physical challenges are not to be refused services or entry to places because of their physical or mental impairment. The act, however, has been the focus of much debate and criticism. Advocates find it's language and the punishments for violation of the policies are much too weak and that despite its passage, individuals living with mental and physical impairments still are treated as second-class citizens living in very powerless situations. For many, the DDA is simply a way to allow power and control to continue to be dominated by the able-bodied hegemonic masculine culture already in place in America. As of this writing, people living with physical challenges have been encouraged to become active participants in sports and to increase their physical activity. In American culture, hospitals and schools continue to use sports as recreation and as a form of treatment.

Few scholarly and empirical studies have been conducted to demonstrate low levels of participation by athletes with physical and mental challenges in sport. While the lack of empirical research on disabled individuals' involvement in sports is regrettable, the few studies that are available are loaded with practical and ethical dilemmas. Research that does exist provides evidence that in terms of participation in sports, when compared to nondisabled cohorts and peers, disabled people are less likely to be active participants in any physical activity. Typically, socialization factors, such as media, coaches, friends and family, and schools, influence and can even perpetuate and reinforce negative ideas presented in messages about people living with disabilities in American sports.

In fact, there is evidence suggesting that the average American ranks people living with disabilities very low in terms of the social hierarchy here in our culture. This low ranking is accompanied by ideas that disabled people are denied prestige and opportunities typically enjoyed by able-bodied individuals. When persons living with disabilities are unable to take part in organized sports, one of the consequences of this obstacle is the low status given to them by members of American society. For the first time in American history, a policy called the National Curriculum for Physical Education was created to offer encouragement for modification and adaptation of activities for teachers to use to address students with special educational needs.

Exclusivity of Able-Bodied Sport

According to Hahn (1984), people who participate in highly visible and recognized sports are often well received and accepted in the larger culture. Comparing this with those who do not participate in sports, Hahn (1984) found over 30 years ago that those individuals are often denied acceptance in our culture. This acceptance based on one's participation in sports also enhances the idea that those who participate are able-bodied and therefore participation in sports results in an exclusive entrance into the part of our culture that exists just for the able-bodied athlete. While we know that participation in sports does not ensure that everyone who participates will be accepted into the larger society, we do know that our culture's preoccupation with looks, physicality, body type, health and fitness, and beauty sets up extreme challenges and obstacles for the "disabled population with the opportunity to challenge and clarify the values that these preoccupations project" (Thomas, 2002).

Classifications of Athletes by Physical and Mental Challenges

In terms of sports, athletes are classified by physical and mental challenges because this is a process that levels the playing field for athletes living with different types of disabilities.

To classify athletes based on disability requires at least three or four steps. All athletes must have a medical evaluation to determine their limitations. Then there is what is referred to as a functional evaluation that involves observing the athlete in training and in competition. This second step involves many trained experts as well as a classification panel and committee. Other selective criteria involve classification based on age, sexual orientation, gender, weight, or size. The selective criteria are included because of the belief that they affect and can predict the athlete's performance. When it comes to classification in the world of disability sports, we find that classification is based less on the athlete's performance, as it is in the larger sports world where athletes are grouped based on skill level, and more on the assurance that the impairment is relevant to the athlete's equality with other athletes living with similar impairments.

Team Sports for Physically Challenged Athletes

Wheelchair Athletics

Athletes who play sports in wheelchairs are those persons whose disabilities include physical and intellectual challenges. Often known as adapted sports, wheelchair sports are related to sporting events where athletes are able to use either manual or powered wheelchairs to participate. In terms of athletes' overall well-being, we know that participation in sports allows those living with disabilities to experience increases in self-esteem and confidence, the same positive consequences obtained

FIGURE 11.1 *Confidence of athletes.*

for older athletes and able-bodied athletes. Figure 11.1 is an illustration of athletes demonstrating confidence in their participation in sports.

In terms of injuries for wheelchair athletics, we find that not only have changes in wheelchair design contributed to athletes' injuries but also new wheelchairs that allow athletes to lower the seat height may actually put their elbows and upper arms in closer contact with the wheels, causing an intense friction burn. As you can tell in Figures 11.2 and 11.3, current wheelchair designs have changed immensely. Notice the lowered seats and position of the wheels. These changes can cause other injuries besides friction burns. Other injuries related to wheelchair athletes are fractures of the metacarpals and phalanges. These fractures are typically observed in athletes who participate in wheelchair basketball. Overuse of the shoulder and rotator cuff are also more likely in athletes who

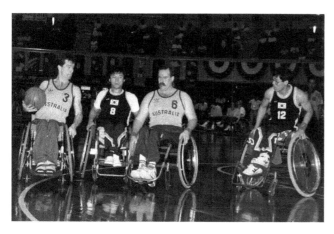

FIGURE 11.2 *Men's wheelchair basketball.*

FIGURE 11.3 *Hannah Cockroft.*

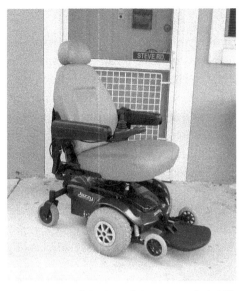

FIGURE 11.4   *Pride Jazzy Select power chair 001.*

FIGURE 11.5   *Wounded warrior Todd Reed hits a softball during the Wounded Warrior Amputee Celebrity Softball Classic at Nationals Park in Washington, DC, on April 3, 2012. The game pitted Washington-area celebrities against veterans and active-duty service members who lost limbs while serving in Iraq or Afghanistan.*

participate in wheelchair sports simply because of their use in athletic activity. Classifications for exercises that help wheelchair athletes have been provided by BlazeSports America (2004). This organization received support from the U.S. Paralympics to complete a training manual. The manual is used to identify and inform classifications of athletes living with challenges.

Athletes With an Amputation

An athlete with an amputation is at risk of developing skin irritations. However, many athletes have found that the use of appropriate equipment and resources, such as padding, can help reduce the friction that comes with wearing a prosthetic. High-impact products that reduce friction make participation in sports much more likely and safe (see Figures 11.4 and 11.5). Other materials that eliminate friction are silicone liners that cover irritated areas. These liners are extremely useful in helping the athlete compete and perform skills and physical feats much more safely.

Athletes With Cerebral Palsy

Seizures are relatively frequent in individuals with cerebral palsy. When an individual participates in any type of physical activity, an increase in lactic acid is likely, especially if the activity is considered an aerobic sport. Lactic acid lowers the pH levels in our bodies and ultimately leads to lowered risk for seizures (Richter, 1989; Richter, Gaebler-Spira, & Mushett, 1996; Richeter, Sherrill, McCann, Mushett, & Kaschalk, 1998). As we see in Figure 11.6, athletes living with cerebral palsy who also use wheelchairs in their sports are much more likely to incur injuries related to the shoulder and upper body extremities (Ferrara & Buckley, 1996; Ferrara & Davis, 1990; Ferrara, Buckley, & McCann, 1992; Ferrara, Buckley, & Messner, 1992; Ferrara, Palutsis, & Snouse, 2000).

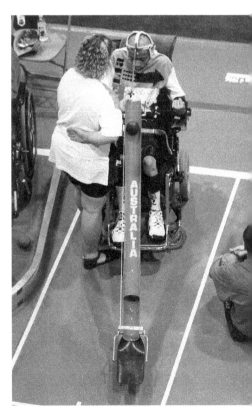

FIGURE 11.6   *Boccia, a sport designed specifically for people with disabilities.*

Athletes With Visual Impairment

Visual impairment in athletes can lead to injuries such as running into walls and other surfaces, as well as conditions that athletes living without visual impairments do not typically encounter. On July 3, 2018, a group of athletes with visual impairments set out to change the way Americans view blindness and other impairments. Six athletes living with visual impairments, also part of a group known as Team Sea to See, an organization made up of people who are blind or visually impaired, decided to participate in the 2018 sporting event known as Race Across America. This nationally and highly visible event involves participants engaged in a cycling route that goes from the Pacific to the Atlantic in less than 9 days.

In fact, the U.S. Paralympic team has focused exclusively on introducing more athletes with visual impairments to other sports, such as cross-country skiing and biathlon. And their efforts are working. As of this writing, sports involving athletes with visual impairments are increasing at rapid rates, which is a positive sign of the support that the U.S. Paralympics Committee has dedicated to this group of athletes (see Figure 11.7).

As illustrated in Figure 11.7, we find that many sporting activities that require visual cues allow guide runners. These guides are specifically there to aid athletes with visual impairments. It is interesting to discover that athletes with visual disabilities expend more energy during the sport, but the extra effort is not due to a "lack of visual cues," but it is related to the fact that the athlete has to rely on his or her other perceptual processes and skills that often result in overuse (BlazeSports America, 2004). The human body expends extra energy when one has to live with visual challenges and disabilities. We learn from research that "visual impairments also lead to fatigue and the potential injuries all related to overuse" (BlazeSports America, 2004). Figures 11.8 and 11.9 illustrate visually impaired athletes with helpers who are competing in the Olympic Games.

Athletes With Mental Challenges and Impairments

Research on the topic of mental health and living with mental challenges reveals that individuals from all walks of life are likely to have some experiences with suffering from some sort of mental illness. In fact, research conducted in 2015 by the National Institute of Mental Health shows that close to 44 million Americans report having some type of mental illness. Medical research takes this statistic and suggests that, while not measured or heavily

FIGURE 11.7   William Groulx, U.S. wheelchair rugby captain, holds the ball as members of the British team try to take it during the 2012 Paralympic Games in London, September 5, 2012.

FIGURE 11.8   Visually impaired track athlete Gerrard Gosens sprints with his guide/lead runner during a race at the 2000 Sydney Paralympic Games.

FIGURE 11.9   *Visually impaired athletes competing in the Olympic stadium.*

researched, athletes may be at a greater risk for experiencing some type of mental illness. Recall in Chapter 10 that we discussed the mental effects that the transition from an active career in sports to the new phase of life known as retirement have on some athletes. In addition to retirement, athletes who suffer from injuries, competitive losses, and/or overtraining are also at risk for some type of mental psychological distress. The NCAA conducted a survey of student-athletes and discovered that over 30% of all student-athletes stated that at some point in their college experience they felt depressed and reported being extremely anxious all of the time.

A search of the literature on mental illness revealed a surprising fact: many issues related to mental health start early in a young athlete's career. Why? Careful study revealed several risk factors that lead to issues with mental health. Scholars have divided the risk factors into two broad categories: intrinsic and extrinsic. Intrinsic risk factors are those elements related to athletic identity (which we discussed in Chapter 10) and identity related to self-worth, self-confidence, and self-esteem. All of these intrinsic factors are almost always related and connected to sports performance. For example, an athlete who is consistently successful from one event to another over a span of years will develop what has been termed a perfectionist personality. Perfectionist personalities constantly seek top performance not only during a competitive sporting event but also when they train.

External risk factors are those influences in an athlete's environment. As mentioned in several chapters in this book, family members, friends, parents, and coaches play a vital role in the development of a young athlete's overall health and well-being. When parents put intense pressure on a young athlete to perform, this pressure leads to negative stress and a decreased interest in competing in a sport. When parents offer negative verbal comments pre- or post-sporting event, it is likely that the young athlete will experience stress and burnout. And as we mentioned in Chapter 10, research

FIGURE 11.10   *Jon Stocklosa, an Elite weightlifter with Down syndrome.*

shows that adolescent athletes tend to report higher levels of emotional harm and negative experiences when their coaches yell, shout, or make negative comments about their athletic performance to manipulate and intimidate.

In terms of mental impairments, we know that Down syndrome is unique because it refers to cognitive and physical symptoms that have resulted from an extra copy of a chromosome. In Chapter 3, we discussed gender and the combination of XX and XY. Down syndrome is tangentially related because the extra chromosome leads to a mild to moderate disability in terms of intellect. "The degree of intellectual disability in people with Down syndrome varies and we know from research that typically children with Down syndrome frequently are delayed in reaching key developmental milestones when compared to other children" (BlazeSports America, 2004).

Jon Stocklosa, an elite athlete with Down syndrome, pictured in Figure 11.10, started competing in weightlifting competitions since 1999. Competing with able-bodied weight lifting elite athletes allows Jon and other athletes with Down syndrome to address and perhaps change attitudes and educate others about people with Down syndrome.

Mental Challenges and Athletic Competition

Mental impairments are not as readily noticeable as other impairments, which can include physical markers such as flattened faces and noses, short necks, eyes that slant upward, and a type of fold stemming from the upper eyelid that spreads to the inner corner of the eyes. Because of their physical appearance, athletes with Down syndrome tend to have features that make this disability one of the most recognized forms of physical and mental challenges (BlazeSports America, 2004). In 2014, sports media introduced us to an adult male athlete living with Down syndrome and told the story of how he overcame certain odds to ultimately become a champion weight lifter. Jon Stoklosa is a 35-year-old old male athlete who not only competes in the Special Olympics but also competes in sports with nondisabled opponents. In 2012, CNN broadcasted a story about a young athlete with

Down syndrome who plays high school football and basketball. Despite the fact that his teammates, coaches, and fellow students welcomed him with open arms, it was the Michigan High School Athletic League that said 19-year-old Eric Dompierre was not allowed to play during his senior year. Because of his Down syndrome, Eric was detained in kindergarten, which ultimately caused him to be a year behind the average high school senior. And in 2017, sports media offered a very low-key story about a man who became the first climber athlete with Down syndrome to conquer the Grand Tetons. It was August 18, 2017, when Bob Harris reached the top of the mountain, which measures approximately 13,776 feet above Jackson Hole, Wyoming.

Athletes With Multiple Sclerosis

In 2011, a young male race car driver became the youngest person to win the NASCAR Daytona 500. What makes this story even more exceptional is that Trevor Bayne was diagnosed earlier in the year with multiple sclerosis (MS). Then in 2012, a professional hockey player in the NHL announced that he had also been diagnosed with MS. As of this writing, Joshua Harding has achieved recognition for being the highest leading goal in the NHL. MS affects an individual's physical, mental, and emotional well-being, so much so that it can cause issues with vision, imbalance, depression, numbness, and extreme fatigue. Some individuals living with MS also experience a numbness or tingling in their extremities.

For athletes living with MS, the one sport that has been identified as a therapeutic sport is swimming. Because of the relatively cool water temperatures of most swimming pools, the water tends to cool the athlete's muscles and eventually prevents an increase in body core temperature.

Athletes and Diabetes

When we partake in exercise and in sports, the activity lowers blood sugar levels for anywhere from 24 to 48 hours after the activity concludes. When blood sugar levels reach more than 250 milligrams, individuals participating in physical activities may experience hyperglycemia. An athlete who has diabetes is vulnerable to injuries and illnesses, particularly if the activity is performed in excessive heat. Diabetic athletes always carry products with them, such as glucose and medical response information, to alert first responders of their condition if something should happen while they are exercising.

Obesity

Obesity is prevalent in American society. When we visit our primary physicians, we are often categorized in one of four categories according to our weight. The four classifications are often based on our body mass index (BMI), or the amount of body fat in relationship to height and weight. Today, research shows that the average American consumes two-thirds over the recommended daily allowance of fats and grain. Research commissioned by the World Health Organization (2016) recorded rises in profits by fast food restaurants and recommended strategies to address critical stages in childhood that help tackle childhood obesity.

Issues in Sports and Ableism

Oscar Pistorius, the first double-leg amputee, competed in the 2012 Summer Olympics and the 2012 Paralympics. Pistorius finished in second place, beating several able-bodied track opponents. The 2012 Olympics allowed us to see many athletes living with physical and mental challenges compete in both the Summer Olympics Games and the Paralympics competition. We saw athletes in sporting events such as archery, table tennis, swimming, and equestrian. Consequently, with technology continually advancing, especially regarding prosthetics and orthotics, it should be no surprise if we start seeing athletes living with physical challenges begin dominating a sport or two.

One issue that has been raised over the last few years is whether technological advances enable persons living with physical challenges unique advantages over able-bodied athletes. For professional athletes involved in the sport of racing, wheelchairs, for example, are extremely customized. For example, the spokes in the wheels often consist of aluminum, a metal that provides narrow profiles. The aluminum spokes ultimately reduce the aerodynamics and allow athletes participating in races to position their chairs in such a way that they are able to manipulate the spokes. This means that when the athlete is racing downhill or on flat terrains, athletes in wheelchairs are able to coast and ultimately recover and conserve energy levels. For able-bodied racers, the benefit of coasting downhill is not possible. Able-bodied runners, when racing downhill, must expend inordinate amounts of energy even on flat terrain. However, it should be noted that the previous section does not mean, nor should you conclude, that the point is to communicate the idea that using a wheelchair in a race is unfair. That is not the case. The point is that athletes who use wheelchairs in races must carefully negotiate roads and surfaces that able-bodied runners do not even have to consider. These features alone make racing particularly tricky for athletes in wheelchairs. Tricky roads and races that take place on hard pavement have fewer curves and are less crowded. These features, according to research, cause athletes racing in wheelchairs to have to adjust to the curvature of the road, and that alone makes the athlete work harder to avoid the curb. To avoid the curb, athletes in wheelchairs must use energy to correct their chairs, and they have to expend energy that puts a strain on their arms and shoulders. Then there is the issue of uneven or poorly maintained road surfaces as depicted in Figures 11.11 and 11.12. The conditions of the races, including thousands of runners in addition to hills and unkept roads, can cause problems for athletes in wheelchairs—problems that are greater

FIGURE 11.11   *David Bizet, Marathon de Paris 2014.*

FIGURE 11.12   *Athletes at the start of a 10-mile race showing the condition of the roads.*

for them than for able-bodied runners. The major challenge of roads that are poorly maintained (e.g., potholes) presents athletes in wheelchairs with the possibility of injury. Keeping this in mind, remember that even though wheelchair competitors may gain a slight advantage when racing on downhill courses, increases in their speed on these downhill routes does not make up for or allow extra time when having to go uphill.

The Role of Mass Media and Sports Media Coverage

We know from published research that active participation in sports by persons living with disabilities is important in terms of enhancement of self-esteem, overall life satisfaction, and health and well-being. Research also shows that athletes with disabilities have much higher self-esteem and tend to fill leadership positions in the sports industry at much greater rates than those people living with physical and mental disabilities who are not active in sports.

We know that mass media has tremendous influence in shaping public attitudes and ideas about an event. We also know that mass media has significant influence in social constructions of reality (refer to Chapter 2 of this text). In terms of language used in media stories, activists have offered tips on how to write about able-bodied athletes and athletes with disabilities in their media messages. Workshops that educate journalists on the language to use also include tabloid media and other vehicles responsible for distributing messages to consumers. Studies from 1988 until 2008 have shown problems with respect to language when sports journalists cover the Olympics and Paralympics. What is needed is more research that analyzes coverage and the various ways that sports media frame athletes with disabilities. Equally important and vital is the need for a study analyzing coverage of the Paralympics.

Research using agenda-setting theory has obtained data showing that readers of the *New York Times* reported having different ideas about what they perceived to be the most important problems facing our country. For agenda-setting theorists, Iyengar and Kinder (1987), these systematic discrepancies prove that uninformed readers are vulnerable and incredibly sensitive to frames and peripheral cues and heuristics contained in a media story. These frames and cues send unintended coverage messages about the level of importance associated with events, issues, and problems in our culture. From an agenda-setting perspective, this finding expects to show the effects of media's agenda-setting influence among uneducated, uninformed readers.

Given the important role that our American media play in the social construction and transmission of ideas and stereotypes transmitted to media consumers, it is imperative that scholars start examining how news and other media frame and cover the Paralympics. Studies that focus on frames found in media can also compare frames with other media coverage. Studies in this area furnish much-needed information that allows closer examination and a better understanding of how media represent athletes living with disabilities when compare to able-bodied athletes.

The Media and Stereotypes

Goffman (1963) noted that the difference between healthy and stigmatized persons is a simple question of perspective, not reality. Research supports the idea that stereotypes of mental illness are created based on selective perceptions that people use to predict, control, and understand events in the world (Byrne, 1997; Philo, 1996; Townsend, 1979). Stereotypes exaggerate differences between groups ("them and us") so that individuals blur perceived and real differences within out-groups (Townsend, 1979). Common knowledge about stereotypes tells us that they help us integrate new incoming information as well as help us control and understand events in our environment. Therefore, what we know is that stereotypes make it easier for people to dismiss conflicting information, or they simply create subcategories, keeping original stereotyped exaggerations about a group of people in place. We also know that mass media actually reinforce and perpetuate stereotypes and depictions. The media perpetuate stigmas/stereotypes, giving the public narrow frame-focused, mediated messages, images, and stories based on these stigmas and stereotypes. We hope that information presented in this chapter encourages many to create healthy campaigns and write and produce more media messages aimed at challenging and replacing current ill-informed stereotypes about mental illness.

Mental Illness

As mentioned previously, people living with mental challenges are stigmatized because they are often saddled with stereotypes of being violent and/or crazy (Hazelton, 1997; Pirkis & Francis, 2012). Mental illness specifically has become so stereotyped in news and entertainment that the average individual finds it hard to delineate and distinguish the reality of mental illness from caricatured media images (Beveridge, 1996; Hodgkinson, 1986; Wilson, Nairn, Coverdale, & Panapa, 2000). Take, for example, popular movies such as *Psycho* and *One Flew Over the Cuckoo's Nest*. These movies, it can be argued, might communicate stereotypes and beliefs to the American culture against mental illness that encourages individuals to group people with such conditions under two stereotypical labels: dangerous or pitiful. Not all people who suffer from mental conditions are as uncontrollably dangerous, pitiful, or sick as media may lead others to believe. Nevertheless, people living with mental illnesses are considered a burden on the nondisabled portion of American society, giving rise to feelings of prejudice, resentment, and blame toward others perceived as or known to be mentally ill.

We know that media perpetuates ideas about people, groups, or things. From depictions in entertainment media, news, magazines, commercials, and sports media, we also know that it is the media that is responsible for perpetuating myths about mental illness. One common stereotype often found in news stories is the idea that mental illness is equated with mass tragedies and violence. Studies have found the most common depiction of mental illness in media is one involving a tragic crime (Donaldson, 1981). However, media-related research shows that in terms of likelihood to be a victim of a violent crime, persons living with mental illness are much more likely to be victims of violent and tragic crime than the perpetrators of a crime (Wolfe, 1996). In fact, it is common for major news media to report that in cases of tragic crime, the alleged shooter's motivation for the crime is often said to be due to a mental illness. Yet we know from research that mental illness alone does not predict violent behavior (Elbogen & Johnson, 2009).

Representations of mental illness in major media are also used as a strategy for comedic relief. We often find situations where the audience is laughing at, rather than laughing with, characters who are dealing with mental illnesses on a program (Byrne, 1997). Hyler, Gabbard, and Schneider (1991) have conducted several studies of films produced in Hollywood where people with mental illnesses are depicted as "over-privileged, oversexed narcissistic parasites." When people with mental illness do appear in media, they are the butt of many jokes and treated as outsiders (Donaldson, 1981). Donaldson's early work (1981) shows that not one character with a mental or physical illness appeared on television in a major role. Instead, the research shows that individuals with disabilities tend to be portrayed as pitiful, inspirational, or threats to society and in other extremely negative roles, especially when the individuals appear in roles juxtaposed with other characters. None were visible, thus reinforcing the "invisible minority" characterization (Nelson, 1996). Research, therefore, concludes, that persons with mental illness are often shown in extremely negative roles, as threats to society, or as an inspiration (Byrne, 1997; de Balcazar, Bradford, & Fawcett, 1998; Donaldson, 1981; Hyler, Gabbard, & Schneider, 1991).

Higgins (1992) argues that news media tend to frame people with disabilities in stories and images actively. The Higgins (1992) study discovered that news stories that feature people with disabilities tend to present this group in soft or what they call feature stories. For example, research shows that stories with references to persons with disabilities tend to be about people with mental retardation or individuals associated with labels such as "handicapped" or "disabled." According to de Balcazar, Bradford, and Fawcett (1998), media tend to frame stories involving persons with disabilities negatively and unrealistically, often relying on the sensational news or pitiful frames with emotionally laden language and accounts that describe disabilities in stereotypical ways. Terms such as "a victim of," "suffers from," and "confined to" are found to frame individuals with these illnesses under a stigmatizing light (Keller, Hallahan, McShane, Crowley, & Blandford, 1990).

Research does find that mental illness is rarely covered, and when it is, the lines are blurred, treating all mental illness as if it is violent. Media messages also appear to suggest that healing from mental illness is achievable, further enhancing the stereotype and stigma that the mentally ill are simply being held back because of public policy and American society's failing mental health system. Past studies have shown a history of media stereotyping and stigmatizing the mentally ill and assuming violence and crime to be correlated to mental illness (Byrne, 1997; de Balcazar, Bradford, & Fawcett, 1998; Donaldson, 1981; Higgins, 1992; Hyler, Gabbard, & Schnceider, 1991). Clarification on how media frames issues surrounding mental illness is vitally important if we want to see improvement in this area. Mental Illness in the News and Information Media conducted an interesting study in 2012 designed to examine media depictions of mental illness and the effects of those depictions on consumer attitudes and behavior (Dietrich, Heider, Matschinger, & Angermeyer, 2006; Francis, Pirkis, Dunt, & Blood, 2001; Hazelton, 1997; Pirkis & Francis, 2012). Research obtained in the study indicates that in terms of obtaining vital information on mental illness, people look to mass media for information to educate themselves about causes and symptoms associated with conditions related to the mental health of individuals. In addition, we find research that shows that for Americans, those living with and without mental illness, the media play a significant role in learning more about mental illness in our culture.

When media frequently depict inaccurate images of and messages about mental illness (e.g., making illusory correlations that lead readers to believe that mental illness and extreme violent behavior are associated), we find an unintentional promotion of stereotypes and stigmas concerning mental illness. In fact, if we survey the recent tragedies involving mass shootings, we find that the events are oftentimes explained in terms of mental illness and access to guns. But what is missing in the news stories is the fact that close to 90% of the violent crimes committed are by White men. And according to recent statistics, approximately 9.8 million Americans, close to 4.0% of our population, experience at some point in time a mental illness that will ultimately interfere with their ability to perform major life activities (Dietrich, Heider, Matschinger, & Angermeyer, 2006; Francis, Pirkis, Dunt, & Blood, 2001; Gordon, 2017; Hazelton, 1997; Pirkis & Francis, 2012). The point here is that mental illness affects every individual regardless of ethnicity, gender, sexual orientation, race, or socioeconomic class.

In terms of media portrayals, research reveals that mental illness and associated misconceptions actually influence individuals to withhold any indication that they may be experiencing issues related to their mental health. Recall that we discussed mental health and the effects of participation in sports. If we consider all the information presented, we find that taken together, studies on the framing of mental illness in the media show that media immortalizes and bolsters several notions about the able-bodied and the disabled. Research on uses and gratifications of media consistently shows that many people in our culture specifically seek out information on mental illness from mass media (Wahl, 1992). The effects of the depictions, research suggests, leads the average American to fear, avoid, and discriminate against people who are living with challenges because of mental illness.

Media Depictions of Paralympic Athletes

According to de Balcazar, Bradford, and Fawcett (1998), media tend to frame stories involving persons with disabilities negatively and unrealistically, often relying on the "sensational news" or "pitiful" frames, which depend on emotionally laden language and accounts that describe disabilities in stereotypical ways. Terms such as "a victim of," "suffers from," and "confined to" are found to frame individuals with these illnesses under a stigmatizing light (Keller, Hallahan, McShane, Crowley, & Blandford, 1990). When not directly related to crime and violence—and the absence is most often seen in stories involving children with mental illness—news stories present individuals with mental illness in soft or what they call feature stories.

Media narratives that present an athlete living with physical challenges as the hero or superman/ woman are often associated with successful athletes living with physical challenges. It appears that the media tend to focus on those athletes in particular who are successful. The reward for these athletes is relatively intense media coverage and exposure. The problem is that those athletes with physical challenges who do win but do not receive similar media hype will often become marginalized simply because of their disabilities. As stated previously, media tend to publish stories where the disabled are depicted as individuals who have overcome a deficit by participating in sports that show their "miraculous, heroic abilities." The messages media seem to convey often attempt to evoke emotions from Americans using inspirational stories of the disabled athlete.

Identity Construction and Able-Bodies

In American culture, participation in a sport is one way for young boys to develop and socially construct a gender identity. We learned in previous chapters that masculinity and ideas of what it means to be a main are established when young boys enjoy relationships with other males. It has been argued that participation in "hyper-masculine sports provides a venue for adult men living with physical impairments to create notions of their ideas of hegemonic masculinity" (Smith, Wedgwood, Llewellyn, & Shuttleworth, 2015, p. 69).

Despite masculinity being a significant focus in research on sport and physical impairment, few studies could be identified that focused on understanding how gender identity is developed through sport for people with intellectual disabilities. It is important to distinguish whether people living with intellectual disabilities experience and negotiate contradictions in our culture. Future research also needs to investigate the development of intellectual disabilities and their relationship with broader theories of masculinity.

For people with intellectual disabilities, media and research can be found that frequently asserts a "relationship between participation in sport and increased social connection, interactions, and acceptance" Now the next challenge for sports media is to attain funding to help create sporting environments that are supportive in working with young athletes' various intellectual disabilities.

Media Portrayals of People With Physical Disabilities

Research tells us that stereotyping is a mental heuristic that all people use in order to understand the world around us. In terms of individuals living with physical disabilities, we know that when people with disabilities are depicted in media, they are frequently portrayed as remarkable, heroic, or dependent victims It is frequently documented that media often present people living with physical disabilities as "individuals are viewed as the objects of pity and depicted as having the same attributes and characteristics no matter what the disability may be" (see Smith, Wegwood, Llewellyn, & Shuttleworth, 2015). Similarly, according to Media and Disability's website, when people living with disabilities are portrayed in media, the representations continue to imply that these are people who are either heroic, violent, or helpless. In terms of the actual people playing roles of characters with disabilities, we find that able-bodied actors often fill these roles. Further, we notice the use of a prop like a wheelchair, which allows consumers to immediately conclude that the actor is the one who is disabled (e.g., James Cameron's *Avatar*).

The victim is a commonly presented as a stereotypical person with physical challenges in that most media depict the individual as someone who is often in situations that make him or her helpless or the object of sympathy or pity. Research has determined that the message that tends to come across in media portrayals is one that draws on our preconceptions of disability, and as a result, it primes attitudes of fear among those exposed to the images. Not only is fear an outcome of exposure but also ignorance of physical disabilities is likely. In other words, producers who are intent on including depictions of persons with physical disabilities know that when they portray a character with a missing leg or a disfigured head and face (e.g., the Elephant Man), these depictions are created mainly to elicit specific feelings from the audience or reader. Consider the 1998 hit movie *Simon Birch* about a 12-year-old boy named Joe Wenteworth and his best friend Simon Birch, who was born with dwarfism. Simon is so small that even at age 12, he can still play the infant Jesus in the church Christmas pageant. The victim stereotype is often used in comedies as well. For example, the character's disability is used to provide humor in a given situation. A perfect illustration of this type of portrayal may be found in the hit movie *Forrest Gump*. Forrest Gump's character was clearly one who might be said to have some sort of intellectual disability. But in this case, the disability was used in ways that allowed the audience opportunities to laugh or chuckle. However, some people living with certain challenges make a career bringing awareness of their physical or mental challenge to others. Although not a comedic film, the 2001 biographical film *A Beautiful Mind* was about economics professor John Nash who won a Nobel Memorial Prize for his work on game theory. This real-life depiction of Nash's personal life story included his struggle with paranoid schizophrenia. From a scholarly and critical perspective, the depiction of the struggles that one goes through when suffering with paranoid schizophrenia received praise and much attention for the fact that the portrayal was a factual and accurate depiction.

Case in point: Josh Blue is an American comedian who won *Last Comic Standing* on NBC in 2006. Josh Blue has cerebral palsy and uses this in what has been described as self-deprecating humor, as many of his jokes center on living with his disability, how he deals with it, and how other people view him. Blue appeared on *Last Comic Standing* so that he could "make people aware of the fact that people with disabilities can make an impact" (Blue, 2009). As a part of his comedic routine, Blue coined the term "palsy punch." It was during his final set on the final show when Blue said that the term "palsy punch" helped to describe a move he found useful in a fight because, according to Blue (2009), they [people] don't know where the punch is coming from, and second of all, he said neither does he (*Last Comic Standing*, Blue, 2006).

Then there is the hero depiction. The hero is a portrayal of a person living with a disability who is seen proving his or her worth by overcoming limitations related to the disability. The term coined for this depiction is known as the "supercrip." Supercrips are individuals who are able to conform and integrate into the larger society, but they do so because they overcome their disabilities and appear normal. An example of a mass media portrayal of the "supercrip" that accurately shows this description is in the top-grossing moving titled *My Left Foot*. Other examples of this stereotype are superhero characters such as Daredevil, who is blinded by a radioactive substance, a substance that amplifies the remaining senses beyond average human abilities. The radioactive substance ultimate gives Daredevil extreme radar-like senses. This ability makes Daredevil reach superhuman levels. Depictions of disabled people with superhuman abilities are not only represented in movies but also found in video games such as *Mortal Kombat*, where a blind fighter is supernaturally gifted.

While some may argue that the "supercrip" hero is a more positive stereotype than the victim, we must understand some of the issues related to this positive stereotype. The stereotype of the supercrip sends a message that the individual "succeeds" in overcoming a disability as opposed to those left to live normal, day-to-day lives. These images also seem to show that living with a physical disability is something that an individual must overcome to be "normal" and gain acceptance and respect in our culture. One effect of exposure to this type of stereotype is the fact that research shows that audiences tend to feel better about the person being depicted who lives with a physical challenge. These stereotypes regarding persons living with physical disabilities also make audiences feel that these individuals do not have to adjust to the living conditions that other people living with disabilities are faced with. Instead, the supercrip depiction reinforces an idea that disabilities are easily overcome when one tries hard enough.

Another common stereotype for this group in media is referred to as the villain. As mentioned briefly in previous sections of this chapter, we know that physical and mental disabilities are often used to depict evil people. These images often portray a character's depravity. Consider the images contained in the movie *Pirates of the Caribbean*. We find that many of the images of the pirates are those that show them missing limbs, eyes, and legs.

Six Forms of Ableism We Need to Retire Immediately

As mentioned in the introduction, ableism extends beyond intentional or unintentional perceptions related to how we recognize disability and disabled people. Ableism in our culture is associated with the idea that a disability can be corrected, overcome, or fixed. Subtle implications of the stereotypes as mentioned previously often imply that an individual living with a disability simply just has "a defect rather than a dimension of difference" (Smith, Foley, & Chaney, 2011, p. 305). The tendency to feel that disability is more of a defect than a difference is at the main core of American ableist attitudes and behaviors. And one consequence of this is that it causes people living with disabilities to feel discriminated against and marginalized, and, ultimately, as if they are of little to no value in American society.

On the website www.everdayfeminism.com, six common forms of ableism were identified that, although mostly normalized, need to be eliminated (Zeilinger, 2015). From this website, one learns that more accommodations can be made than just adding a ramp for people who use wheelchairs. For example, the website lists other accommodations, such as including braille on signs, allowing seeing-eye dogs and assistant dogs to have access to areas inside buildings that are welcoming, and having note takers and recording devices.

Ableist language has become undeniably a part of our English language. For example, it is relatively common for the average American to use words such as "crazy," "bat-stupid crazy," "psycho," "insane," or "retarded" without giving it a second thought. And to make matters worse, many users of these and other words will adamantly defend their use, becoming upset with those who may question their freedom and right to use words that they feel are okay. Some people might argue that opposition to these words is just too "politically correct" or that those in the group are just being too "sensitive." Recall that those opposed to changing the mascot and team names that reference indigenous people also blame the marginalized group for being too sensitive. However, one needs to recognize that this defense is not about the words in and of themselves but has more to do with what the words imply. Another covert difference between what is said and how it is said is the feeling and emotion the speaker exhibits toward the individuals these terms represent. In our culture, the language we use can be full of ethnophaulisms or pejorative metaphors about a group of people. Thus in American culture, we are more likely to view those individuals in a demoralizing, devalued way. And, more importantly, excessive exposure to the stereotyped depictions in media concerning people living with physical and mental challenges result in the idea that this group should not have, nor are they entitled to, resources and programs that will provide them with quality mental health care, opportunities for employment, resources to gain quality education, and, more importantly, integration and inclusion as normal, regular people.

Able-bodied individuals fail to recognize the privileges they have, privileges that allow them to acquire access into any space available. Just as we highlighted in an earlier chapter of this text, privilege is a concept that is difficult for those who experience it to fathom. Many of us may not intentionally and directly engage in discriminatory actions toward those people living with disabilities. But we do discriminate when we use the resources that have been specifically allocated for their use. For example, many able-bodied people use handicapped bathroom stalls, or if in a hurry, or are able to park in the handicapped parking spots. Able-bodied individuals often use handicapped stalls and the other preceding behaviors because they can and often times engage in these behaviors without a second thought. While deciding to take the stairs when the elevator is crowded is not a product of one's ill will toward the disabled, it is evidence of how abled-body individuals use their privileges to be able to enjoy alternatives that people living with physical challenges are not.

Automatically helping people living with physical challenges without asking is one of the most common ableist ideas. Many people who use a wheelchair do not want us to assume that they need a door held when approaching it. Several people have asked that people wait for a person with a disability to ask for help or speak up. As one person living with a handicap said, "Just know, we know how to ask for help, and you just need to wait for us to speak up" (Welker, July 9, 2004).

Able-bodied people express curiosity and interest for those persons who are living with disabilities to talk about and provide details on how they live in their bodies and how they happened to become disabled. Regardless, these conversations are inappropriate, unfair, and insulting. This type of conversation is known to frequently occur among young children. When a 3-year-old dancer with a prosthetic arm takes a dance class, and all the students stare, parents often ask the teacher to allow the child to talk about what happened to his or her arm. It is presumed that answers will immediately accentuate the need for tolerance and accepting difference. But if we are honest as a culture, we inadvertently teach our children that this is just another way for them to learn that they are privileged and entitled, and that they should demand that others who are not able-bodied explain and justify their differences.

We often assume that disability is always visible. This is no doubt one of the biggest mistakes in our schemas. We often forget that people who are living with mental challenges may have no outward sign or characteristic that allows us to identify his or her mental illness. In American culture, there seems to be an embedded and pervasive stigma that mental illness leads to forced institutionalization and extreme and radical medication. And it is possible that ideas delivered in media may result in a lack of concern for quality medical care for illnesses related to mental health. We must also keep in mind that mental illness is not the only disability that is not readily apparent. We must remember those who struggle with learning disabilities and disabilities related to developmental growth may also be dealing with chronic illnesses that can be categorized as a disability. One consequence of frequent portrayals of other "more common" physical and mental challenges may be the denial of treatment and resources needed because they are not predominately recognized.

Reflect on Sports: Ableism and Sports

In recent news, Kylie Jenner was branded as an "ableist" when she appeared in a wheelchair in a magazine ad. The magazine that featured the image received media scrutiny, and several readers were outraged over the gold wheelchair that is used as a prop in many of the photos. And that is not all.

Jenner is portrayed in the ad posing in a wheelchair wearing S&M-type clothing and accessories. She appears to look as if she was a store mannequin, as she is seen staring off into space, frozen. Another photo in the advertising campaign shows her in a sexualized pose and raising her leg provocatively.

Angry readers took to social media as well as disability advocates posting that they believe that the images are offensive. For some, it was unfortunate to think that advertisers felt that they had to rely on the overused idea that being in a wheelchair is limiting. For many wheelchair users, life in a wheelchair is empowering and allows them to live full, satisfied lives. Many advocates for people with disabilities see this advertising campaign as a message that adds to previous messages in which this group is often seen as powerless. However, the magazine that ran the images, *Interview*, says the pictures were intended to play with ideas of power and subjectivity, and that it was not intended to be offensive.

When media select a nondisabled person to pose in a wheelchair as a provocative fashion prop, this depiction will without a doubt offend many who live with wheelchairs. It is a rare moment when media use authentic and aspirational reflections of people who live with physical and mental challenges. For advocates, if media would like to challenge assumptions about disability, particularly about sex and disability, they must use real-life depictions and experiences from those who live day to day with these challenges.

Challenge Magazine is a publication of Disabled Sports USA (http://www.disabledsportsusa.org/about/news/challenge-magazine/). The magazine serves as a resource that provides adaptive sports information to adults and children living with disabilities. The publication also seeks to include individuals who are "visually impaired, paraplegic and quadriplegic." According to their website, they also serve people who have MS, head injuries, cerebral palsy, autism, and other related intellectual disabilities (Disabled Sports of America, 2018).

Conclusion

In this chapter, we learned that the term "ableism" is used to describe the treatment of and discrimination leveled against individuals living with mental health and physical disabilities. Ableism prevents people in this group from full participation in employment, housing, recreation, and sports. While the concept of age has been described here and in Chapter 10 in this textbook as a multidimensional concept, we are learning that athletes with disabilities are a rapidly rising group of individuals who find themselves challenging American culture's system of old beliefs about how an athlete should look. We find that each year, increasing opportunities avail themselves, making sports and physical activity more accessible to young children, adolescents, and adults who are living with disabilities. We also learned in this chapter that benefits involved in active participation in sports and physical activity are numerous and outweigh negatives. In addition, we learned that with proper care and precautions, many, if not most, people with physical and mental disabilities can safely pursue active sporting lifestyles in American culture.

QUESTIONS FOR REFLECTION AND DISCUSSION

1. Define ableism and think of how it is reflected in your life.
2. What are the stereotypes commonly found in media portrayals of persons living with physical and mental challenges?
3. Can you identify the classifications for specific physical challenges?
4. What are the forms of ableism that need to be removed from our language?
5. What is an intellectual disability, and how is that represented in the media?
6. Why is our culture considered an ableist society?

SUGGESTED ACTIVITIES

1. Find time to do some journaling. The purpose of this activity is for you to reflect on the following questions: How has American culture and/or subcultures reaction to persons living with disabilities affected others around them? For 1 week, 7 full days, make observations of

people (yes, engage in people watching) while thinking of this statement. Write a reaction paper of your observations.

2. Sometimes the media influences us to believe that some things are barriers for groups, but in reality, we find out that there is a clear misrepresentation of those barriers. Take a moment to think outside of the box and come up with a list of solutions that sports media might use to dissolve the inaccurate perception of the barriers faced by persons living with disabilities.

3. Watch a week's worth of television. Be sure to watch at various times during the day. How many images or depictions did you find that were of persons living with physical or mental challenges? What other observations did you make?

4. Identify a barrier you once thought would hinder participation in sports but later found that this turned out to be an inaccurate depiction. If you are unable to think of a barrier(s), consider the reasons why you never thought about barriers related to disabilities and participation in sports. What creative solutions were identified that helped to change your perception? Write a brief paper identifying the elements that compelled you to identify the barriers and what it was that led you to change your thoughts?

5. Think of the classroom, lecture hall, or college you attend. Do you notice barriers that prevent people with disabilities from being able to participate in the course fully? What are those barriers? Refer to your list of barriers and describe in detail the ones that might offer creative solutions so that those barriers no longer exist.

6. Conduct research on your community's readiness to assist people who live with physical and mental challenges during natural disasters. Is there a plan for protecting this group? Write a news story that chronicles your research and findings?

7. Write a news story on the paratransportation system available for persons living with physical disabilities in your community. Include interviews with relevant experts, sources, and others who can help educate readers on this experience for people who identify with this group.

8. Write a news story that normalizes people living with depression, manic disorders, and bipolar disorders. Many people, more often than not, struggle with these challenges, yet they are all stigmatized. How can you change the perception of these perceptions?

9. As part of the information provided in a disability workshop for adults, we found the following quotes by Robert M. Hensel, a wheelchair athlete who happens to also hold the Guinness World Record for longest nonstop wheelie in a wheelchair. Hensel, an athlete born with spina bifida wrote a serious of quotes used to motivate and inspire. Go to the website https://www.uua.org/accessibility/aim/workshops/adults-youth/ableism (last accessed July 14, 2018) and review the quotes provided. Next, write a reaction paper on the sentiments expressed by Hensel in the quotes. How should journalists cover an athlete who accomplishes feats such as Robert Hensel did? Remember the discussion on stereotypical portrayals, such as the supercrip, victim, hero, and villain. How would you write a story that does not reflect the common stereotypes used for this group? Provide a copy of your magazine or news story.

10. Study the handout titled "Attitudinal Barriers" and ask yourself if you have observed any of these barriers. Next, determine how you should act the next time you see the barrier. Write a summary of your observations.

11. Victim blaming seems to occur when a member is part of a historically marginalized group. One of the most extreme examples is evident in media stories about rape. More times than not, a victim engages in self-blame and that he/she allowed the event to happen. We find this self-blame in medical literature as well. When diagnosed with cancer, many

survivors, according to doctors, ask the same question: "What did I do to cause this to happen to me?" People living with disabilities tend to look inward and place blame on themselves. People living with impaired vision or hearing loss often report feelings of guilt and embarrassment when they have to ask for help. Asking someone to repeat themselves or speak louder makes some individuals with disabilities internalize blame for a situation they did not cause. With this in mind, reflect on a time in your life when you blamed a failure on yourself and later realized it was not because of your own doing. Write a reaction paper about how that realization felt and what changed that allowed you to recognize where the fault lies.

DISABLED SPORT ORGANIZATIONS

The following list contains a wide variety of sports organizations that make themselves available for athletes with disabilities. Many of these sports resources act as advisors to the United States Olympic Committee. The complete list was acquired on July 15, 2018, from http://www.blazesports.org/wp-content/uploads/2011/02/BSA-Injuries-and-Medical-Issues-Manual.pdf.

United States Olympic Committee—U.S. Paralympics Division

U.S. Paralympics is the National Paralympic Committee of the United States and represents U.S. interests in the international Paralympic movement.

One Olympic Plaza

Colorado Springs, CO 80909

719-866-2030; fax: 719-866-2029

e-mail: paralympicinfo@usoc.org

Website: http://usparalympics.org/

Disabled Sports USA

DSUSA is a multisport organization providing year-round sports and recreation opportunities for people with disabilities.

e-mail: information@dsusa.org

Website: http://www.dsusa.org/

Dwarf Athletic Association of America (DAAA)

The DAAA promotes and provides quality amateur level athletic opportunities for dwarf athletes in the United States.

708 Gravenstein Hwy, North, #18 Sebastopol, CA 95472

888-598-3222

e-mail: Daaa@flash.net

Website: http://www.daaa.org/

National Wheelchair Basketball Association (NWBA)

NWBA provides oversight, development, and opportunities for basketball participation and elite competition for wheelchair athletes.

451 Hungerford Dr., Suite 100, Rockville, MD 20805

301-217-0960; fax: 301-217-0968

Website: http://www.nwba.org

United States Association of Blind Athletes (USABA)

USABA provides opportunities for sports participation and elite competition for blind/ visually impaired athletes.

33 North Institute Street

Colorado Springs, CO 80903

719-630-0422; fax: 719-630-0616

Website: http://www.usaba.org/

United States Quad Rugby Association (USQRA)

USQRA provides oversight, development, and opportunities for rugby participation and elite competition.

Website: www.quadrugby.com

USTA

USTA is the National Governing Body for tennis in the United States and provides oversight, development, and opportunities for tennis participation and elite competition.

70 West Red Oak Lane

White Plains, NY 10604

914-696-7000; fax: 914-696-7029

Website: www.usta.com

Wheelchair Sports USA (WSUSA)

WSUSA provides individuals who use wheelchairs the opportunity to participate in both recreational and competitive sports. WSUSA promotes competition at the regional, national, and international levels for athletes with permanent disabilities affecting mobility.

P.O. BOX 5266

Kendall Park, NJ 08824-5266

732-266-2634; fax: 732-355-6500

e-mail: office@wsusa.org

Website: http://www.wsusa.org/

Special Olympics International (SOI)

SOI is a year-round sports training and athletic participation organization for children and adults with mental retardation.

Washington, DC 20036-3604

202-628-3630; fax: 202-824-0200

e-mail: info@specialolympics.org

Website: http://www.specialolympics.org

USA Deaf Sports Federation (USADSF)

The USADSF (formerly American Athletic Association of the Deaf) provides organized competition for adult deaf and hearing-impaired athletes.

P.O. Box 910338, Lexington, KY 40591-0338

605-367-5760; fax: 605-782-8441

TTY: 605-367-5761

e-mail: HomeOffice@usdeafsports.org

Website: http://www.usdeafsports.org/

ADDITIONAL RESOURCES

Health and Disability Fact Books Guides and Publications, https://www.disabledworld.com/disability/publications/

Adaptive Sports: Staying Active While Living With a Disability, https://www.moveforwardpt.com/Resources/Detail/adaptive-sports-people-with-disabilities

Directory of Organizations for Athletes with Disabilities, http://www.aapmr.org/about-physiatry/about-physical-medicine-rehabilitation/patient-resources/directory-of-organizations-for-athletes-with-disabilites---listing

The Challenged Athletes Foundation List of Resources, http://www.challengedathletes.org/resources/

Resources for Increasing Physical Activity among Adults with Disabilities, https://www.cdc.gov/ncbddd/disabilityandhealth/pa.html

Team CAF Athletes, http://www.challengedathletes.org/athletes/?gclid=Cj0KCQjwvqbaBRCOARIsAD9s1XBKuqNsZT5KWJbOZsmLaVZhW81fjTOFk5mjNPYRbuln9lFU37nVu70aAmpEEALw_wcB

Enabling people of all abilities: JOIN ABLETHRIVE, https://ablethrive.com/?gclid=Cj0KCQjwvqbaBRCOARIsAD9s1XCBgxtXEh0APzGA4g4UtEE7rwqGaiUc3m7VVLjbEI0ZkOrtQVd1sOEaAlYOEALw_wcB

CREDITS

Fig. 11.1: Source: https://commons.wikimedia.org/wiki/File:Invictus_Team_U.S._Wheelchair_Rugby_Semi-Finals_160511-A-NU064-010.jpg.

Fig. 11.2: Copyright © 1989 by Don Worley, (CC BY-SA 3.0) at https://commons.wikimedia.org/wiki/File:XX0989_-_Kobe_FESPIC_Mens_Wheelchair_Basketball_Athlete_shots_-_4_of_5_-_Scan_-_Crop.jpg.

Fig. 11.3: Copyright © 2012 by ian_fromblighty, (CC BY 2.0) at https://commons.wikimedia.org/wiki/File:Hannah_Cockroft_wins_T34_100m_qualifying_heat.jpeg.

Fig. 11.4: Copyright © 2016 by Stephen B Calvert Clariosophic, (CC BY-SA 3.0) at https://commons.wikimedia.org/wiki/File:Pride_Jazzy_Select_power_chair_001.JPG.

Fig. 11.5: Source: https://commons.wikimedia.org/wiki/File:Defense.gov_News_Photo_120403-A-AJ780-014_-_Wounded_Warrior_Todd_Reed_hits_a_softball_during_the_Wounded_Warrior_Amputee_Celebrity_Softball_Classic_at_Nationals_Park_in_Washington_D.C._on.jpg.

Fig. 11.6: Copyright © 2017 by Australian Paralympic Committee/Sport The Library, (CC BY-SA 3.0) at https://commons.wikimedia.org/wiki/File:85_ACPS_Atlanta_1996_Bocciu_Tu_Huynh.jpg.

Inequalities in Ownership, Power, and Sports

After completing this chapter, students should be able to:

- articulate why ownership of a sports league is considered a monopoly or cartel;

- explore the advantages and benefits of professional sports leagues as a monopoly;

- understand the role of a league commissioner;

- discuss team owners and their characteristics;

- understand why teams relocate and their influences on city policy; and

- know the people of color and women who occupy the top positions of authority and power in sports.

Introduction

Professional sports teams operate as institutions that create rules, policies, and regulations; oversee ownerships; and mediate relationships with players, media, broadcasters, advertisers, and marketers. Today, professional sports leagues run almost like unions because of the domination involving owners and ownership of professional sports teams. Unlike other industries, professional sports teams are mostly impervious to intrusion of outside competitive forces. Internationally, the world of supports earns approximately $90 billion in annual revenue. Profits are obtained primarily from negotiations with media and media rights, ticket sales, sponsorships, and sales from copyrighted promotional apparel and other merchandise according to research (Masteralexis, Barr, & Hums, 2018; PwC Sports Outlook, 2016).

In other parts of the world, the sport that we know as soccer in America is referred to as football. In fact, internationally, football (soccer) remains the world's most dominant sport. Research shows that other popular sports internationally are sports such as cricket, baseball, and rugby. Economists predict that if we consider the passion and zeal that sports have in the world, the sports industry may reach revenue that exceeds $110 billion in the near future.

Sports in the United States is by all definitions a monopoly or, as some call it, a "cartel." The professional leagues' monopoly has been used in the past to apply pressure on local governments. Pressure on local governments include extortions related to moving teams to other cities, particularly if local government officials do not agree to build new arenas or stadiums (Parker, 2015; Uberti, 2014).

Research obtained from various sources shows that in the United States, approximately 47 teams changed cities between 1950 and 1997. Research has also found that during the years 1992 and 1998, approximately 34 new stadiums were built or endured major renovations. As a result of negotiations with local government officials, a majority of the costs for building or renovating new stadiums or arenas is covered by taxpayers. Despite the fact that local taxpayers pay for the rebuilt stadium or arena, the professional sports leagues almost always retain the right to keep all or most of the revenue generated by team sales. The question that must be addressed is this: How is it that teams are able to continue to monopolize who owns teams and the power that is sustained in ownership?

Professional Sports as a Monopoly

Unlike other corporate profit-making industries, professional sports leagues are primarily unaffected by competition. In the case of sports leagues, they are considered monopolies because the sports leagues are one large enterprise big enough to own all or nearly most of the franchises' commodities for a league. In the United States, antitrust laws have been put in place to protect consumers, prohibit practices that restrain trade, and ensure a marketplace that is open and competitive. However, unlike other market industries, sports leagues are immune to antitrust laws and regulations that have been put in place to discourage monopolistic operations. Some argue that professional sports teams in the United States are unique because they are the only conglomerate that operates under the same set of rules.

The word monopoly in sports has become a topic of interest as of late. The NBA, NFL, and other leagues consist of a group of competitors that operate very similar to a cartel in that they come together for one common goal: economic benefits. This type of group arrangement offers the best of two worlds: a reduced opportunity to compete yet offering them freedoms and powers not covered in the agreement. While members have to come to a consensus on common interest issues, such as rules of the game, promotions, and the production of promotional campaigns (e.g., the NFL regulates content and overall aesthetics of websites), the total number of professional teams that can be a part of a particular league and where they are allowed to make their home, and the legality and language contained in their media contracts.

Being a cartel brings enormous benefits to a sports league. When teams bid against each other for highly gifted players, for example, the process is regulated by the rules for contracts, drafts, and trades. In the annual college football draft, for instance, professional teams take turns designating the college athletes they prefer to hire. Leagues also decide how many teams can be in the league and where they can reside (Eitzen, 2000; Eitzen, 2001; Eitzen, 2009). A cartel-like structure resembling a monopoly also allows the professional league to negotiate TV contracts. Television contracts actually offer benefits to all involved in the monopoly of a particular league. The Sports Broadcast Act of 1961 was created to give professional leagues the right to negotiate media contracts. The act also made it possible for those media rights to be sold without being subjected to the antitrust laws in our governmental system. Because of the Broadcast Act of 1961, national networks and cable systems were able to bid for the right to broadcast all of the games within a particular sports league (Eitzen, 2000; Eitzen, 2001; Eitzen, 2009). For example, in 1997, Fox Television paid the NFL approximately $17.6 billion for exclusive rights to broadcast all their content until 2005. The contract meant that each team in the NFL stood to earn close to $75 million per season. Recently, the U.S. courts issued a rule stating that the NBA was not able to preclude the Chicago Bulls from selling their media rights to a media vehicle that is not a part of the NBA's contract.

The Power of Monopolies

Professional sports leagues are significantly more powerful than in years past. Currently, there is a professional basketball league (NBA), a football league (NFL), a baseball league (MBA), and a hockey league (NHL). The power of monopolies leads to bullying-like behaviors that allow them to fix prices in such a way that fans will pay more for tickets and other services. In sports, the leagues will even coordinate game schedules so that they can circumvent competition for fan attention. For example, to curtail competition for fans, MLB specifically starts its season in the spring and concludes mid-fall, just when seasons for the NBA and the NFL are starting up. In fact, from all information on the starting dates and times for playoffs, we find that none of the professional leagues have overlapping dates for popular championship tournaments.

Starting a new league is quite tricky. Any corporation or individual that wants to challenge the sports cartels would not only need to secure multiyear stadium leases but also obtain signed contracts with television networks to build loyal fans. To create a new professional team within an existing league, one must obtain approval from all the current team owners affiliated with the league.

Although professional sports teams compete against one another for titles, we have learned that they also work in one accord with the overall goal of ensuring that their business and economic interests are protected. This army-like protection is interestingly another feature of a monopoly or a cartel. The leagues vote together and present a united front when faced with conflicts from external forces. The united front is most visible when the owner of a team is undergoing some type of chaos or economic upheaval. For example, when the New York Mets were struggling to pay expenses, the MLB provided $25 million to help assuage the financial hardship. In another case, the NBA interceded and provided emergency funds to the Charlotte Hornets because the previous team owner, Robert Johnson, did not have enough finances to cover the start-up cost of the expansion franchise in 2004. Public records show that Johnson's team was close to $150 million in debt. Former professional basketball player, Michael Jordan purchased the team for a reported $275 million (Associated Press, 2010), making him the second black majority owner of a major pro sports team (Associated Press, 2010).

Exclusivity is yet another characteristic of a monopoly. Exclusive ownership is obtained when a single owner joins the league and can do what he or she desires without approval from the league. For example, when the New Orleans Pelicans were up for sale, several potential owners showed an interest in buying the team, but only if they were to leave the city of New Orleans. Exclusivity was demonstrated in this instance when the NBA intervened and restricted the purchase of Pelicans to a corporation or individual that would ensure that the team would remain in New Orleans.

Listed next is a summary detailing a few of the ways that sports teams operate like monopolies (aka cartels). In his book *Social Issues in Sports*, Ronald Woods (2016) provides five distinct characteristics that sports leagues have in common with monopolies.

- Team owners have the power to control how teams included in the league will "compete against each other for fans, players, media revenues, sales of licensed merchandise, and sponsorships" (Woods, 2016).
- Like monopolies, leagues are of one accord to eliminate and create barriers for competition or the development of new leagues (Woods, 2016).
- In terms of how players are hired for professional teams, sports leagues use a draft to encourage players to only engage in negotiations with the teams that draft them. This process actually puts a cap on the salaries athletes are able to earn from playing in the professional league.

- New teams or expansion teams are not allowed to join a league without having to pay inordinate fees to all owners in a particular league (Woods, 2016). Also like a monopoly, an owner is not allowed to move the team to another city or state without the approval of all team owners in a league.

- Individual team owners are not allowed to sell merchandise associated with their team. In fact, the NFL markets all merchandise and properties as one single unit. So, basically, if you buy merchandise for one team, the funds are combined into one "account" in the NFL. This profit-sharing benefit of the sports monopoly has proved largely successful in terms of negotiation of licensing agreements, sponsorships, and media rights.

The Role of the League Commissioner

Professional sports are popular and play a huge role in today's culture. Fans often forget or are unaware of the fact that all of the professional sports leagues in America operate like a monopoly. The league commissioner is charged with the task of growing the league and is hired by all of the team owners. The responsibility of a league commissioner is to set game rules and policy, determine salary constraints, pursue marketing and sales increases, and expand the league's brand and value in financial and social ways. The league commissioner might often be needed in the resolution of controversies that reach national media and garner national attention. In April 2014, Donald Sterling, former owner of the Los Angeles Clippers, was barred from the NBA for life. After being recorded making racist comments, Sterling also received a fine of $2.5 million when the recording was released in national media. As a result of Sterling's comments, he was forced to sell the pro ball team (CBS News, 2014b).

Just for a recap of the "Sterling Tape," here is a quick overview: In 2013, *TMZ Sports* obtained a recording of a conversation that Sterling had with a woman named Maria Vanessa Perez. In the recording, Sterling sounded angry and irritated about a photograph that Perez uploaded to her Instagram page. The photograph was of Perez posing with retired basketball player Magic Johnson. On the tape, the male voice, later identified as Donald Sterling's, made statements such as, "It bothers me a lot that you want to broadcast that you're associating with black people," and, "You can sleep with [black people]. You can bring them in, you can do whatever you want," but "the little I ask you is … not to bring them to my games" (CBS News, 2014b). The recording received national media coverage.

The comments Sterling made significantly affected the NBA, one of the professional leagues with predominantly African American players. The Clippers were forced to hold a meeting to discuss the comments. During the meeting, coaches and players were extremely angry over what was said on the recording. Several of the coaches and players even discussed boycotting Game 4 of the series. Instead of instigating a boycott, players protested Sterling's remarks by wearing their jersey's inside out (see Figure 12.1) to conceal the team's logo during the pregame

FIGURE 12.1 *Members of the Los Angeles Clippers listen to the national anthem with shirts turned inside out before Game 4 of an opening round of the NBA basketball playoff series against the Golden State Warriors on April 27, 2014, in Oakland, California.*

FIGURE 12.2   *Miami Heat players turn their shirts inside out.*

and the singing of the national anthem. Later that year, in solidarity with the Clippers protest, the Miami Heat players chose to wear their shirts inside out also, as shown in Figure 12.2. LeBron James was interviewed about his team's decision to support the Clippers; he was quoted as saying, "There's no room for Donald Sterling in the NBA" (NBA.com, 2014). Miami Heat team owner Micky Arison also went on record saying that he found Sterling's comments to be "appalling, offensive and very sad" (Greenberg, 2014; Moore, 2014) In addition to being banned for life and given a fine of $2.5 million, the maximum fine allowed according to rules and policies, the league commissioner also stripped Sterling of all his power, control, and authority, which disallowed him to ever enter a Clippers facility, including attending any of their games. According to historical records, Sterling's punishment was the most severe sanction ever directed toward a team owner in the league's history.

League commissioners have the power to suspend, ban, issue sanctions, and force team owners to sell (Glasspiegel, 2013). The overall mission of the NBL is to determine the best options and alternatives that are for the greater good. In the case of Donald Sterling, any time owners feel that racism, sexism, or other offensive acts might harm profits, regulations have granted league commissioners with the power and authority to suspend, ban and/or force them to see the team (Glasspiegel, 2013).

Influences of Leagues on City Policy

The league and its owners exercise an enormous amount of impact on a city's policy. Team owners often seek new venues because venues have a direct relationship and effect on the team's revenues. Renovated or brand-new stadiums, for example, are very expensive. For instance, a new stadium for the Dallas Cowboys was reported to have cost close to $1.2 million. In the world of sports in the

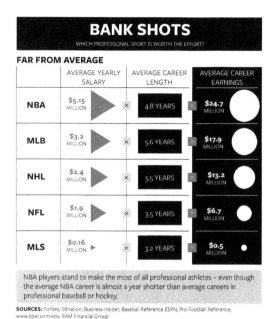

FIGURE 12.3   *Average career earnings for professional athletes.*

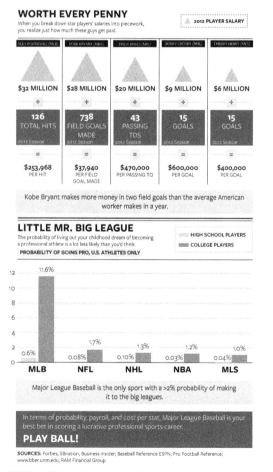

FIGURE 12.4   *Breakdown of player's salaries by game plays.*

United States, the only teams that can afford to pay for billion-dollar stadiums are those with large and loyal fan bases. Other teams often seek funding opportunities from their local cities so that they can afford to build new stadiums or arenas. City politicians on many occasions will agree to the needed cost for the new stadium because it is believed that local citizens like having a national professional sports team in their city. And for many city politicians and sports fans, having a nice, new stadium and a professional sports team in the city not only enhances entertainment options for community members but also city revenue increases are much more likely. Of interest is the finding that city officials are acutely aware that if they do not work with a team, there is a higher chance that negative publicity from major media will result in the team considering a move to another city.

Records show that "70% of stadium construction costs were funded by local taxpayers, mostly in the form of long-term bonds" (Zhou, 2014). Information that details the term limits and effects of long-term bonds on local governments has yet to be determined (Zhou, 2014). At the time of this writing, academic literature and studies showing positive budgetary benefits from supporting new sports facilities have yet to be published.

The value of a team is known to increase significantly when a stadium is new or renovated. Figure 12.3 contains salary data obtained from major leagues sports in America— the NFL, NBA, NHL, MLB and MLS. Interestingly, we learn that of all the major leagues in our culture, NBA players have the highest average career earnings (Schwartz, 2013). Ultimately when a team is sold, the person who gains the most is the team owner, particularly if the team he or she owns has brand equity and immense value. Figure 12.4 is a breakdown of the value of top paid professional athletes. For example, when we divide their annual salaries by game plays or performances, we find that one basketball shot, one hit in baseball, one goal or one passing touchdown play is worth more than the average American makes in a year (Schwartz, 2013). Taken together, Figures 12.3 and 12.4 provide an overall bird's-eye view of all the league's and their average worth as well as average salaries for top athletes in the professional leagues (data are as of 2012).

Over 10 years ago, MLB's Cleveland Indians were reported to be valued at $81 million. The decision was made to build a new ballpark facility, which when it opened immediately propelled the team's brand equity and value to $100 million. In addition to new stadiums, we find increases in revenue also occur when stadiums include luxury suites and VIP club levels. The revenue from these amenities goes straight to the team owners.

In the early 1980s, Memphis, Tennessee, was hoping to find a national basketball team to make Memphis its home. City officials promised the construction of a new Pyramid Arena, estimated to cost approximately $113 million. As a result, the NBA team now known as the Memphis Grizzlies chose to move to Memphis from Vancouver, British Columbia. Team managers convinced government officials in Memphis to build a new stadium in 2004—a facility that was estimated to cost more than double the Pyramid Arena. Interesting note: The Pyramid Arena was left vacant for several years until the city of Memphis added grant funds allowing local businesses to use the space for a new retail center.

Fighting Inequality Within a Cartel

Consider this: If professional sports teams followed the antitrust laws, we would probably have less than half of the teams we have today. And what about those teams that are based in large markets (e.g., the Los Angeles Lakers and New York Knicks)? Sports teams that are centered in larger markets tend to have sizable, loyal fan bases and much higher ticket prices than those teams in smaller markets. Teams in these dominant areas can also afford to pay exorbitant salaries and ultimately recruit and draft the "rock star" players and free agents from smaller less urban, tourist cities, such as Memphis, Atlanta, San Francisco, Phoenix, Denver, and Los Angeles, to name a few. Information located on a website providing data on sports leagues revealed that out of all the professional basketball teams in the United States, the team that has been identified as the most profitable team is, as of this writing, the New York Knicks (Badenhausen, 2018; Statista, 2018). This accolade has been associated with the team despite the fact that they have won a mere 45% of their games and missed several playoff opportunities.

In terms of players associated with teams in smaller cities, we consider teams such as the Kansas City Royals, the Jacksonville Jaguars, and the Milwaukee Bucks. These and other professional sports teams are able to survive because of the way the sports cartel/monopoly handles drafts and player salaries. Leveling the playing field for players is technically one of the greatest benefits of being a part of a monopoly in sports. Sports monopolies or cartels have several rules in place that offer positive competitive sports atmospheres. Because sports in our culture are often viewed as entertainment, even the most attractive, winningest, and richest teams understand that rivalries, close games, and competitive matchups are important for attracting fans and gaining revenue.

Equality is achieved when teams take turns selecting draftees. The teams that have been identified and labeled as "the lowest performing" are typically allowed to make their selections first. Rookies are not allowed to select the teams that draft them. In other words, rookies have no input on the team or location they are asked to join. The team that picks them in the draft ends up being the only team they can join. Information on the draft policy and regulations further shows that the league predetermines a rookie's salary. This process allows those team owners who are housed in smaller markets, such as Kansas City, to have an opportunity to rebuild their team's brand around a new and upcoming superstar. What would happen if the sports leagues allowed players to "interview" with teams like candidates do when in the job market in corporate America? We might speculate that the most sought-after rookies would be attracted to the larger markets and cities, and select the wealthy teams to negotiate higher salaries. Thus the professional sports cartel ensures that each team gets an equal share regarding superstars and talent. As of recent years, we have noticed a vast variety in the competitive equality in that eight distinct professional football teams have won the last 10 Super Bowls.

The Leagues' Effect on Other Businesses

Sports leagues are acquiring growing revenues from cable broadcasting rights. Innovations in technology, such as satellite TV, pay-per-view, HBO, and other media, have become intense competitors for traditional television. Nowadays, cable television and traditional television are fighting for eyes on the screen. Cable channels now appreciate live sports and view them as their most bankable asset. For many cable channels, live sports is media content that is best consumed live. Research shows that regarding certain events, most consumers would rather watch their teams live than via some network program. The desire to observe certain sporting events live provides leverage to professional leagues to negotiate large media contracts. For example, in September of 2012, "the NFL negotiated to pay ESPN 70% more per game than they originally paid for the rights to broadcast Monday Night Football" (Zhou, 2014). Networks such as Fox, ABC, and CBS often try to outbid one another for the most lucrative sports contracts. Revenue from television contracts for sports leagues is a huge source of profits. In broadcast, the amount of revenue earned is largely dependent on the area of dominant influence or the size of the market. While the NFL is known to restrict individual sports teams and team owners from negotiating with local television and media contracts, MLB allows negotiations with local broadcast media. This is why the St. Louis Cardinals sell their broadcast rights for an estimated $75 million a year (e.g., Fox Sports Midwest, local channels in the state of Missouri).

Team Franchise Owners

In terms of an overall qualitative description of sports team owners, research uncovered information that states that many of the team owners are middle-aged, white, male, self-proclaimed billionaires. These individuals are known to purchase a professional sports team in the United States from anywhere between $500 million and $2 billion (Zhou, 2014). Currently, owners of the professional teams in the league are also included in the Fortune 500's list of chief executive officers or chief operating officers. Many are actually born into wealth. And for many sports teams, the franchises become part of a much larger family-owned business. Cablevision, for example, owns the New York Knicks. Cablevision is also a part owner of the Los Angeles Lakers.

Team franchise ownership has many clandestine goals besides the most obvious one: making money from the team. According to news reports, Bruce Ratner moved his professional basketball team to Brooklyn specifically to have an arena constructed. Today, the Barclays Center is now as a historical landmark and is part of a development in the area called Pacific Park Brooklyn (*New York Times*, 2014). Some team owners see owning a sports team as the main component of their enterprise. At the time, the team was owned by Anschutz Entertainment Group who also owns Cablevision. This business currently holds a minority investment in the Laker's home court currently known as the Staples Center (Zhou, 2014). Other team owners believe that owning a franchise is a tangible display of pride. For many, owning a team is the equivalent to a wealthy person's habit of collecting art. Take for instance the owner of the Dallas Mavericks, Mark Cuban. Cuban is so emotionally invested in his team that he has gone on record to say that "losing games hurts a whole lot worse than losing money" (Zhou, 2014). His quote may actually be an understatement. So far, Cuban has been fined close to $2 million for instigating arguments with referees.

(For a compilation of the richest team owners, refer to Mark [2016].)

Most owners of sports teams are wealthy and often accumulate their wealth long before deciding that they want to enter the business of sports. We know from research that owning a sports team results in billionaire status for some investors. As of this writing, there are approximate "63 billionaires who own a franchise in a major sports league around the world" (Badenhausen, 2016). This count was reported in a 2016 Forbes study on billionaires. The investigation revealed that, collectively, billionaires own 81 sports teams and are involved in seven sports and 12 leagues.

NBA's Wealthy Owners

The former chief executive officer of Microsoft, Steve Ballmer, owner of the Los Angeles Clippers, is currently "the world's richest sports team owner with a net worth of $28.5 billion" (Badenhausen, 2016; see also Newcomb, 2014). It was reported that Ballmer paid close to $2 billion in 2014 to buy the Clippers after the team was put up for sale because of racist remarks made by ousted owner, Donald Sterling (Helin, 2014).

The NBA now has approximately 20 billionaires as owners, and they are worth a collective $102 billion. The list of billionaire owners includes Stephen Ross, owner of the Miami Dolphins whose net worth is approximately $12 billion; the owner of the Seattle Seahawks and Portland Trail Blazers, Paul Allen who passed away in October 2018, was stated to be worth about $17.5 billion.

Although Ballmer is said to be the wealthiest of team owners, the second wealthiest owner is real estate mogul Stanley Kroenke, who has an estimated worth of $7.7 billion. Kroenke owns the Denver Nuggets, the Colorado Avalanche, the Colorado Rapids, the Los Angeles Rams, and Arsenal FC. Although he may be the second wealthiest team owner, he has also earned the title of being the most hated team owner (we will go into this in a later section of this chapter). In January 2015, the NFL initiated a lottery for relocation. Kroenke submitted a relocation application and received approval to move his football team from St. Louis back to Los Angeles. Rounding out the top-five wealthiest NBA team owners in order of their net worth are the owner of the Brooklyn Nets, Mikhail Prokhorov ($7.6 billion); owner of the Miami Heat, Micky Arison, who is reported to be worth $7.1 billion; and Charles Dolan, owner of the New York Knicks, whose net worth is estimated to be approximately $5 billion.

NFL's Wealthy Owners

Records show that in terms of wealthy owners in the NFL, there are 19 billionaire team owners. Unlike the NBA, franchises and ownership in the NFL are typically family owned or are shared by multiple shareholders. Years ago, the Green Bay Packers chose to open up its ownership by selling stock to fans. As of this writing, there are approximately 360,760 "owners" of the Green Bay Packers. In terms of wealthy individual team owners, records show that the owner of the Jacksonville Jaguars, Shahid Khan, and Jerry Jones, owner of the Dallas Cowboys are worth $6.4 and $6.7 billion, respectively.

The Most Hated Team Owners

Research on owners took a very interesting turn when Stan Kroenke and Art Modell, two names associated with major sports teams, were deemed the most hated owners ever. Art Modell died in 2012 and is remembered as "the most hated man in the city of Cleveland" (Davis, 2017; Yardbarker, 2017). In one of his last sports media interviews, Modell felt as though "he will always remain the bull's eye on the fans' dartboard for moving the former Browns franchise to Maryland in 1996" (Dyer, 2007; Henkel, 2005). Modell made a decision in 1995 to move his team from Cleveland to Baltimore, Maryland. Fans immediately took to the streets and social media, even showing up at games showing their anger and hurt (see Figure 12.5). Figure 12.5 is a photograph of the former Cleveland Browns owner, giving a press conference around 1983. During this press conference, Modell made a public apology, staying that he was deeply sorry about his decision to move the team, but it did little to assuage the anger felt by the fans. Modell, in an attempt to rationalize with the fans, explained that with the combined expenses associated with the stadium and the expensive

FIGURE 12.5   *Art Modell, the former Cleveland Browns owner, giving a press conference around 1983.*

improvements needed, he lost almost $21 million. Player salaries and other expenses forced Modell to face the reality of his financial decline, and he explained that he felt that moving to another city would be the most beneficial for all those involved. Cleveland Browns fans were not accepting of that rationale. Figure 12.6 shows how Cleveland Brown sports fans reacted to the move and Modell's rationale to move the team to another city.

Fast-forward 20 years, and we find a more recent news story of an owner who surprised a city and the local community by announcing that the beloved franchise team would be moving. In fact, the owner that makes Art Modell appear almost angelic is Stan Kroenke, owner of Kroenke Sports and Entertainment Co. As mentioned in an earlier section of this text, Kroenke is the owner of a lacrosse team, an NFL team, an NBA team, an NHL team, and an MLS team. The problem started in 1995 when Kroenke purchased a share of the Los Angeles Rams and moved them from California to St. Louis, Missouri. In many public sports interviews, Kroenke went on record telling fans and the city of St. Louis that he would do everything in his power to ensure that the Rams stay in St. Louis. Then 10 years later, in January of 2015, an announcement was made that the Rams were returning to

FIGURE 12.6   *Angry Cleveland sports fans.*

California. It was then that Kroenke felt that the stadium located in downtown St. Louis was no longer appropriate for the team. In fact, he went on to say, "St. Louis is no longer a viable market for the National league" (Hunn, 2016; Rosenbaum, 2016; Thomas, 2018). To make the situation even tenser, NFL commissioner Roger Goodell was recorded making statements that St. Louis's revenue had not met the criteria determined by the league. Skepticism was intertwined in that many St. Louis officials and others closely related to the situation felt that Kroenke did not objectively represent the city of St. Louis and that he misrepresented his "facts" during owners' meetings (Hunn, 2016).

Fans and elected officials alike felt that Kroenke was beyond cruel to a city that not only welcomed him and his franchise but also hosted the team for over a decade. The city of St. Louis aggressively tried to keep Kroenke and the team by offering an exclusive plan and blueprint for a new stadium with the promise of funding the costs of building the stadium with taxpayer money. The blueprint for the new stadium was reported to be one of the best plans to be offered to the NFL to keep a team in a city. Kroenke not only disregarded the offer for the new stadium, but several news stories reported that Kroenke had also already started the construction on the team's new stadium in California. It was speculated that Kroenke began construction on the stadium in California without obtaining approval by the NFL. Note: Basically, Kroenke started plans for relocation before the NFL commission actually approved the application for the team's relocation to California. As seen in Figure 12.7, St. Louis Rams fans were angry about the move, and many critics feel that the attitude displayed by Kroenke shows that on a list of what is most important we see that owners and money are first and foremost in importance and fans are last on the list. Some even feel that the Rams and other teams that choose to relocate show that owners will almost always get their way. Then in October of 2015, angry St. Louis Rams fans were invited to a town hall discussion by the NFL to discuss the relocation (Farmer, 2015).

One aspect of the move was not just that Kroenke stated that he felt that St. Louis was not the perfect fit for the Rams, but he went on record saying that St. Louis was not a good place for anyone. The *St. Louis Post-Dispatch* found a report written by Kroenke that was actually a copy of the application and proposal Kroenke sent to the NFL requesting the relocation to Los Angeles.

FIGURE 12.7   *Angry St. Louis Rams fans angry about the move to California.*

In the report, it was said that Kroenke felt that leaving the Edward Jones Dome and breaking his lease to move to Los Angeles was something any owner in his shoes would do. It was in the last section of the proposal that Kroenke essentially burned the bridge with residents of St. Louis and surrounding communities. In the proposal, Kroenke wrote that he believes that the city of St. Louis is what he called a "dead city." He goes on to say that no one should ever want to play football in St. Louis again. To add salt to the injury, Kroenke stated that he believes that the two cities in California, San Diego and Oakland, are "significantly more attractive markets than St. Louis" (Eschman, 2016; Leitch, 2016; Schroetenboer, 2016). Kroenke went on to write "compared to all other U.S. cities, St. Louis is struggling" and that the city "lags, and will continue to lag, far behind in the economic drivers that are necessary for sustained success of an NFL franchise" (Eschman, 2016; Leitch, 2016; Schroetenboer, 2016). He then concluded the proposal to the NFL by asking for a relocation with this statement: "Any NFL Club that signs on to this proposal in St. Louis will be well on the road to financial ruin, and the League will be harmed" (Eschman, 2016; Leitch, 2016; Schroetenboer, 2016). It, therefore, should not come as a surprise when we learn that Stan Kroenke was voted "the most hated man in the NFL" (Eschman, 2016; Leitch, 2016; Schroetenboer, 2016).

Stan Kroenke will go down in professional sports history as the team owner who destroyed every bridge possible on his way out of town. Even when Modell, the owner who was voted as the most hated man in the NBA, moved the Browns from Cleveland in 1995, he went on record referring to Cleveland and the fans and community as wonderful, stating that "Ohio is my home." Modell even apologized to the city and later told the media that "the move and the response to it haunted him." Reports say that Modell felt bad even to his death. Even though some perceived Modell's apology to be disingenuous, many fans felt that it was better than nothing and that he at least pretended to feel bad. Unlike Kroenke, whose comments were made almost two decades later, Modell did not speak ill of Cleveland or its residents.

NHL, MLB, and Their Wealthy Owners

Topping the list of wealthy NHL billionaire owners is Philip Anschutz, who made his fortune in several industries from railroads, oil, and telecommunications to sports and entertainment. He is reported to be worth over $9.7 billion. Currently, Anschutz is the owner of an NHL team known as the Los Angeles Kings. Anschutz also owns an MLS known as the Los Angeles Galaxy. The owner who leads the MLB in terms of wealth is Ted Lerner. Lerner, principal owner of the Washington Nationals baseball team, is unique in that he maintains the largest lead of owners in the MLB by having a net worth of $5.5 billion. Lerner earned his wealth in the real estate industry. In June 2018, Mr. Lerner transferred ownership of the Washington Nationals to his son, Mark (Svrluga, 2018). Major League Baseball approved of the transfer to Mr. Lerner's son during a annual meeting in April of 2018.

Female Wealthy Owners

A survey of the breakdown of wealthy team owners by gender clearly shows that as of 2018, wealthy middle-aged white men own a vast majority of the teams. Yet there is some positive information in that dedicated research revealed that women currently own four professional sports teams, three of which are in the NFL and one in the NBA. Specifically, the female co-owner of the New York Giants was Tisch, whose net worth was approximately $3.3 billion; Denise York's, the owner of the San Francisco 49ers, estimated net worth rings in at around $2.5 billion in 2018 (*Sports Illustrated*, 2018); and rounding out the third female owners of NFL teams is Martha Ford, owner of the Detroit Lions, whose net worth is close to $1.3 billion. The sole female NBA owner, Gail Owens, owns the team known as the Utah Jazz. Miller's estimated worth is close to $1.4 billion. Worthy of note is the fact that the richest person in sports is a man, who, although not an owner of a professional sports team, leads a company involved in every aspect of the sports merchandising and marketing industry. Phil Knight, cofounder of Nike, ranks high in the nation in terms of overall net worth. His net worth is close to $30.4 billion (*Forbes*, 2018). According to media reports, Knight plans to donate $400 million to Stanford University to start a program that will focus on social issues in American culture, such as poverty, global warming, and climate change.

When Teams Relocate

All relocations are not typically as complex or interconnected as the Rams' relocation. Teams have been moving for over a century. During the last 50 years, 36 teams have relocated, which includes teams like the Rams who return their cities of origin. As far as records show, it has been noted that five professional sports teams have reportedly relocated more than once since 1966.

The Pros and Cons of Relocation

Overzealous, die-hard sports fans hold on to their anger and resentments when teams relocate. Over the last 50 years, we find that sports fans never forgive, nor do they forget the experience. Fans experience feelings of deception, anger, cheating, and being taken advantage of when teams leave and then find quick success in a new city. In 1901, MLB's Oakland Athletics moved from Philadelphia to Kansas City and decided to return to Oakland in 1914. While the Kansas City team made it to the World Series, once they moved back to Oakland in 1914, they won the World Series consecutively in their fifth, sixth, and seventh seasons.

Many, many cities in the United States have experienced sports teams coming and going, leaving their towns for other cities at some point in time. But there is one metropolitan city that holds the record for more moves by professional teams: St. Louis, Missouri. Records show that four sports franchises have relocated to and from St. Louis since 1954.

There are instances when relocating does not salvage a floundering team. One of six teams joining the NHL, known as the California Golden Seals, became the first club in its 1967 expansion to relocate. The franchise relocated to Cleveland in 1976 and changed its name to the Cleveland Barons.

One of the reasons owners consider relocating a team is based on perceived success (as

PROFESSIONAL TEAMS THAT HAVE YET TO WIN MAJOR GAMES AFTER RELOCATION TO ANOTHER CITY

MLB

Milwaukee Brewers
Texas Rangers
Washington Nationals

NFL

Arizona Cardinals
Oakland Raiders (although they won in Oakland before leaving for Los Angeles)
Tennessee Titans

NBA

Atlanta Hawks
Sacramento Kings (also never won as the Kansas City Kings, 1972–1985)
Los Angeles Clippers (also never won as the San Diego Clippers, 1978–1984)
Utah Jazz
Memphis Grizzlies
New Orleans Pelicans
Oklahoma City Thunder

NHL

Arizona Coyotes
Winnipeg Jets

Source http://www.sportsonearth.com/article/161900652/la-well as financial rewards). Basically, as some athletes move to join winning teams, owners often perceive that winning major championships are much more likely in a different city. We obtained a list of current professional teams in their respective leagues that have yet to win major games after relocating from one city to another (Delessio, 2016; Ford, 2017; Hartman, 2017; Wilson, 2018).

Does the NFL Care About Fans When Relocating?

For some, Kroenke's sudden announcement that the Rams were moving back to Los Angeles is proof positive that fans are often an afterthought. San Diego Chargers owner Dean Spanos decided in 2016 that he was relocating his team to Los Angeles, leaving the city his team has called home for 56 years (Fenno, 2017). It was reported that Spanos made the decision after the city refused to give him a billion-dollar stadium. Spanos died in October of 2018 at age 95 (Associated Press, 2018).

Critics argue that the Chargers' move should be the latest signal to fans that they are subject to a "next man up" dynamic that essentially means fans are as easily replaceable as the backup player (Waldron, 2017). In the case of the Chargers, many felt that it just did not make sense to relocate. Los Angeles survived well without having a single NFL franchise for more than 20 years. Recall that the Raiders and Rams left for Oakland and St. Louis, respectively, in 1994. As of 2017, Los Angeles has two teams. The Rams returned, somewhat ceremoniously, to Los Angeles before the 2016 season and were coldly greeted with multitudes of empty seats and dismal television ratings (Caesar, 2017).

Now let us compare the Raiders' and Rams' relocations to that of the San Diego Chargers. The city and its people loved the Chargers. According to an article written by Bernie Wilson of *USA Today* (2017), the Chargers made the championship playoffs 17 times in their 56 seasons. They played in one Super Bowl, which they lost (and they were the 1963 AFL Champions). Even though they were considered a bad team for most of their history, the fans were loyal and believed in them. They filled the seats; the team provided a sort of connection that allowed fans to share with the community. Season tickets were treated like family heirlooms passed down to sons and daughters.

So why relocate and take the risk of losing loyal fans to gain absolutely nothing in return? Because from an owner's perspective, the team and players are first and foremost financial assets in their financial plan. From a business model and owner perspective, the value of a player and team is measured more or less by wins and losses. Value increases as teams make memorable and miraculous game plays. For owners, finding ways to increase profit and a team's value is often deemed the most important part of the sports business. If we consider the relocation of the Rams and Chargers despite fan loyalty, we see this bias in the decision to uproot a team. As we mentioned earlier in this chapter, there is no better way to increase the value of an asset than with a new stadium and luxury boxes. Spanos reportedly asked for this. However, it was recorded that San Diego repeatedly declined to give him what he wanted, so he relocated. There are those, even in the Chargers' fan base, who blame what happened on the San Diego taxpayers because the team's proposals were repeatedly rejected (Bauder, 2016).

As of this writing, the Oakland Raiders will leave Oakland for Las Vegas, where Sheldon Adelson and Co. obtained $750 million for a new stadium that will provide "a large profit to a team owner with one of the lowest net worths in the NFL" (Waldron, 2017). Fans of the Oakland Raiders went into mourning, while future fans in Las Vegas celebrated the news of the Raiders' migration to Las Vegas. The Raiders' owner was enticed to consider Las Vegas when the Nevada state legislature approved a $750 million proposal to build a building equipped with a stadium that was estimated to cost $1.9 million, even though the city officials in Oakland also made an attractive offer of 55 acres that could be used for building a new stadium along with funds to complete improvements in the infrastructure that would benefit the team. Instead, the NFL preferred the more lucrative proposal from Las Vegas. The Raiders will play for two seasons in Oakland until their current lease expires and then relocate to Las Vegas in 2020.

Sports leagues argue that new stadiums boost local economies and that the money offered to the owners is a good investment that leads to increases in team value. Regarding investment, sports officials feel that professional sports games provide employment and tax revenue that will only end up in other places when teams relocate. Economists tend to point out that the argument that sports teams create an influx of jobs isn't completely fair because the jobs that are created by ballparks tend to be part time and low paying.

The Minnesota Vikings, Miami Dolphins, and Buffalo Bills—to name just a few—have from time to time played with the idea of leaving their respective cities. Even when they do stay, teams show little regard for the local people who fill their stadium seats (Waldron, 2017). For example, consider the recent news story about the Cincinnati Bengals. The Bengals secured a stadium deal so lucrative for its owner and so financially bad for the city that Cincinnati had to sell its public hospital to pay debts (Bennett, 2017).

The dynamics of lucrative stadium deals for a sports team at the expense of the fans repeatedly plays out in the MLB, NBA, and NHL. Even MLS franchises have tried relocation practices and other strategies to increase profits (Chad, 2017). Take the fan-ownership model. The fan-ownership model has kept a team like the Packers in tiny Green Bay in business for years. Fan ownership has worked for decades in Green Bay and for European soccer teams because it allows fans to show their love for their teams without the constant fear that they will consider relocating (Florio, 2016). However, we must mention that the professional sports leagues have said that fan ownerships are no longer permissible in the NFL.

Labor Disputes in Sports Leagues

Profitability of sports teams is largely and directly related to attendance at the sporting events as well as the number of viewers exposed to the games via a television broadcast. Fans at the games and those watching from home are components magnified by effective marketing and competitive, closely played competitions. In terms of labor disputes, historical research revealed that the MLB is currently the only league that has not experienced a dispute between players and owners in over 20 years.

In 2004–2005, the NHL was forced to cancel its entire season. As a result of the strike, the league was reported to have lost tangible and intangible assets. The NFL endured strikes in 2012–2013 because of a referee lockout that took place in the first three weeks of the fall season.

Why do labor disputes happen in sports? The potential gains for players and owners make it hard for either side to avoid engaging in labor negotiations. Disagreement about where the league spends the massive amounts of revenue it takes in often seems to be at the center of labor disputes in sports leagues. Strikes can occur when there is a perception that excessive amounts of money are being earned by a particular sport. Disagreements about how the funds should be distributed can take place between owners, players and owners, and referees and owners. Players often demand larger revenue shares. The impetus for the demand is based on the idea that players feel that the revenue is partly related to their performance and team membership. Some strikes happen when owners of teams think there is not enough revenue being received and tend to disagree with the appropriate strategies and marketing ploys that can increase revenue. A disagreement among owners on how to fix the decrease in revenue is listed as the reason for the 2011 NBA strike and the 2012–2013 NFL strike.

The MLB Players Association is often considered "one of the strongest labor unions in American professional sports" (Hiatt, 2012). The NFL, NBA, and NHL are said to have the weaker unions. When sports leagues have weak players associations, it becomes extremely challenging for players and owners to bargain with one another. As historical records for the MLB show, a league that has not had labor disputes for 23 years and has a strong players association can negotiate with one voice. Strong players associations offer more capabilities regarding negotiations and are more likely to settle before the dispute reaches the breaking point and results in a strike.

Some sports pundits state that the main reason that the NBA and NFL have weak players associations is the fact that the careers for athletes in these sports are short-lived. As we discussed in Chapter 10 of this text, professional athletes have very short careers; therefore, the threat of a strike might result in financial strains not only for the athletes but also for owners and others who rely on the revenue. Professional athletes in basketball and football may receive high salaries, but the average length of their career is low, especially when compared to athletes in other sports such as golf and tennis (refer to Chapter 9 of this text).

Reflect on Sports: Letting Go

"The Value of a Team Owner Letting Go" by Ian Crouch a contributing writer and producer for NewYorker.com (this is an excerpt from the article by Brooks, 2017)

The New England Patriots were scheduled to play the Green Bay Packers in the 1997 Super Bowl. In the 37-year history of the NFL, the Patriots were considered to be a maligned and mostly irrelevant team. Instead of being able to bask in the glory of achieving national recognition and playing in the Super Bowl, the Patriots were faced with a week of negative press. News coverage of the big game just a week leading up to the Super Bowl was dominated by stories about a heated debate between Robert Kraft, the Patriots' owner, and Bill Parcells, the head coach. Years after media coverage of the dispute, Kraft, blamed himself for his role in the feud. He was recorded stating that the main reason for the public feud was due, in part, to his need to want to micromanage the team. He was quoted as saying: "Look, I was a new owner. I had a lot of debt. I had stardust in my eyes" (Brooks, 2017). During his ownership of the team, "Kraft's team has won eight Super Bowls, one more than any other owner in the history of the league" (Brooks, 2017). We share the story of the owner-coach dispute in the hope that it showcases how important it is for an owner to let go and leave important decisions to the coaches.

Today, Kraft is considered a very wise and optimistic cheerleader for his team. Kraft is one of a few owners (Mark Cuban is another) who knows all of the players' names. Kraft and Cuban are both owners who are known to be extremely responsive to the fans; they respond personally to Twitter and Facebook posts. There are owners who sign the checks and stay out of the way. Jerry Jones is often accused of being a leader/owner who interferes with and micromanages personnel decisions. It was also rumored that his interference negatively affected the value of the Cowboys' brand.

Signs of effective and positive owners in a league show their mark in subtle ways. Good owners show that they trust players and coaches. Effective owners know how to manage their relationships with their fans and can negotiate "complicated high-stakes relationships with other owners and the league commissioner" (Crouch, 2017). Kraft is an owner who has a reputation as an effective contract mediator and negotiator. He remains well liked by a diverse group of people. His skills in mediation and negotiation were evident in 2015 when the Patriots endured what has become known as the Deflategate saga. "Deflategate" refers to the time in 2015 when Tom Brady found himself at the center of accusations stating that he participated in a nefarious scheme that involved deflating footballs during the playoffs. Kraft defended Brady until a report revealed that the team was culpable. In response to the controversy, Kraft said, "I do have to respect the commissioner and believe he's doing what is in the best interest" of the league (Crouch, 2017). After the 2016 Super Bowl game, Kraft accepted the Super Bowl trophy saying to fans, "For many reasons, all of you in this stadium understand how big this win was" (Crouch, 2017).

Minority Ownership

Owners of Color

Robert L. Johnson, the founder of Black Entertainment Television, was the first African American to become the principal owner of a major professional sports team, the Charlotte Hornets, in the NBA. Johnson paid a "$300 million expansion fee for a new franchise in Charlotte, N.C., which began playing in the 2004–5 season" (Sandomir, 2002). In response to comments that implied that the only reason for his ownership was due to race, Johnson wanted it to be known that it was completely "foolish to believe that his race was the primary reason he was unanimously selected by the league's expansion committee over a group that included Larry Bird, the former Boston Celtic" (Sandomir, 2002).

Women in Sports and Owners of Color

Lesa France Kennedy is considered an influential female in the business world of sports. Kennedy manages over 1,000 employees and is said to earn an estimated $700 million in annual revenues. She is chief executive officer of International Speedway Corporation and oversees 13 race tracks. She also plays a significant role in NASCAR by serving as an active member of its board of directors.

Hours spent searching records revealed that there are a very few African Americans who own or have owned shares in professional teams. As of the current writing, Magic Johnson owns a very small percentage of the NBA's Los Angeles Lakers. "Roughly 80 percent of the league's players are black, or members of minority groups; 12 of the 29 coaches are African-American" (Sandomir, 2002).

In July of 2018, history was made in the world of sports when Evelyn Magley became the first African American woman to ever own a male professional sports league in the United States (Hill, 2018). Magley (pictured in Figure 12.8), along with her husband and president of the league, retired NBA player David Magley, are founders of a newly formed league known as "the Basketball League (TBL)." TBL is a minor professional basketball league, which recently acquired the North American Premier Basketball league and is scheduled to make its debut in 2019 (Hill, 2018). As of the time of this writing, the league currently has targeted 40 markets in the United States and Canada and will start the 2019 season with 11 teams. Some of the teams include the "Kansas City Tornadoes, Nevada Desert Dogs, Albany Patroons, Yakima SunKings, Raleigh Firebirds, Tampa Bay Titans, and San Diego Waves" (Hill, 2018). Each team will play 32 games that will be available via livestream (Hill, 2018; Magley, personal communication, 2018).

TBL will offer talented basketball players an opportunity to play professionally and earn anywhere from "$1,500 to $7,500 a month." The league offers an opportunity for those athletes

FIGURE 12.8 *Evelyn Magley, first African American woman to own a league.*

to play on the professional level while honing their life skills by being active in community service, which is a core tenant of Evelyn's vision for the league. All levels of college and professional players will play in this league. According to Magley, TBL is first and foremost dedicated to offering communities and families "affordable and quality entertainment as well as community support through the launch of an upcoming philanthropic arm, youth camps, clinics, and nonprofit organizations" (Hill, 2018).

Celebrity Owners of Sports Teams

Recently, there has been an increase in the trend of celebrities seeking minority ownership of sports teams. For many celebrities, as well as sports franchises, the relationship is mutually beneficial in that the merger results in increased exposure for both parties. Jay-Z owned less than 1/15 of 1% of the Nets in 2012. The hip-hop artist was said to have helped increase the team's brand. "Other celebrity team owners include Magic Johnson (Dodgers), Justin Timberlake (Grizzlies), LeBron James (Liverpool FC), Will Smith and Jada Pinkett Smith (76ers), and Marc Anthony and Gloria Estefan (Dolphins)" (Hanlon, 2015).

In Summary: Minority Ownership, the Good and the Bad

The general thought in our culture that sports leagues would rather have one owner than to deal with group ownership. The dilemma with minority ownership seems to center on the revenue and profit-generating opportunities that result when celebrities and highly publicized groups own shares in teams. According to an article titled "The Perks and Perils of Owning a Small Share of a Sports Team," out of all the professional leagues, the NBA and MLB seem to be the leagues that are more comfortable with large groups of owners. The reason for this, the author argues, is "[the NFL is] an owner-driven league, rather than more commissioner-driven" (Waldron, 2014).

Although obtaining minority ownership has its perks, there are also a few downsides associated with it. First, minority owners usually have no decision-making abilities or a voice when it comes to votes about major changes in the team. Compared to teams with one owner, minority owners often serve on advisory boards as opposed to the controlling board of decision makers of one owner teams. Minority owners are not invited to attend league meetings. Another disadvantage relates to the selling of shares. For minority owners, it is often challenging to sell shares quickly, especially if the team is not being sold.

Breaking Down the Barriers and Stereotypes

Throughout history, we know that women have had to fight for an equal place in our society. We know that when compared to men, women have had fewer legal rights and career opportunities over the last century (Simmons, 2011). Gender roles in our culture seem to imply that women are to serve solely as wives and mothers and are considered to be the weaker sex (Cohen & Huffman, 2007). Despite these barriers, we do currently have women in high positions of power and authority in the sports industry. Take, for example, Michele Roberts, the recently appointed executive director of the NBPA. Roberts is the first woman to lead a major professional sports union in America (Berger, 2014; Belzer, 2015; Gregory, 2014).

Christine Driessen, executive vice president and chief financial officer of ESPN, is solely responsible for managing ESPN's multibillion-dollar programming contracts and rights "with the Southeastern Conference, MLB, Monday Night Football, as well as the College Football Playoff" (Belzer, 2015). Driessen was also instrumental in the start-up of networks now known as ESPN2, ESPNEWS,

ESPNU, ESPN Deportes, and espnW. "While some progress has been made over the last two decades, the glass ceiling for women in the male-dominated sports industry is getting lower in sports than any other industry" (Belzer, 2015; Berger, 2014). Women in top executive positions can be found in approximately 8.5% of all jobs in sports, numbers that are equally low across other careers. This is one reason why the author of this text chose to include a list of the top female executives in sports. We need to be aware that female executives exist in sports and that female athletes are engaged in activities that should be celebrated. These women have overcome obstacles, jumped hoops, and broken barriers to rise to positions of power and influence.

Black Women of Power in Sports

BlackEnterprise.com celebrated the following women who hold positions in executive suites all across this male-dominated industry. These women have broken barriers, raised the bar, and shifted perspective when it comes to who calls the shots in athletics.

Michelle Roberts   Roberts is the first woman to serve as executive director of the NBPA.

Pam El   "El is the chief marketing officer at the NBA where she heads global marketing operations, direct brand development, and advertising for the NBA, WNBA, and NBA Development League" (NBA Careers, 2018). On November 28, 2018, the NBA announced that Ms. El would retired at the end of 2018.

Kerry D. Chandler   Chandler served as the chief human resources officer at Under Armour and as of October 2018 accepted a new position as chief human resources officer at Endeavor, an American talent agency who represents the NFL, NHL, and also owns the Ultimate Fighting Championship and Miss Universe (Sun, 2017; Sun, 2018).

Sarah Mensah   Mensah is the vice president and general manager of the Jordan Brand in North America. Before accepting this position, Mensah was employed with the Trail Blazers serving in roles ranging from Executive Vice President/Chief Operating Officer to Senior Vice President/ Chief Marketing Officer to Corporate Sales Manager.

Sheila Johnson   Johnson made the most influential list because as of 2018, she continues to hold the title of being "the first black American female billionaire" before Oprah Winfrey's success. Johnson served in various leadership roles within the WNBA's Washington Wizards. Johnson also was the first African American woman to be a partner or owner in the NHL (Washington Capitals), NBA (Washington Wizards), and WNBA (Washington Mystics).

Laurel Richie   Richie, served as president of the WNBA, after serving 20 years working for ad agency Ogilvy and Mather. Richie is a trustee of Dartmouth College where she serves as vice chair and chairman of the communications committee.

Sheryl Swoopes   In July 2017, Swoopes was hired as the women's basketball program's Director of Player Development at Texas Tech. Then, in January 1, 2018, Swoopes was promoted to regular assistant coach under interim head coach Shimmy Gray-Miller. Swoopes was "the first player to be signed to the WNBA" and has "won three Olympic Gold Medals" (NBA Careers, 2018).

In America today, women are not only becoming more educated, but they are also breaking the glass ceiling in a male-dominated sports industry. We know that the number of women holding positions in top management has not increased significantly over the years. Simmons (2011) agrees and stated that even though women hold many entry-level and middle-management positions, they are relatively sparse in terms of upper-level leadership positions (NBA, 2011).

Typically, female leaders are told that they must be tough and authoritative (like men) to be taken seriously (Simmons, 2011). However, when they are tough, they are more likely to receive backlash and be labeled a "bitch" (Oakley, 2000). Men who display similar behaviors are often well-received and viewed much more positively, whereas women who display these leadership attributes are vulnerable to harsh criticisms and discriminatory treatment. This hypocritical response to male and female leaders seems to be entrenched in our culture's norms and ideals in relation to what is masculine and what is feminine. In American culture, most women find themselves in situations they cannot win no matter what (Jamieson, 1998, Jamieson, 2000; Oakley, 2000). Basically, the point here is that we have unspoken rules regarding speaking assertively but not too assertively, and dressing "like a woman" but not dressing "too feminine" (Jamieson, 2004; Oakley, 2000). In other words, if a female is perceived to be "too feminine" she is perceived to be incompetent in terms of understanding sports (Jamieson, 1998; Jamieson, 2003). Oakley (2000) argues that when women speak assertively and dress "like women" and are too feminine, she has faces the stereotype that she wants to work in sports for one main purpose—to meet the players. In our society, it seems that assertiveness and femininity are mutually exclusive categories that are difficult for us to reconcile and integrate (Jamieson, 2003; Oakley, 2000; Simmons, 2011).

Conclusion

Professional sports in America are growing and prosperous. In this chapter, we learned that revenue from sports aids in the economic health of the city that they call "home." Professional sports are like cartels or monopolies that are used to control team competition. The protection that a sports cartel provides ensures that not only are players, merchandising, and media reviews protected from competition, but they also ensure that fans are not in situations of having to choose one tournament over another, particularly since in the United States not one final championship for the major leagues has overlapped. We made the point that in terms of professional team sports, the fact that there is only one provider of the service and that provider is the league (i.e., NFL, NBA, MLB, NHL, MLS), is the reason that professional sports in our culture are considered a monopoly.

Owners, advertisers, marketers, and sports media prosper economically because our government allows them to operate as a monopoly to keep competitors at bay. Owners of sports teams earn profits from ticket sales, media contracts, concession and stadium sales, and product licensing and merchandising fees.

QUESTIONS FOR DISCUSSION AND REFLECTION

1. What have you observed in terms of news about teams moving from one city to another? Write a brief reflection detailing your thoughts on the pros and cons of relocation.

2. What are some of the reasons why more women do not own sports franchises?

3. Is it possible for sports stadiums and arenas to generate tangible and positive benefits to the local community? How would those benefits be revealed? What tips might you offer for the media to be sure that their consumers are informed of these economic benefits?

4. Government officials and others involved in enticing teams to come to cities do so by creating blueprints for the newest and most innovative stadiums and arenas. For some, the areas that receive the greatest benefit are those places of business in close proximity to the stadium. Restaurants, hotels, retail stores, and bars are often in prime positions to expand

their businesses by making their products and services convenient for fans to patronize before and after games. If you were preparing ideas for a new or renovated stadium in this day and time, what are some of the features that would make it unique, and what types of businesses other than those listed might you encourage to invest in renting space? Explain your thoughts.

5. While some feel that professional teams relocating to a different city bring jobs to those who are unemployed, others find that the jobs are seasonal and often low-salaried types of work. What are your thoughts about the opportunity for employment? Back up your response with information and data.

6. What are the reasons why women and people of color face advancement barriers in the sports industry?

7. Do women in sports have to be tomboys to be respected in upper management? Why or why not? Did the women in sports mentioned here play sports growing up? If so, which sports? Were they tomboys? Do they have more male friends?

8. Identify barriers to that must be overcome to advance into top positions within the sports industry today for women and people of color.

SUGGESTED ACTIVITIES

1. Create a "how-to" guide for women who might want to own a sports franchise or go into upper management. You will have to conduct research and perform interviews to inform your work.

2. Sometimes the things we think are barriers to access for ownership of teams turn out not to be true barriers. With some creative thinking, identify and write a paper with your proposed solutions that dissolve the barriers for women and people of color to gain authority and power in sports.

3. Interview St. Louis fans who are angry about the relocation of their team. Interview those fans who understand and have accepted the relocation from St. Louis to Los Angeles. Were there common areas of agreement? What can St. Louis do to attract another team to the area? What type of team would you recruit to relocate to St. Louis?

4. Reread the statements that Stan Kroenke made about St. Louis. Write an editorial response to his comments. Be sure to research to inform your editorial with counterarguments that can persuade someone to doubt his statements.

5. Conduct research on the top-10 owners of sports teams. What are some common areas that they all have in their backgrounds? How did they make their millions? Did they play sports growing up? What are their backgrounds? How do they differ? Pretend you are working on a top story, and it will be on the front page of the newspaper or magazine? . What is your angle/lead and why?

6. Consider an application to the IOC encouraging the members to consider an American city for a summer competition. Keeping in mind that oftentimes, the city must ascertain funding to build an Olympic village and competition venues. Do some research and determine the various factors that must be considered to get the Summer Games to come to

your hometown. What types of investments and revenue does a host city have to make and have? What are the costs and benefits involved in hosting the Olympics?

7. Interview one of the women of people of color in top positions in the male-dominated sports world. Find out what she enjoys the most and the things that could be improved.

8. Write an article for the NCAA that discusses ways that more women and minorities can obtain positions of power in the organization. You may want to interview people working for the NCAA (this could be an awesome networking opportunity) and those in positions within your athletic department. Write a lead story or produce a short news segment on your findings.

9. Pretend you are Stan Kroenke's publicist. What strategies would you suggest if he decided he made a mistake leaving St. Louis? What would your objective be and what strategies would you use to meet your objective? Write his speech and submit your public relations promotional plan to create a reactive strategy to the bad publicity resulting from the statements he made about St. Louis and the people of St. Louis.

ADDITIONAL RESOURCES

"If You Build It, They Might Not Come: The Risky Economics of Sports Stadiums," https://www.theatlantic.com/business/archive/2012/09/if-you-build-it-they-might-not-come-the-risky-economics-of-sports-stadiums/260900/

"How Different Types of Ownership Structures Could Save MLB Teams From Contraction," https://scholarlycommons.law.hofstra.edu/cgi/viewcontent.cgi?article=1017&context=jibl

"Professional Sports Teams Need A Better Ownership Model," https://talkingpointsmemo.com/cafe/professional-sports-teams-need-a-better-ownership-model

"NFL Cross-Ownership Rule," http://www.greenberglawoffice.com/nfl-cross-ownership-rule/

"Public Teams, Private Profits: How Pro Sports Owners Run Up the Score on Fans and Taxpayers," http://www.dollarsandsense.org/archives/2000/0300eitzen.html

"The Sale of Professional Sports Franchises," https://edgewortheconomics.com/experience-and-news/edgewords-blogs/edgewords/article:10-29-2014-12-00am-the-sale-of-professional-sports-franchises-a-lesson-in-market-value/

YouTube

10 Most Hated NFL Owners, https://www.youtube.com/watch?v=-HNGOTmWbKI

The New Breed of Sports Owners, https://www.youtube.com/watch?v=3v7n0CE3zbs

Owning a Team Isn't a "Trophy" Anymore, https://www.youtube.com/watch?v=7A61RpsZc_A

Floyd Mayweather Wants to Buy an NBA Team, but Can He Afford One?, https://www.youtube.com/watch?v=JAUySHVyDNk

Buying and Owning a Professional Sports Team—Kenneth Shropshire, https://www.youtube.com/watch?v=GCY4EPgMj2A

Meet the Richest: Billionaire Sports Owners, *Forbes,* https://www.youtube.com/watch?v=3CdA9hdN4-U

How to Buy a Professional Sports Team, https://www.youtube.com/watch?v=wVMLSiW1W4w

CREDITS

Social Class and Sports Participation

After completing this chapter, students should be able to:

- define social class and understand the typology of the social classes;

- understand social class and related concepts when studying sports and participation in sports;

- explain the disparities in sports and how they differ by social class;

- identify who benefits and who is disadvantaged by the way sports are organized; and

- appreciate the fact that the sports we play are determined by a social class stratification system.

Introduction

Our level of participation and interest in sports is heavily influenced by our culture. Cultural norms and values influence the way people live. Where people live, the country they live in, and the socio-economic class they fall into also affect participation in sports. Sports may operate as a representation of the social class. Often, we can identify a person's social class by taking notice of the sports he or she plays. We find that social class is intertwined with sports participation in many ways. In this chapter, we will explore how social class affects the sports that people choose to compete in. For example, we know that people in the upper social class have the choice to compete in those "expensive" sports that rely on equipment, uniforms, membership fees, competition entry fees, and the list goes on. People in the middle to lower classes are often exposed to those sports that, unlike the upper social class, do not require a large budget to participate, such as running, football, soccer, wrestling, baseball, volleyball, and basketball.

As noted in Chapter 3 of this book, participation in sports can serve as the major foundation in self-perception and identity development. Participation in sports, we learned, develops vital life skills such as leadership, how to handle challenges and adversity, and how to work in a team. Sports have such a unifying influence in that they have a strange knack for gathering crowds of people from different backgrounds, ethnicities, social classes, and ages. Our culture's love of sports is a passion shared between almost every individual in American society. In our culture, our shared passions include experiences such as the thrill of victory when our team or favorite athlete wins, and we share the agony of defeat when our favorite team or athlete loses. While sports are a unifying factor in our culture, we know that there is a huge divide in terms of social status in sports.

Social Class and Economic Inequalities

In a broad stroke of the definition, we learn that social class most closely defines the relationship between one's social and cultural economic expression. Social class signifies a group of people who share analogous amounts of affluence, prestige, and social standing. Typically, in our culture, the social class hierarchy is organized around dimensions of professional fame, educational training, income, and assets. These aspects are then used to separate the cultural concept of social status or social class into four main categories: the upper class; "upper-middle class; middle class; and lower class" (Hall, 2016). Research on the distribution of wealth in America shows that close to "15 to 20 percent of most Americans are placed in the poor, lower social class" (Monte Carlo Forum, 2018). Data obtained from the Census Bureau further show that 30% to 40% of Americans are categorized as belonging to the working social class. Data show that "40 to 50 percent of Americans are in the middle social class level; and 1 to 3 percent are reported to be in the upper class" (Pew Research Center, 2015). In our society, the construct of social status is gauged by one's net worth, assets, material possessions, and profession. The focus of sociological research and theory is to examine the relationship between social class indices and a person's identity.

From sociological research, poverty, homelessness, and unemployment are terms that are typically used to describe the lower social class. Individuals who are more aligned with the lower social class are often unable to complete high school, lack medical care and access to resources for health care and are often stereotyped in the media. We know that media often refer to people in the lower class as "the underclass." This descriptor is not only inaccurate but also a perfect illustration of how media may perpetuate stereotypes of individuals. Often, we find media refer to women in the lower class as "welfare mothers" who are lazy and take advantage of the system by having baby after baby (Monte Carlo Forum, 2018).

The working class, according to sociology literature, are minimally educated people who are often considered unskilled workers. Other references to this group identify them as the group that relies on manual labor. Individuals in this class often find employment as dishwashers, cashiers, maids, and waitresses. Referred to in media as "the working poor," research does show that individuals in this social class are often employed as carpenters, plumbers, and electricians, and are often called blue-collar workers.

People in the middle class are typically called "white-collar workers" who have more money than the lower and working-class people below them (Geewax, 2015). This middle class is further "subdivided into levels based on wealth, education, and prestige" (Kraus, Park, & Tan, 2017). According to information on social class, we learn that those persons most aligned with the lower middle class group, a sublevel of the middle class, are often recognized by their occupations. Lower middle class individuals hold jobs that include manager, teacher, businessowner, and administrator. The upper middle class, the other sublevel of the middle class, is frequently identified by occupation. Individuals in the upper middle class are associated with highly educated business and professional occupations with high incomes. People in this social class are often in professions such as "doctors, lawyers, stockbrokers, and CEOs" (Hall, 2016; Monte Carlo Forum, 2018; Pew Research Center, 2015).

Then there is the upper class, which, according to the Census Bureau, is "composed of approximately 1 to 3 percent of the United States population" (U.S. Census Bureau, 2017b). Data show that the upper class "holds more than 25 percent of the nation's wealth and are divided into two groups: lower-upper and upper-upper" (U.S. Census Bureau, 2017b). Researching the topic of social class in America reveals several fascinating statistics on lower upper class individuals. We find that individuals in this social class are further divided based on the "type of money" or wealth obtained. Lower upper class individuals, or people with "new money," have obtained their wealth from investments, business ventures, and start-up companies (Schoenberg, 2016). In contrast to the lower upper class group is the upper-upper class. This social class refers to individuals and high society families that have what has been termed "old money." Aristocrats in the upper-upper class are those who happen to be born into wealth and are able to live off their inheritance (Schoenberg, 2016). Compared to the lower upper class, the upper-upper class is considered in this culture to be more prestigious and esteemed. Wherever their money comes from, both divisions of the upper class—"old money" and "new money"—are extraordinarily wealthy. The upper-upper class and lower upper class groups both live in elite neighborhoods, have memberships at affluent golf and social clubs, and send their children to the finest private academies and schools (Schoenberg, 2016). In American culture, the wealthy also have a great deal of influence and power.

Disparities in Participation in Sports by Social Class

In American culture, it is often presumed that sports and our participation in sports have the ability to transcend social class. We learn from careful analysis of published research that social class is directly related to sports participation. Social class in American sports is used to define the type of sports athletes specifically want to participate in. We also know that social class influences a person's level of participation and positively affects the probability that an individual will be successful in the sport that he or she has selected. It is interesting to think that sports reflect our social class, but they do. In spite of the all-encompassing role that social class plays in our participation in sports, the relationship between sports and social class also presents many complexities and proves to be an extremely difficult concept to explore.

Upper Class

Historically, people in the upper class use sports for two purposes: as entertainment and a way to demonstrate their wealth (Hall, 2016). For members of the upper class, sports participation has always been a popular extracurricular activity and hobby. We learn from research that the reason that sports are popular with the upper class is primarily a result of an abundant amount of leisure time and their enormous wealth. Excessive disposable income allows members of this group exclusive access to those sports that are exceedingly expensive. When it comes to high-contact sports, we find that those individuals most closely aligned with the upper class will avoid engaging in sports that stress physical contact and involve violence, toughness, self-restraint, and hard manual labor—behaviors that are frequently associated with the lower class (Wilson, 2002). Hobbies associated with the upper class tend to be more expensive for individuals in the middle and other social classes to participate in. The expensive sports "hobbies" have been identified as those that are only available at upper class social and private clubs. Most, if not all, of these clubs are not open to the public. Sports associated with these expensive clubs include "tennis, golf, polo, horseback riding, sailing, and skiing" (Hall, 2016). For members of the upper class, sports are oftentimes those activities that are performed simply to build social networks, increase social capital, and negotiate business deals. For members of the upper class, participation in sports serves primarily as a means to escape or an outlet to do something fun. The lifestyle of the "rich" and wealthy generally requires that they have control and freedom, and the time needed to participate in sports. We also know that the wealthy are also free to combine their sports with their jobs, such as taking clients or business partners out to play 18-holes of golf.

Upper Middle Class

We mentioned in a previous section of this chapter, the upper middle class is primarily described as "white-collar" professionals. Again, as stated previously, people in this social class are often professionals with titles such as physician, attorney, business leader, and manager (Schoenberg, 2016). Research on the upper middle class shows that this group accounts for approximately 4.4% of all American households, "earning between $150,000 and $200,000 annually" (Gilbert, 2011; Mishel, Bernstein, & Shierholz, 2009; Snider, 2018). This social class is known to have high amounts of discretionary income as well. Members of the upper middle class tend to enjoy their social experiences through memberships to social and private clubs, country clubs, and other exclusive organizations that only allow members of similar social status (Gilbert, 2011; Mishel et al., 2009; Snider, 2018).

Level of education is highly valued by members of the upper middle class. Members of this social group share numerous qualities and characteristics with members of the upper class. In terms of their sports participation, both the upper middle class and the upper class tend to invest in sports that take place in private clubs. Perhaps they enjoy the exclusivity and the fact that the sports and resources associated with participation in those sports may be too expensive for any of the other social classes (Hall, 2016). Sports of interest to the upper middle class are sports such as archery, gymnastics, figure skating, swimming, and riflery (Hall, 2016). In addition, for the upper middle class, team sports in American culture are viewed as important activities to participate in, especially in sports such as ice hockey and lacrosse. Ice hockey and lacrosse are sports that require membership in clubs rather than participating on a school team. Expenses related to memberships are often considerably costlier than the fees associated with any of the other team sports. Although other sports have high-priced expenses associated with competition (e.g., gymnastics, dance, swimming, and tennis, to name a few), we find that sports such as tennis and lacrosse are exclusively associated with individuals in the upper middle class. American culture is not known to provide these sports in areas where members in the lower social classes reside.

Middle Class

The middle class, according to data obtained by the U.S. Census Bureau (2015), is "the largest economic group and social class in America." The middle class, according to research, includes "46% of all households, reporting incomes ranging from $50,000 to $150,000 annually" (Elwell, 2014). Although the middle class does not have a large amount of discretionary income, we find that they carefully select expenditures related to daily living and leisure spending. Members of the middle class have a vast range in terms of occupations held, income earned, and levels of education. For many researchers and statisticians, the wide range in variety, unlike the previous social classes, makes this group difficult and very challenging to define and characterize. We do know, however, that team sports dominate the middle class. The reason that team sports have more members from the middle class may be due to the idea that team sports are able to accommodate more players. Team sports also provide a social environment. Examples of team sports that are popular with the middle class are "basketball, football, soccer, baseball, softball, and volleyball" (Elwell, 2014). Children are more likely to start their interest in sports by participating in youth leagues and typically have parents who serve as coaches. Middle-class values are associated with sports such as football and baseball because of the emphasis on toughness and hard labor. American culture emphasizes grace and aesthetic performance, values that are frequently associated with sports connected to the upper class. In general, the middle-class involvement with sports often reflects values such as teamwork, determination, and perseverance. Interestingly, these are similar features associated with sustaining a comfortable lifestyle.

Lower Class

In 2016, "a family of four whose annual income is below $24,250 is considered to be living below the poverty line" (Tiderman, 2015). Research shows that the lower class often participate in sports that are high contact and highly violent. Lower class members interested in sports often select those sports that require immense physical strength (Hall, 2016). Consensus on sports participation of the lower class group shows that the sports that are most popular with this group are "boxing, wrestling, and weightlifting" (Hall, 2016). Boxing, wrestling, and weightlifting are high in physical contact and associated with resources that are affordable for members of this social class group. Contact sports are known to have low, affordable expenses associated with participation, and we already know that access to the areas and buildings that allow one to practice these sports are often accessible to lower class individuals. Thus when we compare expenses and resources of these sports to the sports that are the most popular with upper class members, we begin to understand why high-contact sports, such as boxing, is most closing aligned with the lower class (Eime, Charity, Harvey & Payne, 2015; Flanagan, 2017; Thompson & Rowe, 2018).

Sports related to the lower class are a legitimate means of establishing belonging to the lower social class group with confidence, a sense of self-worth, self-perception, and, as we mentioned in other chapters of this text (i.e., Chapters 3, 8, and 9), an immense sense of masculinity. Self-respect and a sense of what it means to be masculine are two traits necessary for survival in low-income neighborhoods. Also, we know that members of the lower class report enjoyment from participating in several of the sports that the middle class are active in (Hall, 2016). The sports that lower class individuals have a definite affinity for are basketball, football, and soccer. The significant difference in the two classes lies in how they choose to participate in their chosen sport. Lower class individuals are often found and report being more open to participating in "spontaneous, unorganized games with neighborhood people" (Hall, 2016). Lower class individuals are also willing to play a sport on disorderly fields and old, worn-out basketball courts. The reason for this seems to be explained by the fact that lower class individuals are drawn to sports that are highly accessible and aligned with resources in the environment (Thompson & Rowe, 2018). Members of the lower class are often flexible when it comes to using whatever resources that may be available. For members of the middle class, sports and their level of participation in sports are one way to demonstrate masculinity and "manliness."

As mentioned at the beginning of this chapter, social class is suggestive of the opportunities and lifestyles we choose. The influence that social class has on lifestyles also includes a massive influence on sports participation and involvement. Members of the higher, upper class tend to engage and participate in extravagant and expensive sports while lower class individuals are most likely to participate in those sports that are not as highly visible in media. Sports that are fast, dangerous, and violent, and that require immense physical strength by participants are the sports that lower class individuals tend to enjoy (Schoenberg, 2016).

Bridging the Social Economic Status Gap in Sports

Social status or another common reference known as SES is a major cause of the disparities and gaps we find when explaining and understanding individual involvement and participation in sports. Research tells us that individuals who live in resource-deficient social and physical environments, and who report having low individual incomes, have been found to be at an increased risk of physical inactivity. It is therefore important to explore the socioeconomic differentials in sports participation among individuals in the United States. In this chapter, we hope to uncover those differentials so that we might identify mechanisms that create and influence such gaps in sports based on social class.

In the previous section on social classes, we learned that individuals in low socioeconomic environments benefit from sports that require manual and physical labor and do not require membership or equipment fees. Thus it may be concluded that the motivations of low-SES individuals' to engage in sports are more influenced by aspects of the neighborhood and environment. By contrast, high-SES individuals might be more reactive to other influences. To narrow the SES gap in sports participation among U.S. citizens, perhaps we could find ways to encourage low-SES families to engage in activities outside of their environment (e.g., tennis, racquetball, golf). That is, if we offer support and access to resources to sporting activities outside of the norm, perhaps we may be able to widen the range of opportunities for people of diverse backgrounds to engage in sports that go beyond the stereotypical sports that we have come to expect.

Extracurricular activities are pastimes that are organized and managed by the school. These activities take place outside of the regular school day and include arts, membership in specific clubs, and sports. Over the years, the expense of managing extracurricular programs has increased dramatically, making it difficult for many students to participate (Burkhardt, 2016). As a result of rising costs, many schools have been forced to charge fees and/or require funds in order for students to participate. In a study conducted over 10 years ago, Hoff and Mitchell (2007) found that "34 states had at least some schools charging fees for extracurricular participation" (Hoff & Mitchell, 2007). In the report, it was stated that "school districts have raised fees from $15 to $50 a year" (Burkhardt, 2016; Hoff & Mitchell, 2007). Records even show that school districts on the West Coast have made fees associated with some extracurricular sports as much as $1,500 per year.

Factors Limiting Participation in Extracurricular Activities

Differences and changes in the cost to participate in extracurricular activities also affect the availability of extracurricular opportunities, particularly for those students in the lower class echelon. We find that in terms of social class, those students in the low socioeconomic class are least likely to be involved in sports and extracurricular activities than are students from the upper class (National Center for Education Statistics, 1995). Statistics on sports participation by social class shows us that "almost three-quarters of low SES students participate in at least one activity, compared with 87 percent of high SES students" (National Center for Education Statistics, 1995). Moreover, we find statistics that inform us that the participation rate of low-SES students is often "consistently lower than that of high SES students in each type of sport" (Walpole, 2003).

Research on the topic of social class and participation in sports shows that the social context of the school may be closely associated with the effective influence (a positive or negative influence) on students' behavior and attitude, particularly their attitudes toward sports and interest in sports. Studies further show that a student's level of involvement in sports depends primarily on whether the student is "in the relative minority or majority in the school" (National Center for Education Statistics, 1995). While we know that covertly the terms "minority" and "majority" actually refer to one's ethnicity and ultimately level of power and wealth, we find that those students from low socioeconomic backgrounds, are more likely to display interest and actively participate in sports. Moreover, when a student from a lower-income SES is placed in an environment where they feel like an outcast, they are less likely to participate in sports (Burkhardt, 2016; Hoff & Mitchell, 2007). Therefore, based on empirical work, we now understand that acceptance and fitting in play a role in how involved students become in sports.

Researchers have identified important barriers that impede student participation in sports. Barriers that impede sports participation include but not limited to cost, time, club fees, community setting, friends, ability, fear of being judged, embarrassment, not being very good at the sport, and accessibility (Somerset & Hoare, 2018). Barriers related to cost to participate, membership or club fees and others make it difficult for students from the lower to middle classes to participate in sports. Barriers related to the family's limited amount of finances and resources that can be used to buy or use equipment, funds to buy team uniforms, fees for competition, and, last but not least, whether the family has reliable transportation that will allow them to get to team practices, fees, lodging and food bills to attend away games, competitions, and championships that take place. All these barriers, as well as others, have a significant effect on an interest in or feeling of belonging versus alienation in school and in sports (Burkhardt, 2016; Hoff & Mitchell, 2007). The participation gap should cause many in this field to have concerns. Many low-SES students participate in sports at significantly lower rates than do their high classmates from high-SES backgrounds. The gap that exists in children's sports participation based on social class should elicit concern. We must, as a society, be concerned with extracurricular activities that might be used to allure the more at-risk students to desire full involvement and commitment at their school. We know a sense of belonging and affiliation with other students at school also enhances a student's chances of school success. Taken together, data collected in this program of research suggest the importance of future research to uncover the role of poverty and family on the influence of a low-income SES students' interest in and level of participation in sports.

We learn from research and medical documents that involvement in extracurricular activities has several positive effects. With the fact that many sports and extracurricular activities require monies for fees, this makes it extremely difficult for many low-income children to afford to participate in a sport. To increase participation rates of low-income children in sports, policy makers and others involved in this area should come up with strategies and innovative ideas that will cut down costs and associated fees, making their participation more likely. As a culture, the reason we need to focus on creative ways to make costs feasible is because research over time shows that after-school sports and extracurricular activities provide opportunities for positive growth and development for a child's overall well-being. However, research tells us that children living in low-income households actually participate in sports at significantly lower rates than other lower SES groups (Burkhardt, 2016; Hoff & Mitchell, 2007). Research also shows that the number of children left unsupervised after school (aka latchkey children) is increasing for single-parent households. For youth who spend time alone and without supervision, we find a significant increase in antisocial behaviors and fewer positive outcomes (see, for example, Afterschool Alliance, 2005; Casey, Ripke, & Huston, 2005; Fredricks & Eccles, 2005; Mahoney, Lord, & Carryl, 2005).

The high costs associated with sports participation create negative consequences and hurdles for those students who come from low-income families (Hoff & Mitchell, 2007). Students from underprivileged families lack the opportunities that other children receive. We know that students from low-income families lack opportunities that give them goals and strategies needed to increase self-confidence. We also know that low-income children are devoid of participation and interest in individual sports that will introduce them to the idea of diversity, especially opportunities to engage in sports that are aligned with the middle and upper social classes (Sheehan & Rall, 2011). Involvement in various sports is important for individual cognitive and behavioral development because sports provide a way for people to release energy and aggression, but in a positive direction (Hoff & Mitchell, 2007). The challenge, though, is how do we encourage people from underprivileged backgrounds to participate in sports? Is it possible to make sports and extracurricular activities in American culture easy and more accessible to low-income students?

Income is a major predictor of the extracurricular activities that children show interest and participate in. In today's culture, we have a "pay-to-play" norm that makes participating in extracurricular activities more of a burden for families (Hoff & Mitchell, 2007). Pay-to-play sports are more popular in this day and time. Sadly, Whitmer (2013) believes that the "pay-to-play" idea has slowly become the norm at many schools in the United States. The reason for this is simply due to the fact that public schools are finding revenue decreasing and are basically short on funds. To offset costs, schools must charge a fee to play and participate in sports simply because it makes it less complicated for the school to offer sports as an extracurricular activity. However, making students pay not only limits participation but also it can have a negative effect on students' motivation and interest. When children cannot afford to participate in a sport, just the knowledge alone that they are "too poor" and unable to participate may negatively affect their attitude toward the sport and sports in general.

Lower income areas typically do not have sports activities with high fees simply because they know that people living in those communities cannot afford to pay the fees. Affordability determines the sports that can be offered in lower income communities. Higher income families are much more likely to be able to expose children to a wide variety of sports. Contrast this with lower income families who may only be able to allow a child to select one sport. Affordability in and of itself is known to prevent a child from being involved with several sporting opportunities and activities. When a family cannot afford the extra expenses associated with a sport, financial assistance from an outside source will be important. We know that extracurricular activities can be quite expensive. Expenses related to sports-related equipment, membership fees to access sports facilities, uniforms, and other items make participation in sports vary based on one's socioeconomic status (Golle, Granacher, Hoffmann, Wick, & Muehlbauer, 2014).

Our culture places emphasis on teams that can purchase high-quality, expensive protective equipment for athletes for safety. This cultural pressure to have the best equipment results in a plethora of programs seeking ways to offset the massive costs (Hoff & Mitchell, 2007).

Although we recognize that fees associated with sports participation are needed and oftentimes mandatory, it is the fees that make it extremely challenging for some families to be able to afford to allow their children to participate, particularly if their children want to be involved in more than one sport. Involvement by parents is another key factor limiting participation. Parental involvement, according to research, is key when we consider a child's overall well-being (National Middle School Association, 2006). We discussed this at length in Chapter 10 on aging.

Parents are often charged with being responsible for the child's level of participation and involvement. Parents carry the burden and responsibility for making sure that the child gets to and from team practices and sporting events, as well as paying fees and other costs associated with participation (Loptinzi, Cardinal, Loprinzi, & Lee, 2012; Merkel, 2013). As stated previously in this chapter, children from low-SES environments have lower participation rates in sports than those from high-SES environments (Wijtzes et al., 2014). For children coming from lower income homes, just making a commitment to a sport can be a struggle. Low-income children often are not able to commit to consistency in their attendance simply because one or both of their parents may work. When parents work, it becomes challenging to get children to and from after-school sporting activities. We also know that some parents who work multiple jobs and have limited transportation are also less likely to allow their children to participate in sports (Holt, Kingsley, Tink, & Scherer, 2011).

Related to our discussion on parental involvement and factors limiting participation in extracurricular activities is the number of children in a household. If there are several children in the home, then it makes sense that this would affect the amount of money that they can provide for participation in specific and multiple sports activities. Having multiple children in multiple sports activities adds more pressure in that this alone requires that parents have several transportation options, which some families living in poverty are unable to provide. For many low-income families, one mode of transportation is challenging let alone finding multiple modes of transportation that will get children to and from sports; this can also decrease the probability and likelihood that children from low-income families will participate in sports activities after school (Merkel, 2013).

Some low-income households, according to Census Bureau statistics (2016) are considered "one-parent households." This attribute alone makes it very difficult for the parent to commit to extracurricular activities for one child, let alone multiple children. Research conducted by Barrett and Turner (2006) revealed that those children from two-parent households are more likely to be found participating in sports activities than those children coming from single-parent households. According to the research, dual parent households allow one parent to be able to take the child to the activity while the other attends to something else, such as work (Barrett & Ollendick, 2004; Barrett & Turner, 2006). It is also a challenge for one parent to pay costs and fees as he or she has a limited amount of disposable income. While we know that being a single parent can be challenging, we also realize that in America, single parent's limited income and resources practically mandate that many of individuals living in that situation simply cannot allow children to participate in extracurricular sports activities.

Families from lower social classes, we find, tend to live in neighborhoods that are considered to be unsafe. Many of these areas are described as having higher crime rates and violence, as well as overcrowding (Engle & Black, 2008). Individuals living in this environment report that they often do not feel safe in their own neighborhoods, but they also report being less interested in participating in extracurricular sports (Howie, Lukacs, Pastor, Reuben, & Mendola, 2010). "When living in unsafe areas, it is difficult to offer and participate in organized activities because, for example, there are limited safe locations to hold events" (Burkhardt, 2016; Hoff & Mitchell, 2007). We find that children from middle-class families often have safe streets to play on. Often you find children playing in cul-de-sacs or playing hopscotch on the sidewalks.

Effect of Limited Participation

Physical activity, as we know, is vital for one's overall health. Research from sociological sources shows that out of all the social classes, physical inactivity is most prevalent among low-income families (Burkhardt, 2016; Hoff & Mitchell, 2007). We also know that limited participation affects children because it not only makes them less active but also it affects overall well-being, obesity, and confidence (Barnett, Morgan, & Van Beurden, 2011; Barnett, Van Beurden, & Morgan, 2009). Lack of physical activity causes increases in obesity, Type II diabetes, and stress. Along with these negative effects of physical inactivity, we also know that inactive children are affected mentally, emotionally, and socially. Research in the area of childhood and adolescence development shows that participation in organized sports is positively associated with increases in academic adjustment. We also know that physical activity for low-income children is related to a child's psychological and social adjustment (Fredricks & Simpkins, 2012). Without an outlet to engage in activity and sports, children will not be afforded the opportunity to learn or enhance essential life skills. We know from child development literature that children who are active in physical sports and activities report higher social skills than those who are inactive or do not participate in an organized sport (Howie, Lukacs, Pastor, Reuben, & Mendola., 2010). Researchers remind us that sports and physical activity are tied intimately to children's ability to integrate into a larger social network, to learn how to work in a team, and to increase their level of confidence (Wijtzes et al., 2014). Teamwork and social integration are two life skills that participation in sports provides. Sports offer opportunities for children to learn how to

Physical activity and mental health

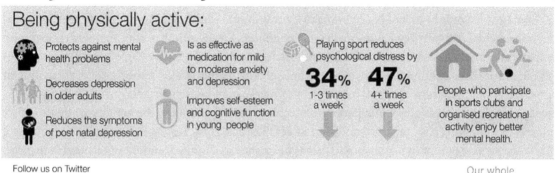

FIGURE 13.1   *Physical activity and mental health.*

not only get along with other children in their age group but also to take instructions from coaches and how to work with adults. Participation in organized sports is a win-win solution in that sports allow youth to get comfortable listening to directions from other adults.

Figure 13.1 is an infographic that portrays the positive benefits of physical activity on mental health. Although we know that regular exercise is good for the body, the infographic illustrates that exercise is also one of the most effective ways to improve depression, anxiety, and other psychological states associated with mental health. Consistent exercise is also known to relieve stress, improve memory, sleep and mood states. And you don't have to be a fitness fanatic to reap the benefits. Research indicates that modest amounts of exercise can make a difference. No matter your age or fitness level, you can learn to use exercise as a powerful tool to feel better.

Another perk of participation in extracurricular activities is a little less overt: it teaches students how to manage their time and schoolwork. We know that children who live in environments with limited resources are often prevented from learning how to develop time management skills. They are also less adept at working under pressure. Extracurricular activities provide these and other benefits, such as personal responsibility, how to work alone or in a team, and how to communicate. Students are also afforded opportunities to exercise and socialize in a safe and supervised environment (Grudeva, 2010). Other lesser known perks of involvement in sports and extracurricular activities include "better and consistent school attendance, higher graduation rates, and improved test scores" (Burkhardt, 2016; Hoff & Mitchell, 2007).

"Poverty can also prevent them from being able to do something enjoyable with their friends, leading to unhealthy emotional health. Depression is high in families in poverty, and activity participation has shown to improve mental health and reduce symptoms of depression" (Burkhardt, 2016; Hoff & Mitchell, 2007). Even more important, we know that participation in organized sports lowers risky behaviors, such as alcohol and drug use (Fredricks & Simpkins, 2012). Studies have gathered data that prove that students from low-income homes and neighborhoods are least likely to participate in crime if they are given the opportunity to engage in an organized youth sport after school. Data also show that low-income students report having a "sense of connectedness to the school, exhibit increased self-esteem, and created positive social networks they might otherwise not have" (Burkhardt, 2016; Hoff & Mitchell, 2007).

Interventions to Increase Access to Activities

For sports promoters who are focused on increasing youth participation in organized sports, the first required step is to conduct extensive research on the youth market to identify interests, activities, and media youth are most interested in. While interests among youth will differ based on environment, influencers, ethnicity, and age, we know that children will participate in events and activities that they feel confident about, good at, and involved in. In terms of influencers, research tells us that children's attitudes and behaviors toward sports are often determined by the sports and activities that those in their social network are most involved in because it makes them feel safe. Research should be conducted that provides insights and useful information for schools and community organizations so that they will have informed knowledge about the popular sporting and extracurricular activities to offer to attract the youth in the neighborhood. As previously mentioned, it is understood that families with limited income and resources make it hard for communities and schools to provide as many events and sports activities as those schools and communities that are composed primarily of higher income residents (Fredricks & Simpkins, 2012). While government and foundation grant funding has increased significantly for low-income areas and the public schools that have been identified as low-performance, few funds have been offered to support the development of facilities and sports clubs that can meet the needs of lower income families with children who desperately need to participate in some sort of physical activity. For example, many facilities and sports clubs could offer flexible, affordable arrangements for fees and memberships to the community. According to research on the topic, allowing affordable financial arrangements is one effective way to increase physical fitness in children (Golle, Granacher, Hoffmann, Wick, & Muehlbauer, 2014). Some communities might offer fee waivers or scholarships to those who qualify and cannot afford to pay membership fees, buy equipment, or pay costs associated with joining a competitive sports team (Hoff & Mitchell, 2007). Communities, local businesses, and sponsors might also join in the effort to increase low-income children's physical activities. Sponsorships, local government offices, and businesses by building recreational and sports facilities that are either supported by tax dollars or by funding from local businesses. Cooperative sponsorships by local governments and businesses might also help to reduce the costs and fees that prevent low-income families from participating in many sports events and activities.

Another idea in addressing the disparities in sports participation by SES might be for schools and after-school programs to use a more personal approach. Starting in elementary school, it is suggested that in attempts to increase participation in sports, young children should be matched with a "sports" mentor, or a role model, or someone who can expose them to diverse sports and sporting events with the goal of nurturing untapped sports potential. The Boys and Girls Clubs of America is one example of an organization that addresses disparities in sports by SES. The oldest, community-based youth organization, the Boys and Girls Clubs of America receives federal funding to help families in need. Since research showed decades ago that many children in low-income neighborhoods do not have places to go after school, the Boys and Girls Clubs of America were created to provide a positive and safe place for children. Programs provided by the Boys and Girls Clubs of America promote skills such as leadership development, health and fitness skills, life skills, the arts, tutoring, and other educational needs, as well as programs in sports and recreation. The Boys and Girls Clubs of America provide all children with a safe environment and a place to go after school. Recall earlier that research found that one reason that low-income children reported for their lack of participation in after-school sports is their fear of danger and the feeling that they are not safe. The Boys and Girls Clubs of America addresses these feelings while also providing opportunities for children to develop positive friendships (Fredricks & Simpkins, 2012.

Some teams offer fundraising and other events to raise money. To subsidize the extra costs, teams look to fundraising tools that help students who cannot afford uniforms or equipment to be able to participate. PlanetHS is a fundraising resource that assists schools and businesses with fundraising techniques specifically to help them figure out how to meet the needs of those children and families who are not able to afford costs associated with expensive equipment and uniforms. Fundraising techniques should be tried more often to help local sports teams be successful. From a sports promotion and public relations perspective, we know that local businesses are willing to sponsor teams because sponsorships are one way to connect with a community. Revenue from sponsorships is often used to pay for uniforms and other needs. The most attractive part of fundraising is that it raises money for the entire team and does not isolate or highlight the children who need the financial assistance from those who do not. There are also tips for those health clubs and other sporting environments to use to bridge the SES gap in sports participation. First and foremost, personnel and others need to make sure that every individual from all backgrounds and ethnicities feels welcome and a part of the sport. The most straightforward example of this are opportunities for owners and coaches to greet each person and learn everyone's names.

Changing the Complexion of Sports

If we examine the stories behind the Williams sisters', Tiger Woods's, and Simone Manuel's success in sports that blacks are not as involved in, we find common elements in their entrance into tennis, golf, and swimming. In 2010, a study was conducted that showed that nearly "70 percent of African-American children and almost 60 percent of Hispanic/Latino children have low or no swim ability, compared to 40 percent of Caucasians" (Almond, 2018). To address these statistics, many swim officials have started intense initiatives to introduce and recruit minorities to the sport of swimming. As a result, swimming officials report a rise in African American swimmers by approximately 55% in the last decade (Almond, 2018). The same source reported increases in Hispanic and Latino swimmers by approximately 77% (Almond, 2018).

Simone Manuel, a 2016 Olympic gold medalist in swimming, struggled in a sport that was dominated by white athletes. Manuel has stated that her parents observed her uncanny interest in the water and later signed her up to receive swimming lessons at age four. Her parents have gone on record saying that their main motivation to place Simone in swimming lessons was so that she would know how to be safe in the water. But Manual also stated that she enjoyed swimming so much that she fully engaged in the sport by the time she was age nine. Manuel's passion for swimming, according to media reports, extends far beyond the pool. Manual currently serves as a mentor for aspiring swimmers. She also recently joined the USA Swimming National Diversity and Inclusion Committee, which she said helped her overcome the loneliness she felt at being one of the few minorities in the sport of swimming (Almond, 2018).

Middle to Upper Class Privilege

Persons who relate and associate more with the middle to upper class are typically receiving lessons and tutelage from individuals who are associated with the middle upper class. One's social class membership is not centered on feelings of shame. Social class membership is about understanding.

Next is a list of middle to upper class privileges. If you are a member of the middle class or upper class economic groups (or, in some cases, perceived to be), listed next are benefits that may be granted based on your group membership—benefits not given to people found in the lower classes of social status.

The following list was obtained from the Internet in July 2018 and found various American cultural behaviors almost inevitably connected with one's level of social class (see Killermann, 2014):

30+ Examples of Middle-to-Upper Class Privilege

1. *Politicians pay attention to your class, and fight for your vote in election seasons.*
2. *You can advocate for your class to politicians and not have to worry about being seen as looking for a handout.*
3. *You can readily find accurate (or non-caricatured) examples of members your class depicted in films, television, and other media.*
4. *New products are designed and marketed with your social class in mind.*
5. *If you see something advertised that you really want, you will buy it.*
6. *You can swear (or commit a crime) without people attributing it to the low morals of your class.*
7. *If you find yourself in a legally perilous situation, you can hire an attorney to ensure your case is heard justly.*
8. *You can talk with your mouth full and not have people attribute this to the uncivilized nature of your social class.*
9. *You can attend a "fancy" dinner without apprehension of doing something wrong or embarrassing the hosts.*
10. *You understand the difference between healthy and unhealthy food, and can choose to eat healthy food if you wish.*
11. *You can walk around your neighborhood at night without legitimate concern for your safety.*
12. *In the case of medical emergency, you won't have to decide against visiting a doctor or the hospital due to economic reasons.*
13. *You have visited a doctor for a "check-up."*
14. *Your eyesight, smile, and general health aren't inhibited by your income.*
15. *If you become sick, you can seek medical care immediately and not just "hope it goes away."*
16. *If you choose to wear hand-me-down or second-hand clothing, this won't be attributed to your social class, and may actually be considered stylish.*
17. *You can update your wardrobe with new clothes to match current styles and trends.*
18. *As a kid, you were able to participate in sports and other extracurricular activities (field trips, clubs, etc.) with school friends.*
19. *As a kid, your friends' parents allowed your friends to play and sleep over at your house.*
20. *You don't have to worry that teachers or employers will treat you poorly or have negative expectations of you because of your class.*
21. *The schools you went to as a kid had updated textbooks, computers, and a solid faculty.*
22. *Growing up, college was an expectation of you (whether you chose to go or not), not a lofty dream.*
23. *Your decision to go or not to go to college wasn't based entirely on financial determinants.*
24. *People aren't surprised if they realize you are intelligent, hard-working, or honest.*
25. *An annual raise in pay at your job is measured in dollars, not cents.*

Sam Killermann, "30+ Examples of Middle-to-Upper Class Privilege," It's Pronounced Metrosexual. 2014.

26. *You've likely never looked into a paycheck advance business (e.g., "Check Into Cash"), and have definitely never used one.*

27. *You are never asked to speak for all members of your class.*

28. *Whenever you've moved out of your home it has been voluntary, and you had another home to move into.*

29. *It's your choice to own a reliable car or to choose other means of transportation.*

30. *Regardless of the season, you can count on being able to fall asleep in a room with a comfortable temperature.*

31. *When you flip a light switch in your house, you don't have to wonder if the light will come on (or if your utilities have been terminated).*

32. *People don't assume you've made an active choice to be in your social class, but instead assume you're working to improve it.*

33. *The "dream" of a house, a healthy family, and a solid career isn't a dream at all, but simply a plan.*

34. *People do not assume based on the dialect you grew up speaking that you are unintelligent or lazy.*

35. *When you choose to use variants of language (e.g., slang terms) people chalk them up to plasticity in the language (rather than assuming your particular dialectical variants deserve ridicule and punishment).*

The aforementioned list and all the previous sections in this chapter have touched the surface of what we know about SES and the effect it has on our lives and participation in sports. The list also shows us how social class is related to certain behaviors and how our social class might accelerate or preclude participation and success in sports. We find interactions with differing amounts of wealth in sports and lifestyles of people with power (Bourdieu, 1986a; Laberge & Sankoff, 1988). For the most part, relationships and associations between social class and sports show clearly intertwined and complex relationships between income and access to resources and opportunities for involvement in various sports and extracurricular activities. For example, individuals in the upper class can participate in sports such as sailing, tennis, racquetball, golf, and other sports that are played at exclusive health clubs and exquisite resorts. Upper class individuals can even participate in these sports during the regular workday, unlike lower and middle class individuals who are confined to jobs that will not allow them to leave for a midday "golf game" or other sporting activity. Sports such as golf, tennis, and racquetball often use expensive equipment and are part of an exclusive fitness or country club. Over time in the United States, these country clubs and health clubs have become closely aligned with the upper class and those who have the power and authority to use their wealth. The people who engage in these "upper class" sports usually have considerable control over their work lives, which also means that they have the freedom to take time off from work that is needed to participate in the sport, or they can combine participation with their work.

Money and Power in Sports

People with more money, education, and power tend to play and watch sports more often than people with little education and fewer financial assets. People coming from low socioeconomic backgrounds tend to work longer hours and do not have the disposable income needed to enjoy leisure activities. Thus it can be concluded that money has a great influence on sports participation. Money not only affects if people play a sport but also what sports people might play.

Reflect on Sports: How Money Interacts With Sports

It was March 13 in the year 2006 when the Duke University lacrosse team "hired two strippers to dance at a party" (Cohan, 2014, https://www.economist.com/news/books-and-arts/21600649-messy-tale-money-sport-and-race-power-punch). One of the strippers was a black single mother, Crystal Mangum. Ms. Mangum claimed that after the party was over, three players from the lacrosse team violated her. News concerning this event produced a scandal that media frequently reported and discussed. The event and rape of Ms. Mangum provoked many discussions about race, ethnicity, and social class. Eventually, the case was dismissed against the three players and Duke University "settled lawsuits for around $20 million each" (Cohan, 2014).

"While lacrosse players made up less than 1% of Duke undergraduates in the fall of 2005, 25% of disorderly conduct cases, 50% of noise ordinance cases and one-third of all open-container violations involved lacrosse players," says William Cohan, a former banker who wrote a book called *The Price of Silence: The Duke Lacrosse Scandal, the Power of the Elite, and the Corruption of Our Great Universities*. Students and other people perceived the administrators to have turned a blind eye, with little expression of concern about the rape—that is, until the rape allegations reached national media and a media storm ensued. The district attorney told the media that a crime had occurred. This validation of the rape persisted even as doubt, skepticism, and inconsistencies were slowing being revealed regarding Ms. Mangum's account of the rape. DNA tests conducted on Mangum were unable to establish a link to Mangum and any of the lacrosse players. The DNA test did show, however, that the victim engaged in sexual intercourse with four other men at approximately the same time as the alleged crime supposedly committed by the three lacrosse players (Cohan, 2014). If the Mangum sex scandal had been the result of consensual sex, the prosecution's case would have been severely weakened. "Mr. Nifong connived with DNA Security to exclude this evidence from their report. He was later disbarred" (Cohan, 2014).

One explanation offered to help us understand how the mix of the upper class or the privileged white players and a black woman from the lower social class who also hailed from the southern region led many to jump to conclusions about the reason the rape took place. Research shows that this rapid need for closure took place long before the facts of the case emerged. Many individuals, along with the mass media, were quick to judge the black female stripper.

The Intersectionality of Social Class, Age, and Gender

If we want to investigate the intersectionality of social class, age, and gender, we might notice even more interesting patterns. Take, for example, married women. A married woman may want to take part in a sport, but she may not have the flexibility or freedom to regularly attend practices and competitive sports events. In American culture, women, particularly those women in lower and middle-class brackets, tend to be confined to very strict gender roles. Gender roles associated with child care, domestic work, and other responsibilities that lead to fewer opportunities to be involved with a sport. Even women who choose to work outside of the home lack the time and may be limited in time to practice. Women from upper class families have few, if any, constraints on their participation in sports. They can afford to find someone to watch their children. They can afford to pay fees. They can buy dinner. Oftentimes, the network for upper class women includes other women who are also active in a sport. Be it playing tennis at the health club or a resort, this group of women seldom experiences the constricted pressure of conservative gender roles that lower and middle-class women experience.

In terms of the intersectionality of social class and race/ethnicity, we find that African American athletes are very visible in sports. Yet, as we discussed in previous chapters, we find fewer opportunities in terms of ownership and management portrayals for women and athletes of color. We also know that African American and some Latin American athletes dominate in boxing and baseball. We further know that African Americans dominate exclusively in basketball, football, and track. Yet the lucrative sports are predominately white—sports such as swimming, golf, and tennis.

Disparities in Salaries

As noted in several chapters in this text, we know that the world of sports has several disparate issues. In terms of salary, we find that the sports world continues to offer unequal funding and salaries to women working in sports. "Paying men more for the same sport gives women in the sport less incentive to push themselves and discourages future female participation in the sport" (Wright, 2017).

Gender Inequity in Collegiate Sports

While female student-athletes consist of close to 60% of the U.S. college student population, "female athletes are recipients of only 43% of all athletic participation opportunities at NCAA schools" (Jackson, 2018). This statistic translates to 63,241 fewer female athletes being afforded athletic participation opportunities when compared to their male athlete counterparts (NCAA, 2018). NCAA statistics show that male student-athletes continue to receive more than half of all scholarship dollars (Jackson, 2018). If we investigate dollars allocated to men's and women's sports, we find that women's sports at most colleges receive less than 40% of athletic departments' operating budgets. Further research on salaries of head coaches averages approximately "$3,430,000 for head coaches of men's teams and $1,172,400 for women's teams" (NCAA, 2018).

Gender Equity in Professional Sports

The World Major Marathon is a large organization that includes international races such as the "New York Marathon, the Boston Marathon, the London Marathon, the Tokyo Marathon, the Berlin Marathon, and the Chicago Marathon" (Jackson, 2018). This is one unique area in sports where both the winning male and winning female athlete are awarded the same amount ($500,0000). In terms of equal pay for men and women, historical records revealed that the United States Open's Grand Slam event in 1873 was the first professional sport to provide its athletes with equal pay. In 2007, Wimbledon also started paying winners in equal amounts (Wimbledon, 2018).

Women surfers now earn the same prize money as their male counterparts. Their championship event, World Surf League Samsung Galaxy Championship Tour, includes 11 stops. The award for the men's championship tour in 2014 was $525,000, compared to only $262,500 for women surfers. In 2016, Swatch Women's Pro made sure the prize money for women surfers was the same as men.

In other sports, the biggest difference in winnings can be found in golf, where the male winner of the Open Championship receives $1.8 million in comparison to just $298,000 for the women's event. The winners of golf's biggest men's tournaments earn $1.8 million for the week out of $10 million. In women's golf, "$4.5 million at the U.S. Women's Open is the largest reward" in the sport for women golfers (Walters, 2016). Prize money in 2015 for the PGA Tour was more than $340 million. That prize, according to experts, "is more than five times that of the new-high for the 2016 LPGA tour at $61.6 million" (Jackson, 2018). For a graphic illustration of the pay gap, Figure 13.2 is an infographic that shows the abysmal differences in pay for the PGA and LGPA athletes.

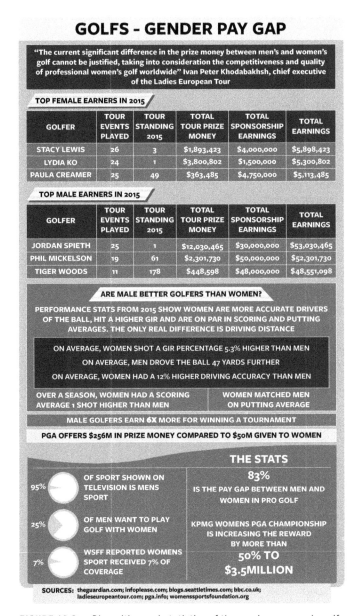

GOLFS – GENDER PAY GAP

"The current significant difference in the prize money between men's and women's golf cannot be justified, taking into consideration the competitiveness and quality of professional women's golf worldwide" Ivan Peter Khodabakhsh, chief executive of the Ladies European Tour

TOP FEMALE EARNERS IN 2015

GOLFER	TOUR EVENTS PLAYED	TOUR STANDING 2015	TOTAL TOUR PRIZE MONEY	TOTAL SPONSORSHIP EARNINGS	TOTAL EARNINGS
STACY LEWIS	26	3	$1,893,423	$4,000,000	$5,898,423
LYDIA KO	24	1	$3,800,802	$1,500,000	$5,300,802
PAULA CREAMER	25	49	$363,485	$4,750,000	$5,113,485

TOP MALE EARNERS IN 2015

GOLFER	TOUR EVENTS PLAYED	TOUR STANDING 2015	TOTAL TOUR PRIZE MONEY	TOTAL SPONSORSHIP EARNINGS	TOTAL EARNINGS
JORDAN SPIETH	25	1	$12,030,465	$30,000,000	$53,030,465
PHIL MICKELSON	19	61	$2,301,730	$50,000,000	$52,301,730
TIGER WOODS	11	178	$448,598	$48,000,000	$48,551,098

ARE MALE BETTER GOLFERS THAN WOMEN?

PERFORMANCE STATS FROM 2015 SHOW WOMEN ARE MORE ACCURATE DRIVERS OF THE BALL, HIT A HIGHER GIR AND ARE ON PAR IN SCORING AND PUTTING AVERAGES. THE ONLY REAL DIFFERENCE IS DRIVING DISTANCE

ON AVERAGE, WOMEN SHOT A GIR PERCENTAGE 5.3% HIGHER THAN MEN

ON AVERAGE, MEN DROVE THE BALL 47 YARDS FURTHER

ON AVERAGE, WOMEN HAD A 12% HIGHER DRIVING ACCURACY THAN MEN

OVER A SEASON, WOMEN HAD A SCORING AVERAGE 1 SHOT HIGHER THAN MEN	WOMEN MATCHED MEN ON PUTTING AVERAGE

MALE GOLFERS EARN **6X** MORE FOR WINNING A TOURNAMENT

PGA OFFERS $256M IN PRIZE MONEY COMPARED TO $50M GIVEN TO WOMEN

THE STATS

95%	OF SPORT SHOWN ON TELEVISION IS MENS SPORT	**83%** IS THE PAY GAP BETWEEN MEN AND WOMEN IN PRO GOLF
25%	OF MEN WANT TO PLAY GOLF WITH WOMEN	KPMG WOMENS PGA CHAMPIONSHIP IS INCREASING THE REWARD BY MORE THAN
7%	WSFF REPORTED WOMENS SPORT RECEIVED 7% OF COVERAGE	**50% TO $3.5MILLION**

SOURCES: theguardian.com; infoplease.com; blogs.seattletimes.com; bbc.co.uk; ladieseuropeantour.com; pga.info; womenssportsfoundation.org

FIGURE 13.2 *Disparities and statistics of the gender pay gap in golf.*

FIGURE 13.3 *Squash racquets.*

Squash

In 2017, for the first time, men's and women's World Squash Championships offered equal prize awards, with both winners receiving $45,000 (Etchells, 2017). Squash is following in the footsteps of Fédération Internationale de Volleyball, the four Grand Slams in tennis, multiple World Major Marathons, and the World Surf League. Figure 13.3 is a picture of the racquets used in squash.

Tennis

Tennis is the only sport in America that places women on Forbes's "World's 100 Highest-Paid Athletes." Known for being the "most gender-equitable sport for women," we know that the sport also idolizes its female players more than other sports (Klenke, 2017). Maria Sharapova earned $23 million in endorsements and $6.7 million in prize money in 2015, and even though her endorsements have reduced, she, along with Serena Williams, are two ladies who have become wealthy through their business guile and sheer talent, thanks to the equitable realm of tennis.

WNBA Versus NBA

Regarding the WNBA, in 2014, former University of Connecticut women's basketball player Diana Taurasi was selected to be a part of the All-WNBA First Team. Her performance while playing with the WNBA's Phoenix Mercury helped score the league's championship. In the same season, the WNBA paid Taurasi the maximum salary allowed for a WNBA player which at the time was $107,500. Currently, the maximum salary in the WNBA is capped at $110,000 which is 20% of the average NBA player's salary (Lamonier, 2018). Compare that number to salaries of male players in the NBA. In the same year, 2014, Dionte Christmas was played with the Phoenix Suns for a total of 198 minutes. "For three hours and thirty-eight minutes—his total tenure playing in the NBA, it was documented that Christmas was paid the league minimum of $490,180" (Berri, 2015).

We know that the WNBA earns revenue from selling rights to broadcast stations. As of this writing, the broadcasting contracts earn the league $12 million per year (Berry, 2015). As of 2016, the WNBA games drew approximately 7,578 fans per game (Berry, 2015). "If the WNBA paid 50 percent of its revenues to its players, the average player—given the above estimates for the WNBA—would receive $114,249, which is more than the current maximum wage in the WNBA" (Berri, 2018). NBA 2016 most valuable player (MVP) Stephen Curry earned $11.4 million in 2016. Meanwhile, Nneka Ogwumike, the reigning WNBA MVP of the 2016 season, who happens to be one of the highest paid WNBA players, earned $95,000 in 2016. the maximum salary in the league, which is not even close to the maximum salary reported in the WNBA in 2014.

Cricket

Cricket men's International Cricket Council World Cup offers a $3.975 million prize, while women's World Cup winners are rewarded $75,000. Darts, some parts of cycling, skiing, and snooker are also sports with gender pay disparities.

Soccer

"The players on the World Cup–winning United States women's national soccer team earn less money than their counterparts on the men's national team" (Das, 2016). "Carli Lloyd, Alex Morgan, Megan Rapinoe, Becky Sauerbrunn and Hope Solo" joined forces in a wage-discrimination complaint filed with the Equal Employment Opportunity Commission in March of 2016. The professional athletes filed a single complaint against U.S. Soccer (Das, 2016). The five soccer stars "accused U.S. Soccer of paying them and their teammates less than their male soccer counterparts on the men's national team receive" (Das, 2016). The athletes obtained most, if not all, of their statistics and facts from the federation's financial reports. Information found in the resources showed clear evidence that male soccer players earn significantly higher salaries than female soccer players. The five soccer athletes also attacked a proposal related to the compensation and bonus structure. The five soccer sensations also said that salaries in the soccer field were skewed heavily toward men, even given the widely publicized fact that female soccer players' success on the team "produced millions of dollars in revenue for U.S. Soccer in 2015 and was projected to do the same in 2016" (Das, 2016). The women's soccer team has also won three World Cups in the seven tournaments held since 1991. The men's soccer team, which has never advanced beyond the quarterfinals of the World Cup, has won four Olympic championships as of the current writing of this chapter.

Salaries for Professional Athletes

The common misperception when it comes to athletes is that they all are millionaires. Although some athletes such as Michael Jordan, LeBron James, and Alex Rodriguez, are millionaires or billionaires, the vast majority of professional athletes do not have the privilege of signing million-dollar contracts. Salary data from across the NFL, NBA, NHL, MLB, and MLS reveal that out of all the leagues, the players who earn significant salaries are in the NBA. NBA players are reported to have the "highest average career earnings by far, whereas most MLS players make just half a million dollars" (Schwartz, 2015).

Highest Paid Female Athletes

Tennis

The most lucrative sport for female athletes is tennis, according to research. Tennis is the rare sport that focuses on gender equity. "Seven of the ten highest-earning female athletes in 2016 were members of the WTA Tour" (Walters, 2016). We learn from research that prize money awarded to competitors is the same for both men and women. This applies to all "four grand-slam events—the Australian Open, the French Open, Wimbledon and the U.S. Open" (Walters, 2016).

Golf

Lydia Ko from New Zealand won the Ladies Professional Golf Association Tour prize money in 2017. Ko received approximately $2.8 million in total for her appearance in the tour. However, Jordan Spieth led the PGA Tour salary list with a record of earning a total of $12 million. Even the player who "ranked 25th on the PGA Tour, Daniel Berger, received more than Ko in 2015" (Walters, 2016).

The Outliers

Two female athletes rank on the highest paid female athlete list in male-dominated sports: Danica Patrick and Ronda Rousey. Although Patrick has never won a NASCAR event in more than 200 races, she is reported to have earned more than $13 million last year, half of those dollars were through endorsements and appearances in ads such as the recent GoDaddy commercials.

In 2015, MMA fighter Ronda Rousey (pictured in Figured 13.4) made the cover of *Sports Illustrated* and "appeared on the cover of a version of the *Sports Illustrated* swimsuit issue" (Walters, 2016). Although Rousey lost one of her three bouts in 2015, records show that she earned $6 million. Records also show that half of her riches came from endorsements.

Ultimately, the issue of the gender gap in pay in sports is pervasively met with a variety of arguments for and against: some argue that the misfortune of gender differences in pay is the direct result of ratings and television viewership. Others argue that women in sports should earn less than men because they are "the weaker vessels," or they do not work hard enough, or their sports are not as "athletic" as men.

Controversy in Salary: Academics Versus Athletics

The average salary for "head coaches at major colleges in 2017 is $1.64 million, up nearly 12% over last season" (Brady, Berkowitz, & Upton, 2012). In both college and professional sports, coaches earn more than professors and teachers, and, according to a new study, coaches' salaries increase year after year at much higher rates. The salary gap between athletics and academics has been an ongoing debate for decades. Many

FIGURE 13.4 *Ronda Rousey.*

FIGURE 13.5   *Nick Saban.*

critics think that our society needs to consider the value being placed on athletics compared to education.

"The top-25 highest-paid college football coaches are reported to earn an average salary of $3.85 million a year, which does not take into account benefits like use of private jets, golf club memberships, and thousands of dollars in other incentives" (Sinha, 2014). Successful athletic programs are used to help attract top student-athletes and allow massive contributions toward academic scholarships. The biggest argument in favor of the salaries given to coaches is that the competitive market drives salaries earned by head coaches. Nick Saban, pictured in Figure 13.5, has been the head coach at Alabama since 2007. His leadership has taken the Alabama Crimson Tide football team to three national championships. Coach Saban earns close to $7 million annually. This begs the question: Is it justifiable that coaches earn such high salaries while professors and instructors barely average $50,000 or even $60,000 and often have to work endless hours writing research grants and hiring?

As many chapters in this textbook have discussed, sports in our culture are male dominated, and discussions of athletic salaries will continue to show disparities. According to data that contrasts increases for cost of living for head coaches versus academics, "coaches have salary increases of 79 percent while professors' salaries increased by just four percent" (Sinha, 2014).

While it is true that coaches have higher salaries than most professors, what is not known is the fact that a good majority of a coaches' salary comes from outside work. Often, head coaches are expected to make media appearances. Monies received from their appearances, television contracts, wardrobe agreements, and other endorsements are primarily where they make their millions. While they may earn a base salary in the six-digit figure range, many coaches make their millions through other financial contracts outside of the athletic department. Coaches' salaries have even surpassed the salaries of many top corporate executives (refer to Figure 13.6). A quick glance of the data presented in Figure 13.6, we find that from 2007 to 2017, chief executive officers' pay increased by 23%. The

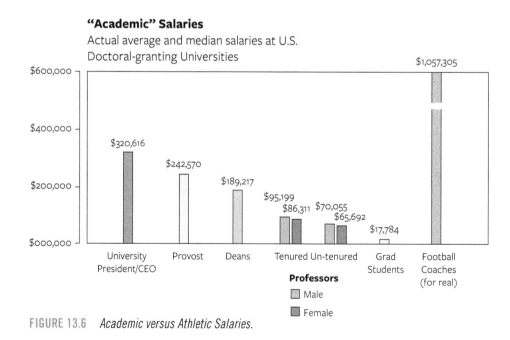

FIGURE 13.6   *Academic versus Athletic Salaries.*

increase includes salaries, stock options, bonuses, and other benefits (Sinha, 2014). In the same 10-year period, statistics showed a 44% increase for head coaches. In a recent study, data showed that some universities in the NCAA are actually "spending more per capita on professors than they are on head coaches—as much as six times more, in some conferences" (Sinha, 2014). The study also suggests that the issue of salary on both sides can be explained by the "revenue theory of cost." The "revenue theory of cost" is a common explanation used in higher education, which states that the more money an athletics program or an academic department make, the more money they will spend.

Some might argue that professors, too, can augment their salaries and make substantial money by writing textbooks. Professors associated with certain disciplines can earn extra compensation by writing the newest textbook. However, the complicated issue with this is that more often than not, millions of faculty members never see the revenue that their textbooks generate. In other words, the number of faculty members who see revenue from writing a textbook is substantially small (Sinha, 2014).

Salaries in academics and athletics are important issues to discuss and monitor; however, it should be noted that we must be careful comparing coaches' salaries to faculty salaries. These direct comparisons only lead to problematic interpretations and ultimately result in neither a favorable impression of the reality concerning compensation in college athletics (Friday, 2001, Toutkoushian & Kramer 2012). Those who recognize and accept the discrepancies in salary often note that "faculty members have the protection of tenure while coaches are employed at will and can be dismissed for lackluster win-loss records or inappropriate behaviors of their players" (Sinha, 2014; Toutkoushian & Kramer 2012). Job security comes by way of winning for coaches at many higher education institutions. And even then, there is still no sense of complete security, particularly if the head coach starts losing after years and years of winning seasons. Often it is asserted that he or she should simply "retire." The takeaway from this discussion is the need to understand how money relates to education and sports. Since much of this chapter has been devoted to SES and participation in sports, it just seemed that we needed to have a discussion on money and salaries in sports.

Figure 13.7 is a graph that shows an average salary of head coaches on a yearly basis. As of the current writing, Nick Saban, head football coach at the University of Alabama, will earn $11.132 million in 2018 (Berkowitz, Shnaars, & Dougherty, 2018; Caron, 2018).

\multicolumn{6}{c}{**2018 NCAAF COACHES SALARIES**}
RK	**SCHOOL**	**CONF**	**COACH**	**SCHOOL PAY**	**TOTAL PAY ▲**
1	Alabama	SEC	Nick Saban	$8,307,000	$8,307,000*
2	Ohio State	Big Ten	Urban Meyer	$7,600,000	$7,600,000*
3	Michigan	Big Ten	Jim Harbaugh	$7,504,000	$7,504,000*
4	Texas A&M	SEC	Jimbo Fisher	$7,500,000	$7,500,000
5	Aubum	SEC	Gus Malzahn	$6,700,000	$6,705,656
6	Georgia	SEC	Kirby Smart	$6,603,600	$6,603,600
7	Clemson	ACC	Dabo Swinney	$6,205,000	$6,543,350
8	Florida	SEC	Dan Mullen	$6,070,000	$6,070,000*
9	Texas	Big 12	Tom Herman	$5,500,000	$5,500,000
10	Nebraska	Big Ten	Scott Frost	$5,000,000	$5,000,000*
11	Oklahoma State	Big 12	Mike Gundy	$5,000,000	$5,000,000
12	Florida State	ACC	Willie Taggart	$5,000,000	$5,000,000*
13	Illinois	Big Ten	Lovie Smith	$5,000,000	$5,000,000*
14	Texas Christian	Big 12	Gary Patterson	$4,840,717	$4,840,717*
15	Penn State	Big Ten	James Franklin	$4,800,000	$4,800,000*

FIGURE 13.7 *The top highest-paid college coaches.*

Conclusion

Socioeconomic status is a person's position within an economic hierarchy. We learned that social status is divided into categories from low income, lower middle, upper middle, middle class, upper class, upper middle, and higher upper class. Where one fits in this hierarchy depends on a number of different variables: occupation, education, income, and where one resides. We also know that SES depends on intangible factors, such as one's attitude, motive, self-concept, and privilege. We also learned how our SES directly influences participation and interest in sports.

We know that attendance at sporting events, consuming media sports, involvement and participation in sports is correlated with income, education, and occupation. Dara Torres trained for the 2008 Olympic Games at age 41. It was noted that Torres had to invest about $100,000 for her general coach, a strength and training coach, a dietician, a physical therapist, and even a nanny to help care for her daughter while she trained. Participation at the elite level requires considerable resources and money. While some athletes get financial relief through sponsorships, others have to use personal funds.

The bottom line: social class and sports are integrally related. Organized sports rely on resources, and those who can afford and gain access to the facilities where the sports are housed find that sports works to their advantage. As we mentioned in the chapter on power and ownership in sports (Chapter 12), we find social class is also intimately related to determining who owns professional sports teams and media coverage of sports, and, ultimately, this intermingled relationship results in an ideology in America that you don't always get what you desire, but you will always deserve what you get. We spoke briefly about the intersectionality of social class, race/ethnicity, and gender. The importance of this discussion was to illustrate that low involvement in sports by lower class and some middle-class youth may be due to resources that are scarce. Other barriers, such as working parents, single parents, transportation, and ability to afford fees associated with facilities, memberships, uniforms, and competition, may discourage some youth from seeking out and becoming involved in a sport. Some suggestions were made with respect to increasing access for lower class youth to participate in sports other than boxing, basketball, football, and track. We must remember that research has proven time and time again that those youth who participate in sports enjoy other benefits besides enhancing a sports skill. They learn how to enhance their leadership skills, manage time, work under pressure, socialize with peers and adults, and other life skills that are not developed if they are not active in a sport. And, yes, let's mention the physical benefits as well—no matter the social class level, physical activity is important for one's overall health and well-being; it helps fight obesity, depression, and can also increase our confidence, self-perceptions, and level of self-esteem.

QUESTIONS FOR REFLECTION AND DISCUSSION

1. How does social class influence sports and sports participation?
2. Does playing sports contribute to occupational success? How and why?
3. How does social class and gender affect young girls and women who may be interested in sports? How does it affect them?
4. What happens when class and gender relations come together in men's lives? How does it generally affect them?
5. Provide examples of sports in low-income high school communities. Then examine the increased club sports in upper income areas. Why do you suppose we see these trends emerge in upper class income areas and neighborhoods? Identify the factors that are able to sustain these clubs?

6. Publicly financed sports stadiums and arenas often state that the main benefit for having the stadium or arena is unity in a city. Do these places unify a city, or are they just avenues for taxpayer money to be transferred into the hands of the upper class? Defend your answer with research.

7. Do money and economic power matter in sports? In what ways?

SUGGESTED ACTIVITIES

1. For sports story ideas, keep an eye out for any local appearances by former student-athletes from your school. Try to find one male and one female, and interview them about their thoughts on salaries.

2. Conduct research on whether student-athletes should be paid. Your answers should be heavily supported with research.

3. Create a marketing campaign for people of color to learn how to swim, play tennis, golf, learn rugby, etc. Many promotional campaigns for fitness focus on showing people the benefits of exercise.

4. Develop a grant proposal and ideas for interventions and programs tailored to increase diversity for sports that lack diversity (e.g., swimming, tennis, rugby)

5. Create a social media marketing campaign aimed at promoting a sport that middle to upper income individuals normally participate in. However, your goal is to promote this among lower SES individuals. Your grade will be based on some "likes" and attendance at the event.

6. Go to your local Boys and Girls Clubs of America. Make observations of the kids and staff and other notable issues. Then go to a health and fitness club. Make observations of people there. Then go to a country club and make observations. Compare your notes from all three places. What evidence did you find that supports information about how social class affects participation and membership in sports? Write it as a news story to educate readers on the objective facts of social class division and how it affects participation and involvement in sports in America.

7. Some argue that the upper class control sports in America? Do they or not? How? Provide evidence.

8. Identify and locate a low-income neighborhood. Make observations and take notes regarding the types of physical activities and facilities that are available. What sports activities are the children playing? Next, create promotional materials to help the community attain sponsors and funds from government officials and business. Be sure to be detailed and specific about the purpose of your proposed center, including the name of your center and its mission. Will you provide free transportation? Why or why not? What type of sports and activities should be included? What about membership fees?

9. Research the low-income youth market. What types of sports are they most interested in? What barriers prevent them from participation in sports? Are the barriers similar to those discussed in this chapter or did they present other more interesting issues that affect their level of participation in sports?

10. Do sports generate jobs that will benefit the working classes in socioeconomic ways? Why or why not? Provide evidence.

ADDITIONAL RESOURCES

"Occupational Employment and Wages, May 2017 Athletes and Sports Competitors," https://www.bls.gov/oes/current/oes272021.htm

"A Look at Male and Female Athlete Salaries, https://sportsmanagement.adelphi.edu/resources/infographics/a-look-at-male-and-female-professional-athlete-salaries/

Emerging Careers in Sports, https://www.learnhowtobecome.org/career-resource-center/careers-in-sports/

"11 Things You Might Not Know About Athlete Salaries" (tells you how athletes are paid, their obligations to their teams, and how taxes differ from state to state), http://mentalfloss.com/article/84792/11-things-you-might-not-know-about-athlete-salaries

"Full List: The World's Highest Paid Athletes 2018," https://www.forbes.com/sites/kurtbadenhausen/2018/06/13/full-list-the-worlds-highest-paid-athletes-2018/#2d80b5437d9f

"100 Women: Is the Gender Pay Gap in Sports Really Closing?" https://www.bbc.com/news/world-41685042

"Gender Pay Gap for Women Athletes," https://inequality.org/great-divide/gender-pay-gap-athletes/

CREDITS

Fig. 13.1: Source: https://www.dsr.wa.gov.au/support-and-advice/research-and-policies/organised-recreational-activity-and-mental-health.

Fig. 13.2: Source: https://golfsupport.com/blog/golfs-gender-pay-gap/.

Fig. 13.3: Source: https://commons.wikimedia.org/wiki/File:Nanoldsquash.jpg.

Fig. 13.4: Source: https://www.flickr.com/photos/sabrebiade/31536890506.

Fig. 13.5: Source: https://commons.wikimedia.org/wiki/File:Nick_Saban,_who_is_the_Alabama_team_coach,_gives_interviews_and_watches_all_the_plays_during_this_important_spring_scrimmage_at_University_of_Alabama,_Tuscaloosa,_Alabama_LCCN2010638313.jpg.

Fig. 13.6: Source: http://phdcomics.com/comics/archive/phd102008s.gif.

Fig. 13.7: Source: http://sports.usatoday.com/ncaa/salaries/.

14

Sports and the Media

LEARNING OBJECTIVES

After completing this chapter, students should be able to:

- determine how sports media messages are distributed and consumed, and what role self- and government regulation play in the sports industry;

- know how athletes are affected by exposure to media hype;

- discuss how sports media works with teams and individuals;

- understand the role of social media in selling sport as a product and brand;

- articulate how social media may be used to aid in branding athletes and sports teams, as well as engaging sports fans; and

- describe the various social media forms and how they work in the sports promotion industry.

Introduction

The aim of this chapter is to find out how media work with the sports industry as well as teams and individuals. Coverage of sports by media is prevalent and pervasive. Stories published or broadcast in media allow American consumers to increase what we know about sports, athletes, coaches, and the art of winning strategies and plays. Before media evolved into a world that includes a thousand or more options, people in our culture relied on either word of mouth or others to tell them about a game. In fact, in terms of broadcast options, radio was the primary means that informed sports fans about a game, a player, wins versus losses, and other play-by-play aspects of a sports competition. With the advances in media such as the Gutenberg Press, America suddenly was introduced to newspapers, which allowed news about sports events to become very popular. Changes in technology and innovations in media altered the way journalists reported and covered sports, and simultaneously changed the way Americans learned about recent news and events happening in the sports world. In terms of the history of sports media, we understand that sports news coverage was picked up from traditional media such as newspapers, radio, and television.

Over the last 50 years, sports journalism and sports reporting have undergone massive changes in process, especially given technological advances. The world of sports has been significantly affected by changes in sports media. In fact, sports are "projected to reach a net worth of $73.5 billion by 2019" (Heitner, 2015). As Figure 14.1 shows, we see that advances in technology-enabled social media have significantly changed journalism and the process of reporting (obtained from UF Online,

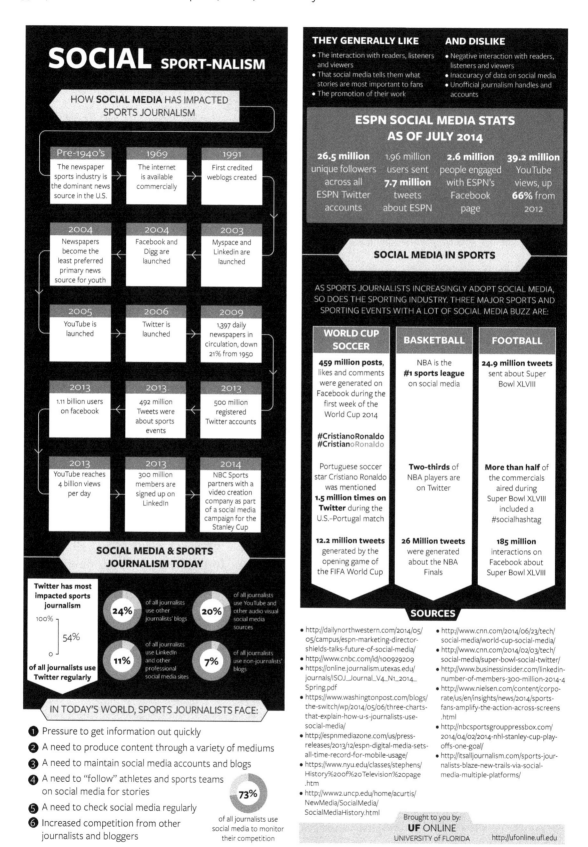

FIGURE 14.1   *Social media and sports journalism.*

University of Florida, March 10, 2015). Figure 14.1 also demonstrates the significant relationship between changes in social media and how sports journalists change writing practices to meet the changes and advances in social media.

Taken together—the data presented in Figure 14.1 along with other information that will be presented in this chapter—it is imperative that we highlight and emphasize media and social media's effect on sports journalism. As a result of the emergence of social media, we will spend some time in this chapter discussing the emergence of the social media trend that has come to change the face of sports media.

In terms of the history of sports media, we know that print media, such as newspapers and magazines, used to be the main sources of sports journalism and reporting. Sports fans also used print media to obtain information about their favorite teams and athletes. The earlier infographic clearly illustrates the effect that social media has had on the sports world. We can tell from the graphic that it was not long before suddenly newspapers became the least preferred media for obtaining information among sports fans.

Suddenly, traditional sports media was quickly replaced by websites such as ESPN.com. A review of published stories on changes in the sports media environment also shows an increasing level of distrust between athletes and sports media. Athletes in this new social media environment realized that they could drive their own content and say what they wanted to say when they wanted to say it. Many athletes felt that sports journalists would take their quotes out of context and maybe mix their words around and create instances of negative publicity. Social media allows athletes to control their own content over the content that is published in sports reports and by traditional sports media.

In terms of the relationship between media and athletes, we know that not only do athletes have to work with media but also sports media often have to deal with criticism and negative attitudes that athletes have toward them. This strained relationship was most evident during Super Bowl 50 when Cam Newton walked out of a postgame interview. In the traditional postgame press conference, it was reported that Newton overheard a player on the opposing team celebrating their victory behind Newton, which upset him and resulted in his quick exit. Newton's exit from the press conference was praised by some and elicited extreme criticism from others. Other instances of tense postgame press conferences are times when coaches, upset with sports media, walk out of interviews when the journalists ask questions about their team's poor performances. Oftentimes, the way the coaches or players handle these interviews is to simply to refuse to answer the journalists' questions. For example, a former coach of the Philadelphia Eagles, Chip Kelly, would consistently ignore the sports journalists' questions about the loss of a game.

Sports media includes newspapers, magazines, books, film, radio, television, the Internet, social media, mobile applications for smartphones, and video games (e.g., *Madden*). The relationship between sports and media is important because sports media frame and influence thoughts, ideas, social constructs, and other beliefs, as was discussed in Chapter 2 of this textbook. Sports media provide important content for fans, and many sports in our culture actually depend on media to increase awareness of them, to generate publicity, and to help increase profit and revenues.

Sports media connect fans with important information, experiences, and images that allow for interactivity among fans, athletes, sports teams, and sports media. In today's sports media environment, we also have the ability to enjoy video games that simulate sports. In fact, the images in many video games have become increasingly lifelike. Video games such as *NHL 18* and *Madden NFL 18* allow sports fans to play their favorite sport from the comfort of their home. Visuals in sports video games are continually improving the realistic physical portrayals of the sporting environment. Tiny replications of reality make the video game athletes look real. Some argue that in today's sports video game, there is not a lot of room left for interpretation. Makers of sports video games have made the video games appear as real as they possibly can be. From athletes' movements, to their uniforms, to the fans in the stadiums, as well as advertising and sponsorships appearing in the stadium or in the landscape almost perfectly (and some say too perfectly). Video game developers go to great lengths to balance a gamer's play experience and the most realistic sports gaming experience possible.

Media's Role in the Sports Industry

What is the role that the media plays in sports? Being a central part of our everyday experience, media brings sporting events straight into our living rooms and shows it to us whenever we choose. One probable answer would be that the media successfully meets our needs for information and entertainment. Watching sports or reading about sports is the best possible entertainment for consumers. Although a football game may take place in San Francisco and a tennis match may take place in London, England, media brings these events into our living rooms. Media makes use of our need to witness the actual thing by serving as a facilitator between the sporting event that is happening miles or countries away and the viewers. Not only do Americans have the convenience of watching worldwide sporting events, but we do not have to pay ticket prices to attend the sporting events live. Since today's sports are available through *and* made attractive by the media, millions of people are now tied to their television, radio, Internet, even the newspapers to find the latest in sporting news.

When we speak of media, we are referring to media that includes newspapers, television, radio, Internet, social media, books, video games, and other ways that information is stored or communicated. We know that the main role of sports media is to inform and educate sports fans about sporting events happening to their favorite team and athlete, and/or events happening in their local communities, the United States, and the world. In fact, in today's media environment, we can use our mobile phone to livestream important sports events as well as get updates from sports media such as ESPN on final scores and winners/losers of highly publicized sporting competitions, championships, and events. And now, because of advances in technology, sports fans can share their opinions in real time on the Internet and on social media.

Media's Effects on Sports

Production of Mediated Messages and Content

This section will explore how the media creates meanings and messages and embeds those elements in mediated content. We will examine the organization and influence of media in their narratives, sound, and images, as well as other aspects and objectives related to the production of sports news. Media staff involved in producing content hold positions and titles ranging from sports editors and reporters, commentators and announcers, photographers, camera operators, sound technicians, and producers. Each of these media professionals is central to what is, in essence, a process of message and ideas that begin with the media. For example, like the Super Bowl, the Olympics and its telecast have expanded much further than being simply another sporting event. For example, opening and closing ceremonies have gone far beyond the status of a sports event to become media spectaculars tailor-made for television and generating revenue and attracting viewers.

Television stations and networks pay massive amounts of money for the exclusive opportunity to broadcast sporting events. And a plethora of advertisers and sponsors also invest money into a sport because of the reach and exposure they obtain from placement in the media. Listed next are the various advantages and disadvantages that are associated with sports and television broadcasts.

Broadcast and Sports: Benefits of the Relationship

While sports organizations benefit from media attention and publicity, sports are important for broadcasters. Live coverage of sports events gives sports media credibility and a profile in the media marketplaces as well as their ability to deliver lucrative audiences to advertisers. For broadcasters, the share that a program earns is extremely vital to the success of a show's tenure. Share requires that media vehicles prove that they can attract a sufficient audience large enough to produce adequate financial resources. The number of viewers exposed to a broadcast program serves as a major index in terms of the extent to which the show and network are popular or not. Low ratings and shares make it impossible for a network to attract advertisers and other investors. To attract viewers, broadcast media find it crucial to create appealing programs that viewers are unable to access on other networks. Sports programs are one of many genres that can deliver an audience and command attention from consumers and advertisers alike.

Programming sports attracts viewers and can reach the hard to reach consumer. The challenge in advertising and media planning in reaching this group is that they are less likely when compared to other consumer groups to watch television than others, making them a difficult and challenging group to reach with television ads. Regarding reaching the hard to reach, market research shows that football has the potential to attract this group better than other programs. When an advertiser places a commercial during the Super Bowl, for example, the research shows that these commercials are the most expensive spots sold during prime time to date. In February 2010, it was recorded that the top commercial placements were sold for more than $3 million. The fight for market share, ratings, and viewers incites sizable pressure for media to obtain exclusive live sports broadcasting rights. And, as we mentioned in Chapter 12, this also results in media contracts for exclusive rights to broadcast popular sports events.

Advertising and the Sports Industry

Demographic market research made available to advertisers also showed the attractiveness of the sports industry. A few crucial facts in the research showed that American males between the ages of 18 and 49 are not heavy viewers of television. Media research shows, however, when men under the age of 49 actually do turn on and watch television, they almost always watch sports. This crucial marketing fact captured advertisers' attention, which led to a further subdivision of the demographic group into different categories. The first group identified was called "sports for the masses" (the big three—football, baseball, and basketball). Advertisers found that advertisements for low involvement products were a perfect match for this group. The other group, the "sports for the classes," was characterized as the upper social class or elite group, which expressed interest in sports such as tennis and golf. It became quickly obvious that the target audience most likely to be interested in advertisements for life insurance and personal computers are viewers aligned with the upper middle and middle-class groups.

"Baseball is not just a sport anymore; we are a business. We are show business. To compete for the entertainment dollar, you have to have more than nine guys playing baseball; you've got to have an attraction." —George Steinbrenner, owner, New York Yankees (http://www.medialit.org/reading-room/play-ballpay-ball-money-and-future-sports)

Advertisers and Marketing Self-Identity

Advertisers make decisions about programs and media placements that are grounded in information that reveals the target market's inner-most needs, interests, and desires. Strategic planners make decisions on the most profitable target audiences based on consumer marketing research that reveals the audience's needs and desires. Then advertisers and marketers focus on aligning their product or service with the needs, desires, wants, and interests of the audience. Strategic researchers and planners also consider the demographics of their target market along with the demographics of media. The ultimate goal is to match the findings of the target audience for a product or service with the demographics of sports media consumed by various demographic groups. Advertising, we know, seeks to learn about a target audience's self-concepts and/or service. Ultimately, advertisers hope to reinforce self-concepts through creative messages about the advertised product and, for example, people who are motivated to achieve (e.g., people who work hard to earn monetary rewards) are said to follow specific sports, such as marathons. Ads placed during wrestling or boxing sports are typically for products and services that achievers tend to positively respond to. Intense and highly aggressive sports attract target audiences who have an interest in economical cars and practical products, such as orange juice and toiletries.

Sports promoters also find financial success when they can promote certain sports events. Unique sporting events, such as the "world's strongest man," are often very popular for promoters to advertise because these events come with a double bargain: they bring a built-in target audience. Currently, in advertising, we notice a trend for these events in becoming preferred packages in the sports media market.

The Growth of Mass Media

Currently, the emphasis in mass media centers on the Internet, social media, radio, and television. In the last 20 years, the media landscape has seen vast changes. Adding to the media environment now are two primary satellite providers. These satellite television providers of subscription-based service are currently known as DirecTV and Dish Network. Presently, satellite TV has made a major entrance into the world of sports media. Other developments that took place toward the end of the 20th century, such as the Internet, also further extended the sports media marketplace. Associated with these new developments, we find broadcast channels that are dedicated to broadcasting one type of content and that is updates and news happening in the sports world. These sports-only broadcast channels are, currently, SEC Network, ESPN, and satellite radio stations, such as Talksport. In the print media category, media devoted to the sports industry are online magazines and news publications, such as *ESPN Magazine* and *Sports Illustrated*. These new sports media outlets have entered into the ever-increasing numbers of the new media environment.

In today's culture, we find that sports media play a progressively more influential role in the world of sports. They are crucial in letting fans know about the recent news and updates related to sporting events and practices. Sports media in American culture are influential in creating new events such as competitions and leagues. Names on the back of athlete's jerseys was first introduced in 1960 by the Chicago White Sox, who added players' names to their road jerseys (Lukas, 2018). Bill Veeck, owner of the Chicago White Sox was one of the first to suggest that player's names be put on jerseys in order to allow television fans to see the names of their favorite White Sox's players (Mansour, 2016). Sponsors' logos have begun to proliferate sports through sponsorship of events and by placement of the logos on uniforms. And to further illustrate the role of media in the world of sports, particularly in sports promotion, we find, for example, increasing numbers in new and renovated sports stadiums. Today, we find stadiums that not only provide video boards with advertisements and better views of game plays but also sponsorships of suites have added to the marketing of American sports.

Numerous examples exist where sports franchises have tried to encourage interest by changing some aspects of the game. Professional football, for example, introduced a new opportunity for football fans to watch their favorite team(s) with the introduction of Thursday Night Football (TNF). TNF began in 2006 on the NFL Network as part of eight overall second-half games, five on Thursdays and three on Saturdays. TNF started out as an attempt to help the NFL Network on satellite leverage viewers and subscribers. They did win those battles for viewers, allowing TNF to broadcast more Thursday night games and fewer Saturday games in 2008. Then in 2014, there was a move to split the time between CBS and the NFL Network. Then in 2016, TNF was further divided when NBC was added to the package. The package, based on increases in satellite subscription fees, has brought in more viewers and more revenue than games on NFL Network alone.

Lack of Coverage of (Some) Sports

Although we know that sports and mass media are interconnected in the lives of their fans and American culture, we find that some sports are either absent in the coverage of sports media, or they are relatively limited in coverage. For example, in January 2017, women's tennis was challenging and even in some cases difficult to see on television. Tennis fans found it extremely challenging to watch their favorite female professional tennis player on television because of changes made to the policy set by the WTA in terms of media rights and broadcasts. For example, one of Serena Williams's matches was not available on television in the United States unless sports fans were knowledgeable about how to pirate live television broadcasts.

Another area depicting the relationship between media and sport is the development of big events in sports, such as the World Cup, March Madness, and the Super Bowl, to name just a few. These high-profile events have allowed sports media to gain access to bigger audiences and immensely larger revenues that are ultimately acquired through revenue from advertisers and sponsors. Sports media, just like other media, are competing for consumer attention. In fact, intense competition among the media is even more so in today's economy because of the fact that it is getting more difficult to get people to attend to messages and media content given the cluttered media environment.

Sports media is a production process. The various ways that media structure, direct, and influence what we see and read with regard to sports and the effect of certain exposures are now key concerns for sports psychologists, sociologists, and others interested in media and sports. Sports and the effects of exposure to sports in various media have become important and relevant topics when we consider the level and significant degree to which people look to media to gain sports knowledge and understanding. We find that in today's media culture, consumers use the media rather than seeking out direct personal involvement when it comes to watching and participating in sports. And, as implied earlier in this section, one main objective for the media to be involved in sports is primarily based on the profit motive they gain from an alliance with sports and sports fans. In today's environment, media professionals must rely on their knowledge and expertise to craft media messages and mediated images that ultimately become sports products used to reflect the media's ability to enhance a sporting organization's status and reputation.

Sports media professionals aim to produce packages that attract, excite, and incite fans while also building their own viewing audiences and increasing their market share. Sports journalists work in a highly competitive media environment, which is a challenge for many. Sports media have to provide media hype or emphasis on making a sports team appear attractive, and this can sometimes be a difficult goal to accomplish. Although when a sporting event is presented in the media as if it is providing viewers with a unique "seat" and perspective, this may be one deception of the production and presentation of the sport in broadcast media. When sports fans opt to watch an event from home instead of going to the game, so many aspects of the sporting ambiance are lost simply because they are not at the event. This is where the role of the sports media professional comes into play in that he or she can add a wealth of information and visual cues to the content. This aspect of sports media production seems to make our sporting experience a little different than if we were to attend and watch the event live.

Sports media interpret games and plays during the sporting event. Media professionals determine what we should know, see, and understand when broadcasting a sporting event. What is often missing is the ability to see the event and draw our conclusions. For example, if we listen to a broadcast of a game on radio or satellite radio, we have to rely on the commentator and analysis to understand what is going on. We rely on these sports professionals to make sense of the events that are happening during a sports event. Sports media help us to integrate events taking place in a sporting event by constructing and framing the activity in such a way that the audience understands what is going on without having to watch the event live. How meanings and messages are organized and influenced by pre-event advertising and during the broadcast of the sporting event are often evident in the sports media's narrative and other production aspects involved in media sports.

Another aspect of media construction of sports as a product is the process of personalization. Sports media seem to enjoy shining the spotlight on individual athletes, building them up, and then keeping them in the forefront of sports media and creating what we may call sports superstars. To illustrate this phenomenon, we can use a current example stripped from today's headlines. Let's consider the athlete known as Odell Beckham Jr. While we will discuss the media's fascination with this athlete a little later in this chapter, we mention Odell Beckham Jr. here and now to set the stage for building the idea that sports media plays a crucial role in creating and highlighting who they consider to be, and who they want the fans to consider to be, media sports superstars.

From Muhammad Ali to Arthur Ashe, to Billie Jean King, to Serena Williams to Terrell Owens, to Cam Newton, sports media are vital in creating these media sports stars. Pre- and postevent/ game/match press conferences, for many athletes, not only become a fact of life but also help them create brand images and personalities. Richard Sherman, for example, would just be another name in football if it were not for his postgame interview with Erin Andrews after Super Bowl 2015. Now the pre- and postevent press conference has become reality for many athletes. For athletes, their sporting and their personal lives have come under the media microscope (Frisby, 2016). An athlete's philanthropic deeds or even crimes and misdemeanors are resurrected, analyzed, discussed, and broadcasted in print and broadcast media. As Frisby's research shows (2016), often, black male athletes are presented in less than favorable media coverage, which further illustrates the sports media's ability to create and produce sports heroes and villains. Sports media thrive on, and seem to invent, interpersonal rivalries (Serena Williams versus John McEnroe). In July 2017, when a sports journalist asked John McEnroe to comment on the best tennis player, and he replied by saying that "Serena Williams is only as good as the male tennis player ranked 700th in the world," we in sports journalism noticed that this was a situation created to stir interest and engagement of sports fans. Certainly, the sports journalist did not need to explore further why McEnroe might have qualified his response when he stated that Serena Williams is the "best female tennis player." Much of sports is qualified by men and women anyway, so it seems that the journalists' follow-up question encouraged the Internet media storm that took place immediately after the news story hit the stands.

Often criticized is the use of expert analysis in media and sports media. The experts carry the title of "color analysts." The color analysts typically lead the sports commentator and are responsible for telling viewers/listeners what is going on in the game/event. They also help explain penalties and other calls and events that take place. Color analysts are now part of the essential staffing in sports broadcasts. Color analysts are often former athletes or coaches who are familiar with educating audiences on events that have transpired during a game. Color analysts are importantly influential in structuring and influencing public opinions (e.g., NFL has Michael Strahan, NBA relies on Shaq).

Media thrive on success (or lack of success) based on ratings (the number of viewers divided by television households x 100) or circulation (the number of people who are exposed to the print media vehicle). Developments in media, such as the use of social media, currently have an extreme effect on sports media and sports media production. New athletes (i.e., rookies) in what is turning into an increasingly competitive, global media sports marketplace can now enhance their brands and images along with the monies that their sport receives simply by relying on social media. We turn to a discussion of social media and its relationship to sports media next.

Revenue-generating sports depend on sports media to promote and provide a combination of coverage and up-to-the-minute news. The sports media then provide the information and at times facilitate discussions between teams, coaches, and the media. This facet of the role of sports media also shows how the media can be used to generate fan interest. For a sports team, the media's influence in sparking interest in new and existing fans plays a vital role in the sale of tickets and the sale of club suites and merchandise and licensing. Sports promoters and owners of teams are well aware of the value that media coverage affords. This may explain why many owners do not argue about reporters' access to athletes. While sports depend on media coverage, we know that some sports in particular pay careful attention to and rely on television media. The heavy reliance on television media is largely due to the fact that television companies pay significant amounts to obtain the exclusive rights to broadcast a team and/or sport.

Broadcast contracts provide the sports industry with significant and increasing sources of revenue and profits. Without exclusive rights to television contracts, many sports would hardly generate revenue and profits. Television revenues have even greater potential for increasing profits than do ticket sales. The viewer size of a program on television (the reach) allows sports to increase their potential fan size in ways that no other media can provide.

With the revenue-generating possibilities that television offers to sports, there are also some areas that cause concern. For example, starting times and pauses during the game for commercial breaks changes the programming lineups for television stations. For some teams, halftime or intermissions have been cut in half to maintain viewers and viewer engagement with the sports program. Time-outs, penalties, and other distractions in a game also create time for television stations to insert more commercials. College football, for example, recently started having Thursday night games in lieu of the typical Saturday competitions to increase revenues. All changes made in a sport because of television contracts have been done willingly and happily by sports teams and organizations.

Social Media in the Sports World

Social media vehicles such as Twitter, Facebook, YouTube have had a tremendous effect on sports, fans, athletes, and teams. In this day and time, media-use studies tell us that more than

80% of all sports fans use social media while they are actually watching sports on television. Media-use studies also show that more than 60% of all sports fans also monitor social media while in attendance at a live sports event. Athletes capitalize on the use of social media and recognize its ability to fuel a massive buzz, resulting in increased exposure and attention. For instance, records show that when Tim Tebow threw an unexpected touchdown pass in the NFL playoffs, greater than 9,000 tweets per second were observed. Another example of the effect of social media was observed when approximately 550,000 sports fans started to follow NBA player Jeremy Lin in one season.

From a sports promotion perspective, sports teams have also learned how to leverage social media. Many leagues and sports franchises have realized the potential that social media has in terms of building a passionate, devoted fan base. Social media, such as Twitter and Facebook, has given sports fans many opportunities to share content and information about their favorite teams and/ or athletes. Social media uses fans' desire to affiliate and belong to a community. Moreover, social media changes and strongly influences the way fans interact with and engage with sports in America.

Key Messages on Social Media in Sports

1. Social media helps sports organizations reach new fans and develop larger and more expansive fan bases, along with being used by sporting organizations to reach new markets, to develop broader and larger fan bases, and, more importantly, to connect with more fans.

2. Social media offers various opportunities to maximize opportunities and minimize risks.

3. Sporting organizations use social media to develop and maintain promotional strategies to create meaningful relationships with their fans.

Almost all major sports teams, competitions, and events have social media accounts and hashtags associated with them. These are displayed and featured prominently to drive engagement and create relationships with audiences. Increasingly, grassroots clubs are also employing these techniques to supplement recruiting efforts and promote club activities to their communities. Social media has already been extremely disruptive for the sports broadcasting and marketing industries by allowing a direct relationship between fans and a sports team or athlete. However, the move by both Facebook and Twitter to broadcast live video content also brings with it a promise to affect major changes in sports media.

Sports teams and athletes also need to consider how to manage their social footprints and brands, and, in particular, how to mitigate the potential risk of athletes, employees, or volunteers causing reputational damage by posting regrettable or inappropriate comments on their profiles. Many of these risks can be mitigated and avoided with an appropriate level of user awareness, effective risk management, guidance, and sound administrative practice.

Facebook

Facebook is, as of this writing, the largest social media network. Using a Facebook page, sports teams have a wealth of opportunities at their disposal to initiate conversations about a sports team, promote sporting events, and offer updates containing newsworthy information. Facebook team pages give sports fans opportunities to interact with their favorite sports team and athlete. Facebook also makes it easy for fans to like and share content posted to their team's page. This characteristic of Facebook is one of the ways that it can be used to increase the reach of a team's content and to some extent a way to increase followers to a page.

Regarding content to share, listed next are just a few ideas for increasing fan engagement with a sports Facebook page:

- Trivia questions about the team and a player
- Results of games and key plays or strategies
- Fans post images and selfies taken at a live event
- Updates about newsworthy events or other behind-the-scenes activities that may interest fans
- Posts and videos from players to fans
- Contests or sweepstakes of season tickets, merchandise, or a visit from a favorite athlete

If an athlete has an upcoming competition or other events, he or she can use the Facebook events feature. Athletes may create an event page that allows followers and fans to invite their friends.

Plus, if it makes sense for the team, a sports promoter or media relations individual who works for the team can now sell tickets, fan club memberships, merchandise, and much more directly from Facebook.

Twitter

Twitter is a microblogging platform that offers another vehicle for promoting a team. Twitter is much more about immediacy. Followers on Twitter can get updates and news on things that are happening with their sports teams or favorite athletes right now. This is what makes Twitter a perfect tool for sports teams to share updates from games and competitions in real time. Twitter allows those fans who were unable to get to the game to watch the live broadcast to know what is happening with their favorite team. When Twitter is used for sports marketing, it has an uncanny way of increasing awareness and engagement of a social media marketing campaign. Teams that take advantage of campaigns that use hashtags and attach hashtags to their marketing and promotional campaigns get their messages in front of their fans and target audiences in a quick and efficient manner. Hashtags help followers find information related to a specific sport, team, athlete, or topic. Apart from that, Twitter allows athletes and team public relations or strategic communications professionals to join conversations and connect with fans and followers.

Pinterest

Pinterest, unlike the other previous social media platforms, motivates increases in product sales. According to 2016 media-use data, more than 70% of consumers reported that they were able to find merchandise on Pinterest. Only 40% of Facebook users reported finding items they wanted to buy. This is the unique feature that Pinterest has that other social media do not: businesses that sell products are finding success on Pinterest. Yet Pinterest is not without its disadvantages. "The fact that between 72% and 97% of Pinterest users are female might initially make it seem like an inappropriate vehicle for some sports" (Hanlon, 2013). However, some sports are finding that they can leverage this social media vehicle to their advantage. For example, the NFL recently discovered that women are a vital part of their market and are loyal fans. This sporting organization is now finding that Pinterest is a viable tool used to reach a market that most would consider nonconventional.

YouTube

The YouTube video network is a social media opportunity available to sports teams for the specific purpose of marketing and promotions. YouTube channels afford a unique opportunity for sports teams to upload practice videos, share game highlights, and allow fans to see firsthand interviews from key players.

Instagram

As of September 2018, Instagram has amassed more 800 million monthly active users (Danjou, 2018). According to online sources, "Instagram is the third biggest social network in the world" (Danjou, 2018). Facebook owns this rising social media platform, and as of this writing, it has added approximately 100 million users between the months of April and September 2017 (Danjou, 2018). Schäferhoff (2016) noted that Instagram users upload "80+ million photos every day with 3.5 billion daily likes." Research on social media use found that compared to a Facebook post, Instagram "averages 60 times more engagement and 120 times more involvement than a tweet" (Schäferhoff, 2016). Figure 14.2 shows Instagram's continued rise in popularity along with other popular social media.

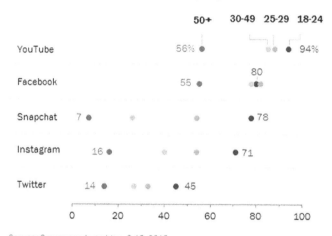

Social platforms like Snapchat and Instagram are especially popular among those ages 18 to 24

% of U.S. adults in each age group who say they use ...

Source: Survey conducted Jan. 3-10, 2018.
"Social Media Use in 2018"

PEW RESEARCH CENTER

FIGURE 14.2   *Facts about Instagram everyone should know*

Instagram Stories, launched in 2017, has become a tool by which sports teams and athletes share information about their personal lives as well as behind-the-scenes video clips and content of their professional athletic lives (Botoon, 2017; Danjou, 2018). Instagram's biggest claim to fame is that it is a vehicle that allows its' users to tell personal stories. Sports teams and athletes rely on Instagram Stories to aid in showcasing live video; to connect with fans before, during, and after games; and to interact during pre- and post-season months.

Research shows that one unique feature that helps propel Instagram usage is the fact that it combines storytelling with live video. Athletes who use Instagram can offer quality information to their fans—information that may be personal and fun. Athletes also can use interactive stickers like location tags and other filters that help them create and/or enhance their public personas via online social media. We know from communication and cognitive psychology that people respond much more effectively to visuals than the written word. The cliché that "actions speak louder than words" or "a picture says more than a thousand words" helps illustrate the thesis that visual images and content are necessary and sufficient to dominate social media. Our love for visuals also helps support the data that shows many journalists and promoters are moving toward social media platforms like those discussed previously: Pinterest, YouTube, and now Instagram. Unlike the other two social media, we know that Instagram's platform makes sharing and interacting with visuals relatively easy to maneuver. Another advantage Instagram has over the other popular social media platforms is that it initially hit the market as a mobile app and has been consecutively listed among "the top 10 most popular smartphone apps for the past couple of years" (Schäferhoff, 2016).

As of recently, athletes and sports organizations use Instagram to send game highlights, behind-the-scenes preparation for events, surveys, and information-qualified content to fans: game highlights, behind-the-scenes content (like athletes used to do), fan surveys, changes or enhancements to arenas or stadiums, and about ticketing/sales (Denjou, 2018; Schäferhoff, 2016). Through Instagram, sporting teams and athletes are able to "provide different kinds of content strategies, from the fun to the commercial" (Denjou, 2018; Schäferhoff, 2016). We find that social media is in a state of flux

Athletes	Clubs	Leagues
Cristiano Ronaldo – 122M	Real Madrid – 56M	NBA – 27M
Neymar JR – 91M	FC Barcelona – 55M	Premier League – 16M
Lionel Messi – 89M	Man United – 21M	NFL – 11M
LeBron James – 36M	Bayern Munich – 12M	La Liga – 6M
James Rodriguez – 35M	PSG – 11M	MLB – 4M
373 million fans accumulated	**156 million fans accumulated**	**64 million fans accumulated**

FIGURE 14.3 *Athlete engagement on Instagram.*

(Botoon, 2017) with Facebook users spending less time on Facebook, Twitter's public relations issues regarding fake Twitter accounts affecting users, and Snapchat's relatively unchanged growth, keeping the platform consistently small in terms of users and followers. These recent situations and user statistics may help to explain why Instagram seems to be the social platform that many, if not most, sports organizations, teams, athletes, and leagues use (Botoon, 2017; Schäferhoff, 2016).

Figure 14.3 shows the popularity and the number of followers of high-profile athletes and the sport they are associated with, along with their affiliated teams. Clearly obvious is the idea that Cristiano Ronaldo leads in the number of followers on Instagram. As we will learn, soccer is the most followed sport on Instagram since it is a global sport, and therefore it seems logical that an athlete in soccer would garner the top spot in athletes and number of followers on Instagram. We also find that in terms of professional leagues, the NBA leads in terms of followers on Instagram—data that tells us that Instagram is a social media vehicle that must garner attention by sports organizations, athletes, and journalists.

Botoon (2017) reports that "a third of Instagram users identify as sports fans and follow an average of 10 sports accounts each, with an average of eight of those accounts belonging to an athlete." We know that users under the age of 25 make up a predominant portion of the Instagram user demographic. This group reportedly spends "an average of 32 minutes a day on Instagram" (Botoon, 2017). We also know that this group tends to follow athletes and sports when compared to older markets. "Soccer is the most popular sport on Instagram by far because of its global reach" (Botoon, 2017).

Best Practices in Sports Social Media Promotion

Listed next are ideas for sports promoters to use to build a fan base and interest in a sports franchise or organization:

- Use color commentary and live play by plays on social media.
- Upload rare pictures that fans are unable to see in traditional sports media. Pictures might, for example, show the team on the way to a sports event or behind the scenes during training and practices. Basically, the idea is to post pictures that will keep fans engaged and interacting with the page. It is one thing for sports marketers and promoters to build excitement using words and another to build excitement with images. You could post pictures from themed events, player and/or player family celebrations, team celebrations and milestones, updates on new recruits who have joined the team, announcements about upcoming themed games, fan focus, "kiss cams," players' birthdays, and fan club members and their events, which should be family friendly for fans with small children (if parents provide permission).
- Ask those in the pictures to tag others, and if possible, ask fans to tag you in photos. This will also get your post in front of others efficiently and effectively.

- Use social media platforms to update fans on newsworthy information. This practice engages fans with the team and upcoming sporting competitions. Keep in mind that quality content beats quantity. Keep the content constant but important. Users judge whether to follow you on social media based on your content.

- Social media offers a unique direct-to-your-fans ability. Fans can ask questions and sports teams can in turn directly interact with fans and followers.

- Use content to connect sports fans to a larger conversation in the sports world. Mention other teams, athletes, and opponents. This feature gives you social media credibility and authenticity.

- Scoreboard contests that ask fans at a live event to tweet using hashtags are now the new thing. Scoreboard contests tied to branded social media applications and promotions are now considered to be the wave of the future. There are guidelines for running a contest on Twitter, but it is without a doubt one major way to engage your audience. Figure 14.1 shows how various teams encourage fans at a live event to use their mobile devices and social media using a scoreboard.

- Make consistent posts that show your team's character. Try creating a collage to tell a story as well.

- Keep your videos short, up to 15 seconds long (Schäferhoff, 2016).

- Create a unique hashtag. "Hashtags are the single most important tool to attract followers" (Schäferhoff, 2016).

- Start following other teams, athletes, and fans. The best way to attract users and followers is to search and find likeminded individuals (Schäferhoff, 2016).

- Post the same content and images to your other social media accounts (e.g., Pinterest, Twitter, YouTube, Instagram).

- Use analytical software and tools to provide insights into the content that garners the most involvement, followers, and engagement. Also, find analytical software that will help you validate your followers (are they real or fake?) Software in this area will allow you to clean up your fan list (followers) and identify those active followers from the nonactive followers on your page.

- Sports promoters can use social media to encourage fans to buy tickets, especially in cases where the sporting event is blacked out by broadcast media. Promoters provide a link to buy tickets and may even offer a special contest or price-off deal for last-minute ticket buyers.

Examples of Sports Teams' Use of Social Media

Here are four examples that illustrate how sports teams use social media to distinguish themselves from other teams and athletic departments. The final result of these marketing efforts led each team to increase its team's brand awareness and ultimately succeed in gaining revenue.

Baylor Athletics

Baylor encourages content sharing: The Baylor Rewards Program encourages fans to use social media by offering incentives when they share content that relates to Baylor Athletics. Baylor fans who post pictures, share videos, tweet or retweet information about Baylor Athletics, use certain hashtags, or check into a Baylor sporting event on social media will earn points toward some "prize." Baylor fans redeem their earned points for prizes, such as tickets to a game of their choice or team merchandise or apparel. The promotion began in November 2011 and has seen tremendous success (Scheiner, 2012). For example, data obtained during the promotion showed that 3 weeks into the promotion, the Facebook page "accumulated more than 4 million impressions" (Scheiner, 2012).

The idea illustrated in the Baylor promotion is the fact that sports promoters must keep fans consistently active A big takeaway is that teams must provide content along with a promotional strategy. The partnership between promotions and content works in that it gives fans a reason to return to the page. In addition, we learned that Baylor Athletics offers incentives for user-generated content. User-generated content cultivates fan involvement and interaction, from blogs to mobile phone uploads to videos and comments.

Louisville Sluggers

The Louisville Sluggers' St. Louis Cardinals' promotional event involved the creation of a scavenger hunt. The main objective for the scavenger hunt was to generate social traffic and foot traffic. When the Cardinals become the World Series champs in 2011, the Louisville Slugger created a promotion around the buzz and produced a 1-day scavenger hunt in St. Louis, Missouri. The manufacturer of baseball bats sought to build awareness for the brand and drive consumers (increasing traffic) to their social media pages. The company hid 45 baseball bats in the city and then posted clues on their Twitter and Facebook. The campaign was a "hit!"

The reason the campaign was successful, according to research, is twofold. First, research on the target audience must be conducted. Promotions will not work if you do not know your target audience well enough. St. Louis is city deeply buried in baseball history. Fans and nonfans were celebrating the World Series win, making the promotion successful. One week before the scavenger hunt began in St. Louis, posts were made to their Facebook and Twitter pages. Baseline data before the promotion showed that 755 followers were "talking about this." Once the scavenger hunt ended, that 755 number jumped to 7,049 different followers who were "talking about" the promotion. "Facebook likes increased by 143%, and their Twitter followers increased to 161%" (Scheiner, 2012). The Louisville Slugger promotion is a perfect example of how a sporting organization used news that was both current and relevant to energize a fan base and a target audience. The Louisville Slugger social media contest demonstrates the value of social media in connecting with nearby fans and potential customers.

New Jersey Devils' "Mission Control"

"Mission Control" was created by this team with the sole purpose of supporting their loyal fan base. Mission Control involved the development of a social media center that was completely maintained by fans. Figure 14.4 shows this control center, which is equipped with the latest in media technology. The goal is to bring fans closer to the team by using social media to boost the team's behind-the-scenes experiences. This social media center is as of present the only media monitoring initiative that is completely run by fans. Although the technical and financial support comes from the team's owners, the fans are the force behind the center. Dedicated and passionate sports fans monitor social media by identifying mentions or discussions about the Devils. Many fans worked up to 12 hours a day, voluntarily, on game days and rotated shifts.

"Mission Control" was created on the premise that dedicated fans seek venues where they are allowed to "voice their

FIGURE 14.4 *Fans inside "Mission Control."*

opinions, ideas, and stories around the NJ Devils brand" (Scheiner, 2012). The social media hub was created in 2011 and within its first 6 months, it had amazing success. For example, the Devils fans on Facebook rose from 100,000 to 170,000. Before the command center started, Devils followers on Twitter were around 25,000. However, 6 months after its appearance, the number of Twitter followers were being added at the rare "high rate of 600 new followers per week" (Scheiner, 2012). While "Mission Control" increased social media fans for the team, the idea also increased the team's revenue. Financial benefits were obtained through two different ticket promotions. The takeaway message from this promotion is that when the team allowed sports fans to have a voice and gave them a sort of "personal" opportunity to communicate instead of making them feel like they were nothing more than dollar signs or worse just part of a crowd.

Michigan Wolverines

At the heart of the success of Mission Control is the idea that it appealed to a passionate group of sports fans whose dream was to pretend to be like sports journalists. However, other sporting organizations might focus on making their zealous fans feel like celebrities. Strategies that allow sports teams to do this include changing profile images to those that are posted by fans, retweets from fans, custom Facebook posts that mention fans' birthdays, anniversaries or other special events that make fans feel closely tied to the team.

As with many businesses, the goal of a sports entity is to make money. This is where the promotions used by the Michigan Wolverines must be highlighted. Before their 2011 football season, the football team used social media to conduct a 1-day presale of tickets. The goal of the promotion was to increase ticket sales. The football team already had an enormous following on Facebook, so the marketers and promoters wanted to take advantage of the large following and generate more revenue from ticket sales before the regular football season began. The 1-day presale season ticket event was exclusively offered on their Facebook page, allowing Michigan to make enthusiastic and loyal fans feel special by providing them with exclusive information and a sense of added value that one can only enjoy as a fan of the team.

Michigan created a landing page that required those visiting to "like" the page if they were not fans or followers. Liking the page would allow them to see content posted on their pages. Once visitors liked the page, they were given a link that took them to a website that included more details about the season ticket sale promotion. Records show that this 1-day preseason promotion was a tremendous success. Evidence showed that the promotion gave the football team "7,000 new Likes and more than $74,000 in ticket sales" (Scheiner, 2012).

As illustrated in these four campaigns, we find that the use of promotions, contests, sweepstakes, and other user-generated content aimed at loyal fans is integral in terms of increasing revenue for a sports team. It takes some out-of-the-box thinking and creative strategy to determine the kind of content or incentive that encourages fans on social media to transition from social media to fans who prefer coming to a sports event and watching it live. "The consensus among sports marketers is that it can be done" (Scheiner, 2012).

Basically, the idea of social media in sports is to determine how a team can differentiate itself from other sports teams. Providing unique content, engaging fans, employing a contest such as a scavenger hunt, and other strategies are illustrations of successful ways that sports teams rely on social media to increase fans or excite a fan base and ultimately increase revenue. Sports teams cannot survive without a solid fans base. Social media in today's culture is vital to a sports team's fans, and interacting with those fans is key, even at the most basic level. Interactions that involve retweets, mentions, and replies to posts demonstrate a team's appreciation of its fans. Other ways that teams can show appreciation is by giving exclusive deals to fans. Promotions and rewards offered on social media are also alternatives that have proven to be effective in terms of retaining fans and adding new ones.

Offline Promotion Ideas

In terms of the social media promotion tips provided in the earlier section, we also know that sports marketers and promoters must realize that a heavy reliance on online media is not the end all be all. Traditional offline promotions are also available to teams with the potential to raise awareness of a sports team.

Rely on Word of Mouth

Depending on the size of the team, use your staff and players to network with their friends, families, and acquaintances of sports club members—these are individuals we know, or others know, who are often happy to help out. Word of mouth in sports is a simple task that may involve asking athletes, fans, and volunteers to share news about upcoming games and events with their network and circle of friends and family. For word of mouth strategies to work, teams must rely on mailing lists and other ways that help their fans stay in the loop. The mailers often ask fans to share the e-mail or social media post with others in their network.

Use Posters and Flyers

Several free desktop publishing sites allow promoters to design professional looking posters and flyers. Relying on flyers and posters is not dependent on hiring specialists in the desktop publishing field. For special sporting events, print media, such as posters and flyers, are an efficient option. Consider adding a quick response code on the poster or flyer that can easily connect the fan to a web page or social media page.

Rely on Local Media

Sports promoters must have a relationship with local radio, newspapers, and magazines. Relationships with local media are one way to ensure that content about a team or athlete will be published. We know that sports marketing, sports promotion, and sports media relations are more about networking and cultivating relationships. Promoters and media relations professionals help these journalists out by providing sports content that is interesting and relevant to their readers. Sports promoters and media relations individuals know, or should know, that to use this tip effectively, they must engage in three behaviors: (1) build rapport with journalists before they are needed, (2) carefully prepare the story/pitch, and (3) write a proper press release.

Some Examples of Media's Effect on Athletes

Kenny Rogers

An athlete known to have a volatile relationship with the media is baseball player Kenny Rogers. In 2005, sports media published a report saying that Rodgers planned to retire if his team did not extend his contract. Upon notification of this story, Rodgers refused to speak with or grant interviews with media. Later that year, Rodgers walked on the baseball field to warm up before a game and ended up having a fight with two cameramen, one was with Fox Sports Southwest. Rodgers shoved the man and grabbed his camera, and then threw the camera to the ground. Rodgers was suspended and fined for his violent behavior. Some speculate that Rodgers's "adversarial relationship with the sports media caused him to publicly lose his temper and become violent" (Ott & Van Puymbroeck, 2008). For Rodgers, these behaviors were ultimately very costly. As a result, Rogers ultimately lost playing time, had a reduction in his salary, and suffered the loss of respect from his fans.

Ricky Williams

Sports media aggressively covered and produced a story about Ricky Williams, an athlete who suffered from a debilitating social anxiety disorder and extreme shyness (Ott & Van Puymbroeck, 2008). Later, we learned from media interviews that the attention and hype made Williams even more uncomfortable and anxious. In his early years as a professional athlete, Williams went on record about how much he dreaded media interviews. Williams said he hated media interviews to the extent that he would put his helmet on and wear an eyeshade inside his face mask specifically so that he could avoid eye contact with sports reporters. In an article, sports media claimed that Williams started smoking marijuana to deal with the media attention. Later in the year, Williams failed three NFL drug tests and found himself at the center of even more embarrassing media coverage. "Ricky Williams walked out on the Miami Dolphins; lost millions of dollars; lost the respect of his teammates and fans; and still finds himself as media fodder" (Ott & Van Puymbroeck, 2008; Swerdlick, 2005).

Mike Tyson

Mike Tyson, one of the most publicized and controversial athletes in recent history, is also known for being one of the most admired professional boxers in American history. He earned the title of most publicized boxer when he was convicted of raping Miss Black America. Sports media also seemed extremely fascinated with Tyson's hot-tempered and explosive antics, such as when he bit the ear of his opponent during a highly televised boxing match. In the early 1990s, Mike Tyson was, according to sports fans and sports media, unbeatable. During his early career, Tyson won several championship titles, including the World Boxing Association Heavyweight Champion and International Boxing Federation Heavyweight Title. But as his professional life and career as a boxer were reaching new heights, his personal life was caught up in drama and legal difficulties. Tyson's relationship with the media was almost always negative. As his personal life spiraled out of control, Tyson eventually lost all of his boxing titles and championships. Some believe that Tyson's decline in the ring may have been related to the excessive media attention and the fact that all the media focus was incredibly negative. This type of negative attention in the media, it is believed, affected Tyson's training and mental state—ultimately ruining his career. For example, just days before Tyson's highly publicized comeback fight, he was asked in a media interview if he was bothered by the negative stories that sports journalists have written about him. Tyson was quoted as saying, "It's my job to beat people and win fights … and it's their job to sell papers. Everything that could've been said about Mike Tyson has already been said. I don't take it personally like I use to" (Ott & Van Puymbroeck, 2008).

FIGURE 14.5   *Mike Tyson*

Cam Newton

Just before the 2016 Super Bowl, the Carolina Panthers' quarterback Cam Newton was quoted on several media sites stating that he has "had his fill of the media" (Newton, 2016). Cam Newton has stated that he believes that sports media tend to ask the same questions over and over again. Mr. Newton was quoted as saying, "You know what's confusing? How can I reword questions I've been asked so many times?" "Nothing pretty much has changed since I had seen you guys 24 hours ago" (Smith, 2016). For Cam Newton, his issue with media was not centered on the pressures that they have to get the interview, but for him, it was the media requirements to have a certain number of interviews that was the most frustrating. As a result of his candid opinions on working with media, Newton quickly became labeled as an athlete who has a negative relationship with media. Newton was quoted as saying, "I think I've got to meet with you guys another time and nothing's going to change. I'll be walking out in this room, walking up those stairs, going to another meeting, going to practice, probably playing a couple of video games, talking to my parents, making sure they make it here on time, waking up, brushing my teeth" (Norris, 2016).

Athletes like Kenny Rogers, Ricky Williams, Mike Tyson, and Cam Newton are just a few of the many examples of athletes whose athletic performances were purported to be negatively associated with the way sports media covered them and their behaviors. Basically, these athletes are just four of many who have been reported to be negatively affected by sports media. Tony Dorsett, a former NFL halfback for the Dallas Cowboys, was quoted as saying, "You can turn the negative around and use it as a motivating force in your life. One of my biggest desires has always been to prove certain people wrong—to prove to them I can do it despite what they think or say" (Ott & Van Puymbroeck, 2008). While some athletes may be negatively affected by media coverage of them and their behaviors, other athletes seem to thrive on media hype.

Venus and Serena Williams

These professional tennis players who are also sisters are often at the heart of sports media coverage that is negative, racist, and sexist. Venus and Serena broke into a sport that typically consists of white female tennis players. What makes the Williams sister's unique in the sport of professional tennis is that they are muscular; they compete to win and win frequently, and they happen to be African American women who win because their athleticism, which involves "hard-hitting returns and power-filled matches" and game strategies) (Ott & Van Puymbroeck, 2008). Sports media often write stories about these professional athletes, but not about their athletic prowess; more stories are written about the fact that the two women do not fit our culture's stereotypical ideals about what a female tennis player should look like. If we consider the beauty bias and idealized images in American culture, then it becomes easy to understand why two of tennis' top female players, Venus and Serena Williams, are often discussed in sports media and even "criticized for their exotic, colorful, and tight-fitting tennis attire worn while on the court" (Ott & Van Puymbroeck, 2008).

In September 2018, an Australian newspaper published a caricature of Serena Williams after her loss at the U.S. Open. As you can see in Figure 14.6, Williams is shown with exaggerated lips and with a huge tongue and curly hair rising from the top of her head. Not only is Williams shown stomping on

FIGURE 14.6 *Caricature of Serena Williams that appeared in an Australian newspaper*

her racket but also her opponent, who actually won the match, was placed in the background and drawn as a blonde Caucasian woman. Williams's opponent, interestingly, was a woman from Japan, named Naomi Osaka. Osaka beat Williams in the U.S. Open women's singles final in New York. The motivation behind the caricature was a heated clash Serena had with chair umpire Carlos Ramos over what he perceived to be code violations. As a result, Williams was fined $17,000 in penalties. While the incident has split our culture regarding her outburst and actions toward the chair umpire, many in the tennis community, including the WTA and U.S. Open men's champion Novak Djokovic, have supported Williams and spoken out about how the chair umpires' penalties show gender bias.

After the match, Williams said male players were held to a lower standard for court conduct.

We know from learning about their background in sports media that Venus and Serena Williams grew up in East Compton Park, a notoriously rough and poor neighborhood in Los Angeles, California. Even though the sisters could not afford tennis lessons or even tennis balls, their father, Richard Williams, who also coached them, was reported to have taught them tennis from books (Davis, 2017). Biographies of the two female players state they had to play and learn the sport of tennis using old, used equipment while also practicing on rundown tennis courts. Richard Williams was quoted at one point saying this about his daughters' training: "It's a radical neighborhood. A lot of dope is sold. We play on two courts—that's all there is—and they look like trash, they're so slippery" (English, 2008; Ott & Van Puymbroeck, 2008).

Few professional female tennis players have been able to match the strength, speed, musculature, and overall athleticism as Venus and Serena Williams (Edmonson, 2005). "Venus and Serena Williams represent in many ways a shift in attitudes concerning women in sports, particularly African American women" (Edmondson, 2005, p. 126). Some argue that because they play tough and are competitive, many find their rise to fame in the tennis world as one that shows it is clearly acceptable for women to be strong, to have muscles, and to compete (Edmonson, 2005). Instead of media writing about their tenacity and ability to overcome disadvantages, it often criticizes these two sister-athletes and negatively depicts them in sports news. Despite the racism and sexism found in sports media coverage of these two amazing and spectacular female tennis players, they continue to demonstrate a tremendous thick skin and mental toughness when it comes to negative and frequent media coverage (Foster, 2015).

Clinton Portis

Clinton Portis was a Washington Redskins running back during the 2005–2006 season. Portis received media attention and became known for wearing shocking costumes and portraying odd characters during media interviews (Ott & Van Puymbroeck, 2008) (see Figure 14.7).

The collage of costumes worn by Portis can be seen in Figure 14.7. One of his most reported costumes was when he dressed up as a character he named "Sheriff Gonna Getcha." For this character, Portis wore a long "black wig, glasses with oversized eyes, a Led Zeppelin T-shirt, a star-shaped badge, and an unusual necklace" For another sports media interview, Portis arrived wearing "a black cape, black Lone Ranger mask, clown-style oversized yellow sunglasses, a shaggy black wig, and fake gold teeth" (Petchesky, 2012). Portis was also known for giving each of his characters outrageous names. We learn from several media sources that names for his costumes included "Dolla Bill," "Dr. Do Itch Big," "Choo-Choo," "Kid Bro Sweets," and "Coach Janky Spanky." A simple scan of the many faces that Portis would use for media interviews along with his reputation for having a very impressive and successful professional football career should communicate that this is a man who is not only talented but also creative and full of personality. The one thing that we can take away from his costumes and various faces is this: Portis clearly

FIGURE 14.7   *The many costumes and faces of Clinton Portis*

demonstrated amazing acting skills that "he polished and refined during his seven-year stay in Washington" (Vingan, 2012).

Portis initially started creating these characters after he was traded to the Washington Redskins in 2004. Portis stated that he was extremely uncomfortable on the Redskins team and as a result found it difficult and challenging to score touchdowns. To take attention away from sports journalists who might ask negative questions about his performance, Portis created characters and started dressing up in costumes to "have fun" with the sports media and his interviews. It was so well received that some of his teammates wanted to join in on the act. For example, during one sports media interview, five of his teammates arrived in costumes calling themselves "Clinton's" Angels. While some critics viewed the characters and interviews as foolish stunts, the strategy was very successful for Clinton Portis. By dressing up in characters and making the sports media interviews fun, he was able to deflect adverse questions and reporting by sports media and replace them with a parade of characters that made the interviews entertaining. The strategy also forced sports media to concentrate on the team's performance instead of one individual athlete. As a result, Portis started scoring touchdown after touchdown, breaking the "Redskins' record for the most rushing yards in a season. Portis went on to become the third running back in the league history to reach 1,500 yards in three of his initial seasons with the new team" (Ott & Van Puymbroeck, 2008). What we witnessed as a result of creative thinking by Clinton Portis was the ability to take a team from a losing record to being contenders for the Super Bowl playoffs in 2006. We mention Clinton Portis in this section of the book to show that this would have initially been a case where negative media interviews could have resulted in an athlete's "poor performance on the football field" (Ott & Van Puymbroeck, 2008). What Clinton Portis did was quite novel and innovative; Portis used sports media interviews to have fun, to motivate himself, and to overcome his own personal anxieties of being traded to a new team as well as making the environment jovial and light for his teammates (Allen, 2014; Ott & Van Puymbroeck, 2008; Vingan, 2012).

Odell Beckham Jr.

New York Giants receiver Odell Beckham Jr. has become the NFL's current king of media, according to news stories published in June 2017. Sources report that Beckham revels in (and profits from) media attention that has created his celebrity while reserving the right to complain about the enhanced awareness that goes with the notoriety territory.

Collegiate athletes experience stress from several sources. They are required to attend endless hours of practice each day, travel to faraway events at various times, and maintain an adequately high grade-point average. Added to this stress is the potential effect of news media coverage. Athletes may be scrutinized by local sports reporters who are expected to be unbiased in their coverage of the athletes. Impartial reporting means, of course, that periodically the coverage will be negative. On one hand, media use could have a negative effect on student-athletes. Media coverage could provide unrealistic expectations about athletic performances by highlighting the stars in sports. Athletes may feel pressured into performing at a level similar to star athletes covered in the media. On the other hand, media use could have a positive effect on student-athletes. Media coverage may provide a distraction or entertainment that could help athletes relieve pressure. Research shows that athletic performance can be reduced by certain distractions that interfere with an athlete's ability to focus on his or her game and performance. According to Dolcos and McCarthy (2006), cognitive interference may stem from a variety of sources. For example, athletes with family or loved ones they want to impress may find this to be a huge mental distraction. Cognitive distractions may also impede athletic performance when athletes are experiencing family or relationship problems or know that scouts are in the crowd to evaluate their performance. Even if none of these variables are present before a game or event, athletes may experience distractions by getting frustrated with mistakes made during a game, or poor refereeing decisions, or criticism and crowd banter.

Frisby and Wanta (2018) conducted a study on the effect of media exposure on college athletes' performance. The findings suggested that media use plays a role in athletes' self-perceptions. In most cases, the role was positive. The researchers surveyed 147 student-athletes and found that newspaper and Internet use had the largest effect on student-athletes. Student-athletes who reported being heavy readers of sports in newspapers tended to be less worried about always being at their best during a sporting event and were less worried about letting emotions get in the way or about trying to get as much sleep as possible. Internet use appeared to have lowered the level of stress among respondents. Student-athletes who reported being heavy users of the Internet for sports information tended to worry less about being distracted by noises or creative thoughts, about letting emotions get in the way, or about taking drugs that may complicate their ability to think clearly. Thus Frisby and Wanta (2018) concluded that newspaper and Internet use are more likely to be a diversionary tool for student-athletes—a way of unwinding and releasing stress associated with their performances. In other words, newspaper and Internet use positively affected student-athletes by affording them with a way to escape from high stress levels that are often accompanied by competing in collegiate sports. Only one regression result showed a negative media effect. The more respondents said they read newspapers for sports information, the more they reported that they tended to put things off (Frisby & Wanta, 2018). This again could be attributed to the diversion aspect of media use. Respondents may read a lot of newspaper sports stories and thus delay taking part in certain activities. Interestingly, television use did not appear to have the same effect. Television use was not related to any of the self-perception measures in the study. In other words, television use was not related to relieving stress among student-athletes.

Conclusion

The sports media relationship will continue to evolve, especially since athlete-negotiated content is emerging. While traditional print media may be losing readership, newspapers and magazines still offer some unique benefits. Although we learned in this chapter that sports media may have positive and negative effects on athletes and their behaviors, we know that external forces may also affect how athletes perceive themselves, their performances, and their abilities. We study the relationship between sports and media because we have learned that the sports media portray sports and athletes to consumers through images, narratives, and coverage that oftentimes conforms to dominant hegemonic masculine ideologies in American culture.

In this chapter, we discussed the innovation of hyperrealistic sports video games. We also find that video games have become an important part of the sports media world. While video games may complement sports media coverage and promotions, we also find that the games offer a unique experience for game players and sports enthusiasts.

We also discussed the fact that sports and media have a codependent relationship in that without media coverage, media publicity, and revenue that broadcast media are willing to pay, several media would be significantly and qualitatively different if they did not have sports news to publish and cover. Sports media know that sports attract audiences. Advertisers who purchase time and space in sports media want to convert those readers into consumers of their products and services. Interactions between advertisers, readers, media, athletes, and sports are also influenced by the relationship between sports and sports media. These relationships are an important feature of the sports and media relationship and therefore make it important to at least understand. Media coverage of sports in America often centers on images and discourses that relate to gender, sexual orientation, social status, race and ethnicity, power and ownership, and media consumption. We spoke in an earlier chapter of this text about the intersectionality of sport and the aforementioned ideologies. We know that media use and gratification, as well as American consumption of media, is ever changing. The changing nature of sports media almost demands that we use research to determine how Americans use media to integrate sports into their everyday lives. For instance, much research is needed that informs us on the conditions by which our consumption of images and messages published in sports media is used to influence our behavior at a sporting event, our participation in sports, and our attendance and desire to attend a live sports event.

Regarding broadcast media, we learned in this chapter that television and radio play significant roles in the sports industry. Many people have access to satellite television and radio, and we know that satellite has significantly increased the broadcast options for sports. With satellite media, sports fans can listen to or watch a broadcast from almost anywhere. We also learned how television and sports rely on each other. By broadcasting a sporting event via television, we find that this allows viewers to watch a big event or sporting event in the comfort of their own homes—offering, for some, the best viewing experience. Lastly, information toward the end of the chapter should be useful for aspiring sports marketers, sports journalists, or sports bloggers. Social media techniques for building a team brand or image for a star player should be useful in your work. From the examples of successful social media marketing campaigns, we learned that there can be a positive relationship between sports media, athletes, sports teams, and social media. We also learned that the sports media and social media have a sort of codependent relationship in that they both have to rely on one another. Both traditional sports media and social media must be willing to help each other succeed (Allums, 2016). Sports teams, as well as the athletes, we found, are turning to social media platforms to keep their fans informed and to interact with fans about their personal lives, performances during athletic events, and other events and activities that may be happening within a team.

QUESTIONS FOR REFLECTION AND DISCUSSION

1. What are some of the unique social media marketing promotions or contests that you have seen used in sports?
2. Do you know of any sports events where cheating was alleged?
3. If so, how was the scandal handled?
4. Are men's and women's sports covered by media differently? If so, how?
5. Why do you think more coverage and attention is paid to men's sports?
6. What is the role of media representation in changing cultural attitudes and values?
7. How does the media create superstars? What attributes do the athletes have that enticed media to sensationalize their behaviors?
8. Why do sports media and athletes have such an adversarial relationship?
9. What are the positive effects of media on a sport? Negative effects?

SUGGESTED ACTIVITIES

1. Create a social media campaign plan for upcoming local appearances by players from the local college and professional team in your area.
2. Identify a high-profile athlete. What characteristics make him or her stand out in media interviews? Are there other athletes like Clinton Portis who try to liven up media interviews?
3. Observe several postgame interviews with athletes. How do they handle the sports journalists' questions concerning their negative performances?
4. Interview an athlete to determine how he or she handles crowd hype, media hype, family and relationship distractions, and other mental distractions.
5. Break down the history of the rivalry between one organization and another.
6. Shine a spotlight on the fans and find a true diehard to interview.
7. Select a televised sport that is qualified by men and women (e.g., tennis, golf). Watch at least two games for both men and women for a total of four games. Compare and contrast elements and attributes of the broadcast, commentator, and analysis comments. Identify the similarities and the differences, and discuss how this might be better.
8. Listen to a live broadcast for at least two different sporting events on satellite radio. Identify themes that were similar and different (you may have to rely on information provided in earlier chapters).
9. Conduct research on how media treat female athletes and how content produced about female athletes may differ from content produced by male athletes. Camera angles? Use of pronouns? Adjectives? Referring to athletes by last name or first name? Anything else?
10. What do you think are potentially positive values that sports media can teach and instill in young people, regardless of whether they are male or female? How can you use this activity in your sports profession?
11. Keep a journal for a month and record your observations about sports media and the various roles (e.g., commentator, analysts, editors, producers, camera/photojournalists). Use this

as an opportunity to explore your exposure to sports and media messages. Keep a detailed record of your observations about media and its relationship with sports.

12. If you are able, attend a sporting event live and then watch the same sport via television. Compare and contrast your experience. Are there benefits that one offers that the other does not? Explain.

13. Do a content analysis on how the coverage differs between male and female sports, paying attention to the following: (a) the frequency of terms used in the article/broadcast; (b) the amount of coverage devoted to the sport, this would include the total time and amount of space devoted to the story as well; (c) where the story appears (front page, lead story, etc.); (d) differences in visuals and images presented in the story (on the field or off, with or without others, etc.); and (e) how the sports journalists use language for male and female athletes and their sporting events. In other words, how do journalists use language to discuss male and female athletes?

14. What differences are there between watching a sport on TV and in person? Take a moment to watch a sport like tennis on television and then go to a live college match. Write a reaction paper that discusses the similarities and differences you observed.

15. Do a study on the marketing of sports by examining sports-related merchandise. Notice patterns on college campuses when teams win "a big game" or lose. How many team-related apparel items are observed the day after a big competition?

ADDITIONAL RESOURCES

Communication Research Trends: Sport and Media covers information regarding spectator sports entertainment, sports and the press, sports pages in daily newspapers, sports papers and magazines, sports and radio, and sports and television, http://cscc.scu.edu/trends/v22/v22_4.pdf

"Edge of Sports," a blog covering the politics of sports, http://www.edgeofsports.com

Real Sports with Bryant Gumbel, https://www.hbo.com/real-sports-with-bryant-gumbel

American Society of News Editors, https://www.asne.org

American Sportscasters Association, resource for those interested in sports journalism and sportscasting, http://www.americansportscastersonline.com

APSE Leadership, http://apsportseditors.com

Association for Women in Sports Leadership, http://www.awsmonline.org

Football Writers Association of America, http://www.sportswriters.net/fwaa/

National Collegiate Baseball Writers Association, http://www.sportswriters.net/ncbwa/

Sports Shooter, an online resource for sports photography, http://www.sportsshooter.com

U.S. Basketball Writers Association, http://www.sportswriters.net/usbwa/

Sports Personalities in Magazine Advertising – Lesson, from MediaSmarts, http://mediasmarts.ca/lessonplan/sports-personalities-magazine-advertising-lesson

CREDITS

Fig. 14.1: Source: http://ufonline.ufl.edu/infographics/social-media-sports-journalism.

Fig. 14.2: Source: http://www.pewinternet.org/2018/03/01/social-media-use-in-2018/pi_2018-03-01_social-media_0-02/.

Fig 14.3: Source: https://www.hookit.com/ranks/.

Fig. 14.4: Source: http://energise2-0.com/wp-content/uploads/2011/06/mission-control-launch-02_16_2011-new-jersey-devils-photos-9.jpg.

Fig. 14.5: Copyright © 2014 by Alfonso Quintero Salazar, (CC BY-SA 4.0) at https://commons.wikimedia.org/wiki/File:WikiMiketyson.jpg.

Fig. 14.6: Source: https://www.springfielddailyrecord.com.au/news/herald-sun-backs-mark-knights-cartoon-on-serena-wi/3517987/.

Fig. 14.7: Source: https://deadspin.com/5936689/clinton-portis-coach-janky-spanky-sheriff-gonna-getcha-southeast-jerome-dolla-bill-dr-do-itch-big-bro-sweets-prime-minister-yah-mon-bud-foxx-coconut-jones-and-choo-choo-announce-their-nfl-retirements.

15

Politics and Religion in Sports

After completing this chapter, students should be able to:

- understand the role of sports in politics,

- trace the history of political activism in the Olympic Games,

- identify the five major political protests of our century,

- define "Tebowing" and other acts of postgame behavior by athletes,

- discuss how politics are integrated into sports in today's culture,

- examine the relationship between religion and sport,

- understand how simple sports objects become sacred,

- recognize sports associated with Native Americans and how sports are perceived, and

- become acquainted with constitutional and biblical laws associated with sports.

Introduction

Sports have always had a conflicted and complex relationship with politics and religion. In the 1936 Berlin Olympics, we saw the relationship between sports and politics when Jesse Owens's four gold medals and record-setting performance destroyed Germany's plan to showcase Aryan superiority in the Olympics. Then in 1938, the first multisport Olympian who also happened to be the first woman to play in a male PGA tournament, Babe Didrikson Zaharias, faced misogynistic criticism of femininity versus athleticism. Muhammad Ali, Jackie Robinson, Billie Jean King, Kareem Abdul-Jabbar, LeBron James, Carmelo Jones, Derrick Rose, and, currently, Colin Kaepernick are just a few athletes who, although it was in different moments in time in our culture, fought for justice, civil rights, and equality for all people. African American athletes, Irish athletes, Italian athletes, female athletes, Jewish and Christian athletes, and many others have battled for centuries so that we can have the right to participate as athletes, regardless of our gender, sexual orientation, religious and spiritual beliefs, and color of our skin. For example, Irish athletes overcame barriers when they appeared in sports such as baseball and boxing early in the 19th century. History tells us that it was during this era that several stores in America would put signs on their doors that read "no Irish need apply." We even found instances in our history when Irish immigrants were depicted in media as terrorists.

At the 1976 Olympics, female athletes, with support from Title IX, achieved silver medals in women's basketball. During this same time, sports media were publishing stories that Condoleezza

Rice, a woman of color who served as the 66th secretary of state under former president George W. Bush, was not allowed to join or purchase a membership to play golf. Published media narratives informed Americans that Rice was unable to join a national golf and country club or purchase a membership because of her gender. Then in 2012, the National Golf Club located in Augusta, Georgia, the golf club that Rice wanted to join but was not allowed to, suddenly began accepting applications from women to join. In this chapter, we will explore the relationship between sports and politics, and sports and religion. We will unpack the idea that sports in our culture have never really been just about sports and how sports media have not been able to just focus on sports in their coverage. By exploring the relationship between sports and politics and religion, we will gain a better understanding of our culture and the role that sports play in our involvement with these two emotionally laden topics.

Sports and Political Activism

Political activism among athletes is not new. As highlighted in the introduction of this chapter, activism and political protests can be traced back to the early 19th century. Then in 1967, we learned about a time when many black athletes met with Muhammad Ali in Cleveland to discuss the legendary fighter's protest against the Vietnam War. We know from historical records that this meeting held in Cleveland eventually helped Ali gain the support of the athletes in attendance and was later referred to as the "Ali Cleveland Summit."

The Cleveland Summit included a group of top black athletes who wanted to express their support to Muhammad Ali. These athletes listened while Ali gave reasons for rejecting the draft during the Vietnam War. The meeting was held in June 1967 and included athletes such as Walter Beach, Willie Davis, Carl Stokes, Bobby Mitchell, Lew Alcindor aka Kareem Abdul-Jabbar (who had not yet converted to Islam), Jim Brown, Bill Russell, Jim Wooten, and Jim Shorter.

The 2016 Olympic Games in Rio de Janeiro, Brazil, is a current example of how the event captured our attention for reasons other than the idea of competition. Politics have been integral to the Olympics since its inception in 1896. Social causes, international rivalries, and protests have been at the core of many if not most of the Summer Olympic Games (Davidson, 2017). In 2016, for example, we saw protests over the lack of concern about the Zika virus and other health risks for athletes participating in Brazil. Before we explore other areas of sports and events involving political protests, we need to review the instances when politics affected sports and the Olympic Games over the last 100 years.

The First Olympics in 1896

The first Olympics were held in Athens, Greece, and was not very popular at the time. Despite its lackluster introduction, the first Olympics Games captured "attention in parts of Western Europe and the United States" (Blackburn-Dwyer & McMaster, 2018). It was at this time that the Olympics began an international sporting tradition, complete with political intrigue.

For example, history tells us that at the time, Germany and France were political rivals, yet they eventually sent teams to compete in the Olympic Games. Then in the 1900s, the first Olympics held in Paris, France, were recorded as the first event that broke barriers when it became the first Olympics to feature female athletes. Charlotte Cooper made history as the first woman to win a medal in tennis for both the singles and doubles categories. Interestingly, female athletes would not compete in the Olympic Games again for another 24 years.

When the IOC voted to admit female athletes formally, many countries did not support this decision. The IOC decision to accept female athletes was "opposed by Turkey, Japan, France, and the

United States" (Blackburn-Dwyer & McMaster, 2018). Despite the political disapproval of female athletes, women became a constant feature of the Olympics from 1924 to the present day. Currently, we know challenges and barriers to overcome gender equality in sports are still an issue around the world. Records show that in 1992, 34 countries were participating in the Olympic Games without any representation by female athletes. To increase participation by female athletes, in 2012, the IOC pressured Saudi Arabia to include female athletes from its country, or it would risk being banned from participating in the Games. Saudi Arabia complied, but as we covered in Chapters 4 and 5 of this text, "Saudi Arabian culture still faces criticism for their domestic bans on female sporting events" (Blackburn-Dwyer & McMaster, 2018).

The politics of race and sports have always been deeply embedded and interconnected in American culture. For centuries, sports have served as a key venue to highlight issues and ideologies concerning what it means to be American and equal. It is in the world of sports where we find African American athletes, Caucasian athletes, Irish athletes, Italian athletes, Jewish athletes, female athletes, LGBTQ athletes, and rich and poor athletes, all of whom come together over decades and centuries to fight for the right to exist as individuals, as athletes. Athletes of all backgrounds use their platforms to correct injustices.

Boycotts and the Olympics

In 1976, athletes were in the news again when a total of 26 African nations decided to boycott the Olympic Games (Bingham, 2016). The boycott was initiated when the IOC made a decision to allow New Zealand to participate in a rugby tour of a South African country, which was a banned country at the time. America is also no foreigner to protests of the Olympic Games. In 1980, the United States protested the Olympic Games held in Moscow because the Soviets invaded Afghanistan. "A total of 62 countries also boycotted the 1980 Olympic Games which also included Japan and West Germany" (Blackburn-Dwyer & McMaster, 2018). The Soviet Union boycotted the 1984 Los Angeles Olympic Games for what they referred to as "security reasons" (Blackburn-Dwyer & McMaster, 2018). The Seoul Olympic Games in 1988 are, as of this date, saw the last known international boycott. The protest involved in the 1988 Games surrounded the fact that North Korea was upset and refused to participate in the Olympics because they were not billed as a cohost of the Summer Games. To show their support for North Korea, two countries, Ethiopia and Cuba, also boycotted the Olympic Games in Seoul.

Over the last 120 years, historical records have shown that the International Olympic Committee has taken on several political stands with the most well-known stand was banning South Africa from participation in the Games from 1964 to 1992 (Blackburn-Dwyer & McMaster, 2018). The reason for the ban was due to South Africa's apartheid policies. The political protests over apartheid resulted in other political arguments, but still, the demonstrations issued a strong statement against the South African nation's racist policies. Political activism is not just about countries or nations at the Olympics. Individual athletes have also made public protests concerning issues including race, identity, and geopolitics. Jesse Owens, an African American athlete, broke racial boundaries in 1936 when he dominated the track and field competitions (Baker, 1986; Dyreson, 1995; Dyreson, 2001; Dyreson, 2006). Owens destroyed ideological claims made by Germany's dictator Adolf Hitler. Hitler had hoped to use the Olympic Games to brag and show off the country's purity concerning whiteness and white supremacy. Jesse Owens's triumph is a story that has become well known throughout history. It is arguably one of the most recognized triumphs from the contentious Olympic Games held in 1924 in Berlin. A less publicized aspect of Owens's performance in the Berlin Olympics is the relationship he

FIGURE 15.1 *John Carlos, Tom-mie Smith, and Peter Norman.*

maintained with his German opponent, Luz Long. As depicted in the 2016 movie about Owens titled *Run*, Long openly encouraged a friendship with Owens during the long jump competition. Long's friendship with Owens was perceived as a snub and rebellion toward Adolf Hitler's Aryan supremacy political ideals. It was said that Jesse Owens maintained a close relationship with Long's family years after Long's death.

U.S. male Olympians Tommie Smith and John Carlos were dismissed during the 1968 Olympic Games in Mexico City for displaying a "black power" salute on the winners' podium (see Figure 15.1). The image of Smith and Carlos with their fists raised instantly became an iconic representation of the civil rights movement in America and made Olympic history. A little over a week before the Mexico City Olympic Games started in 1968, 267 students were murdered by the Mexican government. The killing of these 267 student protestors resulted in some athletes refusing to participate in the Olympics. Few nations or countries boycotted the 1968 Olympic Games because of the massacre by the Mexican government.

Historical records of the Olympic Games held in Munich in 1972 describe a time when Palestinian terrorists snuck into the Olympic Village and took 11 Olympic athletes from Israel hostage (Davis, 2017). According to news coverage at the time, the group known as "Black September" executed two of the 11 hostages (Davis, 2017; Robinson, 2015). The execution took place during a widely viewed international news broadcast (Robinson, 2015). Ultimately, the hostages and three of the captors were killed at a stakeout held in the airport. Historical news accounts describe this as one of the most violent and deadliest events in the history of the Olympic Games (Davis, 2017; Robinson, 2015).

The purpose of the preceding summary of boycotts and other tragic events was to show the complicated relationship between politics and sports, particularly during the Olympics. Even in the 21st century, the Olympic Games in the United States continued to be embroiled in conflicts, political disputes, and protests. For example, the 2008 Beijing Olympics were political in that many were concerned about China's human rights record (Bittnerová, 2014). Canada experienced political unrest when during the 2010 Winter Olympics, the country's complicated history with its indigenous people was highlighted in the media.

As previously mentioned in this chapter, we know that sports can unite people along racial, gender, political, and religious lines. Sports' potential to join Americans from all backgrounds has always been embedded in our nation's most favorite pastime, but we can recognize its ability to show how our disparate worlds might converge.

When Sports and Politics Collide

Currently in American culture, we find that sports and politics once again converge. This convergence of conflicts between race and politics has been shown in the behaviors of those athletes who use their platforms to stand with the Black Lives Matter movement. By kneeling during the playing of the national anthem, Colin Kaepernick used his celebrity to highlight issues which he—and many others—see as injustices that need to be addressed in our country. While Kaepernick's protest may have filled up today's headlines, the idea of athletes taking stances on larger social issues is not new. Let's explore some of the protests by athletes over the years that also highlight the collision of politics and sports.

FIGURE 15.2   *St. Louis Rams: In response to the Michael Brown shooting and to increase awareness of the events that took place in Ferguson, Missouri, players of the then St. Louis Rams raised their arms as they stepped onto the field during their introductions. From left is Stedman Bailey (12), Tavon Austin (11), Jared Cook, (89) Chris Givens (13), and Kenny Britt (81). In response to their "hands up" gesture, several players stated that they participated to acknowledge the events in Ferguson.*

St. Louis Rams: Hands Up

In response to the Michael Brown shooting and to increase awareness of the events that took place in Ferguson, Missouri, players of the then St. Louis Rams raised their arms as they stepped onto the field during their introductions. From the left in Figure 15.2 is Stedman Bailey (12), Tavon Austin (11), Jared Cook, (89) Chris Givens (13), and Kenny Britt (81). In response to their "hands up" gesture, several players stated that they participated to acknowledge the events in Ferguson (CBS News, 2014a).

Muhammad Ali

"I ain't got no quarrel with those Vietcong people" is a statement made by Ali in response to our war in 1967 with Vietnam, which began in April of that year. Muhammad Ali refused to join the armed forces or take part in the draft. Two months later, in June 1967, the professional boxer was indicted on charges of draft evasion, convicted, and then sentenced to 5 years in prison. He was also given a fine of $10,000 and banned from the professional sport of boxing for 3 years.

The Miami Heat: We Are Trayvon Martin Protest

LeBron James, who was playing with the Miami Heat during the George Zimmerman court case over the death of Trayvon Martin. James tweeted a picture of the Miami players "wearing hoodies, with their heads bowed in support of Trayvon Martin" (Demby, 2012). In Figure 15.3 is a photo of

FIGURE 15.3   *Rally for Trayvon Martin.*

FIGURE 15.4 *Billie Jean King and Bobby Riggs.*

Trayvon Martin in a hooded sweatshirt, an article of clothing that has since emerged as symbol of "gansta-rap," "criminals," urban style and race/ethnic membership (Wilson, 2012).

Billie Jean King: Equal Rights for Women

Prize money for women's tennis saw a dramatic increase because of efforts from Billie Jean King's activism for equality. King helped create the first women's players' union. In 1973, in an exhibition tennis match dubbed as "The Battle of the Sexes," she took on Bobby Riggs, who was known as a top tennis player in the 1940s. Years after the King–Riggs match, "Battle of the Sexes" is considered to be a very significant event that helped give recognition and respect for women's tennis. Figure 15.4 is the press photo taken in 1973 of the then 29-year-old Billie Jean King and the 55-year-old Bobby Riggs.

King's effect on women's tennis resulted in the USTA rededicating the tennis center in Flushing Meadows–Corona Park as the USTA Billie Jean King National Tennis Center (Figure 15.5).

FIGURE 15.5 *The USTA National Tennis Center in Flushing Meadows–Corona Park was rededicated as the USTA Billie Jean King National Tennis Center.*

Joe Louis: Challenged the Idea of Racial Superiority of the Aryans

Although the rematch between Louis and German Max Schmeling (Figure 15.6) lasted 2 minutes and 4 seconds, it represented the pinnacle of Louis's career. As discussed in the previous section, German dictator Adolf Hitler was set on promoting the racial superiority of Aryans and presented Schmeling as a perfect example of the Aryan brotherhood. However, Hitler's plans were once again foiled when Joe Louis won a technical knockout in the first round.

Michael Jordan

If Michael Jordan (Figure 15.7) had one fault, it would be the fact that he has

FIGURE 15.6   *Joe Louis versus Max Schmeling.*

often been reluctant to use his high-profile platform to interpose his thoughts and reactions to important political and social issues. Michael Jordan, a hall of famer, the image and source behind Nike's "Air Jordan's," and the owner of the Charlotte Hornets, did decide to speak up in 2014 in response to Donald Sterling's tape-recorded racist comments. Jordan also decided to weigh in on the many killings of young African American boys and men by police in 2016. Jordan said in a statement delivered to sports media, "One of the fundamental rights this country is founded on was freedom of speech, and we have a long tradition of nonviolent, peaceful protest. Those who exercise the right to peacefully express themselves should not be demonized or ostracized" (Spain, 2017).

Since the early 1990s, Jordan has chosen to stay silent during times when his voice would have had influence and impact. Jordan received intense criticism when he sat out of the political race between Harvey Gantt and the then-senator Jesse Helms. For Michael Jordan, the decision not to get involved in the political debated boiled down to his Air Jordan brand and politics. He famously stated, "Republicans buy shoes, too" (Coleman, 2016). Fans, athletes, and nonsports fans were upset and angry because they felt that Jordan chose profit over politics. Some even accused him of choosing "commerce over conscience" (Coleman, 2016).

FIGURE 15.7   *Michael Jordan.*

"We are privileged to live in the world's greatest country—a country that has provided my family and me the greatest of opportunities. The problems we face didn't happen overnight and they won't be solved tomorrow, but if we all work together, we can foster greater understanding, positive change and create a more peaceful world for ourselves, our children, our families and our communities."

(Michael Jordan, quoted in https://www.nbcnews.com/news/us-news/michael-jordan-can-no-longer-stay-silent-n616276, July 22, 2018)

Kareem Abdul-Jabbar

Kareem Abdul-Jabbar (Figure 15.8), a former NBA player who still holds the record for the player with the highest points in the history of the NBA, is often compared to Michael Jordan (McRae, 2017). When it comes to identifying the greatest basketball players of all time in America, two players are consistently listed in the top five: Kareem Abdul-Jabbar and Michael Jordan. Research on athletes and politics surprisingly revealed that Kareem Abdul-Jabbar also holds the record for the athlete who has had the longest record for political activism. Kareem has been a political advocate for over 50 years (Abdul-Jabbar, 2015; McRae, 2017). In fact, in a media interview with *Time* magazine, Abdul-Jabbar is quoted as saying, "I've been writing about politics longer than I played basketball" (Abdul-Jabbar, 2015).

Recall that Abdul-Jabbar was one of many athletes who was involved in the Ali/Cleveland Summit—a meeting of athletes with Muhammad Ali to discuss Ali's protest of the war. Abdul-Jabbar was using his given name, Lew Alcindor, during the summit. At the time, he had not converted to Islam. During the summit, Ali convinced the athletes to stand against the U.S. government, and that is when Abdul-Jabbar stated that he knew he needed to make his voice heard and to speak up for injustices. For Abdul-Jabbar, race has been the main social issue that he confronts daily.

Abdul-Jabbar's first recorded activism was in 1968 when he chose to boycott the Olympic Games that were held in Mexico. Race riots were in full force in major metropolitan cities in response to the assassination of Dr. Martin Luther King Jr. in April 1968. Abdul-Jabbar said that he just could not go to the Olympics and represent a country filled with inequality and mistreatment of blacks. Abdul-Jabbar said in a statement, "I had to make a stand. I wanted the country to live up to the words of the founding fathers—and make sure they applied to people of color and to women. I was trying to hold America to that standard" (Abdul-Jabbar, 2015).

Abdul-Jabbar recently made public his sentiments regarding Colin Kaepernick's take-a-knee protest. When asked if the protest in 2017 mirrors issues in 1968, Abdul-Jabbar was reported as saying, "The whole issue of equal treatment under the law is still being worked out here because for so long our political and legal culture has denied black Americans equal treatment" (Abdul-Jabbar, 2015).

FIGURE 15.8 *Kareem Abdul-Jabbar at the Democratic National Convention in 2016.*

Athletes, Strikes, and Protests: It's All Political

It should be no surprise that as a culture that adores and is passionate about sports that we find that when athletes talk, the public listens. One example is when the University of Missouri's football team threatened to strike to protest the way the university's leaders were handling racial tensions on campus. Combined efforts by faculty, staff, athletes, and students eventually led to the resignation of the university president and chancellor. When the players on the St. Louis Rams football team entered the field with a "hands up, don't shoot" gesture to protest the death of Michael Brown in Ferguson, their actions gained national media attention and became a trending topic on social media. When the Miami Heat players wore black hoodies to show their support for slain Florida teenager Trayvon Martin, their protest statement encouraged a plethora of media coverage and debates on whether athletes should involve themselves in political issues. Should athletes keep their focus on playing sports? Or should athletes use their platforms and celebrity to speak out on social issues? What role, if any, should an athlete play in times of social unrest?

Colin Kaepernick's silent protest has been the focus of many in the sports media world and has been enmeshed in public debate since August 2017. The debate also centers on the question of whether athletes should just "stick to playing sports." The phrase comes from a sentiment frequently aimed at players and coaches who take on a political stance on topics that do not relate to their sport. Figure 15.9 illustrates the kneeling behavior of a few of Kaepernick's former team members. This picture was taken as the player's kneeled during the National Anthem before their game against the Washington Redskins on October 15, 2017, in Landover, Maryland. As of March 2018, the NFL announced that fines will be issued to a team if a player refuses to stand for the flag and national

FIGURE 15.9   *San Francisco 49ers kneeling during the National Anthem.*

anthem. The new rule does allow players to stay in the locker room while the national anthem is being performed, but players are now required to stand proudly for the anthem. The idea is that if players don't stand, then perhaps they should not be allowed to play or even stay in America. If we carefully analyze the NFL policy, we find that out of all the protests that athletes may be involved in, protests that include exercising their First Amendment rights by protesting racial inequality and police violence are only acceptable when athletes engage in the protest out of the media spotlight and behind closed doors.

When famous African American athletes protest in America, one thing we know for sure is this: protests led by athletes of color have had a polarizing effect on our culture and in sports for hundreds of years. In fact, protests led by African American athletes have dominated headlines in sports media for years, dating back to 1910 when Jack Johnson, a black boxer, won a fight against Jim Jeffries, a white boxer. This win was newsworthy because a black boxer beat a white boxer, and in our culture (then and now), the "win" was seen as a symbol of the black man's masculinity and ability to reign over whites. For some, this may be the impetus for the idea that black men pose some type of threat to white supremacy in America. In today's American culture, we still have athletes of color protesting by wearing Black Lives Matter T-shirts, doing a "hands up, don't shoot" pose before games, and now taking a knee during the national anthem. More so today than in the past, we are finding African American athletes using their platforms to expand their athletic voices into the political activism arena.

At the heart of the Kaepernick protest is the idea that he and other athletes refuse to stand up and show pride in a flag for America—a country that clearly demonstrates oppression. Many African Americans and people of color want our country to represent what this country is supposed to represent: liberty and justice for all. The controversy with the take-a-knee protest is currently still explosive and divisive. Facts show that a majority of the NFL players are African Americans. Yet the majority of NFL fans are white (i.e., more than 84% are white). Research also shows that not only is the majority fan base white but also more than 65% of the white fan based is made up of white males. If we elaborate on this demographic fan base, we suddenly realize that these white male sports fans are those who are willing to pay large amounts of money to watch African American men engage in high-contact, physically dangerous plays in the game of football. The shut up and play sentiment is still evident in 2018 in that it seems as if comments about the take-a-knee protest by whites implies that as long as the black athletes run, tackle, win games, wear their helmets, and keep their mouths shut about oppression and inequality, then they are acceptable to be a part of and included in the white mainstream. The very minute that African American athletes make the choice to elucidate systemic racism and other systematic inequalities in American culture, that's when we see anger and extreme backlash toward the athlete.

In the summer of 2018, the NFL initially announced its policy on kneeling during the national anthem. According to news coverage, the NFL's new anthem policy would allow each NFL team to determine if a player should be disciplined for kneeling during the anthem (Maske, 2018). The new policy gives players the option to either stay in the locker room during the anthem or to stand should they choose to be on the field for the anthem. Initially, the NFL required their players to not just appear on the sidelines but did not require them to stand (Maske, 2018). In a controversial move, Dallas Cowboys owner Jerry Jones announced that all the Dallas Cowboys football players must stand with "toes on the line" during the anthem, regardless of the NFL's policy (Jones, 2018). Despite the fact that the NFL has asked owners to "step down" while the NFL and NFLPA create a plan that would allow compromise and proactive steps with respect to the protests, Jerry Jones decided to ignore the request and publicly oppose the NFL and NFLPA's attempt to reach a "compromise" (Stites, 2018).

FIGURE 15.10   *Colin Kaepernick.*

At the time of this writing, the NFL and NFLPA are currently working on a resolution to the protest issue. According to AP news reports, the NFL has stated, "No new rules relating to the anthem will be issued or enforced for the next several weeks while these confidential discussions are ongoing" (Jones, 2018). In September 2018, Nike revealed its newest advertising campaign featuring Colin Kaepernick (Figure 15.10). The campaign honors the athlete who took a knee for justice "even if it means sacrificing everything," including his career with the league (Romero, 2018).

The latest intrusion of politics and sports has had a drastic effect on sports news coverage. The discussion of athletes and protests now seems to bring with it a sense of urgency and relevance that our culture has not seen or experienced since those protests of the '60s and early '70s, when athletes such as Jim Brown, Kareem Abdul-Jabbar, Muhammad Ali, and Arthur Ashe openly talked about civil rights (Kang, 2017). The White House, in an attempt to "make America safe," announced a new travel restriction and ban on individuals from Iran, Libya, North Korea, Somalia, Syria, Venezuela, and Yemen. It was during this time that the Milwaukee Bucks were scheduled to play the Toronto Raptors in Canada. Fans were concerned that Thon Maker, the rookie center playing for the Bucks, would not be allowed to return to the United States because of the travel ban. While the player was directly affected by the travel ban policy (although he reentered the United States without problem), teammates and coaches in the NBA made their support of the Canadian athlete public.

Athletes, especially famous ones, who protest risk being shaded by their politics. When athletes are asked about their political beliefs by sports reporters, they most often will take the opportunity to give voice to injustices. In summer 2015, the WNBA fined several players for supporting Black Lives Matter at pregame practices. Many of the basketball players wore black T-shirts to show their support of Black Lives Matter. It was the next game that the WNBA chose to sanction the players, which led some of them to refuse to discuss basketball. So instead of using postgame media interviews to talk about their game performances and the outcome of the game, players chose to use the media time to discuss police shootings of innocent young black men (The WNBA rescinded the fines soon after.)

Stephen Curry, one of the most popular basketball players, used his celebrity to protest the major sports brand Under Armour. The chief executive of Under Armour referred to newly elected President Trump as a "great asset" for the country (Williams, 2017). Curry, chose to vocalize his disdain for this comment by the executive (Kang, 2017). Curry stated that he spoke out because he felt that Under Armour's positive reference to the president did not align with his ideals. Perhaps more than any other NBA superstar, Curry, knowing that his sponsorships would be at risk, continued to be outspoken about politics.

Following their fifth Super Bowl victory, New England Patriots' key players made a public announcement that they would not visit the White House, which was a traditional victory routine. And in April 2017, photos taken at the White House showed that they did skip the traditional White House visit and the opportunity to be recognized by newly elected president Donald Trump. The Super Bowl victory for the Patriots in 2017 has been called in sports media "the greatest comeback in Super Bowl history" (D'Andrea, 2017). Earlier in the season, many of the Patriot players raised their fists to show support of Colin Kaepernick's national anthem protest. The news coverage of the athletes' decision to reject the White House invitation for political reasons once again incited a "stick to sports" criticism. A Patriots spokesman went on record to provide historical background regarding the White House visit over the years. In 2017, 34 players attended the White House visit, a number very similar to the turnout when President George W. Bush hosted players in 2004 and 2005. Then in 2015, when Barack Obama was president, the number of players approached 50—a key player conspicuously absent was the quarterback Tom Brady. One reason offered as to why so many players did not attend in 2017 as compared to 2015 was that some veteran players did not see the need to go twice in 3 years.

American culture has, for the most part, widely revered athletes. We love sports in this culture. In the United States, sports have allowed athletes to achieve a level of status with which they can express themselves and be heard—a platform that might not be given to the average American. Perhaps this is why many of the athletes who speak out and take activism seriously are often people of color or women. African Americans have been regularly refused access to political, social, and economic positions. As a result, athletes have used their visibility to give voice to the voices that would not otherwise be heard in today's culture. Case in point: the legendary Jackie Robinson, who called for more black managers in baseball. Currently, Kaepernick is just one athlete who exemplifies the idea of exercising his celebrity influence to bring awareness to an issue. Kaepernick uses platforms such as Twitter and other media to address the issue of injustices to men of color in America. There is no doubt that we have athletes who are influential public figures and use their status to articulate and advocate ideas for social change and civil rights.

Religion and Sports

Institutional religions have been a part of the story of religion and sports in America. Americans have somehow transformed the field of sports into religious praying fields. Like politics, religion has also paved its way into the heart and core of American sports. Religion and sports are for some viewed as athletic expressions of our national identity. We find religious themes and ideas deeply embedded in sports now more than ever before. In fact, when it comes to religion, we find that it continues to make its way into the sports world in new and innovative ways. Take for instance a term recently referred to in sports media as "Tebowing." While a college player at the University of Florida, Tim Tebow (Figure 15.11) would kneel in prayer immediately following incredible plays, touchdowns, and victories. In 2011, when Tebow made his debut as the quarterback for the Denver Broncos, several football commentators and analysts thought that the skills that Tebow showed as a quarterback during his college years would not match the skills needed in the professional league. Tebow led the Broncos to a dramatic overtime victory, proving to his critics wrong. During the broadcast of this tremendous victory, we saw many of the Broncos take to the football field in celebration while Tebow remained on the sidelines kneeling in prayer. Broadcast images showed us a picture of Tebow in silent prayer. These images hit the Internet like a storm. Suddenly, the Internet and social media posted memes and other images making fun of the image of Tebow kneeling in silent prayer. And suddenly, just like other terms such as "bootylicious," a new term was introduced in our culture: the verb "Tebowing." "Tebowing" communicates the blending of two American passions: religion and sports.

From his early days in the media spotlight, Tim Tebow has always confidently displayed his Christian faith on the football field (Remillard, 2016). Often, he would be filmed with Bible verses on his eyes in black marker. He would be shown pointing his hands and fingers upward toward the sky, praising God and the Lord and Savior Jesus Christ for blessing him with talents and abilities to play ball.

FIGURE 15.11   *Tim Tebow kneeling in silent prayer.*

Sacred Ground

In the early 20th century, evangelicals created ideals and theologies that would allow us to praise the spiritual and physical benefits of sports (Dator, 2017; Remillard, 2016). It was during this time in our culture that the term "muscular Christians" appeared. At the same time, other denominations and religious groups created similar theologies for sports. The popularity of sports also grew while making America's civil, religious discourse part of our culture's biggest pastime (Remillard, 2016). The relationship between sports and religion has grown over the years, fueling debates and conversations around the sacred aspects of our American patriotic and religious identity. The relationship between religion and sports in the United States goes much further than athletes kneeling in prayer after a winning touchdown. The relationship is more than placing scripture on helmets and foreheads. We find that monuments, stadiums, and other locations have also become sacred in the sports world. Take the "Sacred Ground" exhibit for example. When one visits the Baseball Hall of Fame in Cooperstown, New York, one can find an exhibit on the third floor called Sacred Ground. Upon entering the exhibit, you pass through a threshold that symbolizes the separation of baseball from the outside world (Remillard, 2016).

Sacred Ground, an exhibit at the National Baseball Hall of Fame and Museum, on the Museum's third floor where they find an expansive display of the American baseball ballparks of the past and present. There are more than 200 memorabilia and numerous displays in on the third floor of the building. Some of the most famous and notable memorabilia included in the exhibit are the original ticket booth from Yankee Stadium, the original scoreboard that resembled a "pinwheel" from Comiskey Park, and a view of Walter Johnson's locker from Griffith Stadium, to name just a few of the exhibits. Sacred Ground also includes a special interactive area that is dedicated to the "organ" music frequently played at the ballpark. Sacred Ground allows visitors of the Hall of Fame to hear music from several of the historic ballparks in America. In fact, the exhibit provides background on the classic tune "Take Me Out to the Ball Game."

After entering the third floor, visitors are immediately taken to the ticket booth that was once used in Yankee Stadium. There is a sign above the booth that reads, "Ballparks are baseball's sacred ground.… Ballparks provide the stage for the game, a frame for memories of games past, and the promise of future games enjoyed with family and friends" (Remillard, 2016).

The exhibit of Yankee Stadium opens into themed areas: "Fans," "Ballpark Business," "Evolution of the Ballpark," "The Stadium World," "Reverence," and "Ballpark Entertainment" (Remillard, 2016). Also included in the exhibit are baseball bats, bumper stickers, scorecards, rings, trophies, and bleacher seats (Remillard, 2016).

Sacred Ground is an exhibit that intentionally strikes the senses of all who visit. It allows our sensory perceptions (i.e., ears, eyes, and noses) to come into contact with baseball's history in America. Visitors are also able to "smell" stadiums and other artifacts. The Sacred Exhibit is just one of many illustrations showing how American sports are deeply intertwined with religion. Religious frames and references also influence rituals that we often practice in sports. It is interesting to note that when you visit the exhibit, you can still be Christian, Jewish, Muslim, Buddhist, atheist, agnostic, etc. The exhibit does a nice job of allowing the diverse religions of our nation to connect with the sport that helps them identify and unite as sports fans. Religion, in the context of Sacred Ground then is not merely an expression of ancient theology or one's belief in God. Religion, as many argue, is "what happens when the sport itself becomes spiritual" (Remillard, 2016).

Baseball, in this culture, is a religious ritual. Baseball is often thought of as the sport that serves as an expression of our country's core values. Historical research shows that prior to baseball, "muscular Christians" transformed religion when they included sports in their rituals. It was during this time in American culture that bodily fitness became a necessary component in terms of one's personal holiness and reverence and strength. This is where the term "muscular Christian" was derived. The concerns of this religious sports movement mirrored the ideology and theology of white Protestant founders. As a result of the White Protestants, we noticed that sports began to produce and reinforce the founders' understandings of race/ethnicity, sexual identity and orientation, gender, and class. But, as we noted in Chapter 1 of this text, the 20th century witnessed a growth, and with that growth came more complex and complicated American attitudes that resulted in valuing and respecting the muscular endeavors of sports and male athletes. From historical research and religious literature, it was discovered that this was when Catholics, Jews, African Americans, and women were then able to use their bodily fitness and muscle to insinuate their way into the mainstream sports world. People from all backgrounds also realized that with the introduction of religious ideals, they were now able to use their athletic bodies, and bodily movements represent their own personal religious values. The intersection between religion and sports was also marked by conflict. Conflict and competition arose simply because these new sports and religious voices were starting to challenge our status quo. The challenge caused us to struggle and see America and our values of the past beyond their traditional limits. Some would argue that this may explain why so many of the barriers embedded in sports today (e.g., hegemonic masculinity) are quite difficult to change and challenge.

We know that baseball is as close to a religious ritual as any sport. Baseball has been described as an athletic act that demonstrates the "American way of life" (Remillard, 2016). Patriotism, religion, and baseball started to become a way to honor troops fighting in the Great War. We learn from history that it was during the Great War that "The Star-Spangled Banner" was first performed at a sporting event. The story is that it was "during the seventh inning of the 1918 World Series between the Boston

Red Sox and Chicago Cubs" when it appeared that the fans were getting bored. So the band started to play the national anthem, and all of a sudden people were standing and paying attention (Remillard, 2016). By World War II, "The Star-Spangled Banner" became a standard ritual at the beginning of many sporting events. The sight of large crowds standing and singing in the mass media helped to produce a sense of nationalism, American pride, and unity in a land that was growing in diversity.

Colin Kaepernick is not the first athlete to protest or kneel during the national anthem. In 1995, Mahmoud Abdul-Rauf (known as Chris Jackson), a player on the Denver Nuggets team, decided that he would not stand when the national anthem was performed. Abdul-Rauf, a Muslim convert believed that, for him, the flag and the anthem represent "tyranny and oppression." As soon as the media began taking notice of his protest, the NBA suspended him and fined Abdul-Rauf for the controversial action. Abdul-Rauf eventually came up with a compromise: while he would stand during the anthem, he would pray in silence for those in our country who were suffering from oppression. Some activists believe firmly that Abdul-Rauf's religion and race played a significant part in the conflict and debate over his protest of oppression. Others argue that religion and the religion of Islam and American perceptions about Islam were the major reasons why his protest caused such a ruckus in sports media and with fans alike. After the terrorist attacks on September 11, 2001, Muslim Americans would continue engaging with the ethnic and religious debate on the playing fields. In 2005, a high school football team in Dearborn, Michigan, still continued to pursue playoff victories while honoring the Ramadan fast. This conflict between religion and sports caught the eye of the media, and soon the high school football team was the center of media attention. The high school players' story of faith and football came to typify our culture's counternarrative that tries to tell us that Muslims cannot be "real Americans." The Muslim players on the high school football team in Dearborn worked to find a space for themselves in American culture by adding an Islamic twist to a popular American sport.

Currently, expressions of religion and sports have found a place in America. The Fellowship of Christian Athletes is an American mainstay in high schools, colleges, and professional teams. In a similar vein, the Mormons have gained media attention and national recognition at Brigham Young University through the successes and accomplishments of their male and female student-athletes. Buddhism has been introduced in basketball and golf by basketball coach Phil Jackson and golfer Tiger Woods. And in the sport of distance running, a commune known as Divine Madness in Boulder, Colorado, has introduced the integration of holistic healing, Eastern spirituality, and long-distance running. Religion in this sense is now added to a sport where "members use distance runs as a means of heightening spiritual awareness" (quote taken from Remillard, 2016).

This intersection of sports and religion, however, has also led to some unlikely interfaith conflicts and dialogues. In the NFL, Husain Abdullah, a Kansas City Chiefs football player, was penalized by a referee for "unsportsmanlike conduct." The penalty was issued when Abdulla knelt in prayer after he scored a touchdown (Figure 15.12). Similar to Tim Tebow's kneeling (although he did so on the sidelines), the player sunk to the ground on the field in celebration of the play.

FIGURE 15.12 *Husain Abdullah penalized for bowing in prayer after an interception.*

Abdullah, who is a practicing Muslim, was practicing a gesture that in his religion is considered an act of worship and adoration. In response to the unsportsmanlike penalty, the Council on American-Islamic Relations protested the penalty. And to many fans' surprise, the sports media was even angered about the penalty and published prior images of Tim Tebow Tebowing in comparison. Eventually, the NFL conceded that the penalty was an error and retracted it from the record. This relatively current event and misunderstanding of the Islam religion allowed us as a culture (once again) to explore the new road of enlightenment. We were, again after 9/11, forced to face our misperceptions, unfamiliarity, and confusion about religions. In other instances, efforts to understand other faiths now make some people feel that they come with secret agendas and ulterior motives. "The New York Police Department (NYPD) started a youth soccer league in 2008 as an attempt to connect with Arab Muslims living in the area" (Remillard, 2016). The program was largely successful and encouraged the creation of another league. The success of the youth soccer league for Arab Muslims incited the development of a cricket sports league specifically for Muslims from South Asia (Remillard, 2016). By relying on equipment such as soccer goals and sticky wickets, the police department was making huge progress in terms of developing relationships with Muslims. By 2011, however, information was leaked that revealed a hidden agenda for the creation of the leagues. It was revealed that the leagues were actually created to acquire inside information and facilitate intelligence gathering by the New York Police officers in attendance.

Although the debates concerning politics and sports and religion and sports are polarizing, it is up to journalists, sports promoters, and others in the field to begin careful consideration of all the ways that sports and religion operate here in America in the 21st century. Consider when the University of Mississippi's football team beat the Alabama Crimson Tide in 2014. The loss by the Crimson Tide was said to be the upset among upsets. Immediately after the win, security guards shifted their gaze from the players to the fans only to see that the fans rushed onto the field and took down the goalposts. As a result of the win, what happened after that was mass hysteria. Instead of following time-honored, long-standing rituals of trampling through the goalposts, fans took them out of the ground. This all of a sudden became a symbol, an object of the victory, and was featured in parades and processions. As the crowd hoisted the metal poles, they departed from the stadium and marched onward to the Grove (Figure 15.13), a ten-acre grassy plot at the center of campus.

The Grove at the University of Mississippi is known as "the Holy Grail of tailgating sites." Tailgaters who use the Grove call themselves "grovers." In "the Grove," thousands of "grovers" assemble to socialize, eat, drink, and prepare for the game. After the 2014 victory against the Crimson Tide, fans found a sacred place to erect their sacred object: the goalposts. To further illustrate

FIGURE 15.13   *Tailgating area at Ole Miss known as "the Grove".*

the influence of religion on the victory, days after the victorious game, the goalposts were cut into pieces were sold to fans who could afford the memorabilia. The University of Mississippi received a fine for the destruction of the goalposts. The total fine issued by the Southeastern Conference was set at $50,000. Ole Miss asked fans to help raise funds for the fine and replace the goalposts they tore down. Records show that Ole Miss not only gathered the $50,000 to pay the fines, but they exceeded the goal in just four hours. It seems that the fans preferred to donate hundreds of dollars for the symbolic metal goalposts than to return the pieces. It made complete sense to the fans to spend money on the inanimate piece of metal, now a sacred symbol. The goalposts became a symbol used to celebrate that one moment in time when number 11 Ole Miss beat the number-one football team, the Alabama Crimson Tide. For many of the fans, time stopped and the Ole Miss community united and put away all differences to celebrate the historic win. The honoring of metal poles, we could argue, seems to capture the essence of the true meaning of the word "fan." We learn from history that the word "fan" comes from the Latin word *fanaticus*, which translates to "possessed by a deity" (Patterson, 2014; Remillard, 2016).

Another example of a religious "relic" in sports can be found in Pittsburgh. Visitors to the Pittsburgh International Airport pass two statues standing side by side on their way to baggage claim. One of the statutes is an image of George Washington, our "founding father" and first president. The other is of another "founding father." Hall of Fame running back Franco Harris's likeness is the other statue. The statue honors Harris for creating "Steeler Nation" (Remillard, 2016). A statue of George Washington is a common and well-recognized depiction. The statue of Franco Harris leans forward in a pose that makes him appear to be ready to make a catch. The pose that Harris is demonstrating is now known in Pittsburgh as the "Immaculate Reception," a term born after a winning play (see Figure 15.14). It was in the 1972 playoff game against the Oakland Raiders when Harris caught a deflected pass and scored the winning touchdown (Remillard, 2016).

FIGURE 15.14 *Statues of George Washington and Franco Harris side by side at the Pittsburgh International Airport*

The Pittsburgh Steelers had never won a playoff game until Harris's miraculous, as fans call it, play. But by the end of the 1970s, the Steelers not only earned one but four Super Bowl championships. To this day, Steeler Nation strongly believes that the catch by Franco Harris catapulted a new era of victory for the Steelers. On the fortieth anniversary of the "Immaculate Reception," media described the catch as "the play that changed a city" (Remillard, 2016). And "Children of the Immaculate Reception" have grown up knowing about this catch and they too have transferred the belief that the catch symbolizes the greatness of the city of Pittsburg itself. The way that fans assign sacred meaning to sports is not something unique to football. We see it in other sports such as distance or marathon running when runners use their time and the distance as "a place to commune with God."

Native Americans, Spirituality, and Sports

Navajo leaders in 1998 started Wings of America, a nonprofit group aimed at "promoting running and fitness among the tribal youth" (Remillard, 2016). This organization holds camps and sponsors teams to encourage a running lifestyle for Navajo children. It a mission of the Wings of America that the group will "steer them away from exposure to and threats of alcoholism, obesity, type-2 diabetes, and similar health concerns" (Remillard, 2016). The leaders of Wings of America also stress the importance of participating in the distance running sport. It is believed that distance running is in line with Navajo spirituality, allowing Navajo athletes to recall a time when Navajos were proud and physically fit. Information on religion and sports must include a discussion of Native Americans. For this group, physical activity can assume sacred meaning. For Navajo athletes, running is a way to deal with long-term feelings of despair. For the Cherokee Nation in North Carolina, lacrosse is a sport that continues to be played in Native American cultures. Although lacrosse is not played as frequently, other contact sports, such as football, continue to be a more visible form of tribal identity.

Reflect on Sports: Does God Decide Who Wins?

To answer this question, a survey was distributed by the Public Religion Research Institute (PRRI) and Religion News Service. The survey reported that 1 in 4 Americans believe that God does determine winners and losers. The survey goes on to show that Americans and avid sports fans report believing that God determines and plays a vital role in terms of the winning team. More than 50% of Americans and over 55% of all sports fans reported the idea that God rewards faithful athletes with good health and success (PRRI, 2015).

According to another PRRI study, it was revealed that Americans do pray and ask God to help their teams win. The survey went on to show that 25% of American fans believe that their teams (those with losing records) have been cursed by God. The survey also revealed that most American sports fans feel that on any given Sunday, they are more likely to go to church than to stay home and watch a football game on TV. And it is important to note that when we speak of religion and sports, we would be remiss to omit the fact that the Seattle Seahawks quarterback Russell Wilson is quick to credit his success to divine intervention.

After his team's victory over the Green Bay Packers in the National Football Conference Championship Game in 2014, Wilson told a sideline reporter, "God is too good all the time, man. Every time." Pushed out of the Super Bowl bid that year, Aaron Rodgers, the Packers quarterback, publicly disagreed with the reporter during a broadcast of his weekly radio show. "I don't think God cares a whole lot about the outcome," Rodgers declared. "He cares about the people involved, but I don't think he's a big football fan" (Blumberg, 2015). Wilson told sports reporters, "I think God cares about football. I think God cares about everything he created" (PRRI, 2015).

Sports and religion have always conflicted with one another. The relationship between sports and religion, just like sports and politics, is complicated. Religion loves to borrow from sports, especially when found in themes for sermons, and sport loves to borrow from religion as we saw in the shrines and objects that fans worship (the Hail Mary, the Holy Grail, Tim Tebow's frequent references to God during press conferences). The mix of religion and sports can often become extremely problematic. Consider, for example, Kurt Warner, a former quarterback for the St. Louis Rams. In a speech delivered to a Baptist group, Warner stated that he felt he lost his starting position because of his faith (Lipsyte, 2004). Once the speech hit the media, Warner "suffered" a public scolding by the then head coach Mike Martz.

"I think God wants you to be a winner in life, and that spills over into athletics," according to a statement made by Jerry Falwell (Lipsyte, 2004). "If kicking butts is part of it, that's part of it. Jesus was no sissy. If he played football, you'd be slow getting up after he tackled you" (Pieper, 2015). Falwell's idea of "muscular Christianity" shows how Americans seek a sort of pep talk from God. Sports is no different. In America, God is celebrated, particularly with evidence of our material successes, whether one is successful in obtaining promotions, tenure, selling cars, or scoring touchdowns. The tenet seems to be "if you say you believe in God, then you win." There is an underlying thought that "God must be on your side. If you lose, it's because your faith wasn't strong enough and you must try harder next time" (Lipsyte, 2004).

Religious experience is so varied in American culture that it is complicated and challenging to link all religions, denominations, and religious players into one category, one chapter, and one overall description of its role in sports. Kurt Warner was reported saying that all he wants to do is "use his fame as a platform for God's message" (Lipsyte, 2004). Many athletes pray in silence, while other athletes give thanks to God and Jesus Christ.

Religion and Sports (Constitutional and Biblical Issues)

One of the most controversial issues in sports is the practice of religious beliefs by coaches, athletes, and staff. For example, what happens when prayers are led in public before sports contests? Does the head coach have the freedom to counsel an athlete using Christian principles? One of the fundamental tenets held in America is the separation of church and state. This means that the government is not to promote, endorse, or advance a particular religion. In the late 1700s, the founding fathers developed this tenet in reaction to the Church of England's influence over more Protestant-influenced forms of worship.

While our country appears to be tolerant of various religious beliefs and practices, it is still considered inappropriate and a violation of our constitutional rights when a state or government places more importance on one religion over another. Studies of religion and its effect on sports continue to evolve. According to the First Amendment of the U.S. Constitution, "Congress shall make no law respecting an establishment of religion, or prohibiting the free exercise thereof" (Epstein, 2003).

Prayer Before Sporting Events

A gray area of the law that still brings some controversy concerns whether teams should be allowed to engage in prayer before a game. While prayer ceremonies have been common in American for a century, we find that currently in our culture, we are faced with challenges legally and personally regarding organized prayer. This debate has forced American legal courts to address if prayer ceremonies before a game are constitutional. For example, in terms of separation, the question in this area is whether prayers before a sporting event put one religion over another religion? Other related questions include the following: Do prayers advance any religion? Does it matter who leads the team in prayer? In other words, can a student-athlete lead a prayer or should the coach?

In the mid-1990s, we learned of an account involving a high school Texas student. The student who served as the "school's student council chaplain often shared a prayer over the school's intercom before all home varsity football games" (Green, 2016). A few angry mothers filed a lawsuit challenging this public prayer. The students held elections and showed unanimous support for the prayers before games. The district court modified the policy on prayer and stated that they would permit only nonsectarian, nonproselytizing prayer. Five years later, in 2000, the Supreme Court of the United States vetoed the decision made by the district court and found that any type of student-initiated or student-led prayers that took place in a public high school was unconstitutional.

What happens to elite athletes who publicly express their religious beliefs before, during, and after games, as well as in their personal lives? Does the expression of their religious beliefs violate the notion concerning the separation of church and state? (Remillard, 2016). So the question to be considered is this: When an athlete makes a significant play and then starts to kneel in prayer, or points to the sky, or puts his or her hands together as if in prayer and then looks up to the clouds, should these behaviors be deemed religious, or does our acceptance of them mean that we support one religion while excluding other religious beliefs? (Remillard, 2016). Should it be considered "illegal" when athletes kneel on the field or court after a game? What if they are holding hands in prayer on the field?

Consider the following scenarios:

- Fans are in the stands bowing their heads and praying together.
- Students perform a prayer during sports.
- The head coach of a team tells players to make a circle and join hands in prayer before a game.
- An athlete sits alone in the locker room and reads from a bible or other religious book before or after a game.
- An athlete shares "the Good News" or the gospel of Christ with other teammates or shares the consequences of having faith.

These are all possible scenarios that need to be ironed out in our culture. Players of all sports continue to express their religious beliefs in some form or fashion. Many athletes are not penalized for their public religious expression. Take, for instance, in 1965 when Sandy Koufax, a practicing Jewish professional baseball player, refused to pitch during the first game of the World Series (Rosengren, 2015). Koufax, who played for the Dodgers, did not participate in the game because "the game fell on a Jewish holiday known as Yom Kippur" (Rosengren, 2015). Another example is when Los Angeles Dodgers player Shawn Green did not play in a game because of his Jewish faith and recognition of Yom Kippur. Then there is legendary Vince Lombardi, the former head coach of the Green Bay Packers. Lombardi was known to take his team to Catholic mass before Sunday games.

Prayers before, during, and after a sporting event pose difficult challenges for laws to regulate and determine if an actual violation of the Constitution really took place. American courts use tests such as the "Lemon test, the endorsement test, and the coercion test to determine whether the state may be advancing a particular religion or religion in general" (Epstein, 2003). Should religion be removed from a sport?

Conclusion

Politics, religion, and sports are all topics that you may not want to bring up at a social event. Some organizations have created policies against discussing politics and religion in club meetings simply because of their strange influence on relationships. Religion, for example, has so many divisions and denominational conflicts that it is hard to unite believers, nonbelievers, and denominations on any one aspect of religion. Politics, as we have seen since the 2016 election, can polarize all parties. Presently, we find most, if not all, Americans are divided in terms of politics and religion. There are feelings of hate and anger among everyone about everything in a sort of hyperpartisan way.

Sports for some may be the one aspect in our culture that can be used to unite Americans. Like music, people from all backgrounds come together to cheer on their favorite team or athlete. Sometimes conversations about a sport can generate healthy debate and other times they can generate some debates that are emotional dynamite (e.g., Deflategate). Discussions that talk about our favorite team's performance in a game or championship game, the team's management and/or team owners (e.g., Dallas Cowboys' owner, the man people love to hate), trade rumors, and other ins and outs of the game can be unifying in that they are often topics that are less hostile and least likely to cause division.

But what happens when sports start becoming more about politics and religion? Athletes in America are citizens too. They are individuals with feelings, thoughts, experiences, and interests who hurt and rejoice and have opinions just like every other American. They also have political views and religious views. When the Missouri football team boycotted in response to the protests in November 2015, several Missouri donors were so angry that they threatened to stop donating to the athletic department and scholarships. But why? They are, in reality, student-athletes—students who are also affected by some of the institutional policies that were being contested at the time. It is an interesting discussion that seems to be ongoing even as of this writing.

But what happens when an athlete suddenly is placed in the public eye and makes the decision to talk about religion? Or politics?

Religion in sports is perhaps the most divisive issue in the world of sports. Players are often shown pointing to the heavens to thank God for blessings. Politics in sports is another area where people are divided and take offense. For example, in 2008, fans were offended when Tampa Bay Rays players appeared with (not-yet-elected president) Barack Obama at a campaign appearance. Players endorsing a black presidential candidate caused some fans to be angry and scream that this alliance was "Unfair!" Why would players use their celebrity to back this candidate and not another? It is as if everyone realizes the influence that athletes have on attitudes and behaviors, and the very idea that they would make a public show of support rattles many citizens. The notion is, and has always been, that athletes should not publicly proclaim endorsements for political candidates. That is, it seems that once an athlete becomes a professional, he or she loses his or her American citizenship and is not allowed to show support for anyone or any issue. It's almost as if Americans tell athletes that in this country, while we allow them to vote, we do not want them to have any political beliefs. We just want them to shut up and play and not care about the goings on in America. We do not want athletes of color to protest injustices and unfair treatment of other blacks as in the "hands up, don't shoot" protest. It is as if we are saying subtly, "You are an athlete, and you get special treatment, so you just shut your mouth. Let them worry about themselves." It is believed, in reality, that we are not sending these messages to the athletes. Nor are we saying that they can't have political beliefs. It just seems as if what we are saying is that American culture is one that believes that sports should be free of politics and religion. That is, it seems that Americans are sending subtle messages that tell athletes that the sports world is supposed to be neutral ground. In other words, it seems as if we are telling athletes and other individuals involved in the world of sports that sports should be the one place where Americans can go that is free of discussions of politics (and equality) and religion. But there seems to be one thing that overrides this cultural ideology about what is acceptable and unacceptable for athletes: winning. It is an interesting paradox: winning makes sports fans forget.

QUESTIONS FOR REFLECTION AND DISCUSSION

1. Do you think Kurt Warner was penalized with a reduction in playing time because of his strong religious convictions or his performance? How did sports media report the incident involving Kurt Warner and his presentation?

2. How important is it to you to be involved in a team with others of the same religion? Explain your answer.

3. Should an athlete stay silent about political and religious issues? Why or why not?

4. Do you think sports should have stricter rules regarding protests and religious expression? Why or why not?

5. How is religion defined for you personally? What does religion mean to you? What is the difference between being spiritual versus being religious?

6. In terms of politics in sports, what are other specific political debates outside of kneeling during the national anthem? How do fans react to these protests by athletes? Are there visible differences in how fans react to other protests led by athletes? If so, how? If there are differences, why do you think fans react so differently to protests for equality, justice, and civil rights?

7. Imagine that an object from a sport (e.g., a football, a glove, a bat, a helmet) has become sacred. For example, a baseball bat is rather common, but what if it was the bat that Jackie Robinson used? What if you had the shoes Jesse Owens wore in the 1924 Summer Olympics in Berlin? Should they be included in the Hall of Fame? What if the object you have will never be used again, should it take on characteristics of a sacred object like those discussed earlier in this chapter? Might other objects used in sports fall into this sacred category? Do objects only become sacred because of the symbolic meaning that we give them? Could we make an object sacred?

SUGGESTED ACTIVITIES

1. Make a list of all the objects used in sports that have the potential to become sacred. Then discuss how our society could be altered if many of us believed that object to be sacred.

2. Conduct detailed and lengthy research and literature review on athletes who have professed faith in each of the religions: Christianity, Catholicism, Protestant, Jewish, Muslim, atheism, agnosticism, etc.

3. Write down and discuss in detail how sporting events have become similar to religious events. Write a paper detailing your perspective on religion and sports. Review and analyze your responses, looking for examples of how religion and sports are similar. What shared characteristics do they have? Some examples might include professional football games played on Sundays, high school games played on Fridays, and college games played on Saturdays. Also, consider professional athletes such as LeBron James, Stephen Curry, Michael Jordan, and Tom Brady (just to name a few) who are worshiped as gods.

4. Conduct research on all the churches in your area. Using the phonebook or another directory, identify the churches that appear to be nontraditional. For this activity, you can contact various churches to get information for your story. You are also encouraged to review the churches' website. Make observations of the churches' support for political issues and political leaders.

5. The Gallup organization is a highly respected research firm in America. Sociologists use Gallup polls to obtain useful information. Gallup polls are also used in the States to track religion. Go to Gallup's website and locate all their studies on sports and religion. Be prepared to summarize your findings.

6. Local, state, and federal governments can be involved in sports in a variety of ways. Identify ways that government has shown involvement in sports without violating the separation of church and state. Are there examples of this connection in your hometown? Give specific examples.

7. Some sports fans feel that religion in sports is good. Conduct research that explains this train of thought. Use surveys or interview fans to determine the pros and cons of religion in sports. Is this belief supported by experience for Americans? Explain why or why not.

8. Many athletes (in the United States) combine their religious beliefs with their sports participation. For some fans, this relationship creates tensions or dilemmas for athletes. Consider athletes who play sports that involve brutal body contact and harm to other players. Interview athletes who practice different beliefs. You might want to talk to Christians, Muslims, Jews, atheists, agnostics, Catholics, and Mormons and ask them if their religions present any problems or complications in participating in sports.

9. Athletes use religion to cope with the challenges and problems associated with participation in sports. Coaches and administrators may use religion as a means to bring teams together. Identify examples of how religion and sports have been reported in sports media. Can you think of recent examples where fans, athletes, coaches, or even sports media have used religion as a way to cope with uncertainty? Include a clip of the news article.

ADDITIONAL RESOURCES

Review of Religion and Sports: An Introduction and Case Studies, https://ussporthistory.com/2016/02/21/review-of-religion-and-sports-an-introduction-and-case-studies/

The Biggest Challenge for Muslim Women, http://www.pbs.org/pov/thelightinhereyes/video/the-biggest-challenge-for-muslim-women/

Hiab: A Symbol and an Identity, http://www.pbs.org/pov/thelightinhereyes/video/hijab-a-symbol-and-an-identity/

The Right to Learn, http://www.pbs.org/pov/thelightinhereyes/video/the-right-to-learn/

Young Muslim Women at Lunch, http://www.pbs.org/pov/thelightinhereyes/video/young-muslim-women-at-lunch/

End of Term Speech, http://www.pbs.org/pov/thelightinhereyes/video/end-of-term-speech/

Politics

Teaching the Winter Olympics Across the Curriculum, With Help From *The New York Times*, https://www.nytimes.com/2018/02/07/learning/lesson-plans/teaching-the-winter-olympics-across-the-curriculum-with-help-from-the-new-york-times.html

Teaching Our Athletes How to Deal With Sports Politics, http://nfhs.org/articles/teaching-our-athletes-how-to-deal-with-sports-politics/

Sport as a Tool for Development and Peace: Towards Achieving the United Nations Millennium Development Goals, https://www.un.org/sport2005/resources/task_force.pdf

International Journal of Sport Policy and Politics, https://www.tandfonline.com/toc/risp20/current

CREDITS

Fig. 15.1: Source: https://commons.wikimedia.org/wiki/File:John_Carlos,_Tommie_Smith,_Peter_Norman_1968cr.jpg.

Fig. 15.2: Source: https://www.usatoday.com/story/opinion/2014/12/01/rams-police-butt-heads-hands-up-st-louis-ferguson-opinionline/19753167/.

Fig. 15.3: Copyright © 2013 by Ryan Vaarsi, (CC BY 2.0) at https://www.flickr.com/photos/77799978@N00/9361120423.

Fig. 15.4: Source: https://commons.wikimedia.org/wiki/File:Billie_Jean_King_and_Bobby_Riggs_1973.jpg.

Fig. 15.5: Copyright © 2006 by JonathanRe, (CC BY-SA 3.0) at https://commons.wikimedia.org/wiki/File:Grandpa_Marty_Shoot_Jul-10-06_260A.jpg.

Fig. 15.6: Source: https://commons.wikimedia.org/wiki/File:Joe_Louis_-_Max_Schmeling_-_1936.jpg.

Fig. 15.7: Copyright © 2013 by Bryan Horowitz, (CC BY-SA 2.0) at https://commons.wikimedia.org/wiki/File:MichaelJordan.jpg.

Fig. 15.8: Copyright © 2016 by JefParker, (CC BY-SA 3.0) at https://commons.wikimedia.org/wiki/File:DNC_2016_-_Kareem_Abdul-Jabbar_(cropped).jpeg.

Fig. 15.9: Copyright © 2017 by Keith Allison, (CC BY-SA 2.0) at https://commons.wikimedia.org/wiki/File:San_Francisco_49ers_National_Anthem_Kneeling_(37721041581).jpg.

Fig. 15.10: Source: https://www.youtube.com/watch?v=Fq2CvmgoO7I.

Fig. 15.11: Copyright © 2012 by Ed Clemente Photography, (CC BY-SA 3.0) at https://commons.wikimedia.org/wiki/File:Tim_Tebow_Tebowing.jpg.

Fig. 15.12: Source: https://ftw.usatoday.com/2014/10/husain-abdullah-prayer-penalty-referees-correct-sliding/ap-chiefs-abdullah-penalty-football-s-fbn-usa-mo.

Fig. 15.13: Copyright © 2009 by RebelNation1947, (CC BY-SA 2.0) at https://commons.wikimedia.org/wiki/File:Ole_Miss_The_Grove.jpg.

Fig. 15.14: Source: https://www.buzzfeed.com/dray/the-20-most-pittsburgh-things-that-ever-happened-4666?utm_term=.lc9br9pVB#.eeGVpm1l4.

16

The Professions of Sports Journalism, Marketing, and Promotion

After reading this chapter, students should be able to:

- understand the various jobs available in the sports media/journalism industry;
- identify how the market for televised live sport is changing and the implications for sports journalists;
- explore the intersections of gender and ethnicity in sports organization;
- determine new opportunities for reaching and engaging sports audiences and fans;
- appreciate the shifting balance between free and paid-for sports media; and
- identify innovation opportunities for advertisers, agencies, and investors in sports.

Introduction

For more than 40 years of American history, domination over sports media content has been maintained by sports leagues, franchises, and television networks. Sports media received a jolt when in December of 1993 the NFL announced that it had granted all media rights to the then newly started Fox network. The next largest newsworthy event took place in June of 2017 when the NFL and Verizon announced their multiyear partnership. Details of the partnership involve Verizon and Yahoo sports having exclusive rights to livestream national games, including preseason, regular season, playoff games, and the Super Bowl. This deal allows sports fans to view any and all NFL games regardless of their mobile network provider. The NFL and Verizon partnership started in January of 2018 and began with livestreams of the playoffs. Sports fans could not only see the playoffs on Yahoo and Yahoo Sports, but they were also able to download the NFL mobile app and watch playoffs on their phones.

The Field of Sports Journalism

Sports journalism is a field that reports sporting news and events about elite and amateur sports and athletes. Sports journalists work in all types of media, including newspapers, magazines, television, radio, the Internet, and now social media. Sports journalists fulfill a variety of job responsibilities, such as conducting media interviews with high-visibility athletes and coaches, writing and producing newsworthy stories about games and athletes, updating fans on game statistics, and offering game commentary.

Education and Career Opportunities

To become a journalist, producer, editor, promoter, marketer, or photographer in sports students must complete a postsecondary degree in either journalism, business, or communications, or the legal field. Most professionals working in the fields of sports journalism and marketing must obtain a bachelor's degrees, according to the U.S. Bureau of Labor Statistics (2018). Those interested in these fields as a career have several outlets: One possibility is to enroll in an undergraduate program in journalism; another option is to focus on a communications liberal arts degree and take minor/concentration courses in sports reporting, sports writing, production, and editing, and capstones in sports journalism and marketing. Bachelor's and master's degree programs in sports journalism develop writing, interviewing, and reporting skills that teach students how to write stories and promotions that can be published in multiple media formats. Students must also seek out internships with sports media to build their network and professional contacts in the area. Internships allow students to not only gain insights into the world of sports journalism but also help students gain pregraduation experiences to include on resumes. Once the program in academic sports writing is finished, aspiring sports journalists should seek experience reporting on amateur or school sporting events for local news sources. Interested students might also intern at national sports media publications so that they can have the unique opportunity of providing coverage of professional sporting events for national sports media.

Print and Internet

Sports journalists who work in print media provide detailed previews of upcoming sporting events and postgame analysis. They also offer information on box scores, player statistics, and team standings. Many major national newspapers also cover local and national sports, and provide Internet links to the print content. Sportswriters or reporters often write historical features and get bylines in reoccurring sports columns.

Sportswriters' main duty is to keep sports fans up to date and in touch with their favorite sports teams, athletes, and coaches. While broadcast media provide immediate coverage, today sports reporters have to take time to provide in-depth news and information about what happened in a sporting event and the reasons that a team or athlete won or lost. Besides writing news stories that cover games and events, sportswriters also write about injuries and other team-related news, such as player trades and coaching changes. They write feature stories on players and coaches, and provide insights on trends involving the team or sports they cover. Although a good majority of sportswriters work for traditional media outlets, such as television and radio, many are finding jobs to write stories and publish them on sports websites, sports team websites, or they may even write blog posts to publish on a media's website or for their own professional sports blog.

Broadcast

Broadcast sports journalists provide real-time reporting for sporting events television and radio broadcasts. Sideline sports reporters in broadcast media frequently interview players before, during, and after a game. The sports production team is responsible for directing, editing, and producing athletic events and other sports telecasts. Specialized sports networks, such as ESPN, report sports events, news, and entertainment programming, and offer a wide variety of positions for individuals interested in anything from reporting, to production, to promotions, to development, to other areas, such as accounting, human resources, traffic, and marketing.

Sports broadcasters not only offer play-by-play commentary during a sporting event but also provide on-air live coverage to offer an "in-game" experience for TV viewers and radio listeners. Sports broadcasters for television, radio, and the Internet, or those who are reporting live in the sports arena or stadium, are responsible for sharing their comments, analysis of the game, and experiences with viewers or listeners. Often, sports broadcasters are known as sportscasters or sports announcers. If a student is an avid sports fan, then this career may be his or her dream job—imagine working in a job in which your main duty is to keep the sports fans involved, interested, and entertained during the broadcast of the entire sports event.

Photojournalism

Sports photojournalists are the storytellers. Through photographs, edits, and presentation of images, photojournalists in sports tell the story of sporting events in ways that no other professional in the industry can. Students who aspire to become sports photographers must seek either an associate's degree, bachelor's degree, or certificate from an accredited photography program. Some sports photographers are freelancers who sell their work to a variety of media. Sports photographers take fast action shots at sporting events, while others work for a sporting team or franchise or organization. Oftentimes, sports photographers working for teams take pictures that can be mass produced for commercial merchandising. Sports photojournalists' work can be found in newspapers, television, the Internet and in magazines such as *Sports Illustrated.*

Sports Marketing

Providing scoreboards in athletic stadiums, producing retail-sponsored timeout and halftime contests for fans, and finding top popular athletes to serve as endorsers for advertisers' products or services is the work of a sports marketer. Although sports marketers work long hours, the entry into this profession is brutally competitive. Sports marketing and promotion in a career that offers many intrinsic and extrinsic rewards. Some of the benefits of this career include plentiful and affluent salaries, challenging work tasks and objectives, and unique benefits, such as complimentary tickets to a team's games and other sporting events. Sports marketers have unique opportunities to meet and interview popular athletes.

The main function of marketing in sports is to allow corporations opportunities to link their brands with feelings such as excitement, enjoyment, and admiration that audiences often experience and then transfer those feelings to an advertiser's products or services. Sports marketing, as a whole, obtains its promotional strategies and objectives from other fields of journalism and communications. Sports marketers have bachelor's degrees in advertising, public relations, strategic communication, digital strategy and interactive media, and social media management, to name a few.

The field of sports marketing and promotion is known to have low turnover rates and a wealth of opportunity for career advancement. More often than not, those individuals who begin their careers in entry-level positions can expect to remain in their jobs for many years. Entry-level positions in advertising, for example, often show high rates of turnover. It is almost as if there is a covert notion that the first job in advertising is not your last. Contrast that with sports marketing and promotion jobs. A review of the careers of many mid- and upper level executive positions shows that these jobs become lifetime positions primarily because of high levels of job satisfaction.

Salaries available in this field have been known to vary by region of the country, with most of the salaries being reported for entry-level positions starting on the low end. Wide ranges in salary for upper level executive positions often show the various opportunities for those interested in sports marketing and promotions offered by sports employers. Sports employers, such as sports marketing firms, sports promotion agencies, corporate sports marketing divisions, and sports leagues and associations, report wide salary ranges for those hired to join their companies or agencies. For example, a director of sports marketing working for a major league might earn a salary that is two to three times more than his or her counterpart working in the minor leagues, colleges, and or high schools. Sports marketing and promotion is a fast-paced, exciting, and often hectic job. Promoters, media managers, and event coordinators have to learn how to handle a never-ending stream of requests from sponsors, clients, fans, and coaching staff. To succeed, those with quick personalities, with an ability to handle pressure and manage time, and with a great deal of energy find this career challenging yet extremely exciting as long as they can keep up with all the work.

Reflect on Sports: Breaking Into the Industry

Table 16.1 is a comprehensive presentation of where the jobs are in sports journalism and sports promotion along with salary information and places to start a job search.

TABLE 16.1

Where to Work	Entry-Level Positions
Professional league offices	Group ticket sales representative
Team offices	Customer service representative
Third-party companies	Public relations assistant
Media outlets	Client service assistant (outside agencies)
Nonprofessional sports	E-marketing/database management
Nontraditional sports	Graduate assistant—sports information department
Types of Jobs After College	Account associate (outside marketing agency)
High-level job	Marketing analyst (outside marketing firm)
Entry-level positions	Researcher (television)
After-college programs	**Places to Look for Jobs in Sports**
Internships	Websites
Graduate programs	LinkedIn groups
Different Types of Pay	Twitter
Contract	Recruiters
Hourly	Job boards
Hourly + commission	Listservs
Benefits can accompany any of the above	Graduate programs
	Web sites/job boards
	Networking events
	Listservs to sign up for
	Sports marketing and public relations pros newsletter—e-mail fatherknickerbocker1@yahoo.com
	Sportsnetworker.com and sign up for the e-mail list

Listed next are the skills necessary to have a successful career in sports marketing, sports promotion, ticket sales, and other event planning jobs:

- Focus
- Enthusiasm
- Flexibility
- Communication
- Interpersonal
- Organizational
- Self-confidence

A marketing degree prepares students with the skills that are needed to succeed in an entry-level marketing position in virtually any industry. A degree in sports management extends beyond the sports world. Typically, individuals interested in sports management jobs must compete in a sports marketing and promotions field. It is extremely difficult to gain entry-level sports marketing and promotions jobs immediately after college. Event coordinators often work with the event director both on and off-site. This position requires that individuals are attentive to every detail of planning, coordinating, and preparing for events. Event coordinators also communicate frequently with a team's corporate sponsors.

Public Relations Assistant (Sports League/Association): Most sports teams and leagues have a public relations department. From a sports perspective, it makes sense simply because public relations campaigns, both proactive and reactive, are a very large part of sports and the marketing and promotions of sports. The main job of the public relations specialist or assistant is to garner extensive media attention and coverage—in other words, generating a large number of impressions for an event or sport or athlete is a major determinant that defines success in this job. The individuals trained to obtain media attention are often taught in public relations programs. The public relations assistant works with the top administrators of one or more departments to obtain vital information needed to include in press releases and feature stories to pitch to the media. Public relations assistants employed by professional teams may also oversee events and goings-on in the sky or press box during a game or competition. Public relations assistants employed at sports marketing and promotions agencies are also responsible for tracking any and all stories and other news coverage about athletes and teams. They are expected to gather examples of all news reports.

Reflect on Sports: Virtual Reality in Sports

In 2016, ESPN laid off 100 employees. Although ESPN is notably a sports media that has led the industry in diversity and inclusion issues, the layoffs include a few members of the highly recognizable on-air talent. ESPN often includes stories that focus on the intersectionality of sports and social class, money, and power in sports. ESPN, in an effort to increase revenue, struck a deal with cable companies. Fans and nonsports fans alike had to pay more than $9 a month as part of their cable bills. With viewers now choosing satellite over cable television and opting to do pay-per-view and other specialized viewing options, ESPN is finding that it is losing those dormant cable television subscription dollars it had taken for granted for many years. To combat the financial loss, ESPN has determined other ways to increase revenue by providing unique and newsworthy related sports news on expensive higher tier platforms such as WatchESPN app and ESPN 3, the unique digital-only network. Other sports leagues have found success simulcasting their games digitally,

FIGURE 16.1   *Player using Virtual Reality to play sports*

with Twitter streaming 10 TNF games in 2016. But Twitter won't be streaming these games again in 2017, as Amazon won the rights for $50 million. On top of being broadcast on YouTube, this year, both soccer championships will be available both in 4K ultra high definition and in virtual reality (VR), allowing users to watch a 360-degree view or select the view angle.

Currently, VR is also changing the viewing experience with sports. VR allows sports fans to "watch a game at their house with others who are comfortable in their own homes" (Jason, 2017). VR technology is currently making its entrance into the sports world. VR is already making its impact known in that it is changing the way that many coaches organize and conduct their practices. Researchers from Stanford University have developed STRIVR Labs, "whose client list currently includes NFL teams, college programs, and as of late, NBA, NHL and even WNBA organizations" (Zorowitz, 2017). As illustrated in Figure 16.1, we see that VR captures real, intense movements. Athletes can put on goggles, and in an instant, they are in the huddle in the middle of a major play (see Figure 16.1). A quarterback, for example, can look around and see his tight end and defense. Using VR during practices, athletes can even hear the coaches and the players, and they can listen to the screams and cheers of their fans. This technology might also be beneficial regarding helping athletes learn how to adjust to hype and other emotions during important rival games and competitions. With VR, athletes can get lost, so to speak with the technology. The experiences are so real that the brain translates the experience for the user as if it is real. This example explains why VR is and will be the next step forward in athletic coaching. "Because the mind has no way of distinguishing between a real situation and one generated by the technology, it is the ideal means of supplementing work on the field, on the rink, on the court, to further athletes' skills and knowledge of the game" (Zorowitz, 2017).

Other changes to look for in the future of sports and media include the following:

- Google, Facebook, or other popular social media could join forces and be financially able to outbid traditional media for exclusive rights to sports teams and franchises. Perhaps the result of this merger would be that sports fans will be allowed to watch sports for free. Currently, some major sports are available via pay-per-view.

- Athletes will start to gain more and more control over their postgame media interviews and press conferences (recall Cam Newton's complaint about having to do media press conferences).

- In this current age of digital media, we are already finding that the term "broadcasting" is becoming obsolete. Look for changes to this journalism industry to take place shortly. Sports fans will not only be able to access sports content from multiple places simultaneously but also integrate these streams into increasingly seamless, coherent, and personalized viewer experiences.

- Fans will be able to watch entire games through VR headsets (see "Reflect on Sports: Virtual Reality in Sports" inset). Consider this: one day, fans will be able to watch an entire football game (maybe even the Super Bowl) through a VR headset from the perspective of their favorite quarter. And it may be possible to watch the game with a friend who lives in another state, another town, or around the block. Even more thought provoking, your friend, while watching with you, could watch the VR game from the perspective of a player on the opposing team. Several technological analysts predict that fans will be able to share their comments and highlights in real time, and if they do not like the outcome of a play, viewers will at some point be able to reset the play that they just watched and then engage in a "do-over" by running the play again. This will be fascinating in that so many sports fans love playing referee or coach from the couch or even the stands. This aspect of VR will allow them to put themselves in the shoes of the ref or the coach and perhaps realize that their play may or may not have had a different outcome.

In 2014, pirates generated more than $220 million in ad revenue using stolen digital content. The Periscope personal live casting app allows sports fans to watch pirated sports content with no consequences, no stigma. "More than 50% of Americans between the ages of 18 and 34 admitted to watching pirated content in a recent survey" (Ourand, 2016). The reason pirated sports content is increasing and attracting sports fans is most likely due to rising costs associated with sports media's exclusive content in broadcast. This alone might be the main reason we see a driving increase in piracy (Hutchins, 2015). According to *Sports Business Daily*, "the future of sports media can be seen through apps like the WME-IMG-backed overtime and the live-streaming YouNow, as well as digital media companies like Whistle Sports" (Ourand, 2016).

Social media services that are exclusively focused on sports news are services known as Whistle Sports, Overtime, and Sports Stadium. Whistle Sports, one of the most popular sports social media platforms on YouTube, provides user-generated content on sports teams, athletes, and coaches. The Overtime app and Sports Stadium apps have recently entered the sports social media industry. Facebook has also recently joined these sports services when it launched Sports Stadium during the 2017 NFL playoffs. All of these social media applications created communities and places where sports fans could go to share content about specific games/sports, teams, and players.

Advances in technology are literally forcing major broadcasters to reevaluate how they view themselves. For example, tools such as YouTube and podcasts and other online broadcast vehicles are forcing those in the television broadcast business (e.g., content distribution) to rebrand their image. Are they broadcast or are they digital? With the changing media environment and consumer preferences for new and interactive media, sports broadcasters are feeling pressure (e.g., ESPN), to decide how they will identify with their customers and sponsors/partners/advertisers. Professional sports leagues and teams are now becoming technologically savvy in the ways that they can inter- act and engage with fans. As content providers, sports journalists and those working in the sports leagues and with "teams have more in their favor than broadcast intermediaries who often have to pay for the content" (Pfhal, 2015).

Preparing for a Career in Sports: Skills and Data

For those aspiring to become sports journalists, the basic required skills in terms of writing, editing, shooting, and coding are no-brainers. However, in today's media environment, sports journalists must be able to adapt and problem solve. In fact, more and more, we are finding that because of changes in technology and the way we report the news, journalists must know how to be creative, problem solve, and figure out solutions on their own.

Another key skill is familiarity and a thorough understanding of social media as a journalist. Journalists must learn the ins and outs of social media to brand themselves and use it as a means to connect with readers/viewers and fans. Social media use also helps with researching stories and increases the journalist's writing of headlines for social media, especially when having to write a headline that is less than 140 characters. Journalists need to be proficient at writing stories for a wide range of media platforms. For sports journalists in the 21st century, it is not uncommon to find your work on multimedia platforms such as the Internet, television, magazines, newspapers, and radio.

Many athletes and celebrities have taught us how not to use social media (e.g., Roseanne and Ambien). "Think before you post" is one major tip that should be followed by social media. Jour- nalists and athletes and teams should never (well, almost never) respond in anger or in the moment to an angry fan or an offensive post on Twitter. Examples of athletes and high-profile entertainers who use social media in antisocial ways are vast and many.

For journalists, social media provides the best story leads. Journalists who carefully watch social media posts may on occasion "catch" athletes in impulsive posts of thought and expression that may not be appropriate in a locker room or after a game or match.

The Future: Be the Change Agent

The previous chapters have explored several issues in sports. From race, gender, sexism, social class, politics, and religion to the ways that these various social constructs are portrayed in sports media. The overarching conclusion from all these chapters is that although there have been improvements in some of the disparities concerning gender and race in sports, we still have some areas that need to be addressed and improved. Areas such as pay gaps in certain sports; equity in coverage of all sports, not just the revenue-generating sports; exposure of lower and middle-class youth to sports that are typically out of their purview; and equity of coverage of female athletes and their sports. This chapter started with a discussion of the jobs and skills for those interested in sports and what to expect in the future for sports journalism.

Although progress has been made in increasing diversity initiatives within sports media, we have learned that further efforts are needed to increase representations and level the playing field, pun intended. Many activists and others who have fought for increased voices in sports media (e.g., LGBTQ athletes, women athletes) argue that to achieve true equality in sports media, we must also have representation and equality in the sports media professions. It is no surprise that sport is a white, male-dominated industry. Nor should it be a surprise that sports media is a white, male-dominated industry. Together, these two facts provide a better understanding of some of the issues outlined in this text. It is hoped that after finishing this book readers will come to realize how various groups are portrayed and treated in sports media and that through these representations, we see how some groups have been marginalized or even ignored in the media (e.g., Native American athletes and naming of sports teams). It is hoped that the information presented in this textbook will inspire some, if not most, of its readers to become change agents: individuals who fight for and forge/force changes in the sports industry against status quo notions and ideals that have long persisted in sports media. Change agents interested in impacting the field of sports and sports media will be zealous about forging changes against sustained inequality in sports media.

While traditional print media may be losing readership, newspapers and magazines still offer some unique benefits. Through the stories, pictures, and statistics readers are given important facts and information to evaluate. Although we learned in this chapter that print media may have positive and negative effects on athletes and their behaviors, we know from research that athletes and teams can use framing or priming to influence viewpoints through which people judge them on an issue.

Gender and Racial Imbalances in Sports Journalism: Leveling the Playing Field

As we've mentioned throughout this text, there are vast gender disparities found in print, broadcast, and online platforms. White men, as shown in many chapters in this book, vastly outnumber all women employed in the sports industry, even in 2018. Research conducted in 2017 continues to show the lack of representation of women in leadership roles in sports. Research results continue to show a striking reflection of the exclusive hold that men have in the sports industry. Men can be found in key roles within sports. What we find is that despite the efforts to achieve diversity in sports in positions from chief executive officers to head coaches, there is still a very long way to go.

According to research conducted in 2016, "90 percent of sports editors are white males, the same percentage that was reported in a 2006 report" (Hill, 2013). Most sports columnists in 2016 were white, with 91% of the reporters identifying with the white racial group; this, according to pundits, shows an increase since 2006. And, unfortunately, "the number of Black female sports columnists, however, doubled from one to two since 2006, and that is not a percentage, that is the whole number" (Hill, 2013). One thing is obvious when you research the percentages on diversity and inclusion in sports media: White men still predominately dominate sports journalism, despite recent efforts by the National Association of Black Journalists (NABJ) to increase diversity in this area of journalism. Since 1980, the NABJ has lobbied for diversity, especially given that the current state of minority hiring and promotions appears dismal. We noted in a previous chapter in this text that if it were not for ESPN's intense diversity and inclusion strategic plan in hiring across all of their platforms, the number of people of color and women in sports media would be even more depressing. Of the 12 sports editors who happen to be people of color, a vast majority of them work for ESPN. Of the 52 sports columnists who happen to be people of color, research shows us that 37 of them work for ESPN. In the position of sports editor, research shows that of all the major newspapers in America, only three employ African Americans. The same research further shows that only four Latino/as are employed as editors. And among columnists, "newspapers employ only 19 African-Americans, three Latinos and two Asians" (Guo, 2016; U.S. Bureau of Labor Statistics Reports, 2017). It should be noted that sports editors are the people who decide what content appears in the newspapers. These are the gatekeepers. They make decisions about the critical issues that must be included in a news story, issues such as "who is covered, what is said about them and where the stories are placed" (Hill, 2013).

We know from theories in mass media that the media have the power to shape thoughts, attitudes, and opinions about sports and athletes. When very few of the key decision makers are white, and few are people of color, we find that the lack of diversity in the news staff denies the voices of marginalized communities. Journalists in the 21st and future centuries scratch beyond the surface of a storyline and headlines. Sports journalists and journalists in the other categories must stop searching for lead stories that fit the "if it bleeds it leads" theory to start writing stories that go against the status quo. Some suggested ideas for lead stories include taking the time to cover the accomplishments of female athletes; educating sports fans about religion and the role it plays in sports; going in-depth and offering objective data on controversial issues, such as kneeling during the national anthem; covering athletes who identify in one of the LGBTQ groups; investigating how access to some sports can become more available to diverse participants; and examining athletes who are old and young, rich and poor.

Lapchick, a sports journalist who focuses his work on racism in sports, has suggested that sports media try the "Rooney Rule" for interviewing minority candidates when they have openings in leadership ranks. While many argue that the rule sounds great in theory, it is challenging to execute and lacks practicality. In 2017, we learned that zero people of color were appointed to head coaching or front office jobs when compared to the 15 openings in leadership positions. And if people of color and more women are not majoring in sports journalism, how can we increase the pool of diverse candidates? Thus a Rooney Rule sounds plausible, but all it can do at this moment is punish sports media and journalism schools and programs for their lack of inspiring students to major in the discipline.

What can be done to break the glass ceiling for women and people of color? Organizations such as NABJ and the Sports Journalism Institute are trying. These organizations provide seminars, career fairs, training programs, and other ideas to encourage more interest. Although the statistics and changes in newsrooms and sports journalism (thanks in part to ESPN) regarding diversity seem to be increasing, the pace of the increase regarding diversity still needs to reflect the census statistics from the general population. From all of the issues discussed in this text, disparities in race, gender, sexual orientation, and social class, it is obvious that sports media need to figure out how to do a better job of inspiring people of color and women to go into the profession.

Despite the fact that women are increasing in terms of sports fans and are showing their loyalty to major sports leagues such as the NFL, women in the field of sports journalism are rare. In a report published by the Institute for Diversity and Ethics in Sport, data showed an increase in women of color in the area of sports journalism. In addition, data also show that the "majority of female columnists and editors are employed by ESPN" (U.S. Bureau of Labor Statistics, 2017). As stated previously, without ESPN and their diversity initiative, the employment picture of people of color in sports journalism would be bleak. We know from employment statistics that 90% of sports editors are white, and 90% are male. Research reveals that "95 percent of our sports editors, 87 percent of our assistant sports editors, 90 percent of our columnists and 87.5 percent of our reporters are white" (ESPN Fact Sheet, 2017). And out of the few female reporters currently working in sports, we find news stories or Internet searches that yield the following: "50 Hottest Female Sports Broadcasters From Around the World" "20 Sexiest Sports Reporters of 2012," "20 Sexiest Local Sports Broadcasters," or "40 Hottest College Football Reporters."

Female sports reporters not only have to deal with the male sports reporters who are offended that they have to work with women, but they also have to deal with male athletes who want them out of the locker room and away from male sports. Some female sports reporters even experience negative treatment and harassment from sports fans, harassment from athletes, and even harassment from colleagues working in sports reporting. From a sports reporting perspective, we also need to make mention that the problem of the white, male-dominated sports industry does not just mean that it is the sports journalists who are white men; we know that the sources used in their sports stories are typically white men as well. And regarding bylines, we find that when compared to bylines written by women, a majority of bylines published on the front pages of the *New York Times* are those belonging to men.

Employers are becoming more proactive in adding women and women of color to their employment pools. In fact, in addition to sports media, many universities, schools, and journalists are beginning to work together to promote sports journalism to young women and people of color.

Early in 2017, ESPN announced that Samantha Ponder would be officially taking over as the hostess of the networks *Sunday NFL Countdown* (Lapchick, 2006). Ponder was originally the sideline reporter for ESPN's broadcast of NFL games. This is historic in that a woman never before hosted the popular sports show on ESPN in its 32 years of existence (Daley, 2017). According to thinkprogress. org, ESPN is the leading driver of diversity in sports journalism (Waldron, 2013). According to their website, ESPN believes that "diversity is about who is on the team. Inclusion is about who gets to play" (ESPN, 2018). Research conducted in 2016 shows that at that time, there were 11 female sports editors. However, that isn't saying much when ESPN employs six of the 11 female sports editors. Problematic issues are still rampant when female sportscasters are hired as sideline reporters and remain there as their male counterparts are either initially promoted to more executive positions or are promoted sooner than the female sportscasters performing the same job and executing the same responsibilities (Daley, 2017).

Since 2012, Ponder had been working as a college football reporter. She had 5 years of experience before earning the promotion, tackling on a daily basis the idea that women can discuss football. Ponder is clearly a change agent who battled the stereotype that our culture has that communicates the idea that female sportscasters are unable to understand the game of football and are only on the sidelines to decorate and serve as eye candy (recall the discussion provided in Chapters 7 and 8 of this text).

The increase in depictions and number of women in sports journalism is due to the fact that women are becoming sports reporters for big-name networks is that they have decided that they are not going to wait for the industry to change. More women have decided to change the industry themselves by persevering through trials and situations concerning sexual objectification, sexual harassment, and blatant sexist/misogynistic commentary. Women like Ponder are the role models and inspiration needed to encourage other women to continue to break away at the glass ceiling of sports journalism that was created by men long before they were born.

Top Women of Color in Sports Journalism

The list is not in net worth or alphabetical order. We just listed the top sports journalists of color as presented on the website written by Milligan (2017).

FIGURE 16.2   *Pam Oliver.*

Pam Oliver

Pam Oliver (Figure 16.2) is a sports reporter for Fox Sports. Oliver is a sideline reporter for the NFL and NBA games. She had a recent run-in with "the hair police" just as Gabby Douglas did during the Summer Olympic Games of 2012 and 2016. Oliver directly confronted the hair issue when she reminded viewers of the most important thing to consider when she is reporting from the field. "You're out there trying to catch players, get your reports turned around quickly, and I may or may not have time to put on lip gloss or powder my face" (Sangweni, 2014).

FIGURE 16.3   *Lisa Salters.*

Lisa Salters

Salters (Figure 16.3) is a former collegiate women's basketball player who has covered the NBA and NFL for more than 10 years.

Cheryl Miller

Miller is a sideline reporter for the NBA. She has covered and coached basketball for more than 20 years. This athlete is to be recognized in that although her sexual orientation is often questioned by fans and the media, Miller has never made a public announcement about her sexuality.

FIGURE 16.4   *Jemele Hill.*

Jemele Hill

This Detroit native was the former cohost on ESPN2's *Numbers Never Lie* and the *His & Hers* sports podcast. In September 2017, Jemele Hill (Figure 16.4) tweeted, "Donald Trump is a white supremacist who has largely surrounded himself w/ other white supremacists." Sarah Huckabee Sanders, the White House press secretary, commented on Hill's tweet by asking ESPN to "apologize for untruths" made

by Hill. Then just a month later, ESPN suspended Hill for 2 weeks after she made a series of tweets requesting an advertiser boycott of the Cowboys (owner Jerry Jones had issued a statement saying that players will stand during the anthem, or they will not play). As of February 2018, Hill left her broadcast hosting position on *SportsCenter* and chose to write stories for ESPN's The Undefeated website. She has publicly stated that she chose to move to the website because it is a better platform in terms of allowing her to express her thoughts and opinions. As of August 2018, Hill agreed to a buyout of her contract with ESPN for amicable reasons. And as of September 2018, media report that she is now working for SpringHill Entertainment, a company owned by LeBron James and Maverick Carter (Dumas, 2018).

Cari Champion

Campion (Figure 16.5) engages in heated sports debates daily on the daytime ESPN talk show *First Take.*

FIGURE 16.5   *Cari Champion.*

FIGURE 16.6   *Sage Steel.*

FIGURE 16.7   *Kristina Pink.*

FIGURE 16.8   *Christy Winters Scott.*

Sage Steele

Steele (Figure 16.6) started her career as a sports reporter at a CBS affiliate in Indiana. She rapidly moved up the ranks to sports commentator on shows like *SportsCenter* and *Sports Nation*.

Josina Anderson

The former college track and field star has also won Emmys for her coverage of the NFL and the NBA on ESPN shows such as *SportsCenter* and *Sunday NFL Countdown*. Anderson was also a ballet dancer with the American Youth Ballet. She enjoyed residencies with the Dance Theater of Harlem and Pennsylvania Ballet.

Kristina Pink

Pink (Figure 16.7) works for Fox Sports as a sideline reporter. Her main responsibility is to cover the Los Angeles Clippers (Bucholz, 2017).

Christy Winters Scott

Winters Scott (Figure 16.8) is a basketball color analyst who calls games for the WNBA Washington Mystics, and also provides analysis for several sports stations like ESPN, FSN, The Big Ten Network, NBC Sports Washington, and Raycom Sports as well as the NCAA Women's Basketball Tournament . Currently, she covers events in the NBA, WNBA, and NCAA.

Maria Taylor

A former student-athlete who played volleyball for the University of Georgia, Taylor (Figure 16.9) is currently an ESPN sideline reporter covering college football, basketball, and volleyball.

FIGURE 16.9   *Maria Taylor.*

Tips for Sports Journalists

Listed next are some suggestions for aspiring and practicing sports journalists on how to report, commentate, and cover female athletes and the sports they participate in.

- Female athletes should be referred to in news coverage as "women" or "young women," not as "girls" unless they are under 12 years of age. Female athletes should never be referred to as "ladies."

- Sports journalists should be consistent in using first and last names. That is, use of first and last names must be consistent when writing for both men's and women's sports events.

- Descriptions of an athlete should not place emphasis on physical appearance or skill. The gender of the athlete should not be related to athletic performance, and therefore sports journalists must focus on accomplishment and athleticism for all athletes.

- Watch descriptors of men and women athletes. Both should be described regarding their athletic attributes.

- Based on the type of story you are writing, be sure that you are not framing athletes in categories such as negative versus positive (i.e., thug or criminal versus hero). Be sure to dig deeper and go beyond the fault lines.

- When practical and relevant to the story, ask athletes how they want to be identified and portrayed.

- Identify and engage in activities that highlight and reveal personal biases. Journalists must engage in inner reflections that help elucidate biases that may be getting in the way of the story. Start with taking the implicit bias test (Project Implicit, 2011).

- Although getting the latest "scoop" is ideal, accuracy in a news story is much more important. Journalists should not speculate or make educated guesses about issues or information that is unknown. Sports journalists must remember that readers and consumers of their stories form their impressions from the journalist's speculations.

- Use an appropriate level of specificity when referring to athletes. Choose words and descriptors that are accurate and free of bias.

- Always talk with representatives on both sides of the issue. Use balance in presenting different voices within the story.

- Talk with athletes and take pictures of athletes in their territory so that they feel more comfortable. Be sure to show women and male athletes in their sports and in their athletic environments.

The Future of Sports and Media: A Changing Landscape?

The sports media landscape is rapidly changing and evolving. As technology in American culture moves consumers further and further away from traditional television, all those professionals involved in the sports world from sports reporters, announcers, editors, producers, photojournalists, marketers and promoters, public relations representatives, and community relations personnel, to name a few, must combine their passions for the field to find creative ways to keep a sports team/ brand active in the minds of the sport's fans. Sports journalism is heading into an era where advances in technology and data are becoming more and more important. As stated in the previous section of this chapter, we are finding that sports currently provide more opportunities for those who are interested in entering into sports journalism fields. Sports journalism and marketing have become one of the fastest growing careers in mass media and communications.

Data-driven sports journalism sets a need for journalists to be savvy in terms of understanding numbers and interpretation of those numbers. Sports journalists today must be able to use numbers and go beyond them to provide meaning. In sports, data mean everything, making data-driven journalism very important. Another aspect of successful sports journalism is the ability to conduct audience analysis and analytics. Audience analysis and analytics focus on using data to help shed insights on how and why audiences respond to information when confronted. Sports journalists interested in audience analysis and analytics also enjoy identifying and developing strategies that reach audiences and fans.

With social media increasing in popularity and for some serving as a source for their news, sports journalists need to understand how to communicate on different traditional, nontraditional, and social media forms. As in many sports, numbers and statistics are a major part of the game. Take, for example, baseball. Numbers are frequently used in this sport. Journalists must be aware of the meaning of a player's batting averages (the number of hits divided by the number of at-bats). Knowledge of the sport and the meaning of the number that communicates the player's earned run average (the average number of earned runs allowed by a pitcher per nine innings) must also be understood by sports journalists. Numbers dominate the world of baseball. Sports journalists who understand these numbers must write about them in a way that a baseball fan can understand.

Sports journalists who do not shy away from math and statistics will also find that they will succeed when reporting on football. Sports journalists who can use numbers and statistics will also be equipped with skills to rank players accurately. The focus on advanced analytics and data is just one way that sports media and professional sports journalism will change in the future.

Conclusion

Moving forward, we must consider the idea that a lack of diversity in sports journalism may contribute to the inaccurate reporting of women, LGBTQ, and athletes of color. We must also consider the accurate representation of social class and power, as well as marginalized groups, such as Native Americans, Latina/os, Middle Eastern athletes, athletes living with disabilities, and the aging process for many athletes. Striving for accuracy and objectivity has been and still should be a sports journalist's greatest mission. Let's use the Colin Kaepernick situation again. In a study analyzing partisan media's reporting of the take-a-knee protest, Frisby (2018) revealed that few sports journalists wrote stories about Nate Boyer. Nate Boyer, an ex–Green Beret and former Seahawks player, wrote an open letter to Kaepernick in 2016 admonishing (and that may be putting it nicely) Kaepernick's initial strategy of sitting during the national anthem (Kelly, 2017). A meeting was called between the two men. Boyer said, "Colin wanted to sit. I wanted him to stand, and so we found a common ground on a knee alongside his teammates. I believe that progress and real change happens in this world when you reach across the divide, you build a bridge, you swallow your pride, you open your mind, you embrace what you don't understand, and ultimately you surrender" (Boyer, 2017). For Boyer, the issue was honoring the anthem. It was reported that Boyer told Kaepernick that "soldiers take a knee in front of a fallen brother's grave, you know, to show respect. When we're on a patrol, you know, and we go into a security halt, we take a knee" (O'Donnell, 2017). After the meeting, Kaepernick asked if he would take a picture with him and Boyer said in reply, "Look, I'll stand next to you. I gotta stand though. I gotta stand with my hand on my heart. That's just—that's just what I do and where I'm from" (O'Donnell, 2017). The takeaway message from this story is that in lieu of media "hyping" and focusing on the negative and the kneeling, stories should have been published by the thousands that detailed that meeting between Boyer and Kaepernick. The story, although not highlighted in the media as it should have been, is a perfect example of how two people can come together in a positive and peaceful environment and reach a happy compromise instead of having an emotional conversation that involves screaming and anger. Even Boyer says that he and Kaepernick do not see eye to eye on the matter, but that is not what was important to this veteran. Bridging the gap by speaking face-to-face about the issues that matter to both of them was a start—one that Boyer hopes Americans will start to do.

Next to the "take-a-knee" story and our president's demand that the NFL players be ordered to stand was the next largest news story in sports culture. This story was taken from the sports news sections in 2010. This was the sensational story about NBA star LeBron James's decision to leave the Cleveland Cavaliers to join the Miami Heat. Hours and pages of sports news space were filled with stories of the Cavalier fans' outrage. Many fans were angry in that they felt that James was abandoning Cleveland. Despite that, we found very little coverage that investigated if the anger and uproar had any hints that might be related to race. CNN's Soledad O'Brien interviewed LeBron James and asked him if he thought race played a role in the reaction fans had about his decision to move. James was quoted as saying, "I think so, at times. There's always, you know, a race factor" (Lapchick, 2006). For example, a tweet posted to James's page characterized him as "a big nosed big lipped bug-eyed (racial slur). Ur greedy, u try to hide ur ghettoness" (Rogers, 2011). Few sports reporters asked James questions about his thoughts on how race influenced fan reactions to popular African American athletes. Few, if any, sports reporters have taken the time to do stories exploring how and why white athletes are able to maintain enormous popularity despite well-documented, off-the-field bad behavior and decisions. For a list of 2018's 15 most-hated athletes, see Ballantyne (2018; https://benchlifesports.com/2018/01/31/the-top-15-most-hateable-current-athletes/)

Amid the James story about his move to Miami and then back to Cleveland, a Q Score poll was published. Q-sort data provide public opinion about the ranking of celebrities, products, athletes, and teams (just to name a few of the data they publish). Q-methodology, or Q-sort data, as it is commonly known, is research that gathers data on consumer viewpoints. Q-sort data is used to investigate different opinions on an issue or person. Participants in this survey are presented with a list of statements. Next, they are asked to rank and sort the statements. Often, advertisers and marketers rely on Q-sorts to help identify popular celebrities or athletes to use as endorsers for their products and/or services. In 2010, Q-sort data revealed that the six most-hated athletes were all African Americans. On the list was "Michael Vick, Tiger Woods, Terrell Owens, Chad Ochocinco, Kobe Bryant and LeBron James" (True, 2010). The question posed by a sports journalist writing for the Bleacher Report is, "why do African Americans end up on the most-hated list?"

Careful analysis of the commentary on the six athletes appearing on the list in 2010 shows that two of the six athletes appear simply because fans think they are over the top, cocky, and obnoxious. The list of most-hated seemed to be devoid of athletes who also engaged in similar behaviors. Athletes such as Ben Roethlisberger, who was an alleged perpetrator of domestic and sexual violence; Brett Favre, who like LeBron James moved from one team, the Green Bay Packers, to another, Minnesota; and others who have had negative experiences with the law, had issues with domestic or sexual violence, or otherwise displayed bad behavior on or off the field in recent years did not make the top-10 most disliked athletes in that year. Why? Sports reporters and editors showed no curiosity about this question.

According to Lapchick (2016), diversity in the sports media enhances the overall quality of sports reporting. Diversity in the sports reporter profession may help to put out better news stories that those found with headlines like "When White Fans Turn on Black Athletes," "The #TakeAKnee Protests Have Always Been About Race. Period," "Black Lives or Bottom Line?" "Papa John's CEO Blames NFL Protests for Poor Pizza Sales," "Refusing to Stand for the National Anthem," "Trump Attacks Black Athletes," "How the National Anthem Protest Is Bringing Out the Worst in People," "Black Athletes Are Being Made Scapegoats," and "Black America Blames White America." Headlines like these almost instantly imply conflict and seem to be framed to create a particular emotional reaction from readers. Perhaps diversity in the sports journalism field will mean that we will have fewer headlines and stories pitting blacks against whites and more frequent stories about the things that are more relevant and accurate in terms of sports. Sports is an American pastime that at one point in our culture united us. Sports editors must consider this when assigning stories. Perhaps the editor would take a different angle in sports reporting if the staff at the sports media was diverse and inclusive (True, 2010). We are still left pondering the question as to why more people of color are not found behind sports desks of mainstream news media.

The two biggest issues and the current controversy in the profession of sports media revolve around exposure to sports careers and retention once people of color and women are hired. Media-use research tells us that a majority of our children between the ages of 5 and 12 watch television, on average, for more than 6 hours a day. This means that their constant exposure to football and basketball athletes of color sends a message that the only way they can be involved in sports is by playing or coaching. Those of us in sports journalism should make time and use our talents to show vulnerable children that there is another way for them to love sports and enjoy a career in sports. The bottom line to this chapter is that the disparity in the number of people of color working in sports journalism is not about their choice and the choices that would-be journalists of color make, but it is more about training and education at lower levels adding to the pool of potential journalists that media employers want to recruit, hire, train, and promote.

QUESTIONS FOR REFLECTION AND DISCUSSION

1. How can journalism tackle the subjects of sport, discrimination, and racism in the future?
2. What teams have had the most and least mentions on Twitter? What factors do you think may account for your results? (Hint: There is a correlation between attendance numbers.)
3. What percent of fans use social media to invite friends to games?
4. How many extra dollars are spent via social media by sports fans?
5. Do you think it is even possible to have fair and equal representation in sports media? Why or why not?
6. Have traditional forms of media such as print media, newspapers, and magazines become things of the past? Explain your response.
7. Some say that we as a culture have become reliant on social media and the Internet. Do you think we can use this media as a way of changing what we think about diversity? Why or why not?
8. Thinking long term, say 25 years from now, what changes do you think we will see in sports media regarding its portrayal of women, men, LGBTQ, and sports? Will the groups currently known as minorities change? If so how?
9. What future challenges do you think sports media professionals will face regarding diversity?

10. Is there a role/job in sports, based on your reading of the jobs presented in this chapter, that most appeals to you? Why or why not? Explain in detail.

11. Is invisibility in sports media a good thing? Does invisibility or symbolic annihilation make things worse, better, or problematic in sports media and portrayals of athletes?

12. Are there ways in which you see differences in how women and minorities are depicted in their roles as sports journalists? If so, describe your observations.

SUGGESTED ACTIVITIES

1. How would you increase ticket sales using social media? Suppose you are the manager of ticket sales working for a professional team. First, provide a brief overview of your team and the current state of ticket sales. Next, draft a viable sales proposal plan based on research to use social media to increase sales. Remember, your goal is to get people in seats.

2. Find a job announcement in the sports journalism field that is of interest to you. Next, complete your letter of application and a resume targeted for the job. This could also be for an internship in sports journalism. You will be required to print a copy of this announcement to turn in with your assignment (the announcement should contain the full job description/requirements/skills sought, etc.). Use the links to job sites provided in this chapter. Be sure that you specifically address qualifications and job requirements in your resume and cover letter. The point of this assignment is to help you learn how to strategically market your skills to an employer by highlighting relevant experiences that make you the best candidate for the job. Keep in mind that this is a project that you should use to apply for internships, enter into a major or study abroad program, apply for graduate/law school, or apply for a job after graduation. You will have scheduled time to meet with your professor to discuss these career goals, begin an action plan, and receive guidance for completing this project.

3. Consider the various groups discussed in this text: race/ethnicity, gender, sexual orientation, social class, religion, and politics. Write a paper about your personal experiences with each of these groups in terms of sports and your perception of them in the media.

4. Design and execute a research study that investigates the laws and ethics of sports in terms of policies that have been written to correct some of the disparities, misrepresentations, and unequal treatment.

5. If the subject of discrimination is included in training programs and journalists are made more aware of such issues, they should be more capable of understanding and reporting on such matters. Why have the training programs that are currently being conducted not shown the improvement in numbers in the field of sports journalism? Use your research skills to explore this issue and then write a news story that reports your findings.

6. Create a career interest campaign for sports journalists and aim your campaign at young girls and children of color. How will you determine if your campaign is a success?

7. In this chapter, we make predictions about the changes in technology and the effect the changes will have on sports journalism. If you can, spend some time using VR goggles. Watch sports in 3-D and spend time thinking about how this technology will advance and aid sports—athletes, coaches, and journalists. Regarding your experiences in the future, which media, and why, will be most important in your life as a sports journalist? What will be the most important media for you as a consumer of sports? Explain.

8. How should problems with racism, sexism, sexual orientation, gender pay, and social class be addressed in sports journalism, and how can the media ensure a more balanced coverage of sports events? Which is most important to you, objectivity or diversity, in sports media reporting? Are these incompatible ideals? Why or why not?

9. Conduct an in-depth investigative report on the strengths and weaknesses of affirmative action programs. These programs are designed to help diversity and inclusion initiatives. Is this program an effective program for sports journalism? Why or why not? Which is better, the Rooney Rule or affirmative action in regard to increasing diversity in upper level positions in sports media? Defend your answer with support and sources. Be sure to rely on a diverse set of sources and experts for your coverage.

10. Go to a club where there is a diverse group of young children. A United Way club like the Boys and Girls Club of America or Big Brothers Big Sisters would be ideal. Interview the children on "what do they want to be when they grow up?" What are your findings? Ask them about a career in sports journalism? What were some common ideas? How diverse was your sample? Be sure to include as many children of varied ethnic backgrounds and ages in your work as you can.

11. Create a proposal for a new morning news show that features sports, athletes, and weather for those sporting events that take place outdoors. Considering all the sports media professionals that you can think of, who would you cast to anchor the show? Why? Who would your sports reporters be? Explain. Who would do the weather? Why? Who would you hire to do special guest segments? Again, explain the rationale for your choices. Like all morning shows, you would have special series or themes. What themes or topics would you cover and why? What special guests would you have appear on your show each morning? List them and provide background and rationales for why these guests would be asked to appear on your show. Who would you hire as your producer(s)? Who would be the executive producer? Director? How would you go about hiring for these behind-the-scenes professionals in the sports media industry? What skills or characteristics would you require for the jobs?

12. Consider the various sports journalists and popular athletes who are highlighted in media today. Your list might include, for example, Erin Andrews, Michael Wilbon, Michael Strahan, Michele Tafoya, Samantha Steele, Bob Costas, Hannah Storm, and Mike Tirico. Research their careers and put together a motivational journalistic piece on the common attributes that these, and other, sports journalists and celebrated athletes exhibited in their jobs to get to where they are today, paying particular attention to the minorities and women.

13. Talk to women and persons of color in your local TV area who are doing jobs that are mostly held by men. Obtain information on their experiences in the role, the pros, the cons, and other highlights. How do they handle reading commentary on social media about their appearance while doing their jobs?

14. Design a research project that addresses differences in how women and minorities are depicted in their roles as sports journalists. How would your project answer this very important research question?

ADDITIONAL RESOURCES

Sports Journalism Jobs, https://www.indeed.com/q-Sports-Journalism-jobs.html

Careers in Sports, https://www.learnhowtobecome.org/career-resource-center/careers-in-sports/

Sports Journalists Jobs, http://www.sportsjournalists.com/forum/forums/journalism-jobs.3/

Sports Management, Marketing and Communications Careers, https://www.thebalancecareers.com/sports-management-marketing-and-communications-careers-2059878

Sports Job Listings, http://www.journalismjobs.com/job-listings

Sports Journalist Jobs and Media, https://www.journaliststoolbox.org/category/journalism-job-links/

Sports Anchor Jobs, https://www.ihirebroadcasting.com/t-sport-anchor-jobs.html

Sports Writer Jobs, https://www.jobsinsports.com/sports-writer-jobs

Writing Job Descriptions and Meeting the Requirements for Jobs in Sports Journalism, https://study.com/articles/Sports_Writing_Careers_Job_Description_and_Requirements.html

CREDITS

Bibliography

AARP. (2011). The employment situation, April 2011: Average duration of unemployment for older jobseekers exceeds one year. AARP Public Policy Institute. Retrieved from https://www.aarp.org/work/job-hunting/info-05-2011/fs225-employment.html

Abdal-Haqq, I. (1989). Violence in sports. ERIC Clearinghouse on Teacher Education. Retrieved from https://www.ericdigests.org/pre-9214/sports.htm

Abdul-Jabbar, K. (2015, November 16). The importance of athlete activists. *Time*. Retrieved from http://time.com/4114002/kareem-abdul-jabbar-athlete-activists/

Abernethy, B., Farrow, D., & Berry, J. (2003). Constraints and issues in the development of a general theory of expert perceptual motor performance. A critique of the deliberate practice framework. In J. L. Starkes & K. A. Ericsson (Eds.), *Expert performance in sports. Advances in research on sport expertise* (pp. 349–369). Champaign, IL: Human Kinetics.

Aburaiya, I., Avraham, E., & Wolfsfeld, G. (1998). *The Palestinians in Israel in the eyes of the Hebrew media*. Givat Habiba: The Peace Institute; Nazareth, Israel.

ACES. (2018). Resources for editing stories on transgender individuals. ACES. Retrieved from https://aceseditors.org/news/2015/resources-for-editing-stories-on-transgender-individuals

Acosta, R. V., & Carpenter, L. J. (2008). Women in intercollegiate sport: A longitudinal, national study—Thirty one year update, 1977–2008. Acosta/Carpenter. Retrieved from http://www.acostacarpenter.org

Acosta, R. V., & Carpenter, L. J. (2012). *Women in intercollegiate sport. A longitudinal, national study*. Thirty-five year update. Acosta/Carpenter. Retrieved from http://www.acostacarpenter.org

Adams, A., & Anderson, E. (2011). Homosexuality and sport: Exploring the influence of coming out to the teammates of a small, Midwestern Catholic college soccer team. *Sport, Education and Society, 17*(3), 347–363.

Adams, A., Anderson, E., & McCormak, M. (2010). Establishing and challenging masculinity: The influence of gendered discourses in organized sport. *Journal of Language and Social Psychology, 29*(3), 278–300.

Adams, M., Bell, L. A., & Griffin, P. (2007). *Teaching for diversity and social justice* (pp. 198–199). London, United Kingdom: Routledge.

Addis, M. E. 2008. Gender and depression in men. *Clinical Psychology: Science and Practice, 15*(3), 153–168.

Addis, M.E., & Mahalik, J. R. (2003). Men, masculinity, and the contexts of help seeking. *American Psychologist, 58*(1), 5–14.

Adair, D. (2015, December 15). Athletes of influence—the reality of sports role models. UTS. Retrieved from https://www.uts.edu.au/about/uts-business-school/management/news/athletes-influence-reality-sports-role-models

Adler, R. (2016, October 26). The Jew who wasn't there: Halacha and the Jewish woman. Jewish Women's Archive. Retrieved from https://jwa.org/sites/jwa.org/files/mediaobjects/the_jew_who_wasnt_there_adler.jpg

Afterschool Alliance. (2005). Working families and afterschool. A special report from America After 3PM: A household survey on afterschool in America. After School Alliance. Retrieved from http://www.afterschoolalliance.org/press_archives/Working_Families.Rpt.pdf.

Age Concern. (1999). *Work in an ageing society*. Newcastle, United Kingdom: Age Concern.

Ahmed, S. (2000). *Strange encounters: Embodied others in post-coloniality*. New York, NY: Routledge.

Ahmed, S. (2012, August 2). Arab fans show big support to Saudi-Filipino swimmer Jasmine Alkhaldi. *Al-Arabiya News*, Retrieved from http://muslimwomeninsports.blogspot.com/2012/08/arab-fans-show-big-support-to-saudi.html

Akbarzadeh, S., & Smith, B. (2005). Representation of Islam and Muslim in the Australian media: The "age" and "herald sun." Report to the Asia Institute, Retrieved from the Asia Institute website: http://asianinstitute.unimelb.edu.au/__data/assets/pdf_file/0008/571625/akbarzadeh-islam-media.pdf.

Akers, R. L. (1973). *Deviant behavior*. Belmont, CA: Wadsworth.

al-Ariqi, A. (2009). Middle Eastern women in the media: A battle against stereotypes Al Jazeera: A case study. Reuters Institute. Retrieved from https://reutersinstitute.politics.ox.ac.uk/our-research/middle-eastern-women-media-battle-against-stereotypes

Albarran, A., & Dimmick, J. (1993). An assessment of utility and competition superiority in the video entertainment industries. *Journal of Media Economics, 6*(2), 45–51.

Alchin, L. (2014). Star-Spangled Banner lyrics. American Historama. Retrieved from http://www.american-historama.org/1801-1828-evolution/star-spangled-banner-lyrics.htm

Alden T. V. (1982). From white man to redskin: Changing Anglo-American perceptions of the American Indian. *American Historical Review, 87*(4), 917–953.

Ali Center (2016). Athletes & social change. Ali Center. Retrieved from https://alicenter.org/programs/athletes-social-change/

Ali, S. (2018, May 23). The invisible competition: Athletes & mental health. *Psychology Today*. Retrieved from https://www.psychologytoday.com/us/blog/modern-mentality/201805/the-invisible-competition-athletes-mental-health

Allen, K. & Frisby, C. M. (2017). A content analysis of micro aggressions in news stories about female athletes participating in the 2012 and 2016 summer Olympics. *Journal of Mass Communication and Journalism, 7*, 334–339. doi: 10.4172/2165-7912.1000334

Allen, M., D'Alessio, D., & Brezgel, K. (1995). A meta-analysis summarizing the effects of pornography II. *Human Communication Research, 22*(2), 258–283.

Allen, M., Emmers, T., Gebhardt, L., & Geiry, M. (1995). Pornography and acceptance of rape myths. *Journal of Communication, 45*(2), 5–27.

Allen, S. (2014, August 14). Clinton Portis was either terrible or fabulous in his sideline reporting debut. *Washington Post*. Retrieved from https://www.washingtonpost.com

Allums, J. (2016). Media and sports. *Mass Media and Sports*. Retrieved from https://massmediaandsports.wordpress.com/2016/04/09/mass-media-and-sports/

Almond, E. (2018). Race and swimming: Stanford stars helping change sports complexion. *The Mercury News*. Retrieved from https://www.mercurynews.com/2015/06/18/race-and-swimming-stanford-stars-helping-change-sports-complexion/

Al-Nafjan, E. (2012). Two steps forward … : Do Saudi Arabia's two Olympic female athletes—the kingdom's first ever—represent changing times in the land of the two holy mosques, or will the conservative religious backlash win out? *Foreign Policy*. Retrieved from https://foreignpolicy.com/2012/07/19/two-steps-forward/

Alpert, R. T. (2011). *Out of left field: Jews and black baseball*. New York, NY: Oxford University Press.

Altman, D. (1972). *Homosexual: Oppression and liberation*. Sydney, Australia: Angus and Robertson.

Amara, M. (2008). The Muslim world in the global sporting arena. *Brown Journal of World Affairs, 14*(2), 67–76.

Amara, M. (2012). Veiled women athletes in the 2008 Beijing Olympics: Media accounts. *International Journal of the History of Sport, 29*(4), 638–651.

American Academy of Orthopaedic Surgeons. (1992). Position statement: Support of sports and recreation programs for physically disabled people (Document Number: 1123). Atlanta, GA: BlazeSports America, Retrieved from https://www.blazesports.org/wp-content/uploads/2011/02/BSA-Injuries-and-Medical-Issues-Manual.pdf

American College of Sports Medicine. (1995). *Guidelines for exercise testing and prescription*. Baltimore: Williams and Wilkins.

American College of Sports Medicine. (1987). American College of Sports Medicine position stand on the prevention of thermal injuries during distance running. *Medicine and Science in Sports and Exercise, 19*(5), 529–533.

American College of Sports Medicine. (1998). American College of Sports Medicine position stand and American Heart Association: Recommendations for cardiovascular screening, staffing, and emergency policies at health/fitness facilities. *Medicine and Science in Sports and Exercise, 30*(6), 1009–1018.

American College of Sports Medicine, & American Diabetes Association (Joint Position Statement). (1997). Diabetes mellitus and exercise. *Medicine and Science in Sports and Exercise, 12,* i–vi.

American Psychiatric Association. (2013). *Diagnostic and statistical manual of mental disorders: fifth edition (DSM-5).* Washington, DC: American Psychiatric Association.

American Psychological Association. (2007). *Task force on socio-economic status. Report of the APA task force on socio-economic status.* Washington, DC: American Psychological Association. Retrieved from http://www2.apa.org/pi/ SES_task_force_report.pdf

American Psychological Association. (2008). *Answers to your questions: For a better understanding of sexual orientation and homosexuality.* Washington, DC: American Psychological Association. Retrieved from http://www.apa. org/topics/sexuality/orientation.aspx

American Psychological Association. (2011). Definition of terms: Sex, gender, gender identity, sexual orientation: The guideline for psychological practice with lesbian, gay, and bisexual clients. Washington, DC: American Psychological Association. Retrieved from http://www.apa.org/pi/lgbt/resources/sexuality-definitions.pdf

American Psychological Association. (2012). Guidelines for psychological practice with lesbian, gay, and bisexual clients. *American Psychologist, 67*(1), 10–42. doi: 10.1037/ a0024659

American Psychological Association. (2015). Guidelines for psychological practice with transgender and gender nonconforming people. *American Psychologist, 70*(9), 832–864. doi. org/10.1037/a0039906

Andersen, M., & Hysock, D. (2009). *Thinking about women: Sociological perspectives on sex and gender* (8th ed.). Boston, MA: Allyn & Bacon.

Anderson, C. (2004). An update on the effects of playing violent video games. *Journal of Adolescence, 27,* 113–122.

Anderson, C. & Bushman, B. (2001). Effects of violent video games on aggressive behavior, aggressive cognition,aggressive affect, physiological arousal and prosocial behavior: A meta-analysis. *Psychology and Science, 12,* 353–359.

Anderson, C., Berkowitz, L., Donnerstein, E., Huesmann, L., Johnson, J., Linz, D., Malamuth, N., & Wartella, E. (2003). The influence of media violence on youth. *Psychological Science in the Public Interest, 4*(3), 81–111.

Anderson, C., & Dill, K. E. (2000). Video games and aggressive thoughts, feelings, and behavior in the laboratory and in life. *Journal of Personality & Social Psychology, 78*(4), 772–791.

Anderson, C. A., & Huesmann, L. R. (2003). Human aggression: A social-cognitive view. In M. A. Hogg & J. Cooper (Eds.), *The SAGE handbook of social psychology* (pp. 296–323). Thousand Oaks, CA: Sage.

Anderson, E. (2005a). *In the game: Gay athletes and the cult of masculinity.* New York, NY: State University of New York Press.

Anderson, E. (2005b). Orthodox and inclusive masculinity: Competing masculinities among heterosexual men in a feminized terrain. *Sociological Perspectives, 48*(3), 337–355.

Anderson, E., & Adams, A. (2011). "Aren't we all a little bisexual?": The recognition of bisexuality in an unlikely place. *Journal of Bisexuality, 11,* 1, 3–22. doi: 10.1080/15299716.2011.545283

Anderson, J., & Raine, L. (2012). Millennials will benefit and suffer due to their hyperconnected lives. Pew Research Center Study. Retrieved from http://www.pewinternet.org/2012/02/29/ millennials-will-benefit-and-suffer-due-to-their-hyperconnected-lives/

Andreasen, R. (2000). Race: Biological reality or social construct? *Philosophy of Science, 67,* S653–S666. Retrieved from http://www.jstor. org/stable/188702

Andsager, J. L. (2000). How interest groups attempt to shape public opinion with competing news frames. *Journalism and Mass Communication Quarterly, 77*(3), 577–592.

Andsager, J. L., & Powers, A. (1999). Social or economic concerns: How news and women's magazines framed breast cancer in the 1990s. *Journalism and Mass Communication Quarterly, 76*(3), 531–550.

Andsager, J. L., & Roe, K. (1999). Country music video in country's year of the woman. *Journal of Communication, 49*, 69–82.

Angermeyer, M. C., Dietrich, S., Pott, D., & Matschinger, H. (2005). Media consumption and desire for social distance towards people with schizophrenia. *European Psychiatry, 20*, 246–250.

Angyal, C. (2016, August 16). *Superstar Simone Biles wins her fourth gold medal and makes history*. Huffington Post. Retrieved from https://www.huffingtonpost.com/entry/superstar-simone-biles-wins-her-fourth-gold-medal-and-makes-history_us_57b24c81e4b0c75f49d7e4f5

AnoushkaBhardwaj. (2017, September 12). Gender equality: A living reality. CSR Match. Retrieved from https://csrmatch.org/gender-equality-a-living-reality/

Anshel, M. H. (2004). Sources of disordered eating patterns between ballet dancers and non-dancers. *Journal of Sport Behavior, 27*, 115–133.

Anthony, A. (2000, June 4). White men can't run. *The Guardian*. Retrieved from https://www.theguardian.com/observer/osm/story/0,,328508,00.html

Arab American Institute. (2016). Arab Americans. Retrieved from https://web.archive.org/web/20060601221810/http://www.aaiusa.org/arab-americans/22/demographics

Armstrong, L. E., Costill, D. L., & Fink, W. J. (1985). Influence of diuretic-induced dehydration on competitive running performance. *Medicine and Science in Sports and Exercise, 17*, 456–461.

Armstrong, L. E., Pandolf, K. B. (1988). Physical training, cardiorespiratory physical fitness, and exercise-heat tolerance. In K. B. Pandolf, M. N. Sawka, & R. R. Gonzalez (Eds.), *Human performance physiology and environmental medicine at terrestrial extremes* (pp. 199–226). Indianapolis, IN: Benchmark Press, Inc.

Armstrong, N., Barker, A. R., & McManus, A. M. (2015). Muscle metabolism changes with age and maturation: How do they relate to youth sport performance? *British Journal of Sports Medicine, 49*, 860–864.

Arrowsmith J., McGoldrick, A. E. (1996). HRM service practices: Flexibility, quality and employee strategy. *International Journal of Service Industry Management, 7*(3), 46–62.

Arsenault, P. (2004). Validating generational differences: A legitimate diversity and leadership issue. *Leadership & Organization Development Journal, 25*, 124–141.

Artal, R. & Sherman, C. (1999). Exercise during pregnancy: Safe and beneficial for most. *Physician and Sportsmedicine, 24*(7), 89–95.

Arthur, B. (2002, August 28). Serena reveals and revels in her catsuit: It "is really sexy. I love it." *National Post* (Canada), S1. Retrieved from http://www.lexisnexis.com.ezproxy.lib.indiana.edu/hottopics/lnacademic/

Asphodel, A. (2014, May 8). *Difference between transgender & transsexual*. Available from https://www.youtube.com/watch?v=HK62l3xV-AI&vl=en

Associated Press. (2006, January 7). Tyson says he would "really" rape victim now. ABC News. Retrieved from https://abcnews.go.com/US/story?id=90606&page=1

Associated Press. (2010, March 17). Jordan purchase of Bobcats approved. ESPN.com. Retrieved from http://www.espn.com/nba/news/story?id=5003048

Associated Press. (2018, October 19). Los Angeles Chargers owner Alex Spanos dies at 95. Fox Sports. Retrieved from https://www.foxsports.com/west/story/alex-spanos-los-angeles-chargers-owner-dies-at-95-100918

Associated Press Salon Staff. (2014, September). Another Donald Sterling: NBA owner to sell team after revealing racist email. *Salon*. Retrieved from https://www.salon.com/2014/09/07/another_donald_sterling_nba_owner_to_sell_team_after_revealing_racist_email/

Associated Press Stylebook. (2018). *AP stylebook*. Retrieved from https://www.apstylebook.com

Association for Lesbian Gay, Bisexual, and Transgender Issues in Counseling of Alabama. (2016). Rio Olympics and LGBT athletes. ALGBTICAL. Retrieved from http://www.algbtical.org/2A%20SPORTS.htm

Aswad, C. (2017). Women in sports ad strikes nerve in Arab world. Reuters. Retrieved from www.reuters.com/article/us-arab-women-nike/women-in-sports-ad-strikes-nerve-in-arab-world-idUSKBN1620I7

AthleteAlly. (2018, December 11). The athlete equity index. Retrieved from https://www.athleteally.org/actions/athlete-ally-pledge/

Atkinson, J. A. (2009). Age matters in sport communication. *Electronic Journal of Communication, 19*(3 & 4). Retrieved from http://www.cios.org/EJCPUBLIC/019/2/019341.html.

Atkinson, J. L., & Herro, S. K. (2006, March). *The wise old gnome of tennis: Examining coverage of Andre Agassi at the U.S. Open.* Paper presented at the Communication and Sport Summit, Phoenix, AZ.

Atkinson, M. (2010). It's still part of the game: violence and masculinity in Canadian ice hockey. In L. K. Fuller (Ed.), *Sexual sports rhetoric: historical and media contexts of violence* (pp. 15–30). New York, NY: Peter Lang Publishing.

Atkinson, M., & Young, K. (2008). *Deviance and social control in sport.* Champaign, IL: Human Kinetics.

Attri, D. R. (2013). Personality traits and performance of badminton players in relation to their socio-economic states. *International Journal of Scientific Research, 2*(3), 338–339.

Aubrey, J. S., Henson, J., Hopper, K. M., & Smith, S. (2009). A picture is worth twenty words (about the self): Testing the priming influence of visual sexual objectification on women's self-objectification. *Communication Research Reports, 26*, 271–284.

Auerbach, N. & Martin, J. (2014, February 17). One and done, but never as simple as it sounds. *USA Today.* Retrieved from https://www.usatoday.com/story/sports/ncaab/2014/02/17/college-basketball-nba-draft-early-entry-one-and-done-rule/5552163/

Aufderheide, P. (1993). *Media literacy. A report of the National Leadership Conference on Media Literacy.* Presentation to the National Leadership Conference on Media Literacy, Quenstown, MD.

Aulette, J. R., & Wittner, J. (2012). *Gendered worlds* (2nd ed.). New York, NY: Oxford University.

Aulette, J. R., Wittner, J., & Blakeley, K. (2009). *Gendered worlds.* New York, NY: Oxford University Press.

The Australian. (2012, September 29). Hurdles to Muslim women's rights. Retrieved from http://www.theaustralian.com.au/news/world/hurdles-to-muslim-womens-rights/story-e6frg6ux-1226422876926#mm-premium

Australian Sports Commission Report. (2010). *Annual report: 2010–2011.* Clearinghouse for Sport. Retrieved from https://www.clearinghouseforsport.gov.au/Library/archive/digital_archive/asc_publications/australian_sports_commission_corporate_publications/ASC_Annual_Report_2010-11.pdf

Ava. (2016). The top 15 hottest sideline female sports reporters. The Sportster. Retrieved from http://www.thesportster.com/entertainment/top-15-hottest-sideline-reporters-in-sports/

Avolio, B. J., & Barrett, G. V. (1987). Effects of age stereotyping in a simulated interview. *Psychology and Aging, 2*(1), 56–63.

Ayub, A. (2011). A closer look at FIFA's hijab. *SAIS Review, XXXI*(1), 43–50.

Babb, K., & Rich, S. (2016, October 28). A quietly escalating issue for NFL: Fan violence and how to contain it. *Washington Post.* Retrieved from https://www.washingtonpost.com/sports/redskins/a-quietly-escalating-issue-for-nfl-fan-violence-and-how-to-contain-it/2016/10/28/4ec37964-9470-11e6-bb29-bf2701dbe0a3_story.html?utm_term=.d891c362ca63

Babrow, A. J. (1989). An expectancy-value analysis of the student soap opera audience. *Communication Research, 16*, 155–178.

Badenhausen, K. (2018, February 7). NBA team values 2018: Every club now worth at least $1 billion. *Forbes.* Retrieved from https://www.forbes.com/sites/kurtbadenhausen/2018/02/07/nba-team-values-2018-every-club-now-worth-at-least-1-billion/#21cdc4767155

Bailey, A. (2015, July 17). Five trans athletes who made their mark before Caitlyn Jenner. PRI. Retrieved from https://www.pri.org/stories/2015-07-17/five-trans-athletes-who-made-their-mark-caitlyn-jenner

Bailey, R., Armour, K., Kirk, D., Jess, M., Pickup, I., & Standford, R. The Bera physical education and sport pedagogy, The Educational Benefits Claimed for Physical Education and School Sport: An Academic Review. *Research Papers in Education, 24*, 1–27. http://dx.doi.org/10.1080/19398440802673275

Bain-Selbo, E. (2009). *Game day and god: Football, faith, and politics in the American south.* Macon, GA: Mercer University Press.

Baker G. (2011, June 9). Mariners trying to lay the groundwork for wins later on. *Seattle Times.* Retrieved from http://seattletimes.com

Baker, J. & Côté J. (2006). Shifting training requirements during athlete development: The relationship among deliberate practice, deliberate play and other sport involvement in the acquisition of sport expertise. In D. Hackfort & G. Tenenbaum (Eds.), *Essential processes for attaining peak performance* (pp. 93–110). Oxford, United Kingdom: Meyer and Meyer.

Baker, J., Côté, J., & Abernethy, B. (2003). Learning from the experts: Practice activities of expert decision makers in sport. *Research Quarterly for Exercise and Sport, 74*, 342–347.

Baker, J., & Robertson-Wilson, J. (2003). On the risks of early specialization in sport. *Physical and Health Education Journal, 69*, 4–8.

Baker, W. J. (1986). *Jesse Owens: An American life*. New York, NY: Free Press.

Baker, W. J. (2007). *Playing with god: Religion and modern sport*. Cambridge, MA: Harvard University Press.

Baldassaro, L. (2005). Dashing dagos and walloping wops: Media portrayal of Italian American major leaguers before World War II. *Journal of Baseball History and Culture, 14*(1), 98–106. doi: 10.1353/nin.2005.0033

Bale, J. & Cronin, M. (2003) *Sport and postcolonialism*. Oxford, United Kingdom: Berg.

Ballantyne, B. (2018). The top 15 most hateable current athletes. Bench Life Sports. Retrieved from https://benchlifesports.com/2018/01/31/the-top-15-most-hateable-current-athletes/

Ballard, G. G. (2008). Buick human highlight reel—2012 professional biography interview, documentary. California Indian Education. Retrieved from http://www.californiaindianeducation.org/sports_heros/billy_mills/

Baltes, P. B. (1987). Theoretical propositions of lifespan developmental psychology: On the dynamics between growth and decline. *Developmental Psychology, 23*(5), 611–626.

Bandura, A. (1977). *Social learning theory*. Englewood Cliffs, NJ: Prentice Hall.

Bandura, A. (1978). Social learning theory of aggression. *Journal of Aggression, 28*(3), 12–29. doi: 10.1111/j.1460-2466.1978.tb01621.x

Bandura, A. (1989). Social cognitive theory. In R. Vasta (Ed.), *Annals of child development. Vol. 6. Six theories of child development* (pp. 1–60). Greenwich, CT: JAI Press.

Bandura, A. (2008). Social cognitive theory of mass communication. In J. Bryant & M. B. Oliver (Eds.), *Media effects: Advances in theory and research* (pp. 94–124). New York, NY: Routledge.

Banet-Weiser, S. (1999). *The most beautiful girl in the world: Beauty pageants and national identity*. Berkeley, CA: University of California Press.

Baran, S. B., Chase, L., & Courtright, J. (1979). Television drama as a facilitator of prosocial behavior. *Journal of Broadcasting, 23*(3), 277–284.

Baran, S. J., & Davis, D. K. (2012). *Mass communication theory: Foundations, ferment, and future* (6th ed.). Boston, MA: Wadsworth Cengage Learning.

Baranowski, T., Bouchard, C., Bar-Or, O., Bricker, T., Heath, G., Kimm, S.Y.S., Malina, R., Obarzanek, E., Pate, R., Strong, W.B., Truman, B., & Washington, R. (1992). Assessment, prevalence, and cardiovascular benefits of physical activity and fitness in youth. *Medicine and Science in Sports and Exercise, 24*, S237–S247.

Barash, D. P. (2007). *Natural selections: Selfish altruists, honest liars, and other realities of evolution*. New York, NY: Bellevue Literary Press.

Barclay, K., & Liu, J. H. (2003). Who gets voice? (Re)presentation of bicultural relations in New Zealand print media. *New Zealand Journal of Psychology, 32*(1), 3–12.

Barnes, C. (1992). *Disabling imagery and the media. An exploration of the principles for media representations of disabled people*. Halifax, United Kingdom: The British Council of Disabled People and Ryman Publishing.

Barnes, C. (1997). A legacy of oppression: A history of disability in western culture. In L. Barton & M. Oliver (Eds.), *Disability studies, past present and future* (pp. 45–61). Leeds, United Kingdom: The Disability Press.

Barnas, Jo-Ann (2009, June 4). Muskegon's Abdelkader has golden touch. WZZM 13. Gannett. Retrieved from https://en.wikipedia.org/wiki/Justin_Abdelkader#cite_ref-Barnas_20-0

Barnett, L. M., Morgan, P. J., Van Beurden, E. (2011). A reverse pathway? Actual and perceived skill proficiency and physical activity. *Medical Science of Sports Exercise, 43*(5), 898–904.

Barnett, L. M., Van Beurden E, & Morgan, P. J. (2009). Childhood motor skill proficiency as a predictor of adolescent physical activity. *Journal of Adolescent Health, 44,* 252–259.

Barnett, N. P., Smoll, F. L., & Smith, R. E. (1992). Effects of enhancing coach-athlete relationships on youth sport attrition. *Sport Psychologist, 6,* 111–127.

Bar-Or, O. (1983). *Pediatric sports medicine for the practitioner: From physiologic principles to clinical application.* New York, NY: Springer Verlag.

Barrett, A. E., & Turner, R. J. (2006). Family structure and substance use in adolescence and early adulthood: Examining explanations for the relationship. *Addiction, 101,* 109–120.

Barrett, P. M., & Ollendick , T. H. (2004). *Interventions that work with children and adolescents: Prevention and treatment.* Hoboken, NJ: Wiley.

Barton, L. (1993). Disability, empowerment and physical education. In J. Evans (Ed.), *Equality, education and physical education* (pp. 43–54). London, United Kingdom: The Falmer Press.

Baskin, J. R. (1991). *Jewish women in historical perspective.* Detroit, MI: Wayne State University Press.

Bastone, J. (2011). UFC: Analysis of the Miguel Torres "rape van" tweet and firing by Dana White. Bleacher Report. Retrieved from http://bleacherreport.com/articles/976841-ufc-analysis-of-the-miguel-torres-rape-van-tweet-and-firing-by-dana-white

Bauder, D. (2016). Citizens victors over NFL greed: San Diego expects a different Chargers deal. *San Diego Reader.* Retrieved from https://www.sandiegoreader.com/news/2016/nov/10/ticker-citizens-victors-over-nfl-greed/#

BBC Channel 1. (2012, July 27). *The Olympic opening ceremony. Streamed live on 27.07.2012.* Available from http://www.youtube.com/watch?v= 4As0e4de-rI

BBC Radio 3. (2011). *Fasting and the Olympics: Live Debate.* Retrieved from https://www.theguardian.com/lifeandstyle/2012/jul/22/ramadan-olympics-fasting

BBC Radio 4. (2012). *Woman's hour. Arab women and sport legacy.* Available from http://www.bbc.co.uk/programmes/b01lsyjd

BBC Sports. (2012). IOC urged to ban Saudi Arabia from 2012 over stance on women. Retrieved from http://www.bbc.co.uk/sport/0/olympics/17632782

Beadle, M. (2002, February 20). Mascot display takes aim at stereotypes. *Smoky Mountain News.* Retrieved from http://www.main.nc.us/wncceib/esqEXHIBITsmnews.htm

Beal, F. M. (1970). Black women's manifesto; double jeopardy: To be black and female. In R. Morgan (Eds.), *Sisterhood is powerful: An anthology of writings from the women's liberation movement.* New Nork, NY: Random House. Retrieved from http://www.hartford-hwp.com/archives/45a/196.html

Beamon, K. K. (2009). Are sports overemphasized in the socialization process of African American males? A qualitative analysis of former collegiate athletes' perception of sport socialization. *Journal of Black Studies, 41*(2), 281–300.

Bear, A. (1984). The myth of television violence. *Media Information Australia, 33,* 5–10.

Beasley, C. (2008). Rethinking hegemonic masculinity in a globalizing world. *Men and Masculinities, 11*(1), 86–103.

Becker E. (1973). *The denial of death.* New York, NY: Free Press.

Begley, S. (2009, June 29). Don't blame the caveman. *Newsweek,* pp. 52–62.

Begley, S. (2009, September 14). Pink brain, blue brain: Claims of sex differences fall apart. *Newsweek,* p. 28.

Behr, R., & Iyengar, S. (1985). TV news, real-world clues and changes in the public agenda. *Public Opinion Quarterly, 49*(1), 38–57.

Bellamy, R. V., & James, R. W. (2008). *Center field shot: A history of baseball on television.* Lincoln, NE: University of Nebraska Press.

Belson, W. (1978). *Television violence and the adolescent boy.* Hampshire, United Kingdom: Saxon House.

Belzer, J. (201, December 2). The most powerful women in sports. *Forbes.* Retrieved from https://www.forbes.com/sites/jasonbelzer/2015/12/02/the-most-powerful-women-in-sports/#7949ee523a5f

Benardot, D. (Ed.) (1993). Sports nutrition: A guide for the professional working with active people (p. 41). Chicago, IL: American Dietetic Association.

Bender, J. R., Davenport, L. D., Drager, M. W., & Fedler, F. (2009). *Reporting for the media* (9th ed.). New York, NY: Oxford University Press.

Benedict, J. (2004). *Out of bounds: Inside the NBA's culture of rape, violence, and crime*. New York, NY: Perennial Currents.

Benedict, J., & Yaeger, D. (1998). *Pros and cons: The criminals who play in the NFL*, New York, NY: Warner Books.

Benn, T., & S. D. (2012). The Olympic movement and Islamic culture: Conflict or compromise for Muslim women? *International Journal of Sport Policy and Politics, 1*(1), 1–14.

Bennett, D. (2011, July 12). The worst stadium financing deal ever is still crippling Cincinnati's taxpayers. *Business Insider*. Retrieved from https://www.businessinsider.com/worst-stadium-deal-cincinnati-2011-7

Bennett, W. I. (1995). Beyond overeating. *New England Journal of Medicine, 332*, 673–674.

Bentley, A. (2014). Native Americans in pro sports. Partnership with Native Americans. Retrieved from http://blog.nativepartnership.org/native-americans-in-pro-sports/

Berelson, B. (1949). What missing the newspaper means. In P. Lazarsfeld & F. Stanton (Eds.), *Communication research, 1948–1949*. (pp. 111–129) New York, NY: Harper & Row.

Bergen, A., Presperin, J., & Tallman, T. (1990). *Positioning for function: Wheelchairs and other assistive devices*. Valhalla, NY: Valhalla Rehabilitation Publications, LTD.

Berger, B. G., & Owen, D. R. (1988). Stress reduction and mood enhancement in four exercise modes: Swimming, body conditioning, hatha yoga, and fencing. *Research Quarterly for Exercise and Sport, 59*, 148–159.

Berger, K. (2014, July 29). NBPA makes history with election of Michele Roberts as executive director. *CBS Sports*. Retrieved from https://www.cbssports.com/nba/news/nbpa-makes-history-with-election-of-michele-roberts-as-executive-director/

Berghorn, F. J., Yetman, N. R., & Hanna, W. E. (1988). Racial participation and integration in men's and women's basketball: Continuity and change, 1958–85. *Sociology of Sport Journal, 5*(2), 107–124. doi: 10.1123/ssj.5.2.107

Berk, L. E. (2008). *Child development* (8th ed.). Boston, MA: Bacon & Allyn.

Berkowitz, L., & Rogers, K. H. (1986). A priming effect analysis of media influences. In J. Bryant & D. Zillmann (Eds.), *Perspectives on media effects* (pp. 57–81). Hillsdale, NJ: Lawrence Erlbaum.

Berkowitz, S., Schnaars, C., & Dougherty, S. (2018). NCAA salaries. *USA Today*. Retrieved from http://sports.usatoday.com/ncaa/salaries/

Berman, S. (2009, April 14). Too experienced, overqualified or expensive? The plight of older Americans in today's job market. *Seattle Post Intelligencer*. Retrieved from http://www.seattlepi.com

Berri, D. (2015). Basketball's gender wage gap is even worse than you think, *Vice Sports*, Retrieved from https://sports.vice.com/en_us/article/wn3mmy/basketballs-gender-wage-gap-is-even-worse-than-you-think

Berri, D. (2015, August 12). Basketball's gender wage gap is even worse than you think: While NBA players are paid about 50 percent of league revenue, WNBA players appear to earn 33 percent. Vice Sports. Retrieved from https://sports.vice.com/en_us/article/wn3mmy/basketballs-gender-wage-gap-is-even-worse-than-you-think

Berri, D. (2018). The WNBA—or the NBA—should pay its players more. *Forbes*. Retrieved from https://www.forbes.com/sites/davidberri/2018/07/22/the-wnba-or-the-nba-should-pay-the-wnba-players-more/#28b2cd9740fe

Berry, S. M., & Larkey, P. D. (1999). The effects of age on the performance of professional golfers. In M. Farrally & A. Cochran (Eds.), *Science and golf III: Proceedings of the world scientific congress of golf* (pp. 127–137). Champaign, IL: Human Kinetics.

Berry S. M., Reese C. S., & Larkey, P. D. (1999). Bridging different eras in sports. *Journal of the American Statistical Association, 94*(447), 661–676.

Best, C. (1987). Experience and career length in professional football: The effect of positional segregation. *Sociology of Sport Journal, 4*(4), 410–420.

Beveridge, A. I (1996). Images of madness in the films of Walt Disney. *Psychiatric Bulletin, 20*, 618–620.

Bhana, D. (2009). Boys will be boys: What do early childhood teachers have to do with it? *Educational Review, 61*(3), 327–339.

Bianchi, G. (2006). Age requirement in sport. *Sport Journal*. Retrieved from https://thesportjournal.org/article/age-requirement-in-professional-sport/

Bickenbach, J. E., Chatterji, S., Badley, E. M., & Ustun, T. B. (1999). Models of disablement, universalism and international classification of impairments, disabilities and handicaps. *Social, Science & Medicine, 48*, 1173–1187.

Bilandzic, H. & Busselle, R. (2008). Transportation and transportability in the cultivation of genre-consistent attitudes and estimates. *Journal of Communication, 58*(3), 508–529.

Billings, A. C. (2003). Portraying Tiger Woods: Characterizations of a "black" athlete in a "white" sport. *The Howard Journal of Communications, 14*, 29–37.

Billings, A. C. (2004). Depicting the quarterback in black and white: A content analysis of college and professional football broadcast commentary. *The Howard Journal of Communications, 15*, 201–210.

Billings, A. C., & Angelini, J. R. (2007). Packaging the games for viewer consumption: Gender, ethnicity, and nationality in NBC's coverage of the 2004 summer Olympics. *Communication Quarterly, 55*(1), 95–111.

Billings, A. C., Angelini, J. R., & Eastman, S. T. (2005). Diverging discourses: Gender differences in televised golf announcing. *Mass Communication & Society, 8*, 155–171.

Billings, A. C., & Eastman, S. T. (2002). Selective representation of gender, ethnicity, and nationality in American television coverage of the 2000 summer Olympics. *International Review for the Sociology of Sport, 37*(3–4), 351–370. doi.org/10.1177/101269020203700302

Billings, A. C., & Eastman, S. T. (2003). Framing identities: Gender, ethnicity, and national parity in network announcing of the 2002 winter Olympics. *Journal of Communication, 53*(4), 569–586.

Billings, A. C., Halone, K. K., & Denham, B. E. (2002). "Man, that was a pretty shot": An analysis of gendered broadcast commentary surrounding the 2000 men's and women's NCAA Final Four Basketball Championships. *Mass Communication & Society, 5*(3), 295–315.

Bingham, E. (2016). New Zealand sports stars were robbed of their Moscow Olympics dream. Stuff. Retrieved from https://www.stuff.co.nz/sport/olympics/83316204/new-zealand-sports-stars-were-robbed-of-their-moscow-olympics-dream

Biography.com. (2018, December 13). *Caitlyn Jenner biography: Track and field athlete, Athlete, reality television star (1949–)*. Biography. Retrieved from https://www.biography.com/people/caitlyn-jenner-307180

Birley, D. (2003) *A social history of English cricket*. London, United Kingdom: Aurum Press.

Birrell, S. (1989). Racial relations theories and sport: Suggestions for a more critical analysis. *Sociology of Sport Journal, 6*(3), 12–227.

Birrell, S., & Cole, L. C. (Eds.) (1994). *Women, sport, and culture* (pp. 245–322). Champaign, IL: Human Kinetics.

Birrell, S., & Theberge, N. (1994) Ideological control of women in sport. In D. M. Costa & S. R. Guthrie (Eds.), *Women in sport: Interdisciplinary perspectives* (pp. 341–360). Champaign, IL: Human Kinetics.

Birrell, S., & McDonald, M. G. (2000). *Reading sport: Critical essays on power and representation*. Boston, MA: Northeastern University Press.

Bissell, K. L. (2004). What do these messages really mean? Sports media exposure, sports participation, and body image distortion in women between the ages of 18 and 75. *Journalism and Mass Communication Quarterly, 81*, 108–123.

Bissell, K. L., & Zhou, P. (2004). Must-see TV or ESPN: Entertainment and sports media exposure and body-image distortion in college women. *Journal of Communication, 54*, 5–21.

Bittnerová, A. (2014). The Olympic games as a political tool: Case study Beijing 2008. Unpublished manuscript, Department of International Relations and European Studies, Masaryk University, Brno, Czech Republic. Retrieved from https://is.muni.cz/th/x0c6n/Bakalarska_prace_Bittnerova_Andrea_397711.pdf?so=nx

Blackburn-Dwyer, B., & McMaster, A. (2018). 18 times politics trumped sport in Olympic games' history politics, protests, & bans: The long history of social activism at the Olympic Games. Global Citizen. Retrieved from https://www.globalcitizen.org/en/content/history-political-activism-olympics-rio/

Blackistone, K. (2011, February 12). From the court to Cairo: Alaa Abdelnaby celebrates for Egypt. *SFGate*. Retrieved from https://www.sfgate.com/sports/article/From-the-Court-to-Cairo-Alaa-Abdelnaby-2381177.php

Blanchard-Fields, F. (2007). Everyday problem solving and emotion. *Current Directions in Psychological Science*, *16*(1), 26–31.

Blau, P. M., & Duncan, O. D. (1967). *The American occupational structure*. New York, NY: Wiley.

Blazer, A. (2015). *Playing for god: Evangelical women and the unintended consequences of sports ministry*. New York, NY: New York University Press.

BlazeSports America (2004). Injuries and medical issues. BlazeSports. Retrieved from http://www.blazesports.org/wp-content/uploads/2011/02/BSA-Injuries-and-Medical-Issues-Manual.pdf

Blinde, E. M., & Taub, D. E. (1992). Women athletes as falsely accused deviants: Managing the lesbian stigma. *The Sociological Quarterly*, *33*(4), 521–533.

Block S. (2009, October 9). Layoffs raise social security questions for older workers. *USA Today*. Retrieved from http://www.usatoday.com

Bloom M., Grant, M., & Watt, D. (2005, August). Strengthening Canada—the social-economic benefits of sport participation in Canada. *The Conference Board of Canada*, *13*, 1–9.

Blue, J. (2006). *Josh Blue on last comic standing*. Available from https://www.youtube.com/watch?v=qMSrpZi_6WM

Blue, J. (2009). Comedian Josh Blue: 10 things you should never say to a disabled person. Ditch the Label. Retrieved from https://us.ditchthelabel.org/10-things-disability/

Blumberg, A. (2015). Quarterback Russell Wilson says god cares about football—What do you think? Huffington Post. Retrieved from https://www.huffingtonpost.com/2015/01/29/russell-wilson-god-football_n_6565858.html?utm_hp_ref=religion-and-sports

Blumer, H. (1969). *Symbolic interactionism; perspective and method*. Englewood Cliffs, NJ: Prentice Hall.

Blumstein, A. & Benedict, J. (1999, reprinted in 2012). Criminal violence of NFL players compared to the general population. *Chance*, *12*(3), 12–15. doi: 10.1080/09332480.1999.10542151

Blunt, A. P. (1996). Financial exploitation: the best kept secret of elder abuse. *Aging*, *367*, 62–65.

Boden, S. (2006). Dedicated followers of fashion? The influence of popular culture on children's social identities. *Media, Culture & Society*, *28*, 289–298.

Boeringer, S. B. (1999). Associations of rape-supportive attitudes with fraternal and athletic participation. *Violence Against Women*, *5*(1), 81–90. doi: 10.1177/10778019922181167

Bogert, R., (2010, January 7). Is 60 the new 40? *Chicago Tribune*. Retrieved from http://www.chicagotribune.com

Bohlander, G., & Snell, S. (2001). *Managing human resources* (13th ed.). Nashville, TN: South-Western Publishing.

Bologna, C. (2018). The history of the national anthem in sports: How "The Star-Spangled Banner" became a part of American sports culture. Huffington Post. Retrieved from https://www.huffingtonpost.com/entry/history-national-anthem-sports_us_5afc9bcfe-4b06a3fb50d5056

Boninger, M. L., Robertson, R. N., Wolff, M., & Cooper, R. A. (1996). Upper limb nerve entrapments in elite wheelchair racers. *American Journal of Physical Medicine and Rehabilitation*, *75*, 170–176.

Bonkowski, J. (2014, March 2). Updated: Brad Keselowski will be without crew chief Paul Wolfe for Sunday's Sprint Cup race in Phoenix. *NBC Sports*. Retrieved from https://motorsports.nbcsports.com/2014/03/02/brad-keselowskis-crew-chief-paul-wolfe-returns-to-north-carolina-for-birth-of-child/

Bonnesen, J. L., & Burgess, E. O. (2004). Senior moments: The acceptability of an ageist phrase. *Journal of Aging Studies*, *18*, 123–142.

Boone, E. M., & Leadbeater, B. J. (2006). Game on: Diminishing risks for depressive symptoms in early adolescence through positive involvement in team sports. *Journal of Research on Adolescence*, *16*, 79–90.

Booth, A., & Osgood, D. W. (1993). The influence of testosterone on deviance in adulthood: Assessing and explaining the relationship. *Criminology*, *31*(1), 93–117.

Borden, S. (2012). Observance of Ramadan poses challenges to Muslim athletes. *New York Times*. Retrieved from http://www.nytimes.com/2012/08/01/sports/olympics/ramadan-poses-challenges-for-muslims-at-the-olympics.html?_r = 0

Bornstein, K. (2012). 15 spaces of cultural regulations and the binaries they pretend to be. Kate Bornstein. Retrieved from http://katebornstein.typepad.com/date_bornsteins_blog/2012/09/15-spaces-of-cultural-regulations- and-the-binaries-they-pretend-to-be.html

Botha, U. A., Koen, L., & Niehaus, D. J. H. (2006). Perceptions of a South African schizophrenia population with regards to community attitudes towards their illness. *Social Psychology and Psychiatric Epidemiology*, *41*, 619–623.

Botoon, J. (2017). How Instagram aims to change the face of athlete media. Sport Techie. Retrieved from https://www.sporttechie.com/instagram-facebook-aim-change-athlete-media/

Bouffard, L. A. (2010). Exploring the utility of entitlement in understanding sexual aggression. *Journal of Criminal Justice*, *38*(5), 870–879. doi: http://dx.doi.org/10.1016/j.jcrimjus.2010.06.002!

Bourdieu, P. (1978) Sport and social class. *Social Science Information*, *17*(6), 819–840.

Bourdieu, P. (1980). *The logic of practice*. Stanford, CA: Stanford University Press.

Bourdieu, P. (1984). *Distinction: A social critique of the judgement of taste*. London, United Kingdom: Routledge.

Bourdieu, P. (1986a) *Distinction: A social critique of the judgement of taste*. New York, NY: Routledge & Kegan Paul.

Bourdieu, P. (1986b). The forms of capital. In J. G. Richardson (Ed.), *Handbook of theory and research for the sociology of capital* (pp. 241–258). New York, NY: Greenwood Press.

Bowker, J. (1997). *World religions: The great faiths explored & explained* (pp. 121, 131). London, United Kingdom: Dorling Kindersley Limited.

Boyer, N. (2017). Ex-Green Beret Nate Boyer writes open letter to Trump, Kaepernick, NFL and America. ESPN. Retrieved from http://www.espn.com/nfl/story/_/id/21003968/nfl-2017-ex-green-beret-nate-boyer-writes-open-letter-president-donald-trump-colin-kaepernick-nfl-united-states-america

Boyle, R., & Haynes, R. (2009). *Power play: sport, the media and popular culture* (2nd ed.). Edinburgh, United Kingdom: Edinburgh University Press.

Boyle, T. P. (2001). Intermedia agenda setting in the 1996 presidential election. *Journalism and Mass Communication Quarterly*, *78*(1), 26–44.

Boxing News. (2018, August 23). *The contender*. Pressreader. Retrieved from https://www.pressreader.com/uk/boxing-news/20180823/281535111843106

Boyle, R., & Haynes, R. (2000). *Power play: Sport, the media and popular culture*. Harlow, United Kingdom: Pearson Education.

Bradley, J. R. (2005). *Saudi Arabia exposed*. Basingstoke, United Kingdom: Palgrave Macmillan.

Bradley, J., & Deery, J. (2014, July 16). Panthers' Greg Hardy found guilty on 2 counts of domestic violence. WSOC TV. Retrieved from www.wsoctv.com

Brady, E., Berkowitz, S. S., & Upton, J. (2012). College football coaches continue to see salary explosion. *USA Today*. Retrieved from https://www.usatoday.com/story/sports/ncaaf/2012/11/19/college-football-coaches-contracts-analysis-pay-increase/1715435/

Brand, J., & Greenberg, B. (1994). Commercials in the classroom. *Journal of Advertising Research*, *34*(1), 18–27.

Brasile, F. M., Kleiber, D. A., & Harnisch, D. (1994, January–March). Analysis of participation incentives among athletes with and without disabilities. *Therapeutic Recreation Journal*, pp. 18–33.

Bredemeier, B. J., & Shields, D. L. (1987). Moral growth through physical activity: A structural developmental approach. In D. S. Gould & M. R. Weiss (Eds.), *Advances in pediatric sport sciences* (Vol. 2, pp. 143–165). Champaign, IL: Human Kinetics.

Brettell, C. B., & Sargent, C. F. (Eds.). (2009). *Gender in cross-cultural perspective* (5th ed.). Upper Saddle River, NJ: Prentice Hall.

Brewer, B. W., Van Raalte, J. L., & Linder, D. E. (1993). Athletic identity: Hercules' muscles or Achilles heel? *International Journal of Sport Psychology*, *24*(2), 237–254.

Brewer, G. & Howarth, S. (2012). Sport, attractiveness, and aggression. *Personality and Individual Differences*, *53*(5), 640–643. doi: 10.1016/j.paid.2012.05.010

Brewer, K. (2004). Stern ready to agree on a minor concession. *Washington Times*, Retrieved from https://www.researchgate.net/publication/265863951_Norms_Athletic_Identity_and_Concussion_Symptom_Under-Reporting_

Among_Male_Collegiate_Ice_Hockey_Players_A_Prospective_Cohort_Study

Brewer, M. B., Dull, V., & Lui, L. (1981). Perceptions of the elderly: Stereotypes as prototypes. *Journal of Personality and Social Psychology, 41*(4), 656–670.

Brewer, R. A., & Jones, J. S. (1989). Reporting elder abuse: Limitations of statutes. *Annals of Emergency Medicine, 18*, 1217–1221.

Bristor, J. M., & Fischer, E. (1993). Feminist thought: Implications for consumer research. *Journal of Consumer Research, 19*(March), 518–536.

Brod, H. (Ed.) (1987). *The making of masculinities: The new men's studies*. Boston, MA: Allen & Unwin.

Brod, H. (1994). Some thoughts on some histories of some masculinities: Jews and other others. In D. S. David & R. Brannon (Eds.), *Theorizing masculinities* (pp. 97–110). Thousand Oaks, CA: Sage.

Broder, J. M. (2007, January 21). Shushing the baby boomers. *New York Times*. Retrieved from http://www.nytimes.com

Brooke, L., Taylor, P. (2005). Older workers and employment: Managing age relations. *Ageing and Society, 25*(3), 415–429.

Brookins, G. K. (1993). Culture, ethnicity and bicultural competence: Implications for children with chronic illness and disability. *Pediatrics, 9*(5), 1056–1062.

Brooks, G. A., & Fahey, T. D. (1984). *Exercise physiology: Human bioenergetics and its applications*. New York, NY: John Wiley & Sons.

Brooks, L. (2017, July 2). How the success-hating NHL has destroyed budding dynasties. *NY Post*. Retrieved from https://nypost.com/2017/07/02/how-the-success-hating-nhl-has-destroyed-budding-dynasties/

Brosius, H. B., & Kepplinger, H. M. (1990). The agendasetting function of TV news. *Communication Research, 17*(2), 183–211.

Brosius, H. B., & Kepplinger, H. M. (1992). Linear and non-linear models of agenda setting in television. *Journal of Broadcasting and Electronic Media, 36*(1), 5–24.

Broude, G. J. (2003). Sexual attitudes and practices. In C. R. Ember & M. Ember (Eds.), *Encyclopedia of sex and gender: Men and women in the world's cultures volume 1* (pp. 177–184). New York, NY: Springer.

Brouns, F. (1991). Heat-sweat-dehydration-rehydration: A praxis oriented approach. *Journal of Sports Science, 9*, 143–152.

Brown, G. T. (2014). *Mind, body and sport: Understanding and supporting student-athlete mental wellness*. Indianapolis, IN; National Collegiate Athletic Association.

Brown, M. T. (2012). *Enlisting Masculinity: The Construction of Gender in US Military Recruiting Advertising during the All-Volunteer Force*. New York, NY: Oxford University Press.

Brown, M. T., Murphy, F. T., Radin, D. M., Davignon, I., Smith, M. D., & West, C. R. (2012). Tanezumab reduces osteoarthritic knee pain: results of a randomized, double-blind, placebo-controlled phase III trial. *Journal of Pain, 13*, 790–798.

Brown, T. N., James, S., Jackson, K. T., Brown, R. M., Sellers, S., Keiper, & Manuel, J. L. (2003). There's no race on the playing field—perceptions of racial discrimination among white and black athletes. *Journal of Sport and Social Issues, 27*(2), 162–183.

Browne, K. (2002). *Biology at work: Rethinking sexual equality*. New Brunswick, NJ: Rutgers University Press.

Brownfield, P. (2013). Briefly a rising star, forever a mourning son. *New York Times*. Retrieved from https://www.nytimes.com/2013/01/02/sports/baseball/sam-khalifa-briefly-a-rising-star-forever-a-mourning-son.html?pagewanted=all&_r=0

Bruce, T. (2004) Marking the boundaries of the "normal" in televised sports: The play-by-play of race. *Media, Culture & Society, 26*(6), 861–879.

Brustad, R. J. (1993). Who will go out and play? Parental and psychological influences on children's attraction to physical activity. *Pediatric Exercise Science, 5*, 210–223.

Brustad, R. J. (1996). Attraction to physical activity in urban schoolchildren: Parental socialization and gender influences. *Research Quarterly for Exercise and Sport, 67*, 316–323.

Bryant, J., & Thompson, S. (2002). *Fundamentals of media effects*. New York, NJ: McGraw-Hill.

Bryant, J., & Zillmann, D. (1984). Using television to alleviate boredom and stress. *Journal of Broadcasting, 28*(1), 1–20.

Bryant, J., & Zillmann, D. (Eds.). (1994). *Media effects*. Hillsdale, NJ: Lawrence Erlbaum.

Bryant, J. & Zillmann, D. (Eds.). (2013). *Perspectives on media effects* (pp. 57–82). Hillsdale, NJ: Lawrence Erlbaum.

Bryson, L. (1987). Sport and the maintenance of masculine hegemony. *Women's Studies International Forum*, *10*, 349–360.

Bucholz, A. (2017). One of the only black female sports editors at a U.S. metro daily has joined ESPN. Awful Announcing. Retrieved from http://awfulannouncing.com/espn/lisa-wilson-black-female-sports-editor-espn.html

Bucholz, A. (2018, June 27). Fox will add Kristina Pink as a sideline reporter on Thursday night football, likely in addition to Erin Andrews. MSN. Retrieved from https://www.msn.com/en-us/sports/nfl/fox-will-add-kristina-pink-as-a-sideline-reporter-on-thursday-night-football-likely-in-addition-to-erin-andrews/ar-AAyl5OP

Buffington, D., & Farley, T. (2008). Skill in black and white: Negotiating media images of race in a sporting context. *Journal of Communication Inquiry*, *32*(3), 292–310.

Bufkin, J. L. (1999). Bias crime as gendered behavior. *Social Justice*, *26*(1), 155–176.

Bugental, D. B., & Hehman, J. A. (2007). Ageism: A review of research and policy implications. *Social Issues and Policy Review*, *1*(1),173–216.

Bugg, J. M., Zook, N. A., DeLosh, E. L., Davalos, D. B., & Davis, H. P. (2006). Age differences in fluid intelligence: Contributions of general slowing and frontal decline. *Brain and Cognition*, *62*(1), 9–16.

Buller, D. J. (2006). *Adapting minds: Evolutionary psychology and the persistent quest for human nature*. Cambridge, MA: MIT Press.

Bullock, K. H., and Jafri, G. J. (2000). Media misrepresentations: Muslim women in Canadian nation. *Canadian Women's Studies*, *20*(2), 35–40.

Burfoot, D. (1992). White men can't run. *Runner's World*. Retrieved from http://homepage.westmont.edu/hoeckley/readings/symposium/pdf/301_400/341.pdf

Burge, C. M., Carey, M. F., & Payne, W. R. (1993). Rowing performance, fluid balance, and metabolic function following dehydration and rehydration. *Medicine and Science in Sports and Exercise*, *25*(12), 1358–1364.

Burgess, E. (1950). Personal and social adjustment in old age. In M. Derber (Ed.), *The aged and society* (pp. 138–156). Champaign, IL: Industrial Relations Research Association.

Burk, R. F. (2002). *Much more than a game: Players, owners and American baseball since 1921*. Chapel Hill: University of North Carolina Press.

Burkhardt, R. (2016). The impact of poverty on participation in extracurricular activities. Manuscript submitted in partial fulfillment of the requirements for the degree of master of education. Retrieved from https://mdsoar.org/bitstream/handle/11603/3087/BurkhardtRandi_paper.pdf?sequence=1

Burnham, R., Newell, E., & Steadward, R. (1991). Sports medicine for the physically disabled: the Canadian team experience at the 1988 Seoul Paralympics Games. *Clinical Journal of Sports Medicine*, *1*(3), 193–196.

Burnham, R., Wheeler, G., Bhambhani, Y., Belanger, M., Eriksson, P., & Steadward, R. (1994). Intentional induction of autonomic dysreflexia among quadriplegic athletes for performance enhancement: Efficacy, safety, and mechanisms for action. *Clinical Journal of Sport Medicine*, *4*, 1–10.

Burnham, R. S., May, L., Nelson, E., Steadward, R. D., & Reid, D. C. (1993). Shoulder pain in wheelchair athletes: The role of muscle imbalance. *American Journal of Sport Medicine*. *21*, 238–242.

Burnstein, E., Crandall, C., & Kitayama, S. (1994). Some neo-Darwinian decision rules for altruism: Weighting cues for inclusive fitness as a function of the biological importance of the decision. *Journal of Personality and Social Psychology*, *67*(5), 773–789.

Burgos, A. P. (2007). *Playing America's game: Baseball, Latinos, and the color line*. Berkeley, CA: University of California Press.

Burr, V. (2003). *Social constructionism* (2nd ed.). London, United Kingdom: Routledge.

Burton, L. J., Barr, C. A., Fink, J. S., & Bruening, J. E. (2009). Think athletic director, think masculine? Examination of the gender typing of managerial sub-roles within athletic administration positions. *Sex Roles*, *61*(5–6), 416–426.

Bush, M. E. (2011). *Everyday forms of whiteness: Understanding race in a "post-racial" world* (2nd ed.). New York, NY: Rowman & Littlefield.

Bushman, B. J., & Huesmann, L. R. (2006). Short-term and long-term effects of violent media on aggression in children and adults. *Archives of Pediatrics and Adolescent Medicine, 160*(4), 348–352. doi:10.1001/archpedi.160.4.348

Bushner, B. J. (2002). Does venting anger feed or extinguish the flame? Catharsis, rumination, distraction, anger, and aggressive responding. *Personality and Social Psychology Bulletin, 28*(6), 724–731. doi: 10.1177/0146167202289002

Buss, D. M. (1989). Sex Differences in human mate preferences: Evolutionary hypothesis tested in 37 cultures. *Behavioral and Brain Sciences, 12*(1), 1–49.

Butler, R. N. (1969). Age-ism: Another form of bigotry. *The Gerontologist, 9*, 243–246.

Butler, R. N. (2009). Combating ageism. *International Psychogeriatrics, 21*(2), 211.

Buysse, J. M., & Embser-Herbert, M. S. (2004). Constructions of gender in sport: An analysis of intercollegiate media guide cover photographs. *Gender & Society, 18*(1), 66–81. doi: 10.1177/0891243203257914

Buzinski, J. (2016). Vanderbilt hires Stephanie White, openly lesbian, as women's basketball coach. *Outsports*. Retrieved from https://www.outsports.com/2016/5/26/11790442/vanderbilt-hires-stephanie-white-openly-lesbian--womens-basketball-coach

Buzinski, J. (2017). Homophobia is elephant in room in women's basketball, gay Final Four assistant says. *Outsports*. Retrieved from https://www.outsports.com/2017/3/31/15141800/ncaa-women-final-four-melanie-balcomb-homophobia

Buzzini, S. R. R, & Guskiewicz, K. M. (2006). Sports-related concussion in the young athlete. *Current Opinion in Pediatrics, 18*, 376–382

Byrne, J. (2003). *O god of players: The story of the immaculata mighty macs.* New York, NY: Columbia University Press.

Byrne, P. (1997) Psychiatric stigma: past, passing and to come. *Journal of the Royal Society of Medicine, 90*, 618–620

Byrne, P. (2000). Stigma of mental illness and ways of diminishing it. *Advances in Psychiatric Treatment, 6*(1), 65–72. doi:10.1192/apt.6.1.65

Caesar, D. (2017). An astounding turn: After Rams arrived, fewer people watched the NFL in LA. *St. Louis Post-Dispatch*. Retrieved from https://www.stltoday.com/sports/football/professional/an-astounding-turn-af-ter-rams-arrived-fewer-people-watched-the/article_677f2d53-d614-5968-8930-bf-4180d34ebc.html

Cahn, S. (1994). *Coming on strong: Gender and sexuality in twentieth-century women's sport.* New York, NY: Free Press.

Calkins, H., & Zipes, D. P. (2001). Hypotension and syncope. In E. Brawunwald, E. D. Zipes, & P. Libby (Eds.) *Heart disease: A textbook of cardiovascular medicine* (6th ed., pp. 932–939). Philadelphia, PA: W. B. Sanders Company.

Callahan, M. (2015, June 14). How pro athletes lose everything. *NY Post*. Retrieved from https://nypost.com/2015/06/14/how-pro-athletes-lose-everything-buying-cars-jewels-and-pet-tigers/

Campbell, E., & Jones, G. (1994). Psychological well-being in sport participants and nonparticipants. *Adapted Physical Activity Quarterly, 11*, 404–415.

Campbell, J. A. (2009). Model of consequences of dementia caregivers' stress process: Influence on behavioral symptoms of dementia and caregivers' behavior-related reactions. *Research and Theory for Nursing Practice, 23*(3), 181–202.

Campus Pride Athlete Report. (2012). *2012 LGBTQ national college athlete report.* Campus Pride. Retrieved from https://www.campuspride.org/wp-content/uploads/CampusPride-Athlete-Report-Exec-Summary.pdf

Capraro, R. L. (2000). Review of theorizing masculinities, In S. R. Harper & F. Harris III (Eds.), *College men and masculinities, theory, research, and implications for Practice* (pp. 989–1089). San Francisco, CA: Jossey-Bass.

Capraro, R., & Capraro, M. (2002). Myers-Briggs type indicator score reliability across studies: A meta-analytic reliability. *Educational and Psychological Measurement, 62*(4), 590–602.

Card, N. A., Stucky, B. D., Sawalani, G. M., & Little, T. D. (2008). Direct and indirect aggression during childhood and adolescence: A meta-analytic review of gender differences, intercorrelations, and relations to maladjustment. *Child Development, 79*(5), 1185–1229. doi:10.1111/j.1467-8624.2008.01184.x

Cardinali, R, & Gordon, Z. (2002). Ageism: No longer the equal opportunity stepchild. *Equal Opportunities International, 21*(2), 58–68.

Carey, J. (2002). American journalism on, before, and after September 11. In B. Zelizer & S. Allan (Eds.), *Journalism after September 11* (pp. 71–90). London, United Kingdom: Routledge.

Carleton College Physical Education. (2018). Athletics and recreation transgender policy for intercollegiate athletics, club sports and intramural sports. Retrieved from https://apps.carleton.edu/campus/rec/club/assets/Copy_of_Transgender_Policy__Carleton_PEAR_Feb2017.docx.pdf

Carlon, S., Shields, N., Dodd, K., & Taylor, N. (2013). Differences in habitual physical activity levels of young people with cerebral palsy and their typically developing peers: A systematic review. *Disability Rehabilitation, 35,* 647–655. doi: 10.3109/09638288.2012.715721

Carlston, D. E. (1983). An environmental explanation for race differences in basketball performance. *Journal of Sport and Social Issues, 7,* 30–51.

Caron, E. (2018, October 3). Highest-paid NCAA football coaches: Nick Saban, Urban Meyer … and Lovie Smith? *Sports Illustrated.* Retrieved from https://www.si.com/college-football/2018/10/03/nick-saban-urban-meyer-jim-harbaugh-jimbo-fisher-highest-paid-football-coaches-2018

Carrigan, T., Connell, R. W., & Lee, J. (1985). Toward a new sociology of masculinity. *Theory and Society, 14*(5), 551–604.

Carrington, B. (1986). Social mobility, ethnicity and sport. *British Journal of Sociology of Education, 7*(1), 3–18.

Carrington, B., & McDonald, I. (Eds.). (2001). *Race, sport, and British society.* London, United Kingdom: Routledge.

Carstensen, L. L., & Mikels, J. A. (2005). At the intersection of emotion and cognition. *Current Directions in Psychological Science, 14*(3), 117–121.

Carter, J. E. L. (1970). The somatotype of athletes. *Human Biology, 24,* 534–569.

Carvalho, A. (2000). *Discourse analysis and media texts.* International Conference on Logic and Methodology. International Sociology Association. Köln. Retrieved from https://www.sfu.ca/cmns/courses/marontate/2010/801/1-Readings/Carvahlo_Discourse%20Analysis%203.pdf

Casey, D. M., Ripke, M. N., & Huston, A. C. (2005). Activity participation and the well-being of children and adolescents in the context of welfare reform. In J. L. Mahoney, R. W. Larson, & J. S. Eccles (Eds.), *Organized activities as contexts of development: Extracurricular activities, after-school and community programs* (pp. 65–84). Mahwah, NJ: Erlbaum.

Cashmore, E. (2002). *Sport psychology: The key concepts.* London, United Kingdom: Routledge.

Castillo, D. (2011). Rashad Evans' joke about the Penn State scandal is no laughing matter. Bloody Elbow. Retrieved from https://www.bloodyelbow.com/2011/12/7/2618810/rashad-evans-joke-about-the-penn-state-scandal-is-no-laughing-matter

CBC. (2007). International soccer body to discuss Quebec hijab ban. CBC News. Retrieved from http://www.cbc.ca/canada/story/2007/02/28/soccerhijab.html

CBC. (2012, January 12). Timeline: Same-sex rights in Canada. CBC News. Retrieved from http://www.cbc.ca/news/canada/timeline-same-sex-rights-in-canada-1.1147516

CBS Broadcast Group. (1974). *Fat Albert and the Cosby kids.* New York, NY: CBS Office of Social Research.

CBS News. (2014a). Did Rams apologize to police for hands-up gesture? *CBS News.* Retrieved from https://www.cbsnews.com/news/st-louis-rams-apologize-for-players-ferguson-hands-up-dont-shoot/

CBS News. (2014b). Donald Sterling banned for life by the NBA for "deeply disturbing" comments. *CBS News.* Retrieved from https://www.cbsnews.com/news/donald-sterling-banned-for-life-by-the-nba-for-deeply-disturbing-comments/

Centers for Disease Control and Prevention. (2003). Public health and aging: Trends in aging—United States and worldwide. *Mortality and Morbidity Weekly Report, 52,* 101–106.

Centers for Disease Control and Prevention. (2011, January 25). Lesbian, gay, bisexual, and transgender health. CDC. Retrieved from http://www.cdc.gov/lgbthealth/youth.htm

Chad, N. (2017). The problem with the rapid expansion of professional soccer in America. *Washington Post.* Retrieved from https://www.washingtonpost.com/sports/the-problem-with-the-rapid-expansion-of-

professional-soccer-in-america/2018/05/06/
f690dfe0-50d2-11e8-84a0-458a1aa9ac0a_story.
html?utm_term=.283506e1d875

Chaffee, S. (1984). Defending the indefensible.
Society, 21(6), 30–35.

Chambers, M. (1995). *The unplayable lie: The
untold story of women and discrimination in
American golf*. New York, NY: Golf Digest.

Chandrasekaran, S., Krishnaswamy Anbanandan
Suthakar, A., & Balakrishnan, A. (2010). A study
of socio-economic status and psychological
factors potentates the playing ability among
low and high performers of state level football
players. *Journal of Experimental Sciences*, 1(12),
22–28.

Channon, A., & Matthews, C. R. (2015). "It is
what it is:" Masculinity, homosexuality, and
inclusive discourse in mixed martial arts.
Journal of Homosexuality, 62(7), 936–956. doi:
10.1080/00918369.2015.1008280

Charness, G, & Villeval, M. (2009). Coopera-
tion and competition in intergenerational
experiments in the field and the laboratory.
The American Economic Review, 99(3),
96–978.

Chawansky, M. A. (2011). *Gender and sport fact
sheet*. Retrieved from https://socwomen.org/
wp-content/uploads/2018/03/fact_02-2011-
sport.pdf

Cheong, P. (2007). Gender and perceived Internet
efficacy. *Women's Studies in Communication*,
30(2), 205–228.

Chernoff, H. (1954). On the distribution of the
likelihood ratio statistic. *Annals of Mathematical
Statistics*, 25, 573–578.

Cheung C, & Kwan, A. Y. (2009). The erosion of
filial piety by modernization in Chinese cities.
Ageing and Society, 29, 179–198.

Chidester, D. (2005). *Authentic fakes: Religion and
American popular culture*. Berkeley, CA: University of California Press.

Chu, D., & Segrave, J. (1980). Leadership recruitment and ethnic stratification in basketball.
Journal of Sport and Social Issues, 4, 13–22.

Chu, J., Porche, M. V., & Tolman, D. L. (2005). The
adolescent masculinity ideology in relationships
scale. *Men and Masculinities*, 8(1), 93–115. doi:
10.1177/1097184X03257453

Clair, M., & Denis, J. S. (2015). Sociology of
racism. In J. D. Wright (Ed.), *The international
encyclopedia of the social and behavioral sciences*
(pp. 857–863), Amsterdam, The Neverlands:
Elsevier.

Clark, M. A. (2013). Winning! How important is
it in youth sports? ResearchGate. Retrieved from
https://www.researchgate.net/publication/
267254862_Winning_How_Important_Is_It_
in_Youth_Sports

Clarke, J. (2001). Social problems: Sociological
perspectives. In M. May, R. Page, & E. Brunsdon
(Eds.), *Understanding social problems: Issues in
social policy* (pp. 3–15). Oxford, United Kingdom: Blackwell Publishers Ltd.

Clausell, E., & Fiske, S. T. (2005). When do sub-
group parts add up to the stereotypic whole?
Mixed stereotype content for gay male sub-
groups explains overall ratings. *Social Cognition*,
23, 161–181.

Cleveland, J. N., & Landy, F. J. (1983). The effects
of person and job stereotypes on two personnel
decisions. *Journal of Applied Psychology*, 68(4),
609–619.

Clyne, I. D. (2003). Muslim women: Some western fictions. In H. Jawad & T. C. Benn (pp.
131–150), Muslim women in the United
Kingdom and beyond. Leiden-Boston,
Netherlands: Brill.

CNN News. (2011). FIFA defends hijab ban after
Iranian team forfeits Olympic qualifier. CNN.
Retrieved from http://edition.cnn.com/2011/
SPORT/football/06/07/football.iran.hijab.fifa/
index.html

Coakley, J. (2001). *Sport in Society*. New York: Mc
Graw-Hill.

Coakley, J. J. (1992). Burnout among adolescent
athletes: A personal failure or social problem? *Sociology of Sport Journal*, 9, 271–285.

Coakley, J. J. (2007). *Sports in society: Issues &
controversies*. New York City, NY: McGraw-Hill
Higher Education.

Coakley, J. J. (2009). *Sports in society: Issues and
controversies* (2nd Canadian ed.). New York, NY:
McGraw-Hill.

Cock, A. (2004, September 1). *Serena courts rebel
image. Herald Sun* (Melbourne, Australia).
Retrieved from http://www.lexisnexis.com.
ezproxy.lib.indiana.edu/hottopics/lnacademic/

Cockburn, C. (1983). *Brothers: Male dominance
and technological change*. London, United Kingdom: Pluto.

Coenen, C. R. (2005). *From sandlots to the Super Bowl: The National Football League, 1920–1967*. Knoxville, TN: University of Tennessee Press.

Cohan, W. (2014, July 24). Power of the punch: A messy tale of money, space and race. *The Economist*. Retrieved from http://www.economist.com/news/books-and-arts/21600649-messy-tale-money-sport-and-race-power-punch

Cohen, A. (2009, November 7). Age bias gets second-class treatment. *New York Times*. Retrieved from https://www.nytimes.com/2009/11/07/opinion/07sat4.html?mtrref=www.google.com&gwh=852912212CBE6B8304B2CF5687C13A3C&gwt=pay

Cohen, B. (1963). *The press, the public and foreign policy*. Princeton, NJ: Princeton University Press.

Cohen, P. N., & Huffman, M. L. (2007). Working for the woman? Female managers and the gender wage gap. *American Sociological Review, 72*, 681–704.

Colburn, K. (1986). Deviance and legitimacy in ice hockey: A microstructural theory of deviance. *The Sociological Quarterly, 27*, 63–74.

Coleman, A. (2016). The tragic history behind Michael Jordan's statement on police shootings. *Time*. Retrieved from http://time.com/4424493/michael-jordan-statement-history/

Coleman, R. P., & Rainwater, L. (1978). *Social standing in America*. New York, NY: Basic Books.

Collette-Pratt C. (1976). Attitudinal predictors of devaluation of old age in a multigenerational sample. *Journal of Gerontology, 31*, 193–197.

Collier, R. (1998). *Masculinities, crime, and criminology: Men, heterosexuality and the criminal(ised) other*. London, United Kingdom: Sage.

Collins, D. (1997) *Conference report*. National Disability Sport Conference, Kings Fund Centre, London, United Kingdom.

Comeau, T. D., & Kemp, C. L. (2007). Intersections of age and masculinities in the information technology industry. *Ageing & Society, 27*, 215–232.

Commission on Obscenity and Pornography. (1970). *The report of the commission on obscenity and pornography*. Washington, DC: U.S. Government Printing Office.

Comstock, G. (2008). A sociological perspective on television violence and aggression. *American Behavioral Scientist, 51*(8), 1184–1211.

Comstock, G., Chaffee, S., & Katzman, N. (1978). *Television and human behavior*. New York, NY: Columbia University Press.

Comstock, G., & Paik, H. (1991). *Television and the American child*. New York, NY: Academic Press.

Condry, J. (1989). *The psychology of television*. Hillsdale, NJ: Lawrence Erlbaum.

Connell, R. (2009). *Gender*, 2nd edition. Polity Press, Medord, MA.

Connell, R. W. 1982. Class, patriarchy, and Sartre's theory of practice. *Theory and Society, 11*, 305–320.

Connell, R. W. (1983). *Which way is up? Essays on sex, class, and culture*. Sydney, Australia: Allen and Unwin.

Connell, R. W. (1987). *Gender and power: Society, the person, and sexual politics*. Malden, MA: Polity Press

Connell, R. W., 1995. *Masculinities*. Berkeley, CA: University of California Press.

Connell, R. W. (2001). The social organization of masculinity. In S. Whitehead & F. Barrett (Eds.), *The masculinities reader* (pp. 30–50). Cambridge, United Kingdom: Polity Press.

Connell, R. W. (2002). *Gender*. Cambridge, United Kingdom: Polity Press.

Connell, R. W. (2005). *Masculinities*, 2nd edition. Berkeley, CA: University of California Press.

Connell, R. W., & Messerschmidt, J. W. (2005). Hegemonic masculinity: Rethinking the concept. *Gender and Society, 19*(6): 829–859.

Connell, R. W. (1987). *Gender and power: Society, the person and sexual politics*. Stanford, CA: Stanford University Press

Connelly, C. (2014). Mizzou's Michael Sam says he's gay. ESPN. Retrieved from http://www.espn.com/espn/otl/story/_/id/10429030/michael-sam-missouri-tigers-says-gay

Conroy, D. E., & Coatsworth, J. D. (2006). Coach training as a strategy for promoting youth social development. *Sport Psychologist, 20*, 128–144.

Consalvo, M., (2003). The monsters next door: Media constructions of boys and masculinity. *Feminist Media Studies, 3*(1), 27–45.

Constantine, M. G., & Ladany, N. (2000). Self-reported multicultural counseling competence scales: Their relation to social desirability attitudes and multicultural case conceptualization ability. *Journal of Counseling Psychology, 47,* 155–164.

Constantine, M. G., Smith, L., Redington, R. M., & Owens, D. (2008). Racial microaggressions against black counseling and counseling psychology faculty: A central challenge in the multicultural counseling movement. *Journal of Counseling & Development, 86,* 348–355.

Contemporary Feminist Theories. (2011) Contemporary feminist theories. Retrieved from http://www.umsl.edu/~keelr/3210/3210_lectures/feminism.html

Cook, T., Kendzierski, D., & Thomas, S. (1983). The implicit assumptions of television research. *Public Opinion Quarterly, 47*(2), 161–201.

Cooley, C. H. (1902). *Human nature and the social order.* New York, NY: Scribner.

Cooper, D. and Canepri, Z. (2016). *T-Rex: Her fight for gold.* Available from http://www.pbs.org/independentlens/films/t-rex-her-fight-for-gold/

Cooper, M., Hunt, K., & O'Bryant, C. P. (2007). Women in coaching: Exploring female athletes' interest in the profession. *Chronicle of Kinesiology and Physical Education in Higher Education, 18*(2), 8, 17–19.

Cortese, A. (1997, May 5). A census in cyberspace. *Business Week,* 3525, 84–85.

Côté, J., Baker, J., & Abernethy, B. (in press). Practice and play in the development of sport expertise. In R. Eklund & G. Tenenbaum (Eds.), *Handbook of sport psychology* (3rd edition) (pp. 184–202). Hoboken, NJ: Wiley.

Côté, J., Baker, J., & Abernethy, B. (2003). From play to practice: A developmental framework for the acquisition of expertise in team sport. In J. Starkes & K.A. Ericsson (Eds.), *Recent advances in research on sport expertise* (pp. 89–114). Champaign, IL: Human Kinetics.

Côté, J., & Fraser-Thomas, J. (2007). Youth involvement in sport. In P.R.E. Crocker (Ed.), *Introduction to sport psychology: A Canadian perspective* (pp. 266–294). Toronto, Canada: Pearson Prentice Hall.

Côté, J., & Hancock, D. J. (2016). Evidence-based policies for youth sport programs. *International Journal of Sport Policy and Politics, 8*(1), 51–65.

Côté, J., & Hay, J. (2002). Children's involvement in sport: A developmental perspective. In J.M. Silva & D.E. Stevens (Eds.), *Psychological foundations of sport* (pp. 484–502). Boston, MA: Allyn & Bacon.

Côté, J., MacDonald, D., Baker, J., & Abernethy, B. (2006). When "where" is more important than "when": Birthplace and birthdate effects on the achievement of sporting expertise. *Journal of Sport Sciences. 24*(10), 1065–1073.

Cottrell, C. A., & Neuberg, S. L. (2005). Different emotional reactions to different groups: A socio-functional threat-based approach to prejudice. *Journal of Personality and Social Psychology, 88*(5), 770–789.

Coulomb-Cabagno, G., & Rascle, O. (2006). Team sports players' observed aggression as a function of gender, competitive level, and sport type. *Journal of Applied Social Psychology, 36*(8), 1980–2000. doi: 10.1111/j.0021-9029.2006.00090.x

Council for Europe. (1987). *European charter for sport for all: Disabled persons.* Council of Europe Publishing: Strasbourg Cedex, France.

Coupland, N., Coupland, J. (1993). Discourses of ageism and anti-ageism. *Journal of Aging Studies, 7*(3), 279–301.

Coupland, J., Coupland, N., Giles, H., & Henwood, K. (1991). Formulating age: Dimensions of age identity in elderly talk. *Discourse Processes, 14,* 87–106.

Courier Mail. (2012). Saudi women allowed to compete at London Olympics. *Courier Mail.* Retrieved from http://www.couriermail.com.au/sport/saudi-women-allowed-to-compete-at-london-olympics/story-fn9di2lk-1226407284586

Cournoyer, R. J., & Mahalik, J. R. (1995). Cross-sectional study of gender role conflict examining college-aged and middle-aged men. *Journal of Counseling Psychology, 42*(1), 11–19. doi: 0022-0167/95/$3.00

Course Hero (2018, July 18). Law the principles to which they adhere in other. Course Hero. Retrieved from https://www.coursehero.com/file/p317qmmo/law-the-principles-to-which-they-adhere-in-other-words-he-or-she-must-believe/

Coyne, A. C., Reichman, W. E., & Berbig, L. J. (1993). The relationship between dementia and elder abuse. *American Journal of Psychiatry, 150,* 643–646.

Crasnick, J. (2016, December 22). Did Curt Schilling tweet his way out of Cooperstown? ESPN. Retrieved frorm http://www.espn.com/mlb/story/_/id/18326987/controversy-surrounding-curt-schilling-clouds-cooperstown-case-hall-fame-voters

Creapeau, R. (2014). *NFL football: A history of America's new national pastime.* Urbana, IL: University of Illinois.

Crenshaw, K. W. (1991). Mapping the margins: Intersectionality, identity politics, and violence against women of color. *Stanford Law Review, 43*(6), 1241–1299.

Creswell, J. W. (1998). *Qualitative inquiry and research design: Choosing among five traditions.* Thousand Oaks, CA: Sage.

Critical Media Project. (2017). *Class activities.* Retrieved from http://criticalmediaproject.org/diy-activities/

Crocker, J., Major, B., & Steele, C. (1998). Social stigma. In D. T. Gilbert, S. T. Fiske, & G. Lindzey (Eds.), *The handbook of social psychology* (4th edition, Vol. 2, pp. 504–553). New York, NY: McGraw-Hill.

Crosset, T. W. (1995). *Outsiders in the clubhouse: The world of women's professional golf.* Albany, NY: State University of New York Press.

Crossett, T. (1999). Male athletes' violence against women: A critical assessment of the athletic affiliation, violence against women debate. *Quest, 51*(3), 244–257. doi: 10.1080/00336297.1999.10491684

Crouch, I. (2016, April 21). Curt Schilling, Internet embarrassment. *New Yorker.* Retrieved from https://www.newyorker.com/sports/sporting-scene/good-riddance-curt-schilling

Crouch, I. (2017). Patriots owner Robert Kraft's balancing act. *New Yorker.* Retrieved from https://www.newyorker.com/sports/sporting-scene/patriots-owner-robert-krafts-balancing-act

Csikszentmihalyi, M., Rathunde, K., & Whalen, S. (1993). *Talented teenagers: The roots of success and failure.* Cambridge, United Kingdom: Cambridge University Press.

Cuddy, A.J.C., & Fiske, S. T. (2004). Doddering but dear: Process, content, and function in stereotyping of older persons. In T. D. Nelson (Ed.), *Ageism: Stereotyping and prejudice against older persons* (pp. 3–26). Cambridge, MA: MIT Press.

Cuddy, A.J.C., Fiske, S.T., & Glick, P. (2007). The BIAS map: Behaviors from intergroup affect and stereotypes. *Journal of Personality and Social Psychology, 92*(4), 631–648.

Cuddy, A.J.C., Fiske, S. T., Kwan, V.S.Y., Glick, P., Demoulin, S., Leyens, J. P., et al. (2009). Stereotype content model across cultures: Towards universal similarities and some differences. *British Journal of Social Psychology, 48*(1), 1–33.

Cuddy, A.J.C, Norton, M. I., & Fiske, S. T. (2005). This old stereotype: The pervasiveness and persistence of the elderly stereotype. *Journal of Social Issues, 61*(2), 267–285.

Culpepper, C. (2016, August 1). Sarah Attar, who made history in London, plans to go long in Rio. *Washington Post.* Retrieved from https://www.washingtonpost.com/sports/olympics/sarah-attar-who-made-history-in-london-plans-to-go-long-in-rio/2016/08/01/7d7c10d6-572b-11e6-831d-0324760ca856_story.html?utm_term=.632fd9d75c8e

Cunningham, G. (2015). LGBT inclusive athletic departments as agents of social change. *Journal of Intercollegiate Sport, 8*(1), 43–56. doi:10.1123/jis.2014-0131.

Cunningham, G. B. (2011a). *Consumers' attraction to LGBT-inclusive fitness clubs.* Paper presented at the Annual Conference of the Sport Marketing Association, Houston, TX.

Cunningham, G. B. (2011b). Creative work environments in sport organizations: The influence of sexual orientation diversity and commitment to diversity. *Journal of Homosexuality, 58,* 1041–1057.

Cunningham, G. B. (2011c). The LGBT advantage: Examining the relationship among sexual orientation diversity, diversity strategy, and performance. *Sport Management Review, 14,* 453–461.

Cunnigham, G. B. (2012). Sexual orientation and gender identity in sport. Static. Retrieved from http://static.squarespace.com/static/53e51960e4b0f38ca4081a61/t/53e827c1e4b00c61990ad538

Cunningham, G. B. (2012). A multilevel model for understanding the experiences of LGBT sport participants. *Journal for the Study of Sports and Athletes in Education, 6,* 5–20.

Cunningham, G. B. & Bopp, T. (2010). Race ideology perpetuated: Media representations of newly hired football coaches. *Journal of Sports Media* 5(1), 1–19.

Cunningham, G. B., & Melton, E. N. (2011). The benefits of sexual orientation diversity in sport organizations. *Journal of Homosexuality, 58,* 647–663.

Cunningham, G. B. & Sagas, M. (2008). Gender and sex diversity in sport organizations: Introduction to a special issue. *Sex Roles, 58*(1–2), 3–9. doi: 10.1007/s11199-007-9360-8

Cunningham, G. B., Sartore, M. B., & McCullough, B. P. (2010). The influence of applicant sexual orientation, applicant gender, and rater gender on ascribed attributions and hiring recommendations of personal trainers. *Journal of Sport Management, 24,* 400–415.

Curtis, J., McTeer, W., & White, P. (1999). Exploring effects of school sport experiences on sport participation later in life. *Sociology of Sport Journal, 16,* 348–365.

Cutliffe, J. R., & Hannigan, B. (2001). Mass media, "monsters" and mental health clients: The need for increased lobbying. *Journal of Psychiatric and Mental Health Nursing, 8*(4), 315–321.

CyberStats (1998). Spring '98. Media Mark. Retrieved from www.mediamark.com/pages/cs

D'Andrea, C. (2017, July 14). Patriots White House visit 2017: Recap and highlights from meeting with President Trump: Trump was happy to celebrate his favorite NFL team. SB Nation. Retrieved from https://www.sbnation.com/nfl/2017/4/19/15359100/patriots-visits-white-house-2017-highlightsrecap-donald-trump

D'Angelo, P. & Lombard, M. (2008). The power of the press: the effects of press frames in political campaign news on media perception. *Atlantic Journal of Communication, 16*(1), 1–32.

Daddario, G. (1994) Chilly scenes of the 1992 Winter Games: the mass media and the marginalisation of female athletes. *Sociology of Sport Journal, 11*(3), 275–88.

Daddario, G. (1998). *Women's sport and spectacle: Gendered television coverage and the Olympic Games.* Westport, CT: Praeger.

Dadigan, K. (2016). Professional athletes are affecting our youth. Foot Hill Dragon Press. Retrieved from http://foothilldragonpress.org/athletes-play-an-important-role-on-our-youth/

Daily Mail. (2012). Ramadan "will cause even more transport chaos during the Olympics as worshippers squeeze on to non-Games lanes." *Daily Mail.* Retrieved from http://www.dailymail.co.uk/news/article-2176531/Ramadan-2012-add-Londons-Olympic-transport-woes.html

Daily Mail Sport. (2011). Angry Iran complain to FIFA after women's team banned from playing due to Islamic kit. *Daily Mail.* Retrieved from http://www.dailymail.co.uk/sport/football/article-1394915/Iran-complain-FIFA-womens-team-ban-Islamic-kit.html

Daley, A. (2017). ESPN ponders the future of female sports journalism. *The Stylus.* Retrieved from http://www.brockportstylus.org/news/article/current/2017/03/28/100242/espn-ponders-the-future-of-female-sports-journalism

Dane-Staples, E., Lieberman, L., Ratcliff, J., & Rounds, K. (2013). Bullying experiences of individuals with visual impairment: The mitigating role of sport participation. *Journal of Sport Behavior, 36*(4), 365–386.

Daniels, E. A. (2009). The indivisibility of women athletes in magazines for teen girls. *Women in Sport & Physical Activity Journal, 18*(2), 14–24, Retrieved from https://www.questia.com/library/journal/1G1-220136034/the-indivisibility-of-women-athletes-in-magazines

Daniels, E. A. (2012). Sexy versus strong: What girls and women think of female athletes. *Journal of Applied Developmental Psychology, 33,* 79–90.

Daniels, E. A., & LaVoi, N. M. (2013). Athletics as solution and problem: Sports participation for girls and the sexualization of female athletes. In E. Zurbriggen & T. Roberts (Eds.), *The sexualization of girls and girlhood.* (pp. 63–83). Oxford, United Kingdom: Oxford University Press.

Danielson, M. N. (1997). *Home team: Professional sports and the American metropolis.* Princeton, NJ: Princeton University Press.

Danjou, A. (2018). Why Instagram is the main social platform in sport. Digital Sport. Retrieved from https://digitalsport.co/intagram-sport-clubs-leagues-athletes

Dardis, C. M., Edwards, K. M., Kelley, E. L., & Gidycz, C. A. (2013). Dating violence perpetration: The predictive roles of maternally versus paternally perpetrated childhood abuse and subsequent dating violence attitudes and behaviors. *Journal of Aggression, Maltreatment & Trauma, 2,* 6–25. doi:10.1080/10926771.2013.743948

Dardis, C. M., Murphy, M. J., Bill, A. C., & Gidycz, C. A. (2015). An investigation of the tenets of social norms theory as they relate to sexually aggressive attitudes and sexual assault perpetration: A comparison of men and their friends. *Psychology of Violence, 6*(1). doi: 10.1037/a0039443

Das, A. (2016, April 21). Pay disparity in U.S. soccer? It's complicated. *New York Times.* Retrieved from https://www.nytimes.com/2016/04/22/sports/soccer/usmnt-uswnt-soccer-equal-pay.html

Dator, J. (2017). Are NFL players required to be on the field for the national anthem? SB Nation. Retrieved from https://www.sbnation.com/2017/9/24/16358238/nfl-players-national-anthem-requirement

David, A., & Snow, S. (1991). *Media worlds in the postjournalism era* (pp. 9–11). New York, NY: Walter de Gruyter.

Davidson, K. A. (2017). If you thought sports were ever separate from politics, think again. ESPN Online. Retrieved from http://www.espn.com/espnw/voices/article/18614895/if-thought-sports-were-ever.

Davies, R. O. (2012). *Sports in American life: A history.* West Sussex, U.K.: Wiley-Blackwell.

Davis, D. (2017). The story behind the masked horror of the Munich Olympics. Dead Spin. Retrieved from https://deadspin.com/the-story-behind-the-masked-horror-of-the-munich-olympi-1792823912

Davis, H. (2005). *Hardwood.* DVD produced with the assistance of National Film Board of Canada Filmmaker Assistance Program © Hardwood Pictures Inc. and the National Film Board of Canada.

Davis, L. R., & Harris, O. (1998). Race and ethnicity in US sports media. In L. A. Wenner (Ed.), *Mediasport* (pp. 154–169). London, United Kingdom: Routledge.

Davis, P. H. (2010). *Football, the American intercollegiate game.* London, United Kingdom: Nabu Press.

Davis, R. (2017, July 8). 27 most hated coaches of all time. Cheat Sheet. Retrieved from https://www.cheatsheet.com/sports/most-hated-coaches.html/

Davis, S. (2017). Venus and Serena Williams' childhood coach has an amazing story about realizing they could dominate the first time he met them. Business Insider. Retrieved from https://www.businessinsider.com/venus-and-serena-williams-tennis-coach-story-coaching-them-2017-1

Day, C. (2009, March 12). Update: Tentative settlement reached in Aaron O'Neal suit. *Columbia Missourian.* Retrieved from https://www.columbiamissourian.com/news/local/update-tentative-settlement-reached-in-aaron-o-neal-suit/article_e8bf2829-3cec-523e-9d27-ffd9cfa24158.html

Day, J. (2009, October 14). Former UPEI faculty members fight mandatory retirement. *The Guardian.* Retrieved from http://www.theguardian.pe.ca

Dearing, J., & Rogers, E. (1996). *Agenda-setting.* Thousand Oaks, CA: Sage.

de Balcazar, Y. S., Bradford, B., & Fawcett, S. B. (1998). Common concerns of disabled Americans issues and opinions. *Social Policy, 19*(2), 34.

DeBenedette, V. (1987). Are cheerleaders athletes? *Physician and Sportsmedicine, 15,* 214–220.

DeBenedette, V. (1989). People and horses: the risks of riding. *Physician and Sportsmedicine, 17,* 251–255.

DeBenedette, V. (1990). Are your patients exercising too much? *Physician and Sportsmedicine, 18,* 119–122.

DeBock, H. (1980). Gratification frustration during a newspaper strike and a TV blackout. *Journalism Quarterly, 57*(1), 61–66.

DeFleur, M., & DeFleur, L. (1967). The relative contribution of television as a learning source for children's occupational knowledge. *American Sociological Review, 32,* 777–789.

DeFleur, M. L., & Dennis, E. E. (1994). *Understanding mass communication: A liberal arts perspective* (5th ed.). Boston, MA: Houghton Mifflin Company.

De Knop, P., Engström, L. M., & Skirstad, B. (1996). Worldwide trends in youth sport. In P. De Knop, L.-M. Engström, B. Skirstad, & M. Weiss (Eds.), *Worldwide trends in youth sport* (pp. 276–281). Champaign, IL: Human Kinetics.

Delemeester, G. (2008). Do high player salaries cause high ticket prices. Econ Bonus. Retrieved from http://econbonus.blogspot.com/2008/03/do-high-player-salaries-cause-high.html

Delessio, J. (2016, January 4). Brief history of team relocations. Sports on Earth. Retrieved from http://www.sportsonearth.com/article/161900652/la-rams-relocation-major-sports-guide-nfl-mlb

de Luis-Carnicer, P., Martínez-Sánchez, A., Pérez-Pérez, M., & Vela-Jiménez, M. J. (2008). Gender diversity in management: Curvilinear relationships to reconcile findings. *Gender in Management, 23*(8), 583–597.

Delves, A. (1981). Popular recreation and social conflict in Derby, 1800–1850. In E. Yeo & S. Yeo (Eds.), *Popular culture and class conflict 1590–1914: Explorations in the history of labour and leisure* (pp. 89–127). Brighton, United Kingdom: Harvester Press.

Demby, G. (2012). LeBron James tweets picture of Miami Heat Wearing hoodies in solidarity with the family of Trayvon Martin. WZAK Cleveland. Retrieved from https://wzakcleveland.com/3288064/trayvon-martin-lebron-james-and-miami-heat-wearing-hoodies-in-support/

Demetriou, D. Z. (2001). Connell's concept of hegemonic masculinity: A critique. *Theory and Society, 30*(3), 337–361.

DeNavas-Walt, C., Proctor, B. D., & Smith, J. C. (2010). *Income, poverty, and health insurance coverage in the United States: 2009* (Current Population Report P60-238). Washington, DC: U.S. Census Bureau.

Denborough, D. (1996). *Step by step: Developing respectful and effective ways of working with young men to reduce violence.* In C. McLean, M. Carey, & C. White (Eds.), *Men's ways of being* (pp. 91–115). Boulder, CO: Westview.

Denham, B. E., Billings, A. C., & Halone, K. K. (2002). Differential accounts of race in broadcast commentary of the 2000 NCAA men's and women's Final Four basketball tournaments. *Sociology of Sport Journal, 19*(3), 315–332.

Denny, J. (1999, September 9). Media promotes racism by using racist names. In the circle: News from an American Indian perspective (pp. 5–5). Quoted in E. A. Locklear (2012). Native American mascot controversy and mass media involvement: How the media play a role in promoting racism through Native American athletic imagery *Exploration, 7,* 152–159. Retrieved from https://uncw.edu/csurf/Explorations/documents/ElizabethLocklear.pdf

Department of Health and Human Services. (2013). Adolescent physical health and nutrition resources and publications. HHS. Retrieved from https://www.hhs.gov/ash/oah/resources-and-training/adolescent-health-library/physical-health-and-nutrition-resources-and-publications/index.html

Desmond-Harris, J. (2015). Serena Williams, racism, and sexism (double participation). *Ethnic Studies 101.* Retrieved from https://fall2015ces101.wordpress.com/2015/09/11/serena-williams-racism-and-sexism-double-participation/

Desmond-Harris, J. (2017). Despite decades of racist and sexist attacks, Serena Williams keeps winning; she just claimed her 23rd Grand Slam singles title. *Vox.* Retrieved from https://www.vox.com/2017/1/28/14424624/serena-williams-wins-australian-open-venus-record-racist-sexist-attacks

Desronvil, J. (2016, August 12). NFL African-American head coaches win. Hire them. The Good Men Project. Retrieved from https://goodmenproject.com/featured-content/nfl-african-american-head-coaches-win-hire-them-dg/

de Visser, R. O., & McDonnell, E. J. (2013). Man points: Masculine capital and young men's health. *Health Psychology, 32*(1), 5–14.

Devor, A. (1997). *FTM: Female-to-male transsexuals in society.* Bloomington, IN: Indiana University Press.

Devor, A. (2000). How many sexes? How many genders? When two are not enough. Retrieved from http://web.uvic.ca/~ahdevor/HowMany/HowMany.html

de Vreese, C. H. (2005). News framing: Theory and typology. *Information Design Journal + Document Design, 13,* 48–59.

Diaz, A. (2015). ESPN: Jason Whitlock once wrote about Serena Williams being a fat underachiever and it is worse than you could possibly imagine. Retrieved from http://www.complex.com/sports/2015/07/jason-whitlock-serena-williams

Diefenbach, D., & West, M. (2007). Television and attitudes toward mental health issues. *Journal of Community Psychology, 35*(2), 181–195.

Diefenbach, D. L., & West, M. D. (2001). Violent crime and Poisson regression: A measure and a method for cultivation analysis. *Journal of Broadcasting and Electronic Media, 45*(3), 432–445.

Dietrich, S., Heider, D., Matschinger, H., & Angermeyer, M. C. (2006). Influence of newspaper reporting on adolescents' attitudes toward people with mental illness. *Social Psychology and Psychiatric Epidemiology, 41*, 318–322.

DiMatteo, S. (2014). A timeline of the Adrian Petersen child abuse case. SB Nation. Retrieved from www.sbnation.com

Disabled Sports of America. (2018). Retrieved from http://www.disabledsportsusa.org/about/news/challenge-magazine/

DiSalvo, B. J. (2016). Gaming Masculinity: Constructing masculinity with video games. In Y. B. Kafai, G. T. Richard, & B. M. Tynes (Eds.), *Diversifying Barbie and Mortal Kombat: Intersectional perspectives and inclusive designs in gaming* (pp. 105–117). Retrieved from https://www.researchgate.net/publication/316636252_Gaming_Masculinity_Constructing_Masculinity_with_Video_Games

Dishman, R. K., Sallis, J. F., & Orenstein, D. R. (1985). The determinants of physical activity and exercise. *Public Health Reports, 100*, 158–171.

Dittmar, H., Halliwell, E., & Ive, S. (2006). Does Barbie make girls want to be thin? The experimental exposure to images of dolls on the body image of 5- to 8-year-old girls. *Developmental Psychology, 42*(2), 283–292.

Doherty, M., Mitchell, E. A., & O'Neill, S. O. (2011). Attitudes of healthcare workers towards older people in a rural population: A survey using the Kogan Scale. *Nursing Research and Practice*, published online April 14, 2011. doi: 10.1155/2011/352627.

Dolcos, F., & McCarthy, G. (2006). Brain systems mediating cognitive interference by emotional distraction, *Journal off Neuroscience, 26*(7), 2072–2079.

Dollard, J., Doob, L., Miller, N., Mowrer, O., & Sears, R. (1939). *Frustration and aggression.* New Haven, CT: Yale University Press.

Doll-Tepper, G. (2004). Disability sport. In J. Riordan & A. Kruger (Eds.), *The international politics of sport in the twentieth century* (pp. 177–190). New York, NY: E & FN Spon.

Domonoske, C. (2016). Watch: Andy Murray reminds interviewer that women win gold, too. NPR. Retrieved from http://www.npr.org/sections/thetorch/2016/08/15/490056480/watch-andy-murray-reminds-interviewer-that-women-win-gold-too

Donaldson, J. (1981). The visibility and image of handicapped people on television. *Exceptional Children, 47*(6), 413–416.

Donaldson, M. (1993). What is hegemonic masculinity? *Theory and Society, Special Issue: Masculinities, 22*(5), 643–657.

Donaldson, M. (2003). *Male trouble: Looking at Australian masculinities* (pp. 180–199). Melbourne, Australia: Pluto Press.

Donlon, M. M., Ashman, O., & Levy, B. R. (2005). Re-vision of older television characters: A stereotype-awareness intervention. *Journal of Social Issues, 61*, 307–319.

Donnerstein, E., Linz, D., & Penrod, S. (1987). *The question of pornography: Research findings and policy implications.* New York, NY: Free Press.

Dorfman, L. Wallack, L., & Woodruff, K. (2005). More than a message: framing public health advocacy to change corporate practices. *Health Education Behavior, 32*(3), 320–336. doi: 10.1177/1090198105275046.

Dow, B. J., & Wood, J. T. (Eds.). (2006). *The SAGE handbook of gender and communication.* Thousand Oaks, CA: Sage.

Drake, R.F. (1994). The exclusion of disabled people from positions of power in British voluntary organisations. *Disability and Society, 9*, 461–490.

Dreher, G. (2003). Breaking the glass ceiling: The effects of sex ratios and work-life programs on female leadership at the top. *Human Relations, 56*(5), 541–562.

DuBois, C. (2016). "Soft" affirmative action in the National Football League. OUPblog. Retrieved from https://blog.oup.com/2016/06/affirmative-action-hiring-nfl/

DuBois, C. C. (2017). *The impact of the Rooney Rule: far beyond the NFL.* Post-Gazette. Retrieved from https://www.post-gazette.com/opinion/Op-Ed/2017/04/30/The-impact-of-the-Rooney-Rule-far-beyond-the-NFL/stories/201704300145

Dumas, B. (2018). Former ESPN host Jemele Hill lands gig with LeBron James. *The Blaze.* Retrieved from https://www.theblaze.com/news/2018/09/20/former-espn-host-jemele-hill-lands-gig-with-lebron-james

Duncan, L. A., & Schaller, M. (2009). Prejudicial attitudes toward older adults may be exaggerated when people feel vulnerable to infectious disease: Evidence and implications. *Analyses of Social Issues and Public Policy*, 9(1), 97–115.

Duncan, M. C. (1990). Sports photographs and sexual difference: Images of women and men in the 1984 and 1988 Olympic Games. *Sociology of Sport Journal*, 7(1), 22–43.

Duncan, M. C., & Hasbrook, C. (1988). Denial of power in televised women's sport. *Sociology of Sport Journal*, 5, 1–21.

Duncan, M. C., & Messner, M. A. (1998). The media image of sport and gender. In L. A. Wenner (Ed.), *Mediasport* (pp. 170–185). London, England and New York, NY: Routledge.

Duncan, M. C., Messner, M. A., & Williams, L. (1991). *Coverage of women's sports in four daily newspapers.* Los Angeles, CA: Amateur Athletic Foundation of Los Angeles.

Dunegan, K. J. (1993). Framing, cognitive modes and image theory: Toward an understanding of a glass half full. *Journal of Applied Psychology*, 78(3), 491–503.

Dunn, S. (2009). Candidate and media agenda setting in the 2005 Virginia gubernatorial election. *Journal of Communication*, 59(3), 635–652.

Dunning, E. & Sheard, K. (1979) *Barbarians, gentlemen and players: A sociological study of the development of rugby football.* New York, NY: New York University Press.

Duquin, M. (1989) Fashion and fitness images in women's magazine advertisements. *Arena Review*, 13, 97–109.

Dworkin, J. B., Larson, R., & Hansen, D. (2003). Adolescents' accounts of growth experiences in youth activities. *Journal of Youth and Adolescence*, 32, 17–26.

Dworkin, S. L. (2001). "Holding back": Negotiating a glass ceiling on women's muscular strength. *Sociological Perspectives*, 44(3), 333–350.

Dworkin, S. L., and Wachs, F. L. (2000). The morality/manhood paradox: masculinity, sports, and the media. In M. A. McKay, M. A. Messner, & D. F. Sabo (Eds.), *Masculinities, gender relations and sport* (pp. 47–66). Thousand Oaks, CA: Sage.

Dychtwald K. (1999). *Age power: How the 21st century will be ruled by the new old.* New York, NY: Tarcher/Putnam.

Dyer, B. (2007). *The top 20 moments in Cleveland sports history: Tremendous tales of heroes and heartbreaks* (pp. 277–291). Cleveland, OH: Gray & Company.

Dyreson, M. (1995). Marketing national identity: The Olympic games of 1932 and American culture. *Olympika: The International Journal of Olympic Studies*, 4, 23–48.

Dyreson, M. (2001). American ideas about race and Olympic races from the 1890s to the 1950s: Shattering myths or reinforcing scientific racism? *Journal of Sport History*, 28(Summer), 173–215.

Dyreson, M. (2006). Jesse Owens: Leading man in modern American tales of racial progress and limits. In D. W. Wiggins (Ed.), *Out of the shadows: A biographical history of the African American Athlete* (pp. 111–132). Fayetteville, AR: University of Arkansas Press.

Dyrli, O. E. (1998). Internet stats making news. *Technology & Learning*, 18(9), 60.

Eagly, A. H. (1987). *Sex differences in social behavior: A social-role interpretation.* Hillsdale, NJ: Erlbaum.

Eastman, S. T., & Billings, A. C. (2000) Sportscasting and sports reporting. The power of gender bias. *Journal of Sport and Social Issues*, 24(2), 192–213.

Eastman, S. T., & Billings, A. C. (2001). Biased voices of sports: Racial and gender stereotyping in college basketball announcing. *Howard Journal of Communications*, 12, 183–204.

Eccles, J. S., & Barber, B. L. (1999). Student council, volunteering, basketball, or marching band: What kind of extracurricular involvement matters? *Journal of Adolescent Research*, 14, 10–43.

Eckes, T. (1994). Features of men, features of women: Assessing stereotypic beliefs about gender subtypes. *British Journal of Social Psychology*, 33(1):107–123.

Edelstein, A. (2017). They can watch hockey: Commentary. *The Barre Montepelier Times Argus*. Retrieved from https://www.timesargus.com/opinion/commentary/they-can-watch-hockey/article_fbcef468-a793-5fa3-acb6-049a2eca2212.html

Edgar, A., & Sedgwick, P. (2002). *Cultural theory: The key concepts.* London, United Kingdom: Routledge.

Edmondson, J. (2005). *Venus and Serena Williams: A biography*. Santa Barbara, CA: ABC-Clio Greenwood Publishers.

Edwards, H. (2003). The sources of the black athlete's superiority. In E. Dunning & M. Dominic (Eds.), *Sport and power relations* (pp. 5–18). London, United Kingdom: Routledge.

Edwards, K. L. (2008). *The elusive dream: The power of race in interracial churches*. New York, NY: Oxford University Press.

Egarter, S. (2017). Nike commercial celebrates Arab female athletes "to inspire others." CNN. Retrieved from https://edition.cnn.com/2017/02/21/middleeast/nike-arab-women-commercial/index.html

Eime, R. M., Charity, M. J., Harvey, J. T., & Payne, W. R. (2015). Participation in sport and physical activity: associations with socio-economic status and geographical remoteness. *BMC Public Health*, *15*, 434. doi.org/10.1186/s12889-015-1796-0

Eitzen, D. S. (2000) Slaves of big time college sports. *USA Today*, 26–30.

Eitzen, D. S. (2001) Big-time college sports: Contradictions, crises and consequences. In D. S. Eitzen (Ed.), *Sport in contemporary society* (6th ed., pp. 201–212). New York, NY: Worth Publishers.

Eitzen, D. S. (2005). *Sport in contemporary society: An anthology* (7th ed.). Boulder, CO: Paradigm Publishers.

Eitzen, D. S. (2009). *Fair and foul: Beyond the myths and paradoxes of sport* (4th ed.). Lanham, MA: Rowman and Littlefield.

Eitzen, D. S. & Sanford, D. C. (1977). The segregation of blacks by playing position in football: accident or design? *Social Science Quarterly*, *55*(4), 948–959.

Elbogen, E. B, & Johnson, S. C. (2009). The intricate link between violence and mental disorder: Results from the national epidemiologic survey on alcohol and related conditions. *Archives of General Psychiatry*, *66*(2), 152–161. doi:10.1001/archgenpsychiatry.2008.537

Eliot, L. (2009). *Pink brain, blue brain: How small differences grow into troublesome gaps—and what we can do about it*. Boston, MA: Houghton Mifflin Harcourt.

Elley, D., & Kirk, D. (2002). Developing citizenship through sport: The impact of a sport-based volunteer program on young sport leaders. *Sport, Education and Society, 7*, 151–166.

Ellison, L. (2001). Senior management in chartered surveying: Where are the women? *Women in Management Review*, *16*(5/6), 264–278.

Elmagd, M., Abubakr, M., Manal, S., Elmarsafawy, T. S., Aljadaan, O. (2015). The impact of physical activity participation on the self-esteem of the students. A cross-sectional study from RAKMHSU—RAK—UAE. *International Journal of Physical Education, Sports and Health*, *2*(1), 87–91.

El Menjaoui, M. (2012, July 24). Ramadan brings fasting dilemma for Muslim Olympic athletes. Middle East Voices. Retrieved from http://www.yourmiddleeast.com/features/ramadan-brings-fasting-dilemma-for-muslim-olympic-athletes_8335

Elmer, V. (2009). Age discrimination claims by workers reach record high. *AARP Bulletin Today*. Retrieved from http://www.aarp.org

Elvin, I. T. (1994). A UK perspective in the development and management of sport for people with a disability. In H. V. Coppenolle, Y. Vanlanderwijck, J. Simons, P. Van de Vliet, & E. Neerinckx (Eds.), *First European conference on adapted physical activity and sports: A white paper on research and practice.* (pp. 205–229). Leuven, Belgium: ACCO.

Elwell, C. K. (2014). The distribution of household income and the middle class (RS20811). Congressional Research Service. Retrieved from https://fas.org/sgp/crs/misc/RS20811.pdf

Encyclopedia Brittanica. (2018, February 25). The Sociology of Sport. Retrieved from https://www.britannica.com/sports/sports/Sociology-of-sports

Endresen, I. M., & Olweus, D. (2005). Participation in power sports and antisocial involvement in preadolescent and adolescent boys. *Journal of Child Psychology and Psychiatry*, *46*, 468–478.

Engle, M. J., McFalls, J. A., Jr., Gallagher, B. J., III, & Curtis, K. (2006). The attitudes of American sociologists toward causal theories of male homosexuality. *The American Sociologist*, *37*(1), 68–67.

Engle, P. L., & Black, M. M. (2008). The effect of poverty on child development and educational outcomes, *Annals of The New York Academy of Sciences, 1136*, 243–256.

English Federation of Disability Sport (EFDS). (1999). *Building a fairer sporting society. Sport for disabled people in England. A four year development plan 2000–2004*. Crewe, United Kingdom: EFDS.

English, J. (2008, July 7). Early media coverage of U2 ('81), the Williams sisters ('90) & Jesse Helms ('66). *Mental Floss*. Retrieved from http://mentalfloss.com/article/19007/early-media-coverage-u2-81-williams-sisters-90-jesse-helms-66.

Entine, J. (2000). *Taboo: Why black athletes dominate sports and why we are afraid to talk about it*. New York, NY: BSS Public Affairs.

Entman, R. M. (1992). Blacks in the news: Television, modern racism, and cultural change. *Journalism Quarterly, 69*, 341–361.

Entman, R. M. (1993). Framing: Toward clarification of a fractured paradigm. *Journal of Communication, 43*(4), 51–58.

Entman, R. M. (2007). Framing bias: Media in the distribution of power. *Journal of Communication, 57*, 163–173.

Entman, R. M., & Gross, K. A. (2008). Race to judgement: Stereotyping media and criminal defendants. *Law and Contemporary Problems, 71*, 94–133.

Entman, R. M., & Rojecki, A. (2000). *The black image in the white mind: Media and race in America*. Chicago, IL: University of Chicago Press.

Epstein, A. (2003). *Sports law*. Delmar Publishing. Retrieved from https://sportslaw.uslegal.com/religion-and-sports-constitutional-and-biblicalissues/

Equality Network. (2018). Creating change together. Equality Network. Retrieved from https://www.equality-network.org

Equality Network. (2018). Intersectionality. Equality Network. Retrieved from https://www.equality-network.org/our-work/intersectional/

Ericsson, K. A., Krampe, R. T., & Tesch-Römer, C. (1993). The role of deliberate practice in the acquisition of expert performance. *Psychological Review, 100*, 363–406.

Erikson, J. M., Erikson, E. H., & Kivnick, H. (1986). *Vital involvement in old age*. New York, NY: W.W. Norton & Co.

Eschman, T. (2016, January 5). No NFL club would be interested in new St. Louis stadium, Rams' LA relocation application states. Belleville News-Democrat. Retrieved from https://www.bnd.com/sports/article53249840.html#storylink=cpy

Espelage, D. L., & Holt, M. K. (2012). Understanding and preventing bullying and sexual harassment in school. *APA Psychology Handbook: Individual Differences and Cultural and Contextual Factors, 2*, 391–416. doi: 10.1037/13274-016

ESPN. (2008). 9-year-old boy told he's too good to pitch. ESPN. Retrieved from http://sports.espn.go.com/espn/pring?id+3553475&type=story

ESPN (2017). Fact sheet. ESPN. Retrieved from https://espnmediazone.com/us/espn-inc-fact-sheet/

ESPN. (2018). The body issue. ESPN. Retrieved from http://www.espn.com/espn/bodyissue

ESPN. (2018). Diversity, inclusion & wellness. ESPN. Retrieved from https://espncareers.com/working-here/diversity-inclusion-wellness

Etaugh, C., & and Bridges, J. (2004). *Women's lives: A topical approach*. Boston, MA: Allyn & Bacon.

Etchells, E. (2017). Professional squash players earning more money than ever before, according to PSA figures. Inside the Games. Retrieved from https://www.insidethegames.biz/articles/1045466/professional-squash-players-earning-more-money-than-ever-before-according-to-psa-figures

Evans, J., & Roberts, G. C. (1987). Physical competence and the development of children's peer relations. *Quest, 39*, 25–35.

Ewing, M. E., & Seefeldt, V. (1996). Patterns of participation and attrition in American agency sponsored youth sports. In F. L. Smoll & R. E. Smith (Eds.), *Children and youth in sport: A biopsychosocial perspective* (pp. 31–45). Dubuque, IA: Brown & Benchmark.

Eyal, C., Winter, J., & DeGeorge, W. (1981). The concept of time frame in agenda setting. In G. Wilhoit & H. deBock (Eds.), *Mass communication review yearbook* (Vol. II). Beverly Hills, CA: Sage.

Fackler, M. (2010, August 14). Japan, checking on its oldest, finds many gone. *New York Times*. Retrieved from http://www.nytimes.com

Fainaru, S., & Fainaru-Wada, M. (2013). *League of denial: The NFL, concussions, and the battle for truth*. New York, NY: Crown Archetype.

Fairclough, N. (1995a). *Critical discourse analysis. The critical study of language.* London, England and New York, NY: Longman.

Fairclough, N. (1995b). *Media discourse.* London, United Kingdom: Edward Arnold.

Falcous, M. (1998) TV made it all a new game: not again! Rugby league and the case of the "Super-league." *Occasional Papers in Football Studies, 1*(1), 4–21.

Falsani, C. (2012). Muslim women Olympians: "This is legacy." Faith in Action for Social Justice. Retrieved from http://sojo.net/blogs/2012/08/02/muslim-women-olympians-legacy

Farmer, S. (2015). Angry, mournful fans in St. Louis give NFL officials an earful. *LA Times.* http://www.latimes.com/sports/sportsnow/la-sp-sn-rams-townhall-20151027-story.html

Farrell, C. (1999, August 9). Women in the workplace: Is parity finally in sight? *Business Week,* p. 35.

Farrell, P. A. (2005, June 22). Free press sports: NBA, players reach a deal; lockout avoided; minimum age for players rose to 19. *Detroit Free Press.* Retrieved from https://usatodayhss.com/author/perry-a-farrell-detroit-free-press

Farrington, K., & Chertok, W. (1993). Social conflict theories of the family. In P.G. Boss, W. J. Doherty, R. LaRossa, W. R. Schumm, & S. K. Steinmetz (Eds.), *Sourcebook of family theories and methods: A contextual approach* (pp. 357–381). New York, NY: Plenum.

Featherman, D. L., & Hauser, R. M. (1978). *Opportunity and change.* New York, NY: Academic Press.

Feminist Majority Newsletter. (1996). German women call for Olympic ban on gender apartheid countries. *Feminist Majority Newsletter, 8*(1), 11–18.

Feminist Theory—An Overview. (1996) Feminist theory—An overview. Victorian Web. Retrieved from http://www.victorianweb.org/gender/femtheory.html

Fenno, N. (2017, March 8). Dean Spanos' decision to move the Chargers to L.A. is the biggest he'll ever make and one he won't escape. *LA Times.* Retrieved from https://www.latimes.com/sports/sportsnow/la-sp-spanos-chargers-20170215-story.html

Ferguson, C. (2007). The good, the bad and the ugly: A meta-analytic review of positive and negative effects of violent video games. *Psychiatric Quarterly, 78*(4), 309–316.

Ferguson, D., & Perse, E. (2000). The world wide web as a functional alternative to television. *Journal of Broadcasting and Electronic Media, 44*(2), 155–176.

Fernea, E. W. (1998). *In search of Islamic feminisms: One woman's global journey.* New York, NY: Doubleday.

Ferrara, M. S. & Buckley, W. E. (1996). Athletes with disabilities injury registry. *Adaptive Physical Activity Quarterly, 13,* 50–60.

Ferrara, M. S. & Davis, R. (1990). Injuries to elite wheelchair athletes. *Paraplegia, 28,* 335–341.

Ferrara, M. S., Buckley, W. E., & McCann, B. C. (1992). The injury experience of the competitive athlete with a disability: Prevention implications. *Medicine and Science in Sports and Exercise, 24*(2), 184–188.

Ferrara, M. S., Buckley, W. E., & Messner, D. G. (1992). The injury experience and training history of the competitive skier with a disability. *American Journal of Sports Medicine, 20*(1), 55–60.

Ferrara, M. S., Palutsis, G. R, & Snouse, S. (2000). A longitudinal study of injuries to athletes with disabilities. *International Journal of Sports Medicine, 21*(3), 221–224.

Ferrara, M. S., Richter, K. J., & Kaschalk, S. M. (1997). Sport for the athlete with a physical disability. In G. Scuderi, P. McCann, & P. Bruno (Eds.), *Sports medicine: Principles of primary care* (pp. 598–608). Philadelphia, PA: Mosby-Year Book.

Fetter, H. (2003). *Taking on the Yankees. Winning and losing in the business of baseball, 1903–2003.* New York, NY: W. W. Norton.

Fine, G.A. (1987). *With the boys: Little league baseball and preadolescent culture.* Chicago, IL: University of Chicago Press.

Fine, M. & Weis, L. (1998). *The unknown city: Lives of poor and working class young adults.* Boston, MA: Beacon Press.

Fink, J. S. (1998). Female athletes and the media: Strides and stalemates. *Journal of Physical Education, Recreation, & Dance, 69,* 37–45.

Fink, J. S. (2015). Female athletes, women's sport, and the sport media commercial complex: Have we really "come a long way, baby?" *Sport Management Review, 18*(3), 331–342.

Fink, J. S., & Kensicki, L. J. (2002). An imperceptible difference: Visual and textual constructions of femininity in *Sports Illustrated* and *Sports Illustrated for Women*. *Mass Communication & Society, 5*, 317–339. https://doi.org/10.1207/S15327825MCS0503_5

Finn, J. D. (1993). *School engagement and students at risk*. Washington, DC: National Center for Education Statistics.

Finn, S. (1997). Origins of media exposure. *Communication Research, 24*(5), 507–529.

Firat, A. F. (1994). Gender and consumption: Transcending the feminine? In J. A. Costa (Ed.), *Gender issues and consumer behavior* (pp. 205–228). Thousand Oaks, CA: Sage.

Firestone, J., & Shelton, B. A. (1994). A comparison of women's and men's leisure time: Subtle effects of the double day. *Leisure Sciences, 16*, 45–60.

Fischer, E., & and Gainer, B. (1994). Masculinity and the consumption of organized sports. In J. A. Costa (Ed.), *Gender issues and consumer behavior* (pp. 84–103). Thousand Oaks, CA: Sage.

Fischtein, D., Edward, H., & Serge, D. (2007). How much does gender explain in sexual attitudes and behaviors? A survey of Canadian adults. *Archives of Sexual Behaviour, 36*, 451–461.

Fisher L. A., Knust S. K., & Johnson A. J. (2013). Theories of gender and sport. In E. A. Roper (Ed.), *Gender relations in sport. Teaching gender* (pp. 1–20). Rotterdam, Netherlands: Sense Publishers.

Fisher-French, M. (2009, July 26). Lowering pension age "is a risky business." *Mail & Guardian*. Retrieved from http://www.mg.co.za

Fisher, H. (1999). *The first sex: The natural talents of women and how they are changing the world*. New York, NY: Random House.

Fisher, T. D., Moore, Z. T., & Pittenger, M. (2011). Sex on the brain?: An examination of frequency of sexual cognitions as a function of gender, erotophilia, and social desirability. *Journal of Sex Research, 49*(1), 69–77.

Fiske, S. T., Cuddy, A. J., Glick, P., & Xu, J. (2002). A model of (often mixed) stereotype content: Competence and warmth respectively follow from perceived status and competition. *Journal of Personality and Social Psychology, 82*, 878–902.

Fiske, S. T., Cuddy, A.J.C., & Glick, P. (2007). Universal dimensions of social perception: Warmth and competence. *Trends in Cognitive Science, 11*, 77–83.

Flanagan, L. (2017, September 28). What's lost when only rich kids play sports. *The Atlantic*. Retrieved from https://www.theatlantic.com/education/archive/2017/09/whats-lost-when-only-rich-kids-play-sports/541317/

Flanagin, A. J., & Metzger, M. J. (2000). Perceptions of Internet information credibility. *Journalism and Mass Communication Quarterly, 77*(3), 515–540.

Flanagin, N. (2010). Masculine and feminine constructions in sports. Noah Flanigan. Retrieved from https://noahflanigan.wordpress.com/2010/04/11/masculine-and-feminine-constructions-in-sports/

Florio, M. (2016). Packers ownership structure works well, until it doesn't. Pro Football Talk. Retrieved from https://profootballtalk.nbcsports.com/2016/11/26/packers-ownership-structure-works-well-until-it-doesnt/

Fogarty, D. (2011, January 12). ESPN poll: Black, white sports fans see things differently. Sports Grid. Retrieved from https://www.sportsgrid.com/real-sports/nfl/espn-poll-black-white-fans-see-things-differenty-when-it-comes-to-race-and-sports/

Folkes, V. S. (1988). Recent attribution research in consumer behavior. A review and new directions. *Journal of Consumer Research, 14*, 548–565.

Forbes (2018, December 16) #16 Phil Knight and family. *Forbes*. Retrieved from https://www.forbes.com/profile/phil-knight/#1f7d2b581dcb

Forbes, G. B., Adams-Curtis, L. E., Pakalka, A. H., & White, K. B. (2006). Dating aggression, sexual coercion, and aggression-supporting attitudes among college men as a function of participation in aggressive high school sports. *Violence Against Women, 12*(5), 441–455. doi: 10.1177/1077801206288126

Ford, R. (2017, January 15). Behind the numbers: A look at pro football relocations since 1960. Freep. Retrieved from https://www.freep.com/story/sports/nfl/lions/2017/01/15/nfl-relocations/96609592/

Forge, K. L., & Phemister, S. (1987). The effect of prosocial cartoons on preschool children. *Child Study Journal, 17*(2), 83–86.

Foster, I. (2015). Beauty, strength, and power: The shaming, disciplining, and rejection of black women athletes. Wes Scholar. Retrieved from https://wesscholar.wesleyan.edu/cgi/viewcontent.cgi?article=2369&context=etd_hon_theses

Foucault, M. (1980). *The history of sexuality volume 1: An introduction*. New York, NY: Vintage Books.

Fox, K. & Rickards, L. (2004). *Sport and leisure: Results from the sport and leisure module of the 2002 general household survey*. London, United Kingdom: TSO.

Fox, S. (1998). *Big leagues: Professional baseball, football, and basketball in national memory*. Lincoln: University of Nebraska Press.

France24. (2012a). Fasting Muslim athletes face Olympic hurdle of Ramadan. France24. Retrieved from http://www.france24.com/en/20120717-fasting-muslim-athletes-olympic-games-ramadan-london-2012-islam-uk

France24. (2012b). Saudi teenager makes Olympic history in Judo. France24. Retrieved from http://www.france24.com/en/20120803-saudi-arabia-teenager-female-olympic-history-judo-london-2012-abdulrahim-shahrkhani

Francis, C., Pirkis, J., Blood, R. W., Dunt, D., Borley, B., & Stewart, A. (2005). Portrayal of depression and other mental illnesses in Australian nonfiction media. *Journal of Community Psychology*, 33(3), 283–297.

Francis, C., Pirkis, J., Dunt, D., & Blood, R. W. (2001). Mental health and illness in the media: *A review of the literature*. Canberra, Australia: Commonwealth Department of Health and Aged Care.

Franklin, B. A., Fern, A. & Voytas, J. (2004). Training principles for elite senior athletes, *Current Sports Medicine Reports*, 3(3), 173–179.

Franks, J. S. (2000). *Crossing sidelines, crossing cultures: Sport and Asian Pacific American*. Lanham, MD: University Press of America, Inc.

Fraser-Thomas, J., & Côté, J. (2006, September). Youth sports: Implementing findings and moving forward with research, athletic insight: *The Online Journal of Sports Psychology*, 8(3), 12–27. Retrieved from http://www.athleticinsight.com/Vol8Iss3/YouthPDF.pdf

Fraser-Thomas, J., Côté, J., & Deakin, J. (2005). Youth sport programs: An avenue to foster positive youth development. *Physical Education and Sport Pedagogy*, 10, 19–40.

Fredricks, J. A., & Eccles, J. S. (2005). Family socialization, gender, and sport motivation and involvement. *Journal of Sport & Exercise Psychology*, 27, 3–31.

Fredricks, J. A. & Simpkins, S. D. (2012). Promoting positive youth development through organized after-school activities: Taking a closer look at participation of ethnic minority youth. *Child Development Perspectives*, 6(3), 280–287. doi: 10.1111/j.1750-8606.2011.00206.x

Fredrickson, B. L., & Roberts, T-A. (1997). Objectification theory: Toward an understanding women's lived experiences and mental health risks. *Psychology of Women Quarterly*, 21, 173–206.

Friday, W. (2001). Athletics vs. academics: Both sides. *Matrix: The Magazine for Leaders in Education*. Retrieved from http://findarticles.com/p/articles/mi_6_ai_94510120/

Fridell, N. (2017). The story of the Chicago Bulls' downfall. ESPN. Retrieved from http://www.espn.com/nba/story/_/id/21082183/story-chicago-bulls-downfall

Friedlander, B. (1993). Community violence, children's development and mass media. *Psychiatry*, 56(1), 66–81.

Frisby, C. M. (2015). Race and gender in sports. In M. Len-Rios & E. Perry (Eds.), *Cross cultural journalism: Communicating strategically about diversity* (pp. 298–311). London, United Kingdom: Routledge

Frisby, C. M. (2016). Delay of game: A content analysis of coverage of black male athletes by magazines and news websites 2002–2012. *Advances in Journalism and Communications*, 4(4), 2–15.

Frisby, C. M. (2017a). Sexualization and objectification of female athletes on sport magazine covers: Improvement, consistency, or decline? *International Journal of Humanities and Social Science*, 7(5), 1–23.

Frisby, C. M. (2017b). Sacrificing dignity for publicity: Portrayals of female athletes on *Sports Illustrated* and *ESPN the Magazine* covers from 2012–2016. *Advances in Journalism and Communication*, 5(2), 120–125. doi: 10.4236/ajc.2017.52007

Frisby, C. M. (2017c) A content analysis of Serena Williams and Angelique Kerber's racial and sexist microaggressions. *Open Journal of Social Sciences*, 5, 263–281. https://doi.org/10.4236/jss.2017.55019

Frisby, C. M. (2018). "Oh see what we say": A content analysis of partisan media's framing of the take a knee silent protest by the NFL, *American International Journal of Humanities and Social Science*, *4*(3), 6–18.

Frisby, C. M., & Engstrom, E. (2006). Always a bridesmaid and never a bride: Portrayals of women of color as brides in bridal magazines. *Media Report to Women*, *34*(4), 10.

Frisby, C. M., & Wanta, W. (2017). Media hype and its influence on athletic performance. *Advances in Journalism and Communication*, *6*(1), 1–18. Doi: 10.4236/ajc.2018.61001

Friis, H. (1991). The changing elderly in a changing Danish society. *Ageing International*, *18*(1), 25–32.

Fujioka, Y. (2005) Black media images as a perceived threat to African American ethnic identity: Coping responses, perceived public perception, and attitudes towards affirmative action. *Journal of Broadcasting & Electronic Media*, *49*(4), 450–467. doi: 10.1207/s15506878jobem4904_6

Fujioka, Y., R., Agle, E., Legaspi, M., & Toohey, R. (2009). The role of racial identity in responses thin media ideals: Differences between white and black college women. *Communication Research*, *36*(4), 451–474. https://doi.org/10.1177/0093650209333031

Funk, J. B., & Buchman, D. D. (1996). Playing violent video and computer games and adolescent self-concept. *Journal of Communication*, *46*(2), 19–32.

Gaertner, S. L., Dovidio, J. F. (1986). The aversive form of racism. In J. F. Dovidio & S. L. Gaertner (Eds.), *Prejudice, discrimination, and racism* (pp. 61–89). Orlando, FL: Academic Press.

Gage, E. A. (2008). Gender attitudes and sexual behaviors: Comparing center and marginal athletes and nonathletes in a collegiate setting. *Violence Against Women*, *14*(9), 1014–1032. Doi: 10.1177/1077801208321987

Gaines, C. and Nudelman, M. (2017). The number of minority head coaches in the NFL is back up to an all-time high. Business Insider. Retrieved from https://www.businessinsider.com/nfl-black-head-coaches-rooney-rule-2017–12

Gamson, J. (2000). Sexualities, queer theory, and qualitative research. In N. K. Denzin & Y. S. Lincoln (Eds.), *Handbook of qualitative research* (2nd ed., pp. 347–365). Thousand Oaks, CA: Sage.

Gamson, W. A. (1992). *Talking politics*. Cambridge, United Kingdom: Cambridge University Press.

Gamson, W. A., Croteau, D., Hoynes, W., & Sasson, T. (1992). Media images and social construction of reality. *Annual Review of Sociology*, *18*(2), 373–393.

Gamson, W. A., & Modigliani, A. (1989). Media discourse and public opinion on nuclear power: A constructionist approach. *American Journal of Sociology*, *95*, 1–37.

Gandhi, L. (2013). Are you ready for some controversy?: The history of "Redskin." NPR. Retrieved from https://www.npr.org/sections/codeswitch/2013/09/09/220654611/are-you-ready-for-some-controversy-the-history-of-redskin

Gannon, M. (2016). Race is a social construct. *Scientific American*. Retrieved from https://www.scientificamerican.com/article/race-is-a-social-construct-scientists-argue/

Garber, G. (2012, August 28). Thirty no longer a death sentence. ESPN. Retrieved from http://www.espn.com/tennis/usopen12/story/_/id/8311320/us-open-thirty-no-longer-death-sentence-tennis

Gardyn, R. (2001). A league of their own. *American Demographics*, 23 (March), 12–13.

Garrett, R. & Danziger, J. (2008). *Gratification and disaffection: Understanding personal Internet use at work*. Paper presented to the International Communication Association in Montreal, Quebec, Canada.

Gatta, G., Benelli, P., & Ditroilo, M. (2006). The decline of swimming performance with advancing age: A cross-sectional study. *Journal of Strength and Conditioning Research*, *20*, 932–938.

Gaugler, J. E., Leach, C. R., & Anderson, K. A. (2005). Family. In E. B. Palmore, L. G. Branch, & D. K. Harris (Eds.), *Encyclopedia of ageism* (pp. 147–151). Binghamton, NY: Haworth Press.

Gay, Lesbian, Straight Education Network (2017). *2017 national school climate survey*. GLSEN. Retrieved from https://www.glsen.org/article/2017-national-school-climate-survey-1

Gearhart, S., & Zhang, W. (2015). "Was it something I said?" "No, it was something you posted!" A study of the spiral of silence theory in social media contexts. *Cyberpsychology, Behavior, and Social Networking*, *18*(4), 208–213. https://doi.org/10.1089/cyber.2014.0443

Geewax, M. (2015). The tipping point: Most Americans no longer are middle class. NPR. Retrieved from https://www.npr.org/sections/thetwo-way/2015/12/09/459087477/the-tipping-point-most-americans-no-longer-are-middle-class

Gehring, J. (2004). Education week, American education's newspaper of record. *Editorial Projects in Education, 23*(23), 3.

Geiger, W., Harwood, J., & Hummert, M. L. (2006). College students' multiple stereotypes of lesbians: A cognitive perspective. *Journal of Homosexuality, 51*(3), 165–182.

Gelb, S. (1989). Language and the problem of male salience in early childhood classroom environments. *Early Childhood Research Quarterly, 4*(2), 205–215.

Geoghegan, T. (2011, June 19). Get radical: Raise social security. *New York Times.* Retrieved from http://www.nytimes.com

Gerbner, G. (1970). Cultural indicators: The case of violence in television drama. *Annals of the American Academy of Political and Social Science, 388,* 69–81.

Gerbner, G. (1972). Violence in television drama: Trends and symbolic functions. In G. A. Comstock, & E. Rubinstein (Eds.), *Television and social behavior: Content and control* (Vol. 1, pp. 28–187). Washington, DC: U.S. Government Printing Office.

Gerbner, G., & Gross, L. (1976). Living with television: The violence profile. *Journal of Communication, 26*(2), 173–179.

Gerbner, G., Gross, L., Eleey, M. F., Jackson-Beeck, M., Jeffries-Fox, S., & Signorielli, N. (1977). TV violence profile no. 8. *Journal of Communication, 27*(2), 171–180.

Gerbner, G., Gross, L., Jackson-Beeck, M., Jeffries-Fox, S., & Signorielli, N. (1976). Cultural indicators: Violence profile no. 9. *Journal of Communication, 28*(3), 176–207.

Gerbner, G., Gross, L., Morgan, M., & Signorielli, N. (1986). Living with television: The dynamics of the cultivation process. In J. Bryant & D. Zillmann (Eds.), *Perspectives on media effects* (pp. 17–40). Hillsdale, NJ: Lawrence Erlbaum.

Gerschick, T. J., & Miller, A. S. (1994). Gender identities at the crossroads of masculinity and physical disability. *Masculinities, 2*(1), 34–55.

Gerson, W. (1966). Mass media socialization behavior: Negro-white differences. *Social Forces, 45,* 40–50.

Ghanem, S. (1997). Filling in the tapestry. The second level of agenda setting. In M. McCombs, D. Shaw, & D. Weaver (Eds.), *Communication and democracy* (pp. 3–15). Mahwah, NJ: Lawrence Erlbaum.

Gibson, H., Willming, C., & Holdnak, A. (2002). "We're Gators ... Not just Gator fans": Serious leisure and University of Florida football. *Journal of Leisure Research, 34,* 397–425.

Giddens, A. (1993). *Sociology.* Cambridge, United Kingdom: Polity Press.

Gidén, C. & Houda, P. (2010). Stick and ball game timeline. *Society for International Hockey Research, 4,* 1–12.

Gilbert, D. (2011). *The American class structure in an age of growing inequality* (8th ed.). Thousand Oaks, CA: Pine Forge Press.

Gilbert, W. D., Gilbert, J. N., & Trudel, P. (2001a). Coaching strategies for youth sports. Part 1: Athlete behavior and athlete performance. *JOPERD, 72,* 29–33.

Gilbert, W. D., Gilbert, J. N., & Trudel, P. (2001b). Coaching strategies for youth sports. Part 2: Personal characteristics, parental influence, and team organization. *JOPERD, 72,* 41–46.

Gilboa, E. (2009). Media and Conflict Resolution: A framework for analysis, *Communication and Conflict, 11*(2), 37–51.

Giles, H., Fox, S., Harwood, J., & Williams, A. (1994). Talking age and aging talk: Communicating through the life span. In M. Hummert, J. Wiemann, & J. Nussbaum (Eds.), *Interpersonal communication in older adulthood: Interdisciplinary theory and research* (pp. 192–212). Manchester, United Kingdom: Manchester University Press.

Girl. (2018). In *Merriam Webster.com.* Retrieved from https://www.merriam-webster.com/dictionary/girl

Gitmez, A. S., & Morcol, G. (1994). Socioeconomic status and life satisfaction in Turkey *Social Indicators Research, 31,* 77–98.

Glasspiegel, R. (2013, July 29). Getting owned: 10 sports team owners who were suspended, banned, or forced to sell. *Sports Illustrated.* Retrieved from https://www.si.com/extra-mustard/2013/07/29/

getting-owned-10-sports-team-owners-who-were-suspended-banned-or-forced-to-sell

GLBT Resource Center of Michiana. (2018). The difference between transgender and transsexual. GLBT Resource Center of Michiana. Retrieved from http://www.michianaglbtcenter.org/difference-transgender-transexual/

GLBT Resource Center of Michiana (2018). *The most gay-friendly cities in the world.* GLBT Resource Center of Michiana. Retrieved from http://www.michianaglbtcenter.org

Global Sports Jobs. (2018). Inspiring, educating and innovating for the international business of sport. Global Sports Jobs. Retrieved from https://www.globalsportsjobs.com

Global Sports Jobs Insight Team. (2018). Life after sport: Athlete transition into the working world. Global Sports Jobs. Retrieve from https://www.globalsportsjobs.com/article/how-athletes-transition-from-sport-to-the-working-world/

GLSEN. (2018). GLBT Resource Center game changers. GLSEN. Retrieved from https://www.glsen.org/sports/game-changers

Goffman, E. (1963). *Stigma; Notes on the management of spoiled identity.* Englewood Cliffs, NJ: Prentice-Hall.

Goggin, G. & Newell, C. (2005). *Disability in Australia: Exposing an Australian apartheid.* Sydney, Australia: UNSW Press.

Goffman, E. (1977). The arrangement between the sexes. *Theory and Society*, 4(Fall), 301–331.

Golant, A., Christoforous, D. C., Slover, J. D., & Zuckerman, J. D. (2010). Athletic participation after hip and knee arthroplasty. *Bulletin of the NYU Hospital for Joint Diseases*, 68(2), 76–83.

Goldberg, A. (2017). Gender & sports: female athletes. Competitive Edge. Retrieved from https://www.competitivedge.com/gender-sports-female-athletes

Goldlust, J. (1987) *Playing for keeps: Sport, the media and society.* Melbourne, Australia: Longman.

Golle, K., Granacher, U., Hoffmann, M., Wick, D., & Muehlbauer, T. (2014). Effect of living area and sports club participation on physical fitness in children: A 4 year longitudinal study. *BMC Public Health*, 14(1), 834–850. doi:10.1186/1471-2458-14-499

Goodman, F., Fields, D., & Blum, T. (2003). Cracks in the glass ceiling: In what kinds of organizations do women make it to the top? *Group & Organization Management*, 28(4), 475–501.

Goodman, H. A. (2016). 70 percent of NFL players are black men. Colin Kaepernick: Should be praised, not condemned. Huffington Post. Retrieved from https://www.huffingtonpost.com/entry/70-of-nfl-players-are-black-men-colin-kaepernick_us_57c7b12be4b07addc4114047

González, G. L., Jackson, E. N., & Regoli, R. M. (2007). The transmission of racist ideology in sport: Using photo-elicitation to gauge success in professional baseball. *Journal of African American Studies*, 10(3), 46–57.

Gordon, J. A. (2017, September 21). Transforming the understanding and treatment of mental illnesses. NIMH. Retrieved from https://www.nimh.nih.gov/health/statistics/mental-illness.shtml

Gormley, W. (1975). Newspaper agendas and political elites. *Journalism Quarterly*, 52(2), 304–308.

Gould, D. (1987). Understanding attrition in children's sport. In D. Gould & M. R. Weiss (Eds.), *Advances in pediatric sport sciences: Behavioral issues* (Vol. 2., pp. 61–85). Champaign, IL: Human Kinetics.

Gould, D., Udry, E., Tuffey, S., & Loehr, J. (1996). Burnout in competitive junior tennis players: A quantitative psychological assessment. *Sport Psychologist*, 10, 322–340.

Goyette, B. (2014). LA Clippers owner Donald Sterling's racist rant caught on tape: Report. Huffington Post. Retrieved from www.huffingtonpost.com/2014/04/26/donald-sterling-racist_n_5218572.html

Graham, B. A. (2011). Rashad Evans makes joke about Penn State scandal at UFC on Fox presser. *Sports Illustrated.* Retrieved from https://www.si.com/boxing/counter-punch/2011/12/08/rashad-evans-makes-joke-about-penn-state-scandal-at-ufc-on-fox-presser

Grant, D. (2018, August 28). The Cubs had an awkward LGBTQ fan night with their new homophobic second baseman. Queerty. Retrieved from https://www.queerty.com/cubs-awkward-lgbtq-fan-night-new-homophobic-second-baseman-20180828

Grappendorf, H., Henderson, A., Sanders, S. & Peel, J. (2007). Is it equitable online? The media coverage of the 2007 NCAA division I basketball tournament on foxsports.com. *Smart Journal*, *5*(1), 30–42.

Grasso, M. (2018, March 12). Stick to sports: The character clause, and why Curt Schilling is being blackballed from the Hall of Fame. Retrieved from https://www1.villanova.edu/villanova/law/academics/sportslaw/commentary/sls_blog/2018/0314.html

Gratton, C, & Jones, I. (2010). *Research methods for sports studies*. New York, NY: Routledge.

Grau, S., Roselli, G., & Taylor, C. R. (2007). Where's Tamika Catchings? A content analysis of female athlete endorsers in magazine advertisements. *Journal of Current Issues & Research in Advertising (CTC Press)*, *29*(1), 55–65.

Gray, E. (2016, August 8). Stop attributing the success of women Olympians to men. Huffington Post. Retrieved from https://www.huffingtonpost.in/entry/women-olympians-dont-need-men-to-be-badass_us_57a87489e4b03ba68012ccbb

Gray, H. (1995). *Watching race: Television and struggle over blackness*. Minneapolis: University of Minnesota Press.

Gray, J. J., & Ginsberg, R. L. (2007). Muscle dissatisfaction: An overview of psychological and cultural research and theory. *Muscular Ideal: Psychological Social, and Medical Perspectives*, pp. 15–39.

Green, C. A., & Ferber, M. A. (2008). The long-term impact of labor market interruptions: How crucial is timing? *Review of Social Economy*, *66*, 351–379.

Green, L. (2015). Top ten sports law issues impacting school athletics programs. NFHS. Retrieved from https://www.nfhs.org/articles/top-ten-sports-law-issues-impacting-school-athletics-programs/

Green, L. (2016). Prayer, religion-related activities at school athletics events, national federation of state high schools association. NFHS. Retrieved from https://www.nfhs.org/articles/prayer-religion-related-activities-at-school-athletics-events/

Greenberg, C. (2014, April 28). Heat players protest Donald Sterling in show of solidarity with Clippers players. Huffington Post. Retrieved from https://www.huffingtonpost.com/2014/04/28/heat-players-protest-donald-sterling_n_5229297.html

Greenberg, J., Schimel, J., Mertens, A. (2004). Ageism: Denying the face of the future. In T. D. Nelson (Ed.), *Ageism: Stereotyping and prejudice against older persons* (pp. 27–48). Cambridge, MA: MIT Press.

Gregory, S. (2014, July 30). Meet the first woman to run a major U.S. pro sports union. *Time*. Retrieved from http://time.com/3060207/michele-roberts-nbpa-basketball/

Grenoble, R. (2015). Olympic silver medalist Gus Kenworthy comes out as gay. Huffington Post. Retrieved from https://www.huffingtonpost.com/entry/gus-kenworthy-gay_us_5629013fe-4b0aac0b8fbdc00.

Griffin, E. (1997). *A first look at communication theory*. New York, NY: McGraw-Hill Companies.

Grindstaff, L., & West, E. (2006). Cheerleading and the gendered politics of sport. *Social Problems*, *53*, 500–518.

Grindstaff, L. & West, E. (2011). Hegemonic masculinity on the sidelines of sport. *Sociology Compass*, *5*(10), 859–881.

Groes-Green, C. (2009). Hegemonic and subordinated masculinities: Class, violence and sexual performance among young Mozambican men. *Nordic Journal of African Studies*, *18*(4), 286–304. Retrieved from http://www.njas.helsinki.fi/pdf-files/vol18num4/groes-green.pdf

Groes-Green, C. (2012). Philogynous masculinities: Contextualizing alternative manhood in Mozambique. *Men and Masculinities*, *15*(2), 91–111. Retrieved from http://jmm.sagepub.com/content/15/2/91

Grose, T. K. (2007, March 18). Straight facts about the birds and bees. *US News and World Report*. Retrieved from http://www.usnews.com/usnews/news/articles/070318/26sex.htm

Groshek, J. (2009). The democratic effects of the Internet, 1994–2003. *International Communication Gazette*, *71*(3), 115–136.

Gross, K. (2008). Framing persuasive appeals: Episodic and thematic framing, emotional response, and policy opinion. *Political Psychology*, *29*(2), 169–192. https://doi.org/10.1111/j.1467-9221.2008.00622.x

Gross, L., & Morgan, M. (1985). Television and enculturation. In J. Dominick & J. Fletcher (Eds.), *Broadcasting research methods* (pp. 221–234). Boston, MA: Allyn & Bacon.

Grossmann, I., Na, J., Varnum, M.E.W., Park, D. C., Kitayama, S., & Nisbett, R. E. (2010). Reasoning about social conflicts improves into old age. *Proceedings of the National Academy of Sciences, 107*(16), 7246–7250.

Grudeva, M. (2010). Social aspects of extracurricular activities for youth. *Trakia Journal of Sciences, 8,* 400–405.

Gruneau, R. (1989a). Making spectacle: A case study in television sports production. In L. Wenner (Ed.), *Media, sports and society* (pp. 134–56). London, United Kingdom: Sage.

Gruneau, R. (1989b). Television, the Olympics and the question of ideology. In R. Jackson & T. McPhail (Eds.), *The Olympic movement and the mass media: Past, present and future issues* (pp. 23–34). Calgary, Alberata: Hurford Enterprises.

Gruneau, R., Whitson, D., & Cantelon, H. (1988). Methods and media: Studying the sports/television discourse. *Society and Leisure, 11*(2), 265–281.

Grunert, S. C. (1994). On gender differences in eating behavior as compensatory consumption. In J. A. Costa (Ed.), *Gender issues and consumer behavior* (pp. 63–83). Thousand Oaks, CA: Sage Publications.

The Guardian. (2012, January 14). The Secret Footballer: It is time we gave up on our tackle obsession. *The Guardian.* Retrieved from https://www.theguardian.com/global/blog/2012/jan/13/the-secret-footballer-tackle-obsession

The Guardian. (2012, March 18). Ramadan and the Olympics: To fast or not to fast?" *The Guardian.* Retrieved from http://www.theguardian.com/lifeandstyle/2012/jul/22/ramadan-olympics-fasting

The Guardian. (2018, December 13). Tyson's hatred for rape-case woman. *The Guardian.* Retrieved from https://www.theguardian.com/sport/2003/may/29/boxing.

Guilbert, S. (2006). Violence in sports and among sportsmen: A single or two-track issue? *Aggressive Behavior, 32*(3), 231–240. doi: 10.1002/ab.20121

Gunderson, A., Tomkowiak, J., Menachemi, N., & Brooks, R. (2005). Rural physicians' attitudes toward the elderly: Evidence of ageism? *Quality Management in Health Care, 14*(3), 167–176.

Guo, J. (2016). The real secret to Asian American success was not education. *Washington Post.* Retrieved from https://www.washingtonpost.com/news/wonk/wp/2016/11/19/the-real-secret-to-asian-american-success-was-not-education/?utm_term=.04a26db80049

Guskiewicz, K. M., Weaver, N. L., Padua, D. A., & Garrett, W. E. (2000). Epidemiology of concussion in collegiate and high school football players, *American Journal of Sports Medicine, 28*(5), 643–650.

Guthrie, J. (2004). Congress may need to set baseball's drug-test rules. *San Francisco Chronicle.* Retrieved from https://www.sfgate.com/sports/article/Giambi-admitted-taking-steroids-2631890.php

Gutmann, M. C. (1997). Trafficking in men: The anthropology of masculinity. *Annual Review of Anthropology, 26,* 385–409.

Guttmann, L. (1976). *Textbook of sport for the disabled.* Oxford, United Kingdom: HM & M Publishers.

GVU. (1998). GVU's ninth Internet survey. Retrieved from www.cc.gatech.edu/gvu

Hacker, H. M. (1957). The new burdens of masculinity. *Marriage and Family Living, 19*(3), 227–233.

Hahn, H. (1984). Sport and the political movement of disabled persons examining non-disabled social values. *Arena Review, 8*(1), 1–15.

Halbert, C. (1997). Tough enough and woman enough: Stereotypes, discrimination, and impression management among women professional boxers. *Journal of Sport and Social Issues, 21*(7), 7–36.

Hall, T. A. (2016). Social class and sports. Broken Clipboard. Retrieved from https://brokenclipboard.wordpress.com/2016/04/11/social-class-and-sports-2/

Halliday, P. (1993) Physical education within special education provision—equality and entitlement. In J. Evans (Ed.), *Equality, education and physical education* (pp. 205–217). London, United Kingdom: The Falmer Press.

Hammond, W. P., Gillen, M., & Yen, I. H. (2010). Workplace discrimination and depressive symptoms: A study of multi-ethnic hospital employees. *Race and Social Problems, 2*(1), 19–30. http://doi.org/10.1007/s12552-010-9024-0

Hanke, R. (1992). Redesigning men: Hegemonic masculinity in transition. In S. Craig (Ed.), *Men, masculinity, and the media* (pp. 829–859). Newbury Park, CA: Sage.

Hanlon, A. M. (2013, July 29). The strengths and weaknesses of different social media channels for B2C. Retrieved from https://brainwavegroup.net/2013/07/the-strengths-and-weaknesses-of-different-social-media-channels-for-b2c/

Hanlon, G. (2015, April 9). The perks and perils of owning a small share of a sports team. *Observer*. Retrieved from https://observer.com/2015/04/the-perks-and-perils-of-owning-a-small-share-of-a-sports-team/

Hansberry, M. R., Chen, E., & Gorbien, M. J. (2005). Dementia and elder abuse. *Clinics in Geriatric Medicine, 21*(2), 315–332.

Hanson, M. E. (1995). *Go! fight! win! Cheerleading in American culture*. Bowling Green, OH: Bowling Green State University Popular Press.

Hanson, R. (2009). *Mass communication: Living in a media world* (pp. 80–81). Washington, DC: CQ Press.

Hardin, M., Chance, J., Dodd, J. E., & Hardin, B. (2002). Olympic photo coverage fair to female athletes. *Newspaper Research Journal, 23*, 64–78.

Haridakis, P., & Hanson, G. (2009). Social interaction and co-viewing with YouTube: Blending mass communication reception and social connection. *Journal of Broadcasting & Electronic Media, 53*(2), 317–335.

Hardin, M., Chance, J., Dodd, J. E., & Hardin, B. (2002). Olympic photo coverage fair to female athletes. *Newspaper Research Journal, 23*, 64–78.

Hardin, M., & Greer, J. D. (2009). The influence of gender-role socialization, media use and sports participation on perceptions of gender-appropriate sports. *Journal of Sport Behavior, 32*, 207–226.

Hardin, M., Lynn, S., Walsdorf, K., & Hardin, B. (2002). The framing of sexual difference in *SI for Kids* editorial photos. *Mass Communication & Society, 5*, 341–359.

Hardin, M., Shen, F., & Yu, N. (2008, August 6). *Sex-typing of sports: The influence of gender, participation, and media on visual priming responses*. Paper presented at the annual meeting of the Association for Education in Journalism and Mass Communication, Marriott Downtown, Chicago, IL. Retrieved from http://citation.allacademic.com/meta/p271441_index.html

Harmon, A. (1998, August 30). Internet increases loneliness, researchers find. *Atlanta Journal-Constitution*, p. 18, Section A.

Harper, S. R. (2015, November 11). *Black college football and basketball players are the most powerful people of color on campus*, Retrieved from https://www.washingtonpost.com/posteverything/wp/2015/11/11/black-college-football-and-basketball-players-are-the-most-powerful-people-of-color-on-campus/?utm_term=.0347c5d935cb

Harris, A. H. S., & Thoresen, C. E. (2005). Volunteering is associated with delayed mortality in older people: Analysis of the longitudinal study of aging. *Journal of Health Psychology, 10*, 739–752.

Harrison, K., & Fredrickson, B. L. (2003). Women's sports media, self-objectification, and mental health in black and white adolescent females. *Journal of Communication, 53*(2), 216–232.

Harrison, L., Lee, A. M., & Belcher, D. (1999). Race and gender differences in sport participation as a function of self-schema. *Journal of Sport & Social Issues, 23*(3), 287–307. doi: 10.1177/0193723599233004

Hartman, M. (2017, March 27). Las Vegas Raiders are just latest NFL franchise to gamble on moving. *Daytona Daily News*. Retrieved from https://www.daytondailynews.com/sports/las-vegas-raiders-are-just-latest-nfl-franchise-gamble-moving/t6dlHmCklnFAd97SVUC81O/

Harwood, J. (2000). "Sharp!" Lurking incoherence in a television portrayal of an older adult. *Journal of Language and Social Psychology, 19*, 110–140.

Harwood, J. (2007). *Understanding communication and aging*. Thousand Oaks, CA: Sage Publications, Inc.

Haslam, S. A., Oakes, P. J., Reynolds, K. J., & Turner, J. C. (1999). Social identity salience and the emergence of stereotype consensus. *Personality and Social Psychology Bulletin, 25*, 809–818. http://dx.doi.org/10.1177/0146167299025007004

Hassell, B. L., & Perrewe, P. L. (1995). An examination of beliefs about older workers: Do stereotypes still exist? *Journal of Organizational Behavior, 16*(5), 457–468.

Hatty, S. E. (2000). *Masculinities, violence and culture*, Thousand Oaks, CA: Sage Publications.

Hauptman, J. Lieber, D. L. (Ed.) (2001). "*Women.*" *Etz Hayim: Torah and commentary*. Simi Valley, CA: Jewish Publication Society.

Hautzinger, D. (2018, June 6). The Harlem (Actually Chicago) Globetrotters. Retrieved from https://interactive.wttw.com/playlist/2018/06/06/harlem-actually-chicago-globetrotters

Hawes, K. (1999). History of the NCAA: The NCAA century series. *The NCAA News*. Retrieved from www.ncaa.org/news

Hawkins, R., & Pingree, S. (1981). Using television to construct social reality. *Journal of Broadcasting*, *25*(4), 347–364.

Hazelton, M. (1997). Reporting mental health: A discourse analysis of mental health related news in two Australian newspapers. *Australian & New Zealand Journal of Mental Health Nursing*, *6*(2), 73–89.

Health Education Authority (1999). *Physical activity in our lives. Qualitative research among disabled people*. London, United Kingdom: Health Education Authority.

Hearn, J. (2004). From hegemonic masculinity to the hegemony of men. *Feminist Theory*, *5*(1), 49–72.

Hearn, J., & Morgan, D. H. (1990). *Men, masculinities and social theory*. London, United Kingdom: Unwin Hyman Ltd.

Heath, T. (2006, February 22). Court battle with apparel firm threatens Nats merchandise. *Washington Post*. Retrieved from http://www.washingtonpost.com/wp-dyn/content/article/2006/02/21/AR2006022101721.html

Heeter, C., Brown, N., Soffin, S., Stanley, C., & Salwen, M. (1989). Agenda-setting by electronic text news. *Journalism Quarterly*, *66*(1), 101–106.

Heitner, D. (2015). Sports industry to reach $73.5 billion by 2019. *Forbes*. Retrieved from https://www.forbes.com/sites/darrenheitner/2015/10/19/sports-industry-to-reach-73-5-billion-by-2019/#732b8fa81b4b

Helin, K. (2014, August 13). Court of appeals shoots down Donald Sterling's effort to overturn Clippers sale. *NBC Sports*. Retrieved from https://nba.nbcsports.com/2014/08/13/court-of-appeals-shoots-down-donald-sterlings-effort-to-overturn-clippers-sale/related/

Heller, M., & Polsky, S. (1976). *Studies in violence and television*. New York, NY: American Broadcasting Company.

Helliker, K. (2006, February 11). Older but better. *Wall Street Journal* Online. Retrieved from http://online.wsj.com/article_print/SB113962383641871505.html.

Hellison, D. R. & Cutforth, N. J. (1997). Extended day programs for urban children and youth: From theory to practice. In H. Walberg, O. Reyes, & R. Weissberg (Eds.), *Children and youth: Interdisciplinary perspectives* (pp. 223–249). San Francisco, CA: Jossey-Bass.

Hellstedt, J. C., (1995). Invisible players: A family system model. In S. M. Murphy (Ed.), *Sport psychology interventions* (pp. 117–146). Champaign, IL: Human Kinetics.

Hellsten, J., Dawson, L., & Leydesdorff, L. L. (2010). Implicit media frames: Automated analysis of public debate on artificial sweeteners. *Public Understanding of Science*, *19*(5), 590–608. doi: 10.1177/0963662509343136

Helsen, W. F., Starkes, J. L., & Hodges, N. J. (1998). Team sports and the theory of deliberate practice. *Journal of Sport & Exercise Psychology*, *20*, 12–34.

Helson, R., Kwan, V.S.Y., John, O. P., & Jones, C. (2002). The growing evidence for personality change in adulthood: Findings from research with personality inventories. *Journal of Research in Personality*, *36*, 287–306.

Henderson, K. A. (1996), One size doesn't fit all: The meanings of women's leisure. *Journal of Leisure Research*, *28*(3), 139–154.

Henderson, K. A. (1994). Perspectives on analyzing gender, women, and leisure. *Journal of Leisure Research*, *26*(2), 119–137.

Henkel, F. M. (2005). *Cleveland Browns History*. Mt. Pleasant, SC: Arcadia Publishing.

Henry, P. J., & Sears, D. O. (2000). The symbolic racism 2000 scale. *Political Psychology*, *23*(2), 253–283.

Herdt, G. H. (1981). *Guardians of the flutes: Idioms of masculinity*. New York, NY: McGraw-Hill.

Herzog, H. (1944). What do we really know about daytime serial listeners? In P. Lazarsfeld & F. Stanton (Eds.), *Radio research, 1942–43* (pp. 3–33). New York, NY: Duell, Sloan & Pearce.

Hetsroni, A., & Tukachimski, R. (2006). Television-world estimates, real-world estimates and television viewing. *Journal of Communication*, *56*(1), 133–156.

Hewstone, M., Hantzi, A., & Johnston, L. (1991). Social categorization and person memory: The pervasiveness of race as an organizing principle. *European Journal of Social Psychology*, *21*(6), 517–528, http://dx.doi.org/10.1002/ejsp.2420210606

Hiatt, A. (2012, December 4). Why we should applaud baseball's all-powerful players union. *The Week*. Retrieved from https://theweek.com/articles/469877/why-should-applaud-baseballs-allpowerful-players-union

Higgins, P. C. (1992). *Making disability: Exploring the social transformation of human variation*. Springfield, IL: Charles C. Thomas.

Hilker, A. (1976, November 10). Agenda-setting influence in an off-year election. *ANPA Research Bulletin*, *1*(1), 7–10.

Hill, G. (1988). Celebrate diversity (not specialization) in school sports. *Executive Educator*, *10*, 24.

Hill, G. M., & Hansen, G. F. (1988). Specialization in high school sports—The pros and cons. *Journal of Physical Education, Recreation, & Dance*, *59*, 76–79.

Hill, J. B. (2013). Commentary: Black sports journalists keep hitting the glass ceiling. BET.com. Retrieved from https://www.bet.com/news/sports/2013/03/07/commentary-black-sports-journalists-keep-hitting-the-glass-ceiling.html#!

Hill, R. P., & Kanwalroop, K. D. (1999). Gender inequity and quality of life: A macromarketing perspective. *Journal of Macromarketing*, *19* (December), 140–152.

Hill, S. (2018). Meet the first black woman to own a male professional sports league in the U.S. *Black Enterprise*. Retrieve from https://www.blackenterprise.com/black-woman-own-professional-basketball-league/

Hilton, J. L. & von Hippel, W. (1996). Stereotypes. *Annual Review of Psychology*, *47*, 237–271.

Himebaugh, G. (1994). The image never fades: A survey of tribal college presidents on media stereotyping. *Tribal College*, *I*(1), 32–32. Retrieved from http://search.pro-quest.com/docview/231684493?accountid=13153

Hine, J. (2009). Young people's lives: Taking a different view. In J. Wood & J. Hine (Eds.), *Work with young people* (pp. 27–38). London, United Kingdom: Sage.

Hinton, P. (2017). Implicit stereotypes and the predictive brain: Cognition and culture in "biased" person perception. *Palgrave Communications*, *3*, 1–8, . doi:10.1057/palcomms.2017.86

Hirsch, P. (1980). The "scary world" of the non-viewer and other anomalies. *Communication Research*, *7*, 403–456.

Hirschman, E. C. (1993). Ideology in consumer research, 1980 and 1990: A Marxist and feminist critique. *Journal of Consumer Research*, *19*(March), 537–555.

History of Hockey. (2018). England Hockey. Retrieved from https://www.englandhockey.co.uk/page.asp?section=1147

History of the WNBA. (2018). Women's National Basketball Association. Retrieved from https://www.wnba.com/history/

Ho, I., & Kaskan, E. (2016). Microaggressions and female athletes. *Sex Roles*, *74*, 275–287.

Hobbs, F. B. (2008). The elderly population. U.S. Census Bureau population profile of the United States. Retrieved from http://www.census.gov/population/www/pop-profile/elderpop.html.

Hoberman, J. M. (1997). *Darwin's athletes: How sport has damaged black America and preserved the myth of race*. Boston, MA, and New York, NY: Houghton Mifflin.

Hoberman, J. M. (2005). *Testosterone dreams—Rejuvenation, aphrodisia, doping*. Berkeley, CA: University of California Press.

Hodge, R. W., Siegel, P., & Rossi, P. (1964). Occupational prestige in the United States, 1925–63. *American Journal of Sociology*, *70*, 286–302.

Hodge, T., & Deakin, J. (1998). Deliberate practice and expertise in the martial arts: The role of context in motor recall. *Journal of Sport & Exercise Psychology*, *20*, 260–279.

Hodges, M. J., & Budig, M. J. (2010). Who gets the daddy bonus? Organizational hegemonic masculinity and the impact of fatherhood on earnings. *Gender & Society*, *24*(6), 717–745.

Hodges, N. J., & Starkes, J. L. (1996). Wrestling with the nature of expertise: A sport specific test of Ericsson, Krampe and Tesch-Römer's (1993) theory of deliberate practice. *International Journal of Sport Psychology*, *27*, 400–424.

Hodgkinson, J. (1986). Disney's return to Oz and ECT. *Biological Psychiatry*, *21*, 578.

Hoeber, L., & Shaw, S. (2003). A strong man is direct and a direct woman is a bitch: Analyzing discourses of masculinity and femininity and their impact on employment roles in sport organizations. *Journal of Sport Management, 17,* 347–375.

Hoferek, M. J., & Hanick, P. L. (1985). Woman and athlete: toward role consistency. *Sex Roles, 7*(8), 687–695.

Hoff, D. L. & Mitchell, S. N. (2007). Should our students pay to play extracurricular activities? *The Education Digest, 72*(6), 27–34. Retrieved from https://pdfs.semanticscholar.org/0d38/6a47d098140d3443627fa772021ee-5c16aad.pdf

Hofmann, S. (2005). The elimination of indigenous mascots, logos, and nicknames: Organizing on college campuses. *American Indian Quarterly, 29*(1), 156–177, 354. Retrieved from http://search.proquest.com/docview/216855190?accoun tid=13153

Hogben, H. (1998). Factors moderating the effect of televised aggression on viewer behavior. *Communication Research, 25*(2), 220–247.

Holladay, S. J. (2002). "Have fun while you can," "you're only as old as you feel," and "don't ever get old!": An examination of memorable messages about aging. *Journal of Communication, 52*(4), 681–697.

Hollender, M. (2016). How talking to my dad about sex changed my life. Refinery29. Retrieved from https://www.refinery29.com/talk-about-sex-parents.

Holliday, R. & Hassard, J. (2001). *Contested bodies.* London, United Kingdom: Routledge.

Holmsten, B. and Lubertozzi, A. (2001). *The complete war of the worlds: Mars' invasion of Earth from H.G. Wells to Orson Welles.* Naperville, Illinois: Sourcebooks.

Holt, N. L. (2006). *Positive youth development through sport.* Milton Park, Abingdon, Oxon: Routledge. Retrieved from http://citeseerx.ist.psu.edu/viewdoc/download?doi=10.1.1.454.9870&rep=rep1&type=pdf

Holt, N. L. & Jones, M. I. (2008). Future directions for positive youth development and sport. In N. L. Holt (Ed)., *Positive youth development through sport.* (pp. 122–129). Milton Park, Abingdon, Oxon: Routledge.

Holt, N. L., Kingsley, B. C. Tink, L. N., & Scherer, J. (2011). Benefits and challenges associated with sport participation by children and parents from low-income families, *Psychology of Sport and Exercise, 12*(5), 490–499.

Holter, O. G. (2003). *Can men do it? Men and gender equality—The Nordic experience.* Copenhagen, Denmark: Nordic Council of Ministers.

Hooper, C. (1999). Masculinities, IR and the "gender variable": A cost-benefit analysis for (sympathetic) gender sceptics. *Review of International Studies, 25,* 475–480. doi:10.1017/s0260210599004751.

Hooper, C. (2001). *Manly states: Masculinities, international relations, and gender politics.* New York, NY: Columbia University Press.

Horn, T. S., & Harris, A. (2002). Perceived competence in young athletes: Research findings and recommendations for coaches and parents. In F.L. Smoll & R.E. Smith (Eds.), *Children and youth in sport: A biopsychosocial perspective* (2nd ed., pp. 435–464). Dubuque, IW: Kendall-Hunt.

Horrigan, J. (2006). Hope when the game is over: The effect of exploitation on athletes. In R. Green & J. Horrigan (Eds.), *Hope: probing the boundaries* (pp. 291–331). Oxford, United Kingdom: Interdisciplinary Press.

Hoose, P. (1990). A new pool of talent. *New York Times.* Retrieved from https://www.nytimes.com/1990/04/29/magazine/a-new-pool-of-talent.html

Howie, L. D., Lukacs, S. L., Pastor, P. N., Reuben, C. A., & Mendola, P. (2010). Participation in activities outside of school hours in relation to problem behavior and social skills in middle childhood. *Journal of School Health, 80*(3), 119–125. doi: 10.1111/j.1746-1561.2009.00475.x

Hsu, H. (2007). Exploring elderly people's perspectives on successful aging in Taiwan. *Ageing & Society, 27,* 87–102.

Huesmann, L. R., & Eron, L. D. (1986). *Television and the aggressive child: A cross-national comparison.* Hillsdale, NJ: Lawrence Erlbaum.

Huesmann, L. R., Moise-Titus, J., Padolski, C., & Eron, L. (2003). Longitudinal relations between children's exposure to TV violence and violent behavior in young adulthood. *Developmental Psychology, 39*(2), 201–222.

Huffington Post. (2012a). Olympics: Ramadan poses challenge for Muslim athletes. Retrieved from http://www.huffingtonpost.com/2012/07/19/olympics-ramadan-muslim-athletes_n_1685214.html

Huffington Post. (2012b). The Muslim woman at play: FIFA, the Olympics and the Veil. Retrieved from http://www.huffingtonpost.com/qanta-ahmed/fifa-hijabs_b_1564325.html

Huffington Post. (2012c). Hurdles to Muslim women's rights. Retrieved from http://www.huffingtonpost.com/ida-lichter-md/hurdles-to-muslim-womens-rights_b_1664747.html

Huffman, S., Tuggle, C. A. & Rosengard, D. S. (2004). How campus media cover sports: The gender-equity issue, one generation later. *Mass Communication and Society*, 7(4), 475–489. doi: 10.1207/s15327825mcs0704_6

Hughes, B., & Patterson, K. (1997). The social model of disability and the disappearing body: Towards a sociology of impairment. *Disability and Society*, 12(3), 325–40.

Hughes, M. (1980). The fruits of cultivation analysis: A re-examination of some effects of television viewing. *Public Opinion Quarterly*, 44(3), 287–302.

Hughes, R. & Coakley, J. (1991). Positive deviance among athletes: The implications of overcomformity to the sports ethic. *Sociology of Sport Journal*, 8, 307–325.

Huizinga, J. (1955). *Homo ludens: A study of the play-element in culture*. Boston, MA: Beacon.

Human Rights Campaign (2018). Sexual orientation and gender identity definitions. Retrieved from https://www.hrc.org/resources/sexual-orientation-and-gender-identity-terminology-and-definitions

Human Rights Watch. (2012). Steps of the devil. Denial of women and girls sport in Saudi Arabia. Retrieved from http://www.hrw.org/reports/2012/02/15/steps-devil-0

Hummert, M. L., Shaner, J. L., Garstka, T. A., & Henry, C. (1998). Communication with older adults: The influence of age stereotypes, context, and communicator age. *Human Communication Research*, 25(1), 124–151.

Hummert, M. L., Garstka, T. A., Shaner, J. L., & Strahm, S. (1994). Stereotypes of the elderly held by young, middle-aged, and elderly adults. *Journal of Gerontology: Psychological Sciences*, 49, 240–249.

Hunn, D. (2016, January 13). Goodbye, St. Louis Rams; next stop, LA. *St. Louis Post-Dispatch*. Retrieved from https://www.stltoday.com/sports/football/professional/goodbye-st-louis-rams-next-stop-la/article_ae537abe-8471-5ac3-9edc-2c3174ce7fd9.html

Hunt, C. (2017, January 2). Simone Biles: Making gymnastics history in 2016. AXS. Retrieved from https://www.axs.com/simone-biles-making-gymnastics-history-in-2016-112422

Hunter, C. D. (1997). The uses and gratifications of Project Agora. Retrieved from www.asc.upenn.edu/usr/hunter/agora_uses

Hunter, D. (1996). Race and athletic performance: A physiological review. *Journal of African American Men*, 2(2/3), 23–38. Retrieved from http://www.jstor.org/stable/41819303

Hurley, M. (1997, September 1). But can it lead to the harder stuff? *US News and World Report*, 123(8), 12.

Hurley, S. (2007). Sex and the social construction of gender: Can feminism and evolutionary psychology be reconciled? In J. Browne (Ed.), *The future of gender* (pp. 98–115). New York, NY: Cambridge University Press.

Hutchins, B. (2015). The future of sports broadcasting. The Future of Sports. Retrieved from http://futureof.org/sports-2015/broadcasting/

Hwang, H. (2005). *Predictors of instant messaging use: Gratifications sought, gratifications obtained, and social presence*. Paper presented to the International Communication Association, New York City, NY.

Hyler, S. E., Gabbard, G. O., & Schneider, I. (1991) Homicidal maniacs and narcissistic parasites: stigmatization of mentally ill persons in the movies. *Hospital and Community Psychiatry*, 42, 1044–1048.

Ice Hockey Wiki (2018, December 11). List of ice hockey players of Asian descent. Retrieved from https://icehockey.fandom.com/wiki/List_of_Ice_Hockey_Players_of_Asian_Descent

Institute of Sport and Recreation Management (ISRM). (1999). Disability in sport: The legal framework. The Disability Discrimination Act 1995. Melton Mowbray: ISRM, Ref. 188:12/99.

Internet drawing more women for research, purchases. (1998). *Media Report to Women, 26*(1), 4.

Ireland, K. (2016). The pros & cons of the influence of sports athletes on kids. Livestrong. Retrieved from https://www.livestrong.com/article/371876-the-pros-cons-of-the-influence-of-sports-athletes-on-kids/

Isler, L., Popper, E. T., & Ward, S. (1987). Children's purchase requests and parental response. *Journal of Advertising Research, 27*(5), 28–39.

Iyengar, S., & Kinder, D. R. (1987). *News that matters: Television and American opinion.* Chicago, IL: University of Chicago Press.

Iyengar, S. (1991). *Is anyone responsible? How television frames political issues.* Chicago, IL: University of Chicago Press.

Iyengar, S., & Simon, A. (1993). News coverage of the Gulf crisis and public opinion. *Communication Research, 20*(3), 265–283.

Iyer, E. S. (1988). The influence of verbal content and relative newness on the effectiveness of comparative advertising. *Journal of Advertising, 17*(3), 15–21. doi: 10.1080/00913367.1988.10673119

Jackson, D. Z. (1989, January 22). Calling the plays in black and white. *Boston Globe.*, pp A30, 33. Also refer to https://ecommons.udayton.edu/cgi/viewcontent.cgi?referer=https://www.google.com/&httpsredir=1&article=1039&context=cmm_fac_pub

Jackson, S. A., Kimiecik, J. C., Ford, S., & Marsh, H. W. (1998). Psychological correlates of flow in sport. *Journal of Sport & Exercise Psychology, 20,* 358–378.

Jackson, Y. (2018). Sponsorship of women's sports … is there such a thing? Marketing Female Athletes. Retrieved from https://marketingfemaleathletes.com/tag/womens-sports-foundation/

James, C. (1995). Negotiating school through sports: African Canadian youth strive for academic success. *Avante, 1,* 20–36.

Jamieson, K. (1998). Reading Nancy Lopez: Decoding representations of race, class, and sexuality. *Sociology of Sport Journal, 15,* 343–358.

Jamieson, K. M. (2000). Nancy Lopez: Decoding representations of race, class, and sexuality. In S. Birrell & M. G. MacDonald (Eds.), *Reading sport: Critical essays on power and representation* (pp. 144–165). Boston, MA: Northeastern University.

Jamieson, K. M (2003). Occupying a middle space: Toward a Mestiza sport studies. *Sociology of Sport Journal, 20,* 1–16.

Jansson-Boyd, C. (2010). *Consumer psychology* (pp. 59–62). New York, NY: McGraw-Hill.

Jarvis, M. (2006). *Sport psychology: A students handbook.* Hove East Sussex, United Kingdom: Routledge.

Jason, D. (2017). Ignition 2017: Learn how the future of sports media is being turned on its head. Business Insider. http://www.businessinsider.com/ignition-2017-learn-how-sports-media-is-changing-2017-5

Jay, K. (2004). *More than just a game: Sports in American life since 1945.* New York, NY: Columbia University Press.

Jeffres, L., Neuendorf, K., Bracken, C., & Atkin, D. (2008). Integrating theoretical traditions in media effects. *Mass Communication and Society, 11*(4), 470–491.

Jensen, R. (1994). Banning "Redskins" from the sports page: The ethics and politics of Native American nicknames. *Journal of Mass Media Ethics, 9*(1), 16.

Jhally, S. (2000, January 1). *The codes of gender.* Retrieved from http://www.mediaed.org/discussion-guides/The-Codes-of-Gender.pdf

Johns Hopkins Medicine. (2016, November 29). Evidence of brain injury found in young NFL players. Hopkins Medicine. Retrieved from https://www.hopkinsmedicine.org/news/media/releases/evidence_of_brain_injury_found_in_young_nfl_players

Johnson, A. G. (2006). *Privilege, power, and difference.* New York, NY: McGraw-Hill.

Johnson, J., Cohen, P., Smailes, E., Kagen, S., & Brook, J. (2002). Television viewing and aggressive behavior during adolescence and adulthood. *Science, 295*(5564), 2468–2472.

Johnson, J., Jackson, J., & Gatto, L. (1995). Violent attitudes and deferred academic aspirations. *Basic and Applied Social Psychology, 16*(1/2), 27–41.

Johnson, M. (2016). Let's take the national anthem literally, and the songwriter at his word: A deeper look at the song, the man who wrote it—and the history attached. The Undefeated. Retrieved from https://theundefeated.com/features/lets-take-the-national-anthem-literally-and-the-songwriter-at-his-word/

Johnson, T. J., & Kaye, B. K. (1998). Cruising is believing?: Comparing Internet and traditional sources on media credibility measures. *Journalism and Mass Communication Quarterly, 75*(2), 325–340.

Jones, C. (2016, November 21). Sport: Raising the game. Retrieved from https://callumjones-sportdevelopment.wordpress.com/2016/11/21/raising-the-game/

Jones, E. E., Farina, A., Hastorf, A. H., Markus, H., Miller, D. T., Scout, R. A., & French, R. S. (1984). *Social stigma: The psychology of marked relationships*. New York, NY: Plenum.

Jones, G., Leonard, W., Schmitt, R., Smith, D., & Tolone, W. (1987). Racial discrimination in college football. *Social Science Quarterly*, *68*(1), 70–83. Retrieved from http://www.jstor.org/stable/42862195

Jones, S. (2018). Dallas Cowboys owner Jerry Jones behaves like slave owner over NFL kneeling policy. *Star-Telegram*. Retrieved from https://www.star-telegram.com/opinion/opn-columns-blogs/other-voices/article215982135.html

Jones, M. A. (2016). NBA stars explain how ESPYS awards speech came about. The Undefeated. Retrieved from https://theundefeated.com/features/nba-stars-explain-how-espys-awards-speech-came-about/

Jones, R., Murrell, A. J., & Jackson, J. (1999). Pretty versus powerful in the sports pages: Print media coverage of U.S. women's Olympic gold medal winning teams. *Journal of Sport and Social Issues*, *23*, 183–192.

Jorg, M. (2008). Need for orientation as a predictor of agenda-setting effects. *International Journal of Public Opinion Research*, *20*(4), 440–453.

Just Not Sports. (2016). *#Morethanmean: Women in sports face harassment*. Available from https://www.youtube.com/watch?v=9tU-D-m2JY8

Kaiser Family Foundation (2005). Generation M: Media in the lives of 8–18 year-olds. Retrieved from http://www.kff.org/entmedia/7251.cfm

Kamhawi, R., & Weaver, D. (2002). Mass communication research trends from 1980 to 1999. *Journalism and Mass Communication Quarterly*, *80*(1), 7–27.

Kamphoff, C., & Gill, D. (2008). Collegiate athletes' perceptions of the coaching profession. *International Journal of Sports Science & Coaching*, *3*(1), 55–72.

Kane, E. (1996). *Gender, culture, and learning*. Washington, DC: Academy for Educational Development.

Kane, M. (1971). An assessment of "black is best." *Sports Illustrated*. Retrieved from http://sportsillustrated.cnn.com/vault/article/magazine/MAG1084501/index.htm

Kane, M. J. (1996). Media coverage of the post title IX female athlete: A feminist analysis of sport, gender and power. *Duke Journal of Gender Law and Policy*, *3*(1), 95–127.

Kang, J. C. (2017). Should Athletes Stick to Sports? *New York Times*. Retrieved from https://www.nytimes.com/2017/02/14/magazine/should-athletes-stick-to-sports.html

Kantomaa, M. T., Tammelin, T. H., Näyhä, S., & Taanila, A. M. (2007). Adolescents' physical activity in relation to family income and parents' education. *Prevevntive Medicine*, *44*, 410–415.

Karweit, N., & Hansell, S. (1983). School organization and friendship selection. In J. Epstein & N. Karweit (Eds.), *Friends in school* (pp. 29–38). New York, NY: Academic Press.

Kaskan, E. R., & Ho, I. K. (2014). Microaggressions and female athletes. *Sex Roles*, *74*(7-8), 275–287. doi: 10.1007/s11199-014-0425-1

Kassing, J. W., Billings, A. C., Brown, R. S., & Turman, P. D. (2004). Chapter 10: Communication in the community of sport: The process of enacting, (re)producing, consuming, and organizing sport. *Communication Yearbook*, *28*(1), 373–409. doi: 10.1207/s15567419cy2801_10

Kassing, J. W., Billings, A. C., Brown, R. S., Halone, K. K., Harrison, K., Krizek, R. L., Mean, L. J., & Turman, P. D. 2004). Communication in the community of sport: The process of enacting, (re)producing, consuming, and organizing sport. *Communication Yearbook*, *28*, 373–409.

Katsaros, T., & University of New Haven Foundation. (2004). *International Sports Journal: 8*(2), Summer.

Katz, J. (2011). Advertising and the construction of violent white masculinity: From BMWs to Bud Light. In G. Dines & J. M. Humez (Eds.), *Gender, race and class in media*. (pp. 261–269). Thousand Oaks, CA: Sage.

Katz, E., Blumler, J. G., & Gurevitch, M. (1973). Uses and gratifications research. *Public Opinion Quarterly*, *37*(4), 509–523. https://doi.org/10.1086/268109

Kaufman, M. (1999). *Beyond Patriarchy: Essays by Men on Pleasure, Power and Change*, Toronto, Canada: Oxford University Press.

Keane, T. (2013). The myth about crime and the NFL. *Boston Globe*. Retrieved from https://www.bostonglobe.com/opinion/2013/07/01/

the-myth-about-crime-and-pro-athletes/qln-KoSMkbhuImiS4pO87WJ/story.html

Keister, L. A. (2000). *Wealth in America: Trends in wealth inequality*. Cambridge, United Kingdom: Cambridge University Press.

Kelinske, B., Mayer, B. W., & Chen, K.-L. (2001). Perceived benefits from participation in sports: A gender study. *Women in Management Review, 16*(2), 75–84. https://doi.org/10.1108/09649420110386601

Keller, C., Hallahan, D., McShane, E., Crowley, P., & Blandford, B. (1990). The coverage of persons with disabilities in American newspapers. *Journal of Special Education, 24*(3), 271–282.

Kelly, J. (2017). Taking a knee: Simple phrase, powerful—and changing—meaning. Mashed Radish. Retrieved from https://mashedradish.com/2017/09/25/taking-a-knee-simple-phrase-powerful-and-changing-meaning/

Kelly, L. A., Reilly, J. J., Fisher, A., Montgomery, C., Williamson, A., McColl, J. H., Payton, J. Y., & Grant, S. (2006). Effect of socioeconomic status on objectively measured physical activity. *Archives of Disease in Childhood, 91*, 35–38.

Kennedy, C. L. (2010). A new frontier for women's sports (beyond title IX). *Gender Issues, 78*(1–2), 78–90. doi:10.1007/s12147-010-9091-y

Kerr, J. H. (1993). The role of aggression and violence in sport. A rejoinder to the ISSP position stand. *Sport Psychologist, 13*, 83–88.

Kerr, J. H. (2002). Issues in aggression and violence in sport: The ISSP position stand revisited, *Sport Psychologist, 16*, 68–78.

Kerbo, H. R. (2009). *Social stratification and inequality*. New York, NY: McGraw-Hill.

Kessler, S.J., Ashenden, D. J., Connell, R. W., & Dowsett, G. W. (1982). *Ockers and disco-maniacs*. Sydney, Australia: Inner City Education Center.

Kian, E. M., & Hardin, M. (2009). Framing of sport coverage based on the sex of sports writers: Female journalists counter the traditional gendering of media coverage. *International Journal of Sport Communication, 2*, 185–204.

Kight, K. L. (2017). The history of singing the national anthem before NFL games. Axios. Retrieved from https://www.axios.com/the-history-of-singing-the-national-anthem-before-nfl-games-1513305769-97a4edd0-6748-432d-b1cc-2b377848e712.html

Kilbourne, J. (2000). *Can't buy me love: How advertising changed the way we think and feel*. New York, NY: Touchstone Publishing.

Killermann, S. (2014). 30+ examples of middle-to-upper class privilege, privilege lists/social justice tagged class list privilege. It's Pronounced Metrosexual. Retrieved from http://itspronouncedmetrosexual.com/2012/10/list-of-upperclass-privilege/

Killion, A. (2005, June 21). NBA makes a deal—are you listening, NHL? *San Jose Mercury News*. Quoted in https://thesportjournal.org/article/age-requirement-in-professional-sport/

Kim, J., & Haradakis, P. (2008). *The role of Internet user characteristics and motives in explaining three dimensions of Internet addiction*. Paper presented to the International Communication Association in Montreal, Quebec Canada.

Kim, J. Y., & Parlow, M. J. (2009). Off-court misbehavior: Sports leagues and private punishment. *Journal of Criminal Law and Criminology, 99*(3), 573–596.

Kimball, R. I. (2003). *Sports in Zion: Mormon recreation, 1890–1940*. Urbana, IL: University of Illinois Press.

Kimmel, M. (2000). *The gendered society*. Oxford, United Kingdom: Oxford University Press.

Kimmel, M. S. (1996). *Manhood in America: A cultural history*. New York, NY: Free Press.

Kimmel, M. S. (2010). Masculinity as homophobia: Fear, shame, and silence in the construction of gender identity. In S. R. Harper & F. Harris III (Eds.), *College men and masculinities: Theory, research, and implications for practice* (pp. 23–31). San Francisco, CA: Jossey-Bass.

King, C. (2017). *Training tips to match your body type*. Bodybuilidng.com. Retrieved from https://www.bodybuilding.com/content/training-tips-to-match-your-body-type.html

King, W. C., Jr., Miles, E. W., & Kniska, J. (1991). Boys will be boys (and girls will be girls): The attribution of gender role stereotypes in a gaming situation. *Sex Roles, 25*, 607–623.

Kingston, K. (2018). A brief history of basketball. Street Directory. Retrieved from http://www.streetdirectory.com/travel_guide/41417/recreation_and_sports/a_brief_history_of_basketball.html

Kinkema, K. M., & Harris, J.C. (1998) Mediasport studies: Key research and emerging issues. In

L. A. Wenner (Ed.), *Mediasport* (pp. 27–54). London, United Kingdom: Routledge.

Kinsman, G. (2000). Constructing gay men and lesbians as national security risks, 1950–1970. In G. Kinsman, D. K. Buse, & M. Steedman (Eds.), *In whose national security? Canadian state surveillance and the creation of enemies* (pp. 143–153). Toronto, Canada: Between the Lines Press.

Kiousis, S. & Shields, A. (2008). Inter-candidate agenda setting in presidential elections. *Public Relations Review, 34*(4), 325–330.

Kirk, D. (2002). The social construction of the body in physical education and sport. In A. Laker (Ed.), *The sociology of sport and physical education* (pp. 79–91). London, United Kingdom: Routledge.

Kirk, D. (2005). Physical education, youth sport and lifelong participation: The importance of early learning experiences. *European Physical Education Review, 11*, 239–255.

Kite, M. E., & Wagner, L. S. (2004). Attitudes toward older adults. In T. D. Nelson (Ed.), *Ageism: Stereotyping and prejudice against older persons* (pp. 129–161). Cambridge, MA: MIT Press.

Klapper, J. (1960). *The effects of mass communication*. Glencoe, IL: Free Press.

Kleese, E. J., & D'Onofrio, J. A. (1994). *Student activities for students at risk*. Reston, VA: National Association of Secondary School Principals.

Klein E. (2010, November 27). Good reasons to be uneasy about retirement security. *Washington Post*. Retrieved from http://www.washingtonpost.com

Klein, J. Z. (2008, July 14). The starting line: At the Olympics, age is just a number. *NYTimes.com*. Retrieved from https://www.nytimes.com/2008/07/14/sports/olympics/14olympics.html?mtrref=www.google.com&gwh=A0F59558C00008E2961EBA6F-DA79934F&gwt=pay

Klein, S. S. (Ed.). (2007). *Handbook for achieving gender equity through education* (2nd ed.). Mahwah, NJ: Lawrence Erlbaum Associates.

Klenke, K. (2017). Sports as context for women's leadership. In K. Klenke (Ed.), *Women in leadership* (2nd ed., pp. 251–301), New York City, NY: Oxford University Press.

Knight, C. (2013). Gender and sexuality—Sexuality, cohesion, masculinity and combat motivation: Designing personnel policy to sustain capability. *Australian Army Journal*, Culture edition, *10*(3), 58–78.

Knight, J. L., & Giuliano, T. A. (2001). He's a Laker; she's a "looker": The consequences of gender-stereotypical portrayals of male and female athletes by the print media. *Sex Roles, 45*(3–4), 217–229.

Knight, J. L., & Giuliano, T. A. (2003). Blood, sweat, and jeers: The impact of the on perceptions of male and female athletes. *Journal of Sport Behavior, 26*(3), 272–284.

Ko, D. M. & Kim, H. S. (2010) Message framing and defensive processing: A cultural examination. *Health Communication, 25*(1), 61–68. doi: 10.1080/10410230903473532

Koivula, N. (1995). Ratings of gender appropriateness of sports participation: Effects of gender-based schematic processing. *Sex Roles, 33*, 543–557.

Koivula, N. (1999, October). Gender stereotyping in televised media sport coverage. *Sex Roles: A Journal of Research, 33*, 543–557. Retrieve from http://findarticles.com/p/articles/mim2294/is1999Oct/ai59426460

Koivula, N. (2001). Perceived characteristics of sports categorized as gender-neutral, feminine and masculine. *Journal of Sport Behavior, 24*(4), 377–393.

Kolnes, L. (1995). Heterosexuality as an organizing principle in women's sport. *International Review for the Sociology of Sport, 30*(1), 61–77.

Koss, M. P. & Gaines, J. A. (1993). The prediction of sexual aggression by alcohol use, athletic participation, and fraternity affiliation. *Journal of Interpersonal Violence, 8*(1), 94–108. doi: 10.1177/088626093008001007

Krane, V. (1996). Lesbians in sport: Toward acknowledgment, understanding, and theory. *Journal of Sport & Exercise Psychology, 18*, 237–246.

Krane, V. (2001). We can be athletic and feminine, but do we want to? Challenging hegemonic femininity in women's sport. *Quest, 53*, 115–133.

Krane, V. & Barber, H. (2005). Identity tensions in lesbian intercollegiate coaches. *Research Quarterly for Exercise and Sport, 76*(1), 67–81. doi: 10.1080/02701367.2005.10599263

Krane, V., Barber, H., & McClung, L. R. (2002). Social psychological benefits of gay games participation: A social identity theory explanation. *Journal of Applied Sport Psychology, 14*(1), 27–42.

Krane, V., Choi, P. Y. L., Baird, S. M., Aimar, C. M., & Kauer, K. J. (2004). Living the paradox: Female athletes negotiate femininity and muscularity. *Sex Roles, 50*, 315–329.

Krane, V., Waldron, J., Michalenok, J., & Stiles-Shipley, J. (2001). Body image, and eating and exercise behaviors: A feminist cultural studies perspective. *Women in Sport and Physical Activity Journal, 10*(1), 17–54.

Kraus, M. W., Park, J. W., & Tan, J. J. X. (2017). Signs of social class: The experience of economic inequality in everyday life. *Perspectives on Psychological Science, 12*(3), 422–435. http://doi.org/10.1177/1745691616673192

Kraut, R., Kiesler, S., Bonera, B., Cummings, J., Hegelson, V., & Crawford, A. (2002). Internet paradox revisited. *Journal of Social Issues, 58*(1), 49–75.

Krcmar, M. (1998). The contribution of family communication patterns to children's interpretations of television violence. *Journal of Broadcasting and Electronic Media, 42*(2), 250–264.

Kremarik F. (2000). A family affair: Children's participation in sports. *Canadian Social Trends, 58*, 20–24. Retrieved from /pub/11-008-x/2000002/article/5166-eng.pdf.

Kristjansdottir, G., & Vilhjalmsson, R. (2001). Sociodemographic differences in patterns of sedentary and physically active behaviour in older children and adolescents. *Acta Paediatric, 90*, 429–435.

Krizek, B. (2002). The grayer side of the game: Baseball and the "older" fan. In G. Gumpert & J. Drucker (Eds.), *Take me out to the ballgame: communicating baseball* (pp. 401–428). Cresskill, NJ: Hamptong Press.

Ku, G., Kaid, L., & Pfau, M. (2003). The impact of web campaigning on traditional news media and public information processing. *Journalism and Mass Communication Quarterly, 80*(3), 528–548.

Kupers, T. A. (June 2005). Toxic masculinity as a barrier to mental health treatment in prison. *Journal of Clinical Psychology, 61*(6), 713–724. doi:10.1002/jclp.20105.

Kurzban, R., & Leary, M. R. (2001). Evolutionary origins of stigmatization: The functions of social exclusion. *Psychological Bulletin, 127*, 187–208.

Kytta, M. (2002). Affordances of children's environments in the context of cities, small towns, suburbs, and rural villages in Finland and Belarus. *Journal of Environmental Psychology, 22*, 109–123.

La Corte, R. (2009, October 24). Most state judges in the U.S. must retire in '70s. *Seattle Post-Intelligencer*. Retrieved from http://www.seattlepi.com

La Torre, G., Masala, D., De Vito, E., Langiano, E., Capelli, G., Ricciardi, W. & PHASES collaborative group. (2006). Extra-curricular physical activity and socio-economic status in Italian adolescents. *BMC Public Health, 6*(22), 1–9. doi: 10.1186/1471-2458-6-22

Laberge, S., & Sankoff, D. (1988). Physical activities, body habitus, and lifestyles. Not just a game. *Essays in Canadian Sport Sociology, 14*(2), 267–286.

Lachs, M. S., & Pillemer, K. (2004). Elder abuse. *The Lancelet, 364*, 1263–1272.

Laderman, G. (2009). *Sacred matters: Celebrity worship, sexual ecstasies, the living dead, and other signs of religious life in the United States.* New York, NY: New Press.

Laemmle, J. (2013). Barbara Martin: Children at play: Learning gender in the early years. *Journal of Youth and Adolescence, 42*(2), 305–307.

Lally, P. (2007). Identity and athletic retirement: A prospective study. *Psychology of Sport and Exercise, 8*, 85–99.

Lamborn, S. D., Brown, B. B., Mounts, N. S., & Steinberg, L. (1992). Putting school in perspective: The influence of family, peers, extracurricular participation, and part-time work on academic engagement, in F. M. Newman (Ed.), *Student engagement and achievement in American secondary schools* (pp. 153–181). New York: Teachers College Press.

Lamonier, P. (2018, July 2). The business of being a WNBA player. *Forbes*. Retrieved from https://www.forbes.com/sites/plamonier/2018/07/02/the-business-of-being-a-wnba-player/#71057a885af1

Lampman, B. (2006). Conclusion: Sport, society, and social justice. In S. S. Prettyman &

B. Lampman (Eds.), *Learning culture through sports: Exploring the role of sports in society* (pp. 255–264). Lanham, MD: Rowman & Littlefield Education.

Landers, C. (2017). Why do we sing the national anthem before sporting events? MLB.com. Retrieved from https://www.mlb.com/cut4/the-1918-world-series-and-the-debut-of-the-national-anthem-in-american-sports/c-229202336

Landers, M. A., & Fine, G. A. (1996). Learning life's lessons in tee ball: The reinforcement of gender and status in kindergarten sport. *Sociology of Sport Journal, 13*, 87–93.

Lang, K., & Lang, G. (1966). The mass media and voting. In B. Berelson & M. Janowitz (Eds.), *Reader in public opinion and communication* (pp. 455–472). New York, NY: Free Press.

Langlois, J. A., Rutland-Brown, W., & Wald, M. M. (2006). The epidemiology and impact of traumatic brain injury: A brief overview. *Journal of Head Trauma and Rehabilitation, 21*(5), 375–383.

Langlois, J. H., Kalakanis, L., Rubenstein, A. J., Larson, A., Hallam, M., & Smoot, M. (2000). Maxims or myths of beauty? A meta-analytics and theoretical review. *Psychological Bulletin, 126*, 390–423.

Lapchick, R. (2006). Who's covering whom? Sports sections lag in diversity. ESPN. http://www.espn.com/espn/news/story?id=2496651

Lapchick, R. (2011). The 2011 racial & gender report card: Major League Baseball. University of Central Florida. Retrieved from http://tidesport.org/RGRC/2011/2011_MLB_RGRC_FINAL.pdf&gt

Lapchick, R. (2016). TIDES: The institute for diversity and equity in sports. Retrieved from https://www.tidesport.org

Lapchick, R. (2018, May 3). The 2018 Associated Press sports editors racial and gender report card. ESPN. Retrieved from http://www.espn.com/espn/story/_/id/23382605/espn-leads-way-hiring-practices-sports-media

Lapchick, R. (2018, October 25). WNBA score record marks for hiring practices. ESPN. Retrieved from http://www.espn.com/wnba/story/_/id/25075162/wnba-once-again-sets-record-high-marks-diversity-their-hiring-practices

Lapchick, R., Little, E., Mathew, R., & Zahn, J. (2008). *The 2008 racial and gender report card of the associated press sports editors.* Orlando, FL: Institute for Diversity and Ethics in Sport. Retrieved from http://www.tidesport.org/RGRC/2008/2008_APSE_RGRC_Press_Release.pdf

Lapchick, R. & Matthews, J. K. (2002). *2002 Racial and gender equity report card.* Orlando, FL: Institute for Diversity and Ethics in Sport.

Lapchick, R. E., & Matthews, J. (2001). *Racial and gender report card.* Boston, MA: Northeastern University Center for the Study of Sport in Society.

Lapchick, R., Milkovich, M., & O'Keefe, S. (2012). *The 2012 Women's National Basketball Association Racial and Gender Report Card.* Retrieved from http://web.bus.ucf.edu/documents/sport/2012-WNBA-RGRC.pdf

LaRose, R., Lin, C. & Eastin, M. (2003). Unregulated Internet usage: Addiction, habit, or deficient self-regulation. *Media Psychology, 5*(3), 225–253.

Larson, C. U. (1994). *Persuasion* (7th ed.). Belmont, CA: Wadsworth.

Larson, R.W. (2000). Toward a psychology of positive youth development. *American Psychologist, 55*, 170–183.

Larson, R.W., & Verma, S. (1999). How children and adolescents spent time across the world: Work, play, and developmental opportunities. *Psychological Bulletin, 125*, 701–736.

Laurie, T. (2015). Masculinity studies and the jargon of strategy: Hegemony, tautology, sense. *Angelaki: Journal of the Theoretical Humanities, 20*(1), 17. Retrieved from https://www.academia.edu/10912537/Masculinity_Studies_and_the_Jargon_of_Strategy_Hegemony_Tautology_Sense

Lavallee, D. (2000). Theoretical perspectives on career transitions in sport. In D. Lavallee & P. Wylleman (Eds.), *Career transitions in sport: International perspectives* (pp. 1–28). Morgantown, WV: Fitness Information Technology.

Lavallee, D. (2005). The effect of a life development intervention on sports career transition adjustment. *Sport Psychologist, 19*, 193–202. Retrieved from http://www.storre.stir.ac.uk/handle/1893/7656

Lavallee, D., Golby, J., & Lavallee, R. (2002). Coping with retirement from professional sport. In I. M. Cockeril (Ed.), *Solutions in sport psychology* (pp. 184–187). London, United Kingdom: Thompson. Retrieved from http://dspace.stir.ac.uk/handle/1893/22471

Lavallee, D., Gordon, S., & Grove, J. R. (2008). Retirement from sport and the loss of athletic identity. *Journal of Personal and Interpersonal Loss: International Perspectives on Loss and Coping, 2,* 129–147. doi: 10.1080/10811449708414411

LaVeist, T. A. (1996). Why we should continue to study race … but do a better job: An essay on race. *Racism and Health Ethnicity and Disease, 6*(2), 21–29.

Law, M., Côté, J., & Ericsson, K. A. (2007). The development of expertise in rhythmic gymnastics. *International Journal of Sport and Exercise Psychology.*

Lawrence, G., & Rowe, D. (1986). The corporate pitch: televised cricket under capitalism. In G. Lawrence & D. Rowe (Eds.), *Power play: The commercialization of Australian sport* (pp. 166–178). Sydney, Australia: Hale & Iremonger.

Layer, M. (2015, April 4). We're all screwed. New Ball Park. Retrieved from https://newballpark.org/2015/04/04/were-all-screwed/

Lazarus, N. R., & Harridge, S. D. R. (2007). Editorial. *Scandinavian Journal of Medicine and Science in Sports, 17,* 461–463.

Leach, M. (1994). The politics of masculinity: An overview of contemporary theory. *Social Alternatives, 12*(4), 36–37.

Leal, W., Gertz, M., Piquero, A. R., & Piquero, N. L. (2016). What happens on the field stays on the field: Exploring the link between football player penalties and criminal arrests. *Deviant Behavior, 38*(11). doi: 10.1080/01639625.2016.1248715

Leath, V. M., & Lumpkin, A. (1992). An analysis of sportswomen on the covers and in the feature articles of women's sports and fitness magazine, 1975–1989. *Journal of Sport and Social Issues, 16,* 121–126. https://doi.org/10.1177/019372359201600207

Ledru, A. 2012. Le sport se voile la Face. *Paris Match.* Retrieved from http://www.parismatch.com/Actu/Sport/Le-sport-se-voile-la-face-157679

Lee, J. D. & Eagleman, A. N. (2013). From tennis skirt to catsuit: A qualitative analysis of Serena Williams' impact on women's tennis fashion. *Journal of Contemporary Athletics, 7*(1), 27–36.

Retrieved from https://link.springer.com/article/10.1007%2Fs12111-996-1002-7

Lee, R. E., & Cubbin, C. (2002). Neighborhood context and youth cardiovascular health behaviors. *American Journal of Public Health, 92*(3), 428–436.

Lefkowitz, M., Eron, L., Waldner, L., & Huesmann, L. (1972). Television violence and child aggression. In G. Comstock & E. Rubinstein (Eds.), *Television and social behavior: Vol. III. Television and adolescent aggressiveness* (pp. 253–263). Washington, DC: U.S. Government Printing Office.

Leichenger, A. (2014, May 1). *What's next in the fight for LGBT equality in sports?* Think Progress. Retrieved from https://thinkprogress.org/whats-next-in-the-fight-for-lgbt-equality-in-sports-b63d1e6b3d64/

Leichenger, A. (2018). Protest as sport: The drive to separate politics from sports did not start in 1968, but the year did set many rules still played by. Common Reader. Retrieved from https://commonreader.wustl.edu/c/protest-as-sport/

Leitch, K. (2016, January 6). The most hated man in St. Louis. Sports on Earth. Retrieved from http://www.sportsonearth.com/article/161161120/stan-kroenke-hates-st-louis-rams-proposal

Lemyre, P., Roberts, G. C., & Ommundsen, Y. (2002). Achievement goal orientations, perceived ability, and sportspersonship in youth soccer. *Journal of Applied Sport Psychology, 14,* 120–136.

Lenskyj, H. (1987). Female sexuality and women's sport. *Women's Studies International Forum, 10*(4), 381–386.

Leonard, W. M. (1988). *A sociological perspective of sport* (3rd ed.). New York, NY: Macmillan Publishing Company.

Leonard II, W. M., Ostrosky, A., & Huchendorf, S. (1990). Centrality of position and managerial recruitment: The case of major league baseball. *Sociology of Sport Journal, 7* (3), 299–314.

Levant, R. F., & Wong, Y. J. (2017). *The psychology of men and masculinities.* Washington, DC: American Psychological Association.

Lever, J. (1978). Sex differences in the complexity of children's play and games. *American Sociological Review, 43,* 471–483.

Levin, D. & Arafeh, S. (2002). *The digital disconnect: The widening gap between Internet-savvy students and their schools*. Washington, DC: American Institutes for Research.

Levin, D., Richardson, J. & Arafeh, S. (2002). Digital disconnect: Students' perceptions and experiences with the Internet and education. In P. Barker & S. Rebelsky (Eds.), *Proceedings of ED-MEDIA 2002—world conference on educational multimedia, hypermedia & telecommunications* (pp. 51–52). Denver, Colorado: Association for the Advancement of Computing in Education (AACE). Retrieved from https://www.learntechlib.org/primary/p/9663/

Levine, P. (1985). *Albert Spalding and the promise of American sport*. New York, NY: Oxford University Press.

Levitz, J., & Shishkin, P. (2009, March 11). More workers cite age bias after layoffs. *Wall Street Journal*. Retrieved from http://online.wsj.com

Levy, B. (1996). Improving memory in old age through implicit self-stereotyping. *Journal of Personality and Social Psychology, 71*, 1092–1107.

Levy, B., & Langer, E. (1994). Aging free from negative stereotypes: Successful memory in China among the American deaf. *Journal of Personality and Social Psychology, 66*(6), 989–997.

Levy, B. R., & Banaji, M. R. (2004). Implicit ageism. In T. D. Nelson (Ed.), *Ageism: Stereotyping and prejudice against older persons* (pp, 49–75). Cambridge, MA: MIT Press.

Levy, B. R., & Leifheit-Limson, E. (2009). The stereotype-matching effect: Greater influence on functioning when age stereotypes correspond to outcomes. *Psychology and Aging, 24*, 230–233.

Levy, B. R., Slade, M. D., Kunkel, S. R., & Kasl, S. V. (2002). Longevity increased by positive self-perceptions of aging. *Journal of Personality and Social Psychology, 83*, 261–270.

Levy, B. R., Zonderman, A. B., Slade, M. D., & Ferrucci, L. (2009). Age stereotypes held earlier in life predict cardiovascular events in later life. *Psychological Science, 20*, 296–298.

Levy, M., & Windahl, S. (1984). Audience activity and gratifications. *Communication Research, 11*, 51–78.

Lewis, A. (2014). Is sport sexist? Six sports where men & women are still set apart. BBC.com. Retrieved from https://www.bbc.com/sport/golf/29242699

Lewis, J. J. (2017, June 30). Top women in basketball history: Top American female basketball players, coaches and others. Retrieved from https://www.thoughtco.com/top-women-in-basketball-history-3528492

Li, D. (2007). *Why do you blog?* Paper presented to the International Communication Association in San Francisco, CA.

Libby, L., & Taylor, P. (2005). Older workers and employment: Managing age relations. *Ageing and Society, 25*(3), 415–429.

Libby, O'Brien, Kingsley, & Champion. (2018). Sports law. Retrieved from https://www.lokllc.com/practice-groups/sports-law/

Liben, L. S., & Bigler, R. S. (2002). The developmental course of gender differentiation: Conceptualizing, measuring, and evaluating constructs and pathways. *Monographs of the Society for Research in Child Development, 67*(2), vii–147.

Liden, R. C., Stilwell, D., & Ferris, G. R. (1996). The effects of supervisor and subordinate age on objective performance and subjective performance ratings. *Human Relations, 49*(3), 327–347.

Liebert, R. M., & Sprafkin, J. (1992). *The early window* (3rd ed.). New York, NY: Pergamon Press.

Liebert, R., & Baron, R. (1972). Short-term effects of televised aggression on children's aggressive behavior. In J. Murray, E. Rubinstein, & G. Comstock (Eds.), *Television and social behavior: Vol. II. Television and social learning* (pp. 3–55). Washington, DC: U.S. Government Printing Office.

Lillie-Blanton, M., & LaVeist, T. A. (1996) Race/ethnicity, the social environment and health. *Social Science and Medicine, 43*(1), 83–91.

Lin, C. (1993). Modeling the gratification-seeking process of television viewing. *Human Communication Research, 20*(2), 224–244.

Lin, X. (2008). *Moderation of media issue salience: Retesting the agenda-setting effect within the elaboration likelihood model*. Paper presented to the International Communication Association in Montreal, Quebec, Canada.

Lindsey, L. L. (2011). *Gender roles: A sociological perspective* (5th ed.). Upper Saddle River, NJ: Prentice Hall.

Lindstrom, P. (1997). The Internet: Nielsen's longitudinal research on behavioral changes in use of this counter intuitive medium. *Journal of Media Economics, 10*(2), 35–40.

Lines, G. (2000). Media sport audiences—young people and the summer of sport '96: Revisiting frameworks for analysis. *Media, Culture & Society*, 22, 669–680.

Ling, L. (2011). Transgender child: A parent's difficult choice. Oprah.com. Retrieved from http://www.oprah.com/own-our-america-lisa-ling/Transgender-Child-A-Parents-Difficult-Choice

Linz, D., Donnerstein, D., & Penrod, S. (1984). The effects of multiple exposure to film violence against women. *Journal of Communication*, 34(3), 130–147.

Lipka, S. (2006). Athletes cite stress of balancing sports and academics. *The Chronicle of Higher Education*. Retrieved from https://www.chronicle.com/article/Athletes-Cite-Stress-of/23592

Lipka, S., & Wolverton, B. (2007). Title IX enforcement called "Deeply Troubling." *The Chronicle of Higher Education*. Retrieved from https://www.chronicle.com/article/Title-IX-Enforcement-Called/3779/

Lippmann, W. (1922). *Public opinion*. New York, NY: Macmillan. (Reprint, 1965, New York, NY: Free Press)

Lipshultz, J. (2007). Framing terror. *Electronic News*, 1(1), 21–35.

Lipsyte, R. (2010). Sports, god & religion. ESPN. Retrieved from http://www.espn.com/espn/page2/story?page=bloc/040210

Little, B. (2017). Why the "Star-Spangled Banner" is played at sporting events: The tradition began during a time of national sorrow. History.com. retrieved from https://www.history.com/news/why-the-star-spangled-banner-is-played-at-sporting-events

Little, W., & McGivern, R. (2011). *Introduction to sociology*. Montreal, Quebec: PressBooks Publishing.

Litzky, B., & Greenhaus, J. (2007). The relationship between gender and aspirations to senior management. *Career Development International*, 12(7), 637–659.

Liu, J. H., Ng, S. H., Weatherall, A., & Loong, C. (2000). Filial piety, acculturation, and intergenerational communication among New Zealand Chinese. *Basic and Applied Social Psychology*, 22(3), 213–223.

Liu, C., Comer, L., & Dubinsky, A. (2001). Gender differences in attitudes toward women as sales managers in the people's Republic of China.

Journal of Personal Selling & Sales Management, 21(4), 303–311.

Lo, V., & Weir, R. (2002). Third person effect, gender, and pornography on the Internet. *Journal of Broadcasting & Electronic Media*, 46(1), 13–34.

Lobjois, R., Benguigui, N., & Bertsch, J. (2005). Aging and tennis playing in a coincidence-timing task with an accelerating object: The role of visuomotor delay. *Research Quarterly for Exercise and Sport*, 76, 398–406.

Locklear, E. A. (2009). Native American mascot controversy and mass media involvement: How the media play a role in promoting racism through Native American athletic imagery. Retrieved from https://uncw.edu/csurf/Explorations/documents/ElizabethLocklear.pdf

Locklear, E. A. (2012). Elizabeth A. Locklear, Native American mascot controversy and mass media involvement: How the media play a role in promoting racism through Native American athletic imagery. Class Race Gender. Retrieved from https://classracegender.wordpress.com/2015/04/21/native-american-mascots-the-fight-to-reclaim-a-name/

Logan, A. J., & Baker, J. (2007). Cross-sectional and longitudinal profiles of age related decline in golf performance. *Journal of Sport & Exercise Psychology*, 29, S15–S17.

Lomax, M. E. (Ed.). (2008). *Sports and the racial divide: African American and Latino experience in an era of change*. Jackson, MS: University Press of Mississippi.

Longman, P. (1986). Age wars: The coming battle between young and old. *The Futurist*, 20, 8–11.

Longman, J. (2017). Number of women coaching in college has plummeted in Title IX era. *New York Times*. Retrieved from https://www.nytimes.com/2017/03/30/sports/ncaabasketball/coaches-women-title-ix.html

Longman, J. (2017). Female coaches few and far between. Bend Bulletin. Retrieved from https://www.bendbulletin.com/sports/5193899-151/female-coaches-few-and-far-between

Longman, J. (2012). Saudi Arabia and London 2012: mixed messages of mammoth proportion. *The Age Newspaper*. Retrieved from http://www.theage.com.au/olympics/mixed-messages-of-mammoth-proportions-20120427-1xqlq.html

Lopez, G. (2018). Research says there are ways to reduce racial bias. Calling people racist isn't one of them. Vox. Retrieved from https://www.vox.com/identities/2016/11/15/13595508/racism-research-study-trump

Lopiano, D. A. (2000). Modern history of women in sports: Twenty-five years of Title IX. *Clinics in Sports Medicine, 19*(2), 1–8.

Lopiano, D. (2005). Recruiting, retention and advancement of women in athletics. Women's Sports Foundation. Retrieved from https://www.womenssportsfoundation.org/research/articles-and-reports/?re_cord=878

Loprinzi, P. D., Cardinal, B. J., Loprinzi, K. L., & Lee, H. (2012). Benefits and environmental determinants of physical activity in children and adolescents, *Obesity Facts, 5,* 597–610.

Loretto, W., & White, P. (2006). Employers' attitudes, practices and policies toward older workers. *Human Resource Management, 16*(3), 313–330.

Lukas, P. (2018, February 21). The colorful history of the uniform name game. ESPN. Retrieved from http://www.espn.com/espn/story/_/id/22539880/looking-back-storied-history-uniform-name

Lumpkin, A., & Williams, L.D. (1991). An analysis of *Sports Illustrated* feature articles, 1954–1987. *Sociology of Sport Journal, 8,* 16–32.

Lundy, M. (2013, May 4; updated May 11, 2018). Five female sports reporters and the disrespect they faced. *The Globe and Mail.* Retrieved from https://www.theglobeandmail.com/sports/five-female-sports-reporters-and-the-disrespect-they-faced/article11719668/

Luther, J. (2014, May 7). Changing the narrative. Sports on Earth. Retrieved from http://www.sportsonearth.com/article/74027694/sports

Lyndon, A. E., Duffy, D. M., Smith, P. H., & White, J. W. (2011). The role of high school coaches in helping prevent adolescent sexual aggression: Part of the solution or part of the problem? *Journal of Sport & Social Issues, 35*(4), 377–399. doi: 10.1177/0193723511426292

MacArthur, H. J. & Shields, S.A. (2015). There's no crying in baseball, or is there? Male athletes, tears, and masculinity in North America. *Emotion Review, 7*(1), 39–46. doi: 10.1177/1754073914544476

MacCambridge, M. (Ed.). (2005). *ESPN college football encyclopedia: The complete history of the game.* New York, NY: Hyperion Books.

MacCambridge, M. (2004). *America's game: The epic story of how prof football captured a nation.* New York, NY: Random House.

Macdonald, J. (2014). Examining the growth and popularity of women's mixed martial arts. Bleacher Report. Retrieved from https://bleacherreport.com/articles/2148497-examining-the-growth-and-popularity-of-womens-mixed-martial-arts

Macklon, M. (2011, July 5). The rise of labor unions in pro sports. Investopedia. Retrieved from https://www.investopedia.com/financial-edge/0711/the-rise-of-labor-unions-in-pro-sports.aspx

MacNeil, M. (1988) Active women, media representations and ideology. In J. Harvey & H. Cantelon (Eds.), *Not just a game: Essays in Canadian sport sociology* (pp. 195–211). Ottawa, Canada: University of Ottawa Press.

MacPhail, A., & Kirk, D. (2006). Young people's socialization into sport: Experiencing the specializing phase. *Leisure Studies, 25,* 57–74.

Madensen, T. D., & Eck, J. E. (2008). The problem of spectator violence in stadiums, spectator violence. Center for Problem-Oriented Policing. Retrieved from https://popcenter.asu.edu/problems/spectator_violence

Magd H. (2003). Management attitudes and perceptions of older employees in hospitality management. *International Journal of Contemporary Hospitality Management, 15*(7), 393–401.

Magnay, J. (2012, April 4). IOC faces calls to ban Saudi Arabia after it refuses to send women to the games. *The Telegraph.* Retrieved from https://www.telegraph.co.uk/sport/olympics/9189537/London-2012-Olympics-IOC-faces-calls-to-ban-Saudi-Arabia-after-it-refuses-to-send-women-athletes-to-Games.html

Maguire, J. (1990) More than a sporting "touchdown." The making of American football in Britain 1982–1989. *Sociology of Sport Journal, 7,* 213–37.

Maguire, J. (1999) *Global sport. Identities, societies, civilizations.* Cambridge, United Kingdom: Polity Press.

Maguire, J., & Poulton, E. (1999). European identity politics in EURO 96: invented traditions and national habitus codes. *International Review for the Sociology of Sport, 34*(1), 17–29.

Mahoney, J. L., Lord, H., & Carryl, E. (2005). Afterschool program participation and the development of child obesity and peer acceptance. *Applied Developmental Science, 9,* 201–214.

Malach-Pines A., & Kaspi-Baruch, O. (2008). The role of culture and gender in the choice of a career in management. *Career Development International, 13*(4), 306–319.

Malanga, G., Filart, R., & Cheng, J. (2002). Athletes with disabilities. Medscape. Retrieved from https://emedicine.medscape.com/article/92814-overview

Malloy, M. (2016). Andy Murray gives brilliant response to John Inverdale gaffe about women tennis players. *The Telegraph.* Retrieved from http://www.telegraph.co.uk/olympics/2016/08/15/andy-murray-gives-brilliant-response-to-john-inverdale-gaffe-abo/

Mandell, N. (2014, September 16). Why so many professional athletes accused of domestic violence are still allowed to take the field. *USA Today.* Retrieved from https://ftw.usatoday.com/2014/09/nfl-players-domestic-violence-policy

Manheim, J. B. (1987). A model of agenda dynamics. In M. L. McLaughlin (Ed.), *Communication yearbook* (Vol. 10, pp. 499–516). Beverly Hills, CA: Sage Publications.

Manjone, J. (1998). International youth tour benefits. *The Sport Journal.* Retrieved from www.thesportjournal.org/vol1no1/travel.htm

Mansour, R. (2016, April 27). When did athletes begin putting last names on the back of their jerseys? Quora.com. Retrieved from https://www.quora.com/When-did-athletes-begin-putting-last-names-on-the-back-of-their-jerseys

Mark (2016). Top 10 richest sports team owners. Retrieved from http://topbet.eu/news/top-10-richest-sports-team-owners.html

Marlow, N., Marlow, E., & Arnold, V. A. (1995). Career development and women managers: Does "one size fit all"? *Human Resource Planning, 18*(2), 38–49.

Martens, R. (1993). Psychological perspectives. In B. R. Cahill & A. J. Pearl (Eds.), *Intensive participation in children's sports* (pp. 9–18). Champaign, IL: Human Kinetics.

Martin, A. C. (2008). Television media as a potential negative factor in the racial identity development of African American youth. *Academic Psychiatry, 32,* 338–342.

Martin, J., & Almasy, S. (2014, September 16). Ray Rice terminated by team, suspended by NFL after new violent video. CNN. Retrieved from http://www.cnn.com

Martin, M. C., & Kennedy, P. F. (1994). The measurement of social comparison to advertising models: A gender gap revealed. In J. A. Costa (Ed.), *Gender issues and consumer behavior* (pp. 104–124). Thousand Oaks, CA: Sage.

Martin, P. Y. (1998). Why can't a man be more like a woman? Reflections on Connell's masculinities. *Gender and Society, 12*(4), 472–474.

Martin, S. B., Jackson, A.W., Richardson, P.A., & Weiller, K. H. (1999). Coaching preferences of adolescent youths and their parents. *Journal of Applied Sport Psychology, 11,* 247–262.

Martino, W. (1995). Boys and literacy: Exploring the construction of hegemonic masculinities and the formation of literate capacities for boys in the English classroom. *English in Australia, 112,* 11–24.

Martinson, J. (2012). London 2012 lit a cauldron for gender equality. *The Guardian.* Retrieved from http://www.guardian.co.uk/lifeandstyle/the-womens-blog-with-jane-martinson/2012/jul/30/london-2012-cauldron-gender-equality

Maske, M. (2018). NFL stands by its controversial helmet rule, with one clarification. *Washington Post.* Retrieved from https://www.washingtonpost.com/news/sports/wp/2018/08/22/nfl-reaffirms-helmet-hitting-rule-clarifies-incidental-contact-isnt-a-penalty/?utm_term=.dfe8bd5ed5c3

Mason, T. (1980). *Association football and English society 1863–1915.* Brighton, United Kingdom: Harvester Press.

Massa, M. S. (1999). *Catholics and American culture: Fulton Sheen, Dorothy Day, and the Notre Dame football team.* New York, NY: Crossroad.

Massengale, J., & Farrington, S. (1977). The influence of playing position centrality on the careers of college football coaches. *Review of Sport and Leisure, 2,* 107–115.

Masteralexis, L. P., Barr, C. A., & Hums, M. (2018). *Principles and Practice of Sport Management* (5th ed.). Santa Clara, CA: Chegg, Inc.

Mastro, D., Behm-Morawitz, E., & Ortiz, M. (2007). The cultivation of social perceptions of

Latinos: A mental models approach. *Media Psychology*, 9, 347–365.

Matschiner, M. & Murnen, S. K. (1999). Hyperfemininity and influence. *Psychology of Women Quarterly*, 23(3), 631–642. https://doi.org/10.1111/j.1471-6402.1999.tb00385.x

Matthews, W. (2011, May 15). Posada drama? Ain't seen nothin' yet. ESPN. Retrieved from ESPNNewYork.com

Maurer, T. J., Wrenn, K. A., & Weiss, E. M. (2003). Toward understanding and managing stereotypical beliefs about older workers' ability and desire for learning and development. In J. Martocchio, H. Lioa, A. Joshi (Eds.), *Research in personnel and human resources management* (Vol. 22, pp. 253–285). Bingley, United Kingdom: Emerald Group Publishing.

Maxs (2010, December 3). Did Belmont University force lesbian soccer coach Lisa Howe to quit because she's having a baby? Queerty. Retrieved from https://www.queerty.com/did-belmont-university-force-lesbian-soccer-coach-lisa-howe-to-quit-because-shes-having-a-baby-20101203

Mayeda, D. T. (1999). From model minority to economic threat: Media portrayals of Major League Baseball pitchers Hideo Nomo and Hideki Irabu. *Journal of Sport & Social Issues*, 23(2), 203–217. doi: 10.1177/0193723599232007

Mayer, A. E. (2009). Review of *Women, the Koran and international human rights law: The experience of Pakistan* [book review]. *Human Rights Quarterly*, 31(4), 1155–1158.

Mayo Clinic Staff (2016, October). Human growth hormone (HGH): Does it slow aging? Mayo Clinic. https://www.mayoclinic.org/healthy-lifestyle/healthy-aging/in-depth/growth-hormone/art-20045735

Mazur, A. (2009). Testosterone and violence among young men. In A. Walsh & K. M. Beaver (Eds.), *Biosocial criminology: New directions in theory and research* (pp. 190–204). New York, NY: Routledge.

McCarthy, B. (2012). Consuming sports media, producing sports media: An analysis of two fan sports blogospheres. *International Review for the Sociology of Sport*, 48, 421–434.

McCauley, H. L., Jaime, M.C.D., Tancredi, D. J., Silverman, J. G., Decker, M. R., Austin, S. B., Jones, K., & Miller, E. (2014). Differences in adolescent relationship abuse perpetration and gender-inequitable attitudes by sport among male high school athletes. *Journal of Adolescent Mental Health*, 54(6), 742–744. doi:10.1016/j.jadohealth.2014.01.001

McCombs, M. (1981). The agenda setting approach. In D. Nimmo & K. Sanders (Eds.), *Handbook of political communication* (pp. 121–140.). Beverly Hills, CA: Sage.

McCombs, M. (1994). News influence on our pictures of the world. In J. Bryant and D. Zillmann (Eds.), Media effects (pp. 1–18). Hillsdale, NJ: Lawrence Erlbaum.

McCombs, M., & Shaw, D. (1972). The agenda-setting function of mass media. *Public Opinion Quarterly*, 36(2), 176–187.

Mccreary, J. (2018). Study: Diversity remains low in sports news departments. *US News and World Report*. Retrieved from https://www.usnews.com/news/sports/articles/2018-05-02/study-diversity-remains-low-in-sports-news-departments

McDonald, M. (2006). Muslim women and the veil. *Feminist Media Studies*, 6(1), 7–23.

McDonald, S. N. (2014, August 8). Ron Artest—we mean Metta World Peace—has changed his name again. *Washington Post*. Retrieved from https://www.washingtonpost.com/news/morning-mix/wp/2014/08/08/ron-artest-we-mean-metta-world-peace-has-changed-his-name-again/?noredirect=on&utm_term=.a35807bee20a

McDowell, M. A., Fryar, C. D., Ogden, C. L., & Flegal, K. M. (2008). Anthropometric reference data for children and adults: United States, 2003–2006. *National Health Statistics Reports*, 10, 1–45.

McEvoy, G. M., & Cascio, W. F. (1989). Cumulative evidence of the relationship between employee age and job performance. *Journal of Applied Psychology*, 74(1), 11–17.

McGinnis, L., & Gentry, J. W. (2001). *Analyzing the gender gap in participatory golf using a ritual dramaturgical framework*. Paper presented at the American Marketing Association Summer Educators' Conference, Washington, D.C.

McGoldrick, A. E., & Arrowsmith, J. (1993). Recruitment advertising: Discrimination on the basis of age. *Employee Relations*, 15(5), 54–65.

McGregor, J., & Comrie, M. (1995). *Balance and fairness in broadcasting news*. Wellington, New Zealand: Broadcasting Standards Authority.

McGuffey, S. (2011). Playing in the gender transgression zone: Race, class, and hegemonic masculinity in middle childhood. In J. Z. Spade & C. G. Valentine (Eds), *The kaleidoscope of gender: Prisms, patterns, and possibilities* (3rd ed., pp. 608–627). Thousand Oaks, CA: Sage / Pine Forge Press.

McIntosh, P. (1988). *White privilege and male privilege: A personal account of coming to see correspondences through work in women's studies.* Wellesley, MA: Wellesley College Center for Research on Women.

McIntosh, P. (1989). *White privilege and male privilege. Peace & Freedom* (pp. 10–12). Philadelphia, PA: Women's International League for Peace and Freedom.

McIntosh, P. (1993). The sociology of sport in the ancient world. In E. C. Dunning, J. A. Maguire, & R. E. Pearton (Eds.), *The sports process: A comparative and developmental approach* (pp. 19–38). Champaign, IL: Human Kinetics.

McIntosh, P. (1997). White privilege and male privilege: A personal account coming to see correspondences through work in women's studies. In R. Delgado & J. Stefancic (Eds.), *Critical white studies: Looking behind the mirror* (pp. 291–299). Philadelphia, PA: Temple University Press.

McIntosh, P. (1998). White privilege: Unpacking the invisible knapsack. In M. McGoldrick (Ed.), *Re-visioning family therapy: Race, culture, and gender in clinical practice* (pp. 147–152). New York, NY: Guilford Press. (Reprinted from Peace and freedom, July/August 1989, pp. 10–12. Also reprinted in modified form from *White privilege and male privilege: A personal account of coming to see correspondences through work in women's studies, center working paper* 189, 1989).

McIntyre, A. (1994). Sex makes a difference. *IPA Review, 47*(2), 17.

McKay, J., & Rowe, D. (1987) Ideology, the media and Australian sport. *Sociology of Sport Journal, 4*(3), 258–273.

McKenna, S., & Richardson, J. (2017). Game over: how professional athletes can have a career after sport. The Conversation. Retrieved from https://theconversation.com/game-over-how-professional-athletes-can-have-a-career-after-sport-71555

McKinnon, J. D. (2009, May 5). President's tax proposal riles businesses. *The Wall Street Journal.* Retrieved from http://online.wsj.com.

McKirdy, E. (2017). Racial slur sprayed on LeBron's house: It's tough being black in America. Fox2Now. Retrieved from http://fox2now.com/2017/06/01/racial-slur-sprayed-on-lebrons-house-its-tough-being-black-in-america/

Mclarney, E. (2009). The burqa in Vogue. *Journal of Middle Eastern Women's Studies, 5*(1), 1–20.

McLeod, J., & Becker, L. (1981). The uses and gratifications approach. In D. Nimmo & K. Sanders (Eds.), *Handbook of political communication* (pp. 67–100). Beverly Hills, CA: Sage.

McLeod, J., Atkin, C., & Chaffee, S. (1972). Adolescents, parents and television use. In G. Comstock & E. Rubinstein (Eds.), *Television and social behavior: Vol. III. Television and adolescent aggressiveness* (pp. 274–344). Washington, DC: U.S. Government Printing Office.

McLeod, J., Becker, L., & Byrnes, J. (1974). Another look at the agenda setting function of the press. *Communication Research, 1*(2), 131–166.

McMahan, I. (2015, April 22). Running into old age. *The Atlantic.* Retrieved from https://www.theatlantic.com/health/archive/2015/04/running-into-old-age/390219/

McMillan, J. H., & Reed, D. F. (1994). At-risk students and resiliency: Factors contributing to academic success. *Clearing House, 67*, 137–140.

McRae, D. (2017). Kareem Abdul-Jabbar: "Trump is where he is because of his appeal to racism." *The Guardian.* Retrieved from https://www.theguardian.com/sport/2017/dec/08/kareem-abdul-jabbar-kaepernick-trump-interview

Mead, M. (1935). *Sex and temperament in three primitive societies.* New York, NY: William Morrow.

Meân, L. J., & Kassing, J. W. (2007). Identities at youth sporting events: A critical discourse analysis. *International Journal of Sport Communication, 1*, 42–66.

Meân, L. J., & Kassing, J. W. (2008). "I would just like to be known as an athlete": Managing hegemony, femininity, and heterosexuality in female sport. *Western Journal of Communication, 72*(2), 126–144.

Mennesson, C. (2000). "Hard" women and "soft" women: The social construction of identities among female boxers. *International Review for the Sociology of Sport, 35*(1), 21–33.

Merikangas, K. R., He, J. P., Burstein, M., Swanson, S. A., Avenevoli, S., Cui, L., Benjet, C., Georgiades, K., & Swendsen, J. (2010, October). Lifetime prevalence of mental disorders in U.S. adolescents: Results from the national comorbidity survey replication—adolescent supplement (NCS-A). *Journal of the American Academy of Child and Adolescent Psychiatry, 49*(10), 980–989.

Merkel D. L. (2013). Youth sport: Positive and negative impact on young athletes. *Open Access Journal of Sports Medicine, 4,* 151–160. doi:10.2147/OAJSM.S33556

Merskin, D. (1998). Sending up signals: A survey of Native American media use and representation in the mass media. *Howard Journal of Communications, 9*(4), 333–345. doi:10.1080/106461798246943

Merton, R. K. (1938). Social structure and anomie. *American Sociological Review, 3*(5), 672–682.

Mertz, T. J. (2000). The Harlem Globetrotters. *St. James encyclopedia of popular culture* (Vol. 2). Detroit, MI: St. James Press.

Messerschmidt, J. W. (1993). Masculinities and crime: Critique and reconceptualization of theory. Lanham, MD: Rowman and Littlefield.

Messerschmidt, J.W. (1995). Managing to kill: Masculinities and the space shuttle Challenger explosion. *Masculinities, 3*(4), 1–22.

Messerschmidt, J. W. (2010). *Hegemonic masculinities and camouflaged politics: Unmasking the Bush dynasty and its war against Iraq.* London, United Kingdom: Paradigm Publishers.

Messner, M. (2007). *Out of play: Critical essays on gender and sport.* New York, NY: State University of New York Press.

Messner, M. A. (1992). *Power at play: Sports and the problem of masculinity.* Boston, MA: Beacon.

Messner, M. A., (1990). When bodies are weapons: Masculinity and violence in sport. *International Review for the Sociology of Sport, 25,* 203–220.

Messner, M. A. (2002). *Taking the field: Women, men, and sports.* Minneapolis, MN: University of Minnesota Press.

Messner, M.A., Dunbar, M. and Hunt, D. (2000) The televised sports manhood formula. *Journal of Sport and Social Issues, 24*(4), 380–394.

Messner, M. A., Dunbar, M., & Hunt, D. (2005). The televised sports manhood formula. In D.S.

Eitzen (Ed.), *Sport in contemporary society: An anthology* (pp. 98–111). Boulder, CO: Paradigm Publishers.

Messner, M. A., Duncan, M. C., & Cooky, C. (2003). Silence, sports bras, and wrestling porn: The treatment of women in televised sports news and highlights. *Journal of Sport and Social Issues, 27,* 38–51.

Messner, M. A., Duncan, M. C., and Jensen, K. (1993). Separating the men from the girls: The gendered language of televised sports. *Gender and Society, 7*(1), 121–137.

Messner, M. A., Duncan, M. C., & Wachs, F. L. (1996). The gender of audience-building: Televised coverage of men's and women's NCAA basketball. *Sociological Inquiry, 66,* 422–439.

Messner, M.A., & Sabo, D. (Eds.). (1990). *Sport, men, and the gender order: Critical feminist perspectivces.* Champaign, IL: Human Kinetics Books.

Messner, Michael A. (1992). *Power at play.* Boston, MA: Beacon.

Messner, Michael A. (1990). When bodies are weapons: Masculinity and violence in sport. *International Review for the Sociology of Sport, 25*(3), 203–220.

Meyers-Levy, J., & and Durairaj, M. (1991). Exploring differences in males' and females' processing strategies. *Journal of Consumer Research, 18*(June), 63–70.

Meyers, G. (1996). Selling a man's world to women. *American Demographics, 18*(April), 36–42.

Meyerson, D. E., and Fletcher, J. K. (2000). A modest manifesto for shattering the glass ceiling. *Harvard Business Review, 78* (January–February), 127–136.

Miczek, K. A., Mirsky, A. F., Carey, G., DeBold, J., & Raine, A. (1994). An overview of biological influences on violent behavior. In J. Albert, J. Reiss, K. A. Miczek, & J. A. Roth (Eds.), *Understanding and preventing violence: Biobehavioral influences* (Vol. 2, pp. 1–20). Washington, DC: National Academy Press.

Miedzian, M. (1992). *Boys will be boys: Breaking the link between masculinity and violence.* New York, NY: Doubleday.

Milavsky, J., Kessler, R., Stipp, H., & Rubens, W. (1983). *Television and aggression.* New York, NY: Academic Press.

Milgram, S., & Shotland, R. (1973). *Television and antisocial behavior.* New York, NY: Academic Press.

Milhausen, R., & Herold, E. (1999). Does the sexuality double standard still exist? Perceptions of university women. *Journal of Sex Research, 36*(4), 361–368.

Miliband, R. (1977). *Marxism and politics.* Oxford, United Kingdom: Oxford University Press.

Milillo, D. (2008). Sexuality sells: A content analysis of lesbian and heterosexual women's bodies in magazine advertisements. *Journal of Lesbian Studies, 12*(4), 381–392.

Miller, C. F., Lurye, L. E., Zosuls, K. M., & Ruble, D. N. (2009). Accessibility of gender stereotype domains: Developmental and gender differences in children. *Sex Roles, 60*(11–12), 870–881. http://doi.org/10.1007/s11199-009-9584-x):

Miller, D. (2016). Intersectionality: how gender interacts with other social identities to shape bias. The Conversation. Retrieved from https://theconversation.com/intersectionality-how-gender-interacts-with-other-social-identities-to-shape-bias-53724

Miller, J. (1990). *The baseball business: Pursuing pennants and profits in Baltimore.* Chapel Hill, NC: University of North Carolina Press.

Milligan, R. (2017). The top 10 Black women sports journalists in 2017. Rolling Out.com. Retrieved from https://rollingout.com/2017/12/28/the-top-10-black-women-sports-journalists-in-2017/

Miner, J. W. (2016). Why 70 percent of kids quit sports by age 13. *The Washington Post.* Retrieved from https://www.washingtonpost.com/news/parenting/wp/2016/06/01/why-70-percent-of-kids-quit-sports-by-age-13/

Minister for Sport Review Group. (1989). *Building on ability.* Leeds, United Kingdom: HMSO for Department of Education the Ministers' Review Group.

Minkler M. (2006). Generational equity and the new victim blaming. In H. R. Moody (Ed.), *Aging: Concepts and controversies* (pp. 181–190). Newbury Park, CA: Pine Forge Press. (Reprinted from *Critical perspectives on aging*, pp. 67–79, by M. Minkler & C. Estes, Eds., 1991, Amityville, NY: Baywood).

Minton, J. (1975). The impact of "Sesame Street" on readiness. *Sociology of Education, 48*(2), 141–155.

Mishel, L., Bernstein, J., & Shierholz, H. (2009). *The state of working America 2008/2009.* Ithaca, NY: ILR Press.

Moffett, M. (2013, February 13). As the world turns, so do the wheels of roller derby. WSJ.com. Retrieved from https://www.wsj.com/articles/SB10001424127887324610504578278171721339976?fb_action_ids=10152543496805385&fb_action_types=og.recommends&fb_source=aggregation&fb_aggregation_id=288381481237582

Mohammed, N. S. (2012). Muslim women and the London Olympics. The Canadian Province. Retrieved from http://www2.canada.com/theprovince/news/editorial/story.html?id = ea39b0ba-323d-472d-8f97-70c87f135fae&p = 1

Mohanty, C. T. (1988). Under western eyes: Feminist scholarship and colonial discourses. *Feminist Review, 30*(1), 61–89.

Monte Carlo Forum. (2018). Types of social classes of people. Retrieved from http://montecarloforum.com/forum/archive/index.php/t-6343

Montepare, J. M., & Zebrowitz, L. A. (2004). A social-developmental view of ageism. In T. D. Nelson (Ed.), *Ageism: Stereotyping and prejudice against older persons* (pp. 129–161). Cambridge, MA: MIT Press.

Montepare, J. M., & Lachman, M. E. (1989). "You're only as old as you feel": Self-perceptions of age, fears of aging, and life satisfaction from adolescence to old age. *Psychology and Aging, 4*, 73–78.

Montgomery, K. (1995). *Prosocial behavior in films.* Unpublished master's thesis, University of Georgia.

Montiel, I., & Delgado-Ceballos, J. (2014). Defining and measuring corporate sustainability: Are we there yet? *Organization & Environment, 27*(2), 113–139. https://doi.org/10.1177/1086026614526413

Moore, B., Parisotto, R., Sharp, C., Pitsalidis, Y., & Kayser, B. (2007). Erythropoetic indices in elite Kenyan runners training at altitude. *East African Running, 8*(4), 199–214.

Moore, K. (1990, February). Sons of the wind. *Sports Illustrated*, pp. 72–80.

Moore, M. (2014, April 29). NBA owners speak out against alleged Sterling comments. *CBS Sports.* Retrieved from https://www.cbssports.com/nba/news/nba-owners-speak-out-against-alleged-sterling-comments/

Moore, M. (2017). The question of intersectionality in women's sport. Michelle Moore. Retrieved from http://michellemoore.me/the-question-of-intersectionality-in-womens-sport/

Morgan, M. (1988). The impact of religion on gender-role attitudes. *Psychology of Women Quarterly, 11*, 301–310.

Morgan, M., & Shanahan, J. (1997). Two decades of cultivation research. In B. R. Burleson (Ed.), *Communication yearbook 20* (pp. 1–47). Thousand Oaks, CA: Sage Publications.

Morgan, S. (Ed.). (1989). *Gender and anthropology: Critical reviews for research and teaching.* Washington, DC: American Anthropological Association.

Morris, B. (2014, July 31). The rate of domestic violence arrests among NFL players. Five Thirty Eight. Retrieved from https://fivethirtyeight.com/features/the-rate-of-domestic-violence-arrests-among-nfl-players/

Morrison, S. (2014). Media is failing women—sports journalism particularly so. Poynter. Retrieved from https://www.poynter.org/2014/media-is-failing-women-sports-journalism-particularly-so/240240/

Morrow-Howell N, Hinterlong J, Rozario PA, & Tang F. (2002). Effects of volunteering on the well-being of older adults. *Journals of Gerontology Series B, 58*(3), S137–S145.

Mota, J, & Silva, G. (1999). Adolescent's physica activity: association with socio-economic status and parental participation among a Portuguese sample. *Sport, Education and Society, 4*(2), 193–199.

Mu, H., & Ramirez, A. (2006). *Who, how, and with whom: An exploration of social Internet use and loneliness.* Paper presented to the International Communication Association in Dresden, Germany.

Mueller, C., Donnerstein, E., & Hallam, J. (1983). Violent films and prosocial behavior. *Personality and Social Psychology Bulletin, 9*, 183–189.

Mullin, B. (2016, April 25). Want to get a journalism job? Here are the skills you need, according to a new report. Poynter. Retrieved from https://www.poynter.org/business-work/2016/want-to-get-a-journalism-job-here-are-the-skills-you-need-according-to-a-new-report/

Mullins, E. (1977). Agenda setting and the younger voter. In D. Shaw & M. McCombs (Eds.), *The emergence of American political issues* (pp. 133–148). St. Paul, MN: West.

Murdock, G. (1937). Comparative data on the division of labor by sex. *Social Forces, 15*, 551–553.

Murner, S. K. (2015). A social constructivist approach to understanding the relationship between masculinity and sexual aggression. *Psychology of Men and Masculinity, 16*(4), 370–373. doi: 10.1037/a0039693

Murray, J. (1984). A soft response to hard attacks on research. *Media Information Australia, 33*, 11–16.

Musick, M. A., Herzog, A. R., & House, J. S. (1999). Volunteering and mortality among older adults: Findings from a national sample. *Journal of Gerontology Series B: Psychological Sciences and Social Sciences, 54*, S173–S180.

Nabi, R. (2009). Cosmetic surgery makeover programs and intentions to undergo cosmetic enhancements. *Communication Research, 35*(1), 1–27.

Nabi, R., & Riddle, K. (2008). Personality traits, television viewing and the cultivation effect. *Journal of Broadcasting & Electronic Media, 52*(3), 327–348.

Nafjan, E. A. (2012, July 19). Two steps forward: Do Saudi Arabia's two Olympic female athletes—the kingdom's first ever—represent changing times in the land of the two holy mosques, or will the conservative religious backlash win out? *Foreign Policy.* Retrieved from https://foreignpolicy.com/2012/07/19/two-steps-forward/

Nagel, M. S., Southall, R. M., & O'Toole, T. (2004). Punishment in the four major North American professional sports leagues. *International Sports Journal, 8*(2), 15–27.

Nahhas, P. (2016). Heritage month: Arab Americans as athletes. Arab America.com. Retrieved from https://www.arabamerica.com/heritage-month-arab-americans-athletes/

Nairn, R. G., & Coverdale, J. H. (2005). People never see us living well: An appraisal of the personal stories about mental illness in prospective print media sample. *Australian and New Zealand Journal of Psychiatry, 39*, 281–287.

NAJA calls upon news media to stop "using mascots." (2002, March 1). *Native American Times*, p. 4B. Retrieved from https://web.archive.org/web/20020611210337/http://www.naja.com/pr-stopmascot.html

Nakamura, Y. (2005). The samurai sword cuts both ways: A transnational analysis of Japanese and US media representations of Ichiro. *International Review for the Sociology of Sport*, 40(4), 467–480. doi: 10.1177/1012690205065749

Nanda, S. (1997). Neither man nor woman: The Hirjas of India. In C. B. Brettell & C. F. Sargent (Eds.), *Gender in cross-cultural perspective* (2nd ed., pp. 198–201). Upper Saddle River, NJ: Prentice Hall.

Nathan, D. A. (2003). *Saying it's so: A cultural history of the black Sox scandal.* Urbana, IL: University of Illinois Press.

Nathanson, A. I. (1999). Identifying and explaining the relationship between parental mediation and children's aggression. *Communication Research*, 26(2), 124–143.

Nathanson, A. I. (2001). Parents vs. peer. *Communication Research*, 28(3), 251–274.

National Coalition Against Violent Athletes. (2018). It starts in the locker room. Retrieved from http://www.ncava.org/athletes

National Coalition of Anti-Violence Programs. (2010). Hate violence against lesbian, gay, bisexual, transgender, queer and HIV-affected communities in the United States. Retrieved from http://www.avp.org/storage/documents/Reports/2012_NCAVP_2011_HV_Report.pdf

National Collegiate Athletic Association. (2005). Legislation and governance. Retrieved from http://www2.ncaa.org/legislation_and_governance/

National Golf Foundation. (1998). Golf participation remains steady: New NGF participation report demonstrates that 1997 was no fluke. Retrieved from http://www.ngf.org/whatsnew/OLD/story60.html

National Golf Foundation. (1999). Improving the investment return on women's golf. Retrieved from http://www.ngf.org/whatsnew/story72.html.

National Institute of Mental Health. (1982). *Television and behavior: Ten years of scientific progress and implications for the 1980s.* Washington, DC: U.S. Government Printing Office.

National Institute of Mental Health. (2016). Depression. Mental Health Center. Retrieved from http://www.mentalhealthcenter.org/pushing-the-limits-professional-athletes-and-mental-health/

National Middle School Association. (2003). *This we believe: Successful schools for young adolescents.* Westerville, OH: Author.

The National Post. (2012). Sarah Attar becomes Saudi Arabia's first female Olympian on the track. Retrieved from http://sports.nationalpost.com/2012/08/08/sarah-attar-becomes-saudi-arabias-first-female-olympian-on-the-track/

Native American Mascots. (2008, March 6). National Collegiate Athletic Association. Retrieved from http://www.ncaa.org/wps/portal/ncaahome?WCM_GLOBAL_CONTEXT=/ncaa/NCAA/Media%20and%20Events/Press%20Room/ Current%20Issues/General%20Information/native_american_mascots.html

Navarro, L. (2010). Islamophobia and sexism: Muslim women in the western mass media. *Human Architecture: Journal of the Sociology of Self-Knowledge*, 8(2), 95–114, Available at: https://scholarworks.umb.edu/humanarchitecture/vol8/iss2/10

NBA. (2011). NBA career opportunities. Retrieved from http://www.nba.com/careers/management_team.html

NBA Careers. (2018, June 2). Pam El. Retrieved from https://careers.nba.com/executive/pam-el/

NBA.com (2014). LeBron James: "No room for Donald Sterling in NBA." Retrieved from http://www.nba.com/2014/news/04/26/lebron-james-donald-sterling-comment.ap/

NBC News.com (2018, July 22). Michael Jordan can "no longer stay silent." Retrieved from https://www.nbcnews.com/news/us-news/michael-jordan-can-no-longer-stay-silent-n616276

NCAA. (2018). NCAA inclusion of transgender student-athletes. Retrieved from https://www.ncaa.org/sites/default/files/Transgender_Handbook_2011_Final.pdf

NCAA. (2018). Sports sponsorship and participation research database. Retrieved from http://www.ncaa.org/about/resources/research/sports-sponsorship-and-participation-research

Nelson, J. (1996). The invisible cultural group: Images of disability. In P. Lester (Ed.) *Images that injure: Pictorial stereotypes in the media* (p. 123). Westport, CT: Praeger.

Nelson, M. B. (1994). *The stronger women get, the more men love football: Sexism and the American culture of sports.* San Diego, CA: Harcourt, Brace & Company.

Nelson, T. E., & Clawson, R. A. (1997). Media framing of a civil liberties conflict and its effect on tolerance. *American Political Science Review, 91,* 567–583.

Nelson, M. B. (2001). *The stronger women get, the more men love football.* New York, NY: PerfectBound.

Nelson, T. D. (Ed.) (2004). *Ageism: Stereotyping and prejudice against older persons.* Cambridge, MA: MIT Press.

Nelson, T. D. (2005). Ageism: Prejudice against our feared future self. *Journal of Social Issues, 61*(2), 207–221.

Nelson, T. D. (2009). Ageism. In T. D. Nelson (Ed.), *Handbook of prejudice, stereotyping and discrimination* (pp. 431–440). New York, NY: Psychology Press.

Nelson, M. B. (1998, March). I won, I'm sorry. *Self Magazine,* pp. 145–147.

Neugarten, B. L. (1974). Age groups in American society and the rise of the young-old. *Annals of the American Academy of Political and Social Science, 415*(1), 187–198.

Neverson, N., & White, P. (2002). Muscular, bruise, and sweaty bodies … That is not Barbie territory. *Canadian Woman Studies, 21*(3), 44–49.

New, J. (2016, January 14). Mental health of college athletes. Inside Higher Ed. Retrieved from https://www.insidehighered.com/news/2016/01/14/ncaa-establishes-best-practices-mental-health-college-athletes

Newburn, T., & Stanko, E. A. (1994). *Just boys doing business? Men, masculinities, and crime.* New York, NY: Routledge.

Newhagen, J., & Lewenstein, M. (1992). Cultivation and exposure to television following the 1989 Loma Prieta earthquake. *Mass Communication Review, 19*(1/2), 49–56.

Newport, F., & Saad, L. (1998, July/August). A matter of trust. *American Journalism Review, 20*(6), 30–33.

Newton, D. (2013). Weighty issue follows Danica. ESPN. Retrieved from http://www.espn.com/racing/nascar/cup/story/_/id/8967000/daytona-500-danica-patrick-body-weight-not-plus-driver-seat

Newton, D. (2016, February 2). Cam Newton takes Peyton's "face of the NFL" prediction in stride. ESPN. Retrieved from http://www.espn.com/nfl/story/_/id/14694984/super-bowl-50-cam-newton-carolina-panthers-peyton-manning-flattery-ink-gold

New York Times. (2012a). Observance of Ramadan poses challenges to Muslim athletes. Retrieved from http://www.nytimes.com/2012/08/01/sports/olympics/ramadan-poses-challenges-for-muslims-at-the-olympics.html?_r = 0

New York Times. (2012b). 82 seconds, long enough for history. Retrieved from http://www.nytimes.com/2012/08/04/sports/olympics/wojdan-shaherkani-first-female-saudi-olympian-loses-in-debut.html?_r = 0

The *New York Times* Archive. (1990). Tennis; status: Undefeated. Future: Rosy. Age: 10. *New York Times.* Retrieved from https://www.nytimes.com/1990/07/03/sports/tennis-status-undefeated-future-rosy-age-10.html

Ng, S. H. (1998). Social psychology in an ageing world: Ageism and intergenerational relations. *Asian Journal of Social Psychology, 1,* 99–116.

Ng, S. H. (2002). Will families support their elders? Answers from across cultures. In T. D. Nelson (Ed.), *Ageism: Stereotyping and prejudice against older persons* (pp. 295–309). Cambridge, MA: MIT Press.

Ng, S. H., & McCreanor, T. (1999). Patterns in discourse about elderly people in New Zealand. *Journal of Aging Studies, 13*(4), 473–489.

Niblock, G. (2010, December 12). Report: Faryd Mondragon set to leave Koeln for Philadelphia Union. Goal.com. Retrieved from https://www.goal.com/en-us/news/87/germany/2010/12/09/2253448/report-faryd-mondragon-set-to-leave-koeln-for-philadelphia

Nicholas, S. (2017). Just a number: Meet the 97-year-old bodybuilder who refuses to retire. *Daily Express.* Retrieved from https://www.express.co.uk/entertainment/books/762775/bodybuilder-pensioner-retirement-age-just-number-book

Nie, N. H., & Erbring, L. (2000). *Internet and society: A preliminary report.* Palo Alto, CA: Stanford Institute for the Quantitative Study of Society.

Nielsen Market Research. (2007, March). Consumer insights: Delivering consumer clarity. Retrieved from https://www.nielsen.com/

content/dam/nielsen/en_us/documents/pdf/ Consumer%20Insight/Hispanic%20Fusion%20 Finally%20Hitting%20the%20Bullseye.pdf

Nieporent, D. (2004, February 9). Easterhuh? Jumping to conclusions. Retrieved from http:// oobleck.com/tollbooth/archives/2004_02.html

Nisbett, R. E. (2003). *The geography of thought: How Asians and westerners think differently ... and why.* New York, NY: The Free Press.

Nixon, H. L. (2007). Constructing diverse sports opportunities for people with disabilities. *Journal of Sport and Social Issues, 31*(4), 417–433. https://doi.org/10.1177/0193723507308250

Noakes, T. D., Myburgh, K. H., & Schall, R. (1990). Peak treadmill running velocity during VO2max test predicts running performance. *Journal of Sports Sciences, 8,* 35–45.

Noelle-Neumann, E. (1974). The spiral of silence a theory of public opinion. *Journal of Communication, 24*(2), 43–51.

Norris, M. (2016). Cam Newton comments on Super Bowl media requirements. *Bleacher Report.* Retrieved from https://bleacherreport. com/articles/2613738-cam-newton-comments-on-super-bowl-media-requirements

North, M. S., & Fiske, S. T. (2010, January). *Succession, identity, and consumption: Dimensions of control in age-based prejudice.* Poster presentation at the 11th Annual Society for Personality and Social Psychology Conferences, Las Vegas, NV.

North, M. S., & Fiske, S. T. (2011, January). *A prescriptive, intergenerational scale of ageism: succession, identity, & consumption.* Poster presentation at the 12th Annual Society for Personality and Social Psychology Conference, San Antonio, TX.

North, M. S., & Fiske, S. T. (2012). An inconvenienced youth? Ageism and its potential intergenerational roots. *Psychological Bulletin, 138*(5), 982–997.

North, M. S., & Fiske, S. T. (2013). Act your (old) age prescriptive, ageist biases over succession, consumption, and identity, *Psychological Bulletin, 39*(6), 720–734.

Norton, K. I., Olds, T. S., Olive, S., & Dank, S. (1996). Ken and Barbie at life size. *Sex Roles, 34,* 287–294.

Novak, M. (1976). *The joy of sport: End zones, bases, baskets, balls, and the consecration of the American spirit.* New York, NY: Basic Books.

Nowatzki, R. (2002). Foul lines and the color line: Baseball and race at the turn of the twentieth century. *Nine, 11*(1), 11–15.

Nowlin, B. (2018). Joe Lahoud. Retrieved from https://sabr.org/bioproj/person/c00b38fc

Nucci, C., & Young-Shim, K. (2005). Improving socialization through sport: An analytic review of literature on aggression and sportsmanship. *Physical Educator, 62*(3), 123–129.

Nudd, T. (2015). Always unveils "like a girl" sequel showing girls redefining the phrase for real. *Adweek.* Retrieved from https://www.adweek. com/adfreak/always-unveils-girl-sequel-showing-girls-redefining-phrase-real-163249/

Nuessel, Jr., F. H. (1982). The language of ageism. *The Gerontologist, 22,* 273–276.

Nussbaum, J. F., Pitts, M. J., Huber, F. N., Raup Krieger, J. L., & Ohs, J. E. (2005). Ageism and ageist language across the life span: Intimate relationships and non-intimate interactions. *Journal of Social Issues, 61,* 287–305.

Oakley, J. (2000). Gender-based barriers to senior management positions: Understanding the scarcity of female CEOs. *Journal of Business Ethics, 27*(4), 321–334.

Oates, J. C. (2006). *On boxing.* Garden City, NY: HarperPerennial Modern Classics.

O'Brien, K. S., Kolt, G. S., Martens, M. P. Ruffman, T., Miller, P. G., & Lynott, D. (2012). Alcohol-related aggression and antisocial behavior in sportspeople/athletes. *Journal of Science and Medicine in Sport, 15*(4), 292–297. doi: 10.1016/j.jsams.2011.10.008

O'Brien, N. (2018). Monday motivation: 104 year-old shows no sign of slowing. Irish Runner. Retrieved from http://www.irishrunner.ie/ monday-motivation-104-year-old-shows-no-sign-of-slowing/

O'Connor, V. (2001). Women and men in senior management—a "different needs" hypothesis. *Women in Management Review, 16*(7/8), 400–404.

O'Donnell, A. (2017). Why does Colin Kaepernick kneel? Former Longhorn Nate Boyer says he wrote him a letter. *Austin American-Statesman.* Retrieved from https:// www.statesman.com/events/sports/ why-does-colin-kaepernick-kneel-former-longhorn-nate-boyer-says-wrote-him-letter/ uvJ4bzdMO3uIDvsMtkhTfN/

O'Keefe, G. J., & Reid-Nash, K. (1987). Crime news and real world blues. *Communication Research, 14*(2), 147–163.

Oliffe, J. L., & Phillips, M. J. (2008). Men, depression, and masculinities: A review and recommendations. *Journal of Men's Health,* 5(3), 194–202.

Oliver, M. (1990). *The politics of disablement.* Basingstoke, United Kingdom: Macmillan.

Olmstead, M. (2016, September 2). Title IX and the Rise of Female Athletes in America. Women's Sports Foundation. Retrieved from https://www .womenssportsfoundation.org/education/title-ix-and-the-rise-of-female-athletes-in-america/

Omar, A., & Davidson, M. (2001). Women in management: A comparative cross-cultural overview. *Cross Cultural Management, 8*(3/4), 35–67.

O'Neil, M. (2009). *Invisible structures of opportunity: How media depictions of race trivialize issues of diversity and disparity.* Washington, DC: Frameworks Institute.

Oransky, M., Fisher, C. (2009). The development and validation of the meaning of adolescent masculinity scale. *Psychology of Men & Masculinity, 10*(1), 57–72.

Oriard, M. (2007). Brand NFL: *Making and selling America's favorite sport.* Chapel Hill, NC: University of North Carolina Press.

Orlov, A. (2016). 9 Athletes over 60 who can kick your butt. Daily Burn. Retrieved from https://dailyburn.com/life/fitness/best-athletes-over-60/

Ott, K., & Van Puymbroeck, M. (2008). Does the media impact athletic performance? *The Sport Journal.* Retrieved from https://thesportjournal.org/article/does-the-media-impact-athletic-performance/#post/0

Ourand, J. (2016). The future? Look to apps, live-streaming and digital media firms. *Sports Business Daily.* Retrieved from http://www.sportsbusinessdaily.com/Journal/Issues/2016/02/29/Media/Sports-Media.aspx

Outsports. (2016). A record 56 out LGBT athletes compete in Rio Olympics 54: The Rio Olympics has 56 publicly out LGBT athletes, the most ever for an Olympics. *Outsports.* Retrieved from https://www.outsports.com/2016/7/11/12133594/rio-olympics-teams-2016-gay-lgbt-athletes-record

Paffenbarger, R. S., Hyde, R. T., Wing, A., & Hsieh, C. C. (1986). Physical activity, all-cause mortality, and longevity of college alumni. *New England Journal of Medicine, 314,* 605–613.

Pai, K., & Vaidya, S. (2009). Glass ceiling: Role of women in the corporate world. *Competitiveness Review, 19*(2), 106–113.

Paik, H., & Comstock, G. (1994). The effects of television violence on antisocial behavior: A meta-analysis. *Communication Research, 21*(4), 516–546.

Palmgreen, P. (1984). Uses and gratifications: A theoretical perspective. In R. Bostrom (Ed.), *Communication yearbook 8* (pp. 20–55). Beverly Hills, CA: Sage.

Palmgreen, P., & Lawrence, P. A. (1991). Avoidances, gratifications and consumption of theatrical films. In B. A. Austin (Ed.), *Current research in film* (Vol. 5, pp. 39–55). Norwood, NJ: Ablex.

Palmore, E. (2003). Ageism comes of age. *The Gerontologist, 43*(3), 418–420.

Palmore, E. B. (1999). *Ageism: Negative and positive.* New York, NY: Springer Publishing Company.

Paloian, A. (2018). The female/athlete paradox: Managing traditional views of masculinity and femininity. Stein Hardt. Retrieved from https://steinhardt.nyu.edu/appsych/opus/issues/2012/fall/female

Papacharissi, Z., & Rubin, A. (2000). Predictors of Internet use. *Journal of Broadcasting and Electronic Media, 44*(2), 175–196.

Papacharissi, Z. (2009). Uses and gratifications. In D. Stacks & M. Salwen (Eds.), *An integrated approach to communication theory and research* (pp. 153–154). New York, NY: Routledge.

Pappas, N. T., McKenry, P. C., & Catlett, B. S. (2004). Athlete aggression on the rink and off the ice: Athlete violence and aggression in hockey and interpersonal relationships. *Men and Masculinities, 6*(3), 291–231. doi: 10.1177/1097184X03257433

Parke, R., Berkowitz, L., & Leyens, J. (1977). Some effects of violent and nonviolent movies on the behavior of juvenile delinquents. *Advances in Experimental Social Psychology, 16,* 135–172.

Parker, C. B. (2015). Sports stadiums do not generate significant local economic growth, Stanford expert says. Retrieved from https://news .stanford.edu/pr/2015/pr-stadium-economics-noll-073015.html

Parks, J. B., & Roberton, M. A. (1998). Influence of age, gender, and context on attitudes toward sexist/nonsexist language: Is sport a special case? *Sex Roles*, 38, 477–494.

Parsons, T., Bales, R. F., Olds, J., Zelditsch, M., & Slater, P. E. (1955). *Family, socialization, and interaction process*. New York, NY: Free Press.

Parsons, T. (1958 [1943]). *The kinship system of the contemporary United States in Essays in Sociological Theory* (pp. 177–196). New York, NY: Free Press.

Pastrana, A. J., Battle, J. & Harris, A. (2016, December 22). *An Examination of Latinx LGBT populations across the United States: Intersections of race and sexuality*. New York, NY: Springer Publishing.

Patterson, C. (2014). Ole Miss fans take down goal posts, walk them down the street. *CBS Sports*. Retrieved from https://www.cbssports.com/college-football/news/ole-miss-fans-take-down-goal-posts-walk-them-down-the-street/

Patterson, D. A., Adelv Unegv Waya, S. W., Welte, J. W., Barnes, G. M., Tidwell, M. C., & Spicer, P. (2015). Sociocultural influences on gambling and alcohol use among Native Americans in the United States. *Journal of Gambling Studies*, 31(4), 1387–1404.

Patterson, T., & McClure, R. (1976). *The unseeing eye*. New York, NY: G. P. Putnam's.

Payne, B. K., & Cikovic, R. (1995). Empirical examination of the characteristics, consequences, and causes of elder abuse in nursing homes. *Journal of Elder Abuse and Neglect*, 7(4), 61–74.

PEAR Equity Committee (2014). Transgender policy for intercollegiate athletics, club sports and intramural sports. Trans Student. Retrieved from http://www.transstudent.org/definitions/

Pedersen, P. M. (2002). Examining equity in newspaper photographs: A content analysis of the print media photographic coverage of interscholastic athletics. *International Review for the Sociology of Sport*, 37(3), 303–318.

Pedersen, P. M., & Whisenant, W. A. (2003). Examining stereotypical written and photographic reporting on the sports page: An analysis of newspaper coverage of interscholastic athletics. *Women in Sport and Physical Activity Journal*, 12, 67–86.

Pedersen, P. M., & Whisenant, W. A. (2005, Winter). Successful when given the opportunity: Investigating gender representation and success rates of interscholastic athletic directors. *Physical Educator*, 62(4), 178–186.

Pedersen, P. M., Whisenant, W. A., & Schneider, R. G. (2003). Using a content analysis to examine the gendering of sports newspaper personnel and their coverage. *Journal of Sport Management*, 17(4), 376–393.

Pelletier, L. G., Fortier, M. S., Vallerand, R. J., & Brière, N. M. (2001). Associations among perceived autonomy support, forms of self-regulations, and persistence: A prospective study. *Motivation and Emotion*, 25, 279–306.

Penny, D., & Evans, J. (1995). The national curriculum for physical education: Entitlement for all? *The British Journal of Physical Education*, Winter, pp. 6–13.

Perkinson, M. A. (1980). Alternate roles for the elderly: An example from a midwestern retirement community. *Human Organization*, 39(3), 219–226.

Perrin, T. (1987). *Football: A college history*. Jefferson, NC: McFarland & Co Inc.

Petchesky, B. (2012, August 12). Clinton Portis, Coach Janky Spanky, Sheriff Gonna Getcha, Southeast Jerome, Dolla Bill, Dr. Do Itch Big, Bro Sweets, Prime Minister Yah Mon, Bud Foxx, Coconut Jones, and Choo-Choo all announce their NFL retirements. Retrieved from https://deadspin.com/5936689/clinton-portis-coach-janky-spanky-sheriff-gonna-getcha-southeast-jerome-dolla-bill-dr-do-itch-big-bro-sweets-prime-minister-yah-mon-bud-foxx-coconut-jones-and-choo-choo-announce-their-nfl-retirements

Peter, J., & Valkenburg, P. (2008) Adolescents' exposure to sexually explicit Internet material, sexual uncertainty and uncommitted sexual exploration. *Communication Research*, 35(5), 579–601.

Peters, A. (2018). For Olympic track hopeful, coming out as gay has made him more focused on his sport. *Outsports*. Retrieved from https://www.outsports.com/2018/9/18/17858700/anthony-peters-racewalking-gay-coming-out

Petersen, A. (2003). Research on men and masculinities: Some implications of recent theory for future work. *Men and Masculinities*, 6(1), 54–69.

Peterson, R. W. (1990). *Cages into jump shots: Pro basketball's early years*. New York, NY: Oxford University Press.

Pew Internet and American Life Project. (2003). The ever-shifting Internet population. Retrieved from www.pewinternet.org/PPF/r/88/report_display/asp

Pew Research Center. (2013). The global divide on homosexuality: Greater acceptance in more secular and affluent countries. Retrieved from http://www.pewglobal.org/files/2013/06/Pew-Global-Attitudes, Homosexuality-Report-FINAL-JUNE-4-2013.pdf

Pew Research Center. (2015, December 6). The American middle class is losing ground. Pew Social Trends. Retrieved from http://www.pewsocialtrends.org/2015/12/09/the-american-middle-class-is-losing-ground/

Pfhal, M. (2015). Why the future of sports media is more cord shaving than cord cutting. Media Shift. Retrieved from http://mediashift.org/2015/10/why-the-future-of-sports-media-is-more-cord-shaving-than-cord-cutting/

Pfister, G. (2010). Outsiders: Muslim women and Olympic games. *International Journal of the History of Sport, 27* (16–18), 2925–2957.

PGALinks.Com (2000). Research and statistics. Retrieved from http://www.pgalinks.com/sectinfo.cfm

Phillips, C. (2018). Why diversity must become sports journalism's most important priority. *NY Daily News*. Retrieved from http://www.nydailynews.com/sports/more-sports/diversity-sports-journalism-priority-article-1.3977157

Philo, G. (1996). *Media and mental distress*. New York, NY: Addison Wesley Longman.

Phoenix, C. (2016). Thoughts on "re-imagining the ageing body with Alex Rotas." Ageing Issues. Retrieved from https://ageingissues.wordpress.com/2016/05/13/re-imagining-the-ageing-body-with-alex-rotas/

Phoenix, C., Faulkner, G., & Sparkes, A.C. (2005). Athletic identity and self-ageing: The dilemma of exclusivity. *Psychology of Sport and Exercise, 6*, 335–347.

Physorg.com (2009). Research: Male, female reporters cover sports differently. Retrieved from https://phys.org/news/2009-06-male-female-sports-differently.html#jCp

Pieper, L. (2015). Sport and religion at Jerry Falwell U, Sport in American history. US Sport History. Retrieved from https://ussporthistory.com/2015/02/23/sport-and-religion-at-jerry-falwell-u

Pierce, J. L. (1995). *Gender trials: Emotional lives in contemporary law firms*. Berkeley, CA: University of California Press.

Pilkington, E. (2015, June 2). Caitlyn Jenner: transgender community has mixed reactions to *Vanity Fair* reveal. *The Guardian*. Retrieved from https://web.archive.org/web/20160609015249/https://www.theguardian.com/tv-and-radio/2015/jun/02/caitlyn-jenner-transgender-response-vanity-fair

Pillemer, K. A., & Finkelhor, D. (1988). The prevalence of elder abuse: A random sample survey. *The Gerontologist, 28*, 51–57.

Pillows, A. (2012). Muslim women participation in 2012 London Olympics is the start, not the goal. Bleacher Report. Retrieved from http://bleacherreport.com/articles/1275194-muslim-women-participation-in-2012-london-olympics-is-the-start-not-the-goal

Pinquart, M. (2002). Creating and maintaining purpose in life in old age: A meta-analysis. *Ageing International, 27*(2), 90–114.

Pirkis, J., & Francis, C. (2012). *Mental illness in the news and information media: A critical review*. Canberra, Australia: Commonwealth Department of Health and Aged Care.

Pirkis, J., Blood, R. W., Dare, A., & Holland, K. (2008). *The media monitoring project: Changes in media reporting of suicide and mental health and illness in Australia: 2000/01–2006/07*. Canberra, Australia: Commonwealth Department of Health and Aged Care.

Pirkis, J., Francis, C., Blood, R. W., Burgess, P., Morley, B., & Stewart, A. (2001). *The media monitoring project: A baseline description of how the Australian media reports and portrays suicide and mental health/illness*. Canberra, Australia: Commonwealth Department of Health and Aged Care.

Planned Parenthood. (2017). *Planned Parenthood: 2016–2017 annual report*. Retrieved from https://www.plannedparenthood.org/uploads/filer_public/d4/50/d450c016-a6a9-4455-bf7f-711067db5ff7/20171229_ar16-17_p01_lowres.pdf

Planned Parenthood. (2018). Gender and gender identity. Retrieved from https://www.planned-parenthood.org/learn/sexual-orientation-gender/gender-gender-identity

Plymire, D. C., & Forman, P. J. (2000). Breaking the silence: Lesbian fans, the internet, and the sexual politics of women's sport. *International Journal of Sexuality and Gender Studies, 5*(2), 141–153.

Pockrass, B. (2013, December 23). Controversy, tragedy among NASCAR's top stories in 2013. *Sporting News*. Retrieved from http://www.sportingnews.com/us/nascar/news/controversy-trage-dy-among-nascars-top-stories-in-2013/gda7m5f5xvxk1gwwenwget0iv

Pomeroy, R. (2014). The NFL has a lower rate of domestic violence than the general population. Real Clear Science. Retrieved from https://www.realclearscience.com/blog/2014/09/domestic_violence_crime_much_lower_among_nfl_players.html

Poole, E., & J. E. Richardson (Eds.) (2006). *Muslims and the news media*. London, United Kingdom: I.B. Tauris.

Porter, D. (1997). *Internet culture*. New York, NY: Routledge.

Porter, W. C., & Stephens, F. (1989). Estimating readability: A study of Utah editors' abilities. *Newspaper Research Journal, 10*(2), 87–96.

Potard, C., Courtois, R., & Rusch, E. (2008). The influence of peers on risky sexual behavior during adolescence. *European Journal of Contraception & Reproductive Health Care, 13*(3), 264–270.

Potter, W. J. (1986). Perceived reality and the cultivation hypothesis. *Journal of Broadcasting and Electronic Media, 30*(2), 159–174.

Potter, W. J. (1988). Three strategies for elaborating the cultivation hypothesis. *Journalism Quarterly, 65*(4), 930–939.

Potter, W. J. (1991a). The linearity assumption in cultivation research. *Human Communication Research, 17*(4), 562–583.

Potter, W. J. (1991b). Examining cultivation from a psychological perspective. *Communication Research, 18*(1), 77–102.

Potter, W. J. (1993). Cultivation theory and research. *Human Communication Research, 19*(4), 564–601.

Potter, W. J., & Chang, I. C. (1990). Television exposure and the cultivation hypothesis. *Journal of Broadcasting and Electronic Media, 34*(3), 313–333.

Powell, G., & Butterfield, D. (2003). Gender, gender identity, and aspirations to top management. *Women in Management Review, 18*(1/2), 88–96.

Powell, K. E., Thompson, K. D., Caspersen, C. J., & Kendrick, J. S. (1987). Physical activity and the incidence of coronary heart disease. *Annual Review of Public Health, 8*, 253–287.

Powell, J. W., & Barber-Foss, K. D. (1999). Injury patterns in selected high school sports: A review of the 1995–1997 seasons. *Journal of Athletic Training, 34*(3), 277–284.

Price, J. L. (2006). *Rounding the bases: Baseball and religion in America*. Macon, GA: Mercer University Press.

Primm, E., Preuhs, R. R., & Hewitt, J. D. (2007). The more things change the more they stay the same: Race on the cover of *Sports Illustrated*. *The Journal of American Culture, 30*(2), 239–250.

Professional Football Researchers Association. (2010). Camp and his followers: American football 1876–1889. Retrieved from https://www.webcitation.org/5qRx5vacY?url=http://www.profootballresearchers.org/Articles/Camp_And_Followers.pdf#

Pro Football News. (2018). Mike Tomlin's anti-celebration stance is surprising. The 4519.com. Retrieved from https://the4519.com/tag/professional-athletes/

Project Implicit. (2011). Take a test. Retrieved from https://implicit.harvard.edu/implicit/takeatest.html

Pueschel, S. M., & Scola, F. H. (1984). Atlantoaxial instability in Down's syndrome orthopedic clinics in North America. *Physician and Sportsmedicine, 74*, 152–154.

Putney, C. (2001). *Muscular Christianity: Manhood and sports in Protestant America, 1880–1920*. Cambridge, MA: Harvard University Press.

PwC Sports Outlook. (2016). At the gate and beyond: Outlook for the sports market in North America through 2020. Retrieved from http://www.pwc.com/us/en/industry/entertainmentmedia/publications/assets/pwc-sports-outlook-2016.pdf

Purcell, D. (2016). *Minor injuries: A clinical guide*, Edinborough, United Kingdom: Elsevier.

Purcell, L. K. (2005). Sport readiness in children and youth. *Paediatrics & Child Health, 10*(6), 343–344. https://doi.org/10.1093/pch/10.6.343

Quick, B. (2009). The effects of viewing *Grey's Anatomy* on perceptions of doctors and patient satisfaction. *Journal of Broadcasting & Electronic Media, 53*(1), 38–55.

Quindlen, A. (2009, May). Stepping aside. *Newsweek*. Retrieved from http://www.newsweek.com

Quinn, M. J., & Tomita, S. K. (1997). *Elder abuse and neglect: Causes, diagnosis, and intervention strategies*. New York, NY: Springer Publishing Company.

Raacke, J., & Bonds-Raacke, J. (2008). MySpace and Facebook: Applying the uses and gratifications theory to exploring friend-networking sites. *CyberPsychology & Behavior, 11*(2), 169–174.

Rabiner, D. J., Brown, D., & O'Keeffe, J. (2005). Financial exploitation of older persons: Policy issues and recommendations for addressing them. *Journal of Elder Abuse & Neglect, 16*(1), 65–84.

Rada, J. A. (1996). Color blindsided: Racial bias in network television's coverage of professional football games. *The Howard Journal of Communications, 7*, 231–239.

Rada, J. A. (2000). A new piece to the puzzle: Examining effects of television portrayals of African-Americans. *Journal of Broadcasting & Electronic Media, 44*, 704–715.

Rada, J. A., & Wulfemeyer, K. T. (2002). *Color blindsided in the booth: An examination of the descriptions of college athletes during televised games*. Paper presented at the annual convention of the Association for Education in Journalism and Mass Communication, Miami, FL.

Rada, J. A. & Wulfemeyer, K. T. (2005) Color coded: Racial descriptors in television coverage of intercollegiate sports. *Journal of Broadcasting and Electronic Media, 49*(1), 65–85.

Rader, B. G. (2008). *Baseball: A history of America's game* (3rd ed.). Urbana, IL: University of Illinois Press.

Rader, B. G. (2009). *American sports: From the age of folk games to the age of televised sports* (6th ed.). Englewood Cliffs, NJ: Prentice Hall.

Raedeke, T. D., & Smith, A.L. (2001). Development and preliminary validation of an athlete burnout measure. *Journal of Sport and Exercise Psychology, 23*, 281–306.

Rainey, D. W. (1994). Assaults on umpires: A statewide survey. *Journal of Sport Behavior, 17*, 148–155.

Rainey, D. W., & Duggan, P. (1998). Assaults on basketball referees: A statewide survey. *Journal of Sport Behavior, 21*(1), 113–120.

Raman, P. & Harwood, J. (2008). Accultuartion of Asian-Indian sojourners in America. *Southern Communication Journal, 73*(4), 295–311.

Ramirez, A., Dimmick, J., Feaster, J., & Lin, S.-F. (2008). Revisiting interpersonal media competition: The gratification niches of instant messaging, e-mail, and the telephone. *Communication Research, 35*(4), 529–547.

Rampell, C. (2010). Still few women in management, report says. *New York Times*. Retrieved from http://www.nytimes.com/2010/09/28/business/28gender.html

Rainville, R., & McCormick, E. (1977). Extent of covert racial prejudice in pro football announcers' speech. *Journalism Quarterly, 54*(1), 20–26.

Ramasubramanian, S. (2007). Media based strategies to reduce racial stereotypes activated by news stories. *Journalism and Mass Communication Quarterly, 84*(2), 249–264.

Ramasubramanian, S. (2011). The impact of stereotypical versus counterstereotypical media exemplars on racial attitudes, causal attributions, and support for affirmative action. *Communication Research, 38*(1), 497–516.

Ramirez, T. L., & Blay, Z. (2016, July 5). Why people are using the term "Latinx." Huffington Post. Retrieved from https://www.huffingtonpost.com/entry/why-people-are-using-the-term-latinx_us_57753328e4b0cc0fa136a159

Raney, A. A. & Bryant, J. *Handbook of Sports and Media*, London, United Kingdom: Routledge.

Ranker. (2017). Athletes charged with domestic violence. Retrieved from https://www.ranker.com/list/athletes-charged-with-domestic-violence/people-in-sports?var=2&utm_expid=16418821-310.smDnXTH_QT6V93qtvQFoXw.1&utm_referrer=https:%2F%2Fwww.google.com%2F

Ranker. (2018). The top female MMA fighters. Retrieved from https://www.ranker.com/crowdranked-list/top-female-mma-fighters

Rasanen, P. (2008). The persistence of information structures in Nordic countries. *Information Society*, 24(4), 219–228.

Ready, D. (2001). "Spice girls," "nice girls," "girlies," and "tomboys": Gender discourses, girls" cultures and femininities in the primary classroom. *Gender and Education, 13*(2), 153–167.

Reddy, G. (2006). *With respect to sex: Negotiating Hirja identity in South India*. New Delhi, India: Yoda.

Redman T., & Snape E. (2002). Ageism in teaching: Stereotypical beliefs and discrimination towards the over-50s. *Work, Employment & Society*, 16(2), 355–371.

Reed, K. (2014). LGBT athletes still facing harassment and discrimination. Huffington Post. Retrieved from https://www.huffingtonpost.com/ken-reed/lgbt-athletes-still-facin_b_5648282.html

Reel, J. J., & Gill, D. L. (1996). Psychosocial factors related to eating disorders among high school and college female cheerleaders. *Sport Psychologist, 10*, 195–206.

Reese, S. D. (1990). Setting the media's agenda. In J. Anderson (Ed.), *Communication yearbook, No. 14* (pp. 309–340). Newbury Park, CA: Sage.

Reeves, C. W., Nicholls, A. R., & McKenna, J. (2009). Stressors and coping strategies among early and middle adolescent premier league academy soccer players: Differences according to age, *Journal of Applied Sport Psychology, 21*(1), 31–48 doi: 10.1080/10413200802443768

Regalado, S. O. (2002). Hey Chico! The Latin identity in major league baseball. *NINE, 11*(1), 16–24. doi: 10.1353/nin.2002.0043

Regalado, S. O. (2013). *Nikkei baseball: Japanese American players from immigration and internment to the major leagues*. Urbana-Champagne, IL: University of Illinois Press.

Reid, D. R. (2018). Why the 'Redskins' is a racist name. Retrieved from http://www.darrenreidhistory.co.uk/why-the-redskins-is-a-racist-name

Remillard, A. (2018). Sports and religion in America. *Oxford Research Encyclopedia of Religion*. New York, NY: Oxford University Press, Online Publication Date: Mar 2016. DOI: 10.1093/acrefore/9780199340378.013.145

Reskin, B. F., & Padavic, I. (1994). Sex differences in moving up and taking charge. In L. Richardson, V. Taylor, & N. Whittier (Eds.), *Feminist frontiers* (pp. 253–262). New York, NY: McGraw-Hill.

Reskin, B. F. (1998). Bringing the men back in: Sex differentiation and the devaluation of women's work. In K. A. Myers, C. D. Anderson, & B. J. Risman (Eds.), *Feminist foundations: Toward transforming sociology* (pp. 278–298). Thousand Oaks, CA: Sage.

Resnick, B. (2005) Labor relations in professional sport. Published writings responses to sports violence: media coverage of the, 1987 world junior hockey championship. *Sociology of Sport Journal, 6*, 247–256.

RFI. (2012). Referee refuses to officiate French woman's football match where players wore Muslim headscarves. Retrieved from http://en.rfi.fr/sports/20120319-referee-refuses-officiate-french-womans-football-match-where-players-wore-muslim-hea

Rhodebeck, L. A. (1993). The politics of greed? Political preferences among the elderly. *Journal of Politics, 55*(2), 342–364.

Rhodes, M. (2018). This super cute pro soccer player just came out as gay. Queerty. Retrieved from https://www.queerty.com/super-cute-pro-soccer-player-just-came-gay-20180629?utm_source=Queerty+Subscribers&utm_campaign=1d6fcfd902-20180629_Queerty_Newsletter&utm_medium=email&utm_term=0_221c27272a-1d6fcfd902-430568445

Ricciardelli, R., Clow, K. A, & White. P. (2012). Investigating hegemonic masculinity: Portrayals of masculinity in men's lifestyle magazines. *Sex Roles, 63*, 64–78.

Richards, K. (2018, November 29). NBA CMO Pam El announces plans to retire at the end of 2018. Adweek. Retrieved from https://www.adweek.com/brand-marketing/nba-cmo-pam-el-announces-plans-to-retire-at-the-end-of-2018/

Richardson, J. E. (2004). *Mis/representing Islam: Racism and rhetoric of British broadsheet newspapers*. Amsterdam, The Netherlands: John Benjamins Publishing.

Richcreek, K. (2016). The rise of women's boxing: Two-time Olympic gold medalist Claressa Shields is scheduled to make her pro boxing debut Saturday. The Undefeated. Retrieved from https://theundefeated.com/features/the-rise-of-womens-boxing/

Richter, K. J. (1989) Seizures in athletes. *Journal of Osteopathic Sports Medicine*, (3), 19–23.

Richter, K. J., Gaebler-Spira D & Mushett CA (1996) Annotation: Sport and the person with spasticity of cerebral origin. *Developmental Medicine and Child Neurology*, 38, 867–870.

Richter, K. J., Sherrill, C., McCann, C. B., Mushett, C. A., & Kaschalk, S. (1998). Recreation and sport for people with disabilities. In J. A. DeLisa & B. Gans (Eds.), *Rehabilitation medicine: Principles and practice* (3rd ed., pp. 853–871). Philadelphia, PA: Lippincott-Raven.

Riess, S. A. (1989). *City games: The evolution of American urban society and the rise of sport.* Urbana, IL: University of Illinois Press.

Riess, S. A. (1999). *Touching base: Professional baseball and American culture in the progressive era.* (Rev. ed). Urbana, IL: University of Illinois Press.

Riess, S. A. (2014). *A companion to American sport history.* Chichester, West Sussex, U.K.: Wiley-Blackwell.

Riess, S. (2017). Professional team sports in the United States. *Oxford research encyclopedia of American history.* Retrieved from http://oxfordre.com/americanhistory/view/10.1093/acrefore/9780199329175.001.0001/acrefore-9780199329175-e-198

Risman, B. J. (1998). *Gender vertigo: American families in transition.* New Haven, CT: Yale University Press.

Roberts, D., & Bachen, C. (1981). Mass communication effects. In M. Rosenzweig & L. Porter (Eds.), *The uses of mass communication* (pp. 75–104). Beverly Hills, CA: Sage.

Roberts, D. (2015, November 12). College football's biggest problem with race. *Time.* Retrieved from http://time.com/4110443/college-football-race-problem/

Roberts, G. C. (2001). Understanding the dynamics of motivation in physical activity: The influence of achievement goals on motivational process. In G. C. Roberts (Ed.), *Advances in motivation in sport and exercise* (pp. 1–50). Champaign, IL: Human Kinetics.

Roberts, I. (2006). Taking age out of the workplace: Putting older workers back in? *Work, Employment, & Society*, 20(1), 67–86.

Robertson-Wilson, J., Baker, J., Derbyshire, E., & Côté, J. (2003). Childhood physical activity involvement in active and inactive female adults. *Avante*, 9, 1–8.

Robertson, S. (2003). "If I let a goal in, I'll get beat up": Contradictions in masculinity, sport and health. *Health Education Research*, 18(6), 706–716.

Robertson, T. S., Ward, S., Gatignon, H., & Klees, D. M. (1989). Advertising and children: A cross-cultural study. *Communication Research*, 16(4), 459–485.

Robinson, G. (2006). Harlem Globetrotters, *Encyclopedia of African-American culture and history* (Vol. 3). Detroit, MI: Macmillan Reference USA.

Robinson, J. P., & Godbey, G. (1997). *Time for life: The surprising ways Americans use their time.* University Park, PA: The Pennsylvania State University Press.

Robinson, T. T., & Carron, A. V. (1982). Personal and situational factors associated with dropping out versus maintaining participating in competitive sport. *Journal of Sport Psychology*, 4, 364–378.

Robinson, W. (2015). Revealed: How Palestinian terrorists tortured Israeli hostages before 1972 Munich Olympic massacre—including castrating one athlete while others watched. *Daily Mail.* Retrieved from https://www.dailymail.co.uk/news/article-3341784/New-horrifying-details-emerge-1972-Munich-Olympic-massacre-including-one-athlete-castrated-hostages-watched.html

Rodin, J., & Langer, E. (1980). Aging labels: The decline of control and the fall of self-esteem. *Journal of Social Issues*, 36(2), 12–29.

Roe, K., & Vandebosch, H. (1996). Weather to view or not. *European Journal of Communication*, 11(2), 201–216.

Rogers, D. (2011). NFL, NBA, MLB: The white world of sports journalism. Bleacher Report. Retrieved from http://bleacherreport.com/articles/560608-nfl-nba-mlb-the-white-world-of-sports-journalism

Romero, D. (2018). NFL says issues raised by Colin Kaepernick "deserve our attention and action." NBC News. Retrieved from https://www.nbcnews.com/news/nbcblk/nfl-says-issues-raised-colin-kaepernick-deserve-our-attention-action-n906431

Roos, D. (2017, May 9). Why aren't there more Asian-Americans in pro team sports? Retrieved from https://entertainment.howstuffworks.com/ where-are-asian-american-pro-athletes.htm

Roper, E. (2013). *Gender relations in sports*. Boston, MA: Sense Publishers.

Roper, E. A. (2014). *Gender relations in sport: Teaching gender*. Berlin, Germany:Springer Science & Business Media.

Rose, D. (1998). Television, madness and community care. *Journal of Community & Applied Social Psychology*, *8*(3), 213–228.

Rosen, B. (2016). A historic number of LGBT athletes at Rio: Trend or trendsetter?: The number of openly gay Olympians in Rio are more than twice as many as in London at the 2012 Games. *Christian Science Monitor*. Retrieved from https://www.csmonitor.com/ World/Global-News/2016/0812/A-historic-number-of-LGBT-athletes-at-Rio-trend-or-trendsetter

Rosenbaum, J. (2016, January 12). It's over: Kroenke is moving the Rams to Los Angeles. St. Louis Public Radio. Retrieved from http://news. stlpublicradio.org/post/its-over-kroenke-moving-rams-los-angeles#stream/0

Rosenberg, E. (1980a). Gerontological theory and athletic retirement. In S. Greendorfer A. Yiannakis (Eds.), *Sociology of sport: Diverse perspectives* (pp. 118–126). West Point, NY: Leisure Press.

Rosenberg, E. (1980b). Social disorganizational aspects of professional sports careers. *Journal of Sport and Social Issues*, *4*, 14–25.

Rosenberg, E. (1982). Athletic retirement as social death: Concepts and perspectives. In N. Theberge & P. Donnelly (Eds), *Sport and the sociological imagination* (pp. 245–258). Fort Worth, TX: Texas Christian University Press.

Rosenbloom, C., & Bahns, M. (2005). What can we learn about diet and physical activity from master athletes? *Nutrition Today*, *40*, 267–272.

Rosenfeld, J. P. (1998). Will contest: Legacies of aging and social change. In R. K. Miller & S. J. McNamee (Eds.), *Inheritance and wealth in America* (pp. 173–192). New York, NY: Plenum Press.

Rosengren, J. (2015). Myth and fact part of legacy from Sandy Koufax's Yom Kippur choice. *Sports Illustrated*. Retrieved from https://www.si.com/mlb/2015/09/23/ sandy-koufax-yom-kippur-1965-world-series

Rosengren, K. E. (1974). Uses and gratifications: A paradigm outlined. In J. G. Blumler & E. Katz (Eds.), *The uses of mass communication* (pp. 141–154). Beverly Hills, CA: Sage Publications.

Rosenthal, R. (1986). Media violence, antisocial behavior, and the social consequences of small effects. *Journal of Social Issues*, *42*(3), 141–154.

Ross, J. Andrew. (2015). *Joining the clubs: The business of the National Hockey League to 1945*. Syracuse, NY: Syracuse University Press.

Ross, S. R., & Shinew, K. J. (2008). Perspectives of women college athletes on sport and gender. *Sex Roles*, *58*, 40–57.

Rossen, J. (2016). The German teens who rebelled against Hitler. *Mental Floss*. Retrieved from http://mentalfloss.com/article/73451/ german-teens-who-rebelled-against-hitler

Rowe, D. (1999). *Sport, culture and the media*. Buckingham, United Kingdom: Open University Press.

Rowe, D., McKay, J., & Miller, T. (1998) Come together: Sport, nationalism and the media, 119–133, New York, NY: Routledge/Taylor & Francis.

Rowe, N. (Ed.). (2003). *Driving up participation: The challenge for sport. (Academic review papers commissioned by Sport England as contextual analysis to inform the preparation of the Framework for Sport in England)*. London, United Kingdom: Sport England.

Rubin, R., and Hunter, K. (2011, June 30). Democrats push offshore corporate tax changes in debt bill. *Bloomberg News*. Retrieved from http://www.bloomberg.com

Rubin, A. (1979). Television use by children and adolescents. *Human Communication Research*, *5*(2), 109–120.

Rubin, A. (1985). Uses and gratifications. In J. Dominick and J. Fletcher (Eds.), *Broadcasting research methods* (pp. 97–119). Boston, MA: Allyn and Bacon.

Rubin, A. M. (1994). Media uses and effects. In J. Bryant & D. Zillmann (Eds.), *Media effects* (pp. 417–436). Hillsdale, NJ: Lawrence Erlbaum.

Rubin, A. M., Perse, E. M., & Taylor, D. S. (1988). A methodological examination of cultivation. *Communication Research*, *15*(2), 107–136.

Rubin, A. R., & Bantz, C. R. (1989). Uses and gratifications of videocassette recorders. In J. L. Salvaggio & J. Bryant (Eds.), *Media use in the information age* (pp. 181–195). Hillsdale, NJ: Lawrence Erlbaum.

Rubin, H. (2003). *Self-made men: Identity and embodiment among transsexual men*. Nashville, TN: Vanderbilt University Press.

Ruggiero, T. (2000). Uses and gratifications theory in the 21st century. *Mass Communication and Society*, *3*(1), 3–38.

Runciman, W. G. (1966). *Relative deprivation and social justice: A study of attitudes to social inequality in twentieth-century England*. Berkeley, CA: University of California Press.

Ryan, S. (2017). Lesbian college coaches still face difficult atmosphere to come out. *Chicago Tribune*. Retrieved from http://www.chicagotribune.com/sports/college/ct-lesbian-college-coaches-challenges-spt-0118-20170117-story.html

Ryan, T. L. (2015, March 10). Why do straight men cross-dress? Chicago Now. Retrieved from http://www.chicagonow.com/shades-gender/2015/03/why-do-straight-men-cross-dress/

Ryba, T. V., & Wright, H. K. (2005). From mental game to cultural praxis: A cultural studies model's implications for the future of sport psychology. *Quest*, *57*, 192–212.

Sabo, D., & Gordon, D. F. (Eds.) (1995). *Men's health and illness: Gender, power, and the body*. Thousand Oaks, CA: Sage.

Sabo, D., Curry-Jansen, S., Tate, D., Carlisle-Duncan, M., & Leggett, S. (1995). The portrayal of race, ethnicity, and nationality in televised international athletic events. LA84. Retrieved from https://la84.org/the-portrayal-of-race-ethnicity-and-nationality-in-televised-international-athletic-events/

Sabo, D., & Jansen, S. C. (1998). Prometheus unbound: Constructions of masculinity in the sports media. In L. A. Wenner (Ed.), *Mediasport* (pp. 202–217). London, England, and New York, NY: Routledge.

Sabo, D. F., & Jansen., S. C. (1992). Images of men in sport media: The social reproduction of the gender order. In S. Craig (Ed.), *Men, masculinity, and the media* (pp. 169–l 84). Newbury Park, CA: Sage.

Sabo, D. F., Jansen, S. C., Tate, D., Duncan, M., & Leggett, S. (1995). The portrayal of race, ethnicity, and nationality in televised international athletic events. LA84. Retrieved from https://la84.org/the-portrayal-of-race-ethnicity-and-nationality-in-televised-international-athletic-events/

Said, E. (1995). *Orientalism: Western conceptions of the orient*. London, United Kingdom: Penguin Books.

Said, E. W. (1978). *Orientalism*. New York, NY: Pantheon Books.

Sadker, M., & Sadker, D. (1994). *Failing at fairness: How America's schools cheat girls*. New York, NY: Charles Scribner's.

Saeed, A. (2007). Media, racism and Islamophobia: Representation of Islam and Muslims in media. *Sociology Compass*, *1*(4), 443–462.

Sage, G. H. (1998). *Power and ideology in American sport*. Champaign, IL: Human Kinetics.

Sajoo, E. (2012a). An Olympic first for Muslim women? Hardly! *The Province*. Retrieved from http://www2.canada.com/theprovince/news/editorial/story.html?id = ea39b0ba-323d-472d-8f97-70c87f135fae&p = 1

Sajoo, E. (2012b). Covering Muslim women: The Olympics and beyond. *The Vancouver Sun*. Retrieved from http://www.vancouversun.com/sports/Covering+Muslim+women+Olympics+beyond/7072809/story.html

Saks, A., & Waldman, D. (1998). The relationship between age and job performance evaluations for entry-level professionals. *Journal of Organizational Behavior*, *19*(4), 409–419.

Salgado, G. (2016, December 27). The top ten Latino sports moments of 2016. NBC News. Retrieved from https://www.nbcnews.com/storyline/2016-year-in-review/top-ten-latino-sports-moments-2016-n698676

Salinas, C., & Lozano, A. (2017). Mapping and recontextualizing the evolution of the term Latinx: An environmental scanning in higher education. *Journal of Latinos and Education*, *18*. doi: 10.1080/15348431.2017.1390464

Salisbury, J., & Jackson, D. (1996). *Challenging macho values: Practical ways of working with adolescent boys*. Washington, DC: Falmer.

Salminen, S., & Liukkonen, J. (1996). Coach-athlete relationship and coaching behavior in training sessions. *International Journal of Sport Psychology*, *27*, 59–67.

Salovey, P., & Wegener, D. T. (2003). Communicating about health: Message framing, persuasion, and health behavior. In J. Suls & K. A. Wallston (Eds.), *Social psychological foundations of health and illness* (pp. 54–81). Malden, MA: Blackwell Publishing.

Salovey, P., & Williams-Piehota, P. (2004). Field experiments in social psychology: Message framing and the promotion of health protective behaviors. *American Behavioral Scientist*, 47(5), 488–505, https://doi.org/10.1177/0002764203259293

Saltin, B. (1971). Diet, muscle glycogen, and endurance performance. *Journal of Applied Physiology*, 31, 203–206.

Salwen, M. B. (1988). Effect of accumulation of coverage on issue salience in agenda setting. *Journalism Quarterly*, 65(1), 100–106.

Salwen, M. B., & Wood, N. (1994). Depictions of female athletes on *Sports Illustrated* covers, 1957–1989. *Journal of Sport Behavior*, 17(2), 98.

Samie, S. F. (2013). Hetero-sexy self/body work and basketball: The invisible sporting women of Pakistani Muslim heritage. *Journal of South Asian Popular Culture*, 11(3), 257–270.

Samie, S. F., & Sehlikoglu, S. (2015). Strange, incompetent and out-of-place. *Feminist Media Studies*, 15(3), 363–381. doi: 10.1080/14680777.2014.947522

Samuel, J. (2103, April 4). Philadelphia Union GK Faryd Mondragon named SBI's MLS player of the month. Brotherly Game. Retrieved from https://www.brotherlygame.com/2011/4/4/2090421/philadelphia-union-gk-faryd-mondragon-named-sbis-mls-player-of-the

Sandomir, R. (2002, April 15). Sports media: An unrestrained Venturi exits the masters booth. *New York Times*. Retrieved from https://www.nytimes.com/2002/04/15/sports/sports-media-an-unrestrained-venturi-exits-the-masters-booth.html

Sander, I. (1997). How violent is TV violence? *European Journal of Communication*, 12(1), 43–98.

Sandhu, H. S., & R.Mehta. (2007). Career advancement challenges for women executives in the service sector. *Journal of Advances in Management Research*, 4(2), 69–78.

Sandomir, R. (April 16, 2003). W.N.B.A., going on 7, has grown-up labor dispute. *New York Times*. Retrieved from https://www.nytimes.com/2003/04/16/sports/pro-basketball-wnba-has-a-grown-up-dispute.html

Sangweni, Y. (2014). Play by play: 13 black women sportscasters we love. *Essence*. Retrieved from https://www.essence.com/galleries/play-play-12-black-women-sportscasters-we-love/

Sardar, Z. (1999). *Orientalism*. Philadelphia, PA: Open University Press.

Sartore, M. L., & Cunningham, G. B. (2007). Ideological gender beliefs, identity control and self-limiting behavior within sport organizations. *Quest*, 59, 244–265.

Sartore, M. L., & Sagas, M. (2006). A trend analysis of the proportion of women in college coaching. *International Journal of Sport Management*, 8, 226–244.

Sasaki, J. Y., & Kim, H. S. (2011). At the intersection of culture and religion: A cultural analysis of religion's implications for secondary control and social affiliation. *Journal of Personality and Social Psychology*, 101(2), 401–414. http://dx.doi.org/10.1037/a0021849

Saunders, C., Alhabash, S., & Frisby, C. M. (2011). *What are you talking about? Racial differences in Twitter use*. Paper presented to the Minorities and Communication Division of the Association for Education in Journalism and Mass Communication (awarded top-three faculty paper), St. Louis, MO.

Saunders, J. (2018). How to help athletes adapt to life after sport. The Conversation. Retrieved from https://theconversation.com/how-to-help-athletes-adapt-to-life-after-sport-94584

Savage, D. G. (2009). Supreme Court makes age bias suits harder to win. *Los Angeles Times*. Retrieved from http://www.latimes.com

Sayyid, S. (2003). *A fundamental fear: Eurocentrism and the emergence of Islamism* (2nd ed.). London, United Kingdom: Zed Books.

Scanlan, T. K., & Lewthwaite, R. (1986). Social psychological aspects of competition for male youth sport participants: IV. Predictors of enjoyment. *Journal of Sport Psychology*, 8, 25–35.

Scarrow, A. M., Linskey, M., Asher, A. L., Anderson, V. C., & Selden, N. R. (2009). Neurosurgeon transition to retirement: Results of the 2007 congress of neurological surgeons consensus conference. *Neurosurgery*, 65(2), 231–236.

Schäferhoff, N. (2016, May 12). How to use Instagram for your sports team marketing. Digital

Sport. Retrieved from https://digitalsport.co/intagram-sport-clubs-leagues-athletes

Scheiner, T. (2012). 4 winning sports social media campaigns you can learn from. Brafton. Retrieved from https://www.brafton.com/blog/four-winning-sports-social-media-marketing-campaigns-you-can-learn-from/

Scheper-Hughes, N. (1987). The Margaret Mead controversy: Culture, biology and anthropological inquiry. In H. Applebaum (Ed.), *Perspectives in cultural anthropology* (pp. 443–454). Albany, NY: State University of New York Press.

Scheufele D, A. (1999). Framing as a theory of media effects. *Journal of Communication, 49,* 103–122.

Scheufele, D. A. & Tewksbury, D. (2000). Framing, agenda setting, and priming: The evolution of three media effects models. *Journal of Communication, 57*(1), 9–20.

Schiavone, M. (2015). *Sports and labor in the United States.* Albany, NY: State University of New York Press.

Schmidt-Gotz, E., Doll-Tepper, G., & Lienert, C. (1994) Attitudes of university students and teachers towards integrating students with disabilities into regular physical education classes. *Physical Education Review, 17* (1), 45–57.

Schoenberg, E. R. (2016). On wealth inequality. Schoen Blog. Retrieved from http://schoenblog.com/?p=820

Schramm, W., Lyle, J., & Parker, E. (1961). *Television in the lives of our children.* Stanford, CA: Stanford University Press.

Schroetenboer, B. (2016, January 2016). Rams bash St. Louis in Los Angeles relocation bid. *USA Today.* Retrieved from https://www.usatoday.com/story/sports/nfl/2016/01/06/st-louis-rams-la-relocation-bid-nfl/78344012/

Schumacher, N., Schmidt, M., Wellmann, K., & Braumann, K. M. (2018) General perceptual-cognitive abilities: Age and position in soccer. *PLoS ONE, 13*(8), e0202627. https://doi.org/10.1371/journal.pone.0202627

Schwartz, N. D. (2011, May 27). Easing out the gray-haired. Or not. *New York Times.* Retrieved from http://www.nytimes.com

Schwartz, N. (2013, October 24). The average career earnings of athletes across America's major sports will shock you. *USA Today.* Retrieved from https://ftw.usatoday.com/2013/10/average-career-earnings-nfl-nba-mlb-nhl-mls.

Schwartz, N. (2015). The average career earnings of athletes across America's major sports will shock you. *USA Today.* Retrieved from https://ftw.usatoday.com/2013/10/average-career-earnings-nfl-nba-mlb-nhl-mls

Schwenk, T. L. (2000). The stigmatisation and denial of mental ill-health in athletes. British *Journal of Sports Medicine, 34,* 4–5.

Schwenk, T. L., Gorenflo, D. W., Dopp, R. R., & Hipple, E. (2007). Depression and pain in retired professional football players. *Medicine and Science in Sports and Exercise, 39*(4), 599–605.

Scott-Samuel, A., Stanistreet, D., & Crawshaw, P. (2009). Hegemonic masculinity, structural violence and health inequalities. *Critical Public Health, 19,* 287–292.

Scrutton, S. (1999). *Counselling older people.* London, United Kingdom: Gower Publishing.

Scully, G. (1974). Discrimination: The case of baseball. In R. G. Noll (Ed.), *Government and the sports business* (p. 246). London, United Kingdom: Routledge.

Sedgwick, E. K. (1990). *Epistemology of the closet.* Berkeley, CA: University of California Press.

Seidman, S. A. (1992) An investigation of sex-role stereotyping in music videos. *Journal of Broadcasting & Electronic Media, 36*(2), 209–216. doi: 10.1080/08838159209364168

Seefeldt, C., Jantz, R. K., Galper, A., & Serock K. (1977). Using pictures to explore children's attitudes toward the elderly. *The Gerontologist, 17,* 506–512.

Segrave, J. (1983). Sport and juvenile delinquency. In R. Terjung (Ed.), *Exercise and sport science review* (Vol. 11, pp. 181–209). Philadelphia, PA: Franklin Institute Press.

Sehlikoglu, S. (2012). Portrayal of Muslim female athletes in the media: Diversity in sport. Retrieved from http://blogs.lse.ac.uk/diversity/2012/08/portrayal-of-muslim-female-athletes-in-the-media-diversity-in-sport/

Seiffge-Krenke, I. (1995). *Stress, coping, and relationships in adolescence.* Mahwah, NJ: Lawrence Erlbaum.

Seligman, D. (1988, February 15). Debating dinosaurs, measuring muscles, playing to the yuppies, and other matters. Of fingerprints and other clues. Retrieved from *Fortune* https://money.cnn.com/magazines/fortune/fortune_archive/1988/02/15/70181/index.htm.

Serrano, A. (2007, July 17). Michael Vick indicted by grand jury. CBS News. Retrieved from www.cbsnews.com

Sewart, J. J. (1987). The commodification of sport. *International review for the sociology of sport, 22,* 171–192.

Seymour, H., & Seymour, D. (1960–1989). *Baseball* (3 vols.). New York, NY: Oxford University Press, 1960–1989.

Shaheen, J. G. (1984). *The TV Arab*, Minneapolis, MN: The Board of Regents of the University of Wisconsin System.

Shaheen, J. G. (2008) *Guilty: Hollywood's verdict on Arabs after 9/11*. Northampton, MA: Olive Branch Press.

Shakespeare, T., & Watson, N. (1997) Defending the social model. *Disability and Society, 12* (2), 293–300.

Shanahan, J., & Morgan, M. (1999). *Television and its viewers*. Cambridge, NY: Cambridge University Press.

Shanahan, J., Morgan, M., & Stenbjerre, M. (1997). Green or brown? Television and the cultivation of environmental concern. *Journal of Broadcasting and Electronic Media, 41*(3), 305–323.

Shao, G. (2009). Understanding the appeal of user-generated media: A uses and gratification perspective. *Internet Research, 19*(1), 7–25.

Shapiro, D., R., Pitts, B., G., Hums, M., A. & Calloway, J. (2012). Infusing disability sport into the sport management curriculum. *Sport Management International Journal, 8*(1), 102–118.

Sharps, M. J., Price-Sharps, J. L., & Hanson, J. (1998). Attitudes of young adults toward older adults: Evidence from the United States and Thailand. *Educational Gerontology, 24*(7), 655–660.

Shaw, S. M. (1994). Gender, leisure, and constraint: Towards a framework for the analysis of women's leisure. *Journal of Leisure Research, 26*(1), 8–22.

Sheehan, K., & Rall, K. (2011). Rediscovering hope: Building school cultures of hope for children of poverty. *Phi Delta Kappan, 93*(3), 44–47.

Sheldon, J. P. (2004). Age and gender differences in the sources of self-evaluation valued by adult athletes. *Journal of Adult Development, 11,* 47–53.

Sheldon, J. P., Pfeffer, C. A., Jayaratne, T. E., Feldbaum, M., & Petty, E. M. (2007). Beliefs about the etiology of homosexuality and about the ramifications of discovering its possible genetic origin. *Journal of Homosexuality, 52*(3/4), 111–150.

Shergold, A. (2012). Muslim women who overcame the odds and the prejudice to make history today on the Olympic stage. *Daily Mail.* Retrieved from http://www.dailymail.co.uk/news/article-2183262/Olympics-2012-The-Muslim-women-overcame-odds-make-London.html

Sherice, G., & Zhang, W. (2014). Gay bullying and online opinion expression: Testing spiral of silence in the social media environment. *Social Science Computer Review, 32,* 18–36.

Sherrill, C. & Williams, T. (1996). Disability and sport: psychosocial perspectives on inclusion, integration and participation. *Sport Science Review, 5*(1), 42–64.

Sherrill, C., Heikinaro-Johansson, P. & Slilinger, D. (1994). Equal-status relationships in the gym. *Journal of Physical Education, Recreation & Dance, 65*(1), 27–31.

Sherry J. (2007). Violent video games and aggression: Why can't we find links? In R. Preiss, B. Gayle, N. Burrell, M. Allen, & J. Bryant, *Mass media effects research: Advances through meta-analysis* (pp. 231–248). Mahwah, NJ: L. Erlbaum.

Sherry, J. L. (2001). The effects of violent video games on aggression. *Human Communication Research, 27*(3), 409–431.

Shields, D.L.L., & Bredemeier, B.J.L. (1995). *Character development and physical activity*. Champaign, IL: Human Kinetics.

Shields N, & Synnot, A. J. (2014). An exploratory study of how sports and recreation industry personnel perceive the barriers and facilitators of physical activity in children with disability. *Disability & Rehabilitation. 36*(24), 2080–2084. doi: 10.3109/09638288.2014.892637

Shields, N., & Synnot, A. (2016). Perceived barriers and facilitators to participation in physical activity for children with disability: A qualitative study. *BMC Pediatrics, 16,* 9. doi:10.1186/s12887-016-0544-7

Shirazi, F. (2001). *The veil unveiled: Hijab in modern culture*. Gainesville, FL: University Press of Florida.

Shoemaker, P., Tankard Jr., J., & Lasorsa, D. (2004). *How to build social science theories* (p. 120). Thousand Oaks, CA: Sage.

Shropshire, K., Briley, R., Ezra, M., Fields, S., Hawkins, B., Iber, J. &. Smith, M. (2008). *Sports and the racial divide: African American and Latino experience in an era of change* (Lomax M., Ed.). Jackson, MS: University Press of Mississippi. Retrieved from http://www.jstor.org/stable/j.ctt2tvcq4

Shrum, L. (1996). Psychological processes underlying cultivation effects. Human *Communication Research, 22*(4), 482–509.

Shrum, L. (2001). Processing strategy moderates the cultivation effect. *Human Communication Research, 27*(1), 94–120.

Shrum, L., & O'Guinn, T. (1993). Process and effects in the construction of social reality. *Communication Research, 20*(3), 436–471.

Shrum L. J., Wyler, R. S., Jr., & O'Guinn, T. C. (1998). The effects of television consumption on social perceptions: The use of priming procedures to investigate psychological processes. *Journal of Consumer Research, 24*, 447–458.

Shugarman, L. R., Fries, B. E., Wolf, R. S., & Morris, J. N. (2003). Identifying older people at risk of abuse during routine screening practices. *Journal of the American Geriatrics Society, 51*, 24–31.

Siegel, A. (1958). The influence of violence in the mass media upon children's role expectations. *Child Development, 29*, 35–56.

Siegenthaler, K. L., & Gonzalez, G. L. (1997). Youth sports as serious leisure. *Journal of Sport and Social Issues, 21*, 298–314.

Signorielli, N., & Morgan, M. (1990). *Cultivation analysis: New directions in media effects research.* Newbury Park, CA: Sage.

Silvern, S., & Williamson, P. A. (1987). The effects of video game play on young children's aggressive, fantasy and prosocial behavior. *Journal of Applied Developmental Psychology, 8*, 453–462.

Simmons, K. (2011). Women in top management positions in the sport industry: Breaking down the barriers and stereotypes. Retrieved from http://fisherpub.sjfc.edu/sport_undergrad/22

Sinha, S. (2014). As the average salary of college coaches soar, academics are growing more and more disgruntled with the priorities of American higher learning. Vice Sports. Retrieved from https://sports.vice.com/en_us/article/kbv5zz/so-how-much-is-a-college-coach-really-worth

Skelton, A. (1993). On becoming a male physical education teacher: The informal culture of students and the construction of hegemonic masculinity. *Gender and Education, 5*(3), 289–303.

Smedley, A., & Smedley, B. D. (2005). Race as biology is fiction, racism as a social problem is real: Anthropological and historical perspectives on the social construction of race. *American Psychologist, 60*(1), 16–26. http://dx.doi.org/10.1037/0003-066X.60.1.16

Smiley, C., & Fakunle, D. (2016). From "brute" to "thug:" the demonization and criminalization of unarmed black male victims in America. *Journal of Human Behavior in the Social Environment, 26*(3–4), 350–366.

Smith v. City of Jackson, 544 U.S. 228 (2005).

Smith, A. (2004). The inclusion of pupils with special educational needs in secondary school physical education. *Physical Education and Sports Pedagogy, 9*(1), 37–54.

Smith, A., & Thomas, N. (2006). Including pupils with special educational needs and disabilities in national curriculum physical education: A brief review. *European Journal of Special Needs Education, 21*(1), 69–83.

Smith, A. (2015). Here are some of the greatest Muslim-American athletes. *Business Insider.* Retrieved from https://www.businessinsider.com/some-great-muslim-american-athletes-2015-12

Smith, B. J. (2018). Early beginnings to the current world of sports history. The People History. Retrieved from http://www.thepeoplehistory.com/sports.html

Smith, B. T. (2018). Sports: The history and evolution. The People History. Retrieved from http://www.thepeoplehistory.com/sports.html

Smith, L., Wegwood, N., Llewellyn, G., & Shuttleworth. R. (2015). Sport in the lives of young people with intellectual disabilities: Negotiating disability, identity and belonging. *Journal of Sport for Development, 3*(5): 61–70, https://jsfd.org/2015/12/29/sport-in-the-lives-of-young-people-with-intellectual-disabilities-negotiating-disability-identity-and-belonging/

Smith, M. D. (2016). Cam Newton says Super Bowl media requirements get under his skin. NBC Sports. Retrieved from https://profootballtalk.nbcsports.com/2016/02/03/cam-newton-says-super-bowl-media-requirements-get-under-his-skin/

Smith, R. E., Smoll, F. L., & Curtis, B. (1978). Coaching behaviors in little league baseball. In F. L. Smoll & R. E. Smith (Eds.), *Psychological perspectives in youth sports* (pp. 173–201). Washington, DC: Hemisphere Publishing Corporation.

Smith, S. (2008). Gender stereotypes: An analysis of popular films and TV. Geena Davis Institute on Gender in Media. Retrieved from http://www.thegeenadavisinstitute.org/downloads/GDIGM_Gender_Stereotypes.pdf

Smolak, L., Murnen, S. K., & Ruble, A. E. (2000). Female athletes and eating problems: A metaanalysis. *International Journal of Eating Disorders, 27*, 371–380.

Smoll, F. L., Smith, R. E., Barnett, N. P., & Everett, J. J. (1993). Enhancement of children's self-esteem through social support training for youth sport coaches. *Journal of Applied Psychology, 78*, 602–610.

Snelgrove, R., Taks, M., Chalip, L., & Green, B. C. (2008). How visitors and locals at a sport event differ in motives and identity. *Journal of Sport Tourism, 13*, 165–180.

Snider, S. (2018, July 17). *Where do I fall in the American economic class system?* Retrieved from https://money.usnews.com/money/personal-finance/family-finance/articles/2018-07-17/where-do-i-fall-in-the-american-economic-class-system

Snider, S. (2018, July 17). While you can break down class by income, economic class is more complex, experts say, *US News and World Report.* Retrieved from https://money.usnews.com/money/personal-finance/family-finance/articles/2018-07-17/where-do-i-fall-in-the-american-economic-class-system

Snopes. (2017, October). Are 871 convicted felons currently playing for the NFL? Snopes.com Retrieved from https://www.snopes.com/fact-check/are-there-871-convicted-felons-currently-playing-for-the-nfl/

Snyder, H. N., Cooper, A. D., & Mulako-Wangota, J. (2018). Bureau of Justice Statistics. Generated using the Arrest Data Analysis Tool at www.bjs.gov. Retrieved from https://www.bjs.gov/index.cfm?ty=datool&surl=/arrests/index.cfm

Somerset, S., & Hoare, D. J. (2018). Barriers to voluntary participation in sport for children: a systematic review. *BMC Pediatrics, 18*(1), 47. doi: 10.1186/s12887-018-1014-1

Snyder, M., & Miene, P. K. (1994). Stereotyping of the elderly: A functional approach. *British Journal of Social Psychology, 33*, 63–82.

Sommers-Flanagan, R., Sommers-Flanagan, J., & Davis, B. (1993). What's happening on music television? A gender role content analysis. *Sex Roles, 28*, 745–753.

Sonderlund, A. L., O'Brien, K., Kremer, P., Rowland, B., De Groot, F., Staiger, P., … Miller, P. G. (2014). The association between sports participation, alcohol use and aggression and violence: A systematic review. *Journal of Science and Medicine in Sport, 17*(1), 2–7. doi: 10.1016/j.jsams.2013.03.011

Space Coast Daily. (2014, September). Study: NFL crime rate lower than general population. *Space Coast Daily.* Retrieved from http://spacecoastdaily.com/2014/09/study-nfl-crime-rate-lower-than-general-population/

Spain, K. (2017). Michael Jordan in response to Trump tweets: Peaceful protesters shouldn't be "demonized." *USA Today.* Retrieved from https://www.usatoday.com/story/sports/nba/hornets/2017/09/25/michael-jordan-donald-trump-tweets-peaceful-protesters-demonize/700891001/

Sparks, G., & Ogles, R. M. (1990). The difference between fear of victimization and the probability of being victimized. *Journal of Broadcasting and Electronic Media, 34*(3), 351–358.

Sparks, G., Nelson, C. L., & Campbell, R. G. (1997). The relationship between exposure to televised messages about paranormal phenomena and paranormal beliefs. *Journal of Broadcasting and Electronic Media, 41*(3), 345–359.

Spector-Mersel, G. (2006). Never-aging stories: Western hegemonic masculinity scripts. *Journal of Gender Studies, 15*(1), 67–82.

Spijkerboer, T. (2013). *Fleeing homophobia: Sexual orientation, gender identity and asylum.* London, United Kingdom: Routledge.

Sports Conflict Institute. (2018, December 12). *Sports Conflict News.* Retrieved from https://sportsconflict.org/sports-conflict-in-the-news/

also refer to https://sportsconflict.org/page/2/?s=violence

Sport England. (2001). *Disability survey 2000: Young people with a disability & sport*. London, United Kingdom: Author.

Sporting Equals. (2018). Promoting ethnic diversity in sport and physical activity. Retrieved from http://www.sportingequals.org.uk

Sports Conflict Institute. (2018, July). Sports violence model. Retrieved from https://sportsconflict.org/resource/sports-violence-model/

Sports Council. (1982). *Sport in the community: Into the 90s. A strategy for sport 1988–1993*. London, United Kingdom: Sports Council.

Sports Council. (1988). *Sport in the community: The next ten years*. London, United Kingdom: Sports Council.

Sports Council. (1993). *People with disabilities and sport. Policy and current/planned action*. London, United Kingdom: Sports Council.

Sports Illustrated. (2018). Jed York, Denise Debartolo York, John York, San Francisco 49ers, Retrieved from https://www.si.com/nfl/san-francisco-49ers-owner-jed-york-denise-debartolo-family

Sprafkin, J., & Rubinstein, E. (1979). Children's television viewing habits and prosocial behavior. *Journal of Broadcasting, 23*(7), 265–276.

Srikanth, K., Chavan, U., Singh, B., & Chandrashekhar, S. J. (2012). Socio-economic status of team and individual game players. *Variorum Multi-Disciplinary e-Research Journal, 3*(2), 1–4.

Stahl, J. (2017). Black panthers: How Sean Combs could make his dream of becoming the NFL's first black principal owner a reality. Slate. https://slate.com/culture/2017/12/how-sean-combs-could-become-the-nfls-first-black-principal-owner.html

Staples, R., & Jones, T. (1985). Culture, ideology and black television images. *The Black Scholar, 16*(3), 10–20. doi: 10.1080/00064246.1985.11414338

Staples, R., & Johnson, L. B. (2004). *Black families at the crossroads: Challenges and prospects*. San Francisco, CA: Jossey-Bass.

Starkes, J. L., Deakin, J. M., Allard, F., Hodges, N. J., & Hayes, A. (1996). Deliberate practice in sports: What is it anyway? In K.A. Ericsson (Ed.), *The road to excellence: The acquisition of expert performance in the arts, sciences, sports and games* (pp. 81–106). Mahwah, NJ: Erlbaum.

Statista. (2018). National Basketball Association franchise value by team in 2018 (in million U.S. dollars). Retrieved from https://www.statista.com/statistics/193696/franchise-value-of-national-basketball-association-teams-in-2010/

Statistics Canada. (2011). *Women in Canada: A gender based statistical report*. Ottawa, Canada: Statistics Canada. Retrieved from http://www.statcan.gc.ca/pub/89-503-x/89-503-x2010001-eng.pdf

Statistics Canada. (2006). Detailed average household expenditure by household type, Canada, 2005. Statistics Canada, Catalogue no. 62F0034XDB. Ottawa, Canada: Minister of Industry.

Steadward, R. (1996). Integration and sport in the Paralympic movement, *Sport Science Review, Adapted Physical Activity, 5*(1), 26–41.

Steele, C. M. (1997). A threat in the air: How stereotypes shape the intellectual identities and performance of women and African Americans. *American Psychologist, 52*, 613–629.

Steele, C. M., & Aronson, J. (1995). Stereotype threat and the intellectual test performance of African Americans. *Journal of Personality and Social Psychology, 69*(5), 797–811.

Steinberg, D. (2011). Portis goes out with a [redacted]. *Washington Post*. Retrieved from http://voices.washingtonpost.com/dcsports-bog/2011/02/portis_goes_out_with_a_redacte.html

Steinberg, L. (2015). 5 reasons why 80% of retired NFL players go broke. *Forbes*. https://www.forbes.com/sites/leighsteinberg/2015/02/09/5-reasons-why-80-of-retired-nfl-players-go-broke/#4556109278cc

Steinberg, L. (2016). Does playing the national anthem at sporting events promote unity and patriotism? *Forbes*. Retrieved from https://www.forbes.com/sites/leighsteinberg/2016/09/24/does-playing-the-national-anthem-at-sporting-events-promote-unity-and-patriotism/#51f055e37328

Steinfeldt, J. A., Vaughan, E. L., LaFollette, J. R., & Steinfeldt, M. C. (2012). Bullying among adolescent football players: Role of masculinity and moral atmosphere. *Psychology of Men & Masculinity, 13*(4), 340–353. doi: 10.1037/a0026645

Stempel, G. H., & Hargrove, T. (2003). Despite gains, Internet not major player as news source. *Newspaper Research Journal, 25*(2), 113–116.

Stempel, G. H., Hargrove, T., & Bernt, J. (2000). Relation of growth of use of Internet to changes in media use from 1995 to 1999. *Journalism and Mass Communication Quarterly, 77*(1), 71–79.

Stern, B. B. (1993). Feminist literary criticism and the deconstruction of ads: A postmodern view of advertising and consumer responses. *Journal of Consumer Research, 19*(March), 556–566.

Stern, B. B. (1999). Gender and multicultural issues in advertising: Stages on the research highway. *Journal of Advertising, 28*(Spring), 1–9.

Stern, K. (2009). *Queers in history: The comprehensive encyclopedia of historical gays* (p. 78). Dallas, TX; BenBella Books, Inc.

Stille, A. (2000, October 14). Marshall McLuhan is back from the dustbin of history; with the Internet, his ideas again seem ahead of their time. *New York Times.* Retrieved from http://www.nytimes.com/2000/10/14/arts/marshall-mcluhan-back-dustbin-history-with-internet-his-ideas-again-seem-ahead.html

Stites, A. (2018, July 30). Jerry Jones keeps making the NFL's mishandling of the anthem worse. SB Nation. Retrieved from https://www.sbnation.com/2018/7/25/17614374/jerry-jones-protests-national-anthem-dallas-cowboys

Stoller, R. J. (1968). *Sex and gender: On the development of masculinity and femininity.* New York: Science House.

Stone, J. A., Perry, Z. W., & Darley, J. M. (1997). "White men can't jump": Evidence for the perceptual confirmation of racial stereotypes following a basketball game. *Basic and Applied Social Psychology, 19*(3), 291–306.

Stone, J. A., Sjomeling, M., Lynch, C. I., & Darley, J. M. (1999). Stereotype threat effects on black and white athletic performance. *Journal of Personality and Social Psychology, 77*(6), 1213–1227. https://doi.org/10.1037/0022-3514.77.6.1213

Stone, S. (1995). The myth of bodily perfection. *Disability and Society, 10*(4), 413–24.

Strauss, A., & Corbin, J. (1998). *Basics of qualitative research: Techniques and procedures for developing grounded theory.* Thousand Oaks, CA: Sage.

Strauss, W., & Howe, N. (1991). *Generations: The history of America's future, 1584 to 2069.* New York, NY: HarperPerennial.

Sue, D. W. (2010) *Microaggressions in everyday life: Race, gender, and sexual orientation.* Hoboken, NJ: John Wiley & Sons.

Sue, D. W., Bucceri, J., Lin, A. I., Nadal, K. L., & Torino, G. C. (2007). Racial microaggressions and the Asian American experience. *Cultural Diversity and Ethnic Minority Psychology, 13,* 72–81.

Sue, D. W., Capodilupo, C. M., & Holder, A. (2008). Racial microaggressions in the life experience of black Americans. *Professional Psychology: Research and Practice, 39*(3), 329–336.

Sugden, J. (1987). The exploitation of disadvantage: The occupational sub-culture of the boxer. In J. Horne, D. Jary, & A. Tomlinson, A. (Eds.), *Sport, leisure and social relations* (pp. 187–209). London, United Kingdom: Routledge & Kegan Paul.

Sugden, J., & Tomlinson, A. (2000). Theorizing sport, social class and status. In J. Coakley & E. Dunning (Eds.), *Handbook of sports studies* (pp. 309–321). London, United Kingdom: Sage.

Sun, R. (2017, October 29). WME-IMG renames parent company as Endeavor. *Hollywood Reporter.* Retrieved from https://www.hollywoodreporter.com/news/wme-img-renames-parent-company-as-endeavor-1047094

Sun, R. (2018, October 19). Endeavor hires Kerry D. Chandler as chief human resources officer. *Hollywood Reporter.* Retrieved from https://www.hollywoodreporter.com/news/endeavor-hires-kerry-d-chandler-as-chief-human-resources-officer-1152503

Surdam, D. G. (2012). *The rise of the National Basketball Association.* Urbana, IL: University of Illinois Press.

Surdam, D. G. (2013). *Run to glory and profits: The economic rise of the NFL during the 1950s.* Lincoln, NE: University of Nebraska Press.

Surdam, D. G. (2015). *The big leagues go to Washington: Congress and sports anti-trust.* Urbana, IL: University of Illinois Press.

Surgeon General's Scientific Advisory Committee on Television and Social Behavior. (1972). *Television and social behavior. Television and growing up (summary report).* Washington, DC: U.S. Government Printing Office.

Svrluga, B. (2018, June 14). Nationals owner Ted Lerner, 92, to cede control of club to his son, Mark. *Washington Post*. Retrieved from https://www.washingtonpost.com

Swanson, D. L. (1987). Gratification seeking, media exposure, and audience interpretations. *Journal of Broadcasting and Electronic Media, 31*(3), 237–254.

Sweetser, K., Golan, G., & Wanta W. (2008). Intermedia agenda setting in television, advertising and blogs during the 2004 presidential election. *Mass Communication and Society, 11*(2), 197–216.

Swerdlick, D. (2005, February 2). Ricky Williams— Why can't we just let him be? Retrieved from https://www.popmatters.com/050203-rickywilliams-2496108288.html

Syed, M. (2012). The past, present, and future of Eriksonian identity research: Introduction to the Special Issue. *Identity: An International Journal of Theory and Research, 12*(1), 1–7.

Sykes, H. (1998). Turning the closets inside/out: Towards a queer-feminist theory in women's physical education. *Sociology of Sport, 15*(2), 154–173.

Sykes, H. (2010). *Queer bodies: Sexualities, genders, & fatness in physical education*. Bern, Switzerland: Peter Lang Inc., International Academic Publishers.

Sykes, H. (2014) Un-settling sex: Researcher self-reflexivity, queer theory and settler colonial studies. *Qualitative Research in Sport, Exercise and Health, 6*(4), 583–595. doi: 10.1080/2159676X.2014.893899

Synovitz, R. (2012.) Muslim athletes at London Olympics face Ramadan fasting rules. *Middle East Voices*. Retrieved from http://middleeastvoices.voanews.com/2012/06/muslim-athletes-at-london-olympics-face-ramadan-fasting-rules-69936/

Tai, Z. (2009). The structure of knowledge and dynamics of scholarly communication in agenda setting research, 1996–2005. *Journal of Communication, 59*(3), 481–513.

Talev, M. (2005). Baseball under a shadow; steroid hearings send sport a message: Clean up your act. Washington Bureau of the *Sacramento Bee*.

Tarmarkin, S. (2014, April 28). It's all in their heads: The mental edge of athletes who win. Retrieved from https://greatist.com/fitness/mental-training-tips-professional-athletes

Tan, A. S. (1986). *Mass communication theories and research* (2nd ed.). Columbus, OH: Grid Publications.

Tanenbaum, L. (2009). *Taking back god: American women rising up for religious equality*. New York, NY: Farrar, Straus and Giroux.

Tannen, D. (2001). *You just don't understand: Women and men in conversation*. New York, NY: Quill.

Tannenbaum, P., & Zillmann, D. (1975). Emotional arousal in the facilitation of aggression through communication. In L. Berkowitz (Ed.), *Advances in experimental social psychology* (pp. 1–55). New York, NY: Academic Press.

Tapper, J. (1995). The ecology of cultivation. *Communication Theory, 5*(1), 36–57.

Taub, D. & Greer, K. (2000). Physical activity as a normalizing experience for school-age children with physical disabilities. *Journal of Sport & Social Issues, 24*(4), 395–414.

Taub, D., Blinde, E. & Greer, K. (1999). Stigma management through participation in sport and physical activity: experiences of male college students with physical disabilities. *Human Relations, 52*(11), 1469–84.

Taub, D. E., & Greer, K. R. (1998). Sociology of acceptance revisited: Males with physical disabilities participating in sport and physical fitness activity. *Deviant Behaviour, 19*, 279–302.

Taylor, C. B., Sallis, J. F., & Needle, R. (1985). The relation of physical activity and exercise to mental health. *Public Health Report, 100*, 195–202.

Taylor, J. (2012). London 2012: Wojdan Shaherkani makes history. *The Independent*. Retrieved from http://www.independent.co.uk/sport/olympics/news/london-2012-wojdan-shaherkani-makes-history-competing-as-saudi-arabias-first-ever-female-olympic-athlete-8005090.html

Taylor, P., Lopez, M. H., Martínez, J. H., & Velasco, G. (2012). When labels don't fit Hispanics and their views of identity. Pew Hispanic Center. Retrieved from http://www.pewhispanic.org/2012/04/04/when-labels-dont-fit-hispanics-and-their-views-of-identity/

Team USA. (2018). Claressa Shields. Retrieved from http://www.teamusa.org/Athletes/SH/Claressa-Shields.aspx

Tedx Talks. (2013, February 20). *Be a man: Joe Ehrmann at TEDxBaltimore 2013* [Video file]. Retrieved from https://www.youtube.com/watch?v=jVI1Xutc_Ws

Tenenbaum, G., Stewart, E., Singer, R. N., & Duda, J. (1997). Aggression and violence in sport: An ISSP position stand, *Sport Psychologist, 11*, 1–7.

Tentori, K., Osherson, D. N., Hasher, L., & May, C. (2001). Wisdom and aging: Irrational preferences in college students but not older adults. *Cognition, 81*(3), B87–B96.

Terkildsen, N., & Schnell, F. (1997). How media frames move public opinion: An analysis of the women's movement. *Political Research Quarterly, 50*, 879–900.

Terry, P, C. and Jackson, John J. (1985). The determinants and control of violence in sport. *Quest, 37*(1), 27–37.

Thabet, O. (2013, June 10). Justin Abdelkader: First Arab-American NHL player. Retrieved from https://www.isportsweb.com/2013/06/10/justin-abdelkader-first-arab-american-nhl-player/

Theberge, N. (1985). Toward a feminist alternative to sport as a male preserve. *Quest, 37*, 193–202.

Theberge, N. (2003). No fear comes: adolescent girls, ice hockey, and the embodiment of gender. *Youth & Society, 34*(4), 497–516.

Theory. (2008). Social role theory. Retrieved from http://www.psych- it.com.au/Psychlopedia/article.asp?id=77

Thomas, J. (2018, September 6). Rams football games are long gone from St. Louis, but the legal ones go on. *St. Louis Post-Dispatch*. Retrieved from https://www.stltoday.com/sports/football/professional/rams-football-games-are-long-gone-from-st-louis-but/article_af55e70b-7938-5ce9-bba6-1d405d94dcf5.html

Thomas, K. (2010). Transgender man playing women's basketball at George Washington University. *New York Times*. Retrieved from https://www.nytimes.com/2010/11/02/sports/ncaabasketball/02gender.html

Thomas, N. (2002). Sport and disability. http://www.sagepub.com/sites/default/files/upm-binaries/9462_011233Ch6.pdf

Thomas, N., & Green, K. (1994). Physical education teacher education and the "special needs" of youngsters with disabilities: The need to confront PETE's attitude problem. *British Journal of Physical Education, 25*(4), 26–30.

Thompson, C. J., & Elizabeth, C. H. (1995). Understanding the socialized body: A poststructuralist analysis of consumers' self-conceptions, body images, and self-care practices. *Journal of Consumer Research, 22*(September), 139–153.

Thompson, E. P. (1967). Time, work, discipline and industrial capitalism. *Past and Present, 38*, 56–97.

Thompson, E. P. (1968). *The making of the English working class*. London, United Kingdom: Penguin.

Thompson, E. H., Bennett, K. M. (2015). Measurement of masculinity ideologies: A (critical) review. *Psychology of Men & Masculinity, 16*(2), 115–133. doi: 10.1037/a0038609

Thomson, A.B.R., Bernstein, C.N., & Leddin, D. (2008). Mandatory retirement for gastroenterologists: A viewpoint. *Canadian Journal of Gastroenterology, 22*(2), 125–127.

Thorne, B. (1993). *Gender play: Girls and boys in school*. New Brunswick, NJ: Rutgers University Press.

Thornhill, R., & Palmer, C. T. (2000). *A natural history of rape: Biological bases of sexual coercion*. Cambridge, MA: MIT Press.

Thrane, C. (2001) Sport spectatorship in Scandinavia: A class phenomenon? *International Review for the Sociology of Sport, 36*(2), 149–163.

Tiderman, A. (2015, May 14). *Living below the poverty line in the United States*, Retrieved from https://www.channelone.com/interact_post/living-below-the-poverty-line-in-the-united-states/

Tignor, S. (2013). Martina's moment. Retrieved from http://www.tennis.com/pro-game/2011/11/high-strung-lost-chapter-martinas-moment/45361/

Tipton, L., Haney, R., & Baseheart, J. (1975). Media agenda setting in city and state election campaigns. *Journalism Quarterly, 52*(1), 15–22.

Tomlinson, A. (2007). *The sports studies reader*. New York. NY: Routledge.

Toombs, S. K. (1995). The lived experience of disability. *Human Studies, 18*(9): 9–23.

Toomey, A. & Machado, B. (2015, September 25). Caitlyn Jenner legally changes her name and gender. Eonline. Retrieved from http://www.eonline.com/news/699992/

caitlyn-jenner-legally-changes-her-name-and-gender

Toutkoushian, R. K. & Kramer, D. A. II (2012). Analyzing equity in faculty compensation. In R. D. Howard, G. W. McLaughlin, & W. E. Knight (Eds.), *The handbook of institutional research* (p. 563). San Francisco, CA: Jossey-Bass.

Townsend, J. (1979) Stereotypes of mental illness: a comparison with ethnic stereotypes. *Culture, Medicine & Psychiatry*, *24*, 205–229.

Tracy, A. (2014, September 15). NFL, NBA lead arrest rates across pro sports. Retrieved from https://www.vocativ.com/culture/sport/nfl-arrest-rates/index.html

Tremblay, M. S., Katzmarzyk, P. T., & Willms, J. D. (2002). Temporal trends in overweight and obesity in Canada, 1981–1996. *International Journal of Obesity and Related Metabolic Disorders*, *26*, 538–543.

True, G. (2010). Kobe, LeBron, Tiger, Vick, T. O., Ocho: The six most-hated figures are black. Bleacher Report. https://bleacherreport.com/articles/454479-kobe-lebron-tiger-vick-to-amp-ocho-the-6-most-hated-sports-figures-are-black

Trujillo, N. (1991) Hegemonic masculinity on the mound: Media representations of Nolan Ryan and American sports culture. *Critical Studies in Mass Communication*, *8*(3), 290–308. doi: 10.1080/15295039109366799

Trujillo, N. (1995) Machines, missiles and men: images of the male body on ABC's Monday night football. *Sociology of Sport Journal*, *12*(4), 403–423.

Trujillo, N. (2000). Hegemonic masculinity on the mound: Media representations of Nolan Ryan and American sports culture. In S. Birrell & M. G. McDonald (Eds.), *Reading sport: Critical essays on power and representation* (pp. 14–39). Boston, MA: Northeastern University Press.

Trujillo, N., & Ekdom, L. (1985). Sportswriting and American cultural values: The 1984 Chicago Cubs. *Critical Studies in Mass Communication*, *2*, 262–281.

Tuchman, G. (1978). The symbolic annihilation of women by the mass media In G. Tuchman, A. K. Daniels, & J. Benet (Eds.), *Hearth and home: Images of women in the mass media* (pp. 3–38). New York, NY: Oxford University Press.

Tuchman, G. (1979). Women's depiction in the mass media. *Signs*, *4*, 528–542.

Tuchman, G. & Cabell, B. (2003, December 16). Kobe Bryant charged with sexual assault. CNN. Retrieved from http://www.cnn.com

Tucker Center for Research on Girls & Women in Sport. (2018, December 20). *Game On: Women can coach*. Retrieved from http://www.cehd.umn.edu/tuckercenter/

Tudor, A. (1998). Sports reporting: Race, difference and identity. In K. Brants, J. Hermes, & L. van Zoonen (Eds.), *The media in question* (pp. 146–156). London, United Kingdom: Sage.

Tugend, A. (2011, June 3). Fears, and opportunities, on the road to retirement. *New York Times*. Retrieved from http://www.nytimes.com

Tuggle, C. A., Huffman, S., & Rosengard, D. S. (2002). A descriptive analysis of NBC's coverage of the 2000 Summer Olympics. *Mass Communication & Society*, *5*, 361–375.

Tuggle, C. A., & Owen, A. (1999). A descriptive analysis of NBC's coverage of the centennial Olympics: The "games of the woman"? *Journal of Sport & Social Issues*, *23*(2), 171–182. doi: 10.1177/0193723599232004

Turk, J. V., & Franklin, B. (1987). Information subsidies: Agenda setting traditions. Public *Relations Review*, *13*(4), 29–41.

Turner, B. (2001). Disability and the sociology of the body. In G. Albrecht, K. Seelman, & M. Bury (Eds.), *Handbook of disability studies* (pp. 252–266). Thousand Oaks, CA: Sage.

Twenge, J. M. (2017). *iGen: Why today's super-connected kids are growing up less rebellious, more tolerant, less happy—And completely unprepared for adulthood.* New York, NY: Atria Books.

Twenge, J. M. & Park, H. (2017). The decline in adult activities among U.S. Adolescents, 1976–2016. *Child Development*, *00*(0), 1–17, Retrieved from http://cds.web.unc.edu/files/2017/09/Twenge_et_al-2017-Child_Development.pdf

Tygiel, J. (1983). *Baseball's great experiment: Jackie Robinson and his legacy.* New York, NY: Oxford University Press.

Tyler, M., Fairbrother, P. (2013, April). Bushfires are "men's business": The importance of gender and rural hegemonic masculinity. *Journal of Rural Studies*, *30*, 110–119. doi: 10.1016/j.jrurstud.2013.01.002

Uberti, D. (2014, September 22). How American sports franchises are selling their cities short. *The Guardian*. Retrieved from https://www.theguardian.com/cities/2014/sep/22/-sp-how-american-sports-franchises-sell-cities-short

UNICEF. (2007, August 29). Early gender socialization. Retrieved from http://www.unicef.org/earlychildhood/index_40749.html

United Nations. (2006). Convention on the rights of persons with disabilities, Article 30 C.F.R. Retrieved from www.un.org/disabilities/convention/conventionfull.shtml

United States Bureau of Justice. (2014). Criminal victimization, survey 1993–2014. Retrieved from https://www.bjs.gov/content/pub/pdf/cv14.pdf g

United States Bureau of Justice Statistics. (2018). Arrest data. Retrieved from https://www.bjs.gov/index.cfm?ty=datool&surl=/arrests/index.cfm

United States Social Security Administration. (2011). Full retirement age. Retrieved from http://www.ssa.gov/retirement/1943.html

United States Social Security Administration. (2011). Medicare: Electronic booklet. Retrieved from http://ssa.gov/pubs/10043.html

University of Florida. (2015). Social media & sports journalism. Retrieved from https://ufonline.ufl.edu/infographics/social-media-sports-journalism/

USA Today. (2018, December 13). NFL player arrests. Retrieved from https://www.usatoday.com/sports/nfl/arrests/2018/all/all/

U.S. Bureau of Labor Statistics. (2009). The employment situation: September 2009. United States Department of Labor. Retrieved from http://www.bls.gov

U.S. Bureau of Labor Statistics. (2017). Labor force characteristics by race and ethnicity, 2016. Retrieved from https://www.bls.gov/opub/reports/race-and-ethnicity/2016/home.htm

U.S. Bureau of Labor Statistics. (2018). *Department of Labor occupational outlook handbook, advertising, promotions, and marketing managers*. Retrieved from https://www.bls.gov/ooh/management/advertising-promotions-and-marketing-managers.htm

U.S. Census Bureau. (1995). *Sixty-five plus in the united states,* Retrieved from https://www.census.gov/population/socdemo/statbriefs/agebrief.html

U.S. Census Bureau. (1999). *Keeping up with older adults: Older adults, 1999*. Population profile of the United States. Retrieved from https://www.census.gov/prod/2001pubs/p23-205.pdf

U.S. Census Bureau. (2005). Older adults in 2005. Population profile of the United States: Dynamic version. Retrieved from https://www.census.gov/population/pop-profile/dynamic/profiledynamic.pdf

U.S. Census Bureau. (2008). National population projections (based on Census 2000). Retrieved from http://www.census.gov/population/www/projections/summarytables.html

U.S. Census Bureau. (2016). Asian/Pacific American heritage month: May 2016. Retrieved from https://www.census.gov/newsroom/facts-for-features/2016/cb16-ff07.html

U.S. Census Bureau. (2016). Quick facts. Retrieved from https://www.census.gov/quickfacts/fact/table/US/PST045217

U.S. Census Bureau. (2017). *Income and poverty in the United States: Current population reports*. Retrieved from https://www.census.gov/content/dam/Census/library/publications/2017/demo/P60-259.pdf

U.S. Census Bureau. (2017a). Disability statistics. Retrieved from https://www.disabled-world.com/disability/statistics/cbfff.php

U.S. Census Bureau. (2017b). Quick statistics on population and states. Retrieved from https://www.census.gov/quickfacts/fact/table/US/PST045217

U.S. Census Bureau. (2018a). Hispanic origins. Retrieved from https://www.census.gov/topics/population/hispanic-origin.html

U.S. Census Bureau. (2018b). Older people projected to outnumber children for first time in U.S. history. Retrieved from https://www.census.gov/newsroom/press-releases/2018/cb18-41-population-projections.html

U.S. Department of Health and Human Services. (2001). *Youth violence: A report of the surgeon general*. Rockville, MD: U.S. Department of Health and Human Services.

U.S. Department of Labor Employment Standards Administration Wage and Hour Division. (1984). *Child labor requirements in agriculture under the Fair Labor Standards Act* (Child Labor Bulletin No. 102). WH Publication 1295. Retrieved from www.dol.gov/esa

US News. (2012). No Saudi women qualified for Olympics. Retrieved from http://www.usnews

.com/news/sports/articles/2012/07/09/report-no-saudi-women-qualified-for-olympics

Vaillancourt, T., Hymel, S., McDougall, P. (2003). Bullying is power: Implications for school-based intervention strategies. *Journal of Applied School Psychology, 19*(2), 157–176. doi: 10.1300/J008v19n02_10

Valentino, N. A., Buhr, T. A., & Beckmann, M. N. (2001). When the frame is the game. *Journalism and Mass Communication Quarterly, 78*(1), 93–112.

Valkenburg, P. M., Peter, J., & Walther, J. B. (2016). Media effects: Theory and research. *Annual Review of Psychology, 67*, 315–338.

Valkenburg, P., & Soeters, K. E. (2001). Children's positive and negative experiences with the Internet. *Communication Research, 28*(5), 652–675.

Van den Bulck, J. (2003). Is the mainstreaming effect of cultivation an artifact of regression toward the mean? *Journal of Broadcasting & Electronic Media, 47*(2), 289–295.

van der Dennen, J. M. G. (2005). *Theories of aggression: Frustration-aggression (F-A) theory*. University of Groningen. Retrieved from https://www.rug.nl/research/portal/files/2908668/A-FAT.pdf

Van Dijk, T. (1988a). *News analysis: Case studies of international and national news in the press*. Hillsdale, NJ: Laurence Erlbaum.

Van Dijk, T. (1988b). *News as discourse*. Hillsdale, NJ: Laurence Erlbaum.

Van Dijk, T. A. (1993). Principles of critical discourse analysis. *Discourse & Society, 4*(2): 249–283.

Van Dijk, T. A. (2003). Critical discourse analysis. In D. Schiffrin, D. Tannen, & H. E. Hamilton (Eds.), *Handbook of discourse analysis* (pp. 352–371). Oxford, United Kingdom: Blackwell.

Van Evra, J. (1990). *Television and child development*. Hillsdale, NJ: Lawrence Erlbaum.

Van Ingen, C. (2003). Geographies of gender, sexuality and race: Reframing the focus on space in sport sociology. *International Review for the Sociology of Sport, 38*(2), 201–216.

Veblen, T. (1953). *The theory of the leisure class: An economic study of institutions*. New York, NY: Mentor.

Verhaeghen P. (2011). Aging and executive control: Reports of a demise greatly exaggerated. *Current Directions in Psychological Science, 20*(3), 174–180.

Verme, P. (2010). A structural analysis of growth and poverty in the short-term. *The Journal of Developing Areas, 43*, 19–39.

Vescey, G. (2005, September 8). Epic match had it all, except for the black hat. *New York Times*. Retrieved from https://www.nytimes.com/2005/09/08/sports/tennis/epic-match-had-it-all-except-for-the-black-hat.html?mtrref=www.google.com&gwh=C10E61DDE4E93E63619E-47BA80CB5CC1&gwt=pay

Vescey, G. (1999, July 11). Sports of the times; no goals scored, two champions, a bright future. *New York Times*, Retrieved from https://www.nytimes.com/1999/07/11/sports/sports-of-the-times-no-goals-scored-two-champions-a-bright-future.html?mtrref=www.google.com&gwh=DF7E9A0816B61EE7EF973221D-DAEBD7F&gwt=pay

Vestberg, T., Reinebo, G., Maurex, L., Ingvar, M., & Petrovic, P. (2017) . Core executive functions are associated with success in young elite soccer players. *PLoS ONE, 12*(2), e0170845. https://doi.org/10.1371/journal.pone.0170845

Vickers, E. (2013). Life after sport: Depression in the retired athlete. Retrieved from https://commonlit.s3.us-west-2.amazonaws.com/texts/student_pdfs/000/000/566/original/commonlit_life-after-sport_student.pdf?X-Amz-Algorithm=AWS4-HMAC-SHA256&X-Amz-Credential=AKIAJFHNPJSC66AVBG5Q-%2F20181215%2Fus-west-2%2Fs3%2Faws4_request&X-Amz-Date=20181215T015845Z&X-Amz-Expires=30&X-Amz-SignedHeaders=host&X-Amz-Signature=e78e3373d-aa60e94f83deb82aba5e79aee178cd05ad-ba00b4aa98f968abfebf7

Vickers, E. (2016). Life after sport: Depression in the retired athlete. Retrieved from http://believeperform.com/wellbeing/life-after-sport-depression-in-retired-athletes/

Villanueva, G. C. (2006). *The A to Z feminist philosophy*. Lanham, MD: Scarecrow Press, Inc.

Vincent, J., Imwold, C., Johnson, J. T., & Massey, D. (2003). Newspaper coverage of female athletes competing in selected sports in the 1996 centennial Olympic games: The more things change the more they stay the same. *Women in Sport & Physical Activity Journal, 12*(1), 1–22.

Vincent, R. C. (1989). Clio's consciousness raised? Portrayal of women in rock videos, reexamined. *Journalism Quarterly*, 66, 155–160.

Vingan, A. (2012). The many faces of Clinton Portis: A retrospective. Retrieved from https://www.nbcwashington.com/blogs/capital-games/The-Many-Faces-Of-Clinton-Portis-A-Retrospective-166951856.html

Vogel, L. A., Carotenuto, G., Basti, J. J., & Levine, W. N. (2011) Physical activity after total joint arthroplasty. *Sports Health: A Multidisciplinary Approach*, 3, 441–450. pmid:2301604

Volkmar, J., & Westbrook, K. (2005). Does a decade make a difference? A second look at western women working in Japan. *Women in Management Review*, 20(7/8), 464–477.

Volpi, E., Nazemi, R., & Fujita, S. (2004). Muscle tissue changes with aging. *Current Opinion in Clinical Nutrition and Metabolic Care*, 7(4), 405–410.

Wachs, F. L. (2003). "I was there …": Gendered limitations, expectations, and strategic assumptions in the world of co-ed softball. In A. Bolin & S. Granskog (Eds.), *Athletic intruders: Ethnographic research on women, culture, and exercise* (pp. 177–199). Albany, NY: State University of New York Press.

Wacquant, L. (1995) Pugs at work: Bodily capital and bodily labour among professional boxers. *Body and Society*, 1(1), 65–93.

Wahl, O. F. & Lefkowits, J. Y. (1989). Impact of a television film on attitudes towards mental illness. *American Journal of Community Psychology*, 17, 521–528.

Waldron, T. (2013). The leading driver of diversity in sports journalism? It's ESPN. Retrieved from https://thinkprogress.org/the-leading-driver-of-diversity-in-sports-journalism-its-espn-63577ee5b11e/

Waldron, T. (2014, December 10). NFL owner admits league's new domestic violence policy is a public relations ploy. Retrieved from https://thinkprogress.org/nfl-owner-admits-leagues-new-domestic-violence-policy-is-a-public-relations-ploy-de1240fcc889/

Waldron, T. (2017). Our favorite NFL team doesn't care about you. Huffington Post. https://www.huffingtonpost.com/entry/chargers-los-angeles_us_587799d3e4b092a-6cae57cee

Walker, J. (1988). *Louts and legends: male youth culture in an inner city school*. Sydney, Australia: Allen and Unwin.

Walker, N., Bopp, T, & Sagas, M. (2011). Gender bias in the perception of women as collegiate men's basketball coaches. *Journal for the Study of Sports and Athletes in Education*, 5(2), 157–176.

Wallstein, K. (2007). Agenda setting and the blogosphere. *Review of Policy Research*, 24(6), 567–587.

Walpole, M. B. (2003). Socioeconomic status and college: How SES affects college experiences and outcomes. *Review of Higher Education*, 27(1), 45–73.

Walsh, K. (2018). 5 books for millennials to get ahead. Retrieved from https://www.bentley.edu/impact/articles/5-books-millennials-get-ahead

Walter, C. M. & Du Randt, R. (2011). Socio-cultural barriers to physical activity among black isiXhosa speaking professional women in the Nelson Mandela Metropolitan Municipality. *South African Journal for Research in Sport, Physical Education and Recreation*, 40(3), 143–156.

Walters, J. (2016). Taking a closer look at the gender pay gap in sports. *Newsweek*. Retrieved from https://www.newsweek.com/womens-soccer-suit-underscores-sports-gender-pay-gap-443137

Wandzilak, T. (1988). Values development through physical activity: Promoting sportsmanlike behaviors. Perceptions and moral reasoning. *Journal of Teaching in Physical Education*, 8(1), 13–21.

Wankel, L. M., & Berger, B. G. (1990). The psychological and social benefits of sport and physical activity. *Journal of Leisure Research*, 22, 167–182.

Wankel, L. M., & Kreisel, P. S. (1985). Factors underlying enjoyment of youth sports: Sport and age group comparisons. *Journal of Sport Psychology*, 7, 51–64.

Wankel, L. M., & Mummery, W. K. (1990). The psychological and social benefits of sport and physical activity. *Journal of Leisure Research*, 22, 167–182.

Wanta, W. (1991). Presidential approval ratings as a variable in the agenda-building process. *Journalism Quarterly*, 68(4), 672–679.

Wanta, W. (1997). *The public and the national agenda*. Mahwah, NJ: Lawrence Erlbaum.

Wanta, W., & Hu, Y. (1994a). Time-lag differences in the agenda-setting process. *International Journal of Public Opinion Research, 6*(3), 225–240.

Wanta, W., & Hu, Y. (1994b). The effects of credibility reliance and exposure on media agenda setting. *Journalism Quarterly, 71*(1), 90–98.

Wanta, W., Stephenson, M. A., Turk, J. V., & McCombs, M. E. (1989). How president's state of the union talk influenced news media agendas. *Journalism Quarterly, 66*(3), 537–541.

Warner, W. L., & Lunt, P. S. (1941). *The social life of a modern community*. New Haven, CT: Yale University Press.

Hanke, R. (1998). Theorizing Masculinity With/In the Media. *Communication Theory, 8*(2), 183–201. https://doi.org/10.1111/j.1468-2885.1998.tb00217.x

Washington, R., & Karen, D. (2001). Sport and society. *Annual Review of Sociology, 27*, 187–212.

Waters, J. A., & Bird, F. (1987). The moral dimension of organizational culture. *Journal of Business Ethics, 6*(1), 15–22.

Watson, N. (1998). Enabling identity: disability, self and citizenship. In T. Shakespeare (Ed.), *The disability reader: Social science perspectives* (pp. 147–172). London, United Kingdom: Cassell.

Weaver, A. (1998). Net worth. *Working Woman, 23*(1), 20.

Weaver, D. (1977). Political issues and voter need for orientation. In M. McCombs & D. Shaw (Eds.), *The emergence of American political issues* (pp. 107–119). St. Paul, MN: West.

Weaver, J., & Wakshlag, J. (1986). Perceived vulnerability in crime, criminal victimization experience, and television viewing. *Journal of Broadcasting and Electronic Media, 30*(2), 141–158.

Webber, C. (2007). Revaluating relative deprivation theory. *Theoretical Criminology, 11*(1), 97–120.

Wedgwood, N. (2003). Aussie rules! Schoolboy football and masculine embodiment. In S. Tomsen & M. Donaldson (Eds.), *Male trouble: Looking at Australian masculinities* (pp. 180–199). Melbourne, Australia: Pluto.

Wedgwood, N. (2004). Kicking like a boy: Schoolgirl Australian rules football and bi-gendered female embodiment. *Sociology of Sport Journal, 21*(2), 140–162.

Weed, E. (1996). Introduction. In E. Weed & N. Schor (Eds.), *Feminism meets queer theory* (pp. vii–xiii). Bloomington, IN: Indiana University Press.

Weirsma, L. D. (2000). Risks and benefits of youth sport specialization. *Pediatric Exercise Science, 12*, 13–22.

Weiser, K., & Love, P. (1988, September–October). Who owns your team? *Strategies, 2*(1), 5–8.

Weitzer, J. E. (1989). *Childhood socialization into physical activity: Parental roles in perceptions of competence and goal orientations.* (Unpublished master's thesis). University of Wisconsin-Milwaukee, Miwaukee, WI.

Wenner, L. A. (Ed.). (1998). *Mediasport*. London, United Kingdom: Routledge.

Wenner, M. D. (1995). Group credit: A means to improve information transfer and loan repayment performance. *Journal of Development Studies, 32*(2), 263–281. doi: 10.1080/00220389508422414

Wentling, R. (2003). The career development and aspirations of women in middle management—revisited. *Women in Management Review, 18*(5/6), 311–324.

Wertham, F. (1954). *The seduction of the innocent.* New York, NY: Holt, Rinehart & Winston.

Werthner, P. & Trudel, P. (2006). A new theoretical perspective for understanding how coaches learn to coach. *Sport Psychologist, 20*, 198–212.

West, C., & Zimmerman., D. H. (1987). Doing gender. *Gender & Society, 1*(June), 125–151.

Wetherell, M., & Edley, N. (1999). Negotiating hegemonic masculinity: Imaginary positions and psycho-discursive practices. *Feminism and Psychology, 9* (3), 335–356.

Weyer, B. (2007). Twenty years later: Explaining the persistence of the glass ceiling for women leaders. *Women in Management Review, 22*(6), 482–496.

Whannel, G. (1992). *Fields in vision: Television sport and cultural transformation.* London, United Kingdom: Routledge.

Whannel, G. (2002). *Media sport stars: Masculinities and moralities.* London, United Kingdom: Routledge.

Wharton, D. (2012). London Olympics: Women from three Muslim countries are pioneers. *LA Times*. Retrieved from http://articles.latimes.com/2012/jul/30/sports/la-sp-oly-muslim-20120730

Whisenant, W., Pedersen, P. M., & Obenour, B. L. (2002). Success and gender: Determining the rate of advancement for intercollegiate athletic directors. *Sex Roles, 47*(9–10), 485–491. https://doi.org/10.1023/A:1021656628604

Whisenant, W. A., & Pedersen, P. M. (2004). Analyzing attitudes regarding quantity and quality of sports page coverage: Athletic director perceptions of newspaper coverage given to interscholastic sports. *International Sports Journal, 8*, 54–64.

Whitbourne, S. K., & Sneed, J. R. (2004). The paradox of well-being, identity processes, and stereotype threat: Ageism and its potential relationships to the self in later life. In T. D. Nelson (Ed.), *Ageism* (pp. 242–273). Cambridge, MA: MIT Press.

White, G. E. (1998). *Creating the national pastime: Baseball transforms itself, 1903-1953*. Princeton, NJ: Princeton University Press.

White, P., & Wilson, B. (1999). Distinction in the stands. *International Review for the Sociology of Sport, 34*(4), 245–264.

White, P., & Young, K. (1999). *Sport and gender in Canada*. Toronto, Canada: Oxford University Press.

Whitehead, S. M. (2002). *Men and masculinities: Key themes and new directions*. Cambridge, United Kingdom: Polity.

Whitmer, R. (2013). Athletics for all. *District Administration, 49*(4), 44–49.

WHO (2003). *Health and development through physical activity and sport*. Geneva, Switzerland: World Health.

Widmer, E. D., Judith Treas, & Newcomb, R. (1998). Attitudes toward nonmarital sex in 24 countries. *Journal of Sex Research, 35*(4), 349.

Wiggins, D. K. (1997). Great speed but little stamina: The historical debate over black athletic superiority. In S. W. Pope (Ed.), *The new American sport history: Recent approaches and perspectives* (pp. 312–338). Urbana, IL: University of Illinois Press.

Wijtzes, A., Jansen, W., Bouthoorn, S. H., Pot, N., Hofman, A., Jaddoe, V. W., & Raat, H. (2014). Social inequalities in young children's sports participation and outdoor play. *International Journal of Behavioural Nutrition and Physical Activity, 11*, 155.

Wilber, D. Q. (2007, January 31). FAA to raise retirement age for pilots. *Washington Post*. Retrieved from http://www.washingtonpost.com

Wiley, C. G. E., Shaw, S. M., & Havitz, M. E. (2000). Men's and women's involvement in sports: An examination of the gendered aspects of leisure involvement. *Leisure Sciences, 22*, 19–31.

Wilkins, R, (2003, July). Sacrificing to compete: An interview with Dina Al-sabah. Bodybuilding.com. Retrieved from https://ipfs.io/ipfs/QmXoypizjW3WknFiJnKLwHCnL72vedxjQkDDP1mXWo6uco/wiki/Dina_Al-Sabah.html.

Wilkins, R. (2018, October 20). Edmonton Oilers win third straight with OT victory over Boston in home opener. Global News. Retrieved from https://globalnews.ca/news/4570379/edmonton-oilers-2018-19-home-opener-bruins/

Wilkinson, T. (2004, August 18). Hurdles are their best event. *LA Times*. Retrieved from http://articles.latimes.com/2004/aug/18/world/fg-muslims18

Williams, A. (2001). Basketball's new breed. Tribune Media Services. Retrieved from townhall.com

Williams, A., & Giles, H. (1998). Communication of ageism. In M. L. Hecht & L. Michael (Eds.), *Communicating prejudice* (pp. 136–160). Thousand Oaks, CA: Sage.

Williams D. (2007, July 27). The new face of fitness is getting older. CNN. Retrieved from http://cnn.com

Williams J. E., & Best, D. L. (1990). *Measuring sex stereotypes: A multination study*. Thousand Oaks, CA: Sage.

Williams, L. M., Brown, K. J., Palmer, D., Liddell, B. J., Kemp, A. H., Olivieri, G., Peduto, A., & Gordon, E. (2006). The mellow years? Neural basis of improving emotional stability with age. *Journal of Neuroscience, 26*, 6422–6430.

Williams, B., & Carpini, M. (2004). Monica and Bill all the time and everywhere: The collapse of gatekeeping and agenda setting in the new media environment. *American Behavioral Scientist, 47*(9), 1208–1231.

Williams, C., Lawrence, G., & Rowe, D. (1986) Patriarchy, media and sport. In G. Lawrence &

D. Rowe (Eds.), *Power play: The commercialization of Australian sport* (pp. 215–229). Sydney, Australia: Hale & Iremonger.

Williams, J. (2017). Stephen Curry takes issue with Under Armour leader on Trump. *New York Times*. Retrieved from https://www.nytimes.com/2017/02/08/sports/basketball/stephen-curry-under-armour-donald-trump-warriors.html

Williams, R. (1977) *Marxism and literature.* Oxford, United Kingdom, Oxford University Press.

Williams, R. L. & Youssef, Z. I. (1975). Stereotypes of football players as a function of positions. *Journal of Sports Medicine*, *3*(1), 7–11. https://doi.org/10.1177/036354657500300102

Williams, T. (1994) Sociological perspectives on sport and disability: Structural-functionalism. *Adapted Physical Activity Quarterly*, *17*(1), 14–24.

Williams, T., & Newman, I. (1988). Initial research on integration and involvement in community sport and recreation. *Working Papers of the Everybody Active Demonstration Project No. 4*, Sunderland Polytechnic.

Williams, T. B. (1986). *The impact of television.* New York, NY: Academic Press.

Williams, W. L. (1997). Amazons of America: Female gender variance. In C. B. Brettell & C. F. Sargent (Eds.), *Gender in cross-cultural perspective* (2nd ed., pp. 202–213). Upper Saddle River, NJ: Prentice Hall.

Williams, W., & Semlak, W. (1978). Campaign 76: Agenda setting during the New Hampshire primary. *Journal of Broadcasting*, *22*(4), 531–540.

Williams-Piehota P., Schneider, T. R., Pizarro, J., Mowad, L., & Salovey P. (2003). Matching health messages to information-processing styles: Need for cognition and mammography utilization. *Health Communication*, *15*(4), 375–392.

Willis, P. (1977). *Learning to labor: How working class kids get working class jobs.* Farborough, United Kingdom: Saxon House.

Wilson, B. (2017). Top moments in San Diego Chargers history. *USA Today.* Retrieved from https://www.usatoday.com/story/sports/nfl/2017/01/12/top-moments-in-san-diego-chargers-history/96512538/

Wilson, B. (2018, October 29). Here's the last time every major professional sports team won a championship. Retrieved from https://lancasteronline.com/sports/here-s-the-last-time-every-major-professional-sports-team/article_db16e178-a1ac-11e6-a112-83761c475e29.html

Wilson C., Nairn, R., Coverdale, J., & Panapa, A. (2000). How mental illness is portrayed in children's television: a prospective study, *British Journal of Psychiatry*, *176*, 440–443.

Wilson, C. C., II, Gutierrez, F. & Chao, L. M. (2012). *Racism, Sexism and the Media* (4th ed.). Thousand Oaks, CA: Sage.

Wilson, S. (2012a, August 11). Saudi Arabia not sending women to London 2012. Huffington Post, April 7. Retrieved from https://www.telegraph.co.uk/sport/olympics/9468113/London-2012-Olympics-diary-three-countries-have-failed-to-send-any-female-athletes.html

Wilson, S. (2012b, July 11). Saudi Arabia not sending women to London Olympics: A report. Huffington Post. Retrieved from https://www.telegraph.co.uk/sport/olympics/news/9391927/London-2012-Olympics-Saudi-Arabia-reverses-pledge-to-send-female-athletes-to-the-Games.html

Wilson, T. C. (2002). The paradox of social class and sports involvement: The roles of cultural and economic capital. *International Review for the Sociology of Sport*, *37*(1), 5–16. doi: 10.1177/1012690202037001001

Wimbledon (2018). Prize money and finance: The full breakdown of prize money. Retrieved from http://www.wimbledon.com/pdf/2018_Prize_Money.pdf

Wimmer, R. D., & Dominick, J. R. (1997). *Mass media research: An introduction.* Belmont, CA: Wadsworth Pub.

Windahl, S. (1981). Uses and gratifications at the crossroads. In G. Wilhoit & H. deBock (Eds.), *Mass communication review yearbook* (Vol. 2, pp. 174-185). Beverly Hills, CA: Sage.

Winter, J. (1981). Contingent conditions in the agenda setting process. In G. Wilhoit & H. deBock (Eds.), *Mass communication review yearbook* (Vol. 2, pp. 235–243). Beverly Hills, CA: Sage.

Winter, J., & Eyal, C. (1981). Agenda setting for the civil rights issue. *Public Opinion Quarterly*, *45*(3), 376–383.

WNBPA (2012, April 26). Dressing the part. Retrieved from https://wnbpa.com/dressing-the-part/

Wofford, G. (2001, May 31). Sportscasters honor native people by not mentioning Indian mascot names. *Native American Times*. Retrieved from https://studylib.net/doc/12033342/native-american-mascot-controversy-and-mass-media-involve.

Wolfe, K. (1996). Ordinary people: Why the disabled aren't so different. *The Humanist, 56*(6), 31–34.

Wolf, N. (2009). *The beauty myth: How images of beauty are used against women*. New York: NY: HarperPerennial.

Wolf, R. (2011, May 13). Medicare, social security running out of money faster. *USA Today*. Retrieved from http://www.usatoday.com

Wolf, R., & Le Guin, C. (2003). *Race and racism: Illumination project curriculum materials* (pp. 1–4). Retrieved from https://www.pcc.edu/illumination/wp-content/uploads/sites/54/2018/05/excerpt.pdf

Wolfe, L. (2018, May 29). Latino or Hispanic: What is the difference between Hispanic and Latino? Retrieved from https://www.thebalancecareers.com/which-is-politically-correct-latino-or-hispanic-3514820

Women's Sports Foundation. (2008). Reasons why girls drop out of sports. Retrieved from https://www.fastandfemale.com/girls-in-sport/reasons-girls-drop-sports/

Women's Sports Foundation. (2018). Pay inequity in athletics. Retrieved from https://www.womenssportsfoundation.org/research/article-and-report/elite-athletes/pay-inequity/

Women's Sports Foundation. (2018). Playing in the closet: Homophobia in sports. Retrieved from https://www.womenssportsfoundation.org/research/article-and-report/understudied-populations/playing-in-the-closet/

Wong, P., Lai, C. F., Nagasawa, R., & Lin, T. (1998). Asian Americans as a model minority: Self-perceptions and perceptions by other racial groups. *Sociological Perspectives, 41*(1), 95–118.

Wong, Y. J., Ho, M. R., Wang, S. & miller, S. K. (2017). Meta-analyses of the relationship between conformity to masculine norms and mental health-related outcomes. *Journal of Counseling Psychology, 64*(1), 80–93. doi:10.1037/cou0000176

Wonsek, P. (1992). College basketball on television: A study of racism in the media. *Media, Culture and Society, 14*, 449–461.

Wood, G. (2008). Gender stereotypical attitudes: Past, present and future influences on women's career advancement. *Equal Opportunities International, 27*(7), 613–628.

Wood, J., & Schauer, K. (2017). Coming out while still in the game: More professional athletes are coming out and not just after they retire. Retrieved from https://www.factmonster.com/sports/coming-out-while-still-game.

Wood, R. (2008). Sporting resources. Topend Sports. Retrieved from https://www.topendsports.com/resources/index.htm

Wood, R. J. (2010). Complete guide to fitness testing. Topend Sports. Retrieved from https://www.topendsports.com/testing/

Wood, G., & Lindorff, M. (2001). Sex differences in explanations for career progress. *Women in Management Review, 16*(4), 152–162.

Woods, R. B. (2016). *Social issues in sport* (3rd ed.). Champaign, IL: Human Kinetics.

Workman, L., & Reader, W. (2009). *Evolutionary psychology* (2nd ed.). New York, NY: Cambridge University Press.

World Health Organization (2012). *World report on disability*. Retrieved from http://www.who.int/disabilities/world_report/2011/report/en/index.html

World Health Organization. (2016). Ending childhood obesity. Retrieved from https://www.who.int/news-room/fact-sheets/detail/obesity-and-overweight

Worsnop, C. M. (2003). Media literacy through critical thinking: Student workbook produced by NW Center for Excellence in Media Literacy. Retrieved from https://depts.washington.edu/nwmedia/sections/nw_center/curriculum_docs/stud_combine.pdf

Wright, A. D., & Côté, J. (2003). A retrospective analysis of leadership development through sport. *Sport Psychologist, 17*, 268–291.

Wright, E. O. (2000). *Class counts: Comparative studies in class analysis*. New York, NY: Cambridge University Press.

Wright, M. (2017, July 20). Why we need Title IX now more than ever. Retrieved from https://www.theplayerstribune.com/monica-wright-why-we-need-title-ix/

Wurtzel, A., & Lometti, G. (1984). Researching TV violence. *Society, 21*(6), 22–30.

Wykes, M. & Welsh, K. (2009). Introducing violence, gender, and justice. *Violence, gender, and justice* (pp. 1–8). London, United Kingdom: Sage.

Yang, H. Ramasubramanian, S., & Oliver, M. (2008). Cultivation effects on quality of life indicators. *Journal of Broadcasting & Electronic Media, 52*(2), 247–267.

Yardbarker, F. (2017, August 19). Opinion: The most hated coaches in sports. Retrieved from https://www.msn.com/en-us/sports/more-sports/opinion-the-most-hated-coaches-in-sports/ss-AAqjh2y

Yardley, J. (2004 September 4). Racial "handicaps" and a great sprint forward. *New York Times.* Retrieved from https://www.nytimes.com/2004/09/08/world/asia/racial-handicaps-and-a-great-sprint-forward.html

Yates, C. (2010, December 3). Lesbian college soccer coach outed by partner's unborn child, forced to resign. Retrieved from https://www.autostraddle.com/lesbian-soccer-coach-resigns-68423/

Yeğenoğlu, M. (1998). *Colonial fantasies: Towards a feminist reading of orientalism.* Cambridge, United Kingdom: Cambridge University Press.

Yoder, J. D., Christopher, J., & Holmes, J. D. (2008). Are television commercials still achievement scripts for women? *Psychology of Women Quarterly, 32*(3), 303–311. doi:10.1111/j.1471-6402.2008.00438.x

Young, I. M. (1998). Situated bodies: throwing like a girl. In D. Welton (Ed.), *Body and flesh: A philosophical reader* (pp. 259–273). Oxford, United Kingdom: Blackwell.

Young, J. R. (1998, February 6). Students are vulnerable to Internet addiction, article says. *Chronicle of Higher Education, 44*(22), A25.

Young, K. (2000). Sport and violence. In J. Coakley & E. Dunning (Eds.), *Handbook of sport studies* (pp. 382–407). London, United Kingdom: Sage.

Young, K. S. (1998). *Caught in the net.* New York, NY: John Wiley.

Young, K., & Atkinson, M., (2008). *Deviance and social control in sport.* Champaign, IL: Human Kinetics.

Young, K., & Smith, M.D. (1989). Mass media treatment of violence in sports and its effects. *Current Psychology: Research and Reviews, 7*(4), 298–311.

Young, K., & White, P. (2000). Researching sports injury: Reconstructing dangerous masculinities. In J. McKay, M. A. Messner, D. Sabo (Eds.), *Masculinities, gender relations, and sport* (pp. 259–273). London, United Kingdom: Sage.

Youngmisuk, O. (2009). Packers fan lay Vikings QB Brett Favre to rest in mock funeral as legend returns to Green Bay. *New York Daily News.* Retrieved from http://www.nydailynews.com/sports/football/packers-fan-lay-vikings-qb-brett-favre-rest-mock-funeral-legend-returns-green-bay-article-1.418381

Yows, S. (1995, August). *Towards developing a coherent theory of framing: Understanding the relationship between news framing and audience framing.* Paper presented to Association for Education in Journalism and Mass Communication, Washington, DC.

Yun, D., Nah, S., & McLeod, D. (2008). Framing effects of news coverage of the embryonic stem cell controversy. *Communication Research Reports, 25* (1–4), 312–315.

Zeilinger, J. (2015, July 7). 6 forms of ableism we need to retire immediately. Retrieved from https://mic.com/articles/121653/6-forms-of-ableism-we-need-to-retire-immediately#.YdUOtyvbM

Zhou, J. (2014). Systems & us: Embracing complexity. Retrieved from https://systemsandus.com/2014/06/09/the-american-professional-sports-cartel/

Zhou, Y. (2008). Voluntary adopters vs. forced adopters. *New Media & Society, 10*(3), 475–496.

Ziemer, T. A. (2000). Study says kids emulate athletes. ABC News. Retrieved from https://abcnews.go.com/Sports/story?id=100296

Zillmann, D., & Bryant, J. (1982). Pornography, sexual callousness, and the trivialization of rape. *Journal of Communication, 32*(4), 10–21.

Zillmann, D., & Bryant, J. (1989). *Pornography: Research advances and policy considerations.* Hillsdale, NJ: Lawrence Erlbaum.

Zillmann, D., Hoyt, J., & Day, K. (1979). Strength and duration of the effect of violent and erotic communication on subsequent aggressive behavior. *Communication Research, 1*(3), 286–306.

Zogry, M., & Anetso, J. (2010). *The Cherokee ball game: At the center of ceremony and identity*. Chapel Hill, NC: University of North Carolina Press.

Zorowitz, J. (2017). It just got real: Coaches like Bret Bielema and Bill Belichick are getting on the virtual-reality wave. NBC Sports. Retrieved from http://sportsworld.nbcsports.com/virtual-reality-sports-arkansas-kentucky/

Index